management

Wherever the **Click-Along** icon
appears, go to *www.mhhe.com/kw*

Click Along 1.1

management

A Practical Introduction

Angelo Kinicki
Arizona State University

Brian K. Williams

McGraw-Hill
Irwin

Boston   Burr Ridge, IL   Dubuque, IA   Madison, WI   New York   San Francisco   St. Louis
Bangkok   Bogotá   Caracas   Kuala Lumpur   Lisbon   London   Madrid   Mexico City
Milan   Montreal   New Delhi   Santiago   Seoul   Singapore   Sydney   Taipei   Toronto

McGraw-Hill Higher Education

A Division of The McGraw-Hill Companies

MANAGEMENT

Published by McGraw-Hill/Irwin, a business unit of The McGraw-Hill Companies, Inc., 1221 Avenue of the Americas, New York, NY, 10020. Copyright © 2003 by The McGraw-Hill Companies, Inc. All rights reserved. No part of this publication may be reproduced or distributed in any form or by any means, or stored in a database or retrieval system, without the prior written consent of The McGraw-Hill Companies, Inc., including, but not limited to, in any network or other electronic storage or transmission, or broadcast for distance learning. Some ancillaries, including electronic and print components, may not be available to customers outside the United States.

This book is printed on acid-free paper.

domestic   1 2 3 4 5 6 7 8 9 0 VNH/VNH 0 9 8 7 6 5 4 3 2
international   1 2 3 4 5 6 7 8 9 0 VNH/VNH 0 9 8 7 6 5 4 3 2

ISBN 0-07-230181-3

Publisher: *John E. Biernat*
Sponsoring editor: *John Weimeister*
Developmental editors: *Sarah Reed and Burrston House, Ltd.*
Marketing manager: *Lisa Nicks*
Producer, media technology: *Mark Molsky*
Senior project manager: *Christine A. Vaughan*
Production and Quark makeup: *Stacey C. Sawyer*
Manager, new book production: *Melonie Salvati*
Lead designer: *Pam Verros*
Supplement producer: *Betty Hadala*
Senior digital content specialist: *Brian Nacik*
Cover photograph: *©Ed Gifford/Masterfile*
Typeface: *11/12 Times Roman*
Compositor: *GTS Graphics, Inc.*
Printer: *R. R. Donnelley*

Cover: The Golden Gate Bridge, which spans San Francisco Bay in California. Some great achievements of history were accomplished by individuals working quietly by themselves, such as scientific discoveries or works of art. But so much more has been achieved by people who were able to leverage their talents and abilities—and those of others—by being managers. None of the great architectural wonders of the world, such as this one, was built single-handedly by one person. Rather, all represent triumphs of management.

Library of Congress Cataloging-in-Publication Data

Kinicki, Angelo.
   Management: a practical introduction/Angelo Kinicki, Brian K. Williams.
      p.   cm.
   Includes index.
      ISBN 0-07-230181-3 (alk. paper)—ISBN 0-07-119701-X (international: alk. paper)
      1. Management. I. Williams, Brian K., II. Title.

   HD31 .K474 2003
   658—dc21   2002029517

INTERNATIONAL EDITION ISBN 0-07-119701-X

Copyright © 2003. Exclusive rights by The McGraw-Hill Companies, Inc. for manufacture and export. This book cannot be re-exported from the country to which it is sold by McGraw-Hill. The International Edition is not available in North America.

www.mhhe.com

brief contents

about the authors

ANGELO KINICKI is Professor and Dean's Council of 100 Distinguished Scholars at Arizona State University. He joined the faculty in 1982, the year he received his doctorate in business administration from Kent State University. His specialty is organizational behavior.

Angelo is recognized for both his research and teaching. He has published over 75 articles in a variety of leading academic and professional journals and has coauthored three textbooks. Angelo's success as a researcher also resulted in his selection to serve on the editorial review boards for the Academy of Management Journal, Journal of Vocational Behavior, and the Journal of Management. He also received the All-Time Best Reviewer Award from the Academy of Management Journal for the period of 1996–1999. Angelo's outstanding teaching performance resulted in his selection as the Graduate Teacher of the Year and the Undergraduate Teacher of the Year in the College of Business at Arizona State University. He was also acknowledged as the Instructor of the Year for Executive Education from the Center for Executive Development at Arizona State University.

One of Angelo's strengths is his ability to teach students at all levels within a university. He uses an interactive environment to enhance undergraduates' understanding about management and organizational behavior. He focuses MBAs on applying management concepts to solve complex problems, and PhD students learn the art and science of conducting scholarly research.

Angelo is also a busy consultant and speaker with companies around the world. His clients are many of the Fortune 500 companies as well as a variety of entrepreneurial firms. Much of his consulting work focuses on creating organizational change aimed at increasing organizational effectiveness and profitability. One of Angelo's most important and enjoyable pursuits is the practical application of his knowledge about management and organizational behavior.

Angelo and his wife Joyce have enjoyed living in the beautiful Arizona desert for 20 years, but are natives of Cleveland, Ohio. They enjoy traveling, golfing, and hiking.

BRIAN K. WILLIAMS has been Managing Editor for college textbook publisher Harper & Row/Canfield Press in San Francisco; Editor-in-Chief for nonfiction trade-book publisher J. P. Tarcher in Los Angeles; Publications & Communications Manager for the University of California, Systemwide Administration, in Berkeley; and an independent writer and book producer based in the San Francisco and Lake Tahoe areas. He has a B.A. in English and an M.A. in communication from Stanford University. He has coauthored 19 books, which include such best-selling college texts as *Using Information Technology* with Stacey C. Sawyer, recently published in its fifth edition by McGraw-Hill/Irwin, and several other computer books. He has also written a number of college success books and health books, and is presently working on social science texts. In his spare time, he and his wife, Stacey Sawyer, enjoy travel, music, cooking, and exploring the wilds of the American West.

dedication

To John and Barbara Di Giovanni, two of my "chosen" family members. I value our friendship and admire and respect what you two have accomplished. From starting and growing a business, to raising a wonderful family, you have done it all. You are also the best doggoned godparents that ever lived. Love, A.K.

To Stacey, for her 17 years of steadfast, patient support and for her collaboration and shared adventures; to Sylvia, for her many years of being the apple of her father's eye; to Kirk, for being the son who continues to delight me. Much love, B.K.W.

Kinicki/Williams: Your Guide through the Book's Teaching and Learning Tools

MANAGEMENT: A PRACTICAL INTRODUCTION is intended for use as a concepts book in a one-semester or one-quarter introductory course in management. It is, we hope, a book that will make a difference to our readers. By blending our two strengths—Angelo's scholarship, teaching, and management-consulting experience and Brian's writing and publishing background—we have tried to create a research-based yet highly readable, practical text with an innovative pedagogical approach and an exciting magazine-like layout that appeals to today's visually oriented students. This approach was used in order to accomplish our primary goal of writing a text that students would enjoy reading.

The text covers the principles that most management instructors have come to expect—planning, organizing, leadership, controlling—plus the issues that today's students need to be aware of and know in order to succeed: customer focus, globalism, diversity, ethics, information technology, entrepreneurship, work teams, the service economy, and small business. Beyond these, our book has **five key features that make it unique:**

- **Student approach to learning**
- **Emphasis on practicality**
- **Expandability**
- **Readability**
- **End-of-chapter resources**

A Student Approach to Learning— Reinforce Acquisition

This book takes a student approach to learning, breaking down the subject matter into constituent parts for easier comprehension. In a plan that has been tested since the book's inception, we have not only written the material but have actually determined and controlled how it should be laid out on the page. The first key feature of the book, therefore, is that it has a carefully thought-out strategy that integrates words, pictures, and layout into a program of learning reinforcement. Here's how it works:

"Major Questions" help student read with purpose: Each chapter begins with four to eight **Major Questions**— which correspond to the four to eight sections within the chapter. We worded the Major Questions so that they will be provocative and motivational, not dry and passive. That is, they are written to appeal to students' concern about "what's in it for me?" and to help them read with purpose— to focus their attention while reading the text so as to be able to gain practical knowledge.

These opening questions are followed by **The Manager's Toolbox** feature— which gives students a practical sample pertaining to the material they are about to read—and then by the **Forecast: What's Ahead in This Chapter,** which provides a brief overview of the chapter.

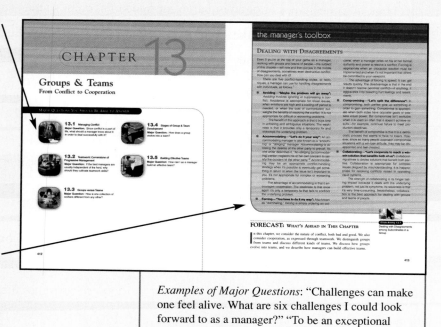

Examples of Major Questions: "Challenges can make one feel alive. What are six challenges I could look forward to as a manager?" "To be an exceptional manager, what roles must I play successfully?" "How do I work with others to make things happen?"

Chapter topics/concepts are arranged in spreads of two, four, or six pages and begin with a Major Question and The Big Picture: These spreads (that is, left and right facing pages) offer **easily manageable units of study** to enhance reader motivation and optimize learning.

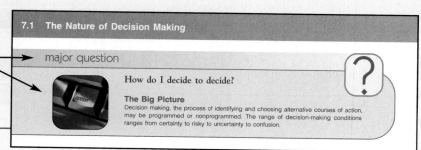

The Major Question is immediately followed by a brief description, The Big Picture, which gives students a preview or overview of the section they are about to read.

"Form Follows Function" Book Design to of Knowledge

Form follows function—subtopics discussed in multiple columns: The **magazine-like layout** within each section is designed both to appeal to today's visually oriented student and, in our student approach, to visually break the subject matter down into its constituent parts to help distinguish it for readers. Accordingly, instructors will observe that within the two-page spreads, text is laid out in multiple columns—that is, as one, two, three, or more columns—in a "form follows function" format appropriate to the subject matter.

Example of form follows function: In Chapter 8, we say organizations are of three types—for-profit, nonprofit, and mutual-benefit—and we describe them in three columns.

Important note: In using this unique pedagogical approach we have carefully avoided forcing substantive coverage into this format and have taken pains to avoid padding or undue compression of the text.

Illustrations are positioned next to discussion: Figures and tables are positioned precisely where they are referenced in the text discussion. Thus, readers will avoid the irritation of having to flip pages back and forth in order to study an important illustration that is closely described in the text.

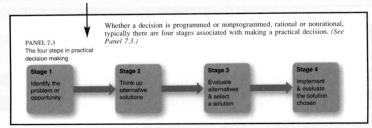

Examples are set off in boxes: It's important to clearly distinguish between concepts and examples, but in many books extended examples are often buried within the text. We have chosen to position 53 examples within boxes, so that these "mini-cases" or verbal illustrations of concepts stand alone in their own right and are highlighted for student readers. (See also page xiii.)

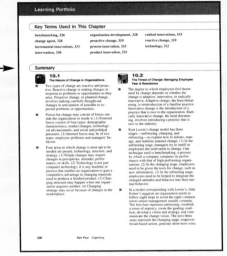

Summarizing topic coverage once again—end-of-chapter list of key terms and summary: To further encourage repetition for learning reinforcement, we give an extensive reprise of the subject matter at the end of the chapter, both in the list of **Key Terms Used in This Chapter** and in the **Summary.** Thus, the reader has several opportunities to focus on what's most important and to grasp the important ideas in the chapter: in the Forecast, in The Big Picture, and in the Key Terms and Summary.

Quizzes reinforce student learning: The student CD contains quizzes for each chapter. These quizzes provide readers with feedback regarding mastery of the subject matter. This completes the student approach to learning.

In sum: We're confident the student approach will induce readers to thoroughly question, preview, and review the material plus scrutinize its component parts in detail. In turn, this will help students acquire a far better knowledge of management principles than is usually the case with conventional textbooks.

Feature #2: Emphasis on Practicality

We would like this book to be a "keeper" for students. Thus, we not only cover fundamental concepts of management but also offer a great deal of **practical advice.** This advice, of the sort found in general business magazines and the business sections of newspapers, is expressed not only in the text but also in the following:

the manager's toolbox

HOW EXCEPTIONAL MANAGERS MAKE DECISIONS

"Failure is a great teacher."

That is one of the life lessons of David Dorman, who at age 45 is the CEO of a $10 billion joint venture between AT&T and British Telecommunications.[1] During his meteoric career, Dorman has had to make many decisions—the subject of this chapter—for which failure is always a possible outcome. But he has learned that that possibility can't stop one from making decisions. And you can probably always learn from the result.

■ **When should you make a decision and when should you delay?** Often you want to stay open-minded before making a decision. But sometimes that can just be a cover for procrastination. (After all, *not* making a decision is in itself a kind of decision.) How do you know when you're keeping an open mind or are procrastinating? Ralph L. Keeney, coauthor of *Smart Choices: A Practical Guide to*

tough choices. "On a daily and weekly basis we can be faced with making hundreds of decisions," says management consultant Odette Pollar. "Most of them are small, but the larger ones where more is at stake can be truly painful." Here are some ways she suggests making decision making easier, some of which resemble Keeney's:[3]

Decide in a timely fashion: "Rarely does waiting significantly improve the quality of the decision," says Pollar. In fact, delay can result in greater unpleasantness in loss of money, time, and peace of mind.

Don't agonize over minor decisions: Postponing decisions about small problems can mean that they simply turn into large ones later.

Separate outcome from process: Does a bad outcome mean you made a bad decision? Not necessarily. The main thing is to go through a well-

The Manager's Toolbox:

Many textbooks open a chapter with a case. Because many students simply skip over this, we've chosen instead to open with **The Manager's Toolbox,** offering readers practical advice pertaining to the chapter they are about to read. Besides providing practical nuts-and-bolts kinds of information they will find useful in their management careers, The Manager's Toolbox is designed to motivate readers for the forthcoming material.

Examples: "Five Rules for Staying Ahead in Your Career." "Being a Successful Road Warrior." "Dealing with Disagreements." "How Exceptional Managers Make Decisions."

Practical Action box:

The **Practical Action** box, which appears one or more times in each chapter, also offers practical advice that students will be able to use in the workplace.

Examples: "Managing Information Overload: Keep Your Eye on the Big Picture." "How to Streamline Meetings." "What Makes a Startup?" "The Challenge of Managing Virtual Teams: Reaching Across Time & Space."

practical action

Toward a More Open Workplace: Treating Employees Right

Some companies are "toxic organizations," Stanford University business professor Jeffrey Pfeffer's name for firms with high turnover and low productivity. Others take a contingency kind of approach, keeping employees through methods such as "open-book management," *Inc.* magazine editor John Case's term for a company's being completely open with employees about its financial status, projections, costs, expenses, and even salaries.[14]

"Companies that manage people right will outperform companies that don't by 30% to 40%.," says Pfeffer. "If you don't believe me, look at the numbers."[15] The author of *The Human Equation: Building Profits by Putting People First,* Pfeffer says that employees' loyalty to employers isn't dead but that toxic companies drive people away.[16] Companies such as Hewlett-Packard, Starbucks, and The Men's Warehouse have had lower turnover—and hence lower replacement and training costs—than their competitors for a reason: They have bent over backward to create workplaces that make people want to stay.

One way of challenging traditional military-style management and empowering employees and increasing earnings is through open-book management. This approach "means training employees in how the company is run," says one account. "It means asking for employee input and acting on it. It means rewarding employees with bonuses when the goals they create are met."[17] By learning the key numbers, employees are able to use their heads instead of just doing their jobs and going home. "Whether or not you have equity ownership, open-book management helps employees to feel, think, and act like owners," says Gary T. Brown, director of human resources for Springfield ReManufacturing Corp., a rebuilder of truck engines in Springfield, Mo.[18] "True open-book management means asking employees what the goals should be."

CompuWorks, a Pittsfield, Mass., computer systems-integration company, cultivates employee loyalty by piling on personal and team recognition, as in giving the Wizard of the Week award to the employee who goes beyond the call of duty. It also operates the Time Bank, into which every month 10 hours of free time is "deposited" for each employee to use as he or she wishes. Employees are trained how to read financial statements and how to chart billable hours and watch cash-flow levels. Regular bonuses are given based on company profits.[19]

Sometimes, despite the mantra that "the customer is always right," companies will even side with employees against clients. For example, The

> **Example of Making Correct Diagnosis:**
> **NASCAR Pit Crew Chief Wins Races**
>
> Former NASCAR race car driver Ray Evernham, now boss of a pit crew for racer Jeff Gordon, heads a crew of seven who change tires and add fuel during pit stops. Using two-way radio communication with the driver, Evernham makes all the decisions as the race proceeds, such as when to make pit stops, how many tires to change, and how much gas to pump. Thus, if a driver says the car is oversteering or understeering, Evernham must determine what kind of repairs must be made at pit stops, such as adjusting weight bolts on tires. By witnessing how other drivers make their pit stops, Evernham plans his, always trying to save a little time.
>
> One day in 1994, for example, Evernham's correct diagnosis shaved crucial seconds off Jeff Gordon's pit stop time, enabling him to overtake Rusty Wallace and win a major race. He watched as Wallace's crew spent 17 seconds changing all four tires. Thus, when Gordon pulled in, Evernham ordered his crew to change just two tires, which took only nine seconds. The eight seconds difference allowed Gordon to win the race by $2^{1}/_{2}$ seconds.[13]

Example boxes:

The theme of practicality also extends to the 53 **"Example of . . ."** boxes in the book, which use real-world situations to help explain text concepts.

Examples: "Example of Open & Closed Systems: Marketing to Generation Y." "Example of Taking Care of the Customer: L. L. Bean's No Questions Asked." "Example of Off-the-Job Training: Practical Courses through Distance Learning."

Web-based "Taking Something Practical Away from This Chapter" essay:

This website feature, which is presented at the end of each chapter, expands a topic introduced in the chapter to enable students to make use of it more thoroughly. The first instance of the "Taking Something Practical Away from This Chapter" essay appears in the text itself at the end of Chapter 1: "Getting Control of Your Time—Dealing with the Information Deluge in College & in Your Career." The essays for all other chapters appear on the Kinicki/Williams website.

Examples: "Encouraging Creativity." "Motivation through Goal Setting." "How to Reduce Stress." "Becoming an Effective Negotiator—Winning Tactics." "Online Job Hunting, Resumes, & Interviews."

> **Taking Something Practical Away from This Chapter**
>
> **Getting Control of Your Time: Dealing with the Information Deluge in College & in Your Career**
>
>
>
> *Except for this first box, "Taking Something Practical Away from This Chapter" appears on the website accompanying this book, with one such box for every chapter. Each box offers you the opportunity to acquire useful experience that directly applies to your career.*
>
> *One great problem most college students face—and that all managers face—is how to manage their time. This first box describes skills that will benefit you in college and later in your career.*
>
> "I've managed to ratchet my schedule down so I can have an outside life," says Doug Shoemaker, a San Francisco architect who tries to be home by 6:00 every night. "I'm a highly organized guy, I really focus on tasks, and I get them done."[38]
>
> Professionals and managers all have to deal with this central problem: how not to surrender their lives to their jobs. The place to start, however, is in college. If you can learn to manage time while you're still a student, you'll find it will pay off not only in higher grades and more free time but also in more efficient information-handling skills that will serve you well as a manager later on.

Feature #3: Expandability through "Click-Along" Connections to Kinicki/Williams Website

Recognizing that a book of this length cannot possibly cover material to suit every instructor's needs, we offer an expandability feature. Approximately 70 "Click-Along" icons appear in the text margins and direct students and instructors to visit the book's website to find additional text regarding that concept. This feature allows expanded topic coverage for those who want to explore subjects in more detail. Wherever the Click-Along icon appears, go to *www.mhhe.com/kw* to access additional text.

Click-Along 6.2

Two Other Strategy Formulations: Driving Force Analysis & Strategies for New Venture Firms

Harvard Business Scho
tant strategist working t
sulting firm McKinsey

Is this high praise (
on competitive strategy
instance, voted him the

Porter's reputation :
that five forces affect in
(2) bargaining power of
substitute products or s
industry firms.[35] An or
ines these five competi
mulate effective strateg

Imaginative Writing for Readability

Research shows that textbooks written in an imaginative, people-oriented style significantly improve students' ability to retain information.

In our book, we have employed a number of journalistic devices—such as the short biographical sketch, the colorful fact, the apt direct quote—to make the material as interesting and memorable as possible.

Having together written over two dozen textbooks and taught thousands of undergraduate students, we are vitally concerned with reinforcing students in acquiring knowledge and developing critical thinking. Accordingly, we offer several other learning aids:

How Organizations Respond to Uncertainty

How do you personally respond to uncertainty? Do you react slowly? conservatively? proactively? Do you watch to see what others do? Organizations in similar ways.

   Scholars **Raymond E. Miles** and **Charles C. Snow** suggest that organizations adapt one of *four positions when responding to uncertainty in their environment.* They become *defenders, prospectors, analyzers, or reactors.*[10]

Defenders—"Let's Stick with What We Do Best, Avoid Other Involvements"   Whenever you hear an organization's leader say that "We're sticking with the basics" or "We're getting back to our core business," that's the hallmark of a defender organization. *Defenders* **are expert at producing and selling narrowly defined products or services.** Often they are old-line successful enterprises—such as Harley-Davidson motorcycles or Brooks Brothers clothiers—with a narrow focus. They do not tend to seek opportunities outside their present markets. They devote most of their attention to making refinements in their existing operations.

Prospectors—"Let's Create Our Own Opportunities, Not Wait for Them to Happen"   A company described as "aggressive" is often a prospector organization. *Prospectors* **focus on developing new products or services and in seeking out new markets, rather than waiting for things to happen.** Like 19th-century gold miners, these companies are "prospecting" for new ways of doing things. The continual product and market innovation has a price: Such companies may suffer a loss of efficiency. Nevertheless, their focus on change can put fear in the hearts of competitors.

- **Key terms and definitions in boldface: Each key term AND its definition is printed in boldface** within the text, in order to help readers avoid any confusion about which terms are important and what they actually mean. *The glossary also contains American slang expressions used in the text,* as an aid to students from other countries.

- *Important people names in boldface:* The names of important management theorists and scholars also appear in boldface, so that readers will know they should pay attention to these names for testing purposes.

- *Material in "bite-size" portions:* Major ideas are presented in bite-size form, with generous use of advance organizers, bulleted lists, and new paragraphing when a new idea is introduced.

- *Plenty of examples:* Extended examples are displayed in the "Example of . . ." boxes. There are also many short examples presented within the body of the text.

End-of-Chapter Resources

Besides Key Terms Used in This Chapter and the Summary, end-of-chapter material includes the following:

Management in Action presents a recent case study or situation along with discussion questions.

Management in Action

Boeing Relies on a Variety of Management Theories to Cut Costs & Increase Profits[31]

Excerpted from J. Lynn Lunsford, "Lean Times: With Airbus on Its Tail, Boeing Is Rethinking How It Builds Planes," The Wall Street Journal, October 5, 2001, pp. A1, A16.

Not far from the steady blatt-blatt of the rivet guns on its 757 assembly line just outside Seattle sits what Boeing Co. calls its moonshine shop. The people here distill work-saving ideas into contraptions that make it easier to build jets.

   Consider the hay loader next to an almost-completed 757. Normally, this cross between a ladder and a metal-spiked conveyor belt would be dumping bales of hay onto waiting trucks. But to veteran mechanic Robert Harms, the hay loader is the perfect way to get bulky passenger seats from the factory floor up 13 feet to the door of the plane without having to use an overhead crane. "It might look funny, but when you see it work, you wonder why we didn't do it this way all along," he says.

   Moonshine shops—so named because they work outside traditional channels and use whatever materials are available—are the essence of Boeing

digit profit margins despite the slowing world economy and sharp decline in aircraft orders from the major airlines. . . . Boeing had been gradually adopting "lean" manufacturing techniques since the early 1990s—a decade after the U.S. auto industry began emulating the Japanese approach. The basic philosophy: Everything from the design of a component to the machine used to build it is examined with the goal of making it as easy as possible for workers to boost output using less space and fewer movements.

   Since late 1998, when the company began applying lean activities on its newest model, the 777, the time it takes to assemble the major components into a finished aircraft has dropped to 37 days from 71. And just since April, the company has trimmed two days out of what was a 20-day final assembly of its best-selling plane, the 737. . . . Seat-

Take It to the Net

During the 20th century the concept of the *learning organization* evolved. This concept posits that organizations and their members must be committed to continuous learning to remain competitive and viable in our turbulent and changing globalized economy.

   One approach to building a learning organization is "Open Book Management." This approach

includes three principles, all of which must be followed if it is to work. Outlined by John Case in his *Open Book Experience* (Perseus Books, 1998, pp. 2–3), they are (1) create a *transparent* company, a company in which everyone, not just those at the top, sees and understands the real numbers; (2) create a system of *joint accountability*, a system that holds everybody responsible for his or her part in

Take It to the Net provides online assignments requiring students to go online to research applicable concepts and topics discussed in the chapter.

Group Exercise

Who Are the Most Admired Companies & Why

Objectives

1. To assess your group's awareness of the most admired companies in the United States (as of 2001).

2. To discover the different perceptions of these companies and their management practices.

3. To understand how companies achieve the reputation they have earned.

Introduction

For decades *Fortune* magazine has asked top managers who they think are the most-admired and best-managed companies in the United States. Over the years we have moved from a time when Frederick Taylor and Henry Ford tied productivity to profit to the current understanding of the effect of the other "bottom lines" that must be considered to assess how well a company is managed (for example, companies' effect on the environment). Only five companies have held the number 1 spot on this *Fortune* list since 1983. They are IBM (5 times), Merck (15 times), Rubbermaid (11 times), Coca-Cola (13

times), and General Electri
only one of these was in th

Instructions

Eight key attributes of repu
the companies (there are 50

  innovation

  financial soundness

  employee talent

  use of corporate assets

  long-term investment va

  social responsibility

  quality of management

  quality of products/servi

Following is a list, in rand
most-admired companies for
your group is to guess thes
based on the attributes liste
the highest ranking and nu
ranking.) Group members
their rankings and come to

This exercise was adapted from http://www.leadersdirect.com/howareyou/html.

Video Case

The Exceptional Entrepreneur

Four entrepreneurs in three companies share their insights. Syl Tang of Hipguide.com, Dale Gray of Communications Services, and Debbie and Les Busfield of Strongfield-Trimco explain what it takes to be a successful entrepreneur. Common themes emerge from their experiences. All convey a passion and excitement at the prospect of going to work each day. They discuss the personality characteristics of an entrepreneur, the highs and lows of owning a business, and the payoffs of success. All relish "being your own boss" but also recognize that they still answer to others. At the business level, these owners discuss the role of a business plan, the need to rely on the expertise of others, and the importance of hiring the right people.

Discussion Questions:

1. Describe the personality characteristics entrepreneurs.

2. What's the biggest challenge faced by ea trepreneur? What is their biggest payoff port your responses with evidence from case.

3. Why is hiring the right people so import these business owners?

4. What makes these entrepreneurs success when so many others fail?

5. What are the common beliefs shared by the entrepreneurs?

Ethical Dilemma

Recycling Automobile Air Bags Is a Common Practice

From Kimberly Weisul, "Car Talk: One Time Not to Recycle," Business Week, August 6, 20

BusinessWeek One unreported casualty of [July 2001] floods in Houston: 95,000 cars. Many of their air bags were water-damaged and should be junked. But because the damage isn't visible, many of the bags are ending up in repair shops as secondhand parts. Add the tens of thousands of air bags stolen each year, and the market for air bags is hot. There's plenty of incentive: A new air bag can cost up to $1,500; a secondhand one might sell for $400.

There's nothing illegal about air bags as secondhand parts. But there are also no regulations requiring repair shops to test them for safety or determine where they came from, and no requirement that drivers replace them after accidents.

That's causing growing safety concerns. Air bags with flood damage are dangerous because of residual moisture. They take up to a third of a second longer to inflate than new ones. By that time, "you've had your head buried in the steering wheel," says Peter Byrne, president of Airbag Testing Technology, which inspects recycled air bags.

Then there are the body shops and car owners who knowingly circumvent air-bag safety. Owners of

banged-up cars may tell body shop
ing the air bags, since they can tack
repair bill for even a fender-bend
knows there's no air bag in there,"
baker, senior vice-president at the
Data Institute. "The next buyer do
require used cars to come equipped

The National Highway Traffic
tration, alert to safety concerns, is
issue and is expected to report
doubt, that will be too late for s
drivers.

Solving the Dilemma

What would you do if you were a
National Highway Traffic Safety A

1. Leave the laws as they are.

2. Create regulations requiring that
fessionals test all recycled air ba

3. Do not allow secondhand air ba

4. Invent other options. Discuss.

Self-Assessment

What Is Your Level of Self-Esteem?

Objectives

1. To get to know yourself a bit better.

2. To help you assess your self-esteem.

Introduction: Self-esteem, confidence, self-worth, and self-belief are all important aspects of being a manager in any organizational structure. However, the need for strong self-esteem is especially vital today because organizations demand that a manager manage people not as appendages of machines (as in Scientific Management) but as individuals who possess skills, knowledge, and self-will. Managers used to operate from a very strong position of centralized power and authority. However, in our modern organizational settings power is shared, and knowledge is to some extent "where you find it." To manage effectively in this situation, mangers need strong self-esteem.

Instructions: To assess your self-esteem, answer the following questions. For each item, indicate the extent to which you agree or disagree by using the following scale. Remember, there are no right or wrong answers.

    1 = strongly disagree

    2 = disagree

    3 = neither agree nor disagree

    4 = agree

    5 = strongly agree

Questions

1. I generally feel as competent as my peers.	1	2	3	4	5
2. I usually feel I can achieve whatever I want.	1	2	3	4	5
3. Whatever happens to me is mostly in my control.	1	2	3	4	5
4. I rarely worry about how things will work out.	1	2	4	4	5
5. I am confident that I can deal with most situations.	1	2	3	4	5

How Can the Internet Help Me Keep My Course Up to Date?

Keeping your course current can be a job in itself, and now McGraw-Hill does that job for you. PowerWeb extends the learning experience beyond the core textbook by offering all of the latest news and developments pertinent to your course, brought to you via the Internet without all the clutter and dead links of a typical online search.

PowerWeb is a robust website that offers these *course-specific* features:

- Current articles related to management and organizations
- Daily and weekly updates with assessment tools
- Informative and timely world news qualified by a content expert and professor
- Refereed Web links
- Online handbook to researching, evaluating, and citing online sources

In addition, PowerWeb provides a trove of helpful learning aids, including self-grading quizzes, interactive glossaries, and exercises. Students may also access study tips, conduct online research, and learn about different career paths.

Visit the **PowerWeb** site at **http://www.dushkin.com/powerweb** and see firsthand what **PowerWeb** can mean to your course.

How Can I Easily Create an Online Course?

For the instructor needing to educate students online, we offer **Management** content for complete online courses. To make this possible, we have joined forces with the most popular delivery platforms currently available. These platforms are designed for instructors who want complete control over course content and how it is presented to students. You can customize the **Management** Online Learning Center content and author your own course materials. It's entirely up to you.

Products like **WebCT** and **Blackboard** expand the reach of your course. Online discussion and message boards will now complement your office hours. Thanks to a sophisticated tracking system, you will know which students need more attention—even if they don't ask for help. That's because online testing scores are recorded and automatically placed in your grade book, and if a student is struggling with coursework, a special alert message lets you know.

Remember, **Management's** content is flexible enough to use with any platform currently available. If your department or school is already using a platform, we can help.

PageOut

McGraw-Hill's Course Management System

PageOut is the easiest way to create a website for your management course.

There's no need for HTML coding, graphic design, or a thick how-to book. Just fill in a series of boxes with simple English and click on one of our professional designs. In no time, your course is online with a website that contains your syllabus!

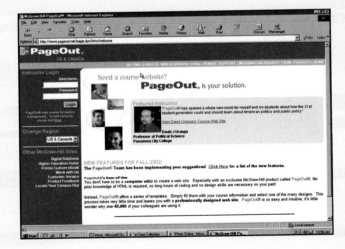

If you need assistance in preparing your website, we can help. Our team of product specialists is ready to take your course materials and build a custom website to your specifications. You simply need to contact a McGraw-Hill/Irwin PageOut specialist to start the process. Best of all, PageOut is free when you adopt **Management!** To learn more, please visit **http://www.pageout.net**.

Supplements for Students and Instructors

Instructor's Manual

The Instructor's Manual is easy to use for new instructors. The Instructor's Manual is unique in its integration with both the text and package. Each chapter opens with a repeat of the major questions that begin each chapter of the text. Following that is a brief overview of the chapter. To make this system even easier to use, the detailed lecture outline contains marginal notes recommending where to include examples, Power-Point slides, figures, and Practical Action boxes.

Key terms are then presented along with their definition. An additional critical thinking exercise is included in each chapter, requiring students to analyze and apply chapter concepts, a great way to get students involved in the learning process. Lecture enhancers—short article summaries that provide additional examples for classroom use—are provided in each chapter to help you implement the latest business and social issues in your course. Suggested answers are also given for the Management in Action case study discussion questions, and Video Case notes are provided for each video in the six parts of the text. This new Instructor's Manual has been constructed by Gayle Ross, a respected expert in preparing such guides.

Test Bank

Each chapter of the print test bank includes multiple choice, true/false, and essay questions. Approximately 80–100 questions are included in each chapter. Each question also consists of a rationale and page number for the correct answer, as well as an indication of whether the question tests knowledge, understanding, or application. Eileen Hogan of Kutztown University authored the 1st edition Test Bank.

Instructor's Resource CD-ROM

This multimedia CD-ROM allows instructors to create dynamic classroom presentations by incorporating PowerPoint, videos, and every available print supplement.

Videos

Six new videos on management issues accompany this edition. The accompanying Video Cases are included in the text at the end of each part. Video notes are also included in the Instructor's Manual.

PowerPoint

This presentation program features two presentations for each chapter. One presentation includes a more typical lecture outline consisting of main concepts from the chapter, key terms, figures, and Ethical Dilemmas and Management in Action cases. The supplemental presentation includes such "extras" to include in your presentation as figures that expand upon the Click-Alongs in the text and slides that illustrate and apply the chapter concepts. The PowerPoint presentation was created by Mandi Goretcki and Angelo Kinicki.

Online Learning Center

www.mhhe.com/kw
This text-specific website follows the text chapter by chapter and also includes professional resources that apply to the course as a whole. Go online to access a Career Corner, the Click-Along materials highlighted in the book, self-grading quizzes to review material in each chapter, an instructors' bulletin board to share ideas, and additional exercises. The OLC can be delivered in multiple ways—professors and students can access it directly through the textbook website, through PageOut, or within a course management system (WebCT, Blackboard).

Student CD-ROM

This Student Resource CD-ROM contains chapter quizzes to help students study, crossword puzzles to help them review key terms, video clips that cover important text topics, a Career Corner, a learning style assessment, and links to Build Your Management Skills and Management Online—discussed below.

Build Your Management Skills

With this interactive resource (accessible through the Student CD included with each new book) students can access self-assessments on topics such as active listening, corporate culture preferences scale, identify their preferred organizational structure, and their conflict-handling style. Also included in the Test Your Knowledge section is the ability to participate in practice or test mode, depending on the students' level of comfort with the subject matter. Topics here include communicating, international management, leadership, motivation, and operations management.

Management Online

Applying the benefits of Flash Technology, students can choose exercises from a list of topics to run interactivities and self-assessments. Topics include planning and decision making, organizing, and leading. This resource can only help them evaluate and improve their skills in the principles of management course.

PowerWeb

Harness the assets of the Web to keep your course current with PowerWeb! This online resource provides high-quality, peer-reviewed content including up-to-date articles from leading periodicals and journals, current news, weekly updates with assessment, interactive exercises, Web research guide, study tips, and much more! Visit *www.dushkin.com/powerweb* or access it through the OLC at *www.mhhe.com/kw*. Your passcode is included with each new book.

Acknowledgments

We could not have completed this product without the help of others. This book was signed by Karen Mellon, to whom we are very grateful. Sincere thanks and gratitude go to our editor, John Weimeister, and his top-rate team at McGraw-Hill/Irwin. Key contributors include Sarah Reed, developmental editor; Lisa Nicks, marketing manager; Christine Vaughan, senior project manager; Pam Verros, senior designer; and Mark Molsky, media producer. We also benefited from the extensive developmental effort of the talented Glenn Turner and his colleagues at Burrston House. His work resulted in the most extensively developed principles of management text. We would also like to thank Stacey Sawyer for her tireless work in laying out this complicated text, Amanda Goretcki for her wonderful work on the PowerPoint presentation and end-of-chapter materials, Gayle Ross for her excellent work on the Instructor's Manual, Eileen Hogan of Kutztown University for authoring the Test Bank, Bob Boothe of University of Southern Mississippi for authoring the quiz questions for the website and Student CD, Anne Cowden of Sacramento State University for her efforts in helping to develop end-of-chapter materials, and Kim Wade for authoring the Video Cases for the text.

Warmest thanks and appreciation go to the individuals who provided valuable input during the developmental stages of this product and to the following colleagues who served as manuscript reviewers:

G. Stoney Alder, Western Illinois University

Phyllis C. Alderdice, Jefferson Community College

Maria Aria, Camden County College

Jim Bell, Southwest Texas State University

Danielle Beu, Louisiana Tech University

Robert S. Boothe, University of Southern Mississippi

Roger Brown, Western Illinois University

Pamela Carstens, Coe College

Rod Christian, Mesa Community College

Mike Cicero, Highline Community College

Jack Cichy, Davenport University

Anthony Cioffi, Lorain County Community College

Deborah Clark, Santa Fe Community College

Sharon Clinebell, University of Northern Colorado

Kathleen DeNisco, Erie Community College

David Dore, San Francisco City College

Steven Dunphy, University of Akron

Subhash Durlabhji, Northwestern State University

Jack Dustman, Northern Arizona University

Joyce Guillory, Austin Community College

Charles T. Harrington, Pasadena City College

Santhi Harvey, Central State University

Jack Heinsius, Modesto Junior College

Edward Johnson, University of North Florida

Marcella Kelly, Santa Monica College

Rebecca Legleiter, Tulsa Community College

Mary Lou Lockerby, College of DuPage

Paul Londrigan, *Charles S. Mott Community College*
Tom McFarland, *Mount San Antonio College*
Christine Miller, *Tennessee Tech University*
Rob Moorman, *Creighton University*
Robert Myers, *University of Louisville*
Francine Newth, *Providence College*
Jack Partlow, *Northern Virginia Community College*
Don A. Paxton, *Pasadena City College*
John Paxton, *Wayne State College*
Sheila Petcavage, *Cuyahoga Community College*
Antoinette S. Phillips, *Southeastern Louisiana University*
Barbara Rosenthall, *Miami Dade Community College/Wolfson Campus*
Gary Ross, *Barat College of DePaul University*
Cindy Ruszkowski, *Illinois State University*
Diane R. Scott, *Wichita State University*
Marianne Sebok, *Community College of Southern Nevada*
Gerald F. Smith, *University of Northern Iowa*
Mark Smith, *University of Southwest Louisiana*
Jeff Stauffer, *Ventura College*
Virginia Anne Taylor, *William Patterson University*
Jerry Thomas, *Arapahoe Community College*
Robert Trumble, *Virginia Commonwealth University*
Anthony Uremovic, *Joliet Junior College*
Barry Van Hook, *Arizona State University*
Susan Verhulst, *Des Moines Area Community College*
Bruce C. Walker, *University of Louisiana at Monroe*
Allen Weimer, *University of Tampa*
John Whitelock, *Community College of Baltimore/Catonsville Campus*

The following professors also participated in an early focus group that helped drive the development of this text. We appreciate their suggestions and participation immensely:

Rusty Brooks, *Houston Baptist University*
Kerry Carson, *University of Southwestern Louisiana*
Sam Dumbar, *Delgado Community College*
Subhash Durlabhji, *Northwestern State University*
Robert Mullins, *Delgado Community College*
Carl Phillips, *Southeastern Louisiana University*
Allayne Pizzolatto, *Nicholls State University*
Ellen White, *University of New Orleans*

We would also like to thank the following students for participating in a very important focus group to gather feedback from the student reader's point of view:

Marcy Baasch, *Triton College*
Diana Broeckel, *Triton College*
Lurene Cornejo, *Moraine Valley Community College*
Dave Fell, *Elgin Community College*
Lydia Hendrix, *Moraine Valley Community College*
Kristine Kurpiewski, *Oakton Community College*
Michelle Monaco, *Moraine Valley Community College*
Shannon Ramey, *Elgin Community College*
Arpita Sikand, *Oakton Community College*

Finally, we would like to thank our wives, Joyce and Stacey, for being understanding, patient, and encouraging throughout the process of writing this first edition. Your love and support helped us endure the trials and tribulations of completing this text.

We hope you enjoy reading and applying the book. Best wishes for success in your career.

—Angelo Kinicki
—Brian K. Williams

contents

part two

The Environment of Management

part three Planning

CHAPTER 5
Planning:
The Foundation of Successful Management 144

CHAPTER 6
Strategic Management:
How Star Managers Realize a Grand Design 176

CHAPTER 7
Individual & Group Decision Making: How Managers Make Things Happen 208

Organizing (part four

CHAPTER 8
Organizational Culture, Structure, & Design: Building Blocks of the Organization 244

CHAPTER 14
Power, Influence, & Leadership: From Becoming a Manager to Becoming a Leader   446

CHAPTER 15
Interpersonal & Organizational Communication   482

part six) Control

CHAPTER 16
Control Techniques for Enhancing Organizational Effectiveness   520

A ONE-MINUTE GUIDE TO SUCCESS IN THIS CLASS

Got one minute to read this section? It could mean the difference between getting an A instead of a B. Or a B instead of a C.

Four Rules for Success   There are four rules that will help you be successful in this (or any other) course.

■ **Rule 1:** Attend every class. No cutting allowed.

■ **Rule 2:** Don't postpone studying, then cram the night before a test.

■ **Rule 3:** Read or review lectures and readings more than once.

■ **Rule 4:** Learn how to use this book.

How to Use This Book Most Effectively   When reading this book, follow the steps below:

■ Get an overview of the chapter by reading over the first page, which contains the section headings and Major Questions.

■ Read "Forecast: What's Ahead in This Chapter."

■ Look at the Major Question at the beginning of each section before you read it.

■ Read the "The Big Picture," which summarizes the section.

■ Read the section itself (which is only 2–6 pages), *trying silently to answer the Major Question.* This is important!

■ After reading all sections, use the Key Terms and Summary at the end of the chapter to see how well you understand the major concepts. Reread any material you're unsure about.

If you follow these steps consistently, you'll probably absorb the material well enough that you won't have to cram before an exam; you'll need only to lightly review it before the test.

Using the Book's "Click-Along" Feature: Multitasking That Reinforces Learning
Many students like to do so-called multitasking while studying. That is, while reading a textbook they will also listen to music, watch TV, talk on the phone, surf the Web, or do all simultaneously. Doing several tasks at once may help alleviate boredom. But because the brain has limits, the distraction in attention usually means less learning takes place.

　　One form of multitasking, however, may reinforce learning. This follows the principle that *the more widely you can apply, analyze, synthesize, and evaluate the facts to which you've been exposed, the better you're apt to remember them.* Thus, when you see the Click-Along icon (shown at right) in the margin of this book, you are invited to use your computer mouse to go online to the book's website (*www.mhhe.com/kw*) and read additional material that will update, illustrate, elaborate, elucidate, and otherwise expand on material in the text.

Click-Along 1.1

Understanding Your Personal Multitasking: How Many Tasks Do You Juggle at Once While You're Studying?

The Exceptional Manager
What You Do, How You Do It

TO BE A STAR MANAGER, YOU NEED A PERSONAL COACH

Some day maybe you can afford to have a *personal career coach*—the kind long used by sports and entertainment figures and now adopted in the upper ranks of business.[1] These individuals "combine executive coaching and career consulting with marketing and negotiations," says one account. "They plot career strategy, help build networks of business contacts, . . . and shape their clients' images."[2]

Because planning a career is increasingly bewildering in today's work world, in the following pages we are going to try to act much like your personal career coach. In that spirit, it is our desire *to make this book as practical as possible for you.* For instance, the **Manager's Toolbox,** like this one, which appears at the beginning of every chapter, offers practical advice appropriate to the subject matter you are about to explore.

Five Rules for Staying Ahead in Your Career

The purpose of this book is to help you become a successful manager—indeed, a *star manager*—an *exceptional manager,* as this chapter's title has it, whose performance is far superior to that of other managers. The first thing star managers learn is how to stay ahead in their careers.

The following strategies for staying ahead in the workplace of tomorrow are adapted from rules offered by professional career counselor Richard L. Knowdell, president of Career Research and Testing in San Jose, Calif.[3]

- ■ **Take charge of your career, and avoid misconceptions:** Because you, not others, are in charge of your career, and it's an ongoing process, you should develop a career plan and base your choices on that plan. When considering a new job or industry, find out how that world *really* works, not what it's reputed to be. When considering a company you might want to work for, find out its corporate "style" or culture by talking to its employees.

- ■ **Develop new capacities:** "Being good at several things will be more advantageous in the long run than being excellent at one narrow specialty," says Knowdell. "A complex world will not only demand *specialized knowledge* but also *general and flexible skills.*"

- ■ **Anticipate and adapt to, even embrace, changes:** Learn to analyze, anticipate, and adapt to new circumstances in the world and in your own life. For instance, as technology changes the rules, *embrace* the new rules.

- ■ **Keep learning:** "You can take a one- or two-day course in a new subject," says Knowdell, "just to get an idea of whether you want to use those specific skills and to see if you would be good at it. Then, if there is a match, you could seek out an extended course."

- ■ **Develop your people and communications skills:** No matter how much communication technology takes over the workplace, there will always be a strong need for effectiveness in interpersonal relationships. In particular, learn to listen well.

FORECAST: WHAT'S AHEAD IN THIS CHAPTER

We describe the rewards, benefits, and privileges managers might expect. We also describe the six challenges to managers in today's world—not only staying ahead of rivals but also managing for diversity, globalization, information technology, ethical standards, and personal happiness and life goals. You'll be introduced to the four principal functions of management—planning, organizing, leading, and controlling—and levels and areas of management. We describe the three types of roles (interpersonal, informational, and decisional) and three skills (technical, conceptual, and human) required of a manager.

What are the rewards of being an exceptional manager—of being a star in my workplace?

The Big Picture

Management is defined as the pursuit of organizational goals efficiently and effectively. Organizations, or people who work together to achieve a specific purpose, value managers because of the multiplier effect: Good managers have an influence on the organization far beyond the results that can be achieved by one person acting alone. Managers are well paid, with the CEOs and presidents of even small and midsize businesses earning good salaries and many benefits.

Debby Krenek, when she was Editor in Chief of the *New York Daily News*, was the first woman in that management post in the newspaper's nearly eight decades of history. What brought about her rise, at age 43, to the top of the macho culture of daily journalism?

Here's one trait she demonstrated: While escorting a visitor through the cavernous newsroom in which she started 10 years before and later came to command, she stopped and pointed to a jumble of electrical cords behind a reporter's desk. "See this?" she said. "I'm the only person in the room who can tell you where all the electrical outlets are."

This knowledge might seem trivial, but in the newspaper business nothing must be allowed to prevent the presses from rolling on time. If a reporter's computer crashes shortly before deadline, for instance, it's vital that a new working terminal be found right away. Thus, Krenek made it a point to memorize the precise locations of all plugs and wires. "If everybody dropped dead," she said, "I could sit down and put the paper out."[4]

Attention to detail is not always a necessary attribute for success, but being prepared for surprises and change is. Continuing change—in the world and in the workplace—is a major theme of this book.

Another necessary attribute: people skills. Besides showing a mastery of the technical aspects of her profession, from reporting to presses to circulation, Krenek also had "emerged as a soft voice of reason and efficiency amid huge dysfunction," according to a magazine profile about her. "In an often anxious newsroom—rocked by a nasty . . . strike, two ownership changes, and a cavalcade of editors . . . —she's gently coaxed headline writers to move faster and nursed endangered projects, plus soothed tempers riled by her big-footed boss."[5]

If you had to put out this newspaper day after day, what would you consider a necessary component of managerial success? Attention to detail? Or only if that helps you achieve your important goals?

The Art of Management Defined

Is being an exceptional manager—a star manager—a gift, like a musician having perfect pitch? Not exactly. But in good part it may be an art. Fortunately, it is one that is teachable.

Management, said one pioneer of management ideas, is "the art of getting things done through people."[6]

Getting things done. Through people. Thus, managers are task oriented, achievement oriented, and people oriented. And they operate within an *organization*—**a group of people who work together to achieve some specific purpose.**

More formally, *management* **is defined as (1) the pursuit of organizational goals efficiently and effectively by (2) integrating the work of people through (3) planning, organizing, leading, and controlling the organization's resources.**

Note the words *efficiently* and *effectively,* which basically mean "doing things right."

■ *Efficiency—the means:* Efficiency is the means of attaining the organization's goals. **To be *efficient* means to use resources—people, money, raw materials, and the like—wisely and cost-effectively.**

■ *Effectiveness—the ends:* Effectiveness is the organization's ends, the goals. **To be *effective* means to achieve results, to make the right decisions and successfully carry them out so that they achieve the organization's goals.**

Good managers are concerned with trying to achieve both qualities. Often, however, organizations will erroneously strive for efficiency without being effective.

Example of Efficiency versus Effectiveness: Won't Someone Answer the Phone—*Please?*

We're all now accustomed to having our calls to companies answered not by people but by a recorded "telephone menu" of options. Certainly this arrangement is *efficient* for the companies, since they no longer need as many telephone receptionists. But it's not *effective* if it leaves us, the customers, fuming and not inclined to continue doing business.

This happened to Brian McConnell, but unlike a lot of us, he was able to do something about it. McConnell, of Roanoke, Va., found that he couldn't get past a bank's automated telephone system to talk to a real person. This was not the fault of the phone technology so much as of the bank's managers.

McConnell, president of a software firm, thereupon wrote a computer program that automatically phoned eight different numbers at the bank. People picking up the phone heard the recording, "This is an automated customer complaint. To hear a live complaint, press . . ."[7]

How often do you encounter organizations using their telephone systems more efficiently then effectively?

Why Organizations Value Managers: The Multiplier Effect

Good managers create value. Bad managers deplete it. The reason is that in being a manager you have a *multiplier effect:* Your influence on the organization is multiplied far beyond the results that can be achieved by just one person acting alone.

Of course, some great achievements of history, such as scientific discoveries or works of art, were accomplished by individuals working quietly by themselves. But so much more has been achieved by people who were able to leverage their talents and abilities by being managers. For instance, of the top 10 great architectural wonders of the world named by the American Institute of Architects, none was built single-handedly by one person. All were triumphs of management, although some reflected the vision of an individual. (The wonders are the Great Wall of China, the Great Pyramid, Machu Picchu, the Acropolis, the Coliseum, the Taj Mahal, the Eiffel Tower, the Brooklyn Bridge, the Empire State Building, and Frank Lloyd Wright's Falling Water house in Pennsylvania.)

Thus, while a solo operator such as a salesperson might accomplish many things and incidentally make a very good living, his or her boss could accomplish a great deal more—and could well earn two to seven times the income. And the manager will undoubtedly have a lot more influence.

Mouse master. The pay package for Michael Eisner, CEO of Walt Disney Co., was $738 million over five years, which put him in the Forbes top 10 executive compensation list for 2000. Eisner has been criticized for receiving bonuses out of all proportion to performance, but he received none for 2001, when Disney stock fell more than 50%. Still, his base salary was $1 million, up from $813,000.

Financial Rewards of Being a Star Manager

How well compensated are managers? According to the U.S. Bureau of Labor Statistics, the median weekly wage in 2001 for American workers of all sorts was $597—roughly $31,000 a year. (Education pays: According to the Census Bureau, holders of high-school diplomas average $22,895 a year, holders of bachelor's degrees $40,478 a year.)

Business magazines frequently report on the astronomical earnings of top chief executive officers (CEOs), such as Walt Disney Co. CEO Michael Eisner's millions of dollars a year, but this kind of compensation isn't common. The average annual salary and bonus for corporate CEOs and presidents of small and midsize businesses—that is, public and private firms with annual revenue up to $200 million, which make up the majority of companies—is $246,000 and $324,000, depending on the region.[8] *(See Panel 1.1.)*

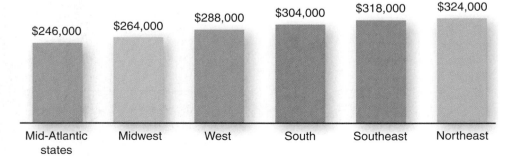

PANEL 1.1
Executive pay. Average yearly income for CEOs and presidents of small and midsize firms, by region

Mid-Atlantic states	Midwest	West	South	Southeast	Northeast
$246,000	$264,000	$288,000	$304,000	$318,000	$324,000

Managers farther down in the organization usually don't make this much, of course; nevertheless, they do fairly well compared to most workers. At the lower rungs, managers may make between $25,000 and $50,000 a year, in the middle levels, between $35,000 and $110,000.

There are also all kinds of fringe benefits and status rewards that go with being a manager, ranging from health insurance to stock options to large offices. And the higher you ascend in the management hierarchy, the more privileges may come your way: personal parking space, better furniture, lunch in the executive dining room, on up to—for those on the top rung of big companies—company car and driver, corporate jet, and even executive sabbaticals (months of paid time off to pursue alternative projects).

Psychological Rewards of Being a Manager

The rewards of being a manager go beyond money and status. Every successful goal accomplished provides you not only with personal satisfaction but also the satisfaction of all those employees you directed who helped you accomplish it.

Every promotion up the hierarchy of an organization stretches your abilities, challenges your talents and skills, and magnifies the range of your accomplishments. Every product or service you provide—the personal Hoover Dam or Empire State Building you build, as it were—becomes a monument to your accomplishments.

Points out Odette Pollar, who owns Time Management Systems, a productivity-improvement firm in Oakland, Calif.:[9]

> *Managers are able to view the business in a broader context, to plan and grow personally. Managers can play more of a leadership role than ever before. This is an opportunity to counsel, motivate, advise, guide, empower, and influence large groups of people.*
>
> *These important skills can be used in business as well as in personal and volunteer activities. If you truly like people and enjoy mentoring and helping others to grow and thrive, management is a great job.*

One of the rewards of being a manager is providing counseling, advice, and empowerment to employees.

Challenges can make one feel alive. What are six challenges I could look forward to as a manager?

The Big Picture

Six challenges face any manager: You need to manage for competitive advantage—to stay ahead of rivals. You need to manage for diversity in race, ethnicity, gender, and so on, because the future won't resemble the past. You need to manage for the effects of globalization and of information technology. You always need to manage to maintain for ethical standards. Finally, you need to manage for the achievement of your own happiness and life goals.

The ideal state that many people seek is an emotional zone somewhere between boredom and anxiety, in the view of psychologist Mihaly Csikzentmihalyi.[10] Boredom, he says, may arise because skills and challenges are mismatched: You are exercising your high level of skill in a job with a low level of challenge, such as licking envelopes. Anxiety arises when one has low levels of skill but a high level of challenge.

As a manager, could you achieve a balance between these two states? Certainly managers have enough challenges to keep their lives more than mildly interesting. Let's see what they are.

Challenge #1: Managing for Competitive Advantage—Staying Ahead of Rivals

Competitive advantage **is the ability of an organization to produce goods or services more effectively than competitors do, thereby outperforming them.** This means an organization must stay ahead in four areas: (1) in being responsive to customers, (2) in innovating, (3) in quality, and (4) in efficiency.

1 Being Responsive to Customers The first law of business is: *take care of the customer.* Without customers—buyers, clients, consumers, shoppers, users, patrons, guests, investors, or whatever they're called—sooner or later there will be no organization. Nonprofit organizations are well advised to be responsive to their "customers," too, whether they're called citizens, members, students, patients, voters, rate-payers, or whatever, since they are the justification for the organizations' existence.

2 Innovation Finding ways to deliver new or better goods or services is called *innovation.* No organization, for-profit or nonprofit, can allow itself to become complacent—especially when rivals are coming up with creative ideas. "Innovate or die" is an important adage for any manager.

We discuss innovation along with entrepreneurship in Chapter 3.

3 Quality If your organization is the only one of its kind, customers may put up with products or services that are less than stellar (as they have with some airlines whose hub systems give them a near-monopoly on flights out of certain cities), but only because they have no choice. But if another organization comes along and offers a better-quality travel experience, TV program, cut of meat, computer software, or whatever, you may find your company falling behind. Making improvements in quality has become an important management idea in recent times, as we shall discuss.

4 Efficiency Whereas a generation ago organizations rewarded employees for their length of service, today the emphasis is on efficiency: Companies strive to produce goods or services using as few employees (and raw materials) as possible. While a strategy that downgrades the value of employees will probably backfire—resulting in the loss of essential experience and skills and even customers—an organization that is overstaffed may not be able to compete with leaner, meaner rivals. This is the reason why, for instance, today many managers—aided by their desktop computers—do much of their own correspondence and filing: Secretarial staffs have been reduced, but of course the secretarial work remains.

Challenge #2: Managing for Diversity—The Future Won't Resemble the Past

During the next half-century, the mix of American racial or ethnic groups will change considerably. Whites are projected to decrease from 82% of the population at the turn of the 21st century to 75% in 2050. African-Americans will increase from 13% to 15%, Asians and Pacific Islanders from 4% to 9%, and Hispanics (who may be of any race) from 11% to 25%.[12] In addition, in the coming years there will be a different mix of women, immigrants, and older people in the general population, as well as in the workforce.

Clearly, the challenge to the manager of the near future is to maximize the contributions of employees diverse in gender, age, race, and ethnicity. We discuss this matter in more detail in Chapter 3.

The famous golden arches. This McDonald's store in Beijing is an example of globalization.

Challenge #3: Managing for Globalization—The Expanding Management Universe

"Imagine how you would react if you logged onto a website and were greeted by a hand flashing an obscene gesture," writes international marketer Wei-Tai Kwok. "You would probably be upset. . . . At the very least you probably wouldn't visit the site again."[13]

But this is exactly what some foreign visitors might have felt if they had visited a pair of American websites (one a technical magazine, the other an online brokerage) featuring a "thumbs up" icon—a rude gesture to Iranians. The point: Icons and symbols don't have the same meaning to everyone throughout the world. Not understanding such differences can affect how well organizations manage globally.

American firms have been going out into the world in a major way. At the same time, the world has been coming to us. Managing for globalization will be a complex, ongoing challenge, as we discuss at length in Chapter 4.

Challenge #4: Managing for Information Technology

"If you think 'doing business on the Net' means setting up a website with cool graphics and tons of corporate information, hold on to your socks," says technology writer Don Tapscott. "That's merely the digital equivalent of handing out your business card in today's networked economy."[14]

In just a few short years, more than $100 billion worth of transactions have been carried out over the Internet, Tapscott points out, and most are businesses selling to other businesses. This kind of e-commerce—electronic commerce—is reshaping entire industries and revamping the very notion of what a company is.

The challenge of managing for information technology, not to mention other technologies affecting your business, will require your unflagging attention. We discuss this subject throughout the book.

Challenge #5: Managing for Ethical Standards

With the pressure to meet sales, production, or other targets, managers can find themselves confronting ethical dilemmas.

What do you do when you learn an employee dropped a gyroscope but put it in the helicopter anyway in order to hold the product's delivery date? How much should you allow your sales reps to knock the competition? (Rivals could sue for confusing or deceptive statements, according to one attorney.[15]) How much leeway do you have in giving gifts to prospective clients in a foreign country to try to land a contract? (American companies need to walk a fine line between observing the realities of the local business culture and complying with the Foreign Corrupt Practices Act, which prohibits bribery.)

Ethical behavior is not just a nicety. It is a very important part of doing business, as we shall discuss in Chapter 3.

Ethical Standards. Bridgestone/Firestone CEO Masatoshi Ono testifies before Congress about tire recalls following several vehicle accidents traced to faulty tires. If you knew your company's product had this kind of problem, would you have covered it up if you thought you could get away with it?

Challenge #6: Managing for Your Own Happiness & Life Goals

Matt Scott, 29, a software engineer whose first love was designing and writing computer code, gave up his title of team manager in a Pittsburgh software development company after trying it for a year. "I'm sick and tired of planning," he had said. "That's not what I came here for."[16]

Regardless of how well paid you are, you have to consider whether in meeting the organization's challenges you are also meeting the challenge of realizing your own happiness. Many people simply don't find being a manager fulfilling. They may feel they have to give up too much of the rest of their lives. They may complain that they have to go to too many meetings, that they can't do enough for their employees, that they are caught in the middle between bosses and subordinates.

They may feel, at a time when Dilbert cartoons have created such an unflattering portrayal of managers, that they lack respect.[17] (Indeed, many students in business schools report they would rather be entrepreneurs, consultants, business partners, or venture capitalists than managers—overlooking the fact that even these occupations require many management skills.[18]) They may decide that, despite the great income, money cannot buy happiness, as the adage goes.

In the end, however, recall what Odette Pollar said: "If you truly like people and enjoy mentoring and helping others to grow and thrive, management is a great job." And it helps to know, as she points out, that "one's experience in management is greatly affected by the company's culture."[19] Culture, or style, is indeed an important matter as it affects your happiness within an organization, and we discuss it in detail in Chapter 8.

What would I actually *do*—that is, what would be my four principal functions as a manager?

The Big Picture

Management has four functions: *planning, organizing, leading,* and *controlling.*

What do you as a manager do to "get things done"—that is, achieve the stated goals of the organization you work for? You perform what is known as the ***management process***, also called the ***four management functions***: **planning, organizing, leading, and controlling.** (The abbreviation "POLC" may help you to remember them.)

As the diagram below illustrates, all these functions affect one another, are ongoing, and are performed simultaneously. *(See Panel 1.2.)*

PANEL 1.2

The management process. What you as a manager do to "get things done"—to achieve the stated goals of your organization.

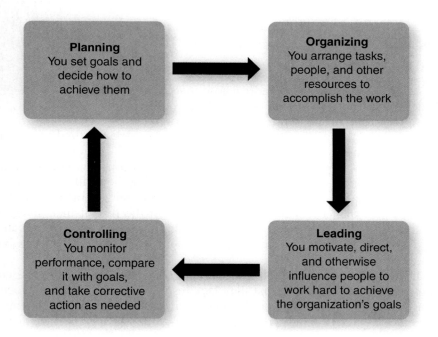

Planning You set goals and decide how to achieve them

Organizing You arrange tasks, people, and other resources to accomplish the work

Controlling You monitor performance, compare it with goals, and take corrective action as needed

Leading You motivate, direct, and otherwise influence people to work hard to achieve the organization's goals

These four functions are very important. Indeed, as a glance at our text's table of contents shows, they form four of the part divisions of the book. Let's consider what the four functions are, using the management (or "administration," as it is called in nonprofit organizations) of your college to illustrate them.

Planning: Discussed in Part 3 of This Book

Planning **is defined as setting goals and deciding how to achieve them.** Your college was established for the purpose of educating students, and its present managers, or administrators, now must decide the best way to accomplish this. Which of several possible degree programs should be offered? Should the college be a residential or a commuter campus? What sort of students should be recruited and admitted? What kind of faculty should be hired? What kind of buildings and equipment are needed?

Organizing: Discussed in Part 4 of This Book

Organizing **is defined as arranging tasks, people, and other resources to accomplish the work.** College administrators must determine the tasks to be done, by whom, and what the reporting hierarchy is to be. Should the institution be organized into schools with departments, with department chairpersons reporting to deans who in return report to vice-presidents? Should the college hire more full-time instructors than part-time instructors? Should English professors teach just English literature or also composition, developmental English, and "first-year experience" courses?

Leader. Steve Ballmer, CEO of Microsoft, in 2001 was named the No. 1 CEO by _Worth_ magazine.

Leading: Discussed in Part 5 of This Book

Leading **is defined as motivating, directing, and otherwise influencing people to work hard to achieve the organization's goals.** At your college, leadership begins, of course, with the president (who would be the chief executive officer, or CEO, in a for-profit organization). He or she is the one who must inspire faculty, staff, students, alumni, wealthy donors, and residents of the surrounding community to help realize the college's goals. As you might imagine, these groups often have different needs and wants, so an essential part of leadership is resolving conflicts.

Controlling: Discussed in Part 6 of This Book

Controlling **is defined as monitoring performance, comparing it with goals, and taking corrective action as needed.** Is the college discovering that fewer students are majoring in nursing than they did five years previously? Is the fault with a change in the job market? with the quality of instruction? with the kinds of courses offered? Are the Nursing Department's student recruitment efforts not going well? Should the department's budget be reduced? Under the management function of controlling, college administrators must deal with these kinds of matters.

Which one of the four functions might this manager be performing?

What are the levels and areas of management I need to know to move up, down, and sideways?

The Big Picture

Within an organization, there are managers at three levels: *top, middle,* and *first-level.* Managers may also be *general managers,* or they may be *functional managers,* responsible for just one organizational activity, such as Research & Development, Marketing, Finance, Production, or Human Resources.

One of the most original management thinkers, Peter Drucker is also a prolific book writer.

The workplace of the future may resemble a symphony orchestra, says famed management theorist Peter Drucker.[20] Employees, especially so-called "knowledge workers"—those who have a great deal of technical skills—can be compared to concert musicians. Their managers can be seen as conductors.

In Drucker's analogy, musicians are used for some pieces of music—that is, work projects—and not others, and they are divided into different sections (teams) based on their instruments. The conductor's role is not to play each instrument better than the musicians but to lead them all through the most effective performance of a particular work.

This model is in sharp contrast to the traditional pyramid-like organizational model, where one leader sits at the top, with layers of managers beneath. We therefore need to take a look at the traditional arrangement first.

The Traditional Management Pyramid: Levels & Areas

A new Silicon Valley technology startup company staffed by young people in sandals and shorts may be so small and so loosely organized that only one or two members may be said to be a manager. General Motors or the U.S. Army, in contrast, has thousands of managers doing thousands of different things. Is there a picture we can draw that applies to all the different kinds of organizations that describes them in ways that make sense? Indeed, there is: by levels and by areas, as the following pyramid shows. *(See Panel 1.3.)*

In high-tech industries, technology and competition change so rapidly that often traditional forms of organization simply won't work. They are being replaced with project management teams and other arrangements that bring together employees from many different areas of the firm. What do you see as the benefits and the drawbacks of constant change for employees in high-tech industries?

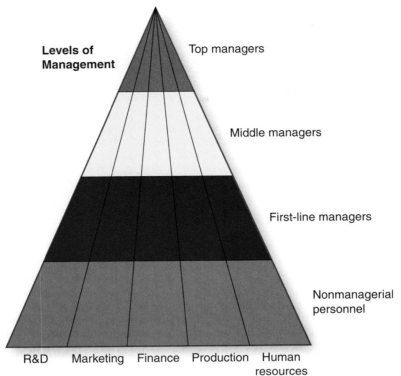

Levels of Management

Top managers

Middle managers

First-line managers

Nonmanagerial personnel

Functional Areas

R&D Marketing Finance Production Human resources

PANEL 1.3
The levels and areas of management. Top managers make long-term decisions, middle managers implement those decisions, and first-line managers make short-term decisions.

Three Levels of Management

Not everyone who works in an organization is a manager, of course, but those who are may be classified into three levels—top, middle, and first-line.

Top Managers Their offices may be equipped with expensive leather chairs and have lofty views. Or, as with one Internet service provider, they may have plastic lawn chairs in the CEO's office and beat-up furniture in the lobby. Whatever their decor, an organization's top managers tend to have titles such as "chief executive officer (CEO)," "chief operating officer (COO)," "president," and "senior vice-president."

Some may be the stars in their fields, the men and women whose pictures appear on the covers of *Business Week* and *Fortune*, people such as Michael Eisner, head of Walt Disney, or Sherry Lansing, who rebuilt Paramount into Hollywood's No. 1 studio. Their salaries and bonuses can average $290,000 a year for CEOs and presidents of small and midsize companies to far over $1 million for top executives in large companies.

Top managers **make long-term decisions about the overall direction of the organization and establish the objectives, policies, and strategies for it.** They need to pay a lot of attention to the environment outside the organization, being alert for long-run opportunities and problems and devising strategies for dealing with them. Thus, executives at this level must be future oriented, dealing with uncertain, highly competitive conditions.

These people stand at the summit of the management pyramid. But the nature of a pyramid, as business consultant Jack Falvey observes, is that the farther you climb, the less space remains at the top. Thus, most pyramid climbers never get to the apex.[21] However, that doesn't mean that you shouldn't try. Indeed, you might end up atop a much smaller pyramid of some other organization than the one you started out in—and happier with the result.

One kind of top manager. Robert L. Nardelli, who was recruited from outside the company, tries on a Home Depot apron on being named president and CEO of the No. 1 home improvement chain. Home Depot owns and operates 1,103 do-it-yourself warehouse retail stores offering building materials and related furnishings and is aiming to top $100 billion in yearly revenue by 2005. Why do you think a highly successful company like Home Depot would go outside the organization to hire a top manager?

Middle Managers *Middle managers* **implement the policies and plans of the top managers above them and supervise and coordinate the activities of the first-line managers below them.** In the non-profit world, middle managers may have titles such as "clinic director," "dean of student services," and the like. In the for-profit world, the titles may be "division head," "plant manager," and "branch sales manager." Their salaries may range from $35,000 to $110,000 a year.

In recent times, the titles have become more creative, in accordance with the changing face of management. For instance, Barb Karlin, 40, of Intuit, a California software company, has the title Director of Great People, which reflects the nature of her challenge—to recruit and retain programmers and other high-technology stars for her company. "I spent 19 years in marketing, bringing in new customers and keeping them," she says. "Now I do it with employees instead of customers. The stakes are equally high: If you lose great people, you lose success. It's that simple."[22]

First-Line Managers The job titles at the bottom of the managerial pyramid tend to be on the order of "department head," "foreman" or "forewoman," "team leader," or "supervisor"—clerical supervisor, production supervisor, research supervisor, and so on. Indeed, *supervisor* is the name often given to first-line managers as a whole. Their salaries may run from $25,000 to $50,000 a year.

Following the plans of middle and top managers, *first-line managers* **make short-term operating decisions, directing the daily tasks of non-managerial personnel,** who are, of course, all those people who work directly at their jobs but don't oversee the work of others.

No doubt the job of first-line manager will be the place where you would start your managerial career. This can be a valuable experience because it will be the training and testing ground for your management ideas.

Top managers of another sort. Entrepreneurs Tony Hsieh, (left) and Afred Lin, who run a venture capital firm, opened up a restaurant next door (called Venture Frogs) for the sake of convenience. They already have a gym and a movie theater in the building where their apartments and offices are. Do you think a top manager is always adventurous?

Areas of Management: Functional Managers versus General Managers

We can represent the levels of management by slicing the organizational pyramid horizontally. We can also slice the pyramid vertically to represent the organization's departments or functional areas, as we did in Panel 1.3 (page 15).

In a for-profit technology company, these might be *Research & Development, Marketing, Finance, Production,* and *Human Resources*. In a nonprofit college, these might be *Faculty, Student Support Staff, Finance, Maintenance*, and *Administration*. Whatever the names of the departments, the organization is run by two types of managers—functional and general. (These are line managers, with authority to direct employees. Staff managers mainly assist line managers, as we discuss later.)

Functional Managers If your title is Vice President of Production, Director of Finance, or Administrator for Human Resources, you are a functional manager. **A *functional manager* is responsible for just one organizational activity.**

Brennen O'Brien, 34, who works for Rosenbluth International, used to have the title Director, Global Marketing and Product Development, but now (indicative of the trend in some companies toward more flexible job titles) she's called Chief Travel Scientist. Her job is heading a research team that is developing services designed to turn reservation agents into travel consultants. The goal: not just cheaper travel but better travel.[23] Leading this specialized sort of research-and-development activity makes her a functional manager.

General Managers If you are working in a small organization of, say, 100 people and your title is Executive Vice President, you are probably a general manager over several departments, such as Production and Finance and Human Resources. **A *general manager* is responsible for several organizational activities.** At the top of the pyramid, general managers are those who seem to be the subject of new stories in magazines such as *Business Week, Fortune, Forbes, Inc.,* and *Fast Company*. Examples are big-company CEOs Kenneth I. Chenault of American Express, Craig Barrett of Intel, and Anne Mulcahy of Xerox Corp. It also includes small-company CEOs such as Gayle Martz, who heads Sherpa's Pet Trading Co., a $4 million New York company with 10 employees that sells travel carriers for dogs and cats. But not all general managers are in for-profit organizations.

Eleanor Josaitis, 67, is cofounder and head of Focus:Hope in Detroit, a nonprofit organization that feeds 48,000 people and runs a day-care center, a training program for machinists, and several for-profit companies with plant and equipment worth $10 million. In the role of a general manager, Josaitis oversees all aspects of the organization, including 850 employees, 51,000 volunteers, and a $72 million annual budget. "We made a conscious decision to run this organization with the sophistication of a business," says Josaitis. Thus, three principles govern Focus:Hope's approach to social change: *Think big. Demand results. Invite people to help.* All these principles reflect the strategic vision characteristic of a top-level general manager.[24]

A general manager is responsible for several organizational activities. Eleanor Josaitis of Focus:Hope oversees a nonprofit organization with a $72 million budget.

To be an exceptional manager, what roles must I play successfully?

The Big Picture

Managers tend to work long hours at an intense pace; their work is characterized by fragmentation, brevity, and variety; and they rely more on verbal than on written communication. According to management scholar Henry Mintzberg, managers play three roles—*interpersonal, informational,* and *decisional.* Interpersonal roles include figurehead, leader, and liaison activities. Informational roles are monitor, disseminator, and spokesperson. Decisional roles are entrepreneur, disturbance handler, resource allocator, and negotiator.

The Manager's Roles: Mintzberg's Useful Findings

Clearly, as *New York Daily News* Editor in Chief Debby Krenek's experience suggests, being a successful manager requires playing several different roles and exercising several different skills. What are they?

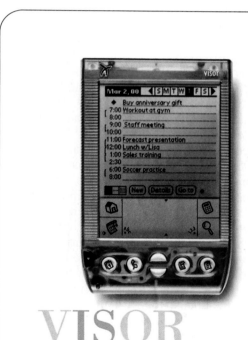

VISOR
having a nice day.

More than just an electronic organizer.

Visor is technology that relieves stress instead of causing it.

handspring
www.handspring.com

Maybe, you think, it might be interesting to shadow some managers to see what it is, in fact, they actually do. That's exactly what management scholar **Henry Mintzberg** did when, in the late 1960s, he followed five chief executives around for a week and recorded their working lives.[25] And what he found is valuable to know, since it applies not only to top managers but also to managers on all levels.

Consider this portrait of a manager's workweek: "There was no break in the pace of activity during office hours," reported Mintzberg about his subjects. "The mail (average of 36 pieces per day), telephone calls (average of five per day), and meetings (average of eight) accounted for almost every minute from the moment these executives entered their offices in the morning until they departed in the evening."[26]

Only five phone calls per day? And, of course, this was back in an era before e-mail, which nowadays can shower some executives with 100, even 300, messages a day. Obviously, the top manager's life is extraordinarily busy. Here are three of Mintzberg's findings, important for any prospective manager:

Multiple activities are characteristic of a manager—which is why so many managers carry a personal digital assistant to keep track of their schedules.

1 A Manager Relies More on Verbal Than on Written Communication Writing letters, memos, and reports takes time. Most managers in Mintzberg's research tended to get and transmit information through telephone conversations and meetings. No doubt this is still true, although the technology of e-mail now makes it possible to communicate almost as rapidly in writing as with the spoken word.

2 A Manager Works Long Hours at an Intense Pace "A true break seldom occurred," wrote Mintzberg about his subjects. "Coffee was taken during meetings, and lunchtime was almost always devoted to formal or informal meetings."

Long hours at work are standard, he found, with 50 hours being typical and up to 90 hours not unheard of. A 1999 survey by John P. Kotter of the Harvard Business School found that the general managers he studied worked just under 60 hours per week.[27]

Are such hours really necessary? Three decades following the Mintzberg research, Linda Stroh, Director of Workplace Studies at Loyola University Chicago, did a study that found that people who work more also earn more. "Those managers who worked 61 hours or more per week had earned, on average, about two promotions over the past five years," she reported.[28] However, researchers at Purdue and McGill universities have found that more companies are allowing managers to reduce their working hours and spend more time with their families yet still advance their high-powered careers.[29]

3 A Manager's Work Is Characterized by Fragmentation, Brevity, & Variety Only about a tenth of the managerial activities observed by Mintzberg took more than an hour; about half were completed in under 9 minutes. Phone calls averaged 6 minutes, informal meetings 10 minutes, and desk-work sessions 15 minutes. "When free time appeared," wrote Mintzberg, "ever-present subordinates quickly usurped it."

No wonder the executive's work time has been characterized as "the interrupt-driven day" and that many managers—such as the late Mary Kay Ash, head of the Mary Kay Cosmetics company—get up as early as 5 A.M. so that they will have a quiet period in which to work undisturbed.[30] No wonder that finding balance between work and family lives is an ongoing concern and that many managers—such as Dawn Lepore, executive V.P. of discount broker Charles Schwab & Co.—have become "much less tolerant of activities that aren't a good use of my time" and so have become better delegators.[31]

It is clear from Mintzberg's work that *time and task management* is a major challenge for every manager. The Practical Action box on the next page (page 20), "Managing Information Overload," offers some suggestions along this line, as does the box at the end of this chapter (page 23), "Getting Control of Your Time: Dealing with the Information Deluge in College & in Your Career."

Charles Schwab, founder of the financial services firm that bears his name. He relies more on verbal than on written communication, works long hours, and experiences an "interrupt-driven day." Interestingly, Schwab has achieved his success despite having had lifelong dyslexia, the common language-related learning disability characterized by difficulty sounding out letters and distinguishing words that sound familiar.

Managing Information Overload: Keep Your Eye on the Big Picture

Chris Peters is a vice president of Microsoft, a company famous for its killer workdays, but he's known for keeping reasonable hours. How does he do it? Like other high achievers, he's able to get more work done in shorter time because he stays focused on things he *has* to do instead of unimportant things he might be doing.[32]

Stars like Peters keep their eye on the big picture. They "have this grasp of what the bottom line is, what 'the critical path' is, and they stay there rather than getting pulled off it all the time," says Carnegie Mellon professor Robert E. Kelley.[33] Stars keep their priorities straight by seeing projects through the eyes of the customers or the coworkers who depend on them. Says star manager Brian Graham, who sits out routine meetings and relies on coworkers to keep him informed, "The key for me is to know what not to do, and to always be looking for the path of quickest resolution."[34]

As a manager, how are you going to deal with information overload? College students already wrestle with this problem. Clearly, if you can come to grips with this beast now, you'll have developed some skills that can save your life in your career. Some strategies are given in the "Taking Something Practical Away from This Chapter" box at the end of this chapter.

Three Types of Managerial Roles

Three Types of Managerial Roles: Interpersonal, Informational, & Decisional From his observations and other research, Mintzberg concluded that managers play three broad types of roles or "organized sets of behavior": *interpersonal*, *informational*, and *decisional*.

1 Interpersonal Roles—Figurehead, Leader, & Liaison In their **_interpersonal roles_, managers interact with people inside and outside their work units. The three interpersonal roles include *figurehead*, *leader*, and *liaison* activities.**

- **Figurehead role:** In your *figurehead role*, you show visitors around your company, attend employee birthday parties, and present ethical guidelines to your subordinates. In other words, you perform symbolic tasks that represent your organization.

- **Leadership role:** In your role of *leader*, you are responsible for the actions of your subordinates, since their successes and failures reflect on you. Your leadership is expressed in your decisions about training, motivating, and disciplining people.

- **Liaison role:** In your *liaison* role, you must act like a politician, working with other people outside your work unit and organization to develop alliances that will help you achieve your organization's goals.

2 Informational Roles—Monitor, Disseminator, & Spokesperson The most important part of a manager's job, Mintzberg believed, is information handling, because accurate information is vital for making intelligent decisions. In their three **_informational roles_—as *monitor*, *disseminator*, and *spokesperson*— managers receive and communicate information** with other people inside and outside the organization.

- **Monitor role:** As a *monitor*, you should be constantly alert for useful information, whether gathered from newspaper stories about the competition or gathered from snippets of conversation with subordinates you meet in the hallway.

- **Disseminator role:** Workers complain they never know what's going on? That probably means their supervisor failed in the role of *disseminator*. Managers need to constantly disseminate important information to employees, as via e-mail and meetings.

- **Spokesperson role:** You are expected, of course, to be a diplomat, to put the best face on the activities of your work unit or organization to people outside it. This is the informational role of *spokesperson*.

3 Decisional Roles—Entrepreneur, Disturbance Handler, Resource Allocator, & Negotiator In their <u>*decisional roles*</u>, managers use information to make decisions to solve problems or take advantage of opportunities. The four decision-making roles are *entrepreneur, disturbance handler, resource allocator,* and *negotiator*.

- **Entrepreneur role:** A good manager is expected to be an *entrepreneur*, to initiate and encourage change and innovation.

- **Disturbance handler role:** Unforeseen problems—from product defects to international currency crises—require you be a *disturbance handler*, fixing problems.

- **Resource allocator role:** Because you'll never have enough time, money, and so on, you'll need to be a *resource allocator*, setting priorities about use of resources.

- **Negotiator role:** To be a manager is to be a continual *negotiator*, working with others inside and outside the organization to accomplish your goals.

Did anyone say a manager's job is easy? Certainly it's not for people who want to sit on the sidelines of life. Above all else, managers are *doers*.

Frederick Smith (left), chairman and CEO of FedEx, is an example of a doer. When given a low grade on a graduate-school paper outlining his ideas for an overnight delivery service, he used his family's money to found that company.

To be a terrific manager, what skills should I cultivate?

The Big Picture

Good managers need to work on developing three principal skills. The first is *technical*, the ability to perform a specific job. The second is *conceptual*, the ability to think analytically. The third is *human*, the ability to interact well with people.

At the *New York Daily News*, Debby Krenek, introduced in the first section of this chapter, was preceded as Editor in Chief by a journalism legend, Pete Hamill, who exhorted his staff to make the tabloid newspaper a reflection of the exciting, ethnically diverse New York City that he saw on the streets. By contrast, Krenek was criticized by some subordinates for not having a grand vision for the paper. Does this mean that she lacks the right management stuff? Let's see what the "right stuff" might be.

In the mid-1970s, researcher **Robert Katz** found that through education and experience managers acquire three principal skills—*technical, conceptual*, and *human*.[35]

1 Technical Skills—The Ability to Perform a Specific Job

Krenek clearly had acquired the job-specific knowledge needed to function in the world of newspapers (as opposed to another industry—tax law, engineering, or restaurant work, say). Indeed, she has a college degree in journalism from Texas A&M and worked as a copy editor and reporter for two Texas newspapers before moving to New York.

Technical skills **consist of the job-specific knowledge needed to perform well in a specialized field.** Having the requisite technical skills seems to be most important at the lower levels of management—that is, among first-line managers.

2 Conceptual Skills—The Ability to Think Analytically

Krenek also had the "big picture" knowledge of all the steps that had to happen for the *Daily News* to be daily news—for the paper to be off the presses and on the trucks at the same time every day. Indeed, she suggested that she could almost get the *News* out by herself, if she had to.

Conceptual skills **consist of the ability to think analytically, to visualize an organization as a whole and understand how the parts work together.** Conceptual skills are particularly important for top managers, who must deal with problems that are ambiguous but that could have far-reaching consequences.

3 Human Skills—The Ability to Interact Well with People

This may well be the most difficult set of skills to master. ***Human skills*** **consist of the ability to work well in cooperation with other people to get things done.** These skills—the ability to motivate, to inspire trust, to communicate with others—are necessary for managers of all levels. But because of the range of people, tasks, and problems in an organization, developing your human-interacting skills may turn out to be an ongoing, lifelong effort. Krenek has an easy-going manner, and she had tried to improve the paper's morale with such simple gestures as compliments and champagne toasts. Although she was criticized for lacking the magnetism and flair of her predecessor, Pete Hamill himself observed that she was able to resist "the pervasive sourness" of the company culture of the *News*. One veteran reporter praised her for having a skill that other managers "don't have: an ability to get along with people. And, unlike the others, she actually listens."[36]

But how successful was she with her boss, real-estate magnate and publisher Mortimer Zuckerman? At first, perhaps because early on she adopted a "no surprises" policy of talking with him regularly throughout the day, Zuckerman praised her as both a "wonderful person" and an adept manager. In fact, he lauded her as being capable enough to run a Fortune 500 company—indeed, even the Pentagon.

But ultimately Zuckerman seems to have lost confidence in her. This shows that in real life even the most talented and skillful of managers can find themselves on the wrong side of their boss if they let their guard down. Despite all Zuckerman's praise, a few years later Krenek found herself fired. And she learned about it not from her boss but from a *Daily News* editor who read the news in a gossip column of a rival publication and called her about it at 1 A.M. When she telephoned Zuckerman to ask about the rumor, the publisher replied, "I can neither confirm nor deny it."[37]

What happened? The dismissal was apparently related to the fact that the *Daily News*'s fierce rival, the *New York Post*, had gained circulation as a result of a per-copy newsstand price cut. This was not a matter over which Krenek had much control. Still, could her people skills have somehow been better?

In nearly all respects, Krenek had what it takes to be a star manager. But all it takes is failure in one area to lose this status.

A star manager. One of the more successful leaders in business today is Tom Siebel, founder and head of software maker Siebel Systems, shown here on his Montana ranch. He is described as being very demanding and unwilling to take "no" for an answer. Few executives are as effective when measured by company performance. Have you had experience with similar leaders?

Taking Something Practical Away from This Chapter

Getting Control of Your Time: Dealing with the Information Deluge in College & in Your Career

Except for this first box, "Taking Something Practical Away from This Chapter" appears on the website accompanying this book, with one such box for every chapter. Each box offers you the opportunity to acquire useful experience that directly applies to your career.

One great problem most college students face—and that all managers face—is how to manage their time. This first box describes skills that will benefit you in college and later in your career.

"I've managed to ratchet my schedule down so I can have an outside life," says Doug Shoemaker, a San Francisco architect who tries to be home by 6:00 every night. "I'm a highly organized guy, I really focus on tasks, and I get them done."[38]

Professionals and managers all have to deal with this central problem: how not to surrender their lives to their jobs. The place to start, however, is in college. If you can learn to manage time while you're still a student, you'll find it will pay off not only in higher grades and more free time but also in more efficient information-handling skills that will serve you well as a manager later on.

Developing Study Habits: Finding Your "Prime Study Time"

Each of us has a different energy cycle. The trick is to use it effectively. That way your hours of best performance will coincide with your heaviest academic demands. For example, if your energy level is high during the evenings, you should plan to do your studying then.

Make a Study Schedule First make a master schedule that shows all your regular obligations—especially classes and work—for the entire school term. Then insert the times during which you plan to study. Next write in major academic events, such as term paper due dates and when exams will take place. At the beginning of every week, schedule your study sessions. Write in the specific tasks you plan to accomplish during each session.

Find Some Good Places to Study Studying means first of all avoiding distractions. Avoid studying in places that are associated with other activities, particularly comfortable ones, such as lying in bed or sitting at a kitchen table.

Avoid Time Wasters, but Reward Your Studying While clearly you need to learn to avoid distractions so that you can study, you must also give yourself frequent rewards so that you will indeed be *motivated* to study. You should study with the notion that, after you finish, you will give yourself a reward. The reward need not be elaborate. It could be a walk, a snack, a television show, a video game, a conversation with a friend, or some similar treat.

Improving Your Memory Ability

Memorizing is, of course, one of the principal requirements of staying in college. And it's a great help for success in life afterward.

Beyond getting rid of distractions, there are certain techniques you can adopt to enhance your memory.

Space Your Studying, Rather Than Cramming Cramming—making a frantic, last-minute attempt to memorize massive amounts of material—is probably the least effective means of absorbing information. Indeed, it may actually tire you out and make you even more anxious before the test. Research shows that it is best to space out your studying of a subject on successive days. This is preferable to trying to do it all during the same number of hours on one day.[39] It is repetition that helps move information into your long-term memory bank.

Review Information Repeatedly—Even "Overlearn" It. By repeatedly reviewing information—what is known as "rehearsing"—you can improve both your retention and your understanding of it.[40] Overlearning can improve your recall substantially. Overlearning is continuing to repeatedly review material even after you appear to have absorbed it.

Use Memorizing Tricks. There are several ways to organize information so that you can retain it better. In the following panel we present some methods of establishing associations between items you want to remember. *(See Panel 1.4.)*

PANEL 1.4
Some memorizing tricks

■**Mental and physical imagery:** Use your visual and other senses to construct a personal image of what you want to remember. Indeed, it helps to make the image humorous, action-filled, sexual, bizarre, or outrageous in order to establish a personal connection. Example: To remember the name of the 21st president of the United States, Chester Arthur, you might visualize an author writing the number "21" on a wooden chest. This mental image helps you associate chest (Chester), author (Arthur), and 21 (21st president).

■**Acronyms and acrostics:** An acronym is a word created from the first letters of items in a list. For instance, Roy G. Biv helps you remember the colors of the rainbow in order: red, orange, yellow, green, blue, indigo, violet. An acrostic is a phrase or sentence created from the first letters of items in a list. For example, *Every Good Boy Does Fine* helps you remember that the order of musical notes on the stave is E-G-B-D-F.

■**Location:** Location memory occurs when you associate a concept with a place or imaginary place. For example, you could learn the parts of a computer system by imagining a walk across campus. Each building you pass could be associated with a part of the computer system.

■**Word games:** Jingles and rhymes are devices frequently used by advertisers to get people to remember their products. You may recall the spelling rule "*I* before *E* except after *C* or when sounded like *A* as in *neighbor* or *weigh*." You can also use narrative methods, such as making up a story.

How to Improve Your Reading Ability: The SQ3R Method

SQ3R Stands for *survey, question, read, recite, and review*[41] The strategy behind SQ3R is to break down a reading assignment into small segments and master each before moving on. The five steps of the SQ3R method are as follows:

Survey **the Chapter before You Read It** Get an overview of the chapter or other reading assignment before you begin reading it. If you have a sense what the material is about before you begin reading it, you can predict where it is going. You can also bring your own experience to it and otherwise become involved in ways that will help you retain it. Many textbooks offer some "preview"-type material. Examples are a list of objectives or an outline of topic headings at the beginning of the chapter. Other books offer a summary at the end of the chapter. This book offers "The Big Picture" at the beginning of each section. It also offers a Summary at the end of each chapter. The strategy for reading this book is presented on page 1.

Question **the Segment in the Chapter before You Read It** This step is easy to do, and the point, again, is to get involved in the material. After surveying the entire chapter, go to the first segment—section, subsection, or even paragraph, depending on the level of difficulty and density of information. Look at the topic heading of that segment. In your mind, restate the heading as a question.

After you have formulated the question, go to steps 3 and 4 (read and recite). Then proceed to the next segment and restate the heading here as a question. For instance, consider the section heading in this chapter that reads "What Managers Do: The Four Principal Functions." You could ask yourself, "What *are* the four functions of a manager?" For the heading in Chapter 2 "Types of Management Theories & Practical Reasons for Studying Them," ask "What *are* the types of management theories, and what are reasons for studying them?"

Read **the Segment about Which You Asked the Question** Now read the segment you asked the question about. Read with purpose, to answer the question you formulated. Underline or color-mark sentences you think are important, if they help you answer the question. Read this portion of the text more than once, if necessary, until you can answer the question. In addition, determine whether the segment covers any other significant questions, and formulate answers to these, too. After you have read the segment, proceed to step 4. (Perhaps you can see where this is all leading. If you read in terms of questions and answers, you will be better prepared when you see exam questions about the material later.)

Recite **the Main Points of the Segment.** Recite means "say aloud." Thus, you should speak out loud (or softly) the answer to the principal question about the segment and any other main points. If you wish, make notes on the principal ideas, so you can look them over later. Now that you have actively studied the first segment, move on to the second segment and do steps 2–4 for it. Continue this procedure through the rest of the segments until you have finished the chapter.

Review **the Entire Chapter by Repeating Questions** After you have read the chapter, go back through it and review the main points. Then, without looking at the book, test your memory by repeating the questions.

Clearly the SQ3R method takes longer than simply reading with a rapidly moving color marker or underlining pencil. However, the technique is far more effective because it requires your *involvement and understanding*. This is the key to all effective learning.

Learning from Lectures

Does attending lectures really make a difference? Research shows that students with grades of B or above were more apt to have better class attendance than students with grades of C- or below.[42]

Regardless of the strengths of the lecturer, here are some tips for getting more out of lectures.

Take Effective Notes by Listening Actively Research shows that good test performance is related to good note taking.[43] And good note taking requires that you *listen actively*—that is, participate in the lecture process. Here are some ways to take good lecture notes:

- **Read ahead and anticipate the lecturer:** Try to anticipate what the instructor is going to say, based on your previous reading. Having background knowledge makes learning more efficient.

- **Listen for signal words:** Instructors use key phrases such as "The most important point is . . . ," "There are four reasons for . . . ," "The chief reason . . . ," "Of special importance . . . ," "Consequently . . . ." When you hear such signal phrases, mark your notes with an asterisk (*), or write *Imp* (for "Important").

- **Take notes in your own words:** Instead of just being a stenographer, try to restate the lecturer's thoughts in your own words. This makes you pay attention to the lecture and organize it in a way that is meaningful to you. In addition, don't try to write everything down. Just get the key points.

- **Ask questions:** By asking questions during the lecture, you necessarily participate in it and increase your understanding. Although many students are shy about asking questions, most professors welcome them.

Becoming an Effective Test Taker

Besides having knowledge of the subject matter, you can acquire certain skills that will help during the test-taking process. Some suggestions:[44]

Review Your Notes Regularly   The good news is that most students, according to one study, do take good notes. The bad news is that they don't use them effectively. That is, they wait to review their notes until just before final exams, when the notes have lost much of their meaning.[45] Make it a point to review your notes regularly, such as the afternoon after the lecture or once or twice a week. We cannot emphasize enough how important this kind of reviewing is.

Reviewing: Study Information That Is Emphasized & Enumerated   Because you won't always know whether an exam will be an objective test or an essay test, you need to prepare for both. Here are some general tips.

- **Review material that is emphasized:** In the lectures, this consists of any topics your instructor pointed out as being significant or important. It also includes anything he or she spent a good deal of time discussing or specifically advised you to study. In the textbook, pay attention to key terms (often emphasized in *italic* or **boldface** type), their definitions, and their examples. In addition, of course, material that has a good many pages given over to it should be considered important.

- **Review material that is enumerated:** Pay attention to any numbered lists, both in your lectures and in your notes. Enumerations often provide the basis for essay and multiple-choice questions.

- **Review other tests:** Look over past quizzes, as well as the discussion questions or review questions provided at the end of chapters in many textbooks.

Prepare by Doing Final Reviews & Budgeting Your Test Time   Learn how to make your energy and time work for you. Whether you have studied methodically or must cram for an exam, here are some tips:

- **Review your notes:** Spend the night before the test reviewing your notes. Then go to bed without interfering with the material you have absorbed (as by watching television). Get up early the next morning, and review your notes again.

- **Find a good test-taking spot:** Make sure you arrive at the exam with any pencils or other materials you need. Get to the classroom early, or at least on time, and find a quiet spot. If you don't have a watch, sit where you can see a clock. Again review your notes. Avoid talking with others, so as not to interfere with the information you have learned or to increase your anxiety.

- **Read the test directions:** Many students don't do this and end up losing points because they didn't understand precisely what was required of them. Also, listen to any verbal directions or hints your instructor gives you before the test.

- **Budget your time:** Here is an important point of test strategy: Before you start, read through the entire test and figure out how much time you can spend on each section. There is a reason for budgeting your time, of course. You would hate to find you have only a few minutes left and a long essay still to be written. Write the number of minutes allowed for each section on the test booklet or scratch sheet and stick to the schedule. The way you budget your time should correspond to how confident you feel about answering the questions.

Objective Tests: Answer Easy Questions & Eliminate Options   Some suggestions for taking objective tests, such as multiple-choice, true/false, or fill-in, are as follows:

- **Answer the easy questions first:** Don't waste time stewing over difficult questions. Do the easy ones first, and come back to the hard ones later. (Put a check mark opposite those you're not sure about.) Your unconscious mind may have solved them in the meantime, or later items may provide you with the extra information you need.

- **Answer all questions:** Unless the instructor says you will be penalized for wrong answers, try to answer all questions. If you have time, review all the questions and make sure you have written the responses correctly.

- **Eliminate the options:** Cross out answers you know are incorrect. Be sure to read all the possible answers, especially when the first answer is correct. (After all, other answers could also be correct, so that "All of the above" may be the right choice.) Be alert that subsequent questions may provide information pertinent to earlier questions. Pay attention to options that are long and detailed, since answers that are more detailed and specific are likely to be correct. If two answers have the opposite meaning, one of the two is probably correct.

Essay Tests: First Anticipate Answers & Prepare an Outline Because time is limited, your instructor is likely to ask only a few essay questions during the exam. The key to success is to try to anticipate beforehand what the questions might be and memorize an outline for an answer. Here are the specific suggestions:

- **Anticipate 10 probable essay questions:** Use the principles we discussed above of reviewing lecture and textbook material that is *emphasized* and *enumerated*. You will then be in a position to identify 10 essay questions your instructor may ask. Write out these questions.

- **Prepare and memorize informal essay answers:** For each question, list the main points that need to be discussed. Put supporting information in parentheses. Circle the key words in each main point and below the question put the first letter of the key word. Make up catch phrases, using acronyms, acrostics, or word games, so that you can memorize these key words. Test yourself until you can recall the key words the letters stand for and the main points the key words represent.

Key Terms Used in This Chapter

Summary

1.1
Management: What It Is, What Its Benefits Are

■ Management is defined as the pursuit of organizational goals. These goals should be pursued efficiently and effectively. Efficiently means to use resources wisely and cost-effectively. Effectively means to achieve results, to make the right decisions and successfully carry them out to achieve the organization's goals.

1.2
Six Challenges to Being a Star Manager

■ Challenge #1, managing for competitive advantage, means an organization must stay ahead in four areas: in being responsive to customers; in innovating new products or services; in offering better quality; and in being more efficient.

■ Challenge #2 is managing for diversity among different genders, ages, races, and ethnicities.

■ Challenge #3 is managing for globalization, the expanding universe.

■ Challenge #4 is managing for computers and telecommunications—information technology.

■ Challenge #5 is managing for right and wrong, or ethical standards.

■ Challenge #6 is managing for your own happiness and life goals.

1.3
What Managers Do: The Four Principal Functions

■ The four management functions are represented by the abbreviation POLC. It stands for *planning, organizing, leading,* and *controlling.*

■ The first function is defined as setting goals and deciding how to achieve them.

■ The second function is defined as arranging tasks, people, and other resources to accomplish the work.

■ The third function is defined as motivating, directing, and otherwise influencing people to work hard to achieve the organization's goals.

■ The fourth function is defined as monitoring performance, comparing it with goals, and taking corrective action as needed.

1.4
Pyramid Power: Levels & Areas of Management

■ Within an organization, there are managers at three levels: top, middle, and first-level.

- Managers at the highest level make long-term decisions about the overall direction of the organization and establish the objectives, policies, and strategies for it.

- The managers below them implement the policies and plans of their superiors and supervise and coordinate the activities of the managers below them.

- The managers farthest down make short-term operating decisions, directing the daily tasks of nonmanagement personnel.

- The organizational pyramid may be sliced vertically to represent its departments or functional areas, such as Marketing or Human Resources. Whatever the departments, they may be run by functional managers, who are responsible for just functional organizational activity, or by general managers, who are responsible for several organizational activities.

1.5
Roles Managers Must Play Successfully

- Scholar Henry Mintzberg shadowed managers in the 1960s to see what they do. Three of his key findings are that, first, a manager relies more on verbal than on written communication; second, managers work long hours at an intense pace; and, third, a manager's work is characterized by fragmentation, brevity, and variety.

- From this, the scholar concluded that managers play three broad types of roles. They are interpersonal, informational, and decisional.

- In the first role, the manager acts as figurehead, leader, and liaison.

- In the second role, the manager acts as monitor, disseminator, and spokesperson.

- In the third role, the manager acts as entrepreneur, disturbance handler, resource allocator, and negotiator.

1.6
The Skills Star Managers Need

- The three skills that star managers cultivate are technical, conceptual, and human.

- The first set of skills consists of job-specific knowledge needed to perform well in a specialized field.

- The second set of skills consists of the ability to think analytically, to visualize an organization as a whole, and to understand how the parts work together.

- The third set of skills consists of the ability to work well in cooperation with other people to get things done.

Management in Action

Aftermath of the Terrorist Attacks: Fundamental Management Skills & Functions Are Needed During a Crisis[48]

The following article was written nearly a month after the September 11, 2001, terrorist-hijacked airplanes crashed into the Twin Towers of New York's World Trade Center and into the Pentagon outside Washington, D.C. Excerpted from Carol Hymowitz, "Companies Experience Major Power Shifts as Crises Continue," The Wall Street Journal, October 9, 2001, p. B1.

These are times that make—and break—leaders. As businesses respond to continuing political and economic crises, power shakeups are occurring in management ranks. Executives with crisis-leadership talents—from making decisions that will need to be constantly revised to keeping rattled employees calm—are gaining more authority at their companies, while others find themselves with less responsibility.

"However power was balanced before, it gets reshuffled in a time of crisis," says David Bliss, vice chairman of Mercer Delta Consulting in New York.

Such is the case at Merrill Lynch & Co., where President E. Stanley O'Neal has taken over more and more of the day-to-day responsibilities of running the securities firm. Mr. O'Neal, 49 years old, was named to the No. 2 spot in July and isn't expected to take over duties from the chief executive, 62-year-old David Komansky, for several years.

But since the terrorist hijackers struck the Twin Towers across the street from Merrill's headquarters, Mr. O'Neal has asserted more control at the firm. As he and two other top executives dashed to the street from their offices, he told his colleagues to split up. "We shouldn't be together, just in case," he said. In subsequent days, he oversaw the company's efforts to relocate 9,000 brokers, traders, and other employees who worked at headquarters to three temporary sites in the area. [After that] he . . . jettisoned several top executives close to Mr. Komansky, including his rival for the president's post, whom Mr. Komansky had favored.

At other companies, executives have stepped forward to fill voids left by those killed in the attacks. Keefe, Bruyette & Woods, the investment bank whose offices were on the 88th and 89th floors of 2 World Trade Center, lost 67 of it 220 employees, including Co-Chief Executive Joseph J. Better and Christopher Duffy, the son of John Duffy, now the firm's sole CEO. While Mr. Duffy took time off to mourn his son's death and visit the families of other victims, he relied on two other executives—Thomas B. Michaud, executive vice president in charge of equity sales, and Vice Chairman Andy Senchak—to manage day-to-day operations.

Mr. Michaud and Mr. Senchak led efforts to relocate surviving employees to temporary offices and to get computer systems running again. They assured clients that the firm would carry on but also acknowledged the grief and trauma suffered by employees. When the New York Stock Exchange resumed trading on Monday, September 17, Keefe Bruyette decided to wait until Tuesday. "I think people needed an extra day," Mr. Michaud said.

This ability to show empathy toward employees while also giving them confidence to carry on is a key challenge for leaders during crises. "Executives who only talk about resuming business at a time like this can strike a mortal wound to employee morale," says Mercer's Mr. Bliss

Some executives won't rise to the occasion, Mr. Bliss predicts. "Good leaders aren't sending out e-mails. They are jumping on airplanes and visiting plants and offices, and standing in front of people who are highly anxious and want answers when they don't have the answers. But that is the challenge—to be able to stand up there and 'I don't know, but I'll find out,' and to convey that we're all in the same boat together," he says

Power is also moving down the ranks at many companies, to managers directly in charge of making and selling products and keeping communications systems running.

Front-line managers who remain focused and able to get things done—rather than panicking and freezing—stand out during crises and gain new respect from both subordinates and superiors.

"What's enabled us to get through this are middle managers who are willing to act independently and who didn't need to be together to work well," says Michael Stocker, chief executive of Empire Blue Cross and Blue Shield, which had offices in the World Trade Center. All but nine of Empire's 1,900 employees safely evacuated the company's offices. Since then, managers have formed informal work teams at various locations to keep departments operating. "We've told people that if they want to rent hotel rooms or go to a restaurant to do it, and if they need grief counselors or laptops or whatever, we'll provide them," says Mr. Stocker.

He points to numerous managers who have acted heroically to keep Empire operating in recent weeks. "They are the stars," he says. Among these are a communications manager who, from the moment he fled the collapsing Twin Towers, worked around the clock to get phone lines and voice mail working again "so we could start talking to each other," says Mr. Stocker. "He acted on his own and knew what to do, even though we'd never anticipated losing all our exchanges," he adds

Mr. Stocker now believes that his past efforts to create a culture "where you can make mistakes and don't always have to ask someone above you if you can try something" now appear to be his most important contributions to Empire.

For Discussion

1. What unique managerial skills were needed during the crisis? Explain your rationale.

2. To what extent were Mr. Michaud, Mr. Senchak, Mr. Stocker, and middle managers at Blue Cross and Blue Shield efficient and effective? Was either of these criteria—efficiency and effectiveness—more important than the other?

3. Using Panel 1.2 as a guide, describe which of the four functions of management were displayed in the case.

4. Which of the three types of managerial roles did Mr. O'Neal, Mr. Duffy, and middle managers at Blue Cross and Blue Shield display?

5. The leaders depicted in this case displayed which of the three critical skills identified by Robert Katz—technical, conceptual, human? Explain.

Take It to the Net

The Internet has become one of the most important managerial tools. You can access research, career potentials, knowledge concerning organizations, papers about a vast variety of subjects, and a host of interactive applications. The Internet can be especially useful in the area of careers and career assessment. At the MAPP (Motivational Appraisal of Personal Potential) site, you can take a MAPP Assessment online for free. Click on the free assessment to assess what seems to best fit you in terms of a career. Go to *http://www.assessment.com/ MAPPMembers/Welcome.asp?accnum= 06-5150-000.00.*

For assessment you can also go to *http://www. myfuture.com/career/interest_quiz.html*. Please take this test and then submit it. You can also explore your career interests at Self-Directed Search. Go to *http://www.sdstest2.com/Home2.html*. Here you can learn more about careers or fields of study that match your own skills and interests. A large site that contains lots of great career information, industry guides and facts about hundreds of careers is available at *http://www.WetFeet.com*.

In addition to these sites, you can look up and research many of the concepts presented in the chapter. Choose a search engine, input a company you want to research or a general management area presented in the chapter, and you will find a wealth of information brought up by the search engine. Not all will be of use or relevant, but if you search through what appear to be good sites, you will learn a great deal. For example, if you go to a site such as *http://www.workteams.unt.edu/links.htm,* you will find not only a great deal of information on teams but links to sites on topics from conflict management to organizational development.

Questions for Discussion

1. What did you learn about your career interests?
2. How would you use the Internet as a tool in your managerial toolbox?
3. How might being technologically savvy in a knowledge-based economy make you a "star"?
4. How do you think the Internet and the Web will change over the next 10 years?

Self-Assessment

Can You Pass the CEO Test?

Objectives

1. To assess whether or not you have "it" at this time to be a CEO.
2. To assess whether or not you want to be a CEO.
3. To see what seems to be expected of a CEO.

Introduction: The Chief Executive Officer of a company is the person in charge, the top STAR. This person has tremendous power and, consequently, experiences incredible pressures. Not everyone is cut out to be a CEO or aspires to be one. Many people would not want the stress and expectations for greatness that come with the job.

Instructions: Take the following quiz at *http://www.mbajungle.com/monthlysurvey/ceotest.cfm* to "test" whether you have "it" or not. Leading a successful company requires a combination of talents and skills that few people seem to have—some people have it, some don't. Here's your chance to find out where you stand.

Accompanying the quiz is an article by John Scaizi for the MBA Jungle Online magazine. Read it; then take the test and see if you are a potential rising star. Once you have completed the test, and submitted your responses, ask yourself the following questions and be prepared to discuss them.

Questions for Discussion

1. Do you want to be a CEO? Explain.
2. Do you want to climb the corporate ladder to become a star?
3. At what level in the organization do you think you would be comfortable?
4. What are the ethics behind #7, #8, #11, # 15, and #16?
5. How would you describe what it takes to be a CEO?

Group Exercise

How Well Do Managers Manage Their Time?

Objectives
To see how time is allocated in a top management position.

1. To start to think about how you might spend your time in a top management position.

2. To see what you think about this kind of job and what functions are performed.

Introduction
Managers must allocate their time appropriately. If as a manager you continuously misallocate your time in terms of work coordination, your company will not reach its goals or, at the very least, you will not achieve your own goals and may become a liability to the organization. So, you must understand how to allocate your time wisely.

Instructions
The following is from Charles Handy's *Understanding Organizations**:

A senior manager's diary: One senior division manager sat down to review what he regarded as the major responsibilities of his job. He listed six key areas for himself:

A. Relations with head office: communicating with the top managers.

B. Long-term and strategic planning: the plans that position the company over time.

C. Operational responsibilities for particular ongoing activities: the day-to-day activities of the company.

D. Co-coordinating function: working with other parts of the company to complete a task or tasks.

E. Standard setting, performance, morale priorities: setting up quality standards and other types of standards, operationalizing performance appraisals, and developing a climate where employees want to work.

F. External relations: working with customers, watching what competitors are doing, dealing with pressure groups, working with suppliers.

As a group, estimate in percentages how you think this senior manager allocated his time to these six key areas. (The senior manager's percentages are included at the end of this exercise.)

A. _____ %

B. _____ %

C. _____ %

D. _____ %

E. _____ %

F. _____ %

What areas would you add to his list? Why?

Questions for Discussion

1. How do your percentages compare to the senior division manager's time allocation?

2. Why do you think that A, C, and D take so much of his time?

3. In this changing world do you think that more time should be spent on B, E, and F?

4. How do managers "know" how to allocate their time? In his position, would you allocate your time differently? Why or why not?

Answers

After outlining the six key areas of responsibility in his job, the division manager then analyzed his diary for the previous three months and came up with the following approximate percentages of time spent on each of the key areas:

A. 20 %		D. 25%
B. 10 %		E. 5 %
C. 35 %		F. 5 %

*Adapted and modified by Anne Cowden, Ph.D., from Charles Handy's *Understanding Organizations* (New York: Penguin, 1993), p. 338.

Ethical Dilemma

Waddell & Reed Financial Inc. Attempt to Keep the Clients of a Fired Employee

Excerpted from Susanne Craig and Kara Scannell, "Settling Accounts: How Spat over Clients Cost a Securities Firm Record Punitive Award," The Wall Street Journal, *September 29, 2001, pp. A1 and A2.*

On February 3, 1997, Waddell & Reed Financial Inc. asked star broker Stephen Sawtelle to chair an elite club made up of the firm's top 12 producers. "Your distinguished service to your clients and our company is unmeasurable," the mutual fund company wrote in a note. Tucked in the envelope was a check for $5,000.

Seven days later, Waddell & Reed fired him for "personality conflicts."

What followed was an extraordinary struggle for control of Mr. Sawtelle's 2,800 clients. Waddell hired a telemarketing firm to place rapid-fire calls to the customers. The firm sent letters saying Mr. Sawtelle, a 47-year-old former Green Beret, was "not authorized" to handle their accounts. Mr. Sawtelle says some clients were told that if they filed complaints against him they could get a lower-fee mutual fund. One client was so alarmed that he asked the police to find out if the broker "had been reported missing or if there were any outstanding warrants" for his arrest.

Waddell lost the battle: Mr. Sawtelle, a 17-year veteran of the firm, retained 2,600 of his clients. Then it lost the war: An arbitration panel ruled this month that the firm must pay $27.6 million in damages to Mr. Sawtelle for "reprehensible conduct" in smearing the broker's reputation. . . .

Questionable tactics long have been common on Wall Street in the behind-the-scenes scuffles that erupt over investor accounts when brokers leave their firms. Remaining brokers start making their pitches to get the business—and sometimes they are less than upfront about their former colleagues. . . .

After the firing, things got really nasty. Mr. Sawtelle says many of his clients received a letter from Waddell on February 10, 1997—the day he was fired—saying: "You may be aware that your representative, Steve Sawtelle, is no longer with our firm, and therefore not authorized to service your accounts with Waddell & Reed." The letter added that investors could face tax penalties if they transferred money from Waddell, a tactic Mr. Sawtelle believes was used to prevent customers from changing firms. Letters such as these are common in the securities industry when a broker leaves a firm. . . .

Waddell brought out big guns. In addition to the letters, Waddell hired Adecco SA, a staffing company to provide telemarketers, which contacted hundreds of customers. About 10 temporary workers set up camp in a Waddell conference room telling clients Mr. Sawtelle was gone and a new broker had been assigned to them.

Solving the Dilemma

What would you do to prevent this situation from happening again at Waddell & Reed?

1. Aggressively pursue the clients of a fired broker, but not use false statements in letters or phone conversations.

2. Send clients a letter informing them that the broker no longer worked in the firm, and ask them if they would like to be reassigned to another broker.

3. Let the fired employee retain his or her clients.

4. Invent other options. Discuss.

CHAPTER 2

Management Theory
Essential Background for the Successful Manager

2.1 Evolving Viewpoints: How We Got to Today's Management Outlook

Major Question: What's the payoff in studying different management perspectives, both yesterday's and today's?

2.5 The Systems Viewpoint

Major Question: How can the exceptional manager be helped by the systems viewpoint?

2.2 The Classical Viewpoint: Scientific & Administrative Management

Major Question: If the name of the game is to manage work more efficiently, what can the classical viewpoint teach me?

2.6 The Contingency Viewpoint

Major Question: In the end, is there one best way to manage in all situations?

2.3 The Behavioral Viewpoint: Behaviorism, Human Relations, & Behavioral Science

Major Question: To understand how people are motivated to achieve, what can I learn from the behavioral viewpoint?

2.7 The Quality-Management Viewpoint

Major Question: Can the quality-management viewpoint offer guidelines for true managerial success?

2.4 The Quantitative Viewpoints: Management Science & Operations Research

Major Question: If the manager's job is to solve problems, how might the two quantitative approaches help?

2.8 The Learning Organization

Major Question: Organizations must learn or perish. How do I build a learning organization?

MINDFULNESS OVER MINDLESSNESS: BEING A LEARNER IN A LEARNING ORGANIZATION

Learn or die. Isn't that the challenge for us as individuals? It's the same with organizations. Thus has arisen the concept of the "learning organization," in which employees continually expand their ability to achieve results by obtaining the right knowledge and changing their behavior.

Throughout your career, you will have to constantly be a learner, evaluating all kinds of beliefs and theories—including those described in this chapter. However, one barrier to learning that all of us need to be aware of is *mindlessness.* Instead we need to adopt the frame of mind that Harvard psychology professor Ellen Langer has called *mindfulness,* a form of active engagement.

We've all experienced mindlessness. We misplace our keys. We write checks in January with the previous year's date. Mindlessness is characterized by the three following attributes:

■ **Entrapment in old categories:** An avid tennis player, Langer says that at a tennis camp she, like all other students, was taught *exactly* how to hold her racquet and toss the ball when making a serve. But later, when watching a top tennis championship, she observed that none of the top players served the way she was taught and that all served slightly differently.[1]

The significance: There is no one right way of doing things. In a conditional, or mindful, way of teaching, an instructor doesn't say "This is THE answer" but rather "This is ONE answer." Thus, all information—even in the hard sciences and mathematics, where it may seem as though there is just one correct answer—should be regarded with open-mindedness, since there may be exceptions. That is, you should act as though the information is true only for certain uses or under certain circumstances.

■ **Automatic behavior:** Langer tells of the time she used a new credit card in a department store. Noticing that Langer hadn't signed the card yet, the cashier returned it to her to sign the back. After passing the credit card through the imprinting machine, the clerk handed her the credit card receipt to sign, which Langer did. Then, says Langer, the cashier "held the form next to the newly signed card to see if the signatures matched."[2]

In automatic behavior, we take in and use limited signals from the world around us without letting other signals penetrate as well. By contrast, mindfulness is being open to new information—including that not specifically assigned to you. Mindfulness requires you engage more fully in whatever it is you're doing.

■ **Acting from a single perspective:** Most people, says Langer, typically assume that other people's motives and intentions are the same as theirs. For example, she says, "If I am out running and see someone walking briskly, I assume she is trying to exercise and would run if only she could," when actually she may be intending to get her exercise only from walking.

For most situations, many interpretations are possible. "Every idea, person, or object is potentially simultaneously many things depending on the perspective from which it is viewed," says Langer.[3] Trying out different perspectives gives you *more choices in how to respond;* a single perspective that produces an automatic reaction reduces your options.

Developing mindfulness means consciously adapting: Being open to novelty. Being alert to distinctions. Being sensitive to different contexts. Being aware of multiple perspectives. Being oriented in the present.

FORECAST: WHAT'S AHEAD IN THIS CHAPTER

This chapter gives you a short overview of the three principal *historical* perspectives or viewpoints on management—*classical, behavioral,* and *quantitative.* It then describes the three principal *contemporary* viewpoints—*systems, contingency,* and *quality-management.* Finally, we consider the concept of *learning organizations.*

major question

What's the payoff in studying different management perspectives, both yesterday's and today's?

The Big Picture

Management began as an art but is evolving into a science. Two principal perspectives are the *historical* and the *contemporary*. Studying management theory provides a guide to action, a source of new ideas, clues to the meaning of your managers' decisions, and clues to the meaning of outside events.

It's a story seen over and over again in the movies: The amateur comes onto the scene and confounds the experts by achieving the goal everyone has been working for—catching the killer, winning the client, finding the Aztec gold, or whatever. And he or she usually does so not because of experience but because of a combination of wits, intuition, alertness, and luck.

Does this happen in real life? Of course—at least sometimes. Indeed, innovations sometimes come from people who aren't experts. The first workable personal computer, for instance, was invented by two college dropouts, Steve Jobs and Stephen Wozniak, not by the engineers at IBM or Hewlett-Packard. Unlike in the movies, however, most of the time to be a good manager it usually helps to have knowledge—to be an expert.

Is Management an Art or a Science?

There's no question that the practice of management can be an art. Debby Krenek, formerly of the *New York Daily News,* has a background in journalism, not business. Bill Gates, the founder of Microsoft Corp. and today the richest man in the world, had no training in management—in fact, he was a college dropout (from Harvard) with a background in computer science. Great managers, like great painters or actors, are those who have the right mix of intuition, judgment, and experience.

But management is also a science. That is, rather than being performed in a seat-of-the-pants, trial-and-error, make-it-up-as-you-go-along kind of way—which can lead to some truly horrendous mistakes—management can be approached deliberately, rationally, systematically. That's what the scientific method is, after all—a logical process, embodying four steps:

1 You observe events and gather facts.

2 You pose a possible solution or explanation based on those facts.

3 You make a prediction of future events.

4 You test the prediction under systematic conditions.

Throughout the book, we describe various scientific tools that managers use to solve problems.

Two Overarching Perspectives about Management & Four Practical Reasons for Studying Them

In this chapter, we describe two overarching perspectives about management:

■ **Historical: The _historical perspective_ includes three viewpoints—_classical_, _behavioral_, and _quantitative_.**

■ **Contemporary: The _contemporary perspective_ also includes three viewpoints—_systems_, _contingency_, and _quality-management_.**

This is supposed to be a practical book. But what could be more practical than studying different approaches to management to see which seem to work best? After all, as philosopher George Santayana said, "Those who cannot remember the past are condemned to repeat it."

Indeed, there are four good reasons for studying theoretical perspectives:

1 Guide to action: Knowing management perspectives helps you develop a set of principles, a blueprint, that will guide your actions.

2 Source of new ideas: Being aware of various perspectives can also provide new ideas when you encounter new situations.

3 Clues to meaning of your managers' decisions: It can help you understand the focus of your organization, where the top managers are "coming from."

4 Clues to meaning of outside events: Finally, it may allow you to understand events outside the organization that could affect it or you.

Example of How Understanding Theory Can Help You: Is the Pyramid Hierarchy Useful or Useless?

Is there a reason for having the kind of management hierarchy that we described in Chapter 1? The idea that the company is shaped like a pyramid, with the CEO at the top and everybody else in layers below, is a legacy with strong roots in the military bureaucracy. German sociologist Max Weber thought bureaucracy was actually a rational approach to organizations, and in his day it probably was an improvement over the organizational arrangements then in place, as we'll discuss. The traditional pyramid hierarchy and bureaucracy have had a past history of great success in large corporations such as the Coca-Cola Company.

Knowing what you know about the pyramid hierarchy, can you think of any problems posed by the traditional organization chart? Could a hierarchy of boxes with lines showing who works in what department and who reports to whom actually become a corporate straitjacket?

That's what Lars Kolind, CEO of Danish digital hearing-aid producer Oticon, thought. He took Oticon's organization chart and simply threw it away. "He unilaterally abolished the old pyramid," says one account. "Today there is no formal organization, no departments, no functions, no paper, no permanent desks."[4] All employees work at mobile workstations, all desks are on wheels, and everybody works on projects, which are always subject to reorganization. Why such deliberate disorganization? Because if you want to have a company that is fast, agile, and innovative, as CEO Kolind does, you might want to have a flexible organizational structure that allows for fast reaction time.

Oticon has only 150 employees, however. Here's the challenge: Could the same be done with a large company such as Coca-Cola, with its hundreds of thousands of employees?

If the name of the game is to manage work more efficiently, what can the classical viewpoint teach me?

The Big Picture

The *three historical management viewpoints* we will describe include (1) the classical, described in this section; (2) the behavioral; and (3) the quantitative. The classical viewpoint, which emphasized ways to manage work more efficiently, had two approaches: (a) scientific management and (b) administrative management. *Scientific management,* pioneered by Frederick W. Taylor and Frank and Lillian Gilbreth, emphasized the scientific study of work methods to improve the productivity of individual workers. *Administrative management,* pioneered by Henry Fayol and Max Weber, was concerned with managing the total organization.

Bet you've never heard of a "therblig," although it may describe some physical motions you perform from time to time—perhaps when you have to wash dishes. A made-up word you won't find in most dictionaries, *thirblig* was coined by Frank Gilbreth and is, in fact, "Gilbreth" spelled backward, with the "t" and the "h" reversed. It refers to one of 17 basic motions. By identifying the therbligs in a job, as in the tasks of a bricklayer (which he had once been), Frank and his wife, Lillian, were able to eliminate motions while simultaneously reducing fatigue.

The Gilbreths were a husband-and-wife team of industrial engineers who were pioneers in one of the classical approaches to management, part of the historical perspective. As we mentioned, there are *three historical management viewpoints* or approaches *(see Panel 2.1, opposite page):*

■ Classical   ■ Behavioral   ■ Quantitative

In this section, we describe the classical perspective of management, which originated during the early 1900s. **The *classical viewpoint*, which emphasized finding ways to manage work more efficiently, had two branches—*scientific* and *administrative*—each of which is identified with particular pioneering theorists. In general, classical management assumes that *people are rational*. Let's compare the two approaches.

Adam Smith. Another voice in the classical viewpoint, the Scottish economist authored *The Wealth of Nations* (1776), in which he suggested that wealth was created through the efforts of entrepreneurs working to improve their lives, which led to the provision of goods and services and jobs for others.

Classical Viewpoint
Emphasis on ways to manage work more efficiently

Scientific management
Emphasized scientific study of work methods to improve productivity of individual workers

Proponents:
Frederick W. Taylor

Frank and Lillian Gilbreth

Administrative management
Concerned with managing the total organization

Proponents:
Henry Taylor

Max Weber

Behavioral Viewpoint
Emphasis on importance of understanding human behavior and motivating and encouraging employees toward achievement

Early behaviorists
Proponents:
Hugo Munsterberg

Mary Parker Follet

Elton Mayo

Human relations movement
Proposed better human relations could increase worker productivity

Proponents:
Abraham Maslow

Douglas McGregor

Behavioral science approach
Relies on scientific research for developing theory to provide practical management tools

Quantitative Viewpoint
Applies quantitative techniques to management

Management science
Focuses on using mathematics to aid in problem solving and decision making

Operations management
Focuses on managing the production and delivery of an organization's products or services more effectively

PANEL 2.1 **The historical perspective.** Three viewpoints are shown.

Scientific Management: Pioneered by Taylor & the Gilbreths

The problem for which scientific management emerged as a solution was this: In the expansive days of the early 20th century, labor was in such short supply that managers were hard pressed to raise the productivity of workers. ___Scientific management___ **emphasized the scientific study of work methods to improve the productivity of individual workers.** Two of its chief proponents were **Frederick W. Taylor** and the team of **Frank and Lillian Gilbreth.**

Frederick Taylor & the Four Principles of Scientific Management   No doubt there are some days when you haven't studied, or worked, as efficiently as you could. This could be called "underachieving," or "loafing," or what Taylor called it—*soldiering,* deliberately working at less than full capacity. Known as "the father of scientific management," Taylor was an engineer who believed that managers could eliminate soldiering by applying four principles of science:

1 Evaluate a task by scientifically studying each part of the task (not use old rule-of-thumb methods).

2 Carefully select workers with the right abilities for the task.

3 Give workers the training and incentives to do the task with the proper work methods.

4 Use scientific principles to plan the work methods and ease the way for workers to do their jobs.

Frederick W. Taylor, called the father of scientific management.

Taylor based his system on *motion studies*, in which he broke down each worker's job at a steel company, say, into basic physical motions and then trained workers to use the methods of their best-performing coworkers. In addition, he suggested employers institute a *differential rate system*, in which more efficient workers earned higher wages.

Although "Taylorism" met considerable resistance from employees fearing that working harder would lead to lost jobs except for the highly productive few, Taylor believed that by raising production both labor and management could increase profits to the point where they no longer would have to quarrel over them. If used correctly, the principles of scientific management can enhance productivity, and such innovations as motion studies and differential pay are still used today.

Frank & Lillian Gilbreth & Industrial Engineering As mentioned, Frank and Lillian Gilbreth were a husband-and-wife team of industrial engineers. Their experiences in raising twelve children—to whom they applied some of their ideas about improving efficiency (such as printing the Morse Code on the back of the bathroom door so that family members could learn it while doing other things)—later were popularized in a book, a movie, and a TV sitcom, *Cheaper by the Dozen*. The Gilbreths expanded on Taylor's motion studies—for instance, by using movie cameras to film workers at work in order to isolate the parts of a job.

Lillian Gilbreth, who received a Ph.D. in psychology, ultimately became a professor at Purdue University and the first woman to be a major contributor to management science.

Lillian and Frank Gilbreth, industrial engineers who pioneered time and motion studies.

Administrative Management: Pioneered by Fayol & Weber

Scientific management is concerned with the jobs of individuals. **Administrative management is concerned with managing the total organization.** Among the pioneering theorists were **Henry Fayol** and **Max Weber.**

Henry Fayol & the Functions of Management Fayol was not the first to investigate management behavior, but he was the first to systematize it. A French engineer and industrialist, he became known to American business when his most important work, *General and Industrial Management,* was translated into English in 1930.

Fayol was the first to identify the major functions of management—planning, organizing, leading, and controlling, as well as coordinating—the first four of which you'll recognize as the functions providing the framework for this and most other management books.

Click-Along 2.1

Management Functions: Fayol's 14 Points

Max Weber & the Rationality of Bureaucracy In our time, the word "bureaucracy" has come to have negative associations: impersonality, inflexibility, red tape, a molasseslike response to problems. But to German sociologist Max Weber, a *bureaucracy* was a rational, efficient, ideal organization based on principles of logic. After all, in Weber's Germany in the late 19th century, many people were in positions of authority (particularly in the government) not because of their abilities but because of their social status. The result, Weber wrote, was that they didn't perform effectively.

A better-performing organization, he felt, should have five positive bureaucratic features:

1 A well-defined hierarchy of authority   **2** Formal rules and procedures   **3** A clear division of labor   **4** Impersonality   **5** Careers based on merit

Weber's work was not translated into English until 1947, but, as we mentioned in the box on page 37, it came to have an important influence on the structure of large corporations, such as General Motors.

The Problem with the Classical Viewpoint: Too Mechanistic

The essence of the classical viewpoint was that work activity was amenable to a rational approach, that through the application of scientific methods, time and motion studies, and job specialization it was possible to boost productivity. Indeed, these concepts are still in use today, the results visible to you every time you visit McDonald's or Pizza Hut.

The flaw in the classical viewpoint, however, is that it is mechanistic: It tends to view humans as cogs within a machine, not taking into account the importance of human needs. Behavioral theory addressed this problem, as we explain next.

Carmakers have broken down automobile manufacturing into its constituent tasks. This reflects the contributions of the school of scientific management. Is there anything wrong with this approach? How could it be improved?

major question

To understand how people are motivated to achieve, what can I learn from the behavioral viewpoint?

The Big Picture
The second of the three historical management perspectives was the *behavioral* viewpoint, which emphasized the importance of understanding human behavior and of motivating employees toward achievement. The behavioral viewpoint developed over three phases: (1) *Early behaviorism* was pioneered by Hugo Munsterberg, Mary Parker Follett, and Elton Mayo. (2) The *human relations movement* was pioneered by Abraham Maslow (who proposed a hierarchy of needs) and Douglas McGregor (who proposed a Theory X and Theory Y view to explain managers' attitudes toward workers). (3) The *behavioral science approach* relied on scientific research for developing theories about behavior useful to managers.

The ***behavioral viewpoint*** emphasized the importance of understanding human behavior and of motivating employees toward achievement. The behavioral viewpoint developed over three phases: (1) early behaviorism, (2) the human relations movement, and (3) behavioral science.

The Early Behaviorists: Pioneered by Munsterberg, Follett, & Mayo

The three people—two men and one woman—who pioneered behavioral theory were **Hugo Munsterberg, Mary Parker Follett,** and **Elton Mayo.**

Hugo Munsterberg & the First Application of Psychology to Industry
Called "the father of industrial psychology," German-born Hugo Munsterberg had a Ph.D. in psychology and a medical degree and joined the faculty at Harvard University in 1892. Munsterberg suggested that psychologists could contribute to industry in three ways. They could:

1 Study jobs and determine which people are best suited to specific jobs

2 Identify the psychological conditions under which employees do their best work

3 Devise management strategies to influence employees to follow management's interests

His ideas led to the field of *industrial psychology,* the study of human behavior in workplaces, which is still taught in colleges today.

Mary Parker Follett & Power Sharing Among Employees & Managers
A Massachusetts social worker and social philosopher, Mary Parker Follett was lauded on her death in 1933 as "one of the most important women America has yet produced in the fields of civics and sociology." Instead of following the usual hierarchical arrangement of managers as order givers and employees as order takers, Follett thought organizations should become more democratic, with managers and employees working cooperatively.

Among her most important ideas were the following:

1 Organizations should be operated as "communities," with managers and subordinates working together in harmony.

2 Conflicts should be resolved by having managers and workers talk over differences and find solutions that would satisfy both parties—a process she called *integration*.

3 The work process should be under the control of workers with the relevant knowledge, rather than of managers, who should act as facilitators.

With these and other ideas, Follett anticipated some of today's concepts of "self-managed teams," "worker empowerment," and "interdepartmental teams"—that is, members of different departments working together on joint projects.

Elton Mayo & the Supposed "Hawthorne Effect" Do you think workers would be more productive if they thought they were receiving special attention? This was the conclusion drawn by a Harvard research group in the late 1920s.

Conducted by Elton Mayo and his associates at Western Electric's Hawthorne (Chicago) plant, what came to be called the *Hawthorne studies* began with an investigation into whether workplace lighting level affected worker productivity. (This was the type of study that Taylor or the Gilbreths might have done.) In later experiments, other variables were altered, such as wage levels, rest periods, and length of workday. Worker performance varied but tended to increase over time, leading Mayo and his colleagues to hypothesize what came to be known as the *Hawthorne effect*—namely, that employees worked harder if they received added attention, if they thought managers cared about their welfare and that supervisors paid special attention to them.

Ultimately, the Hawthorne studies were faulted for being poorly designed and not having enough empirical data to support the conclusions. Nevertheless, they succeeded in drawing attention to the importance of "social man" (social beings) and how managers using good human relations could improve worker productivity. This in turn led to the so-called *human relations movement* in the 1950s and 1960s.

Mary Parker Follett thought managers and employees should work together cooperatively.

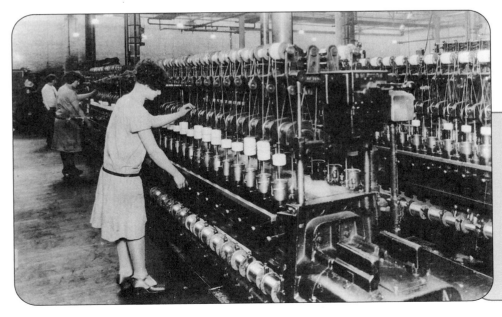

Western Electric's Hawthorne plant, where Elton Mayo and his team conducted their studies in the 1920s. Do you think you'd perform better in a robotlike job if you thought your supervisor cared about you and paid more attention to you?

The Human Relations Movement: Pioneered by Maslow & McGregor

The two theorists who contributed most to the ***human relations movement***—**which proposed that better human relations could increase worker productivity**—were Abraham Maslow and Douglas McGregor.

Douglas McGregor suggested managers need to be aware of their own attitudes toward their employees.

Abraham Maslow & the Hierarchy of Needs   What motivates you to perform: Food? Security? Love? Recognition? Self-fulfillment? Probably all of these, Abraham Maslow would say, although some needs must be satisfied before others. The chairman of the psychology department at Brandeis University and one of the earliest researchers to study motivation, in 1943 Maslow proposed his famous *hierarchy of human needs:* physiological, safety, social, esteem, and self-actualization[5] (as we discuss in detail in Chapter 12).

Douglas McGregor & Theory X versus Theory Y   Having been for a time a college president (at Antioch College in Ohio), Douglas McGregor came to realize that it was not enough for managers to try to be liked; they also needed to be aware of their attitudes toward employees.[6] Basically, McGregor suggested in a 1960 book, these attitudes could be either "X" or "Y."

Theory X represents a pessimistic, negative view of workers. In this view, workers are considered to be irresponsible, to be resistant to change, to lack ambition, to hate work, and to want to be led than to lead.

Theory Y represents the outlook of human relations proponents—an optimistic, positive view of workers. In this view, workers are considered to be capable of accepting responsibility, self-direction, and self-control and of being imaginative and creative.

The principal contribution offered by the Theory X/Theory Y perspective is that it can help managers avoid falling into the trap of the *self-fulfilling prophecy.* This is the idea that if a manager expects a subordinate to act in a certain way, the worker may, in fact, very well act that way, thereby confirming the manager's expectations: The prophecy that the manager made is fulfilled.

Theory Y? Debra Stark (third from left) built her Concord, Mass.--based Debra's Natural Gourmet store into a $2.5 million business by assigning each of her 26 employees, whom she calls "coworkers," a management role, such as monitoring product turnover. Each quarter, Stark distributes 20% of her after-tax profits among everyone, divided according to not only hours worked and salary level but also "how I see they're interacting with customers, each other, and me."

Theory X? Marlene Dolan's job at InsightShare, a software-and-services company based in Andover, Mass., is to keep her coworkers on schedule—using any means necessary. Her title: Project Meanie. "I don't know if I *have* to be mean," she says, "but I am. . . . When I do a good job, I'm like the tough coach everybody loves to hate."

The Behavioral Science Approach

The human relations movement was a necessary correction to the sterile approach used within scientific management, but its optimism came to be considered too simplistic for practical use. More recently, the human relations view has been superseded by the behavioral science approach to management. ***Behavioral science*** **relies on scientific research for developing theories about human behavior that can be used to provide practical tools for managers.** The disciplines of behavioral science include psychology, sociology, anthropology, and economics.

Example of Application of Behavioral Science Approach: Which Is Better—Competition or Cooperation?

A widely held assumption among American managers is that "competition brings out the best in people." From an economic standpoint, business survival depends on staying ahead of the competition. But from an interpersonal standpoint, critics contend competition has been overemphasized, primarily at the expense of cooperation.[7]

One strong advocate of greater emphasis on cooperation, Alfie Kahn, reviewed the evidence and found two reasons for what he sees as competition's failure.

First, he said, "success often depends on sharing resources efficiently, and this is nearly impossible when people have to work against one another." Competition makes people suspicious and hostile toward each other. Cooperation, by contrast, "takes advantage of all the skills represented in a group as well as the mysterious process by which that group becomes more than the sum of its parts."

Second, Kahn says, competition does not promote excellence, "because trying to do well and trying to beat others simply are two different things." Kahn points out the example of children in class who wave their arms to get the teacher's attention, but when they are finally recognized they then seem befuddled and ask the teacher to repeat the question—because they were more focused on beating their classmates than on the subject matter.[8]

What does the behavioral science research suggest about the question of cooperation versus competition? One team of researchers reviewed 122 studies encompassing a wide variety of subjects and settings and came up with three conclusions: (1) Cooperation is superior to competition in promoting achievement and productivity. (2) Cooperation is superior to individualistic efforts in promoting achievement and productivity. (3) Cooperation without intergroup competition promotes higher achievement and productivity than cooperation with intergroup competition.[9]

If it's the manager's job to solve problems, how might the two quantitative approaches help?

The Big Picture

The third and last category under historical perspectives consists of *quantitative viewpoints*, which emphasize the application to management of quantitative techniques, such as statistics and computer simulations. Two approaches of quantitative management are *management science* and *operations management*.

During the air war known as the Battle of Britain in World War II, a relative few Royal Air Force fighter pilots and planes were able to successfully resist the overwhelming might of the German military machine. How did they do it? Military planners drew on mathematics and statistics to determine how to most effectively allocate use of their limited aircraft.

When the Americans entered the war in 1941, they used the British model to form *operations research (OR)* teams to determine how to deploy troops, submarines, and other military personnel and equipment most effectively. For example, OR techniques were used to establish the optimum pattern that search planes should fly to try to locate enemy ships.

After the war, businesses also began using these techniques. One group of former officers, who came to be called the Whiz Kids, used statistical techniques at Ford Motor Co. to make better management decisions. Later Whiz Kid Robert McNamara, who had become Ford's president, was appointed Secretary of Defense and introduced similar statistical techniques and cost-benefit analyses throughout the Department of Defense. Since then, OR techniques have evolved into ***quantitative management*, the application to management of quantitative techniques, such as statistics and computer simulations. Two branches of quantitative management are *management science* and *operations management*.**

Management Science: Using Mathematics to Solve Management Problems

How would you go about deciding how to assign utility repair crews during a blackout? Or how many package sorters you needed and at which times for an overnight delivery service such as FedEx or UPS? You would probably use the tools of management science.

Management science is not the same as Taylor's scientific management. ***Management science* focuses on using mathematics to aid in problem solving and decision making.** Sometimes management science is called *operations research*.

FedEx. What management tools do you use to schedule employees and aircraft to deal with wide variations in package volume—such as December 23 versus December 26?

Example of Management Science: Renting Hotel Rooms at Half the Price

"Anyone who spends more than a few nights in hotels each year should join a half-price hotel program," says travel writer Ed Perkinson.[10] Such programs, like that available by buying the annual *Ultimate Travel and Savings Directory*, which has more than 5,000 participating hotels, offer discounts of 50% or so.

Why would hotels want to sign up for half-price deals? "For the same reasons that airlines sell a few of their seats for half (or even less than half) of the top price," says Perkinson. "The idea is called 'yield management,' and it's based on the simple economic principle that selling a room for half the price is better than having it remain empty."

All it takes for the hotels to work out a half-price program is to do some management science-style math. Research shows that 80% occupancy is the standard for profitability. If the hotel is booked beyond that, half-price members don't get their discount; lower than 80%, they do. In addition, there may be blackout periods at some city locations during weekdays (the most popular days for business travelers) and at resorts during weekends (the most popular times for leisure travelers).

Operations Management: Helping Organizations Deliver Products or Services More Effectively

How does a warehouse store such as Costco decide when to reorder supplies? How does American Airlines decide which planes are to fly where and when? Managers use the techniques of operations management.

Operations management could be considered a less sophisticated version of management science. *Operations management* **focuses on managing the production and delivery of an organization's products or services more effectively.** It thus is concerned with work scheduling, production planning, facilities location and design, and decisions about the optimum levels of inventory a company should maintain, among other tasks.

Example of Operations Management: If Your Electricity Goes Out, Will Work Crews Have What They Need to Restore It?

Immediately restoring electricity to houses gone dark from a storm is a situation every utility company has to be ready for. But how long should work crews take to round up parts before going to the job? ("Quickly!" you'd say, if it were your house without power.)

At Alabama Power, the linemen and women usually have everything they need when they need it, yet the company has reduced the amount of expensive material kept in inventory. The utility readies materials for jobs by assembling "kits" of hardware and electrical components in blue plastic bins at one of four regional warehouses. The kits are then put on shrink-wrapped pallets, which are trucked to the garages where the work crews meet to pick up the bucket trucks that hoist them to the tops of poles. The line people need only crack open the pallets and load the prepacked bins onto their service trucks.[11]

This is an example of supply-chain efficiency brought about by the use of operations research techniques that are making companies more efficient while also saving them money.

Click-Along 2.2

Operations Research: Another Example

How can the exceptional manager be helped by the systems viewpoint?

The Big Picture

Three contemporary management perspectives are (1) the *systems*, (2) the *contingency*, and (3) the *quality-management* viewpoints. The *systems viewpoint* sees organizations as a system, either open or closed, with inputs, outputs, transformation processes, and feedback. The *contingency viewpoint* emphasizes that a manager's approach should vary according to the individual and environmental situation. The *quality-management viewpoint* has two traditional approaches: *quality control*, the strategy for minimizing errors by managing each stage of production, and *quality assurance*, which focuses on the performance of workers, urging employees to strive for zero defects. A third quality approach is the movement of *total quality management (TQM)*, a comprehensive approach dedicated to continuous quality improvement, training, and customer satisfaction.

Being of a presumably practical turn of mind, could you run an organization or a department according to the theories you've just learned? Probably not. The reason: People are complicated. To be an exceptional manager, you need to learn to deal with individual differences in a variety of settings.

Thus, to the historical perspective on management (classical, behavioral, and quantitative viewpoints), let us now add the *contemporary perspective,* which consists of three viewpoints. *(See Panel 2.2, opposite page.)* These consist of:

- Systems
- Contingency
- Quality-management

In this section, we discuss the systems viewpoint.

The Systems Viewpoint

The 52 bones in the foot. The monarchy of Great Britain. A weather storm front. Each of these is a system. **A _system_ is a set of interrelated parts that operate together to achieve a common purpose.** Even though a system may not work very well—as in the inefficient way the Russian government collects taxes, for example—it is nevertheless still a system.

The _systems viewpoint_ regards the organization as a system of interrelated parts. By adopting this point of view, you can look at your organization both as (1) a collection of _subsystems_—**parts making up the whole system**—and (2) a part of the larger environment. A college, for example, is made up of a collection of academic departments, support staffs, students, and the like. But it also exists as a system within the environment of education, having to be responsive to parents, alumni, legislators, nearby townspeople, and so on.

The Systems Viewpoint
Regards the organization as systems of interrelated parts that operate together to achieve a common purpose

The Contingency Viewpoint
Emphasizes that a manager's approach should vary according to—i.e., be contingent on—the individual and environmental situation

The Quality-Management Viewpoint
Three approaches

Quality control
Strategy for minimizing errors by managing each state of production

Proponent:
Walter Shewart

Quality assurance
Focuses on the performance of workers, urging employees to strive for "zero defects"

Total quality management
Comprehensive approach dedicated to continuous quality improvement, training, and customer satisfaction

Proponents:
W. Edwards Deming

Joseph M. Juran

PANEL 2.2 **The contemporary perspective.** Three viewpoints

The Four Parts of a System

The vocabulary of the systems perspective is useful because it gives you a way of understanding many different kinds of organizations. There are four parts:

1 *Inputs* **are the people, money, information, equipment, and materials required to produce an organization's goods or services.** Whatever goes into a system is an input.

2 *Outputs* **are the products, services, profits, losses, employee satisfaction or discontent, and the like that are produced by the organization.** Whatever comes out of the system is an output.

3 *Transformation processes* **are the organization's capabilities in management and technology that are applied to converting inputs into outputs.** The main activity of the organization is to transform inputs into outputs.

4 *Feedback* **is information about the reaction of the environment to the outputs that affects the inputs.** Are the customers buying or not buying the product? That information is known as *feedback*.

Feedback. In focus groups, participants are asked to give responses or feedback about various proposals.

The four parts of a system are illustrated below. *(See Panel 2.3.)*

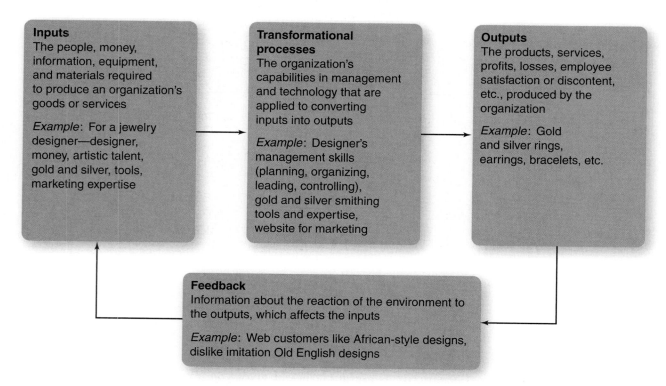

Inputs
The people, money, information, equipment, and materials required to produce an organization's goods or services

Example: For a jewelry designer—designer, money, artistic talent, gold and silver, tools, marketing expertise

Transformational processes
The organization's capabilities in management and technology that are applied to converting inputs into outputs

Example: Designer's management skills (planning, organizing, leading, controlling), gold and silver smithing tools and expertise, website for marketing

Outputs
The products, services, profits, losses, employee satisfaction or discontent, etc., produced by the organization

Example: Gold and silver rings, earrings, bracelets, etc.

Feedback
Information about the reaction of the environment to the outputs, which affects the inputs

Example: Web customers like African-style designs, dislike imitation Old English designs

PANEL 2.3 The four parts of a system

Open & Closed Systems Nearly all organizations are, at least to some degree, open systems rather than closed systems. **An _open system_ continually interacts with its environment. A _closed system_ has little interaction with its environment;** that is, it receives very little feedback from the outside. The classical management viewpoint often considered an organization a closed system. So does the management science perspective, which simplifies organizations for purposes of analysis. However, any organization that ignores feedback from the environment opens itself up to possibly spectacular failures.

The history of management is full of accounts of organizations whose services or products failed because they weren't open enough systems and didn't have sufficient feedback. One of the most famous gaffes was the introduction of the 1959 Edsel by the Ford Motor Co. despite mixed reactions about the car's eccentric styling by customers given a preview look at the vehicle.

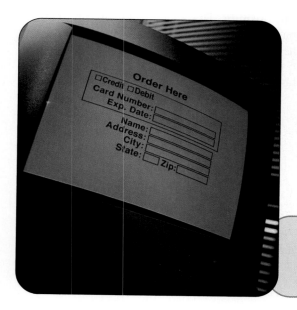

Closed system. The results of failure. Computer equipment from failed companies sits in a warehouse waiting to be auctioned off. Were these companies operating without enough interaction with their environments, so there was insufficient feedback?

Example of Open & Closed Systems: Marketing to Generation Y

Are generations really different? However fuzzy the notion of what a "generation" is, we have been accustomed to hearing them labeled: the Baby Boomers (born between 1945 and 1962), then Generation X (born 1963 to 1978), and now Generation Y (born 1979 to 1994). Generation Y—also tagged the Echo Boomers and the Millennium Generation—consists of 60 million people. While this is not as huge as the 72 million Baby Boomers, it is a great deal larger than the 17 million in Gen X, and no marketer can afford to ignore a demographic bulge of this size. But how to discover what's cool and what's not to this generation?

Growing up with the Internet, Gen Yers are accustomed to high-speed information, research shows, which has made fashions faster changing, with young consumers inclined to switch brand loyalties in a millisecond. So far, however, Tommy Hilfiger has stayed ahead of the style curve. "When Hilfiger's distinctive logo-laden shirts and jackets started showing up on urban rappers in the early '90s," says a *Business Week* account, "the company started sending researchers into music clubs to see how this influential group wore the styles. It bolstered its traditional mass-media ads with unusual promotions. . . . Knowing its customers' passion for computer games, it sponsored a Nintendo competition and installed Nintendo terminals in its stores." By having constant feedback—an open system—with young consumers, Hilfiger has been rewarded: Its jeans are the No. 1 brand in this age group.[12]

By contrast, Levi's, a veritable icon of Baby Boomer youth, was jolted awake in 1997 when its market share slid, and the company's researchers found the brand was losing popularity among teens. "We all got older, and as a consequence, we lost touch with teenagers," said David Spangler, director of market research. Levi's thereupon opened up its relatively closed system by instituting ongoing teen panels to keep tabs on emerging trends. Generation Y "is a generation that must be reckoned with," says Spangler. "They are going to take over the country."

Open system. How do you stay successful? So far Tommy Hilfiger clothes have stayed popular because the firm constantly interacts with its prospective customers.

In the end, is there one best way to manage in all situations?

The Big Picture

The second viewpoint in the contemporary perspective, the contingency viewpoint, emphasizes that a manager's approach should vary according to the individual and environmental situation.

The classical viewpoints advanced by Taylor and Fayol assumed their approaches had universal applications—that they were "the one best way" to manage organizations. The contingency viewpoint began to develop when managers discovered that under some circumstances better results could be achieved by breaking the one-best-way rule.

The *contingency viewpoint* **emphasizes that a manager's approach should vary according to—that is, be contingent on—the individual and the environmental situation.**

A manager subscribing to the Gilbreth approach might try to get workers to build a better mousetrap, say, by simplifying the steps. A manager of the Theory X/Theory Y persuasion might try to use motivational techniques to boost worker productivity. But the manager following the contingency viewpoint would simply ask, "What method is the best to use under these particular circumstances?"

Example of the Contingency Viewpoint: Does Web Access Really Boost Productivity?

Most managers believe that technology increases productivity, a notion that Taylor and the Gilbreths might subscribe to. But does it always? This is a question you might ponder if you were managing a small business and were considering introducing World Wide Web connections for your employees.

According to a survey by SurfWatch Software of Los Altos, Calif., which makes software that restricts access to specified websites, small-business employees spend an average of 20% of their online time on nonwork-related activities. "General news, investment, and sexually explicit sites rated the highest in frequency of use," reports *Fortune* magazine.[13]

So, should you or should you not introduce the Web to your office? The answer, according to the contingency viewpoint: It depends.

Toward a More Open Workplace: Treating Employees Right

Some companies are "toxic organizations," Stanford University business professor Jeffrey Pfeffer's name for firms with high turnover and low productivity. Others take a contingency kind of approach, keeping employees through methods such as "open-book management," *Inc.* magazine editor John Case's term for a company's being completely open with employees about its financial status, projections, costs, expenses, and even salaries.[14]

"Companies that manage people right will outperform companies that don't by 30% to 40%," says Pfeffer. "If you don't believe me, look at the numbers."[15] The author of *The Human Equation: Building Profits by Putting People First*, Pfeffer says that employees' loyalty to employers isn't dead but that toxic companies drive people away.[16] Companies such as Hewlett-Packard, Starbucks, and The Men's Warehouse have had lower turnover—and hence lower replacement and training costs—than their competitors for a reason: They have bent over backward to create workplaces that make people want to stay.

One way of challenging traditional military-style management and empowering employees and increasing earnings is through open-book management. This approach "means training employees in how the company is run," says one account. "It means asking for employee input and acting on it. It means rewarding employees with bonuses when the goals they create are met."[17] By learning the key numbers, employees are able to use their heads instead of just doing their jobs and going home. "Whether or not you have equity ownership, open-book management helps employees to feel, think, and act like owners," says Gary T. Brown, director of human resources for Springfield ReManufacturing Corp., a rebuilder of truck engines in Springfield, Mo.[18] "True open-book management means asking employees what the goals should be."

CompuWorks, a Pittsfield, Mass., computer systems-integration company, cultivates employee loyalty by piling on personal and team recognition, as in giving the Wizard of the Week award to the employee who goes beyond the call of duty. It also operates the Time Bank, into which every month 10 hours of free time is "deposited" for each employee to use as he or she wishes. Employees are trained how to read financial statements and how to chart billable hours and watch cash-flow levels. Regular bonuses are given based on company profits.[19]

Starbucks. It's become PR routine for companies to brag about how much they value their employees. Starbucks, however, really does seem to have bent over backward to create workplaces that make employees want to stay, offering pay that is better than that for most entry-level food-service jobs, as well as health insurance, and even stock options. As a result, annual employee turnover is 60%, compared with an average of 140% for hourly workers in the fast-food business.

Sometimes, despite the mantra that "the customer is always right," companies will even side with employees against clients. For example, The Benjamin Group, a California public relations agency, has fired clients who have been arrogant and hard to work with. This reflects management theories that troublesome customers are often less profitable and less loyal and so aren't worth the extra effort.[20]

All these approaches reflect the application of knowledge derived from management theory and research.[21]

Can the quality-management viewpoint offer guidelines for true managerial success?

The Big Picture

The quality-management viewpoint, the third category under contemporary perspectives, consists of *quality control, quality assurance,* and especially the movement of *total quality management (TQM),* dedicated to continuous quality improvement, training, and customer satisfaction.

The Malcom Baldrige National Quality Award is presented in 2000 by George W. Bush to Los Alamos National Bank executives in recognition of exceptional quality.

During the 1960s and 1970s, word got around among buyers of American cars that one shouldn't buy a "Monday car" or a "Friday car"—cars built on the days when absenteeism and hangovers were highest among dissatisfied auto workers. The reason, supposedly, was that, despite the efforts of quantitative management, the cars produced on those days were the most shoddily made of what were coming to look like generally shoddy products.

The energy crisis of 1973 showed different possibilities, as Americans began to buy more fuel-efficient cars made in Japan. Consumers found they could not only drive farther on a gallon of gas but that the cars were better made and needed repair less often. Eventually American car manufacturers began to adopt Japanese methods, leading to such slogans as "At Ford, Quality Is Job One." Today the average American car lasts eight or nine years compared to five or six 20 years ago.[22]

Although not a "theory" as such, the *quality-management viewpoint*, **which includes quality control, quality assurance, and total quality management**, deserve to be considered because of the impact of this kind of thinking on contemporary management perspectives.

Quality Control & Quality Assurance

Quality **refers to the total ability of a product or service to meet customer needs.** Quality is seen as one of the most important ways of adding value to products and services, thereby distinguishing them from those of competitors. Two traditional strategies for ensuring quality are quality control and quality assurance.

Quality Control *Quality control* **is defined as the strategy for minimizing errors by managing each stage of production.** Quality control techniques were developed in the 1930s at Bell Telephone Labs by **Walter Shewart,** who used statistical sampling to locate errors by testing just some (rather than all) of the items in a particular production run.

Quality Assurance Developed in the 1960s, *quality assurance* **focused on the performance of workers, urging employees to strive for "zero defects."** Quality assurance has been less successful because often employees have no control over the design of the work process.

Total Quality Management: Creating an Organization Dedicated to Continuous Improvement

In the years after World War II, the imprint "Made in Japan" on a product almost guaranteed that it was cheap and flimsy. That began to change with the arrival of two Americans, **W. Edwards Deming** and **Joseph M. Juran.**

W. Edwards Deming   Desperate to rebuild its war-devastated economy, Japan eagerly received mathematician W. Edwards Deming's lectures on "good management." Deming believed that quality stemmed from "constancy of purpose"—steady focus on an organization's mission—along with statistical measurement and reduction of variations in production processes. However, he also emphasized the human side, saying that managers should stress teamwork, try to be helpful rather than simply give orders, and make employees feel comfortable about asking questions.

In addition, Deming proposed his so-called "85–15 rule"—namely, when things go wrong, there is an 85% chance that the system is at fault, only a 15% chance that the individual worker is at fault. (The "system" would include not only machinery and equipment but also management and rules.) Most of the time, Deming thought, managers erroneously blamed individuals when the failure was really in the system.

W. Edwards Deming (right), shown with Kenzo Sasaoka, president of Yokogawa Hewlett Packard, in Japan, 1982.

Joseph M. Juran   Another pioneer with Deming in Japan's quality revolution was Joseph M. Juran, who defined quality as "fitness for use." By this he meant that a product or service should satisfy a customer's real needs. Thus, the best way to focus a company's efforts, Juran suggested, was to concentrate on the real needs of customers.

TQM: What It Is   From the work of Deming and Juran has come the strategic commitment to quality known as total quality management. ___Total quality management (TQM)___ **is a comprehensive approach—led by top management and supported throughout the organization—dedicated to continuous quality improvement, training, and customer satisfaction.**

The four components of TQM are as follows:

1 Make Continuous Improvement a Priority
TQM companies are never satisfied. They make small, incremental improvements an everyday priority in all areas of the organization. By improving everything a little bit of the time all the time, the company can achieve long-term quality, efficiency, and customer satisfaction.

2 Get Every Employee Involved To build teamwork and trust, TQM companies see that every employee is involved in the continuous improvement process. This requires that workers must be trained and empowered to find and solve problems. The goal is to build teamwork, trust, and mutual respect.

3 Listen to & Learn from Customers & Employees TQM companies pay attention to their customers, the people who use their products or services. In addition, employees within the companies listen and learn from other employees, those outside their own work areas.

4 Use Accurate Standards to Identify & Eliminate Problems
TQM organizations are always alert to how competitors do things better, then try to improve on them—a process known as benchmarking. Using these standards, they apply statistical measurements to their own processes to identify problems.

Organizations must learn or perish. How do I build a learning organization?

The Big Picture

Learning organizations actively create, acquire, and transfer knowledge within themselves and are able to modify their behavior to reflect new knowledge. There are three ways you as a manager can help build a learning organization.

Ultimately, the lesson we need to take from the theories, perspectives, and viewpoints we have described is this: We need to keep on learning. Organizations are the same way: Like people, they must continually learn new things or face obsolescence. A key challenge for managers, therefore, is to establish a culture that will enhance their employees' ability to learn—to build so-called learning organizations.

Learning organizations, says Massachusetts Institute of Technology professor **Peter Senge,** who coined the term, are places "where people continually expand their capacity to create the results they truly desire, where new and expansive patterns of thinking are nurtured, where collective aspiration is set free, and where people are continually learning how to learn together."[23]

The Learning Organization: Handling Knowledge & Modifying Behavior

More formally, a *__learning organization__* **is an organization that actively creates, acquires, and transfers knowledge within itself and is able to modify its behavior to reflect new knowledge.**[24] Note the three parts:

1 Creating & Acquiring Knowledge In learning organizations, managers try to actively infuse their organizations with new ideas and information, which are the prerequisites for learning. They acquire such knowledge by constantly scanning their external environments, by not being afraid to hire new talent and expertise when needed, and by devoting significant resources to training and developing their employees.

2 Transferring Knowledge Managers actively work at transferring knowledge throughout the organization, reducing barriers to sharing information and ideas among employees.

Electronic Data Systems (EDS), for instance, practically invented the information-technology services industry, but by 1996 it was slipping behind competitors—missing the onset of the Internet wave, for example. When a new CEO, Dick Brown, took the reins in 1999, he changed the culture from "fix the problem yourself" to sharing information internally.[25]

3 Modifying Behavior Learning organizations are nothing if not results oriented. Thus, managers encourage employees to use the new knowledge obtained to change their behavior to help further the organization's goals.[26]

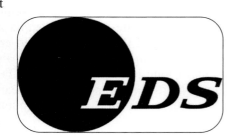

Example of a Learning Organization: An Automaker's Experimental Mindset

Experimental mindset—support for trying new things—is an important factor in facilitating learning. Before it was acquired by Daimler and became DaimlerChrysler, an example of a company employing this learning factor was American automaker Chrysler Corp.

Although it used most of the same 150 suppliers as its larger rivals General Motors and Ford, it did not purchase as much in volume and so did not receive the same kinds of quantity discounts. To cut costs, Chrysler therefore increased its learning capability by involving its suppliers earlier in the car-design process, soliciting ideas on cost savings and technological innovations, thereby finding out about new materials, parts, and other technologies before its competitors.

"When it comes to new technology," a supplier was quoted as saying, "Chrysler winds up getting a peek under the tent early. None of the other car companies we work with are as accessible or willing to take advice from suppliers."[27]

How to Build a Learning Organization: Three Roles Managers Play

To create a learning organization, managers must perform three key functions or roles: (1) *build a commitment to learning*, (2) *work to generate ideas with impact*, and (3) *work to generalize ideas with impact*.[28]

1 You Can Build a Commitment to Learning To instill in your employees an intellectual and emotional commitment to the idea of learning, you as a manager need to lead the way by investing in it, publicly promoting it, creating rewards and symbols of it, and similar activities. In publicly promoting it, for example, you can disseminate videos and readings to employees, be a presenter or participant at training seminars, or share with other managers management practices you've learned.

2 You Can Work to Generate Ideas with Impact As a manager, you need to try to generate ideas with impact—that is, ideas that add value for customers, employees, and shareholders—by increasing employee competence through training, experimenting with new ideas, and engaging in other leadership activities.

Soon after Dick Brown became new CEO of EDS, he saw that the company had to be reinvented as a cool brand to make people feel good about working there. His marketing director decided to launch a new campaign at the biggest media event of all: the Super Bowl. EDS ran an ad showing rugged cowboys riding herd on 10,000 cats. The message: "We ride herd on complexity."[29]

3 You Can Work to Generalize Ideas with Impact Besides generating ideas with impact, you can also generalize them—that is, reduce the barriers to learning among employees and within your organization. You can create a climate that reduces conflict, increases communication, promotes teamwork, rewards risk taking, reduces the fear of failure, and increases cooperation.[30] In other words, you can create a psychologically safe and comforting environment that increases the sharing of successes, failures, and best practices.

Click-Along 2.3

Taking Something Practical Away from This Chapter: Learning Styles & Styles

We consider the learning organization again in Chapter 8.

Key Terms Used In This Chapter

administrative management, 40

behavioral science, 45

behavioral viewpoint, 42

classical viewpoint, 38

closed system, 50

contemporary perspective, 37

contingency viewpoint, 52

feedback, 49

historical perspective, 37

human relations movement, 44

inputs, 49

learning organization, 56

management science, 46

open system, 50

operations management, 47

outputs, 49

quality, 54

quality assurance, 54

quality control, 54

quality-management viewpoint, 54

quantitative management, 46

scientific management, 39

subsystems, 48

system, 48

systems viewpoint. 48

total quality management (TQM), 55

transformation process, 49

Summary

2.1
Evolving Viewpoints: How We Got to Today's Management Outlook

■ Management is an art, but it is also a science. In this chapter we describe two overarching perspectives about management: (1) The historical perspectives includes three viewpoints—classical, behavioral, and quantitative. (2) The contemporary perspective also includes three viewpoints—systems, contingency, and quality-management.

■ There are four good reasons for studying theoretical perspectives. They provide (1) a guide to action, (2) a source of new ideas, (3) clues to the meaning of your managers' decisions, and (4) clues to the meaning of outside ideas.

2.2
The Classical Viewpoint: Scientific & Administrative Management

■ The first of the historical perspectives includes the classical viewpoints, which emphasized finding ways to manage work more efficiently. It had two branches, scientific and administrative.

■ Scientific management emphasized the scientific study of work methods to improve pro-

ductivity of individual workers. It was pioneered by Frederick W. Taylor, who offered four principles of science that could be applied to management, and by Frank and Lillian Gilbreth, who refined motion studies that broke job tasks into physical motions.

■ Administrative management was concerned with managing the total organization. Among its pioneers were Henry Fayol, who identified the major functions of management (planning, organizing, leading, and controlling), and Max Weber, who identified five positive bureaucratic features in a well-performing organization.

■ The problem with the classical viewpoint is that it is too mechanistic, viewing humans as cogs in a machine.

2.3
The Behavioral Viewpoint: Early Behaviorism, Human Relations, & Behavioral Science

■ The second of the historical perspectives, the behavioral viewpoint emphasized the importance of understanding human behavior and of motivating employees toward achievement. It developed over three phases.

- The first phase, early behaviorism, had three pioneers. Hugo Munsterberg suggested that psychologists could contribute to industry by studying jobs, identifying the psychological conditions for employees to do their best work, and devising strategies to influence employees to follow management's interests.

- Mary Parker Follett thought organizations should be democratic, with employees and managers working together. Organizations, she felt, should be operated as communities, conflicts should be resolved by talking over differences, and the work process should be controlled by workers with relevant knowledge.

- Elton Mayo hypothesized a so-called Hawthorne effect, suggesting that employees worked harder if they received added attention from managers.

- The second phase was the human relations movement, which suggested that better human relations could increase worker productivity. It was pioneered by Abraham Maslow, who proposed a hierarchy of human needs (physiological, safety, social, esteem, and self-actualization). Another pioneer was Douglas McGregor, who proposed a Theory X (managers have pessimistic, negative view of workers) versus Theory Y (managers have optimistic, positive view of workers), and suggested that managers could avoid the self-fulfilling prophecy of expecting workers to behave a certain way and then being unsurprised when they acted that way.

- The third phase was the behavioral science approach, which relies on scientific research for developing theories about human behavior that can be used to provide practical tools for managers.

2.4
The Quantitative Viewpoints: Management Science & Operations Research

- The third of the historical perspectives consists of quantitative viewpoints, which emphasized the application to management of quantitative techniques. Two approaches of quantitative management are management science and operations management.

- Management science focuses on using mathematics to aid in problem solving and decision making.

- Operations management focuses on managing the production and delivery of an organization's products or services more effectively.

2.5
The Systems Viewpoint

- We turn from study of the historical management perspectives to the contemporary management perspectives, which includes three viewpoints: (1) systems, (2) contingency, and (3) quality-management.

- The systems viewpoint regards the organization as a system of interrelated parts or collection of subsystems. A system is defined as a set of interrelated parts that operate together to achieve a common purpose. A system has four parts: inputs, outputs, transformation processes, and feedback. A system can be open, or continually interacting with its environment, or closed, having little such interaction.

2.6
The Contingency Viewpoint

- The second viewpoint in the contemporary perspective is the contingency viewpoint, which emphasizes that a manager's approach should vary according to the individual and the environmental situation.

2.7
The Quality-Management Viewpoint

- The third category in the contemporary perspective is the quality-management viewpoint, which includes (1) quality control, (2) quality assurance, and (3) total quality management.

- Quality refers to the total ability of a product or service to meet customer needs. Two traditional strategies for ensuring quality are quality control and quality assurance. Quality control is defined as the strategy for minimizing errors by managing each stage of production; quality-control techniques were developed by Walter Shewart. Quality assurance focuses on the performance of workers, urging employees to strive for "zero defects."

■ Total quality management (TQM) is a comprehensive approach—led by top management and supported throughout the organization—dedicated to continuous quality improvement, training, and customer satisfaction. The four components of TQM are (1) make continuous improvement a priority, (2) get every employee involved, (3) listen to and learn from customers and employees, and (4) use accurate standards to identify and eliminate problems.

2.8
The Learning Organization

■ A term coined by Peter Senge, a learning organization is an organization that actively creates, acquires, and transfers knowledge within itself and is able to modify its behavior to reflect new knowledge.

■ Three roles that managers must perform to build a learning organization are (1) build a commitment to learning, (2) work to generate ideas with impact, and (3) work to generalize ideas with impact.

Management in Action

Boeing Relies on a Variety of Management Theories to Cut Costs & Increase Profits[31]

Excerpted from J. Lynn Lunsford, "Lean Times: With Airbus on Its Tail, Boeing Is Rethinking How It Builds Planes," The Wall Street Journal, *October 5, 2001, pp. A1, A16.*

Not far from the steady blatt-blatt of the rivet guns on its 757 assembly line just outside Seattle sits what Boeing Co. calls its moonshine shop: The people here distill work-saving ideas into contraptions that make it easier to build jets.

Consider the hay loader next to an almost-completed 757. Normally, this cross between a ladder and a metal-spiked conveyor belt would be dumping bales of hay onto waiting trucks. But to veteran mechanic Robert Harms, the hay loader is the perfect way to get bulky passenger seats from the factory floor up 13 feet to the door of the plane without having to use an overhead crane. "It might look funny, but when you see it work, you wonder why we didn't do it this way all along," he says.

Moonshine shops—so named because they work outside traditional channels and use whatever materials are available—are the essence of Boeing Chairman Phil Condit's campaign to boost profits by driving out costly manufacturing techniques and the decades-old thinking behind them. From using materials developed for military aircraft to pulling its big planes onto moving assembly lines for the first time, Boeing is retooling itself to confront tougher times. . . . Boeing executives are counting on this revamp to enable the company's commercial-airplane division to continue posting double-

digit profit margins despite the slowing world economy and sharp decline in aircraft orders from the major airlines. . . . Boeing had been gradually adopting "lean" manufacturing techniques since the early 1990s—a decade after the U.S. auto industry began emulating the Japanese approach. The basic philosophy: Everything from the design of a component to the machine used to build it is examined with the goal of making it as easy as possible for workers to boost output using less space and fewer movements.

Since late 1998, when the company began applying lean activities on its newest model, the 777, the time it takes to assemble the major components into a finished aircraft has dropped to 37 days from 71. And just since April, the company has trimmed two days out of what was a 20-day final assembly of its best-selling plane, the 737. . . . Seattle-area workers got their stronger taste yet of where Boeing is going in April. That's when the company began converting one of its three 737 assembly lines in Renton to a moving line from the traditional bays in which planes are parked among fixed catwalks and other machinery for days at a time. Now, once the wings and landing gear are attached, each plane is dragged by a giant tug toward the door at two inches a minute for two shifts a day. The goal is to shove the aircraft out the door in about five days, down from the 11 days it now takes.

The workers move with the airplane on a float-like contraption. Rather than having mechanics waste time walking back and forth to retrieve tools or parts, specific items for each job are wheeled to waiting spots along the line.

"The moving line adds a sense of urgency because you can look at the airplane and tell when the work is even just a few minutes behind schedule," says Carolyn Corvi, 737 program manager. At several places along the line, devices resembling emergency call boxes with traffic lights on top have been set up so that workers can alert support departments to problems that might slow or stop the line. In one engineering group, the flashing light is accompanied by a recording of Aretha Franklin's "Rescue Me" to bring help running. . . . Already on edge since the moving company announced that it would be moving its headquarters to Chicago from Seattle this month, rank-and-file workers were at first reluctant to accept the changes in the Renton plant, venting some of their frustration at the moonshine workers. The union has filed several grievances against work turned out by the moonshine shops, alleging that the freewheeling nature of the shops' operations has resulted in the failure to use union electricians and toolmakers to do specialized work. The company says it is working to resolve the union's complaints, but it contends that the ability of the hand-picked moonshine teams to move quickly is paramount. . . . Boeing executives acknowledge that many of the improvements so far have been the result of picking low-hanging fruit—changing practices that were obviously wasteful but had endured because of long-standing habits and bureaucratic resistance.

In many cases, the design of the airplanes dictates much of the inefficiency in production. For example, on all of Boeing's planes, smaller work-ers are trained to crawl into confined spaces, such as fuel tanks, to attach wires and paint sealant. In other parts of the factory, workers can spend their entire careers sandwiched inside a labyrinth of jigs holding parts together while they repeatedly drill and set rivets. For Boeing, the Holy Grail is replacing these traditional, labor-intensive production methods with new, cutting edge materials.

Across the country at Boeing Phantom Works research facility in St. Louis, scientists and engineers are experimenting with some of the latest composites and metallurgy. One aim is to take subassemblies such as the dome-like rear pressure bulkhead, which keeps the plane pressurized, and reduce it to a single part, eliminating hundreds of components and thousands of rivets.

"The whole concept is to look for quantum leaps in efficiency, to the tune of 50%," says David Swain, president of the Phantom Works division. "We are looking for whole new ways to build airplanes."

For Discussion

1. Is Boeing making changes more reflective of managerial art or managerial science? Explain your rationale.

2. What advice would Frederick Taylor and Frank and Lillian Gilbreth probably offer managers at Boeing?

3. How might Boeing managers reduce resistance to change by using the behavioral viewpoints and the human relations movement?

4. To what extent is Boeing using management science and operations management to reduce costs and increase productivity? Explain.

5. Are the changes being made at Boeing consistent with recommendations derived from qualitative viewpoints? Provide evidence to support your opinions.

Take It to the Net

During the 20th century the concept of the *learning organization* evolved. This concept posits that organizations and their members must be committed to continuous learning to remain competitive and viable in our turbulent and changing globalized economy.

One approach to building a learning organization is "Open Book Management." This approach includes three principles, all of which must be followed if it is to work. Outlined by John Case in his *Open Book Experience* (Perseus Books, 1998, pp. 2–3), they are (1) create a *transparent* company, a company in which everyone, not just those at the top, sees and understands the real numbers; (2) create a system of *joint accountability,* a system that holds everybody responsible for his or her part in the company's performance; and (3) give people a *stake in success* as well as pay them for their time.

To learn more about Open Book Management, go to *http://www.nceo.org/library/obm_games.html* and read the information on "Open-Book Management Games." Then answer the following questions and be prepared to present your answers to the class:

Questions for Discussion

1. How is this approach different from the Scientific Management approach?
2. How would you describe motivation in this type of organization?
3. Why might some people not like this type of organization?
4. Would you like to work in this type of organization? Why or why not?
5. Could this type of model be adapted to your college?
6. Is this a type of learning organization? Why or why not?

For more information on employee-owned companies, click on the home page at the top of this site, which will take you to NCEO (the National Center for Employee Ownership).

Self-Assessment

What Is Your Level of Self-Esteem?

Objectives

1. To get to know yourself a bit better.
2. To help you assess your self-esteem.

Introduction: Self-esteem, confidence, self-worth, and self-belief are all important aspects of being a manager in any organizational structure. However, the need for strong self-esteem is especially vital today because organizations demand that a manager manage people not as appendages of machines (as in Scientific Management) but as individuals who possess skills, knowledge, and self-will. Managers used to operate from a very strong position of centralized power and authority. However, in our modern organizational settings power is shared, and knowledge is to some extent "where you find it." To manage effectively in this situation, mangers need strong self-esteem.

Instructions: To assess your self-esteem, answer the following questions. For each item, indicate the extent to which you agree or disagree by using the following scale. Remember, there are no right or wrong answers.

    1 = strongly disagree
    2 = disagree
    3 = neither agree nor disagree
    4 = agree
    5 = strongly agree

Questions

1. I generally feel as competent as my peers.	1	2	3	4	5
2. I usually feel I can achieve whatever I want.	1	2	3	4	5
3. Whatever happens to me is mostly in my control.	1	2	3	4	5
4. I rarely worry about how things will work out.	1	2	4	4	5
5. I am confident that I can deal with most situations.	1	2	3	4	5
6. I rarely doubt my ability to solve problems.	1	2	3	4	5
7. I rarely feel guilty for asking others to do things.	1	2	3	4	5
8. I am rarely upset by criticism.	1	2	3	4	5
9. Even when I fail, I still do not doubt my basic ability.	1	2	3	4	5

10. I am very optimistic about my future.		1	2	3	4	5
11. I feel that I have quite a lot to offer an employer.		1	2	3	4	5
12. I rarely dwell for very long on personal setbacks.		1	2	3	4	5
13. I am always comfortable in disagreeing with my boss.		1	2	3	4	5
14. I rarely feel that I would like to be somebody else.		1	2	3	4	5

TOTAL SCORE_____

Arbitrary Norms

High Self-esteem = 56-70

Moderate Self-esteem = 29-55

Low Self-esteem = 14-28

Questions for Discussion

1. Do you agree with the assessment? Why or why not?

2. How might you go about improving your self-esteem?

3. Can you survive today without having relatively good confidence in yourself?

Group Exercise

Who Are the Most Admired Companies & Why?*

Objectives

1. To assess your group's awareness of the most admired companies in the United States (as of 2001).

2. To discover the different perceptions of these companies and their management practices.

3. To understand how companies achieve the reputation they have earned.

Introduction

For decades *Fortune* magazine has asked top managers who they think are the most-admired and best-managed companies in the United States. Over the years we have moved from a time when Frederick Taylor and Henry Ford tied productivity to profit to the current understanding of the effect of the other "bottom lines" that must be considered to assess how well a company is managed (for example, companies' effect on the environment). Only five companies have held the number 1 spot on this *Fortune* list since 1983. They are IBM (5 times), Merck (15 times), Rubbermaid (11 times), Coca-Cola (13 times), and General Electric (8 times). However, only one of these was in the top 10 in 2001.

Instructions

Eight key attributes of reputation are used to rank the companies (there are 500 in all):

innovation

financial soundness

employee talent

use of corporate assets

long-term investment value

social responsibility

quality of management

quality of products/services

Following is a list, in random order, of the top 10 most-admired companies for 2001. Each member of your group is to guess these companies' rankings based on the attributes listed above. (Number 1 is the highest ranking and number 10 is the lowest ranking.) Group members should then compare their rankings and come to a consensus. (If time

*This exercise was adapted from *http://www.leadersdirect.com/howareyou/html.*

permits, locate additional information about each company on the Internet before you complete your group rankings.)

Here are the companies, in random order:

1. Intel
2. Berkshire Hathaway
3. Southwest Airlines
4. Wal-Mart
5. Citigroup
6. Home Depot
7. General Electric
8. FedEx
9. Microsoft
10. Johnson & Johnson

Questions for Discussion

1. Why did you as an individual rank the companies as you did? Explain.

2. How different was the group ranking from your own ranking? Why?

3. Why did the group order its ranking in the way it did?

4. What concepts from the chapter could you use to explain why these companies are so well managed and admired?

Answers:

1. General Electric
2. Southwest Airlines
3. Wal-Mart
4. Microsoft
5. Berkshire Hathaway
6. Home Depot
7. Johnson & Johnson
8. FedEx
9. Citigroup
10. Intel

Ethical Dilemma

Recycling Automobile Air Bags Is a Common Practice

From Kimberly Weisul, "Car Talk: One Time Not to Recycle," Business Week, *August 6, 2001, p. 10.*

BusinessWeek One unreported casualty of [July 2001] floods in Houston: 95,000 cars. Many of their air bags were water-damaged and should be junked. But because the damage isn't visible, many of the bags are ending up in repair shops as secondhand parts. Add the tens of thousands of air bags stolen each year, and the market for air bags is hot. There's plenty of incentive: A new air bag can cost up to $1,500; a secondhand one might sell for $400.

There's nothing illegal about air bags as secondhand parts. But there are also no regulations requiring repair shops to test them for safety or determine where they came from, and no requirement that drivers replace them after accidents.

That's causing growing safety concerns. Air bags with flood damage are dangerous because of residual moisture. They take up to a third of a second longer to inflate than new ones. By that time, "you've had your head buried in the steering wheel," says Peter Byrne, president of Airbag Testing Technology, which inspects recycled air bags.

Then there are the body shops and car owners who knowingly circumvent air-bag safety. Owners of banged-up cars may tell body shops to skip replacing the air bags, since they can tack $3,000 onto the repair bill for even a fender-bender. "The owner knows there's no air bag in there," says Kim Hazelbaker, senior vice-president at the Highway Loss Data Institute. "The next buyer doesn't." No laws require used cars to come equipped with air bags.

The National Highway Traffic Safety Administration, alert to safety concerns, is looking into the issue and is expected to report by yearend. No doubt, that will be too late for some unfortunate drivers.

Solving the Dilemma

What would you do if you were a member of the National Highway Traffic Safety Administration?

1. Leave the laws as they are.

2. Create regulations requiring that certified professionals test all recycled air bags for safety.

3. Do not allow secondhand air bags to be reused.

4. Invent other options. Discuss.

The Exceptional Entrepreneur

Four entrepreneurs in three companies share their insights. Syl Tang of Hipguide.com, Dale Gray of Communications Services, and Debbie and Les Busfield of Strongfield-Trimco explain what it takes to be a successful entrepreneur. Common themes emerge from their experiences. All convey a passion and excitement at the prospect of going to work each day. They discuss the personality characteristics of an entrepreneur, the highs and lows of owning a business, and the payoffs of success. All relish "being your own boss" but also recognize that they still answer to others. At the business level, these owners discuss the role of a business plan, the need to rely on the expertise of others, and the importance of hiring the right people.

Discussion Questions:

1. Describe the personality characteristics of these entrepreneurs.

2. What's the biggest challenge faced by each entrepreneur? What is their biggest payoff? Support your responses with evidence from the case.

3. Why is hiring the right people so important to these business owners?

4. What makes these entrepreneurs successful when so many others fail?

5. What are the common beliefs shared by all of the entrepreneurs?

CHAPTER 3

The Manager's Changing Work Environment & Responsibilities

MAJOR QUESTIONS YOU SHOULD BE ABLE TO ANSWER

3.1 The Community of Stakeholders Inside the Organization

Major Question: Stockholders are only one group of stakeholders. Who are the stakeholders important to me inside the organization?

3.2 The Community of Stakeholders Outside the Organization

Major Question: Who are stakeholders important to me outside the organization?

3.3 The Ethical Responsibilities Required of You as a Manager

Major Question: What does the successful manager need to know about ethics and values?

3.4 The Social Responsibilities Required of You as a Manager

Major Question: Is being socially responsible really necessary?

3.5 The New Diversified Workforce

Major Question: What trends in workplace diversity should managers be aware of?

3.6 The Entrepreneurial Spirit

Major Question: Do I have what it takes to be an entrepreneur?

IN DEMAND: PROBLEM-SOLVING, CONSCIENTIOUS MANAGERS WHO CAN DEAL WITH CHANGE

The world is changing, and changing fast. Thus, the greatest challenge to organizations is finding managers who can manage change. Yet despite great efforts, organizations can't seem to find enough managers and professionals with the qualities they want.

Consider the conclusions of a nationwide study by Caliper, a human-resources consulting firm based in Princeton, N.J. as reported by *Fortune* columnist Anne Fisher. It seems, says Fisher, that "people who do the serious hiring in companies these days are desperate—and no, that's not too strong a word—for candidates with two traits: (1) A talent for problem solving. By which they mean: If I give you a Serious Situation to fix, can you figure it out? . . . And (2) conscientiousness. That is, do you know what a deadline is, and will you meet it? . . . Will you try to do a good job even when you're having a bad day?"[1]

Why are these attributes in such strong demand? Because organizations today are being buffeted by tremendous changes of the sort we describe in this chapter—economic, technological, sociocultural, demographic, political-legal, and international.

How do you achieve and manage success in a workplace being rapidly transformed by change? Here is a new set of ABCs—for accountability, balance, and control:[2]

■ **A is for Accountability:** "The job you are doing now might not have even existed six months ago and may be gone again next year," says time management consultant Odette Pollar. Even so, you need to take responsibility and be accountable for you and your team's performance. The days when you could say "It's not my job" are long gone.

■ **B is for Balance:** In many industries, there are managers who work 60 or even 80 hours a week. Pressures to do more, learn more, create more may make you feel you should take your work home with you every evening and weekend instead of using the time to recharge your batteries. But now, more than ever, it's important to maintain balance in your life.

■ **C is for Control:** If the work environment keeps changing, you may feel you can't keep up. But there are some things you can control. The way to do so is to distinguish between urgent tasks and important tasks. "Things with deadlines—the ringing phone, a person at your desk with a question—are all urgent," says Pollar. But they may not be important. Important tasks add value and are closely tied to long-term organizational success.

It's important to know when to say "No" to distracting activities so that you can say "Yes" to the important work. Otherwise you're not managing change. It's managing you.

FORECAST: WHAT'S AHEAD IN THIS CHAPTER

This chapter sets the stage for understanding the new world in which managers must operate and the responsibilities they will have. We begin by describing the community of stakeholders that managers have to deal with—first the internal stakeholders (of employees, owners, and directors), then the external stakeholders in two kinds of environments (task and general). We then consider the ethical and social responsibilities required in being a manager, the new diversified workforce and the barriers and approaches to managing diversity, and the contributions of entrepreneurship—taking risks in the creation of new enterprises.

major question

Stockholders are only one group of stakeholders. Who are stakeholders important to me inside the organization?

The Big Picture

Managers operate in two organizational environments—internal and external—both made up of stakeholders, the people whose interests are affected by the organization. The first, or internal, environment consists of employees, owners, and the board of directors, as described in this section

Al Dunlap. That the former Sunbeam CEO delighted in his notorious reputation is shown by the title of his autobiography: *Mean Business.*

He was known as Chainsaw Al or The Shredder, for the tens of thousands of people he had fired, but Al Dunlap preferred the nickname Rambo in Pinstripes (he once posed for a photo wearing an ammo belt across his chest). Dunlap became a hero to Wall Street after he was hired as CEO to restore profitability to troubled Scott Paper Co., where the stock tripled during his 18-month tenure. Profitability was achieved through massive cost-cutting efforts that centered on dismissing thousands of workers. As a result, the word "Dunlaping" became a workplace synonym for layoffs.

A self-promoting "turnaround specialist"—he had previously exercised his cutting philosophy at Crown-Zellerbach and Lily-Tulip—he was next hired as board chairman and CEO to rescue Sunbeam Corp., maker of barbecue grills, electric blankets, and blenders. During two years at Sunbeam, he fired half the 12,000 employees, closed two-thirds of the company's factories, and moved production to cheap-labor sites in Mississippi, Mexico, and Asia. But Wall Street loved it, as the small-appliance maker's stock moved from $12 to $53 a share.

Then Dunlap himself was fired—"Dunlaped"—and thousands cheered. "I couldn't think of a better person to deserve it," said the mayor of a town of 2,200 that lost two Sunbeam plants. "It tickled me to death. We may need to have a rejoicing ceremony."

Dunlap was given the pink slip by Sunbeam's board of directors for failing to deliver profits three quarters in a row. He was accused of "channel stuffing," making sales look artificially high by pushing retailers to take products—such as barbecues in the wintertime—that wouldn't be sold for months. His successor vowed to set realistic sales goals, instead of simply ordering employees to boost the numbers 50%.

But consider: Does the source of all this pain really lie with Dunlap, a throwback to yesterday's iron-fisted school of management? Or was he only a "hired assassin," as one commentator put it, brought on board to give a rapid boost to the price of the stock by any means possible? Sunbeam's principal stockholder, after all, was a mutual fund. And mutual-fund money managers are concerned with short-term profits. The social costs are borne by employees, towns affected by plant closings, the rest of us.[3]

Internal & External Stakeholders

The mutual-fund owner was one of Sunbeam's stockholders. But should a company be responsible to just its stockholders? Perhaps we need a broader term to indicate all those with a stake in an organization. That term, appropriately, is _stakeholders_—**the people whose interests are affected by an organization's activities.**

Managers operate in two organizational environments, both made up of various stakeholders. *(See Panel 3.1.)* As we describe in the rest of this section, the two environments are these:

■ Internal stakeholders   ■ External stakeholders

PANEL 3.1

The organization's environment. The two main groups are internal and external stakeholders

The General Environment

Economic forces

The Task Environment

International forces

Customers

Technological forces

Media

Competitors

INTERNAL STAKEHOLDERS

Interest Groups

Employees

Suppliers

Owners

Governments

Distributors

Board of directors

Lenders

Allies

Political-legal forces

Unions

Sociocultural forces

Demographic forces

EXTERNAL STAKEHOLDERS

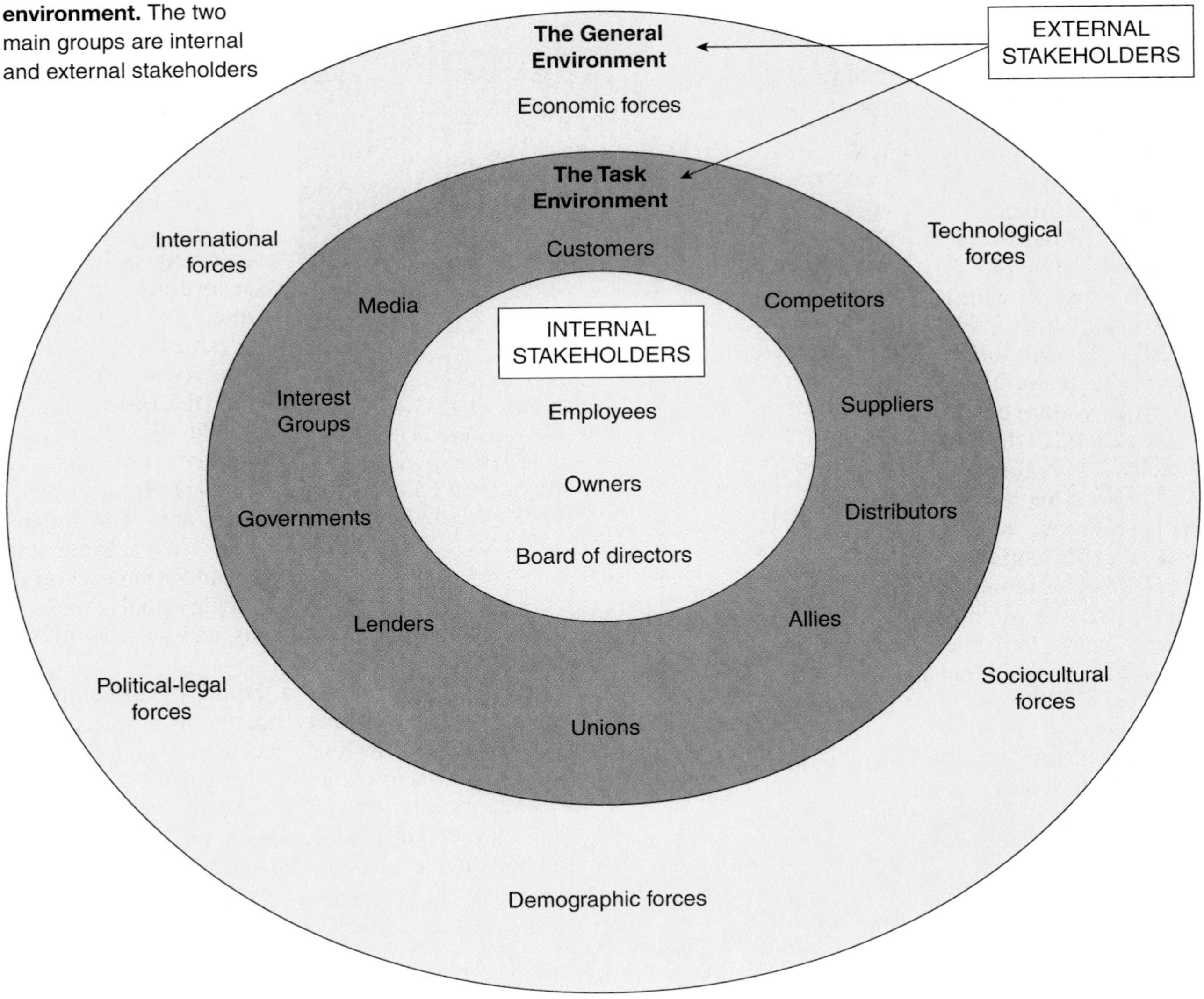

Internal Stakeholders

Whether small or large, the organization to which you belong has people in it that have an important stake in how it performs. These *internal stakeholders* **consist of employees, owners, and the board of directors, if any.** Let us consider each in turn.

Employees As a manager, could you run your part of the organization if you and your employees were constantly in conflict? Labor history, of course, is full of accounts of just that. But such conflict may lower the performance of the organization, thereby hurting everyone's stake. In many of today's forward-looking organizations, employees are considered "the talent"—the most important resource.

For instance, at Trilogy Software, a small, fast-growing software firm in Austin, Texas, workers aren't really considered "employees." "They're all shareholders," says former U.S. Labor Secretary Robert Reich in an article about cutting-edge kinds of companies. "They're all managers. They're all partners. That's how [Joe] Liemandt, Trilogy's CEO, has chosen to run his company—and that's what makes it successful."[4]

Owners The *owners* **of an organization consist of all those who can claim it as their legal property,** such as Sunbeam's stockholders. In the for-profit world, if you're running a one-person graphic design firm, the owner is just you—you're what is known as a sole proprietorship. If you're in an Internet startup with your brother-in-law, you're both

owners—you're a partnership. If you're a member of a family running a car dealership, you're all owners—you're investors in a privately owned company. If you work for an airline that is partly owned by its employees, as United Airlines is (55% employee owned), you are one of the joint owners—you're part of an Employee Stock Ownership Plan (ESOP). And if you've bought a few shares of stock in a company whose shares are listed for sale on the New York Stock Exchange, such as General Motors, you're one of thousands of owners—you're a stockholder. In all these examples, of course, the goal of the owners is to make a profit.

Employees or owners? United Airlines is 55% employee-owned, through a device known as the Employee Stock Ownership Plan, in which employees become owners by buying a company's stock. Although the idea was conceived nearly 50 years ago, there are only about 11,500 ESOPs today out of the hundreds of thousands of publicly and privately owned businesses. Why do you suppose more companies aren't owned by their employees?

Board of Directors Who hires the chief executive of a for-profit or nonprofit organization? In a corporation, it is the *board of directors*, whose members are elected by the stockholders to see that the company is being run according to their interests. In nonprofit organizations, such as universities or hospitals, the board may be called the *board of trustees* or *board of regents*. Board members are very important in setting the organization's overall strategic goals and in approving the major decisions and salaries of top management.

Not all firms have a board of directors. A lawyer, for instance, may operate as a sole proprietor, making all her own decisions. A large corporation might have eight or so members of its board of directors. Some of these directors (inside directors) may be top executives of the firm. The rest (outside directors) are elected from outside the firm.

Click-Along 3.1

Treating Employees as Real Stakeholders

practical action

Managing Information Overload: Keep Your Eye on the Big Picture

As a manager, it's not enough that you be aware of all the changing trends and responsibilities in the workplace. You also need to have a sense of where you're going.

No doubt what you're looking for is something about which you can say "It's not just a job, it's a career," as the slogan goes. Your *career path* is the sequence of jobs and occupations you follow during your career.

Michael J. Driver has suggested there are different possible career paths, among them the *linear career, the steady-state career,* and the *spiral career.*[5]

The Linear Career: Climbing the Stairs The *linear career* resembles the traditional view of climbing the stairs in an organization's hierarchy. That is, you move up the organization in a series of jobs—generally in just one functional area, such as finance—each of which entails more responsibility and requires more skills.

The legendary Roberto C. Goizueta of Coca-Cola Co., who started out as a chemist with a Havana-based Coke subsidiary, spent his entire career with the company, rising through the technical side before he became chairman and CEO. Some top executives may change companies during their ascent, as Lee Iaccoca did from Ford to Chrysler, but their careers are still always upwardly mobile—that is, linear.

Of course, it's possible that a linear career will *plateau.* That is, you'll rise to a certain level and then remain there; there will be no further promotions. Career plateaus actually happen a lot and need not signify disgrace, since they happen even to very successful managers. After all, the higher you get in the hierarchy, the fewer the managerial positions above you and the more intense the competition for them.

Another possibility, of course, is the *declining career,* in which a person reaches a certain level and then after a time begins descending back to the lower levels. This could come about, for instance, because technology changes the industry you're in and you're not willing or able to learn the necessary new skills. It can also happen because people have addiction problems, for example, causing them to take their eye off the career ball. Or they are victims of age, gender, or racial discrimination.

The Steady-State Career: Staying Put The *steady-state career* is almost the opposite of a linear career: you discover early in life that you're comfortable with a certain occupation and you stay with it. Or you accept a promotion for a while, decide you don't like the responsibility, and take a step down.

This kind of career is actually fairly commonplace: sales representatives, computer programmers, graphic artists, accountants, insurance agents, or physicians, for example, may decide they are perfectly happy being "hands-on" professionals rather than managers.

The Spiral Career: Holding Different Jobs That Build on One Another The *spiral career* is, like the linear career, upwardly mobile. However, on this career path, you would have a number of jobs that are fundamentally different yet still build on one another, giving you more general experience and the skills to advance in rank and status. Nowadays this route may actually give you a better chance of reaching the top than the linear career because it provides such a broad base of experience.

For example, an engineer might start out in a company's research and development department, then become a product manager in the marketing department, then move into sales, all the while gradually moving up the organization chart.

Of course, it's possible that you might (like some salespeople, actors, chefs, or construction workers) favor a variant called the *transitory career.* That is, you're the kind of person that doesn't want the responsibility that comes with promotion. You're a free spirit that likes the variety of experience that comes with continually shifting sideways from job to job or place to place (or you're afraid of making the commitment to doing any one thing).

Who are stakeholders important to me outside the organization?

The Big Picture

The external environment of stakeholders consists of the task environment and the general environment. The task environment consists of customers, competitors, suppliers, distributors, strategic allies, employee associations, local communities, financial institutions, government regulators, special-interest groups, and the mass media. The general environment consists of economic, technological, sociocultural, demographic, political-legal, and international forces.

In the first section we described the environment inside the organization. Here let's consider the environment outside it, which consists of *external stakeholders*—**people or groups in the organization's external environment that are affected by it.** This environment consists of:

- The task environment
- The general environment

The Task Environment

The *task environment* **consists of 11 groups that present you with daily tasks to handle: customers, competitors, suppliers, distributors, strategic allies, employee organizations, local communities, financial institutions, government regulators, special-interest groups, and mass media.**

1 Customers The first law of business, we've said, is *take care of the customer.* *Customers* **are those who pay to use an organization's goods or services.** Customers may be the focus not only of for-profit organizations but also nonprofit ones. A 1998 survey found that, with crime rates falling, police forces scored the biggest four-year gain in customer (citizen) satisfaction of all industries and services.[6]

Example of Taking Care of Customers: L.L. Bean's No Questions Asked

Click-Along 3.2

Companies with Lifetime Product Guarantees

Only a handful of companies stand by their products for a lifetime—Parker Pens, Williams-Sonoma cookware, Zippo cigarette lighters, for example. For more than 90 years, L.L. Bean, the Freeport, Maine, mail-order seller of clothing and outdoor gear, has had an unconditional guarantee that it will give a replacement, refund, or charge credit and even pay shipping on a Bean product if a customer is dissatisfied with it—no matter when it was bought. No proof of purchase is required. No product defect need be cited. Even 30-year-old worn-out hiking boots can be exchanged.

Why don't more companies have such lifetime warranties or total-satisfaction guarantees? "Companies are worried about customers cheating them," says one writer. "That's nonsense. People cheat bad companies, because they think the companies have cheated them. Nobody cheats top companies."[7]

2 Competitors Is there any line of work you could enter in which there would *not* be <u>**competitors**</u>—**people or organizations that compete for customers or resources,** such as talented employees or raw materials? Every organization has to be actively aware of its competitors. Florist shops and delicatessens must be aware that customers can buy the same products at Safeway or Kroegers.

Gateway manufactures and sells its personal computers not only over the Internet but also through its own stores. Does doing so give the company a competitive advantage over Internet sellers of PCs, such as Dell and IBM?

3 Suppliers A <u>*supplier*</u> **is a person or an organization that provides supplies—that is, raw materials, services, equipment, labor, or energy—to other organizations.** Suppliers in turn have their own suppliers: The publisher of this book buys the paper on which it is printed from a paper merchant, who in turn is supplied by several paper mills, who in turn are supplied wood for wood pulp by logging companies with forests in the United States or Canada.

4 Distributors A <u>*distributor*</u> **is a person or an organization that helps another organization sell its goods and services to customers.** Publishers of magazines, for instance, don't sell directly to newsstands; rather, they go through a distributor, or wholesaler. Tickets to a Lauryn Hill, Chuck D., or other hiphop artist's performance might be sold to you directly by the concert hall, but they are also sold through such distributors as TicketMaster, Tower Records, and Blockbuster Video.

Distributors can be quite important because in some industries (such as movie theaters and magazines) there is not a lot of competition, and the distributor has a lot of power over the ultimate price of the product. However, the rise in popularity of the Internet has allowed manufacturers of personal computers, for example, to cut out the "middleman"—the distributor—and to sell to customers directly.

5 Strategic Allies Companies, and even nonprofit organizations, frequently link up with other organizations (even competing ones) in order to realize strategic advantages. <u>*Strategic allies*</u> **describes the relationship of two organizations who join forces to achieve advantages neither can perform as well alone.**

In 1999, several major drug companies, normally fierce competitors, discussed joining to pursue basic research out of fear that small biotech firms might monopolize crucial gene information and then charge the big companies huge fees for access to it.[8]

6 Employee Organizations: Unions & Associations As a rule of thumb, labor unions (such as the United Auto Workers or the Teamsters Union) tend to represent hourly workers; professional associations (such as the National Education Association or the Newspaper Guild) tend to represent salaried workers. Nevertheless, during a labor dispute, the salary-earning reporters in the Newspaper Guild might well picket in sympathy with the wage-earning circulation-truck drivers in the Teamsters Union.

In recent years, the percentage of the labor force represented by unions has steadily declined (to 13.5% in 2000).[9] Moreover, union agendas have changed. Strikes and violence are pretty much out. Benefits, stock ownership, and campaigns for "living-wage" ordinances are in.[10]

7 Local Communities North Dakota farm wife Susan Horner works the phones for a travel company in the town of Linton, booking vacations for clients all over the United States while her husband milks their 50 cows on his own. "When this office opened, every fourth business on Main Street was closed. Linton was headed to becoming a ghost town," she says. "My paycheck makes our house payment and our farm payment."[11] The Horners and Linton clearly are grateful for the 4,600 miles of high-speed fiber-optic lines that were recently laid in the state, which brought it several telemarketing, data processing, and reservations centers.

Local communities are obviously important stakeholders, as becomes evident not only when a big organization arrives but also when it leaves, sending government officials scrambling to find new industry to replace it. Schools and municipal governments rely on the organization for their tax base. Families and merchants depend on its employee payroll for their livelihoods. In addition, everyone from the United Way to the Little League may rely on it for some financial support.[12]

8 Financial Institutions Want to launch a small start-up company? As Visa, MasterCard, and Discover continue to flood mailboxes with credit-card offers, some entrepreneurs have found it convenient to use multiple cards to fund new enterprises. Joe Liemandt of Trilogy Software charged up 22 cards to finance his startup.

Established companies also often need loans to tide them over when revenues are down or to finance expansion, but they rely for assistance on lenders such as commercial banks, investment banks, and insurance companies.

9 Government Regulators The preceding groups are external stakeholders in your organization since they are clearly affected by its activities. But why would *government regulators*—**regulatory agencies that establish ground rules under which organizations may operate**—be considered stakeholders?

We are talking here about an alphabet soup of agencies, boards, and commissions that have the legal authority to prescribe or proscribe the conditions under which you may conduct business. To these may be added local and state regulators on the one hand and foreign governments and international agencies (such as the World Trade Organization, which oversees international trade and standardization efforts) on the other.

Such government regulators can be said to be stakeholders because not only do they affect the activities of your organization, they are in turn affected by it. The Federal Aviation Agency (FAA), for example, specifies how far planes must stay apart to prevent midair collisions. But when the airlines want to add more flights on certain routes, the FAA may have to add more flight controllers and radar equipment, since those are the agency's responsibility.

Click-Along 3.3

California Air Resources
Board as Important Regulator

From investor to CEO. Peter Thiel was a money man, running a hedge fund, when Max Levchin, then working in on-line security, approached him in 1998 about investing in a company that would specialize in safeguards for transferring money through wireless devices. Thiel thought it would be fun to run a company and became CEO. Their company, PayPal, has evolved from a person-to-person site (as for enabling people to pay each other back online for dinner) to a person-to-business site that enables almost anything to be bought and sold over the Internet.

10 Special-Interest Groups   "The Gap, a San Francisco-based national clothing chain, was slammed with high-profile demonstrations on Saturday by activists protesting its labor policies in the Mariana Islands . . . ," read the newspaper account.[13] Any organization can become the target of a special-interest group, as The Gap was by an outfit called Global Exchange, which denounced the chain's use of below-minimum-wage labor (so-called sweatshop labor) in its factory on Saipan, which is U.S. territory.

Special-interest groups **are groups whose members try to influence specific issues,** some of which may affect your organization. Examples are Mothers Against Drunk Driving, the National Organization for Women, and the National Rifle Association. Special-interest groups may try to exert political influence, as in contributing funds to lawmakers' election campaigns or in launching letter-writing efforts to officials. Or they may organize picketing and *boycotts*—holding back their patronage—of certain companies, as some African-American groups did in recent years to protest reports of racism at Texaco and at Denny's restaurants.

11 Mass Media   On March 24, 1989, when the tanker *Exxon Valdez* ran aground in Prince William Sound, it dumped 11 million gallons of North Slope crude oil into the water, blackening 1,500 miles of magnificent Gulf of Alaska coastline. This was not only one of the nation's worst environmental disasters; for the Exxon Corporation it was the start of a gigantic public-relations nightmare that never seemed to end. Even 10 years later, the *New York Times* and *USA Today* were running prominent articles on the effects of the incident, once again bringing it to public attention.[14]

Exxon's troubles were not the fault of the press. But no manager can afford to ignore the power of the mass media—print, radio, TV, and the Internet—to rapidly and widely disseminate news both bad and good. Thus, most companies, universities, hospitals, and even government agencies have a public-relations person or department to communicate effectively with the press. In addition, top-level executives often receive special instruction on how to best deal with the media.

The Million Mom March. In May 2000, thousands of mothers from across the U.S. gathered in Washington, D.C. to try to convince lawmakers to take action on gun-control legislation that had languished in Congress for nearly a year. The marchers were opposed by a smaller group known as the Second Amendment Sisters, which objects to gun licensing and registration. Many managers have to deal with "external stakeholders" of special-interest groups such as these.

The General Environment

Beyond the task environment is the _**general environment,**_ or _macroenvironment,_ **which includes six forces: economic, technological, sociocultural, demographic, political-legal, and international.**

You may be able to control some forces in the task environment, but you can't control those in the general environment. Nevertheless, they can profoundly affect your organization's task environment without your knowing it, springing nasty surprises on you. Clearly, then, as a manager you need to keep your eye on the far horizon because these forces of the general environment can affect long-term plans and decisions.

1 Economic Forces _Economic forces_ **consist of the general economic conditions and trends—unemployment, inflation, interest rates, economic growth—that may affect an organization's performance.** These are forces in your nation and region and even the world over which you and your organization probably have no control.

Are banks' interest rates going up in the United States? Then it will cost you more to borrow money to open new stores or build new plants. Is your region's unemployment rate rising? Then maybe you'll have more job applicants to hire from, yet you'll also have fewer customers with money to spend. Are natural resources getting scarce in an important area of supply? Then your company will need to pay more for them or switch to alternative sources.

One indicator that managers often pay attention to is productivity growth. Numbers from the Bureau of Labor Statistics released in May 2002 show that in 1990–2000 productivity rose 9% among nonstore retailers, including online and catalog sales, but fell in several service sector industries, such as grocery stores (down 0.2%) and cable TV (down 0.06%).[15]

2 Technological Forces _Technological forces_ **are new developments in methods for transforming resources into goods or services.** For example, think what the U.S. would have been like if the elevator, air-conditioning, the combustion engine, and the airplane had not been invented. No doubt changes in computer and communications technology—especially the influence of the Internet—will continue to be powerful technological forces during your managerial career. But other technological currents may affect you as well.

For example, biotechnology may well turn health and medicine upside down in the coming decades. Researchers can already clone animals, and they may someday do the same with humans.

3 Sociocultural Forces "I have one client who has tattoos of all kinds of stuff on her body," says Doug, owner of Doug's Tattoos in Oakland, Calif. "There's no theme to it. She has favorite cartoon names, her children's and grandchildren's names—just anything she likes at the time."[16]

Some day, of course, our descendants will view these customs as old-fogyish and quaint. That's how it is with sociocultural changes. _Sociocultural forces_ **are influences and trends originating in a country, society, or culture's human relationships and values that may affect an organization.**

Entire industries have been rocked when the culture underwent a lifestyle change that affected their product or service. The interest in health and fitness, for instance, led to a decline in sales of cigarettes, whiskey, red meat, and eggs. And it led to a boost in sales of athletic shoes, spandex clothing, and Nautilus and other exercise machines.

Trending downward. Any industry can be affected by changes in sociocultural forces. Increasing health awareness in the United States forced tobacco companies to seek expanded markets overseas to make up for the decline in domestic consumption.

4 Demographic Forces Age, gender, race, sexual orientation, occupation, income, family size, and the like are known as demographic characteristics when they are used to express measurements of certain groups. _**Demographic forces**_ **are influences on an organization arising from changes in the characteristics of a population, such as age, gender, or ethnic origin.** In the United States, for instance, more women and minorities continue to join the workforce, making it more diverse.

Ten years ago, for instance, the part of South-Central Los Angeles that experienced urban riots (following the acquittal of four white cops in the beating of black motorist Rodney King) was dominated by African-Americans. Today nearly two thirds of South-Central is Hispanic, with many recent immigrants from Mexico and Central America. The area also is the first rung on the ladder of success for immigrants from Russia, Korea, China, Thailand, Israel, Iran, Italy, and Jamaica.[17]

5 Political-Legal Forces _**Political-legal forces**_ **are changes in the way politics shape laws and laws shape the opportunities for and threats to an organization.** In the United States, whatever political view tends to be dominant at the moment may be reflected in how the government handles antitrust issues, in which one company tends to monopolize a particular industry. Should Microsoft be allowed to dominate the market for personal-computer operating systems?

As for legal forces, some countries have more fully developed legal systems than others. And some countries have more lawyers per capita. (The United States has an estimated 25% of the world's lawyers, according to University of Wisconsin law professor Marc Galanter—not the 70% figure repeated for years by some conservative political figures.[18]) American companies may be more willing to use the legal system to advance their interests, as in suing competitors to gain competitive advantage. But they must also watch that others don't do the same to them.

6 International Forces _**International forces**_ **are changes in the economic, political, legal, and technological global system that may affect an organization.**

This category represents a huge grab bag of influences. How does the economic integration of the European Union create threats and opportunities for American companies? How much risk does the ease with which terrorists cross borders mean for American executives working abroad? We consider global concerns in Chapter 4.

How well Americans can handle international forces depends a lot on their training. The American Council on Education says there is a "dangerous" shortage of experts in non-European cultures and languages. The council urges that schools teach a wider variety of languages and that instruction begin as early as kindergarten, since waiting until students are in college to begin instruction in more obscure languages hinders their ability to become fluent speakers.[19]

Three CEOs. Bill Gates of Microsoft (left), Scott McNally of Sun Microsystems, and Craig Bartlett of Netscape testify before Congress about competitive practices in the computer software industry. The outcome of these hearings played a role in making the antitrust division of the U.S. Justice Department, which is charged with enforcing laws that keep markets open and competitive, with filing suit against Microsoft for anticompetitive practices. Why is competition so important to a free-market system?

major question

What does the successful manager need to know about ethics and values?

The Big Picture

Managers need to be aware of what constitutes ethics, values, the four approaches to ethical dilemmas, and how organizations can promote ethics.

Olympics on the carpet. Robert Garff, who chaired the Salt Lake Organizing Committee, which brought the 2002 Olympic Winter Games to Utah, holds his head as he releases a report investigating the ethics of his committee's actions. The committee was alleged to have bribed Olympic officials (with Donny Osmond photos, music CDs, and cash). Do you think ethical behavior is the most important part of doing business?

"It's a tough issue, choosing between being a law-abiding person and losing your job," says lawyer Gloria Allred, who represented a woman fired for complaining about running her boss's office football pool.[20] Imagine having to choose between *economic performance* and *social performance*, which in business is what most ethical conflicts are about.[21] This is known as an ***ethical dilemma***, **a situation in which you have to decide whether to pursue a course of action that may benefit you or your organization but that is unethical or even illegal.**

Defining Ethics & Values

Most of us assume we know what "ethics" and "values" mean, but do we? Let's consider them.

Ethics *Ethics* **are the standards of right and wrong that influence behavior.** These standards may vary among countries and among cultures. ***Ethical behavior*** **is behavior that is accepted as "right" as opposed to "wrong" according to those standards.**

What are the differences among a tip, a gratuity, a gift, a donation, a commission, a consulting fee, a kickback, a bribe? Regardless of the amount of money involved, each one may be intended to reward the recipient for providing you with better service, either anticipated or performed. However, while giving a member of the International Olympic Committee (IOC) several thousand dollars to help steer the Olympic Winter Games to Salt Lake City may be considered unethical behavior in the United States, it may be considered perfectly ethical under the standards of the IOC member's own country.

Values Ethical dilemmas often take place because of an organization's ***value system***, **the pattern of values within an organization.** ***Values*** **are the relatively permanent and deeply held underlying beliefs and attitudes that help determine a person's behavior,** such as the belief that "Fairness means hiring according to ability, not family background." Values and value systems are the underpinnings for ethics and ethical behavior.

Organizations may have two important value systems that can conflict: (1) the value system stressing financial performance versus (2) the value system stressing cohesion and solidarity in employee relationships.[22]

Four Approaches to Deciding Ethical Dilemmas

How do alternative values guide people's decisions about ethical behavior? Here are four approaches, which may be taken as guidelines:

1 The Utilitarian Approach: For the Greatest Good Ethical behavior in the *utilitarian approach* **is guided by what will result in the greatest good for the greatest number of people.** Managers often take the utilitarian approach, using financial performance—such as efficiency and profit—as the best definition of what constitutes "the greatest good for the greatest number."[23]

Thus, a utilitarian "cost-benefit" analysis might show that in the short run the firing of thousands of employees may improve a company's bottom line and provide immediate benefits for the stockholders. The drawback of this approach, however, is that it may result in damage to workforce morale and the loss of employees with experience and skills—actions not so readily measurable in dollars.

What's fair? CEO Charles B. Wang of Computer Associates International earned $698 million from 1998 to 2000. Was this fair when he produced a shareholder return of *minus* 63%?

2 The Individual Approach: For Your Greatest Self-Interest Long Term, Which Will Help Others Ethical behavior in the *individual approach* **is guided by what will result in the individual's best *long-term* interests, which ultimately are in everyone's self-interest.** The assumption here is that you will act ethically in the short run to avoid others harming you in the long run.

The flaw here, however, is that one person's short-term self-gain may *not,* in fact, be good for everyone in the long term. After all, the manager of an agribusiness that puts chemical fertilizers on the crops every year will always benefit, but the fishing industries downstream could ultimately suffer if chemical runoff reduces the number of fish. Indeed, this is one reason why Puget Sound Chinook, or king salmon, are now threatened with extinction in the Pacific Northwest.[24]

3 The Moral-Rights Approach: Respecting Fundamental Rights Shared by Everyone Ethical behavior in the *moral-rights approach* **is guided by respect for the fundamental rights of human beings,** such as those expressed in the U.S. Constitution's Bill of Rights. We would all tend to agree that denying people the right to life, liberty, privacy, health and safety, and due process is unethical. Thus, most of us would have no difficulty con-

demning the situation of immigrants illegally brought into the United States and then effectively enslaved—as when made to work seven days a week as maids.

The difficulty, however, is when rights are in conflict, such as employer and employee rights. Should employees on the job have a guarantee of privacy? Actually, it is legal for employers to listen to business phone calls and monitor all nonspoken personal communications.[25]

4 The Justice Approach: Respecting Impartial Standards of Fairness Ethical behavior in the *justice approach* **is guided by respect for impartial standards of fairness and equity.** One consideration here is whether an organization's policies—such as those governing promotions or sexual harassment cases—are administered impartially and fairly regardless of gender, age, sexual orientation, and the like.

Fairness can often be a hot issue. For instance, many employees are loudly resentful when a corporation's CEO is paid a salary and bonuses worth hundreds of times more than what they receive—even when the company performs poorly—and when fired is then given a "golden parachute," or extravagant package of separation pay and benefits.

How Organizations Can Promote Ethics

There are three ways an organization may foster high ethical standards:

1 Support by Top Managers of a Strong Ethical Climate   The "tone at the top is critical—and it's always monkey see, monkey do," says Martha Clark Goss, VP and chief financial officer for consulting firm Booze Allen & Hamilton. At her firm, she says, "we have the sunshine rule, which asks employees to consider how they would feel if they had to stand in front of partners [that is, top managers] and explain a particular business expense. It's a good rule, but only a guideline. People almost always follow the example of the senior partners."[26]

If top executives "wink at the problem" or "look the other way" in ethical matters, so will employees farther down the organization.

2 Ethics Codes & Training Programs   A _code of ethics_ **consists of a formal written set of ethical standards guiding an organization's actions.** Most codes offer guidance on how to treat customers, suppliers, competitors, and other stakeholders. The purpose is to clearly state top management's expectations for all employees. As you might expect, most codes prohibit bribes, kickbacks, misappropriation of corporate assets, conflicts of interest, and "cooking the books"—making false accounting statements and other records. Other areas frequently covered in ethics codes are political contributions, workforce diversity, and confidentiality of corporate information.[27]

Click-Along 3.4

Johnson & Johnson's Ethics Code

In addition, about 45% of the 1,000 largest U.S. corporations now provide ethics training.[28] The approaches vary, but one way is to use a case approach to present employees with ethical dilemmas. By clarifying expectations, this kind of training may reduce unethical behavior.[29]

Nike Code of Conduct

NIKE INC. WAS FOUNDED ON A HANDSHAKE.

Implicit in that act was the determination that we would build our business with all of our partners based on trust, teamwork, honesty and mutual respect. We expect all of our business partners to operate on the same principles.

At the core of the NIKE corporate ethic is the belief that we are a company comprised of many different kinds of people, appreciating individual diversity, and dedicated to equal opportunity for each individual.

NIKE designs, manufactures and markets products for sports and fitness consumers. At every step in that process, we are driven to do not only what is required by law, but what is expected of a leader. We expect our business partners to do the same. NIKE partners with contractors who share our commitment to best practices and continuous improvement in:

1. Management practices that respect the rights of all employees, including the right to free association and collective bargaining.
2. Minimizing our impact on the environment.
3. Providing a safe and healthy work place.
4. Promoting the health and well-being of all employees.

Contractors must recognize the dignity of each employee, and the right to a work place free of harassment, abuse or corporal punishment. Decisions on hiring, salary, benefits, advancement, termination or retirement must be based solely on the employee's ability to do the job. There shall be no discrimination based on race, creed, gender, marital or maternity status, religious or political beliefs, age or sexual orientation.

Wherever NIKE operates around the globe we are guided by this Code of Conduct and we bind our contractors to these principles. Contractors must post this Code in all major workspaces, translated into the language of the employee, and must train employees on their rights and obligations as defined by this Code and applicable local laws.

While these principles establish the spirit of our partnerships, we also bind our partners to specific standards of conduct. The core standards are set forth below.

Forced Labor
The contractor does not use forced labor in any form – prison, indentured, bonded or otherwise.

Child Labor
The contractor does not employ any person below the age of 18 to produce footwear. The contractor does not employ any person below the age of 16 to produce apparel, accessories or equipment. If at the time Nike production begins, the contractor employs people of the legal working age who are at least 15, that employment may continue, but the contractor will not hire any person going forward who is younger than the Nike or legal age limit, whichever is higher. To further ensure these age standards are complied with, the contractor does not use any form of homework for Nike production.

Compensation
The contractor provides each employee at least the minimum wage, or the prevailing industry wage, whichever is higher; provides each employee a clear, written accounting for every pay period; and does not deduct from employee pay for disciplinary infractions.

Benefits
The contractor provides each employee all legally mandated benefits.

Hours of Work/Overtime
The contractor complies with legally mandated work hours; uses overtime only when each employee is fully compensated according to local law; informs each employee at the time of hiring if mandatory overtime is a condition of employment; and on a regularly scheduled basis provides one day off in seven, and requires no more than 60 hours of work per week on a regularly scheduled basis, or complies with local limits if they are lower.

Environment, Safety and Health (ES&H)
The contractor has written environmental, safety and health policies and standards, and implements a system to minimize negative impacts on the environment, reduce work-related injury and illness, and promote the general health of employees.

Documentation and Inspection
The contractor maintains on file all documentation needed to demonstrate compliance with this Code of Conduct and required laws; agrees to make these documents available for Nike or its designated monitor; and agrees to submit to inspections with or without prior notice.

Nike's Code. Despite its code of conduct, the athletic-shoe company had to deal with negative websites questioning its treatment of workers in less-developed countries. The company responded with a website of its own showing pictures of its overseas manufacturing facilities and describing the benefits offered employees. Still, a code of ethics is not always a guarantee of ethical behavior. A collector's item is the 64-page "Enron Code of Ethics," which includes sections on conflicts of interest. The Houston-based energy company was greatly criticized for its irregular financial dealings, which brought tremendous losses to shareholders and employees. If you were considering being hired by a new company, how could you tell whether it really tended to act ethically?

Whistleblower. Tobacco industry whistleblower Jeffrey Wigand (right) testifies in March 2000 before a Rhode Island Senate committee as the state's Lt. Gov. Jeffery J. Fogarty looks on. Wigand was a chemist for Brown & Williamson who had learned about the tobacco company's discovery of the relationship between nicotine and addiction, which it had consistently denied. Despite having signed a confidentiality agreement, Wigand decided to make his knowledge public. The case became the basis for the 1999 movie *The Insider*, with Russell Crowe and Al Pacino. Whistleblowing is not for everyone; close to half of all whistleblowers are fired. Given this fact, what would it take for you to become a whistleblower?

3 Rewarding Ethical Behavior: Protecting Whistleblowers It's not enough to simply punish bad behavior; managers must also reward good ethical behavior, as in encouraging (or at least not discouraging) whistleblowers.

A _whistleblower_ **is an employee who reports organizational misconduct to the public,** such as health and safety matters, waste, corruption, or overcharging of customers. For instance, the law that created the Occupational Safety and Health Administration allows workers to report unsafe conditions, such as "exposure to toxic chemicals; the use of dangerous machines, which can crush fingers; the use of contaminated needles, which expose workers to the AIDS virus; and the strain of repetitive hand motion, whether at a computer keyboard or in a meatpacking plant."[30]

The law prohibits employers from firing employees who report workplace hazards, although one study found that about two-thirds of those who complained lost their jobs anyway.[31] Clearly, top managers have to stress that the organization's ethics policy is more than just window dressing.

Click-Along 3.5

Model Code for Whistleblowers

major question

Is being socially responsible really necessary?

The Big Picture

Managers need to be aware of the viewpoints supporting and opposing social responsibility, four managerial approaches to social responsibility, and whether being and doing good pay off financially for the organization.

If ethical responsibility is about being a good individual citizen, social responsibility is about being a good organizational citizen. More formally, _**social responsibility**_ **is a manager's duty to take actions that will benefit the interests of society as well as of the organization.** An example of social responsibility is _**philanthropy**_, **donating money to worthwhile recipients,** such as charities and schools. Companies may also make donations of their products, services, expertise, or employees' time.

Example of Social Responsibility: Good Works Work for Bagel Works

Bagel Works, a nine-store bagel chain headquartered in Keene, N.H., has an unusual December ritual: Its 140 employees nominate five local charities they think deserve help, and the winners are selected by secret ballots cast in the stores by the customers. Then for a year the winning charities get financial support, promotional space in the stores, and often free bagels. And this isn't the only socially responsible thing Bagel Works does: It also donates 10% or so of pretax profits to homeless shelters and other worthy causes.

What's in it for Bagel Works and its cofounders, Richard French, 34, and Jennifer Pearl, 31? "Some could argue that we may be able to make more money," says French. "But if we weren't doing some of those things, we might have a lesser quality of employee or more turnover." Moreover, he says, it has increased customer loyalty.[32]

The Bagel Works experience of decreased employee turnover and increased customer attachment seems to be a common payoff for socially conscious businesses. At the least, such businesses aren't any less profitable as a group. Often they have a competitive edge: In a 1996 survey of 2,000 people, 76% said they'd switch from their current brand to one associated with a good cause if price and quality were equal.[33]

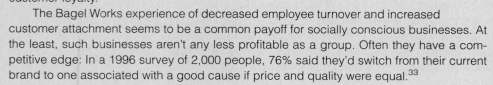

Social responsibility rests at the top of a pyramid of a corporation's obligations, right up there with economic, legal, and ethical responsibilities. That is, while some people might consider that a company's first duty is to make a profit, most would hold that it is equally important that it obey the law, be ethical, and be a good corporate citizen.[34]

Is Social Responsibility Worthwhile?
Opposing & Supporting Viewpoints

In the old days of cutthroat capitalism, social responsibility was hardly thought of. A company's most important goal was to make money pretty much any way it could, and the consequences be damned. Today for-profit enterprises generally make a point of "putting something back" into society as well as taking something out.

Not everyone, however, agrees with these new priorities. Let's consider the two viewpoints.

Against Social Responsibility "Few trends could so thoroughly undermine the very foundations of our free society," argues free-market economist Milton Friedman, "as the acceptance by corporate officials of social responsibility other than to make as much money for their stockholders as possible."[35]

Friedman represents the view that, as he says, "The social responsibility of business is to make profits." That is, unless a company focuses on maximizing profits, it will become distracted and fail to provide goods and services, benefit the stockholders, create jobs, and expand economic growth—the real social justification for the firm's existence.

This view would presumably support the Chainsaw Dunlaps of business life. It would presumably support the efforts of companies to set up headquarters in name only in offshore Caribbean tax havens (while keeping their actual headquarters in the U.S.) in order to minimize their tax burden.

For Social Responsibility "A large corporation these days not only may engage in social responsibility," says famed economist Paul Samuelson, "it had damned well better to try to do so."[36] That is, a company must be concerned for society's welfare as well as for corporate profits.

Beyond the fact of ethical obligation, the rationale for this view is that since businesses create problems (environmental pollution, for example), they should help solve them. Moreover, they often have the resources to solve problems in ways that the nonprofit sector does not. Finally, being socially responsible gives businesses a favorable public image that can help head off government regulation.

Crisis of conscience? Bridgestone/Firestone CEO Masatoshi Ono (center), flanked by executive vice presidents Gary Crigger (left) and Robert Wyant, listens during a September 2000 panel discussion at a congressional hearing regarding recall of Firestone tires. Congress was looking into frequent rollovers of Ford sport-utility vehicles equipped with Firestone tires. If you had been with Ford or Firestone, how many rollovers (and deaths) would you think were acceptable before the company should put out a massive recall of all such vehicles?

Four Managerial Approaches to Social Responsibility

The two extremes in managers' approaches to social responsibility range from "Do nothing" to "Do a lot."[37] Or, stated another way, from "obstructionist" to "proactive," as follows.[38]

Four Approaches to Social Responsibility

Obstructionist: "Just make money, forget any social responsibility."

Defensive: "Just do what the law requires, no more."

Accommodative: "Do the minimum that's ethically required."

Proactive: "Be a leader in social responsibility."

1 The Obstructionist Manager Managers in an obstructionist organization not only resist being socially responsible, they also behave unethically—maybe even illegally—whenever they think they can get away with it, or deny wrongdoing if found out. In the ___obstructionist approach___, **managers put economic gain first and resist social responsibility as being outside the organization's self-interest.**

Illegal drug dealers certainly represent the obstructionist approach. But so do some entirely legal companies. In 1999, according to a grand jury indictment, Waste Management, the largest trash hauler in the United States, hired Joseph Lauricella, who tried to undermine another company by swiping confidential data, sabotaging potential deals, and spreading rumors that tied the other company to illegal dumping and drug trafficking.[39]

Click-Along 3.6

Examples of Defensive Companies

2 The Defensive Manager In the ___defensive approach___, **managers make the minimum commitment to social responsibility—obeying the law but doing nothing more.** The defensive approach probably represents Milton Friedman's position: Companies are in business to make money, and they shouldn't distract themselves by doing anything else.

3 The Accommodative Manager In the ___accommodative approach___, **managers do more than the law requires, if asked, and demonstrate moderate social responsibility.** For months in 1998, Intel battled privacy groups that claimed its new Pentium III chip's hardwired identification number would give websites the power to monitor a user's every move online, until the company finally yielded and released the chip with the ID number turned off.[40]

4 The Proactive Manager In the ___proactive approach___, **managers actively lead the way in being socially responsible for all stakeholders, using the organization's resources to identify and respond to social problems.** For example, Merck & Co., the pharmaceutical concern, spent millions developing a drug (Mectizan) to fight river blindness, then distributed it free in the West African countries in which the disease is mainly found.[41]

Sorry Sears. Sometimes even major companies are obstructionist. In the most serious ethical breach in its history, Sears, Roebuck and Co. was discovered in 1999 to have secretly violated federal law for a decade. It even, suggested U.S. Justice Department lawyers, may have put their illegal practice in its procedures manual. Sears allegedly used unenforceable agreements to collect debts that legally no longer existed with some bankrupt credit-card holders. "The company's 111 years old," said the relatively new CEO at the time, Arthur Martinez, "and I'm the guy in the chair when we plead guilty to a criminal offense. Wonderful."

Enron demise detailed. Attorney William Lerach at a news conference shows the rising and falling share price for the Texas energy company. Lerach was representing Amalgamated Bank, which was suing Enron executives and directors and the company's auditor, Arthur Andersen. The suit alleged that Enron executives inflated earnings to drive up share prices, resulting in $1.1 billion in proceeds for them. What would you expect Enron's stock price to be today as you read this—higher or lower than in 2002?

Bottom Line: Does Being Good Pay Off Financially?

From a hard-headed manager's point of view, does ethical behavior and high social responsibility pay off financially? Here's what the research shows.

Effect on Stock Price Not all illegalities by a company will hurt its stock price, but the announcement of certain kinds of illegalities will—specifically tax evasion, bribery, or violations of government contracts.[42] In general, however, the damage to the stock price lasts for only a few days, as investors turn their attention to the company's future prospects.

Effect on Sales Growth The announcement of a company's conviction for illegal activity may have only a short-term effect on the stock price. However, it has been shown to diminish a company's sales growth for a much longer period of time—indeed, for several years.[43]

Effect on Customers According to one survey, 88% of the respondents said they were more apt to buy from companies that are socially responsible than from companies that are not.[44]

Effect on Job Applicants Another study found that as a company's reputation is enhanced by acts of social responsibility, making it seem to be a more attractive employer, it attracts more applicants.[45]

Ethical behavior and social responsibility are more than just admirable ways of operating. They give an organization a clear competitive advantage.

major question

What trends in workplace diversity should managers be aware of?

The Big Picture

One of today's most important management challenges is working with stakeholders of all sorts who vary widely in diversity—in age, gender, race, religion, ethnicity, sexual orientation, capabilities, and socioeconomic background. Managers should also be aware of the differences between internal and external dimensions of diversity and barriers to diversity.

"Coors Cares," says one of the beer company's slogans.

Didn't it always? Actually, in the 1980s the Coors family's funding of right-wing causes—they helped start the conservative Heritage Foundation—gave the brewer such a bad reputation with minorities and unions that it devastated it financially. Today Coors still gives steady support to the political right. Ironically, however, the company goes far beyond government requirements in embracing sensitivity, diversity, and other politically left policies.

Inside Coors, workers get training in sexual harassment and attend diversity workshops. "Employees can choose among eight 'resource councils'—groups representing gays, women, and Native Americans, among others," says a *Time* article. It also claims to offer "the first corporate mammography program in the country." In addition, it sets aside a specific share of purchases for minority-owned firms. Outside it provides sponsorship of such programs as the Mi Casa resource center for women, a black-heritage festival, and a marathon gay dance party. It is one of the three out of four Fortune 500 companies to have diversity programs to help attract and keep minorities.[46]

Coors and other companies have discovered they can benefit from a singular fact: Minority markets buy more goods and services than any country that trades with the United States.[47] In this section, we describe one of the most important management challenges—dealing with diversity.

How to Think about Diversity: Which Differences Are Important?

Diversity represents all the ways people are unlike and alike—the differences and similarities in age, gender, race, religion, ethnicity, sexual orientation, capabilities, and socioeconomic background. Note here that diversity is not synonymous with differences. Rather, it encompasses both differences and similarities. This means that as a manager you need to manage both simultaneously.

How can we tell which differences among people are the most important? One way is to divide them into *external* and *internal* dimensions. The kind of person you are—your self-image, values, and goals—is influenced by the interaction of these two dimensions. Indeed, the special mix of external and internal dimensions defines your *diversity identity* and affects how you are perceived by others.

Internal Dimensions of Diversity *Internal dimensions of diversity* **are those human differences that exert a powerful, sustained effect throughout every stage of our lives.**[48] The primary dimensions are those shown in the box. For some individuals, we might add other categories. For example, religion has a powerful effect on some people.

What characterizes internal dimensions of diversity is that they are visible and salient in people. And precisely because these characteristics are so visible, they may be associated with certain stereotypes—for example, that black people work in menial jobs.

For instance, an African-American female middle manager reports that, while on vacation and sitting by the pool at a resort, she was approached by a 50ish white male who "demanded that I get him extra towels. I said, 'Excuse me?' He then said, 'Oh, you don't work here,' with no shred of embarrassment or apology in his voice."[49]

External Dimensions of Diversity *External dimensions of diversity* **include an element of choice; they consist of the personal characteristics that people acquire, discard, or modify throughout their lives.** Education, marital status, and geographic location, for example, are generally speaking less visible than internal-dimension characteristics. External-dimension characteristics are also less constant in influencing your life than are internal-dimension characteristics.

Internal dimensions	External dimensions
Gender	Personal habits
Ethnicity	Educational background
Race	Religion
Physical abilities	Income
Age	Marital status
Sexual orientation	Geographic location
	Work experience
	Recreational habits
	Appearance

Trends in Workforce Diversity

How is the U.S. workforce apt to become more diverse in the early years of the new century? Let's examine five categories on the internal dimension—*age, gender, race/ethnicity, sexual orientation, and physical/mental abilities*—and one category on the external dimension, *educational level*.

Age: More Older People in the Workforce The most significant demographic event, suggests management philosopher Peter Drucker, "is that in the developed countries the number and proportion of younger people is rapidly shrinking. . . . Those shrinking numbers of younger people will have to both drive their economies and help support much larger numbers of older people."[50] In Europe and Japan, births are not keeping pace with deaths. Italy, for example, could drop from 60 million to 20 million by the end of the 21st century.

The United States is the only developed economy to have enough young people, suggests Drucker, and that is only because immigrants to the United States still have large families. Even so, the median age of the American worker is expected to reach 40.6 years by 2005, quite a change from 34.3 in 1980.[51]

Diversity enriches. A diverse population in a company can provide ideas, experience, and points of view that strengthen the business culture.

Gender: More Women Working Nearly half the new entrants into the workforce in the years 1990–2005 were expected to be women.[52] In addition, the percentage of women in executive, managerial, and administrative jobs has been increasing—42.9% in 1994, up from only 27% thirteen years earlier.[53] Indeed, women made up 11.2% of Fortune 500 corporate officers in 1998, and for the first time more than half of those companies had more than one woman corporate officer.[54]

Traditionally, however, women have been concentrated in relatively low-paying occupations; the average working woman's family would earn $4,205 more per year if women were paid as much as men with comparable job qualifications, according to one study.[55] In general, women earn 76 cents for every $1 a man is paid. Women executives do even less well: 68 cents for every dollar made by a male executive.[56] The obstacles to women's progress are known as the so-called *glass ceiling* —the metaphor for an invisible barrier preventing women and minorities from being promoted to top executive jobs. For instance, women hold only 83 top jobs in corporate America versus 2,184 men who hold posts as chairman, vice chairman, CEO, president, or senior or executive vice president.[57]

What factors are holding women back? Three that are mentioned are negative stereotypes, lack of mentors, and limited experience in line or general management.[58]

Interestingly, however, several studies have suggested that female managers outshine their male counterparts on almost every measure, from motivating others to fostering communication to producing high-quality work to goal-setting to mentoring employees.[59] We discuss this further in a later chapter.

The color of Coca-Cola. Kimberly Orton (left) speaks during a November 2000 news conference in Atlanta, where Coke is headquartered. The company agreed to pay $192.5 million to settle a class-action racial discrimination suit that alleged that it had discriminated against blacks in pay, promotions, and performance evaluations. Looking on are Linda Ingram (second from left), Elvenyia Barton-Gibson, and George Eddings Jr. Do you think a lawsuit is the best wake-up call for an organization practicing discrimination?

Race & Ethnicity: More People of Color in the Workforce In the years 1990–2005, people of color are expected to contribute 34.7% of new entrants to the workforce (Hispanics 15.7%, African-Americans 13%, Asians and other races 6%).[60] Unfortunately, three trends show that American businesses need to do a lot better by this population.

First, people of color, too, have hit the glass ceiling. For example, African-Americans held only 6.7% and Hispanics only 4.9% of all executive, managerial, and administrative jobs in 1994.[61]

Second, they have not been paid equally with whites. In 1993, for example, college-educated black men employed as executives, administrators, and professionals had a median income that was 86% of that for their white peers.[62]

Third, their chances for success have been hurt by perceived discrimination, as shown, for example, by a study of 200 black managers and 139 Hispanic employees.[63] African-Americans also have been found to receive lower performance ratings than whites have.[64]

In the wake of the September 11, 2000, terrorist attacks on New York's World Trade Center and the Pentagon, Arab Americans also alleged discrimination. "We have people being targeted at work who have lived in this country for 25 years with no record of any violation," said one regional director of the American-Arab Anti-Discrimination Committee. Among the complaints: getting fired after they had been questioned—but cleared—by the FBI, employers disregarding religious and racial slurs at work, bans on turbans and head scarves, and prohibitions of daily prayer and foot-washing rituals.[65]

Sexual Orientation: Gays & Lesbians Become More Visible Gays and lesbians make up 3%–10% of the U.S. population. Between a quarter and two-thirds report being discriminated against at work (with negative attitudes directed toward them held more by men than by women[66]). They also report higher levels of stress compared to heterosexual employees. Finally, gay and bisexual male workers were found to earn 11%–27% less than equally qualified heterosexual counterparts.[67]

How important is the issue of sexual preference? Once again, if managers are concerned about hiring and keeping workplace talent, they shouldn't ignore the motivation and productivity of 3%–10% of the workforce.

People with Differing Physical & Mental Abilities

One out of six Americans has a physical or mental disability, according to the U.S. Department of Labor. Since 1992 we have had the *Americans with Disabilities Act*, **which prohibits discrimination against the disabled** and requires organizations to reasonably accommodate an individual's disabilities. Despite what we've all heard about organizations having to spend hundreds of thousands of dollars building wheelchair ramps and the like, the costs actually aren't that great: Half the disability accommodations cost less than $50 and 69% cost less than $500.[68]

Even so, disabled people have difficulty finding work. Although two-thirds of people with disabilities want to work, roughly two-thirds are unemployed. (Among blind adults, for example, about 70% are out of work.[69]) Those who are working tend to be in part-time, low-status jobs with little chance for advancement. Moreover, they earn up to 35% less than their more fully abled counterparts.[70] Here, too, is a talent pool that managers will no doubt find themselves tapping into in the coming years.

Educational Levels: Mismatches Between Education & Workforce Needs. Two important mismatches between education and workplace are these:

- **College graduates may be in jobs for which they are overqualified:** About 27% of people working have a college degree. But some are *underemployed*—**working at jobs that require less education than they have**—such as tending bar, managing video stores, or other jobs that someone with lesser education could do.

  It is estimated that a quarter of the workforce (not all of them college graduates) is underemployed, a condition associated with higher absenteeism, arrest rates, and unmarried parenthood and with lower motivation, job involvement, and psychological well-being.[71]

- **High-school dropouts and others may not have the literacy skills needed for many jobs:** The high-school dropout rate in the United States is 9.2%, and an estimated 73 million adult Americans are illiterate, meaning unable to use "printed and written information to function in society, to achieve one's goals, and to develop one's knowledge and potential."[72] In addition, more than two-thirds of the American workforce reads below ninth-grade level—a problem because about 70% of on-the-job reading materials are written at or above that level.[73]

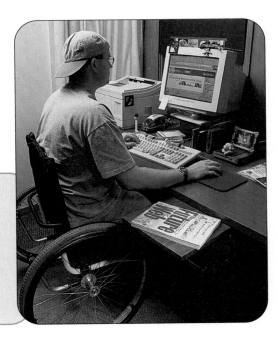

Disability. Everyone recognizes the wheelchair as signifying that a person is partly disabled, but other disabilities are not so easily identified—and may not invite understanding. Do you think that mental disabilites, for example, should be accommodated in employment? If you were subject to mood swings, would you think that would prevent you from doing your job effectively?

Barriers to Diversity

Some barriers are erected by diverse people themselves. In the main, however, most barriers are put in their paths by organizations.[74] When we speak of "the organization's barriers," we are, of course, referring to the *people* in the organization—especially those who may have been there for a while—who are resistant to making it more diverse.

Resistance to change in general is an attitude that all managers come up against from time to time, and resistance to diversity is simply one variation. It may be expressed in the following six ways.

1 Stereotypes & Prejudices *Ethnocentrism* ("eth-no-*sen*-trizm") is the belief that one's native country, culture, language, abilities, or behavior is superior to those of another culture. (An example is embodied in the title of the Wesley Snipes/Woody Harrelson movie about urban basketball hustlers: *White Men Can't Jump*.) When differences are viewed as being weaknesses— which is what many stereotypes and prejudices ultimately come down to—this may be expressed as a concern that diversity hiring will lead to a sacrifice in competence and quality.

2 Fear of Reverse Discrimination Some employees are afraid that attempts to achieve greater diversity in their organization will result in reverse discrimination—that more black or Asian employees will be promoted to fire captain or police lieutenant, for example, over the heads of supposedly more qualified whites.

3 Resistance to Diversity Program Priorities Some companies such as 3M offer special classes teaching tolerance for diversity, seminars in how to get along.[75] Some employees may see diversity programs as distracting them from the organization's "real work." In addition, they may be resentful of diversity-promoting policies that are reinforced through special criteria in the organization's performance appraisals and reward systems.

Diversity determines a company's success.

Eastman Kodak Company is committed to becoming a truly diverse corporation. Embracing the ideals of diversity enables us to better meet the needs of our customers, employees, suppliers, and the communities in which we live and work. All of which ensures our continued success in the global marketplace.

Picture what we can do together!

Interested suppliers please go to: www.kodak.com/go/supplierdiversity   © Eastman Kodak Company, 2002

Picture what we can do together. Kodak ran this ad expressing the company's viewpoint on diversity. Can you think of occasions when you may have resisted change in any of the six ways described in the text?

The look of things to come? In the late 1990s, labor shortages became so profound that employers had to offer day-care centers, flexible work hours, and training programs. Some even allowed parents to bring their children to work. Get ready for a replay. Prime-age employees—those between 25 and 54—grew 35% in the years 1980–2000. In the years 2000–2020, they are expected to grow only *3%*, predicts Harvard University economist Dale W. Jorgenson. To address chronic labor shortages, would you expect employers to offer more flexibility to working mothers and more help with child care needs? What other things do you think they'll have to do?

4 Unsupportive Social Atmosphere Diverse employees may be excluded from office camaraderie and social events.

5 Lack of Support for Family Demands In most families (63%, according to the Bureau of Labor Statistics), both parents work; in 29.5% only the father works, and in 4.5% only the mother works. But more and more women are moving back and forth between being at-home mothers and in the workforce, as economic circumstances dictate.[76] Yet in a great many households, it is still women who primarily take care of children, as well as other domestic chores. When organizations aren't supportive in offering flexibility in hours and job responsibilities, these women may find it difficult to work evenings and weekends or to take overnight business trips.

6 Lack of Support for Career-Building Steps Organizations may not provide diverse employees with the types of work assignments that will help qualify them for positions in senior management. In addition, organizations may fail to provide the kind of informal training or mentoring that will help them learn the political savvy to do networking and other activities required to get ahead.

major question

Do I have what it takes to be an entrepreneur?

The Big Picture

Entrepreneurship, a necessary attribute of business, means taking risks to create a new enterprise. It is expressed through two kinds of innovators, the entrepreneur and the intrapreneur.

In 1995, Jason Levinthal, 21, of Albany, N.Y.—snowboarder, in-line skater, and SUNY Buffalo architecture and design major—cobbled together a pair of what he called "skiboards" for a senior project. (He got an A.) Made from old skis, these were "a pair of stubby planks that resemble miniature skis but [were] tipped together at both ends to let users 'ride fakey'—that is, backward in the style of snowboarders," writes reporter Jeff Weiss.[77]

Levinthal then invested $10,000 and a year of 14-hour days to come up with 35-inch-long, steel-edged wooden planks made of resin-coated fiberglass around a wooden core. He then let his hard-core thrasher friends put the skiboards to the test—180s, 360s, grinds—and they came away impressed. A year later, at a snow sports trade show, he received an order for 1,000 skiboards. To build buzz for his product, he kept after extreme-skiing magazine *Freeze* until it ran a story on skiboarding.

In 1997, skiboarding came to the attention of sports TV channel ESPN2, and the next year the X Games Slopestyle Skiboarding competition was broadcast to 800,000 homes, with Levinthal's skiboards taking bronze and gold medals. As a result of this exposure, the general media began running stories, and ski resorts, determined not to miss the boat as they had with snowboards, began to support the new technology. By the end of the 1999 ski season, an estimated 50,000 pairs of skiboards were sold—"peanuts compared with sales of actual skis," says Weiss, "but impressive for a pastime that didn't even exist five years ago."

The entrepreneur. Jason Levinthal, inventor of the skiboard, admires the mountain views. "Skiboarding is the natural evolution of skiing, snowboarding, and skateboarding," he says. Is visionary thinking a key attribute of entrepreneurs?

Entrepreneurship Defined: Taking Risks in Pursuit of Opportunity

Levinthal is an entrepreneur ("on-treh-pren-*oor*"), a man with an idea, a risk taker.

So is Chip Conley, who has made a success in the offbeat but expanding business of "boutique" hotels, which, unlike Hiltons and Hyatts, each have their own one-of-a-kind charm. Conley likes magazines because they provide inspired themes for the hotels he buys and renovates. For instance, he says the Nob Hill Lambourne in San Francisco, which is oriented toward health-conscious travelers, resembles the magazine *Men's Health*; the hotel offers algae shakes, vitamins instead of chocolates on the pillows, and an on-call psychologist. The Hotel Rex, modeled on *The New Yorker*, features a book-lined cocktail lounge, old leather furniture, and poetry readings.[78]

The most successful entrepreneurs become wealthy and make the covers of business magazines: Fred Smith of Federal Express. Debbie Fields of Mrs. Field's Cookies. Anita Roddick of The Body Shop. Michael Dell of Dell Computers. Failed entrepreneurs may benefit from the experience to live to fight another day—as did Henry Ford, twice bankrupt before achieving success with Ford Motor Co.

What Entrepreneurship Is   *Entrepreneurship* is the process of taking risks to try to create a new enterprise. There are two types of entrepreneurship:

- **The entrepreneur: An *entrepreneur* is someone who sees a new opportunity for a product or service and launches a business to try to realize it.** Jason Levinthal is an example of an entrepreneur. Most entrepreneurs run small businesses with fewer than 100 employees.

- **The intrapreneur: An *intrapreneur* is someone who works inside an existing organization who sees an opportunity for a product or service and mobilizes the organization's resources to try to realize it.** This person might be a researcher or scientist but could also be a manager who sees an opportunity to create a new venture that could be profitable.

Organization on the run.

Now the Post-it® Notes and Flags you depend on to help you stay organized can travel with you. The handy, refillable case can go in your briefcase, purse, backpack, or can be part of your planner. It's an idea you can run with: Post-it® Portable Flags & Notes.

Post-it® Portable Flags & Notes

3M *Innovation*

Example of an Intrapreneur: Art Fry & 3M's Post-it Notes

One of the most famous instances of intrapreneurship occurred at 3M Corp., a company famous for pumping out new products, when 3M employee Art Fry conceived of Post-it Notes, those bright-colored "sticky notes" that people use to post messages on walls and mark books. The company had invented an experimental adhesive for which it could find no use. Meanwhile, when attending church, Fry found that the bits of paper he used to mark hymns in his hymnbook kept slipping out. It dawned on him that 3M's experimental glue could provide adhesive-backed paper that would stick for a long time but could be easily removed without damaging the book.

Coming up with the product was only the first step. Market surveys were negative. Office-supply distributors thought the notion useless. Fry thereupon started giving samples to executives and secretaries at 3M, who began using the sticky paper and soon were hooked. Later Fry used the same approach with other executives and secretaries throughout the United States. After 12 years, the orders began to flow, and Post-its became a winning product for 3M.[79]

How Do Entrepreneurs & Managers Differ? While the entrepreneur is not necessarily an inventor, he or she "always searches for change, responds to it, and exploits it as an opportunity," Peter Drucker points out.[80] How does this differ from being a manager?

Being an entrepreneur is what it takes to *start* a business; being a manager is what it takes to *grow or maintain* a business. As an entrepreneur/intrapreneur, you initiate new goods or services; as a manager you coordinate the resources to produce the goods or services.

The examples of success we mentioned above—Chip Conley, Fred Smith, Debbie Fields, Anita Roddick, Michael Dell—are actually *both* entrepreneurs and effective managers. Some people, however, find they like the start-up part but hate the management part. For example, Stephen Wozniak, entrepreneurial co-founder with Steve Jobs of Apple Computer, abandoned the computer industry completely and went back to college. Jobs, by contrast, went on to launch another business, Pixar, which among other things became the animation factory that made the movie *Toy Story*.

Entrepreneurial companies have been called "gazelles" for the two attributes that make them successful: *speed and agility.* "Gazelles have mastered the art of the quick," says Alan Webber, founding editor of *Fast Company* magazine. "They have internal approaches and fast decision-making approaches that let them move with maximum agility in a fast-changing business environment."[81]

Is this the kind of smart, innovative world you'd like to be a part of? Most people prefer the security of a job and a paycheck. Indeed, even young people—those ages 25–34—who might be expected to be attracted to the entrepreneurial life, are about 40% less likely to be self-employed than their parents, according to the Bureau of Labor Statistics.[82]

Entrepreneurs do seem to have psychological characteristics that are different from managers, as follows:[83]

Up and away. Gary Ream, president and partner of Woodward Camp, transformed this aging gymnastics camp in central Pennsylvania into an extreme-sports summer retreat. First he offered BMX lessons, then coached in-line skaters and skateboarders, then began hosting competitions, which attracted the attention of sports TV channel ESPN and generated further publicity. In 2002, 200 pro athletes coached 10,000 campers, and the camp generated $6 million in revenue.

- **Characteristic of both—high need for achievement:** Both entrepreneurs and managers have a high need for achievement. However, entrepreneurs certainly seem to be motivated to pursue moderately difficult goals through their own efforts in order to realize their ideas and, they hope, financial rewards. Managers, by contrast, are more motivated by promotions and organizational rewards of power and perks.

- **Also characteristic of both—belief in personal control of destiny:** If you believe "I am the captain of my fate, the master of my soul," you have what is known as *internal locus of control*, **the belief that you control your own destiny,** that external forces will have little influence. (External locus of control means the reverse—you believe you don't control your destiny, that external forces do.) Both entrepreneurs and managers like to think they have personal control over their lives.

- **Characteristic of both, but especially of entrepreneurs—high energy level and action orientation:** Rising to the top in an organization probably requires that a manager put in long hours. For entrepreneurs, however, creating a new enterprise may require an extraordinary investment of time and energy. In addition, while some managers may feel a sense of urgency, entrepreneurs are especially apt to be impatient and to want to get things done as quickly as possible, making them particularly action oriented.

- **Characteristic of both, but especially of entrepreneurs—high tolerance for ambiguity:** Every manager needs to be able to make decisions based on ambiguous—that is, unclear or incomplete—information. However, entrepreneurs must have more tolerance for ambiguity

Meg Whitman, eBay CEO. Pierre Omidyar was the entrepreneurial founder of the online auction company, but Whitman is the professional manager who, in one fan's words, "has taken a brilliant idea, and with execution, monitoring, and constant improvement, made it infinitely better."

because they are trying to do things they haven't done before.

- **More characteristic of entrepreneurs than managers—self-confidence and tolerance for risk:** Managers must believe in themselves and be willing to make decisions; however, this statement applies even more to entrepreneurs. Precisely because they are willing to take risks in the pursuit of new opportunities—indeed, even risk personal financial failure—entrepreneurs need the confidence to act decisively.

Of course, not all entrepreneurs have this kind of faith in themselves. So-called *necessity* entrepreneurs are people such as laid-off corporate workers, discharged military people, immigrants, and divorced homemakers who suddenly must earn a living and are simply trying to replace lost income and are hoping a job comes along. These make up about 11% of entrepreneurs. However, so-called *opportunity* entrepreneurs—the other 89%—are those who start their own business out of a burning desire rather than because they lost a job. Unlike necessity types, they tend to be more ambitious and to start firms that can lead to high-growth businesses.

Which do you think you would be more happier doing—being an entrepreneur or being a manager?[84]

Click-Along 3.7

Taking Something Practical Away from This Chapter: Previewing the Steps in Your Management Career—Being the Author of Your Own Life

Key Terms Used in This Chapter

Summary

3.1
The Community of Stakeholders Inside the Organization

■ Managers operate in two organizational environments—internal and external—both made up of shareholders, the people whose interests are affected by the organization's activities. The first, or internal, environment, consists of employees, owners, and the board of directors.

3.2
The Community of Stakeholders Outside the Organization

■ The external environment of stakeholders consists of the task environment and the general environment.

■ The task environment consists of 11 groups that present the manager with daily tasks to deal with. (1) Customers are those who pay to use an organization's goods and services. (2) Competitors are people or organizations

that compete for customers or resources. (3) Suppliers are people or organizations that provide supplies—raw materials, services, equipment, labor, or energy—to other organizations. (4) Distributors are people or organizations that help another organization sell its goods and services to customers. (5) Strategic allies describe the relationship of two organizations who join forces to achieve advantages neither can perform as well alone. (6) Employee organizations consist of labor unions and employee associations. (7) Local communities consist of residents, companies, governments, and nonprofit entities that depend on the organization's taxes, payroll, and charitable contributions. (8) Financial institutions are commercial banks, investment banks, and insurance companies that deal with the organization. (9) Government regulators are regulatory agencies that establish the ground rules under which the organization operates. (10) Special-interest groups are groups whose members try to influence specific issues that may affect the organization. (11) The mass media are print, radio, TV, and Internet sources that affect the organization's public relations.

■ The general environment includes six forces. (1) Economic forces consist of general economic conditions and trends—unemployment, inflation, interest rates, economic growth—that may affect an organization's performance. (2) Technological forces are new developments in methods for transforming resources into goods and services. (3) Sociocultural forces are influences and trends originating in a country, society, or culture's human relationships and values that may affect an organization. (4) Demographic forces are influences on an organization arising from changes in the characteristics of a population, such as age, gender, and ethnic origin. (5) Political-legal forces are changes in the way politics shapes laws and laws shape the opportunities for and threats to an organization. (6) International forces are changes in the economic, political, legal, and technological global system that may affect an organization.

3.3
The Ethical Responsibilities Required of You as a Manager

■ Managers need to be aware of what constitutes ethics, values, the four approaches to ethical dilemmas, and how organizations can promote ethics.

■ Ethics are the standards of right and wrong that influence behavior. Ethical behavior is behavior that is accepted as "right" as opposed to "wrong" according to those standards.

■ Ethical dilemmas often take place because of an organization's value system, the pattern of values within an organization. Values are the relatively permanent and deeply held underlying beliefs and attitudes that help determine a person's behavior.

■ There are four approaches to deciding ethical dilemmas. (1) In the utilitarian approach, ethical behavior is guided by what will result in the greatest good for the greatest number of people. (2) In the individual approach, ethical behavior is guided by what will result in the individual's best long-term interests, which ultimately is in everyone's self-interest. (3) In the moral-rights approach, ethical be-

havior is guided by respect for the fundamental rights of human beings, such as those expressed in the U.S. Constitution's Bill of Rights. (4) In the justice approach, ethical behavior is guided by respect for the impartial standards of fairness and equity.

■ There are three ways an organization may foster high ethical standards. (1) The top managers must support a strong ethical climate. (2) The organization may have a code of ethics, which consists of a formal written set of ethical standards guiding an organization's actions. (3) An organization must reward ethical behavior, as in not discouraging whistleblowers, employees who report organizational misconduct to the public.

3.4
The Social Responsibilities Required of You as a Manager

■ Managers need to be aware of the viewpoints supporting and opposing social responsibility, four managerial approaches to responsibility, and whether being and doing good pays off financially for the organization.

■ Social responsibility is a manager's duty to take actions that will benefit the interests of society as well as of the organization. An example of social responsibility is philanthropy, donating money to worthwhile recipients.

■ For-profit companies generally make a point of "putting something back" into society as well as taking something out, but the idea of social responsibility has opposing and supporting viewpoints. The opposing viewpoint is that the social responsibility of business is to make profits. The supporting viewpoint is that since business creates some problems (such as pollution) it should help solve them.

■ There are four approaches to social responsibility. (1) In the obstructionist approach, managers put economic gain first and resist social responsibility as being outside the organization's self interest. (2) In the defensive approach, managers make the minimum commitment to social responsibility—obeying the law but doing nothing more. (3) In the accommodative approach, managers will do more than the law requires, if asked, and will demonstrate moderate social responsibility. (4) In the proactive approach, managers actively lead the way in being socially responsible for all stakeholders, using the organization's resources to identify and respond to social problems.

■ Negative ethical behavior and social responsibility can have certain negative financial effects—on the organization's stock price, sales growth, and customer loyalty. Practicing social responsibility can make a company attract more job applicants.

3.5
The New Diversified Workforce

■ One of today's most important management challenges is working with stakeholders of all sorts who vary widely in diversity. Diversity represents all the ways people are alike and unlike—the differences and similarities in age, gender, race, religion, ethnicity, sexual orientation, capabilities, and socioeconomic background.

■ There are two dimensions of diversity—internal and external. Internal dimensions of diversity are those human differences that exert a powerful, sustained effect throughout every stage of our lives: gender, ethnicity, race, physical abilities, age, and sexual orientation. External dimensions of diversity have an element of choice; they consist of the personal characteristics that people acquire, discard, or modify throughout their lives: personal habits, educational background, religion, income, marital status, and the like.

■ There are five categories in the internal dimension and one category in the external dimension in which the U.S. workforce is becoming more diverse. (1) Age: There are more older people in the workforce. (2) Gender: More women are working, and more are making progress in penetrating the glass ceiling—the metaphor for an invisible barrier preventing women and minorities from being promoted to top executive jobs. (3) Race and ethnicity: More people of color are in the workforce, such as Hispanics, African-Americans, and Asians. (4) Sexual orientation: Gays and lesbians are becoming more visible. (5) People with differing physical and mental abilities: Spurred by the Americans with Disabilities Act, which prohibits discrimination against the disabled, organiza-

tions are trying to accommodate disabled workers. (6) Educational levels: College graduates may be in jobs for which they are overqualified—that is, they are underemployed, working at jobs that require less education than they have. Many high school dropouts and others may not have the literacy skills needed for many jobs.

■ There are six ways in which employees and managers may express resistance to diversity: (1) Some express stereotypes and prejudices based on ethnocentrism, the belief that one's native country, culture, language, abilities, or behavior is superior to those of another country. (2) Some employees are afraid of reverse discrimination. (3) Some employees see diversity programs as distracting them from the organization's supposed "real work." (4) Diverse employees may experience an unsupportive social atmosphere. (5) Organizations may not be supportive of flexible hours and other matters that can help employees cope with family demands. (6) Organizations may show lack of support for career-building steps for diverse employees.

3.6
The Entrepreneurial Spirit

■ Entrepreneurship, a necessary attribute of business, is the process of taking risks to try to create a new enterprise. There are two types of entrepreneurship: (1) An entrepreneur is someone who sees a new opportunity for a product or service and launches a business to try to realize it. (2) An intrapreneur is someone who works inside an existing organization and sees an opportunity for a product or service and mobilizes the organization's resources to try to realize it.

■ Entrepreneurs, who are needed to start a business, and managers, who are needed to grow or maintain a business, differ somewhat. Both have a high need for achievement and a belief in personal control of their own destiny (internal locus of control). Both have a high energy level and action orientation as well as high tolerance for ambiguity, but these characteristics are especially true of entrepreneurs. Entrepreneurs are more self-confident than managers are and they have a higher tolerance for risk.

New Roles are Required in Employee-Owned Companies

Excerpted from Laird Harrison, "We're All the Boss," Time *Bonus Section, April 2002, pp. 92–93.*

The theory behind employee-ownership programs is that they will transform workers from clock punchers to partners who will be motivated to better serve customers and make things run more efficiently. . . .

On average, worker-owned companies survive longer, lose fewer workers, enjoy bigger profits and are more productive than their non-employee owned competitors, says Rutgers University economist Douglas Kruse, who compiled data from more than 30 studies of worker-owned firms. Employees at these firms earn higher wages and better benefits. And they get a crack at big money if the stock takes off. . . .

What's even more important to the success of employee-owned companies, says Jack Stack, 53, CEO of Springfield Remanufacturing in Springfield, Mo., is openness of information and decision making. Springfield Remanufacturing started in 1983 when 13 supervisors took on heavy debt to buy a division of International Harvester that rebuilt big-vehicle engines. Stack argued that the company's only chance was for every worker to have a stake in its success and understand its finances.

Employees got shares of stock worth a dime apiece. And every week Stack held "huddles" in which everyone from top managers to janitors pored over financial data. Those who couldn't read the data got training. That helped them make day-to-day decisions such as whether a mechanic should repair an engine's connecting rod or install a new one. . . . Within three years of its founding, Springfield Remanufacturing was turning a profit, and today its stock is worth $13.60 a share—82% of it owned by the workers.

As at Stack's firm, each worker at W. L. Gore enjoys broad discretion to make minor decisions. Bigger ones—hiring and firing, setting compensation—are made by committees whose members constantly shift with the demands of the business.

Anyone can start a new project simply by persuading enough people to go along with the idea. Even Bob Gore, 64, chairman and son of the founders, has his compensation set by a committee.

The arrangement has its costs. Above all, workers are forced to devote a lot of time to building relationships. Says process technology manager Michael Jones, 45: "At a traditional company, you have one boss to please. Here, you have everyone to please." And few companies go so far; most of the 3,500 or so American firms in which workers own a majority of the stock are organized as conventional hierarchies. But evidence is growing that the most successful firms are those that find some consistent way of empowering workers.

Corey Rosen, executive director of the National Center for Employee Ownership, says workers "don't necessarily have to have a vote on the board. What's really important is to have an influence on the way you do your day-to-day job." In exchange for that little bit of power and a stake in using it well, most workers will do whatever they can for their company.

For Discussion

1. How do the stakeholders vary between a publicly held firm and an employee-owned company?

2. Do employees have different ethical responsibilities in an employee-owned firm? Discuss.

3. To what extent do managers have different roles in an employee-owned firm? Explain.

4. Given the trends in workforce diversity discussed in this chapter, to what extent will future employees want to be affiliated with an employee-owned company? Discuss your rationale.

5. Would you like to work in an employee-owned company? Why or why not?

Take It to the Net

In early 2002 American newspaper headlines told the unfolding story of the Enron debacle. This scandal raised issues about ethics in the workplace, managers' relationships with stakeholders, the social responsibility of companies to their environment, the role of the government in overseeing corporate activities, and the entrepreneurial spirit gone awry. Managers of companies have been put on notice that ethics and social responsibility are important and need attention.

The OD-Online Organization Health Survey at http://www.od-online.com/toxic_org.asp? redirect=htm lets you assess your company and its activities. If you are not currently working, think of an organization you have worked for in the past and assess that one. Answer the questions on the website and then submit the results for your score and an interpretation of that score.

Questions for Discussion

1. Should all companies have a form such as this filled out by employees regularly so there is feedback from all stakeholders within the company? Explain.

2. Can companies be ethical and socially responsible in these competitive "survival of the fittest" days? Why or why not?

Self-Assessment

What Is My Guiding Ethical Principle?*

Objectives

1. To understand your ethical approach.

2. To understand that there are different ways to perceive ethics in the workplace.

Introduction: Over the centuries human beings have grappled with defining ethics and behaving ethically. Many different principles have evolved to deal with ethics from different perspectives. None is better or worse than the other—they are simply perspectives. You may choose one to be your guiding principle while your friend follows another. This is also true of companies and their employees. For example, Johnson & Johnson has a valued reputation for being very ethical and socially responsible, whereas actions by companies like Ford and Arthur Andersen have placed a large question mark on their ethical conduct and social responsibility.

Instructions: Rank each of the following principles in order from 1 (my most important guiding principle) to 3 (least relevant to my ethical principles).

1. *Utilitarianism:* The greatest good for the greatest number, or any view that holds that actions and policies should be evaluated on the basis of benefits and costs they will impose on society.
   Violation? The Ford Motor Company knew of the problems with its tires six years before they became known in the United States, but this was information from Europe, and U.S. law did not require that the company report it if it did not happen here.

2. *Rights Theory:* A right is an individual's entitlement or claim to something. A person has a right when he or she is entitled to act in a certain way or is entitled to have others act in a certain way toward him or her. It can be a legal right, a moral right, or a human right.
   Violation? Many stockholders at Microsoft want the company to adopt the "U.S. Business Principles for Human Rights of Workers in China," a statement supported by other companies such as Levi Strauss and Reebok. Microsoft management did not agree, arguing that its own principles and code of ethics covered the important points and that the statement principles were too broad and vague. Other companies also thought that American companies should not promote human rights in China because they would be abandoning a position of political neutrality.

*Developed by Anne C. Cowden, Ph.D. See Manuel G. Velasquez, *Business Ethics: Concepts and Cases* (Upper Saddle River, NJ: Prentice Hall, 2002) for a detailed discussion of each approach.

3. *Justice as Fairness:* A principle that aims to protect those least able to protect themselves. *Examples:* Companies should establish strong affirmative action plans to redress the wrongs of discrimination; or, if a company introduces pay cuts, the workers paid the least should receive the smallest pay cut and those who are paid the most should get the largest pay cut.

Questions for Discussion

1. What are the pros and cons of your primary ethical principle in terms of advancing up the corporate ladder? Discuss.
2. Why do you think ethical principles are important in the workplace? Explain.
3. Which of the previous three principles would you want the company that you work for to adopt? Why?
4. In such a competitive world, how ethical can any company really be?

Group Exercise

Ethical Application*

Objectives
1. To assess how you apply your primary ethical principle (from the previous exercise) to a case.
2. To see how group members using different ethical principles approach a case.

Introduction
Because "perception is reality" people see situations differently and thus make different decisions. The subjectivity of perception makes it difficult for organizational members to reach a consensus on what the ethical conduct of the company should be—but consensus must be reached if the company is to be able to make coherent, consistent decisions concerning ethical issues.

Instructions
Divide your class into three groups: those who ranked Utilitarianism as their first choice (in the previous exercise); those who selected Rights Theory as their first choice; and those who ranked Justice as Fairness as their first choice. Each group is to read the following scenario and then discuss how they would manage it, according to their chosen principle. Next each group must in turn try to convince the other two groups that their approach is the best one. Finally, all three groups should try to agree on one approach.

Scenario
You are a U.S. pharmaceutical firm that has discovered a drug that will stop a terrible disease epidemic on the African continent. You have spent a great deal of time (5 years) and an immense amount of money ($100 million) on the drug's development. It has tied up the time of 25 specialists and a lot of lab space. To recoup costs, you are going to have to charge a high price for each pill. You have another, similar product in process, which your scientists are very excited about. Given the competitive nature of the drug market, your stockholders are asking for justification for the time and money spent on these and other such products.

Your marketing and salespeople are now looking for buyers and find that no one wants to meet your price of $10 per pill. The African people need it badly but cannot afford it. The disease causes early blindness in millions of children, and your drug would greatly improve the quality of living for these children as well as increase their society's human resources. What would you do and why? Explain in detail.

Questions for Discussion

1. Did your group easily agree on a solution? Explain why or why not.
2. Did the three groups propose similar or different solutions to the case? Why did this happen? Discuss.
3. What did you learn about the relationship between ethical principles and decision making from this exercise? Discuss.
4. How can people who possess competing ethical principles reach consensus when making decisions?

*Developed by Anne C. Cowden, Ph.D.

Ethical Dilemma

A Teacher Faces the Problem of Dealing with Cheating Students

Excerpted from Clayton Bellamy, "Teacher Resigns as School Backs Plagiarizing Kids,"
The Arizona Republic, *February 10, 2002, p. A 21.*

High school teacher Christine Pelton wasted no time after discovering that nearly a fifth of her biology students had plagiarized their semester projects from the Internet. She had received her rural Kansas district's backing when she accused students of cheating once before, and she expected it again this time after failing the 28 sophomores. Her principal and superintendent agreed: It was plagiarism, and the students should get a zero for the assignment.

But after parents complained, the Piper School Board ordered her to go easier on the guilty. The board ordered her to give the students partial credit and to decrease the project's value from 50% of the final course grade to 30%.

One of the complaining parents, Theresa Woolley, told the Kansas City Star that her daughter did not plagiarize but was not sure how much she needed to rewrite research material.

But Pelton said the course syllabus, which she required students to sign, warned of the conse-quences of cheating and plagiarism. What is worse, according to Donald McCabe, professor of management at Rutgers University, is that tolerance of dishonesty disheartens other students, who have to compete with the cheaters to get into college. "If they see teachers looking the other way, students feel compelled to participate even though it makes them uncomfortable," McCabe said.

Solving the Dilemma

What would you do if you were Christine Pelton?

1. Resign your position in protest over the school board's lack of support.

2. Do what the school board ordered.

3. Ignore the school board's order and give the failing grades.

4. Invent other options. (Explain.)

CHAPTER 4

Global Management
Managing Across Borders

4.1 Globalization: The Collapse of Time & Distance

Major Question: What three important developments of globalization will probably affect me?

4.2 You & International Management

Major Question: Why learn about international management, and what characterizes the successful international manager?

4.3 Why & How Companies Expand Internationally

Major Question: Why do companies expand internationally, and how do they do it?

4.4 Economic & Political-Legal Differences

Major Question: How may foreign countries differ in their economic, political, and legal characteristics?

4.5 The World of Free Trade: Regional Economic Cooperation

Major Question: What are barriers to free trade, and what major organizations and trading blocs promote trade?

4.6 The Importance of Understanding Cultural Differences

Major Question: What are the principal areas of cultural differences?

BEING A STAR ROAD WARRIOR

Since business travelers who fly 100,000-plus miles a year are no longer a rare breed, should you prepare for the possibility of joining them?

As we discuss in this chapter, globalization has collapsed time and distance. Managers must be prepared to work for organizations that operate not only country-wide but worldwide. To stay connected with colleagues, employees, clients, and suppliers, you may have to travel a lot.

Business travel can have its rewards. Many people enjoy going to different cities, meeting new people, encountering new cultures. In one survey, people who took business trips of five nights or more said that being on the road provided certain escapes, as from: their everyday workplace (35% of those polled), putting out work "fires" (20%), frequent meetings (12%), and coworker distractions (11%).[1]

Two lessons that business travelers have learned are the following.

■ **Frequent travel may be needed because personal encounters are essential for teamwork:** "Flying is a waste of time, but it's a necessary evil," says management consultant Jeff Bowden, 52, who flies about 500,000 miles a year. "I've done well financially, so I've been very lucky. I laugh at people who think they can be successful without flying."[2]

Scott Collins, 33, lives in Michigan, where his $100,000 salary goes far. But he works at Netscape Communications in Mountain View, Calif., in the heart of Silicon Valley, and travels the 2,000 miles between home and workplace a couple of times a month. The reason: Phones, e-mail, and videoconferencing aren't entirely feasible. Teamwork requires personal encounters.

"Paradoxically, location matters more than ever in high-tech," says futurist Paul Saffo. "To be a player in Silicon Valley, you have to be in people's faces."[3]

The same is true in most other industries.

■ **Frequent travel requires frequent adjustments:** How do you cope if you travel all the time? Management consultant Bowden keeps sets of clothes in Tampa, Los Angeles, and Vancouver, British Columbia. He is away so much that he has a problem getting rid of his household trash. If he puts his garbage cans out Tuesday morning, he may not be home to wheel them in. So he has learned to dispose of the trash in a trash can en route to the airport.

Vicki Schubert-Martin, who works in the software industry, travels about 250,000 miles a year, which keeps her away from her Denver home about five days a week. To keep up her health, she maintains a high-fiber diet while on the road. She keeps a close relationship with her husband by phoning him daily and spending weekends hiking, biking, and seeing movies with him. "It's a matter of keeping a healthy attitude about it," she says.[4]

FORECAST: WHAT'S AHEAD IN THIS CHAPTER

This chapter covers the importance of globalization—the rise of the global village, of one big market, of both worldwide megafirms and minifirms. We also describe the characteristics of the successful international manager, why and how companies expand internationally, and some of the economic and political-legal differences between countries. We describe the barriers to free trade and the major organizations promoting trade. Finally, we describe some of the cultural differences you may encounter if you become an international manager.

What three important developments of globalization will probably affect me?

The Big Picture

Globalization, the trend of the world economy toward becoming a more interdependent system, is reflected in three developments: the rise of the "global village" and e-commerce, the trend of the world's becoming one big market, and the rise of both megafirms and Internet-enabled minifirms worldwide.

Barry Salzman, president of DoubleClick International, a worldwide Internet advertising firm headquartered in New York, spends about 75% of his time traveling. "He takes a laptop and four battery packs so that he can wade through the 200 e-mail messages he averages daily," says one description. "He carries two mobile phones because he is on call, day or night, to handle problems anywhere in the world."[5]

Here is a manager who heads an Internet company—which can reach all corners of the globe in milliseconds. Yet he spends most of his time traveling because it's the only way he can see to manage his 13 offices worldwide.

Can you visualize yourself operating like this? Like Salzman, you are living in a world being rapidly changed by *__globalization__*—**the trend of the world economy toward becoming a more interdependent system.** Time and distance, which have been under assault for 150 years, have now virtually collapsed, as reflected in three important developments we shall discuss:[6]

1 The rise of the "global village" and electronic commerce.

2 The world's becoming one market instead of many national ones.

3 The rise of both megafirms and Internet-enabled minifirms worldwide.

The Rise of the "Global Village" & Electronic Commerce

The hallmark of great civilizations has been their great systems of communications. In the beginning, communications was based on transportation: The Roman Empire had its network of roads. Later the great European powers had their far-flung navies. In the 19th century, the United States and Canada unified North America by building transcontinental railroads. Later the airplane reduced travel time between continents.

Interacting internationally. Applied Materials CEO James Morgan (left) talks with his foreign counterpart, Samsung Electronics president Yoon-Won Lee, in Austin, Texas. Both are wearing a "yellow rose of Texas" in their lapels. What foreign products are you aware of that are now made in the United States?

From Transportation to Communication Transportation began to yield to the electronic exchange of information. Beginning in 1844, the telegraph ended the short existence of the Pony Express and, beginning in 1876, found itself in competition with the telephone. The amplifying vacuum tube, invented in 1906, led to commercial radio. Television came into being in England in 1925. During the 1950s and 1960s, as television exploded throughout the world, communications philosopher Marshall McLuhan posed the notion of a "global village," where we all share our hopes, dreams, and fears in a "worldpool" of information. **The _global village_ refers to the "shrinking" of time and space as air travel and the electronic media have made it easier for the people of the globe to communicate with one another.**

Then the world became even faster and smaller. Fifteen years ago, cellphones, pagers, fax, and voice-mail links barely existed. When AT&T launched the first cellular communications system in 1983, it predicted fewer than a million users by 2000. By the end of 1993, however, there were more than 16 million cellular phone subscribers in the United States.[7] And as of 2001, there were more than 131 million.

The Net, the Web, & the World And then came the Internet, the worldwide computer-linked "network of networks," where today 544 million people log on every week throughout the world (181 million in Canada and the United States). The Net might have remained the province of academicians had it not been for the contributions of Tim Berners-Lee, who came up with the coding system, linkages, and addressing scheme that debuted in 1991 as the World Wide Web. "He took a powerful communications system [the Internet] that only the elite could use," says one writer, "and turned it into a mass medium."[8]

The arrival of the Web quickly led to _e-commerce_, **or electronic commerce, the buying and selling of products and services through computer networks.** Total U.S. e-commerce sales to consumers were expected to top $100 billion by 2003, or 6% of consumer retail spending.[9] Indeed, online shopping is growing even faster than the increase in computer use.[10]

Example of Worldwide E-Commerce: Amazon.com

In 1994, Jeffrey Bezos left a successful career on Wall Street with a plan to exploit the potential for electronic retailing on the World Wide Web by launching an online bookstore called Amazon.com.

Bezos realized that no bookstore with four walls could possibly stock the more than 2.5 million books that are now active and in print. Moreover, he saw that an online bookstore wouldn't have to make the same investment in retail clerks, store real estate, or warehouse space (in the beginning, Amazon.com ordered books from the publisher *after* Amazon took an order), so it could pass savings along to customers in the form of discounts. In addition, he appreciated that there would be opportunities to obtain demographic information about customers in order to offer personalized services, such as books of interest to them. Finally, Bezos saw that there could be a good deal of online interaction: customers could post reviews of books they read and could reach authors by e-mail to provide feedback.

Amazon.com sold its first book in July 1995 and by the end of 1998 had served 6.2 million customers in more than 100 countries. Later the firm began expanding into nonbook areas, such as online retailing of music CDs, toys, electronics, drugs, cosmetics, and pet supplies. It turned a profit late in 2001.

One Big World Market: The Global Economy

"We are seeing the results of things started in 1988 and 1989," said Rosabeth Moss Kantor of the Harvard Business School a decade later.[11] It was in the late 1980s when the Berlin Wall came down, signaling the beginning of the end of communism in Eastern Europe. It was also when countries of the Pacific Rim began to open their economies to foreign investors. Finally, the trend toward governments deregulating their economies began sweeping the globe. These three events set up conditions by which goods, people, and money could move more freely throughout the world—a global economy. **The _global economy_ refers to the increasing tendency of the economies of the world to interact with one another as one market instead of many national markets.**

The economies of the world have never been more entangled. As Kevin Maney writes in *USA Today*, "They're tied together by instantaneous information arriving via everything from currency trading databases to websites to CNN broadcasts. Capital—the money used to build businesses—moves globally and moves in a matter of keystrokes."[12]

Positive Effects Is a global economy really good for the United States? U.S. exports, international trade, and U.S. workers are connected, points out Nancy Birdsall, executive vice president of the Inter-American Development Bank in Washington, D.C. "As consumers in other regions of the world see their income go up, they are going to be more interested in U.S. products," she said in 1995. "The bottom line is that growth of jobs and income in other countries will mean growth of jobs and income in [the United States]. It's a win-win situation."[13]

Negative Effects However, global economic interdependency can also turn into a lose-lose situation. Its double-edged nature was shown when, following the devaluation of Thailand's currency in July 1997, the previously fast-growing "Asian Tiger" economies—Thailand, Indonesia, South Korea, Japan—became the "Asian crisis." (*Devaluation* means that a nation's currency is lowered relative to other countries' currencies.) The economic catastrophes of the Pacific Rim began affecting the economies of emerging nations from Latin America to Eastern Europe, eventually hurting Australia, Canada, and certain sectors of the United States.[14] National governments were powerless to stop the flight of capital from weakened economies to stronger ones. U.S. stock markets reacted, for a time losing one-fifth of their value.

But the global economy isn't going to go away just because we don't like some of its destabilizing aspects. "The process is irreversible, if only because of the information technology and communications revolutions," says Claude Smadja, managing director of the World Economic Forum in Switzerland. "The problem also is that, contrary to some illusions, one cannot pick and choose in the package. . . . The new globality means a tremendous emphasis on speed, flexibility, versatility, and permanent change—in some respects, insecurity."[15]

The global economy. This purveyor of souvenirs and antiques is located in Bejing. It welcomes American Express cards. In China and other parts of the world, you can use your U.S. credit card or debit card in local cash machines to obtain the currency of your host country. You will see the amount deducted, in dollars, from your credit-card or bank account when you get home.

Cross-Border Business: The Rise of Both Megamergers & Minifirms Worldwide

The global market driven by electronic information "forces things to get bigger and smaller at the same time," suggests technology philosopher Nicholas Negroponte. "And that's so ironic, when things want to do both but not stay in the middle. There will be an increasing absence of things that aren't either very local or very global."[16]

If Negroponte is correct, this means we will see more and more of two opposite kinds of businesses: mergers of huge companies into even larger companies, and small, fast-moving startup companies.

Megamergers Operating Worldwide Exxon + Mobil. British Petroleum + Amoco. Bell Atlantic + GTE. Daimler-Benz + Chrysler. Ford + Volvo. Volkswagen + Rolls-Royce. Travelers Group + Citicorp. Glaxco Wellcome + SmithKine Beecham.

The late 1990s were megamerger time, "corporations on steroids," in one writer's phrase.[17] Oil, telecommunications, automobiles, financial services, and pharmaceuticals aren't suited to being midsize, let alone small and local, so companies in these industries are trying to become bigger and cross-border. The means for doing so is to merge with other big companies. In telecommunications, for instance, Bell Atlantic and GTE teamed up in what's called a "size and scope" deal so that they could deliver worldwide voice, video, data, wireless, Internet, and the like, and be able to compete with other giant companies that are also getting bigger.[18]

Daimler-Benz + Chrysler. The 1998 $41 billion merger of Germany's Daimler-Benz and the U.S.A.'s Chrysler Corp. created a global automotive giant, DaimlerChrysler. Dieter Zetsche, shown here, is the president and CEO of Chrysler USA. In 2001, Zetsche announced as part of the Chrysler turnaround plan that the company would reduce its U.S. workforce by approximately 20%, amounting to the loss of some 26,000 jobs over the next three years. Do you think cross-border megamergers are good for the United States?

Minifirms Operating Worldwide The Internet and the World Wide Web allow almost anyone to be global, which Kevin Maney points out has two important results:

1 Small Companies Can Get Started More Easily Because anyone can put goods or services on a website and sell worldwide, this wipes out the former competitive advantages of distribution and scope that large companies used to have.

2 Small Companies Can Maneuver Faster Little companies can change direction faster, which gives them an advantage in terms of time and distance over large companies.

The most famous example of these two phenomena is Amazon.com, which has scared major retail store chains. But many small firms, such as online auction companies, have also come from nowhere to collapse time and distance. For instance, so-called "Bay-traders" make a living selling things on eBay, the online auction company. Bay traders find they get higher prices at Internet auctions than at swap meets or collectibles shows because bidding generates excitement and because the Internet's worldwide reach makes multiple bids more likely. Ray and Ann Geeck used to sell antique dolls at shows or at their Lake Panasoffkee, Fla., store, but they started auctioning online and now stick just with that. "We were getting $300 and $400 on eBay for things we couldn't sell for $125 at the shows," says Geeck.[19]

major question

Why learn about international management, and what characterizes the successful international manager?

The Big Picture
Studying international management prepares you to work with foreign customers or suppliers, for a foreign firm in the United States or for a U.S. firm overseas. Successful international managers aren't ethnocentric or polycentric but geocentric.

Part of the action. If "all of the action in business is international," as one expert says, what role do you think you might play in it? Do you think cultural bias against women in some foreign countries contributes to the low percentage of U.S. female executives working abroad?

Working overseas "is an advantage to your career," says Lyric Merrie Hughes, head of a Chicago international marketing firm. "All of the action in business is international."[20]

This is true for managers of both genders, but women especially may benefit by taking overseas assignments, whether for a few weeks or a year. Only about 15% of the American executives working outside the United States are women, in one estimate, and few of them are married or have children.[21]

This presents an opportunity, although it means breaking through some male executives' stereotypes about women. Research has found that male top managers believe that women don't want to work overseas because it disrupts their and their families' personal lives. They also were skeptical that women would be accepted in foreign cultures.[22] Nevertheless, gender barriers are crumbling, and there are ways for women to demonstrate their value overseas.

Hughes goes to Europe and Asia every two weeks, relying on a nanny and "a good support system" to care for her three children. "Just do it," she says, in urging women to accept overseas assignments. "It's going to enrich you and your family and enhance your career. Get on the plane!"

Why Learn about International Management?

International management is management that oversees the conduct of operations in or with organizations in foreign countries, whether it's through a multinational corporation or a multinational organization.

- A *multinational corporation*, or multinational enterprise, is a business firm with operations in several countries. Our publisher, McGraw-Hill, is one such "multinational" (see the 17 foreign cities listed on our book's title page). The real behemoths in multinational corporations include the American firms General Electric, Exxon, AT&T, and Coca-Cola and the foreign companies Royal Dutch/Shell (Netherlands/ Britain), Toyota (Japan), Nestlé (Switzerland), and Allianz (Germany).

- A *multinational organization* is a nonprofit organization with operations in several countries. Examples are the World Health Organization, the International Red Cross, the Church of Latter Day Saints.

practical action

What You Can Do to Prepare for Overseas Assignments That Will Boost Your Career

What do you need to do to prepare for a career overseas that can advance your career? This is a question for readers of both sexes but particularly for women, who make up only 15% of the American overseas workforce.

Some skills to develop are mentioned in the box below. Some other suggestions:

Persuade Your Boss That You Can Handle Overseas Duty & That the Organization Will Benefit First be sure your family supports you. Then let your boss know you want to work overseas at some point and that you can handle all family responsibilities. If you're female, suggest that being a woman can even be an advantage in some cultures, especially in Asia and Latin America, which place strong emphasis on the family.[24]

Study Up on Your Host Country Study up on the host country's cultural landmarks, and shrines, painters, writers, and other outstanding personalities to show you respect their cultural heritage.

Before you go, "Spend at least 10% of preparation time on interpersonal skills," suggests executive coach Arlene B. Isaacs.[25]

Learn rituals of respect, including exchange of business cards. Understand that shaking hands is always permissible, but social kissing may not be.

Learn (perhaps from the hotel concierge) the art of gift giving. You don't want to give a gift that's inappropriate or too pricey and risk bribery charges.

Know how to dress professionally. For women, this means no heavy makeup, no flashy jewelry, no short skirts or sleeveless blouses (particularly in Islamic countries).

Whether male or female, if you learn to adapt appropriate behavior—finesse, consideration, tact, awareness of standards of behavior and cultural values—"you will be perceived as respectful and worthy of a relationship," says Isaacs.

Know Your Field If you know your field and behave with courtesy and assurance, Asian colleagues will respect your authority, whatever your gender. "They assume you've proven to other people that you deserve respect," says Lorne Walker, who represented a health-care organization in Singapore, "and so they give it to you."[26]

For Women: Realize When You Can't Be One of the Boys Gender equality is often not a reality overseas. While you may be respected at work, after-hours socialization may remain a males-only prerogative. For instance, if you're single, don't invite your male host to dinner, which can be viewed as being in very bad taste.

"Women can conduct business successfully, but they shouldn't expect to be treated like one of the guys," says Sanjyot Dunung author of *Doing Business in Asia: The Complete Guide.*[27] In other words, don't expect to be invited out to any karaoke bars. If anything, you may have the advantage in doing business the next day because you can go back to your hotel and rest up while the men are whooping it up into the late hours.

Become Skilled in the Language Whatever foreign country you're in, at the very least you should learn a few key phrases, such as "hello," "please," and "thank you," in your host country's language.

However, successful international managers have learned there is no adequate substitute for knowing the local language. Indeed, half the top executives in one survey say that among the skills most needed "to maintain a competitive edge" that they find lacking in employees, the one most deficient is knowledge of a foreign language.[28]

In conclusion: Want to know how to really prepare for an overseas job? *Learn a foreign language.*

Skills Most Lacking for Managers Overseas[23]	For men	For women
Foreign language	31%	27%
Interpersonal skills	14%	7%
Administrative	11%	5%
Management	8%	8%
Technical	8%	15%
Basic computer	7%	9%
Problem solving	5%	6%

Even if in the coming years you never travel to the wider world outside North America—an unlikely proposition, we think—the world will assuredly come to you. That, in a nutshell, is why you need to learn about international management.

More specifically, consider yourself in the following situations:

You May Deal with Foreign Customers or Partners While working for a U.S. company you have to deal with foreign customers. Or you have to work with a foreign company in some sort of joint venture. The people you're dealing with may be outside the United States or visitors to it. Either way you would hate to blow a deal—and maybe all future deals—because you were ignorant of some cultural aspects you could have known about.

A typical scenario is that described by *Fortune* columnist Anne Fisher: "You, a hotshot of either sex, show up alone in Tokyo to meet with the head honchos of a prospective joint-venture partner. You don't know how to say 'hello' or 'thank you' in Japanese, you don't have a proper business card, and you plop yourself down in any old seat at the conference table. Pretty soon your counterparts won't look you in the eye, and before you know it, you're on the plane home and the deal is off."[29] All because you didn't know some details of the culture.

The challenge of interacting successfully with foreign customers. Beyond speaking the language of your host country, what *cultural* skills and awareness might help you gain an advantage over your international competitors?

of the software made in India goes to the United States. Many U.S. software companies—Microsoft, IBM, Oracle, Motorola, Novell, Hewlett-Packard, and Texas Instruments—have opened offices in India to take advantage of high-quality labor.[30]

You May Work for a Foreign Firm in the United States You may sometime take a job with a foreign firm doing business in the United States, such as an electronics, pharmaceutical, or car company. And you'll have to deal with managers above and below you whose outlook is different from yours. For instance, Japanese companies, with their emphasis on correctness and face saving, operate in significantly different ways from American companies.

Sometimes it is even hard to know that an ostensibly U.S. company actually has foreign ownership. For example, many American book publishers (though not McGraw-Hill) are British, German, or Canadian owned.

You May Deal with Foreign Suppliers While working for an American company you have to purchase important components, raw materials, or services from a foreign supplier. And you never know where foreign practices may diverge from what you're accustomed to.

Some services you might not suspect are currently being performed overseas. For example, 58%

You May Work for an American Firm Outside the United States You might easily find yourself working abroad in the foreign operation of a U.S. company. Most big American corporations have overseas subsidiaries or divisions. For example, General Motors has plants in Mexico. Vodaphone AirTouch, the mobil telecommunications company, has operations in Spain and Hungary.

Exports. These American cereal products are being sold in a convenience store in Dublin, Ireland. With 6 billion people in the world, the global market contains over 6 billion potential customers for goods and services. Almost any good or service used in the United States can be used in other countries as well, although sometimes adapting products to specific global markets can be difficult. However, competition overseas may not be nearly as strong as it is in the U.S. An additional benefit of exporting is that it can help the American economy: According to the U.S. Department of Commerce, every $1 billion in U.S. exports generates 25,000 jobs at home. Can you visualize how one of these jobs might be yours?

The Successful International Manager: Geocentric, Not Ethnocentric or Polycentric

Maybe you don't really care that you don't have much understanding of the foreign culture you're dealing with. "What's the point?" you may think. "The main thing is to get the job done." Certainly there are international firms with managers who have this perspective. They are called *ethnocentric*, one of three primary attitudes among international managers, the other two being *polycentric* and *geocentric*.[31]

Ethnocentric Managers—"We Know Best" _Ethnocentric managers_ **believe that their native country, culture, language, and behavior are superior to all others.** Ethnocentric managers tend to believe that they can export the managers and practices of their home countries to anywhere in the world and that they will be more capable and reliable. Often the ethnocentric viewpoint is less attributable to prejudice than it is to ignorance, since such managers obviously know more about their home environment than the foreign environment.

Is enthnocentrism bad for business? It seems so. A survey of 918 companies with home offices in the United States, Japan, and Europe found that ethnocentric policies were linked to such problems as recruiting difficulties, high turnover rates, and lawsuits over personnel policies.[32]

Polycentric Managers—"They Know Best" _Polycentric managers_ **take the view that native managers in the foreign offices best understand native personnel and practices, and so the home office should leave them alone.** Thus, the attitude of polycentric managers is nearly the opposite of that of ethnocentric managers.

Geocentric Managers—"What's Best Is What's Effective, Regardless of Origin" _Geocentric managers_ **accept that there are differences and similarities between home and foreign personnel and practices and that they should use whatever techniques are most effective.** Clearly, being an ethno- or polycentric manager takes less work. But the payoff for being a geocentric manager can be far greater.

The lessons seem clear. If you become an _expatriate manager_—**a manager living or working in a foreign country**—it's imperative that you try to learn everything you can about the local culture so that you can deal effectively with it and avoid being beaten by your competitors.

major question

Why do companies expand internationally, and how do they do it?

The Big Picture

Multinationals expand to take advantage of availability of supplies, new markets, lower labor costs, access to finance capital, or avoidance of tariffs and import quotas. Five ways they do so are by global outsourcing; importing, exporting, and countertrading; licensing and franchising; joint ventures; and wholly owned subsidiaries.

In Austria, Indonesia, and South Korea, you can find Big Macs in the McDonald's franchises just like in the United States. However, there are also variations for the locals. In Vienna, "McCafés" offer coffee blended for local tastes. In Jakarta, you can get rice as well as French fries. And in Seoul, you can get roast pork on a bun with a garlicky soy sauce.

There's an important lesson here. Says a *New York Times* writer, "That combination of a globally recognized brand with a flexible menu that caters to local palates has helped McDonald's navigate the global economic turbulence that has knocked most of the other big corporations operating around the world way off course."[33]

Clearly, we could all benefit from learning why the McDonald's international division accounts for nearly 60% of the burger chain's profits. Let us consider why and how companies expand overseas.

Why Companies Expand Internationally

Many a company has made the deliberate decision to restrict selling its product or service to just its own country. Is anything wrong with that?

The answer is: It depends. It would probably have been a serious mistake for NEC, Sony, or Hitachi to have limited their markets solely to Japan during the 1990s, a time when the country was in an economic slump and Japanese consumers weren't consuming. During that same period, however, some American banks might have been better off not making loans abroad, when the U.S. economy was booming but foreign economies were not. Going international or not going international—it can be risky either way.

Why, then, do companies expand internationally? There are at least five reasons, all of which have to do with making or saving money.

Where is this? Since 1979, home-improvement retailer Home Depot has grown from four stores in Atlanta to 1,301 in four countries. The store shown here is in Laual, Quebec, Canada. Why do you think Home Depot probably felt it had to expand internationally?

A Japanese farmers' market. Americans are accustomed to shopping for food in supermarkets, though many U.S. cities also have farmers' markets, where customers and restaurant buyers can obtain fresh produce directly from growers. In many foreign countries, however, shoppers are not always able to avail themselves of a supermarket. Many American managers and families living abroad find going to farmers' markets one of the most delightful parts of the overseas experience. Do you think you're adaptable enough to enjoy working in a foreign country?

1 Availability of Supplies Antique and art dealers, mining companies, banana growers, sellers of hard woods—all have to go where their basic supplies or raw materials are located. For years oil companies, for example, have expanded their activities outside the United States in seeking cheaper or more plentiful sources of oil.

2 New Markets Elsewhere in this book (Chapter 6) we discuss the *product life cycle,* the natural rise and fall in the sales life of a product. Sometimes a company will find, as cigarette makers have, that the demand for their product has declined domestically but that they can still make money overseas. Or sometimes a company will steal a march on its competitors by aggressively expanding into foreign markets, as did Coca-Cola over PepsiCo under the leadership of legendary CEO Robert Goizuelta. (Recently, however, Coke has slipped behind Pepsi—14% to 22% in 2001—in the United States in the new growing market of noncarbonated beverages.)[34]

3 Lower Labor Costs The decline in manufacturing jobs in the United States is directly attributable to the fact that American companies have found it cheaper to do their manufacturing outside the States. For example, the rationale for using *maquiladoras*—**manufacturing plants allowed to operate in Mexico with special privileges in return for employing Mexican citizens**—is that they provide less expensive labor for assembling everything from appliances to cars. However, even professional or service kinds of jobs may be shipped overseas. As mentioned, some makers of software applications programs are taking care of their programming needs by sending their jobs to India.

4 Access to Finance Capital Companies may be enticed into going abroad by the prospects of capital being put up by foreign companies. Or sometimes a foreign government will offer a subsidy in hopes of attracting a company that will create jobs, as Ireland did in the 1970s for Lotus sports-car maker John DeLorean.

5 Avoidance of Tariffs & Import Quotas Countries place tariffs (fees) on imported goods or impose import quotas—limitations on the numbers of products allowed in—for the purpose of protecting their own domestic industries. For example, Japan imposes tariffs on agricultural products, such as rice, imported from the United States. To avoid these penalties, a company might create a subsidiary to produce the product in the foreign country. General Electric and Whirlpool, for example, have foreign subsidiaries to produce appliances overseas.

How Companies Expand Internationally

Most companies don't start out to be multinationals. Generally, they edge their way into international business, making minimal investments and taking minimal risks, as shown in the drawing below. *(See Panel 4.1.)*

PANEL 4.1
Five ways of expanding internationally. These range from lowest risk and investment (left) to highest risk and investment (right).

| Global outsourcing | Importing, exporting, & countertrading | Licensing & franchising | Joint ventures | Wholly owned subsidiaries |

Lowest risk & investment   *Highest risk & investment*

Let's consider these five ways.

1 Global Outsourcing A common practice of many companies, *outsourcing* **is defined as using suppliers outside the company to provide goods and services.** Management philosopher Peter Drucker believes that in the near future organizations may be outsourcing all work that is "support"—such as information systems—rather than revenue producing.

Global outsourcing (or simply *global sourcing*) extends this technique outside the U.S. *Global outsourcing* **is defined as using suppliers outside the United States to provide labor, goods, or services.** The reason may be that the foreign supplier has resources not available in the United States, such as Italian marble. Or the supplier may have special expertise, as do Pakastani weavers. Or—more likely these days—the supplier's labor is cheaper than American labor. As a manager, your first business trip outside the U.S. might be to inspect the production lines of one of your outsourcing suppliers.

2 Importing, Exporting, & Countertrading When *importing*, **a company buys goods outside the country and resells them domestically.** Nothing might seem to be more American than Jeep Wranglers, but they are made not only in the United States but also in Canada, from which they are imported and made available for sale in the United States. Many of the products we use are imported, ranging from Heineken beer (Netherlands) to Texaco gasoline (Saudi Arabia) to Honda snowblowers (Japan).

When *exporting*, **a company produces goods domestically and sells them outside the country.** One of the greatest U.S. exports is American pop culture, in the form of movies, CDs, and fashion. The United States is also a leader in exporting computers and other information technology.

Sometimes other countries may wish to import American goods but lack the currency to pay for them. In that case, the exporting U.S. company may resort to *countertrading*—**that is, bartering goods for goods.** When the Russian ruble plunged in value in 1998, some goods became a better medium of exchange than currency.

3 Licensing & Franchising Licensing and franchising are two aspects of the same thing, although licensing is used by manufacturing companies and franchising is used more frequently by service companies.

In **_licensing_, a company allows a foreign company to pay it a fee to make or distribute the first company's product or service.** For example, the Du Pont chemical company might license a company in Brazil to make Teflon, the nonstick substance that is found on some frying pans. Thus, Du Pont, the licensor, can make money without having to invest large sums to conduct business directly in a foreign company. Moreover, the Brazilian firm, the licensee, knows the local market better than Du Pont probably would.

Franchising is a form of licensing in which a company allows a foreign company to pay it a fee and a share of the profit in return for using the first company's brand name and a package of materials and services. For example, Burger King, Hertz, and Hilton Hotels, which are all well-known brands, might provide the use of their names plus their operating know-how (facility design, equipment, recipes, management systems) to companies in Greece in return for an upfront fee plus a percentage of the profits.

By now Americans traveling throughout the world have become accustomed to seeing so-called U.S. franchises everywhere: Popeye's Chicken & Biscuits in China, DKNY and The GAP stores in Turkey, Coca-Cola in Mexico, Intercontinental hotels in Hungary.

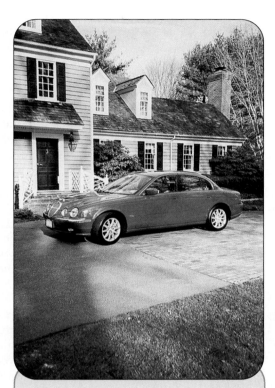

Jaguar. A number of formerly British-owned carmakers have gone over to foreign ownership. Jaguar is a subsidiary of Ford Motor Co., as is Land Rover. Ford also has provided the financial assistance to keep Aston-Martin going. Vauxhall is owned by General Motors. The rights to make Rolls-Royce cars (but not aircraft engines) are now held by German automaker Volkswagen, but Volkswagen's German rival BMW holds the rights to the name and the "RR" marque. Volkswagen owns the Rolls-Royce sister Bentley brand. Do you think American companies General Motors and Ford could ever wind up under foreign ownership?

4 Joint Ventures _Strategic allies_ (described in Chapter 3) are two organizations that have joined forces to realize strategic advantages that neither would have if operating alone. A U.S. firm may form a **_joint venture_, also known as a _strategic alliance_, with a foreign company to share the risks and rewards of starting a new enterprise together in a foreign country.** For instance, General Motors operates a joint venture in Canada with Suzuki Motor Corp. and an assembly plant called NUMMI in California with Toyota.

Sometimes a joint venture is the only way an American company can have a presence in a certain country, whose laws may forbid foreigners from ownership.

General Motors found that the best way to do business in the new nation of Nambia (after it became independent of South African control) was to ship GM vehicles to a plant in that country. The Nambians, who wanted to be producers, not just consumers, then converted them from U.S.-style left-hand drive to right-hand drive, as required in parts of Africa.

5 Wholly-Owned Subsidiaries A **_wholly-owned subsidiary_ is a foreign subsidary that is totally owned and controlled by an organization.** The foreign subsidiary may be an existing company that is purchased outright. A **_greenfield venture_ is a foreign subsidiary that the owning organization has built from scratch.**

General Motors owns Adam Opel AG in Germany, Vauxhall Motor Cars Ltd. in the United Kingdom, Holden's in Australia, and half of Saab Automobile AB in Sweden.

major question

How may foreign countries differ in their economic, political, and legal characteristics?

The Big Picture

Countries' economies vary among free-market, command, and mixed economies, as well as in infrastructure and resources and currency exchange rates. Political systems may vary between democratic versus totalitarian, in political risk, and in laws and regulations.

As an international manager, you might well have to operate amid many complexities. What should you be on the lookout for? First let us consider (1) *economic differences*, then (2) *political-legal differences*.

India. This New Delhi street scene suggests India's greatest challenge: raising living standards for 1 billion people. Is its mixed economy the way to accomplish this?

Economic Differences: Adjusting to Other Countries' Economies

How will you, as an international manager, adjust to economic changes? Let's discuss the following important topics: *economic systems, economic development, infrastructure and resources*, and *currency exchange rates*.

Principal Economic Systems: Free Market, Command, & Mixed Economies How is doing business in Taiwan different from doing business in China? One is a *free-market economy*, the other traditionally a *command economy* (but changing). These are two of the three principal types of economic systems around the globe, the third being a *mixed economy*:

Click-Along 4.1

Doing Business in a Communist Country

1 Free-Market Economy This is the kind of economy found, for example, in the United States and in Great Britain. In a *free-market economy*, **the production of goods and services are controlled by private enterprise and the interaction of the forces of supply and demand, rather than by the government.** As a manager you may prefer dealing with countries with this kind of system because there will be fewer hassles with government regulators. Moreover, in general the citizens of such countries may have higher incomes, which means there may be more markets for your product or service.

2 Command Economy This is the kind of economy found in the old communist countries in and around the former Soviet Union. It is still found in Cuba and North Korea and, to a certain extent, in China and Vietnam. **In a *command economy*, or *central-planning economy*, the government owns most businesses and regulates the amounts, types, and prices of goods and services.** The failure of communism in Europe is largely because such economies proved to be unworkable. Other communist countries (Cuba, North Korea) have experienced great economic difficulties, and still others (China, Vietnam) have begun moving away from command economies.

3 Mixed Economy   This type of economy is found in many countries of Europe. **In a _mixed economy_, most of the important industries are owned by the government, but others are controlled by private enterprise.** This used to be the case in Britain, where the government once owned the railroads, airlines, steel, telecommunications, and health industries. However, in recent years most of these industries underwent _privatization_—**that is, state-owned businesses were sold off to private enterprise.** Russia, too, has been moving away from state-ownership of big utilities and other sectors of the economy.

Whatever the type of economy, some countries have _indigenization laws_, which require that citizens within the host country must own a majority of whatever company is operating within that country.

Developed versus Less Developed Countries   It used to be that the United States, Canada, western Europe, Australia, New Zealand, and Japan were known as "first-world" countries. The communist nations were called "second-world" countries. Pretty much all the rest, especially those in the southern hemisphere, were known as "third-world" or developing countries. With the end of the Cold War, the world now seems to be divided between _developed countries_ and _less-developed countries_.

■ **Developed countries:** These are the first-world countries: the United States, Canada, most European countries, Australia, New Zealand, and Japan. _**Developed countries**_ **are those with a high level of economic development and generally high average level of income among their citizens.**

Most international organizations, whether International Paper Co. or the International Red Cross, Royal Dutch/Shell or the World Health Organization, are headquartered in developed countries. Also, about three-quarters of foreign investment has been directed toward developed countries.[35]

■ **Less-developed countries:** These are the third-world countries, such as Brazil, China, Haiti, Mexico, and Zambia, to name just a handful of the scores of nations in this category.

**Less-developed countries****, also known as** _developing countries,_ **consist of nations with low economic development and low average incomes.** They also are usually characterized by high birth rates.

Today the five largest countries in population size are China, India, the United States, Indonesia, and Brazil. By the middle of the 21st century, because of population growth (most of it owing to birth rates, not immigration), the five largest will be India, China, Pakistan (today's No. 6), the United States, and Nigeria (today's No. 10).[36]

First world or third world? Many "third-world" or less-developed countries have "first-world" or developed parts in them. This upscale store, United Colors of Benetton, is located on Oficios Street, Old Havana, Cuba, an impoverished country. However, the reverse is also true: Many countries that we think of as being highly developed have less-developed parts. In the United States, such "third-world" pockets of rural or urban poverty are found everywhere from within miles of West Virginia's scenic rivers to within blocks of the White House in Washington, D.C.

Caller I.D.? A man talks on a cellphone as former China leader Mao Zedong appears to be looking on. The cellphone represents a boon to less-developed countries because this kind of telephone infrastructure does not entail the costly process of installing miles of telephone poles and land lines.

Infrastructure & Resources In the United States, Canada, and much of Europe, we pretty much take the phone system for granted. In less-developed countries, getting a phone installed may take weeks, even months, and then it may still be inefficient. The significance of the cellphone is that countries with underdeveloped wired telephone systems can use cellular phones as a fast way of installing better communications, giving Pakistan, China, Nigeria, and others a chance of joining the world economy.

Telephone networks are an essential part of a country's infrastructure, especially since they are important to the development of information technology. **A country's _infrastructure_ consists of the physical facilities that form the basis for its level of economic development.** Examples are schools, roads, airports, railroads, harbors, utilities, hospitals, and telecommunications systems. Before you as a manager begin getting involved in major projects in a particular foreign country, you need to be aware of any drawbacks in its infrastructure.

In addition, you'll need to be concerned about resources. If you've set up an apparel plant in Mexico, for example, you need to think about where the fabric and the sewing equipment are going to come from—whether you'll be able to get them from suppliers in that country or you'll have to import them.

Currency Exchange Rates The _exchange rate_ **is the rate at which one country's currency can be exchanged for another country's currency.** International managers have to keep a close eye on currency exchange rates because a change of just a few percentage points can have major implications. For example, if one year the American dollar is worth 1.10 Canadian dollars and the next year it is worth 1.20 Canadian dollars, this means that U.S. goods have become more expensive for Canadians, so they are apt to buy less. If the American dollar drops to the equivalent of 1.00 Canadian dollars, they will probably buy more.

Political-Legal Differences: Adjusting to Other Countries' Governments & Laws

When in the early 1990s McDonald's opened an outlet in Belgrade in the former Yugoslavia, should it have tried to anticipate the possibility that the restaurant might someday be wrecked by angry crowds of Serbs (as happened following air strikes by American and other NATO bombers on Serbia in 1999)? Perhaps someone was foresighted enough to take out political risk insurance, which is available for corporations investing in unstable areas.[37]

Such is one of the considerations of a company hoping to develop new markets overseas. A star international manager needs to always be aware of political-legal differences, including different government systems, political risks, and unfamiliar laws and regulations, as we discuss.

Governmental Systems: Democratic versus Totalitarian No doubt you will have to deal with unfamiliar political systems. There are two extremes:

■ **Democratic:** _**Democratic governments**_ **rely on free elections and representative assemblies.** The government is supposed to represent the society as a whole, or at least the majority of its citizens.

    From the standpoint of ease in doing business, democratic systems of government, such as those in western Europe, generally seem more familiar to an American international manager. Nevertheless, different national attitudes toward bureaucracy, monopolies, and the acceptance of "gratuities" can make it difficult to do business.

■ **Totalitarian:** _**Totalitarian governments**_ **are ruled by a dictator, a single political party, or a special-membership group,** such as a handful of ruling families or a military junta (such as Cuba under Fidel Castro or Indonesia under Sukarno). The risk for you as an international manager is that the political tides may change and through no fault of your own you may find yourself somehow on the wrong side.

    Some governments fall in between democratic and totalitarian. Mexico, for example, regularly features free elections, but for decades it was ruled by a single political party.

Political Risk It's possible that a democratic country in which your company has started up an overseas operation could overnight become a totalitarian country, accompanied by a sudden change in all the rules. Thus, every firm contemplating establishing itself abroad must calculate its _**political risk**_—**the risk that political changes will cause loss of a company's assets or impair its foreign operations.** Two political risks an organization planning to do business abroad might anticipate are these:

■ **Instability:** Even in a developed country a company may be victimized by political instability, such as riots or civil disorders, as happened during the 1989 Rodney King riots in Los Angeles. Overseas an international company may also have to try to anticipate revolutions or changes in government. Italy, for example, has had 57 governments since World War II.

■ **Expropriation:** _**Expropriation**_ **is defined as a government's seizure of a foreign company's assets.** After Fidel Castro overthrew the Batista government in Cuba in 1959, he expropriated millions of dollars worth of assets of American companies. Early in the 20th century, Mexico expropriated American-owned oil fields and production facilities.

Laws & Regulations "Ignorance of the law is no excuse," one hears. That assumes you're supposed to keep up with the important laws in your own country, which can be complicated enough. Now try keeping up with the laws in another country.

    International companies have to work with numerous laws and regulations on subjects ranging from labor to libel to labeling. The United States, for instance, has legislation under the _**Foreign Corrupt Practices Act**_ **of 1977, which makes it illegal for employees of U.S. companies to bribe political decision makers in foreign nations,** an acceptable practice in many countries.

    Many of the laws and regulations have to do with tariffs, import quotas, and the like, as we discuss in the next section.

major question

What are barriers to free trade, and what major organizations and trading blocs promote trade?

The Big Picture

Barriers to free trade are tariffs, import quotas, and embargoes. Organizations promoting international trade are the World Trade Organization, the World Bank, and the International Monetary Fund. Major trading blocs are NAFTA, the EU, ASEAN, and Mercosur.

If you live in the United States, you see foreign products on a daily basis—cars, appliances, clothes, foods, beers, wines, and so on. Based on what you see every day, which countries would you think are our most important trading partners? Japan? Germany? England? South Korea? France?

These five countries do indeed appear among the top ten leading U.S. trading partners. Interestingly, however, our No. 1 and No. 3 trading partners are our immediate neighbors—Canada and Mexico, whose products may not be quite so visible. (Others at the top: 2. Japan; 4. China; 5. Germany; 6. Britain; 7. Taiwan; 8. France; 9. South Korea; 10. Singapore.)

Let's begin to consider *free trade*, **the movement of goods and services among nations without political or economic obstruction.**

Barriers to International Trade

Countries often use *trade protectionism*—**the use of government regulations to limit the import of goods and services**—to protect their domestic industries against foreign competition. The justification they often use is that this saves jobs. Actually, protectionism is not considered beneficial, mainly because of what it does to the overall trading atmosphere.

The three devices by which countries try to exert protectionism consist of *tariffs, import quotas*, and *embargoes*.

Going bananas. Stevedores unload Chiquita bananas from a ship in Antwerp harbor. The Netherlands is a member of the European Union, which had imposed a duty on bananas, including those grown by Cincinnati-based Chiquita Brands Inc. The reason for the duty was that Chiquita's bananas undercut those of the EU's longstanding suppliers. For retaliation, Chiquita successfully lobbied the U.S. government to place duties on European goods (such as paper products) imported into the United States. Such activities among governments are known as a "trade war."

1 Tariffs A *tariff* is a trade barrier in the form of a customs duty, or tax, levied mainly on imports. At one time, for instance, to protect the American shoe industry, the United States imposed a tariff on Italian shoes.

Actually, there are two types of tariffs: One is designed simply to raise money for the government (revenue tariff). The other, which concerns us more, is to raise the price of imported goods to make the prices of domestic products more competitive (protective tariff). For example, in 1999 the U.S. government imposed protective tariffs of 18%–67% on low-priced Japanese steel to effectively make it more expensive for Japan to sell steel in the United States compared to the products of American steel producers.[38]

2 Import Quotas An *import quota* is a trade barrier in the form of a limit on the numbers of a product that can be imported. Its intent is to protect domestic industry by restricting the availability of foreign products.

In 1999, Congress voted to roll back steel imports to 1997 levels to protect U.S. steelworkers worried about losing their jobs to foreign companies selling cheap steel in the United States.[39]

Quotas are designed to prevent *dumping*, the practice of a foreign company's exporting products abroad at a lower price than the price in the home market—or even below the costs of production—in order to drive down the price of the domestic product.

3 Embargoes Ever had a Cuban cigar? They're difficult for Americans to get, since they're embargoed. An *embargo* ("em-*bar*-go") is a complete ban on the import or export of certain products. It has been years since anyone was allowed to import Cuban cigars and sugar into the United States or for an American firm to do business in Cuba.

The U.S. government also tries to embargo the export of certain supercomputers and other high-tech equipment with possible military uses to countries such as China.

Organizations Promoting International Trade

In the 1920s, the institution of tariff barriers did not so much protect jobs as depress the demand for goods and services, thereby leading to the loss of jobs anyway—and the massive unemployment of the Great Depression of the 1930s.[40] As a result of this lesson, after World War II the advanced nations of the world began to realize that if all countries could freely exchange the products that each could produce most efficiently, this would lead to lower prices all around. Thus began the removal of barriers to free trade.

Tea from China. The experience of drinking Dragon Well, a variety of Chinese green tea, "is very intense," says one tea fancier, "completely entrancing and entirely unpredictable. I've had the same tea come out one time sweet and gentle, and another time roaring and full of dense, dark, beautiful bitterness." China has had thousands of years to perfect the process of making tea, and experts rate the country's green teas as among the best in the world. Most of it is laboriously dried and processed by hand, one reason why only government officials and the new business class can afford it in China. In the U.S., however, it costs $50–$150 a pound—only a dollar a cup at the most expensive. Why is it so much more affordable to us?

The three principal organizations designed to facilitate international trade are the *World Trade Organization*, the *World Bank*, and the *International Monetary Fund*.

1 The World Trade Organization (WTO)

Consisting of 132 member countries, the ***World Trade Organization (WTO) is designed to monitor and enforce trade agreements.*** The agreements are based on the *General Agreement on Tariffs and Trade (GATT)*, an international accord first signed by 23 nations in 1947, which helped to reduce worldwide tariffs and other barriers. Out of GATT came a series of "rounds," or negotiations, that resulted in the lowering of barriers; the latest, the Uruguay Round, was implemented in 1996 and cut tariffs by one-third.

Founded in 1995 and headquartered in Geneva Switzerland, WTO succeeded GATT as the world forum for trade negotiations and has the formal legal structure for deciding trade disputes. WTO also encompasses areas not previously covered by GATT, such as services and intellectual property rights. A particularly interesting area of responsibility covers telecommunications—cell phones, pagers, data transmission, satellite communications, and the like—with half of the WTO members agreeing in 1998 to open their markets to foreign telecommunications companies.[41]

2 The World Bank

The World Bank was founded after World War II to help European countries rebuild. Today the purpose of **the *World Bank* is to provide low-interest loans to developing nations for improving transportation, education, health, and telecommunications.** The bank has 135 member nations, with most contributions coming from the United States, Europe, and Japan.

Most recently, the bank has concentrated on bringing the Internet to less-developed and developing countries, such as those in Africa, in hopes that it will attract more companies to those areas and lead to more rapid economic development.[42]

In recent years, the World Bank has been the target of demonstrations in Seattle, Washington, D.C., and elsewhere. Some protestors believe it finances projects that could damage the ecosystem, such as the Three Gorges Dam on China's Yangztse River. Others complain it supports countries that permit low-paying sweatshops or that suppress religious freedom. Still others think it has dragged its feet on getting affordable AIDS drugs to less-developed countries in Africa. Many of the same protests were leveled against the International Monetary Fund, discussed next. The World Bank has responded by trying to support projects that are not harmful to the environment and that are aimed at helping lift people out of poverty.

3 The International Monetary Fund

Founded in 1945 and now affiliated with the United Nations, the International Monetary Fund is the second pillar supporting the international financial community. Consisting of 150 member nations, **the *International Monetary Fund (IMF)* is designed to assist in smoothing the flow of money between nations.** The IMF operates as a last-resort lender that makes short-term loans to countries suffering from unfavorable balance of payments (roughly the difference between money coming into a country and money leaving the country, because of imports, exports, and other matters).

For example, during the late 1990s "Asian crisis," the value of Thailand's currency dropped until at the end of 1997 it was worth half what it was at the start of the year. Because Thailand owed other countries, they, too, were affected: Indonesia's currency dropped 70% and South Korea's 45%. In response to pleas for help, the IMF loaned Asian countries billions of dollars—$57 billion to South Korea alone in 1997.

Major Trading Blocs: NAFTA, EU, ASEAN, & Mercosur

A _trading bloc_, also known as an _economic community,_ is a group of nations within a geographical region that have agreed to remove trade barriers with each other. The four major trading blocs are the _NAFTA nations_, the _European Union_, the _ASEAN countries_, and the _Mercosur._

1 NAFTA—the Three Countries of the North American Free Trade Agreement Formed in 1994, **the _North American Free Trade Agreement (NAFTA)_ is a trading bloc consisting of the**  **United States, Canada, and Mexico,** encompassing 400 million people. The agreement is supposed to eliminate 99% of the tariffs and quotas among these countries, allowing for freer flow of goods, services, and capital in North America. Since 1994, trade both ways between the United States and Mexico has increased 23%.

Is NAFTA a job killer for Americans, as some have complained? Since 1994, the United States has gone from a trade surplus with Mexico to a trade deficit (our imports exceed our exports) as many U.S. jobs have shifted south of the border. However, supporters insist NAFTA ultimately will result in more jobs and a higher standard of living among all three trading partners.

2 The EU—the 15 Countries of the European Union Formed in 1957, **the _European Union (EU)_ consists of 15 trading partners in Europe,** covering 375 million consumers.

Nearly all internal trade barriers have been eliminated (including movement of labor between countries), making the EU a union of borderless neighbors and the world's largest free market.

By 2002, such national symbols as the franc, the mark, the lira, the peseta, and the guilder had been replaced with the EU currency, the euro.[43] There is even speculation that someday the euro could replace the dollar as the dominant world currency.[44]

3 ASEAN—Nine Countries of the Association of Southeast Asian Nations Members of this group were once known as the "Asian tigers," although, as mentioned, in the late 1990s their situation degenerated into the "Asian crisis." **The _Association of Southeast Asian Nations (ASEAN)_ is a trading bloc consisting of nine countries in Asia:** Brunei, Indonesia, Laos, Malaysia, Myanmar (Burma), the Philippines, Singapore, Thailand, and Vietnam. Like other trading blocs, ASEAN is working on reducing trade barriers among member countries, promoting the role of private investment, stimulating the free flow of capital, and assisting in access to technology.

4 Mercosur—Four Countries of Latin America The _Mercosur_ is the largest trade bloc in Latin America and has four members: Argentina, Brazil, Paraguay, and Uruguay. Besides reducing tariffs by 75%, Mercosur nations are striving for full economic integration, and the alliance is also negotiating trade agreements with NAFTA, the EU, and Japan.

Most Favored Nation Trading Status

Besides joining together in trade blocs, countries will also extend special, "most favored nation" trading privileges to one another. **_Most favored nation_ trading status describes a condition in which a country grants other countries favorable trading treatment such as the reduction of import duties.** The purpose is to promote stronger and more stable ties between companies in the two countries.

major question

What are the principal areas of cultural differences?

The Big Picture

Managers trying to understand other cultures need to understand four basic cultural perceptions embodied in language, nonverbal communication, time orientation, and religion.

Americans living near San Jose, Calif., didn't like it when an Australian company acquired the local Valley Fair shopping center and renamed it Shoppingtown.[45]

"The first time I saw the word Shoppingtown, I nearly choked," complained one letter writer to the local paper. "The more I see it, the more it annoys me."

"We aren't the penny-pinchers this name indicates we are," said another. "What happened to that survey about Valley Fair customers having the area's most upscale lifestyle and money to back it up?"

Said a third: "These are the same people—Australians—who did not get [the U.S. television comedy] 'Seinfeld'; the show failed miserably there. 'Shoppingtown' is a brand name in Australia. They are trying too hard to accomplish the same thing here in the U.S. Do you really care that your mall is a 'brand'. . . ? They have not done their homework, and do not understand Americans just yet."

Don't Australians and Americans speak the same language? Could a shopping center risk failing simply because of a name change? And if there can be such misperceptions in English, what might it be like in trying to communicate in a different language? *Training* magazine offers some blunt advice: "The lesson for those [managers] plying foreign markets or hosting business visitors is: Slow down. Shut up. Listen."[46]

The Importance of National Culture

Would you shop at "Shoppingtown"? That was the name new Australian owners gave to a California shopping center known as Valley Fair.

Some of the problems resulting from the experiences of companies such as that described above are the result of cultural differences. A nation's ***culture*** **is the shared set of beliefs, values, knowledge, and patterns of behavior common to a group of people.**

We begin learning our culture starting at an early age through everyday interaction with people around us. This is why, from the outside looking in, a nation's culture can seem so intangible and perplexing. As cultural anthropologist Edward T. Hall puts it, "Since much of culture operates outside our awareness, frequently we don't even know what we know. . . . We unconsciously learn what to notice and what not to notice, how to divide time and space, how to walk and talk and use our bodies, how to behave as men or women, how to relate to other people, how to handle responsibility. . . ."[47] Indeed, says Hall, what we think of as "mind" is really internalized culture.

And because a culture is made up of so many nuances, this is why visitors to another culture may experience culture shock—the feelings of discom-

Culture shock. The "Culture Shock!" line of books (there's even one on the USA) offers readers guidance on understanding people in foreign countries. For instance, among the dos and don'ts for France, the guidebook suggests: "DON'T speak or laugh loudly in public places" and "DO return a compliment or praise with an expression of admiration for that person's judgment." Based on your upbringing, would you have guessed that these were nuances of good behavior in France?

fort and disorientation associated with being in an unfamiliar culture. According to anthropologists, culture shock involves anxiety and doubt caused by an overload of unfamiliar expectations and social cues.[48]

What Are Different Cultural Perceptions of Language, Nonverbal Communication, Time Orientation, & Religion?

How do you go about bridging cross-cultural gaps? It begins with understanding. Let's consider variations in four basic cultural areas: (1) *language*, (2) *nonverbal communication*, (3) *time orientation*, and (4) *religion*.[49]

Note, however, that such cultural differences are to be viewed as *tendencies* rather than absolutes. We all need to be aware that the *individuals* we are dealing with may be exceptions to the cultural rule. After all, there *are* talkative and aggressive Japanese, just as there are quiet and deferential Americans, stereotypes notwithstanding.[50]

1 Language More than 3,000 different languages are spoken throughout the world. However, even if you are operating in the English language, there are nuances between cultures that can lead to misperceptions. For instance, in Asia, a 'yes' answer to a question "simply means the question is understood," says a well-traveled writer. "It's the beginning of negotiations."[51]

In trying to communicate across cultures you have three options:

■ **Speak your own language:** The average American believes that about half the world can speak English, when actually it's about 20%.[52] No doubt you would prefer speaking English, but doing so will put you at a considerable competitive disadvantage.

■ **Use a translator:** Live translations, translations of written documents and advertisements, and computer e-mail translations are helpful but plagued by accuracy problems.[53] If you do use a translator, try to get one that will be loyal to you rather than to your overseas hosts.

■ **Learn the local language:** When you don't know the language, you miss such subtle yet crucial meanings, risk unintentionally insulting people, and jeopardize your business transactions.

2 Nonverbal Communication _Nonverbal communication_ **consists of messages sent outside the written or spoken word.** Says one writer, it includes such factors as "use of time and space, distance between persons when conversing, use of color dress, walking behavior, standing, positioning, seating arrangement, office locations, and furnishings."[54] Nonverbal communication is responsible for perhaps as much as 60% of a message being communicated.[55]

Five ways in which nonverbal communication is expressed are through _interpersonal space, eye contact, facial expressions, body movements and gestures_, and _touch_. A sample of different international norms for nonverbal communications is shown below.[56] _(See Panel 4.2.)_

PANEL 4.2
Different norms.
Variations in meaning of different types of nonverbal communication around the world

■ **China**
Hugging or taking someone's arm is considered inappropriate. Winking or beckoning with one's index finger is considered rude.

■ **Indonesia**
Handshaking and head noddings are customary greetings.

■ **Japan**
Business cards are exchanged before bowing or handshaking. A weak handshake is common. Lengthy or frequent eye contact is considered impolite.

■ **Malaysia**
Touching someone casually, especially on the top of the head (even a child's), is considered impolite.
It's best to use your right hand to eat and to touch people and things.

■ **The Philippines**
Handshaking and a pat on the back are common greetings.

■ **South Korea**
Men bow slightly and shake hands, sometimes with two hands. Women refrain from shaking hands.
It is considered polite to cover your mouth when laughing.

■ **Thailand**
Public displays of temper or affection are frowned on.
It is considered impolite to point at anything using your foot or to show the soles of your feet.

■ **Interpersonal space:** People of different cultures have different ideas about what is acceptable interpersonal space—that is, how close or far away one should be when communicating with another person. For instance, the people of North America and Northern Europe tend to conduct business conversations at a range of 3–4 feet. For people in Latin American and Asian cultures, the range is about 1 foot. For Arabs, it is even closer.

This can lead to cross-cultural misunderstandings. "Arabs tend to get very close and breathe on you," says anthropologist Hall. "The American on the receiving end can't identify all the sources of his discomfort but feels that the Arab is pushy. The Arab comes close, the American backs up. The Arab follows, because he can interact only at certain distances."[57] However, once the American understands that Arabs handle interpersonal space differently and that "breathing on people is a form of communica-

tion," says Hall, the situation can sometimes be redefined so that the American feels more comfortable.

■ **Eye contact:** Eye contact serves four functions in communication:

(1) It signals the beginning and end of a conversation; there is a tendency to look away from others when beginning to speak and to look at them when done.

(2) It expresses emotion; for instance, most people tend to avoid eye contact when conveying bad news or negative feedback.

(3) Gazing monitors feedback because it reflects interest and attention.

(4) Depending on the culture, gazing also expresses the type of relationship between the people communicating. For instance, Westerners are taught at an early age to look at their parents when spoken to. However, Asians are taught to avoid eye contact with a parent or superior to show obedience and subservience.[58]

■ **Facial expressions:** Probably you're accustomed to thinking that smiling represents warmth, happiness, or friendship, whereas frowning represents dissatisfaction or anger. But these interpretations of facial expressions don't apply across all cultures.[59] A smile, for example, doesn't convey the same emotions in different countries.

■ **Body movements and gestures:** An example of a body movement is leaning forward; an example of a gesture is pointing. Open body positions, such as leaning backward, express openness, warmth, closeness, and availability for communication. Closed body positions, such as folding one's arms or crossing one's legs, represent defensiveness.

Some body movements and gestures are associated more with one sex than the other, according to communication researcher Judith Hall. For instance, women nod their heads and move their hands more than men do. Men exhibit large body shifts and foot and leg movements more than women do.[60]

We need to point out, however, that interpretations of body language are subjective, hence easily misinterpreted, and highly dependent on the context and cross-cultural differences.[61] Be careful when trying to interpret body movements, especially when you're operating in a different culture.

■ **Touch:** Norms for touching vary significantly around the world. In the Middle East, for example, it is normal for two males who are friends to walk together holding hands—not commonplace behavior in the United States.

People tend to touch those they like, and women tend to do more touching during conversations than men do.[62] It needs to be noted, however, that men and women interpret touching differently, and in the United States, at least, sexual harassment claims might be reduced by keeping this perceptual difference in mind.

Still, women clearly have the advantage here, at least in the U.S. One study found that, whereas men are "largely boxed into the formality of a handshake," women are freer to emphasize a point with a brief (nonsexual) touch to the forearm of a man or a woman, give a playful mock push to a man's shoulder, and even place a firm hand on a man's shoulder to signal, if necessary, who is in charge. The risk of touching for a woman however, is that she may appear flirtatious.[63]

Working together. From this photo, one can't tell whether this room is in North America or the Middle East, but it could be either. Still, do you think the terrorist attacks of September 11, 2001, on the World Trade Center and the Pentagon would make it more difficult for Americans to work successfully with their counterparts from Arab countries? How important are good international relations to global business success?

3 Time Orientation Time orientation is different in many cultures. Anthropologist Hall makes a useful distinction between monochronic time and polychronic time:

- **Monochronic time:** This kind of time is standard American business practice. That is, _**monochronic time**_ **is a preference for doing one thing at a time.** In this perception, time is viewed as being limited, precisely segmented, and schedule driven. This perception of time prevails, for example, when you schedule a meeting with someone and then give the visitor your undivided attention during the allotted time.[64]

  Indeed, you probably practice monochronic time when you're in a job interveiw. You work hard at listening to what the interviewer says. You may well take careful notes. You certainly don't answer your cellphone or gaze repeatedly out the window.

- **Polychronic time:** This outlook on time is the kind that prevails in Mediterranean, Latin American, and especially Arab cultures.[65] _**Polychronic time**_ **is a preference for doing more than one thing at a time.** Here time is viewed as being flexible and multidimensional.

  This perception of time prevails when you visit a Latin American client, find yourself sitting in the waiting room for 45 minutes, and then find in the meeting that the client is dealing with three other people at the same time. (The American variant these days is referred to as "multitasking," as when you talk on the phone while simultaneously watching television and doing a crossword puzzle.)

As a manager, you will probably have to reset your mental clock when doing business across cultures.

Example of Cultural Differences in Time: A Garment Factory in Mexico

Harry Mehserjian and his brothers own a garment factory near Los Angeles, and they still do the high-fashion work there. However, the T-shirts and other low-budget knitware are sent deep into Mexico, to a factory in a suburb of Guadalajara, where wages are one-seventh those in Los Angeles.[65]

"I never wanted to go to Mexico," Harry says. But since NAFTA removed quotas limiting how much clothing could be brought in from Mexico, that country has shot from sixth place to first place (passing China) in exporting garments to the U.S. The changes caused by NAFTA, along with a rise in minimum wage in California, aggressive unionization, and more regulations, made it difficult for the Mehserjians to continue doing all their business in the United States.

One of the challenges to the Mehserjians is to change their workers' attitudes about time. "If they come on Monday, they're out on Tuesday. If they come on Tuesday, they're out on Wednesday," says a plant manager. To try to overcome absenteeism, the Mehserjians offer a 10% bonus to those who come to work faithfully for the entire week. Even so, their factory is still plagued by absenteeism and turnover. The workplace culture in the interior of Mexico is looser than in the United States—or even in northern Mexico, such as Juarez.

Says one UCLA expert, "These workers don't necessarily see their lives revolving around a job. There's a great deal of informality that they have come to expect from factory employment. You work hard during certain periods of time, and relax during others."[63]

4 Religion Are you a Protestant doing business in a predominantly Catholic country? Or a Muslim in a Buddhist country? How, then, does religion influence the work-related values of the people you're dealing with?

A study of 484 international students at a Midwestern university uncovered wide variations in the work-related values for different religious affiliations.[67] For example, among Catholics, the primary work-related value was found to be consideration. For Protestants, it was employer effectiveness; for Buddhists, social responsibility; for Muslims, continuity. There was, in fact, virtually *no agreement* among religions as to what is the most important work-related value. This led the researchers to conclude: "Employers might be wise to consider the impact that religious differences (and more broadly, cultural factors) appear to have on the values of employee groups."

Current Followers of the Major World Religions	
Christianity	1.7 billion
Islam	950 million
Hinduism	719 million
Buddhism	309 million
Judaism	18 million
Confucianism	5.9 million

After what some World War II veterans have been through, one can sympathize with their outrage over drivers who fly American flags from cars made by their former enemies—Toyotas, Mitsubishis, BMWs, Porsches, and other Japanese and German cars. "I drive all-American," boasts one vet.

But just what *is* an American car nowadays? "Is it a Honda Accord built by Americans in the Midwest," asks a newspaper reader, "or is it a Chrysler built in Mexico with parts from Canada by a company owned by Daimler-Benz?"[68] Perhaps the lesson is this: In a global economy, cultural arrogance is a luxury we can no longer afford.

Click-Along 4.2

Five Dimensions of National Culture

Who made this car? The assembly line producing these Mercedes-Benz SUVs is located in Alabama, but these days an automobile plant may be located nearly anywhere.

Click-Along 4.3

Taking Something Practical Away from This Chapter: You as a Manager in the World—Can You Handle the Challenges of Global Management?

Learning Portfolio

Key Terms Used in This Chapter

Summary

4.1
Globalization: The Collapse of Time & Distance

■ The world is rapidly being changed by globalization, the trend of the world economy toward become a more interdependent system. Globalization is reflected in three developments: (1) the rise of the global village and e-commerce; (2) the trend of the world's becoming one big market; and (3) the rise of both megafirms and Internet-enabled minifirms worldwide.

■ The rise of the "global village" refers to the "shrinking" of time and space as air travel and the electronic media have made it easier for people of the globe to communicate with one another. The arrival of the Internet and the World Wide Web have led to e-commerce (electronic commerce) the buying and selling of products and services through computer networks.

■ The global economy is the increasing tendency of the economies of the nations of the world to interact with one another as one market instead of many national markets. The positive effect is that growth of jobs and income in other countries could mean growth of jobs and income in the U.S. The negative effects are that national governments are powerless to prevent the flow of capital from weak economies to stronger ones.

■ The rise of cross-border business has led to the rise of megamergers, as giant firms have joined forces, and of minifirms, small companies in which managers can use the Internet and other technologies to get enterprises started more easily and to maneuver faster.

4.2
You & International Management

■ Studying international management prepares you to work with foreign customers or partners, with foreign suppliers, for a foreign firm in the U.S., or for a U.S. firm overseas. International management is management that oversees the conduct of operations in or with organizations in foreign countries, whether through a multinational corporation or a multinational organization. A multinational corporation is a business firm with operations in several countries. A multinational organization is a nonprofit organization with operations in several countries.

■ The successful international management is not ethnocentric or polycentric but geocentric. Ethnocentric managers believe that their native country, culture, language, and behavior are superior to all others. Polycentric managers take the view that native managers in the foreign offices best understand native personnel and practices, and so the home office should leave them alone. Geocentric managers accept that there are differences and similarities between home and foreign personnel and practices, and they should use whatever techniques are most effective. If you become an expatriate manager—a manager living or working in a foreign country—you should learn everything you can about the local culture so you can deal effectively with it.

4.3
Why & How Companies Expand Internationally

■ Companies expand internationally for at least five reasons, all of which have to do with making or saving money. (1) They seek cheaper or more plentiful supplies. (2) They seek new markets. (3) They seek lower labor costs, which explains the rise of the maquiladoras on Mexico's side of the U.S. border—manufacturing plants allowed to operate in Mexico with special privileges in return for employing Mexican citizens. (4) They seek access to finance capital. (5) They seek to avoid tariffs (fees) on imported goods or import quotas (limitations on the number of products a country allows in).

■ There are five ways in which companies expand internationally. (1) They engage in global outsourcing. Outsourcing is defined as using suppliers outside the company to provide goods and services, and global outsourcing is extending this practice outside the U.S. (2) They engage in importing, exporting, and countertrading. When importing, a company buys goods outside the country and resells them domestically. When exporting, a company produces goods domestically and sells them outside the country. When countertrading, a company practices bartering for goods. (3) They engage in licensing and franchising. In licensing, a company allows a foreign company to pay it a fee to make or distribute the company's product or service. Franchising is a form of licensing in which a company allows a foreign company to pay it a fee and a share of the profit in return for using the first company's brand name and a package of materials and services. (4) They engage in joint ventures, a strategic alliance with a foreign company to share the risks and rewards of starting a new enterprise together in a foreign country. (5) They become wholly-owned subsidiaries, or foreign subsidiaries that are totally owned and controlled by an organization. The foreign subsidiary may be an existing company that is purchased outright. A Greenfield venture is a foreign subsidiary that the owning organization has built from scratch.

4.4
Economic & Political-Legal Differences

■ Among the differences with which international managers must cope are (1) economic differences and (2) political-legal differences.

■ Four economic differences that managers must deal with include (1) different economic systems, (2) economic development, (3) infrastructure and resources, and (4) currency exchange rates.

■ The principal economic systems are free market, command, and mixed economies. (1) In a free-market economy, the production of goods and services are controlled by private enterprise and the interaction of the forces of supply and demand, rather than by the government. (2) In a command economy, or central-planning economy, the government owns most businesses and regulates the amounts, types, and prices of goods and services. (3) In a mixed economy, most of the important industries are owned by the government, but others are controlled by private enterprise. Some countries, such as Russia, have undergone privatization, with state-owned businesses being sold off to private enterprise. Whatever the economy, some countries have indigenization laws, which require that citizens within the host country must own a majority of whatever company is operating within that country.

■ Countries may be divided between developed countries and less-developed countries. Developed countries are those with a high level of economic development and generally high average level income among their citizens. Less-developed countries consist of nations with low economic development and low average incomes.

■ International companies are concerned about a foreign country's infrastructure and resources. A country's infrastructure consists of the physical facilities that form the basis for its level of economic development, such as roads and schools. Resources consist of labor and equipment, which may have to be imported.

■ Companies operating internationally also have to be concerned about currency exchange rates. The exchange rate is the rate at which one country's currency can be exchanged for another country's currency.

■ Managers operating internationally also need to be concerned about three kinds of political-legal differences: (1) democratic versus totalitarian political systems (2) political risk, and (3) laws and regulations.

■ Governmental systems may be democratic or totalitarian. Democratic governments rely on free elections and representative assemblies. Totalitarian governments are ruled by a dictator, a single political party, or a special-membership group, such as a handful of ruling families.

■ Political risk is defined as the risk that political changes will cause loss of a company's assets or impair its foreign operations. Two political risks a company doing business abroad might anticipate are instability, such as riots or civil disorders, and expropriation, defined as a government's seizure of a foreign company's assets.

■ International companies have to work with numerous laws and regulations. The United States has legislation under the Foreign Corrupt Practices Act of 1977, which makes it illegal for employees of U.S. companies to bribe decision makers in foreign nations.

4.5
The World of Free Trade: Regional Economic Cooperation

■ Free trade is the movement of goods and services among nations without political or economic obstructions.

■ Countries often use trade protectionism—the use of government regulations to limit the import of goods and services—to protect their domestic industries against foreign competition. Three barriers to free trade, or devices by which countries try to exert protectionism, are tariffs, import quotas, and embargoes. (1) A tariff is a trade barrier in the form of a customs duty, or tax, levied mainly on imports. (2) An import quota is a trade barrier in the form of a limit on the numbers of a product that can be imported. Quotas are designed to prevent dumping, the practice of a foreign company's exporting products abroad at a lower price than the price in the home market—or even below the costs of production—in order to drive down the price of the domestic product. (3) An embargo is a complete ban on the import or export of certain products.

■ Three principal organizations exist that are designed to facilitate international trade. (1) The World Trade Organization is designed to monitor and enforce trade agreements. (2) The World Bank is designed to provide low-interest loans to developing nations for improving transportation, education, health, and telecommunications. (3) The International Monetary Fund is designed to assist in smoothing the flow of money between nations.

■ A trading block, also known as an economic community, is a group of nations within a geographical region that have agreed to remove trade barriers with each other. There are four major trading blocs. (1) The North American Free Trade Agreement (NAFTA) consists of the U.S., Canada, and Mexico. (2) The European Union (EU) consists of 15 trading partners in Europe. (3) The Association of Southeast Asian Nations (ASEAN) consists of nine countries in Asia. (4) The Mercosur consists of Argentina, Brazil, Paraguay, and Uraguay.

■ Besides joining together in trade blocs, countries also extend special, "most favored nation" trading privileges—that is, grant other countries favorable trading treatment such as the reduction of import duties.

4.6
The Importance of Understanding Cultural Differences

■ A nation's culture is the shared set of beliefs, values, knowledge, and patterns of behavior common to a group of people. Because a culture is made up of so many nuances, visitors to another culture may experience culture shock—the feelings of discomfort and disorientation associated with being in an unfamiliar culture.

■ Managers trying to understand other cultures need to understand four basic cultural per-

ceptions embodied in (1) language, (2) nonverbal communication, (3) time orientation, and (4) religion.

■ Regarding language, when you are trying to communicate across cultures you have three options: speak your own language (if others can understand you), use a translator, or learn the local language.

■ Nonverbal communication consists of messages sent by means other than the written or the spoken word, and these nonverbal messages can vary according to culture. Five ways in which nonverbal communication is expressed are through interpersonal space, eye contact, facial expressions, body movements and gestures, and touch.

■ Time orientation of a culture may be either monochronic or polychronic. Monochronic time is a preference for doing one thing at a time. Polychronic time is a preference for doing more than one thing at a time.

■ Managers need to consider the effect of religious differences. In order of size (population), the major world religions are Christianity, Islam, Hinduism, Buddhism, Judaism, and Confucianism.

Management in Action

The Daimler-Benz & Chrysler Merger Is a Difficult Management Challenge

Excerpted from Joan Miller and Christine Tierney, "Can This Man Save Chrysler?"
Business Week, September 17, 2001, pp. 86–94.

 Not so long ago—in 1998 say, when Daimler-Benz and Chrysler linked up—Chrysler earned more on each vehicle than any other major carmaker, and it had a well-deserved reputation for eye-catching design. Today, it is bleeding money: It will lose at least $2 billion this year and by its own calculations probably won't make a dollar of profit until 2003. Although it offers huge discounts, Chrysler's mar-

ket share is shrinking. Since the merger, it has fallen from 16.2% to just 13.5% . . . The merger didn't lead to this sorry state, but the turmoil that followed didn't help either. For the first two years, Chrysler executives floundered as they tried to work with their German colleagues, and almost two-thirds of the senior management was fired or reassigned . . . Now, Zetsche [Dieter Zetsche is Chrysler Group's current CEO], 48, has to turn Chrysler into something it hasn't been for a while: a low-cost producer. "I'm pretty confident we'll get our act together," says Zetsche. "But it's taking longer than I thought when I first came in."

For Daimler, the acquisition has proved costly indeed. In 2000, Chrysler's operating profit tumbled 90%, to just $500 million, on $64.2 billion in sales. As a result, Stuttgart itself reported only $4.9 billion in profits, a 49% drop, on sales of $152 billion. It will probably take two more years before DaimlerChrysler even comes close to the profit level it enjoyed during the first full year of the merger . . . It is Zetsche who has to prove that Schrempp [Jürgen Schrempp is DaimlerChrysler's CEO] is right about Chrysler. In February, he started a three-year, $3.9 billion restructuring. He has announced 26,000 layoffs and has wrested big concessions from dealers and suppliers. Zetsche is also driving inefficiencies in Chrysler's vehicle-development process to reduce costs and boost quality: DaimlerChrysler ranks only fifth among the seven largest automakers, according to J. D. Power & Associates Inc. . . .

Along the way, the German engineer has confounded his critics in Detroit, who included almost everybody he works with, by turning out to be a decent, even likable fellow. He has spread a lot of misery, but he has done it with such sensitivity— and often in person—that potential antagonists usually decide to cooperate instead . . . Making Chrysler more efficient is a manageable, if time-consuming, problem for Zetsche. Making Daimler-Chrysler the carmaker that Schrempp had in mind, however, is another sort of challenge altogether. The $36 billion deal was the biggest ever among carmakers, and it pushed rivals around the globe to seek out partners of their own. Schrempp's idea was to create a company that would couple Mercedes's engineering with Chrysler's marketing and design savvy to develop a vehicle for every kind of driver, a colossus that would sell cars everywhere from Buenos Aires to Beijing. It would be extremely competitive: Chrysler and Mercedes could share parts and the cost of developing expensive new technologies. It would be an unprecedented combination of prestige and market power. It would be the global standard.

But so far, the merger has fallen disastrously short of that goal. Distrust between Auburn Hills and Stuttgart has made cooperation on even the simplest of matters difficult. Coming to terms with such prickly issues as deciding which parts image-conscious Mercedes-Benz would share with scrappy, mass-market Chrysler was deteriorating quickly By the time Schrempp sent Zetsche over,

Chrysler had become Daimler's biggest problem. Predictably enough, that's what seems to have finally forced the two to attempt to make their union work. Of course, for the Germans it helps that one of their own is now in charge in Detroit. The first Chrysler vehicle to use Mercedes parts extensively will be the Crossfire, a sensuous two-seat roadster that will be available in 2003 . . . But the Germans and the Americans have been out of sync from the start: The two proud management teams resisted working together, were wary of change, and weren't willing to compromise. Daimler and Chrysler have combined nothing beyond some administrative departments, such as finance and public relations. Talk of synergy might as well have been verboten. Mercedes executives worried their buyers might feel cheated if they shared parts with the American automaker; Chrysler resented the implication that its technology was inferior.

The strange truth today is that only a German can save the American icon. Even Holden [James Holden was the former CEO at Chrysler] admits Zetsche has a better chance of succeeding at Chrysler than any U.S. executive would. Zetsche wants to be called a "Chrysler guy," but the fact that he worked at Daimler for 25 years makes all the difference. First, he has Schrempp's confidence: Holden was fired after predicting that Chrysler wouldn't turn a profit until 2003. When Zetsche made the same forecast, Schrempp accepted it. And Zetsche's relationship with managers in Stuttgart— especially Mercedes boss Jürgen Hubbert—have made it easier for him to pry loose technologies and components that no American can get his hands on. Of course, the crisis helped. For example, Daimler-Chrysler may save $100 million in engineering costs by cloning a Mercedes transmission for Chrysler sedans coming out in 2004. "Being in trouble makes it easier to understand that you have to change," says Zetsche. "In Germany, they understand that we are in one boat." But it took a German to make them understand . . . As it turned out, Zetsche had just the combination of humility and warmth to ease tensions among Chrysler's demoralized staff. He eats in the cafeteria, interrupts plant tours to talk with workers, and even promised to shave his head (he's already half-bald) if the new Dodge Ram again topped the J. D. Power & Associates quality survey. His town hall meetings are so popular that plant officials resort to a lottery to choose participants.

Zetsche's decisive leadership is welcome relief for an outfit that drifted aimlessly after the merger. "There's not an employee around her who didn't know this company was in trouble," says James D. Donlon III, senior vice-president and controller. "They just needed somebody to get up and tell it like it is." That's true for those outside Chrysler as well. Three weeks into the job, Zetsche demanded that suppliers swallow an immediate 5% price cut. That alone should save Chrysler $2 billion this year. And to keep Chrysler's business, suppliers must wring out a further 10% by 2003, which should cut Chrysler's costs by an additional $4 billion. Zetsche has explained to many suppliers just how dire things are . . . In terms of product development, Zetsche wants Chrysler to balance style with thrift—an approach he calls "disciplined pizzazz." He is overhauling the vehicle-development process to put more focus on the earliest stages. By pulling together teams from all areas of the company—design, engineering, marketing, manufacturing, and purchasing—Zetsche hopes to reduce waste and resolve nagging quality problems without diminishing Chrysler's creative instincts. It's an approach that Chrysler itself pioneered in 1989 but couldn't stick with. Zetsche is also borrowing Mercedes' system of "quality gates." This allows Zetsche and his team to review a vehicle at each of the 11 checkpoints throughout the three-year development cycle. If they don't think the vehicle is ready to pass through, they send it back for work. "If he can combine Chrysler's passion for design with German engineering and drivability, he may pull it off," says Christopher W. Cedergren, an analyst at Nextrend Inc., a Thousand Oaks (Calif.) research firm . . . Zetsche is also devoting a good deal of time to making sense of the merger. DaimlerChrysler is expected to announce soon that by year-end Chrysler will offer Mercedes diesel engines in the

Grand Cherokees and the PT Cruisers it sells in Europe. The Crossfire will be only a nice model, but it wowed enthusiasts at this year's auto shows, and Chrysler hopes it will generate excitement about the company's full-size sedan and its next generation Jeep Grand Cherokee, which will borrow parts from the updated Mercedes M-Class SUV.

Zetsche admits that a "not-invented-here" syndrome kept Chrysler and Mercedes from sharing much in the beginning. It took a group of senior executives several months to put together what Schrempp calls the company's bran bible, which decrees what is sacred about both Mercedes and Chrysler. In fact, it was Zetsche and Holden who led the effort; Zetsche jokingly called himself the "brand pope." And while each request is still carefully debated in Stuttgart by a newly established executive automotive committee, "certainly the momentum is stronger now," he says. Schrempp agrees: "It's as if somebody took their foot off the brake."

For Discussion

1. Why did Daimler-Benz merge with Chrysler?

2. What were the key sources of conflict that kept employees at Chrysler and Daimler-Benz from cooperating with each other?

3. To what extent are cultural differences between the United States and Germany contributing to problems associated with the merger? Explain.

4. How is Dieter Zetsche trying to overcome sources of conflict between DaimlerChrysler's U.S. employees and their German counterparts?

5. Why is it so difficult to successfully create a megamerger between two international firms?

Take It to the Net

Globalization is a reality of our lives. The electronic world has brought us closer. The fall of old regimes, the spread of capitalism and democracy have altered political and economic relationships. But people still cling to their roots and their religion. In *The Lexus and the Olive Tree* journalist Thomas Friedman captures the old and the new. He drew the title from an experience he had at a Lexus factory where robots were assembling the cars, representative of modern life, as well as from his travels all over the world, where he saw how deeply rooted people are

still to their own cultures no matter how much electronic technology is introduced. Many places rely on new technology, using computers and robots and wireless communication, but some people still adhere to centuries-old practices such as hand-planting crops.

Management on an international scale is different than it is on a domestic scale. You cannot automatically apply in other countries what worked at your home company, steeped in U.S. culture, and expect others from various backgrounds and cultures to respond positively. Americans and American companies that go abroad must learn about different cultures and adapt accordingly if they are to succeed.

While no one website can provide all you need to know about other nations, the *Journal of Comparative International Management* is a good place to start. At this writing, full-text issues are available from June 1998–2001. Go to *http://www/lib.unb.ca/ Texts/JCIM/* and click on *June 1998*. Then click on *The Impact of Culture on the Management Values and Beliefs of Korean Firms*. Read the article, and then write an assessment test like the ones in this textbook. Trade tests in class and see how everyone does. What seem to be the class members' weak points?

General Questions

1. How are Korean management values and beliefs different from yours? Explain.

2. What did you learn about Korea?

3. Would you feel comfortable working with international firms? Why or why not?

Self-Assessment

How Well Am I Suited to Becoming a Global Manager?*

Objectives

1. To see if you are ready to be a global manager.

2. To help you assess your comfort level with other cultures.

Introduction: As our business world becomes increasingly globalized, U.S. companies need more managers to work in other countries. This usually means vast adjustments for the manager and her or his family during this job assignment. Flexibility is critical as is the ability to adjust to new ways, new people, new foods, different nonverbal communication, a new language, and a host of other new things.

Before agreeing to such an assignment, you need to know more about yourself and how you function in such situations.

Instructions: Are you prepared to be a global manager? Rate the extent to which you agree with each of the following 14 items by circling your response on the rating scale shown below. If you do not have direct experience with a particular situation (for example, working with people from other cultures), respond by circling how you *think* you would feel.

1 = Very strongly disagree
2 = Strongly disagree
3 = Disagree
4 = Neither agree nor disagree
5 = Agree
6 = Strongly agree
7 = Very strongly agree

	1	2	3	4	5	6	7
1. When working with people from other cultures, I work hard to understand their perspectives.	1	2	3	4	5	6	7
2. I have a solid understanding of my organization's products and services.	1	2	3	4	5	6	7
3. I am willing to take a stand on issues.	1	2	3	4	5	6	7
4. I have a special talent for dealing with people.	1	2	3	4	5	6	7

5. I can be depended on to tell the truth regardless of circumstances.	1	2	3	4	5	6	7
6. I am good at identifying the most important part of a complex problem or issue.	1	2	3	4	5	6	7
7. I clearly demonstrate commitment to seeing the organization succeed.	1	2	3	4	5	6	7
8. I take personal as well as business risks.	1	2	3	4	5	6	7
9. I have changed as a result of feedback from others.	1	2	3	4	5	6	7
10. I enjoy the challenge of working in countries other than my own.	1	2	3	4	5	6	7
11. I take advantage of opportunities to do new things.	1	2	3	4	5	6	7
12. I find criticism hard to take.	1	2	3	4	5	6	7
13. I seek feedback even when others are reluctant to give it.	1	2	3	4	5	6	7
14. I don't get so invested in things that I cannot change when something doesn't work.	1	2	3	4	5	6	7

Interpretation: This exercise assesses factors associated with being a successful global manager. These factors include general intelligence, business knowledge, interpersonal skills, commitment, courage, cross-cultural competencies, and the ability to learn from experience.

Total your scores, which will fall between 14 and 98. The higher your score, the greater your potential for success as an international manager.

Arbitrary Norms

High Potential for Success	70–98
Moderate Potential for Success	40–69
Low Potential for Success	39 and below

Questions for Discussion

1. What do the results suggest about your preparedness to be a global manager? Do you agree with these results?

2. How comfortable would you be going to another country at this time in your life?

3. How have your experiences as a citizen of a very diverse nation helped you to understand the other cultures of the world?

4. How might you improve your preparedness to one day assume an international position? Explain.

*Modified and adapted from G. M. Spreitzer, M.W. McCall Jr., and J. D. Mahoney, "Early Identification of International Executive Potential," *Journal of Applied Psychology*, February 1997, pp. 6–29.

Group Exercise

When in Rome, Do as the Romans Do!*

Objectives

1. To raise your awareness regarding appropriate behavior in different nations.
2. To emphasize that different nations have truly different customs.

Introduction

Globalization means that people in business must know the customs of other nations. A mistake can alienate a potential business partner; rudeness, even if unconscious or unknowing, can create a lasting bad impression of Americans; and lack of knowledge about the country you're in shows disrespect for its people. For example, many people in the United States signal "ok" by making a round sign with the thumb and the first finger; however, in Brazil the same gesture is a very crude one, comparable to raising the middle index figure in the U.S.

Instructions

Divide the class into teams of five students. Everyone in each team should individually try to match each of the following countries to the custom/gesture described in the list below. Then score choices according to the answer key at the end of this exercise. After each team member has individually completed his or her answers and scored them, compare them and then share your results with other teams in the class. Which items were incorrectly matched the most times? What do you think are the reasons for this?

Country	Custom/Gesture
	associated with each country
1. Chile	_____
2. France	_____
3. Italy	_____
4. South Korea	_____
5. Denmark	_____
6. Thailand	_____
7. Poland	_____
8. Egypt	_____
9. Pakistan	_____
10. Germany	_____

Gesture/Custom:

a. Never show the bottom of your foot; it is considered offensive.

b. While imported liquor is appropriate, a gift of locally available wine can be interpreted as saying that your host's wine cellar is inadequate.

c. Beckoning is done with the palm down rather than up, moving the fingers toward the body.

d. The "thumbs up" sign means zero.

e. The gesture North Americans use to indicate that someone is crazy—index finger circling while pointed at one's temple—is used here to insult other drivers while on the road.

f. At a meal, keep your hands above the table at all times.

g. Men greet each other with a slight bow and sometimes an accompanying handshake while maintaining eye contact.

h. Press your hands together as though in prayer, keeping arms and elbows close to your body, bow your head to touched fingers, and say Wai (pronounced "why").

i. You may see a disgruntled man quickly stoke his fingertips under his chin and thrust them forward. This is a sign of defiance and/or derision.

j. In social situations, when a man flicks his finger against his neck, he is inviting you to join him for a drink.

Interpretation & Scoring

If you matched the correct country with the correct gesture/custom 8–10 times, you are very cosmopolitan, or international; if you matched the correct country with the correct gesture/custom 4–7 times, you are moving toward becoming cosmopolitan; if you matched 0 to 3 accurately, you probably need to read more about other nations and travel outside the United States.

Questions for Discussion:

1. What does it mean to you to be cosmopolitan or international? Explain.
2. Do you believe that it is important to know about diverse cultures? Why or why not?
3. Do you value knowledge about other cultures? Why or why not?
4. Does the knowledge provided in this exercise encourage to you to learn more about other cultures? Why or why not?

*Anne C. Cowden, Ph.D., developed this assessment. The information came from Terri Morrison, Wayne A. Conaway, and George Borden, *Kiss, Bow, or Shake Hands: How to Do Business in Sixty Countries* (Holbrook, MA: Adams Media Corporation, 1994).

Ethical Dilemma

Dawn Raids Are Used by the European Union Antitrust Authorities

Excerpted from Philip Shishkin, "Tough Tactics: European Regulators Spark Controversy with 'Dawn Raids'," The Wall Street Journal, *February 1, 2002, pp. A1, A6.*

European Union antitrust investigators showed up unannounced at Coca-Cola Co.'s London offices early one morning in 1999.

They were looking for evidence that Coke and its bottlers had shut out rival soft-drink makers by offering questionable discounts to retailers. Even though they didn't have a search warrant, the investigators scoured desktop computers and searched e-mail servers. They sifted through hundreds of messages and left with copies of those that contained such key words as "confidential," "competition," and "discount." They also took copies of confidential legal documents prepared by Coke's in-house lawyers.

Coke didn't try to stop the investigators. It couldn't; EU antitrust agents can walk without warning into any company doing business in the 15-nation union to look for whatever they think might be proof of illegal activity. Then they use the evidence to levy fines as steep as 10% of a company's world-wide revenue. EU investigators say the Coke investigation is still continuing, and the company says it's cooperating.

There is no judicial review before what's known as a dawn raid and no statute prescribing when the raids should be conducted. In fact, judges don't have the authority to question, or even see, the justification for a raid. The only approval needed is from the EU's antitrust chief, Mario Monti, who usually bases his decision on whether the haul of evidence will likely be big enough to justify the time and expense. . . .

Now Mr. Monti is taking big steps to expand this controversial practice. Currently, his investigators are limited to searching corporate offices for evidence of price fixing and abuse of market power, but he is pushing to extend raids to executives' homes. He is also seeking the power to interrogate employees about antitrust violations without guaranteeing they would be entitled to consult a lawyer. . . .

Mr. Monti says investigators need still more power. . . . Investigators would be able to search executives' homes, he proposed, not only their offices. During raids, they could conduct broad-ranging interrogations of employees, rather than being limited to asking only technical questions about documents, such as clarifying the dates and names. . . .

The proposals have sparked concern among European and U.S. companies, which believe the EU wasn't paying enough attention to their rights of defense. . . . Before Mr. Monti's proposals become law, they must be approved by the EU's national governments [who were expected to vote later in 2002].

Solving the Dilemma

What would you do if you were a voting member of an EU national government?

1. Allow Mr. Monti the expanded powers he desires.

2. Not allow Mr. Monti any additional power and authority.

3. Reduce the amount of power and authority possessed by Mr. Monti's investigators.

4. Invent other options.

Video Case

Video Case: Earth First Pharmaceutical

Senior supervisor Sylvia Tang is faced with a difficult dilemma. As the video case opens, Syl is wrapping up a meeting with Dr. Daniel Simmons, Vaccines Manager, and Dr. Robert (Bob) Franklin, Natural Resources Manager. As an aside, Daniel asks Syl for further information regarding benefits for his future spouse. Bob is unaware of the upcoming nuptials and interrupts to congratulate Daniel. He asks, "who's the lucky lady?" to which Daniel responds, "it's not a she." Bob is clearly unaware of Daniel's sexual preference and as the ramifications of Daniel's response sink in, Bob is immediately uncomfortable.

Bob feels "out of the loop" regarding Daniel's upcoming wedding. Daniel initially interprets this to mean that Bob is upset at not having been invited to the wedding. However, he quickly realizes that Bob is actually upset by the knowledge of Daniel's sexual orientation and not at being excluded from the invitation list! Syl interrupts in an attempt to diffuse what is becoming a tense situation and suggests they put aside any personal discussion. Bob admits he'd "like to feel relaxed about this" but he's not. Bob continues to assert that he won't be able to continue working with Daniel as a partner. Daniel is incredulous at Bob's reaction, and again the situation becomes heated. Syl again interrupts to diffuse the situation. She proposes individual meetings with both Daniel and Bob. Bob and Daniel agree that this is an important issue for both of them, and it "isn't going to go away with a meeting." The discussion between Daniel and Bob again becomes heated, and Syl must stress the need for individual meetings and the need to manage the remainder of the business project.

Privately, Syl provides her interpretation of the situation. Bob clearly was unaware of Daniel's sexual orientation and reacted emotionally to the news. Daniel became personally offended, and neither liked the idea of separate meetings to address the issue. As manager, Syl outlines her responsibilities to both Daniel and Bob. To Daniel, her responsibilities include providing benefits information and also keeping the business project moving forward. Her responsibilities to Bob include attempting to make him feel comfortable in the work setting, requesting that he adjust his behavior and "quell some of his discomfort." She needs to provide Bob with coaching regarding how to deal with situations that cause

discomfort and how to keep personal feelings from interfering in business settings. Finally, she sees an obligation to Bob to help him move forward and complete the remainder of the project.

The three parties reconvene with the sole purpose of deciding the best way to complete the remainder of the project. Syl puts forward a proposal. Tasks that would have been allocated to Bob will instead be delegated to two team members. Daniel disagrees with this potential solution and feels he is being discriminated against. Syl reassures Daniel that their workplace is one of equal opportunity. Daniel proposes working together with Bob to finish the project just as they were before. Daniel and Bob both feel they are each being personally attacked and exchange heated words. Yet again Syl must tone down the tense discussion.

Privately, Syl shares her perceptions. Daniel has a valid point: Bob probably will not remain quite regarding Daniel's sexual orientation. Syl sees her role as maintaining a delicate balance between finishing the project on time and helping employees deal with personal issues. She realizes that Daniel likely feels discriminated against and could bring a lawsuit against the company. Syl believes part of an ideal solution includes Bob attending some form of counseling or sensitivity training to help him become more accepting and less judgmental. However, she recognizes the likelihood of this occurring is small.

Discussion Questions:

1. One of Syl's primary obligations is to ensure completion of the work project. Suggest three potential solutions to this problem. How do you predict each of the parties will react to each of the alternative solutions? Use information from the case to justify your response.

2. Critique Syl's handling of the two meetings. What did she do well? Is there room for improvement?

3. Put yourself in Syl's place. How would you bring about a resolution to the personal tension between Daniel and Bob?

4. Does Daniel have sufficient cause for a discrimination suit? Why or why not?

CHAPTER 5

Planning
The Foundation of Successful Management

5.1 Planning & Uncertainty
Major Question: How do I tend to deal with uncertainty, and how can planning help?

5.4 Promoting Goal Setting: Management by Objectives
Major Question: What is MBO, and how can it be implemented successfully to achieve results?

5.2 Fundamentals of Planning
Major Question: What are mission and vision statements, three types of planning and goals, and SMART goals?

5.5 Project Planning
Major Question: What is project planning, why is it important, and what is the project life cycle?

5.3 The Planning/Control Cycle
Major Question: How does the planning/control cycle help keep a manager's plans headed in the right direction?

5.6 A Project-Planning Tool: Break-Even Analysis
Major Question: How can break-even analysis help a manager turn a profit?

HOW DO EXCEPTIONAL MANAGERS MAKE THEIR OWN LUCK?

Risk and luck are two aspects of life that can't be ignored. But planning can improve your odds.

Many people think what happens to them is the result of fickle fate. However, with knowledge and planning, you can better learn what's risky and what's not.

What determines the way people perceive risk? The context in which the risk occurs is often important.[1] For example, you may tend to view something as more risky if you're not in control (as when traveling on an airplane). Another factor is trust: When a company or agency has a shady record, people conclude it can't be trusted and view what it's doing as more risky.

As a manager, you need to be aware of such outside factors when making plans about new endeavors involving some risk. You also need to be aware of how you yourself think about your luck.

Bad luck is when a flaming meteor hits you on the head. But failed business deals, lost promotions, and the like can't be blamed on just bad luck. "We're responsible for a good deal more of what happens to us than we realize," says research psychologist William F. Vitulli.[2]

People who are prone to bad luck are often impulsive. "They routinely speak before they think, make investments and purchases based on passing whims, and put themselves in dangerous spots by failing to plan ahead," says one writer.[3] Other people have bad luck in just one area (such as relationships) in which they are incapable of seeing life realistically. Still others have self-expectations that they will fail, and so they generally do. Or they exaggerate their setbacks to gain sympathy.

How do you improve your luck? Some steps:[4]

■ **Make a list and consider your motives:** If you think you could be the victim of self-induced misfortune, make a written list of specific examples in which you contributed to your own bad luck. Then fight it by putting Post-it reminders (such as the word "Impulse?") on your phone, computer monitor, dashboard, and so on.

■ **Cultivate optimism and confidence:** Can you actually *will* yourself to be in control of your life? The chances are that if you act like the person you want to become, you will become that person. Indeed, you are more apt to ACT your way into a new way of thinking than to THINK your way into it.[5] Thus, try to cultivate optimism. Don't automatically expect the worst in any situation.

■ **Ask for help:** Many of us can't see ourselves objectively. If you have trouble figuring out a pattern of bad luck, the best solution is to talk to a counselor.

FORECAST: WHAT'S AHEAD IN THIS CHAPTER

In this chapter, we describe planning, the first of the four management functions. We consider the benefits of planning and how it helps you deal with uncertainty. We deal with the fundamentals of planning, including the mission and vision statements and the three types of planning—strategic, tactical, and operational. We consider goals and action plans, SMART goals, the planning/control cycle, and management by objectives (MBO). We then consider project planning. Finally, we show a project-planning tool, break-even analysis.

major question

How do I tend to deal with uncertainty, and how can planning help?

The Big Picture

Planning, the first of four functions in the management process, involves setting goals and deciding how to achieve them. Planning helps you check your progress, coordinate activities, think ahead, and cope with uncertainty. Uncertainty is of three types—state, effect, and response. Organizations respond to uncertainty in various ways.

Uncertainty. Managers must plan to deal with surprises. Here demonstrators protest sweatshop conditions for workers in front of Gap Kids in San Francisco.

What is known as the *management process*, you'll recall (from Chapter 1), involves the four management functions of *planning, organizing, leading*, and *controlling*, which form four of the part divisions of this book. In this and the next two chapters we discuss **_planning_, which we previously defined as setting goals and deciding how to achieve them. Another definition: *Planning* is coping with uncertainty by formulating future courses of action to achieve specified results.**[6] When you make a plan, you make a blueprint for action that describes what you need to do to realize your goals.

Why Not Plan?

On the face of it, planning would seem to be a good idea—otherwise we would not be devoting three chapters to the subject. But there are two cautions to be aware of:

1 Planning Requires You to Set Aside the Time to Do It Time-starved managers may be quite resentful when superiors order them to prepare a five-year plan for their work unit.

"What?" they may grouse. "They expect me to do that and *still* find time to meet this year's goals?" Somehow, though, that time for planning must be found. Otherwise, managers are mainly just reacting to events.

Planning means that you must involve the subordinates you manage to determine resources, opportunities, and goals. During the process, you may need to go outside the work unit for information about products, competitors, markets, and the like.

2 You May Have to Make Some Decisions without a Lot of Time to Plan In our time of Internet connections and speedy-access computer databases, can't nearly anyone lay hands on facts quickly to make an intelligent decision? Not always. A competitor may quickly enter your market with a highly desirable product. A change in buying habits may occur. A consumer boycott may suddenly surface. An important supplier may let you down. The caliber of employees you need may not be immediately available at the salary level you're willing to pay. And in any one of these you won't have the time to plan a decision based on all the facts.

Nevertheless, a plan need not be perfect to be executable. While you shouldn't shoot from the hip in making decisions, often you may have to "go with what you've got" and make a decision based on a plan that is perhaps only three-quarters complete.

How Planning Helps You: Four Benefits

You can always hope you'll luck out or muddle through the next time a hurricane, earthquake, tornado, or other natural disaster strikes your area. Or you can plan for it by stocking up on flashlight batteries and canned food. Which is better? The same consideration applies when you're a manager. Some day, after you've dealt with some crisis, you will be very happy that you had a plan for handling it. The benefits of planning are fourfold:

1 Planning Helps You Check on Your Progress

The preprinted score card that golfers use when playing 18 holes of golf isn't blank. For each hole, the card lists the standard number of strokes ("par"), such as three or five, that a good player should take to hit the ball from the tee to the cup. The score card is the plan for the game, with objectives for each hole. After you play the hole, you write your own score in a blank space. At the end of the 18 holes, you add all your scores to see how you performed compared to the standard for the course.

How well is your work going in an organization? You won't know unless you have some way of checking your progress. That's why, like a golfer, it's important to have some expectations of what you're supposed to do—in other words, a plan.

2 Planning Helps You Coordinate Activities

"The right hand doesn't know what the left hand is doing!"

We may hear that expression used, for example, when a crisis occurs and an organization's public relations department, legal department, and CEO's office all give the press separate, contradictory statements. Obviously, such an embarrassment can be avoided if the organization has a plan for dealing with the media during emergencies. A plan defines the responsibilities of various departments and coordinates their activities for the achievement of common goals—such as, at minimum, making an organization not look confused and disorganized.

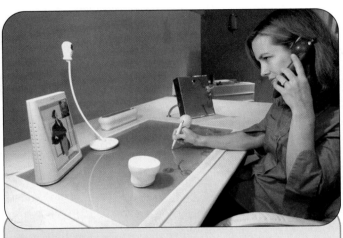

Cutting edge. Unknown to you, a business competitor may be developing a product or service that will revolutionize the industry you are in, as this flat-screen videophone (and drawing tablet) may change the telephone industry. How do you plan for revolutionary developments?

3 Planning Helps You Think Ahead

CEO and founder Michael Dell, of Dell Computer, which makes personal computers, says, "In my business, the life cycle of a product is six months, and so there are two types of people: the quick and the dead."[7] Dell is always trying to look into the future to try to plan for what might be the next big change in microcomputer products.

Similarly, as we describe under product life cycle (Chapter 6), the service or product with which you're engaged will probably at some point reach maturity, and sales will begin to falter. Thus, you need to look ahead, beyond your present phase of work, to try to be sure you'll be one of the quick rather than one of the dead.

4 Above All, Planning Helps You Cope with Uncertainty

You don't care for unpleasant surprises? Most people don't. (Pleasant surprises, of course, are invariably welcome.) That's why trying to plan for unpleasant contingencies is necessary (as we'll describe in Chapter 6). Planning helps you deal with uncertainty, as we discuss next.

Three Types of Uncertainty: State, Effect, & Response

Experts tend to classify uncertainty as being of three types—*state, effect*, and *response*:[8]

State Uncertainty—"What Possible Harmful Event Could Occur?" On a summer day, you're setting out for a hike in the mountains. You scan the skies. Could it rain? Are you at a high enough elevation, and is it cold enough that it could even snow? This is an example of *state uncertainty*, **when the environment is considered unpredictable.**

Effect Uncertainty—"What Possible Harmful Effect Might an Environmental Change Have?" An unexpected summer rainstorm in the mountains could be just a slight inconvenience, forcing you to take cover until it passes. However, a snowstorm could cause you to lose the trail and perhaps risk freezing and hypothermia. This is an example of *effect uncertainty*, **when the effects of environmental changes are unpredictable.**

Response Uncertainty—"What Possible Harmful Consequence Might a Decision Have?" Which would be better to have in a mountain snowstorm, warm clothes or a cellphone? The clothes would help you survive the weather. The cellphone could help summon emergency aid—if anyone could receive your call from a wilderness area. This is an example of *response uncertainty*, **when the consequences of a decision are uncertain.**

Example of Planning for Uncertainty: Nokia Cellphones

In 1993, Motorola dominated the mobile-phone market, selling a third of all cellphones in the world. Today it is Finland-based Nokia that sells more than a third of all cellphones. How did this reversal occur?

Two influential Nokia decision makers were Americans Frank Nuovo and Erik Anderson. A former jazz drummer, Nuovo, 40, is vice-president of design. He has never moved to Finland, preferring to live in Los Angeles, where he thinks beauty and style matter most. Anderson, who is in charge of production, does live in Finland.

In the early 1990s, mobile-phone makers tried to pack their phones with every possible feature. That is, of course, one way to plan for uncertainty. But after designing and producing "one perfect phone" for Nokia, Nuovo and Anderson began to champion the idea of "many perfect phones," each different and each doing one thing well. "A product needs to be *about* something," says Nuovo. "I would rather have five phones that do five things than one that does a little bit of everything." That is another way of planning for uncertainty.

Not that this planning is easy. "[I]f you make too many phones you go bankrupt," observes Anderson. "If you make lots of products but none are the best in their class, you will go bankrupt. If you make one good product, you might do really well with it, but there won't be enough profit, so you'll go bankrupt. In the end, it all really comes back to balance."[9]

Click-Along 5.1

Examples of Three Types of Uncertainty

How Organizations Respond to Uncertainty

How do you personally respond to uncertainty? Do you react slowly? conservatively? proactively? Do you watch to see what others do? Organizations act in similar ways.

Scholars **Raymond E. Miles** and **Charles C. Snow** suggest that organizations adapt one of *four positions when responding to uncertainty in their environment.* They become *defenders, prospectors, analyzers,* or *reactors.*[10]

Defenders—"Let's Stick with What We Do Best, Avoid Other Involvements" Whenever you hear an organization's leader say that "We're sticking with the basics" or "We're getting back to our core business," that's the hallmark of a defender organization. **_Defenders_ are expert at producing and selling narrowly defined products or services.** Often they are old-line successful enterprises—such as Harley-Davidson motorcycles or Brooks Brothers clothiers—with a narrow focus. They do not tend to seek opportunities outside their present markets. They devote most of their attention to making refinements in their existing operations.

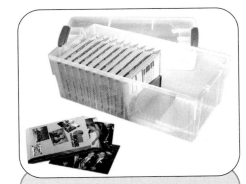

New Rubbermaid products. In the 1990s, Rubbermaid had the goal of producing one new product a *day*. The product here is a media box for CDs or DVDs. Which response is the company taking to uncertainty?

Prospectors—"Let's Create Our Own Opportunities, Not Wait for Them to Happen" A company described as "aggressive" is often a prospector organization. **_Prospectors_ focus on developing new products or services and in seeking out new markets, rather than waiting for things to happen.** Like 19th-century gold miners, these companies are "prospecting" for new ways of doing things. The continual product and market innovation has a price: Such companies may suffer a loss of efficiency. Nevertheless, their focus on change can put fear in the hearts of competitors.

Analyzers—"Let Others Take the Risks of Innovating, & We'll Imitate What Works Best" Analyzers take a "me too" response to the world. By and large, you won't find them called "trendsetters." Rather, **_analyzers_ let other organizations take the risks of product development and marketing and then imitate (or perhaps slightly improve on) what seems to work best.**

Reactors—"Let's Wait Until There's a Crisis, Then We'll React" Whereas the prospector is aggressive and proactive, the reactor is the opposite—passive and reactive. **_Reactors_ make adjustments only when finally forced to by environmental pressures.** In the worst cases, they are so incapable of responding fast enough that they suffer massive sales losses and are even driven out of business. Schwinn bicycles, for instance, failed to respond quickly enough to the sudden popularity of mountain bikes and lost its stature as the leading manufacturer of bicycles.

Click-Along 5.2

Examples of Defenders, Prospectors, Analyzers, & Reactors

What are mission and vision statements, three types of planning and goals, and SMART goals?

The Big Picture

Planning consists of translating an organization's mission into objectives. The organization's purpose is expressed as a mission statement and what it becomes is expressed as a vision statement. From these are derived strategic planning, then tactical planning, then operational planning. Each kind specifies goals and action plans for accomplishing the goals, which should be S-M-A-R-T.

"Everyone wants a clear reason to get up in the morning," writes journalist Dick Leider. "As humans we hunger for meaning and purpose in our lives."[11]

And what is that purpose? "Life never lacks purpose," says Leider. "Purpose is innate—but it is up to each of us individually to discover or rediscover it."

An organization has a purpose, too—a mission. And managers must have an idea of where they want the organization to go—a vision. The approach to planning can be summarized in the following diagram, which shows how an organization's mission becomes translated into objectives. *(See Panel 5.1.)*

PANEL 5.1

Making plans. An organization's reason for being is expressed in a *mission statement.* What the organization wishes to become is expressed in a *vision statement.* From these are derived *strategic planning*, then *tactical planning*, and finally *operational planning.* The purpose of each kind of planning is to specify *goals* and *action plans* for accomplishing those goals.

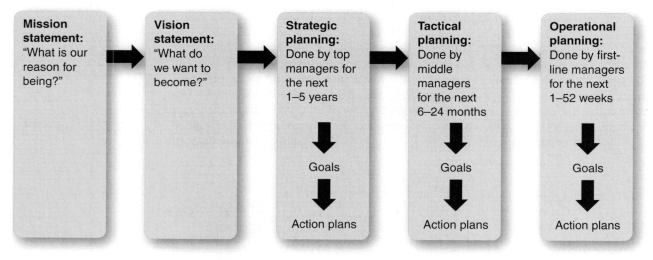

Mission & Vision Statements

The planning process begins with two attributes: a mission statement (which answers the question "What is our reason for being?") and a vision statement (which answers the question "What do we want to become?").

The Mission Statement—"What Is Our Reason for Being?" **An organization's _mission_ is its purpose or reason for being.** Determining the mission is the responsibility of top management and the board of directors. It is up to them to formulate a _mission statement_, **which expresses the purpose of the organization.**

"Only a clear definition of the mission and purpose of the organization makes possible clear and realistic . . . objectives," says Peter Drucker.[12] Whether the organization is for-profit or nonprofit, the mission statement identifies the goods or services the organization provides and will provide, and the reasons for providing them (to make a profit or to achieve humanitarian goals, for example).

> Intel's mission statement:
>
> Do a great job for our customers, employees, and stockholders by being the preeminent building block supplier to the worldwide internet economy.

Example of a Mission Statement: Amazon.com

In less than four years—from July 1995 to June 1999—Internet retailer ("e-tailer") Amazon.com went from zero to 10 million customers. "If anyone had predicted in 1995 that we'd have 10 million Amazonians by now, they'd have been locked up as dangerous," said a jubilant Jeff Bezos, Amazon's founder and CEO.[13]

That, of course, was a victory statement rather than a mission statement. The mission, as expressed on the company's website, is to "use the Internet to offer products that educate, inform, and inspire. We decided to build an online store that would be customer friendly and easy to navigate and would offer the broadest possible selection."[14] More prosaically, since Amazon is a for-profit organization, the mission is to make money: "We believe that a fundamental measure of our success will be the shareholder value we create over the long term," states one of the company's annual reports. "This value will be a direct result of our ability to extend and solidify our current market leadership position. . . . Market leadership can translate directly to higher revenue, higher profitability. . . ."[15]

amazon.com

The Vision Statement—"What Do We Want to Become?" **A _vision_ is a long-term goal describing "what" an organization wants to become. It is a clear sense of the future and the actions needed to get there.** "[A] vision should describe what's happening to the world you compete in and what you want to do about it," says one *Fortune* article. "It should guide decisions."[16]

Before Roger Enrico moved up to CEO of PepsiCo, the company thrived on "big-idea, renegade thinking," according to one report.[17] The problem was that the culture of autonomous business units led to decentralized control and managers who "were ricocheting off each other in search of their next promotion, or chasing new restaurant chains or joint ventures in far-flung parts of the world." Because Enrico had a clear sense of the future and the actions needed to get there—that is, a vision—he recentralized control and offered managers compensation schemes to encourage them to get their present jobs done rather than look for the next one.

After formulating a mission statement, top managers need to develop a ***vision statement*, which expresses what the organization should become, where it wants to go strategically.**

Example of a Vision Statement: Amazon.com

Jeff Bezos started out selling books as Amazon's first online product for the reason that, as one article reports, "there are far more of them in and out of print than any physical bookstore could ever line up on its shelves and that, unlike his second choice, music, the industry is not dominated by a cartel of half a dozen mega-distributors."[18]

However, his vision goes beyond books. "Our vision is to build a place to find and discover anything our customers might want to buy . . . [including] car parts and spark plugs," says Bezos.[19] The company expanded into several endeavors, including a music CD store, a video store, and an online auction business, and was offering a free electronic greeting card service, an Internet movie database, and international websites in the United Kingdom and Germany. It had also invested in several Internet retailers, including drugstore.com, Pets.com, and HomeGrocer.com.

As an extension of the vision, Bezos says that Amazon intends "to build the world's most customer-centric company. . . . I constantly remind our employees to be afraid, to wake up every morning terrified. Not of our competition, but of our customers. . . . We're proud of the differentiation we've built through constant innovation and relentless focus on customer experience. . . ."[20]

Three Types of Planning for Three Levels of Management: Strategic, Tactical, & Operational

Inspiring, clearly stated mission statements and vision statements provide the focal point of the entire planning process. Then three things happen:

- **Strategic planning:** Once the mission and vision statements are developed, it is top management's job to do strategic planning.
- **Tactical planning:** The strategic priorities and policies are then passed down the organizational pyramid to middle management, which needs to do tactical planning.
- **Operational planning:** Middle managers then pass these plans along to lower management to do operational planning.

Each type of planning has different time horizons, although the times overlap since the plans are somewhat elastic. Let's consider these three types of planning.

Strategic Planning by Top Managers: 1–5 Years Top managers make long-term decisions about the overall direction of the organization. The CEO, the vice presidents, the division heads need to pay attention to the environment outside the organization, being alert for long-run opportunities and problems. These executives must be future oriented, dealing with uncertain, highly competitive conditions.

Using their mission and vision statements, top managers do _strategic planning_—**they determine what the organization's long-term goals should be for the next 1–10 years with the resources they expect to have available.** "Strategic planning requires visionary and directional thinking," says one authority.[21] It should communicate not only general goals about growth and profits but also ways to achieve them.

Tactical Planning by Middle Managers: 6–24 Months Middle managers implement the policies and plans of the top managers above them and supervise and coordinate the activities of the first-line managers below them. In for-profit organizations, middle managers are the functional managers and department managers. Their decisions often must be made without a base of clearly defined informational procedures, perhaps requiring detailed analysis and computations.

Middle managers do _tactical planning_—**that is, they determine what contributions their departments or similar work units can make with their given resources during the next 6 months to 2 years.** Often the top and first-line managers will have a hand in developing the tactical plans.

Operational Planning by First-Line Managers: 1–52 Weeks The job titles of first-line managers tend to be on the order of "foreman" or "forewoman," "team leader," or "supervisor." These are the managers at the bottom of the pyramid who direct the daily tasks of nonmanagerial personnel. Their decisions often are predictable ones that follow a well-defined set of routine procedures.

Following the plans of middle and top managers, first-line managers do _operational planning_—**that is, determine how to accomplish specific tasks with available resources within the next 1-week to 1-year period.**

Employees may take part in formulating operational plans, as may middle managers.

Goals & Action Plans

Whatever its type—strategic, tactical, or operational—the purpose of planning is to achieve a goal. A _goal_, also known as an _objective_, is a specific commitment to achieve a measurable result within a stated period of time. The goal should be followed by an action plan, which defines the course of action needed to achieve the stated goal.

When you board a plane going from Los Angeles to New York, you know that the goal of the flight is to deliver you to a specific East Coast airport at a specific time. The fact that so many planes arrive late shows how elusive some goals are, but the airlines never stop trying to achieve them. They know the goal of on-time arrival represents a promise to their customers, and achieving it is an expectation the customers have of them.

As with planning, goals are of the same three types—strategic, tactical, and operational. Also, like planning, goals are arranged in a hierarchy known as a _means-end chain_ **because in the chain of management (operational, tactical, strategic) the accomplishment of low-level goals are the means leading to the accomplishment of high-level goals or ends.**

Communications

No hands? Or no hands on? In the five years leading up to 2002, the U.S. telecommunications industry spent nearly $400 billion on building and improving giant networks. Then the volumes of phone, video, and data traffic that was supposed to pay for them never materialized. Some two dozen American telephone companies have filed for bankruptcy, among them Global Crossing and Teligent. Shouldn't strategic planning have anticipated this possibility?

1 Strategic Goals *Strategic goals* are set by and for top management and focus on objectives for the organization as a whole.

2 Tactical Goals *Tactical goals* are set by and for middle managers and focus on the actions needed to achieve strategic goals.

3 Operational Goals *Operational goals* are set by and for first-line managers and are concerned with short-term matters associated with realizing tactical goals.

Examples of Strategic, Tactical, & Operational Goals: Southwest Airlines

Strategic Goals The goal of top managers of Dallas-based Southwest Airlines is to ensure that the airline is highly profitable, following the general strategy of (a) keeping costs and fares down and (b) offering a superior on-time arrival record. One of the most important strategic decisions Southwest made was to fly just one type of airplane—Boeing 737s. (The fleet has 362 such planes.) Thus, it is able to hold down training, maintenance, and operating expenses.[22] As of this writing, the airline is achieving its strategic goals: By the end of 2001, it had made money for 29 consecutive years, and its stock had averaged 29% annual gains during the last 10 years. It has continually lowered its costs, and it leads the industry in on-time performance. In 2002, Southwest launched non-stop, coast-to-coast flights twice a day between Baltimore/Washington International and Los Angeles, thereby taking on the routes long dominated by higher-fare airlines. In doing so, however, it planned to stick with 737s, but the newer generation that would travel longer distances.[23]

Tactical Goals Cutting costs and keeping fares low is a key tactical goal for Southwest's middle managers. For example, the organization cut costs in its maintenance program by doing more work on a plane when it's in for a check instead of bringing it in three different times. In addition, it gets more use out of its planes every day by limiting the turnaround time between flights to 20 minutes, compared to up to an hour for other airlines. Southwest also usually flies to less-congested airports, thus saving time and money by avoiding traffic. There is just one class of seating, doing away with the distinction between coach and first class. Even the boarding passes are reusable, being made of plastic. Finally, the airline saves by not feeding passengers: It serves only peanuts, no in-flight meals.

How do you make arrival times more reliable? To achieve this second tactical goal, middle managers did away with guaranteed seat reservations before ticketing, so that no-shows won't complicate (and therefore delay) the boarding process. In addition, as mentioned, the airline is religious about turning planes around in exactly 20 minutes, so that on-time departures are more apt to produce on-time arrivals.

Operational Goals Consider how Southwest's first-line managers can enhance productivity in the unloading, refueling, and cleaning of arriving planes. "One example [of productivity] customers mention all the time," said former CEO Herb Kelleher, "is if you look out the window when the airplane is taxiing toward the jetway, you see our ground crews charging before the airplane has even come to rest. Customers tell me that with other airlines nobody moves until the airplane has turned off its engines."[24]

First-line managers also make sure that seat assignments (boarding passes) are not given out until an hour before the plane is due to leave to make sure that the maximum number of passengers will be on hand to fill the seats available.

Setting SMART Goals

Anyone can define goals. But the five characteristics of a good goal are represented by the acronym SMART. A _SMART goal_ is one that is **S**pecific, **M**easurable, **A**ttainable, **R**esults-oriented, and has **T**arget dates.

Specific Goals should be stated in _specific_ rather than vague terms. The goal that "As many planes as possible should arrive on time" is too general. The goal that "Ninety percent of planes should arrive within 15 minutes of the scheduled arrival time" is specific.

Measurable Whenever possible, goals should be _measurable_, or quantifiable (as in "90% of planes should arrive within 15 minutes . . ."). That is, there should be some way to measure the degree to which a goal has been reached.

Of course, some goals—such as those concerned with improving quality—are not precisely quantifiable. In that case, something on the order of "Improve the quality of customer relations by instituting 10 follow-up telephone calls every week" will do. You can certainly quantify how many follow-up phone calls were made.

Attainable Goals should be challenging, of course, but above all they should be realistic and _attainable_. It may be best to set goals that are quite ambitious so as to challenge people to meet high standards. Always, however, the goals should be achievable within the scope of the time, equipment, and financial support available. _(See Panel 5.2.)_

If too easy (as in "half the flights should arrive on time"), goals won't impel people to make much effort. If impossible ("all flights must arrive on time, regardless of weather"), employees won't even bother trying. Or they will try and continually fail, which will end up hurting morale.

Results-Oriented It's important only a few goals be chosen—say, five for any work unit. And they should be _results-oriented_—they should support the organization's vision.

In writing out the goals, start with the word "To" and follow it with action-oriented verbs—"complete," "acquire," "increase" ("to decrease by 10% the time to get passengers settled in their seats before departure").

Some verbs should not be used in your goal statement because they imply activities—the tactics used to accomplish goals (such as having baggage handlers waiting). For example, you should not use "to develop," "to conduct," "to implement."

Target Dates Goals should specify the _target dates_ or deadline dates when they are to be attained. For example, it's unrealistic to expect an airline to improve its on-time arrivals by 10% overnight. However, you could set a target date—three to six months away, say—by which this goal is to be achieved. That allows enough time for lower-level managers and employees to revamp their systems and work habits and gives them a clear time frame in which they know what they are expected to do.

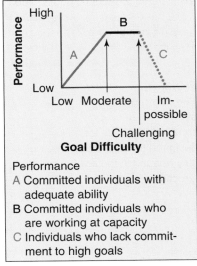

PANEL 5.2

Relationship between goal difficulty and performance[25]

Performance

A Committed individuals with adequate ability

B Committed individuals who are working at capacity

C Individuals who lack commitment to high goals

How does the planning/control cycle help keep a manager's plans headed in the right direction?

The Big Picture
The four-step planning/control cycle helps you keep in control, to make sure you're headed in the right direction.

Once you've made plans, how do you stay in control to make sure you're headed in the right direction? Actually, there is a continuous feedback loop known as the planning/control cycle. (The "organizing" and "leading" steps within the Planning-Organizing-Leading-Controlling sequence are implied here.) **The *planning/control cycle* has two planning steps (1 and 2) and two control steps (3 and 4), as follows: (1) Make the plan. (2) Carry out the plan. (3) Control the direction by comparing results with the plan. (4) Control the direction by taking corrective action in two ways—namely, (a) by correcting deviations in the plan being carried out, or (b) by improving future plans.** *(See Panel 5.3.)*

PANEL 5.3
The planning/control cycle. This describes a constant feedback loop designed to ensure plans stay headed in the right direction.[26]

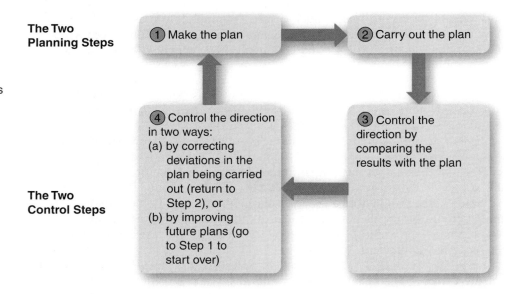

The Two Planning Steps

1 Make the plan

2 Carry out the plan

The Two Control Steps

4 Control the direction in two ways:
(a) by correcting deviations in the plan being carried out (return to Step 2), or
(b) by improving future plans (go to Step 1 to start over)

3 Control the direction by comparing the results with the plan

The planning/control cycle loop exists for each level of planning—strategic, tactical, and operational. The corrective action in Step 4 of the cycle (a) can get a project back on track before it's too late or (b) if it's too late, can provide data for improving future plans.

Example of a Faulty Planning/Control Cycle: The Golden Books Path to Bankruptcy[27]

Richard Snyder was one of the most well-known figures in book publishing—he had built Simon & Schuster into the largest U.S. publisher—when in May 1996 he became chairman and CEO of Golden Books, a publisher since 1942 of children's classics such as *Scruffy the Tugboat* and Mickey Mouse stories. However, in less than three years, the $400 million company was on the brink of bankruptcy.

What happened? **First**, there was the faulty plan. Probably the plan should have been just to stick with and improve the core business, children's books—at least at the beginning. But simply as a children's book company, says writer Michael Shnayerson, Golden held little interest for Snyder. He dreamed of taking Golden, the brand, and making an empire. Not just Golden Books for kids but also Golden books on parenting, Golden family videos, Golden play centers, even Golden theme parks.

Second, there was the faulty carrying out of the plan. While at Simon & Schuster, Snyder had published award-winning children's books that sold for $16 and up in regular bookstores. But Golden's largest customer was Wal-Mart, which treated the $1.29 books like any other class of discount consumer goods. ("We made books for the children of the masses, not the classes," said one Golden executive. "We sold tonnage.") Snyder learned a new term: fill rate—the rate at which a publisher is able to keep store shelves filled. Wal-Mart told Snyder it would be just as happy if Golden pulled out for good, since the publisher was so disorganized that it couldn't keep store shelves filled with successful books or take away those that didn't sell.

Blowing a Golden opportunity?

Third, there was flawed control of the execution of the plan (or what should have been the plan—to improve customer service with the children's books). Snyder found out that, remarkably, Golden Books had no sales reports at all. It knew how many books went out but not what happened to them. But Snyder compounded the problem by firing virtually all Golden's managers because he felt they were stuck in their ways, thereby eliminating the very mass-market children's-books veterans who might have helped him. Meanwhile, for two years, he was "flying blind," as he later admitted, because the company was without a good financial system.

Fourth, there seems to have been a lack of corrective action. Instead of concentrating on finding a quick and simple approach to the sales-report and fill-rate problems, Snyder ordered up a whole new integrated financial system that was later found to be too complex and too expensive for the company's needs. In addition, he pursued his larger brand-extending ideas for Golden. He started an adult Golden Books line (and also paid $40 million for a brand-new printing plant). He paid $81 million for a video company. He looked into Golden theme parks and Golden play centers. He moved the company's headquarters at great expense from Racine, Wisc., to New York City.

"Unfortunately," says Shayerson, "all the empire-building schemes sapped cash—eventually $300 million. And though millions of Golden books were selling, the margin of profit on each was very, very small. Much money out, very little in; quarter by quarter, the losses grew." Finally, in April 1998, it became clear that the company was going bankrupt.

major question

What is MBO, and how can it be implemented successfully to achieve results?

The Big Picture
A technique for setting goals, management by objectives (MBO) is a four-step process for motivating employees.

Click-Along 5.3

Example of MBO at Cypress Semiconductor

Do you perform better when you set goals or when you don't? What about when you set difficult goals rather than easy ones?

Research shows that if goals are made more difficult ("increase study time 30%"), people may achieve them less often than they would easy goals ("increase study time 5%"), but they nevertheless perform at a higher level. People also do better when the objectives are specific ("increase study time 10 hours a week") rather than general ("do more studying this semester").[28]

These are the kinds of matters addressed in the activity known as *management by objectives*. First suggested by **Peter Drucker** in 1954, MBO has spread largely because of the appeal of its emphasis on converting general objectives into specific ones for all members of an organization.[29]

What Is MBO? The Four-Step Process for Motivating Employees

PANEL 5.4
Three types of objectives used in MBO

Management by objectives (MBO) **is a four-step process in which (1) managers and employees jointly set objectives for the employee, (2) managers develop actions plans, (3) managers and employees periodically review the employee's performance, and (4) the manager makes a performance appraisal and rewards the employee according to results.** The purpose of MBO is to *motivate* rather than control subordinates. Let's consider the four steps.

- **Improvement objectives:** "Increase sport-ute sales by 10%." "Reduce food spoilage by 15%." Such *improvement objectives* express performance to be accomplished in a specific way for a specific area.

- **Personal development objectives:** "Attend five days of leadership training." "Learn basics of Microsoft Office XP software by June 1." *Personal development objectives* express personal goals to be realized.

- **Maintenance objectives:** "Continue to meet the increased sales goals specified last quarter." "Produce another 60,000 cases of wine this month." *Maintenance objectives* express the intention to maintain performance at previously established levels.

1 Jointly Set Objectives   You sit down with your manager and the two of you jointly set objectives for you to attain. Later you do the same with each of your own subordinates. Joint manager/subordinate participation is important to the program. It's probably best if the objectives aren't simply imposed from above ("Here are the objectives I want you to meet"). Managers also should not simply approve the employee's objectives ("Whatever you aim for is okay with me"). It's necessary to have back-and-forth negotiation to make the objectives practicable. One result of joint participation, research shows, is that it impels people to set more difficult goals—to raise the level of their aspirations—which may have a positive effect on their performance.[30] The objectives should be expressed in writing and should be SMART. There are three types of objectives, shown at left. *(See Panel 5.4.)*

2 Develop Action Plan Once objectives are set, managers at each level should prepare an action plan for attaining them. Action plans may be prepared for both individuals and for work units, such as departments.

Acting jointly. Because the point of MBO is to motivate employees, manager and employee jointly set objectives and review results.

3 Periodically Review Performance You and your manager should meet reasonably often—either informally as needed or formally every three months—to review progress, as should you and your subordinates. Indeed, frequent communication is necessary so that everyone will know how well he or she is doing in meeting the objectives.

During each meeting, managers should give employees feedback, and objectives should be updated or revised as necessary to reflect new realities. If you were managing a painting or landscaping business, for example, changes in the weather, loss of key employees, or a financial downturn affecting customer spending could force you to reconsider your objectives.

4 Give Performance Appraisal & Rewards, If Any At the end of 6 or 12 months, you and your subordinate should meet to discuss results, comparing performance with initial objectives. *Deal with results*, not personalities, emotional issues, or excuses.

Because the purpose of MBO is to *motivate* employees, performance that meets the objectives should be rewarded—with compliments, raises, bonuses, promotions, or other suitable benefits. Failure can be addressed by redefining the objectives for the next 6- or 12-month period, or even by taking stronger measures, such as demotion. Basically, however, MBO is viewed as being a learning process. After Step 4, the MBO cycle begins anew.

Cascading Objectives: MBO from the Top Down

For MBO to be successful, three things have to happen:

1 The **Commitment of Top Management Is Essential** "When top-management commitment [to MBO] was high," said one review, "the average gain in productivity was 56%. When commitment was low, the average gain in productivity was only 6%."[31]

2 It Must Be Applied Organizationwide The program has to be put in place throughout the entire organization. That is, it cannot be applied in just some divisions and departments; it has to be done in all of them.

3 Objectives Must "Cascade" MBO works by *__cascading__* **objectives down through the organization; that is, objectives are structured in a *unified hierarchy*, becoming more specific at lower levels of the organization.** Top managers set general *organizational* objectives, which are translated into *divisional* objectives, which are translated into *departmental* objectives. The hierarchy ends in *individual* objectives set by each employee.

Cascading. MBO objectives should be set by company directors and top managers and then cascade down through the organization.

Click-Along 5.4

Strengths & Limitations of MBO

What is project planning, why is it important, and what is the project life cycle?

The Big Picture

Project planning, designed to prepare single-use plans called projects, consists of a four-stage project life cycle-definition, planning, execution, and closing.

When you write a term paper, is that a *task*, a *work assignment, a program,* or a *project*—or are they all the same thing? Actually, they're different.[32]

Task or Work Assignment This is the simplest plan—it is something you (or you and others) might do using a simple "to-do" list. A term paper is a task or work assignment.

In your management career, you will direct many task/work assignments. To a contractor building a house, pouring concrete for the foundation is one example. Doing the framing is another. Installing the plumbing is another. Putting on the roof is another. And so on.

Program A program is the most complex plan—a large-scale endeavor that includes many projects. More specifically, a *program* **is defined as a single-use plan encompassing a range of projects or activities.**

For example, the U.S. government space *program* has several *projects,* including the *Challenger* project and the Hubble Telescope project. When Disney built Walt Disney World and Eurodisney, each of those were programs that included several projects (the various rides, for instance).

Project A project is in between a task and a program. **A *project* is defined as a single-use plan of less scope and complexity than a program.**

A project is unique—it is a one-time set of events. It includes numerous, complex, goal-oriented, sequenced activities aimed at delivering a product or a service. It has a start date and an end date. It has limited resources and budget. It involves many people, usually drawn from different areas of the organization.

Why Project Planning Is Important Today

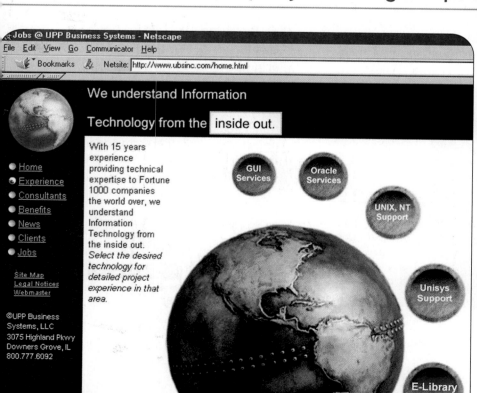

Why care about project planning? Because more and more, this is becoming the fastest way of getting things done. Technology has speeded everything up, including the process of getting a new product or service to market. To complete specific projects quickly, companies will now draw together people with different skills to work together on a temporary basis, then disband once the job is done. Since project management works outside an organization's usual chain of command, project managers need to be adept at people skills, able to communicate, motivate, and negotiate (as we discuss in later chapters).

Project management has long been a standard way of operating for movie production companies, which will pull together a talented team of people to make a film, then disband when the picture is "wrapped." It's also a familiar approach for professional sports teams, construction companies, and even some types of legal teams. However, it is just beginning to be employed by other for-profit organizations, such as manufacturers and insurance companies, as well as non-profit organizations, such as those in health care and education.

An example of project planning is the **_skunkworks_**, **the term given to a project team whose members are separated from the normal operation of an organization and asked to produce a new, innovative product.**

Example of Project Planning: Skunkworks for the IBM PC

In a skunkworks, says futurist Alvin Toffler, "a team is handed a loosely specified problem or goal, given resources, and allowed to operate outside the normal company rules. The skunkworks group thus ignores both the cubbyholes and the official channels—that is, the specialization and hierarchy of the existing corporate bureaucracy."[33]

One famous skunkworks was the project team assembled by International Business Machines to develop its first microcomputer. Rival Apple Computer, which had been launched in 1976, had by 1982 reached $583 million in sales.[34] Once the microcomputer became defined as a business machine in 1980, IBM reacted "with surprising speed" for a monolithic company, says one writer. In 1981, it launched its own version of the microcomputer, the IBM Personal Computer (a brilliant marketing stroke, incidentally, since the term "personal computer," or PC, in fact became the generic name for microcomputers).

Although IBM was the world's largest maker of computers, to get its PC to market quickly it decided to abandon its traditional slow, methodical development process. Instead, development of the PC was given to a nearly autonomous group in Boca Raton, Fla., whose members were reviewed quarterly by corporate headquarters in Armonk, N.Y., but otherwise permitted to operate as they wished. Moreover, in a significant break with corporate policy, the project team was allowed to buy hardware and software components from outside suppliers, including the microprocessor (from Intel) and the operating system (from Microsoft).[35] The result was that the skunkworks was able to deliver IBM's new microcomputer in only 12 months.

The Project Life Cycle: The Predictable Evolution of a Project

Being a project manager is a challenging job if for no other reason than that you have to be attentive both to the big picture *and* to the details. Let us therefore look at the big picture—the four-stage project life cycle that any project goes through, whether it's developing an online magazine or staging a Farm Aid music benefit.

The *project life cycle* has four stages from start to finish: **definition, planning, execution, and closing.** *(See Panel 5.5.)* As we will see, the graph of the rise and fall of the *project* life cycle resembles that for the *product* life cycle, which we discuss in Chapter 6.

PANEL 5.5

The project life cycle[36]

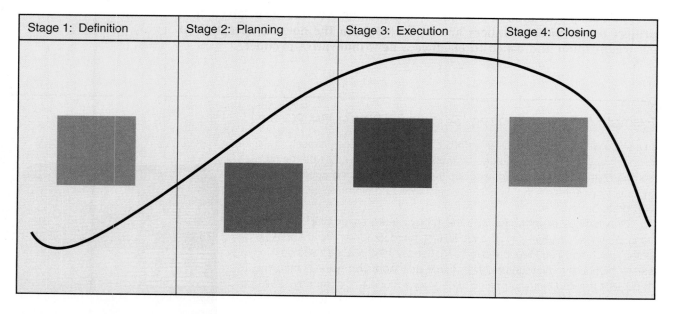

| Stage 1: Definition | Stage 2: Planning | Stage 3: Execution | Stage 4: Closing |

Stage 1 Definition

In the *definition* stage, you look at the big picture. You state the problem, look at the assumptions and risks, identify the project's goals and objectives, and determine the budget and schedule. You may also write a project proposal.

Stage 2 Planning

In the *planning* stage, you consider the details needed to make the big picture happen. You identify the facilities and equipment, the people and their duties, and the schedule and coordination efforts needed.

Stage 3 Execution

The *execution* stage is the actual work stage. You define the management style and establish the control tools. You will need to monitor progress, review the project schedule, issue change orders, and prepare status reports to the "client" (boss or customer) for whom the work is being done

Your main focus is to complete the project on time and under budget while trying to meet the client's expectations.

Stage 4 Closing

The *closing* stage occurs when the project is accepted by the client. This stage can be abrupt but could be gradual, as when you're required to install deliverables (such as a complete computer system) and carry out training.

You may also be required to write a report about the project in which you document everything that happened.

Planning. Many companies use computers to help with planning, such as CAD (computer-assisted design) systems.

Example of Project Life Cycle: Writing a Research Paper

An example of a project is the approach recommended by one college-success book for producing a research paper.[37]

Stage 1: Definition In the definition stage, you concentrate on picking a topic. That is, you set a deadline for when you will have decided on the topic, by which time you will have picked three alternative topics that are important to the instructor and interesting to you. You next refine the three proposed topics into three questions that your paper will be designed to answer. You then check the topic ideas with your instructor to see if he or she considers them satisfactory in importance and in scope.

Stage 2: Planning When writing a term paper, in your planning stage you do initial research in the library to see if there is enough material available to you so that you can adequately research your paper. You then develop a rough outline so that you know the direction your paper will take.

Stage 3: Execution When you're developing a research paper, the execution stage is the longest and most labor-intensive stage. This is when you do extensive research, sort your research notes, revise the outline to reflect changes suggested by your research, write a first draft, and then write and proofread your final draft.

Stage 4: Closing The closing stage for your research paper occurs when you hand in your paper to your "client"—your instructor.

The Importance of Project Deadlines

There's no question that college is a pressure cooker for many students. The reason, of course, is the seemingly never-ending deadlines. But consider: Would you do all the course work you're doing—and realize the education you're getting— if you *didn't* have deadlines?

As we saw under the "T" in SMART ("has Target date"), deadlines are as essential to project planning as they are to your college career. Because the whole purpose of a planned project is to deliver to a client specified results within a specified period of time, deadlines become a great motivator, both for you and for the people working for you.

It's possible, of course, to let deadlines mislead you into focusing too much on immediate results and thereby ignore project planning—just as students will focus too much on preparing for a test in one course while neglecting others. In general, however, deadlines can help you keep your eye on the "big picture" while simultaneously paying attention to the details that will help you realize the big picture. Deadlines can help concentrate the mind, so that you make quick decisions rather than put them off.

Deadlines help you ignore extraneous matters (such as cleaning up a messy desk) in favor of focusing on what's important—achieving the project on time and on budget. Deadlines provide a mechanism for giving ourselves feedback.

major question

How can break-even analysis help a manager turn a profit?

The Big Picture
A tool in the project planner's toolkit is break-even analysis, a way of identifying how much revenue is needed to cover the total costs of developing and selling a product.

If you're in a business that makes a product—toys, paint, steel, or whatever—how do you know how many items you have to sell to turn a profit? Selling 10,000 blouses for $100 each may sound impressive, but you'll literally lose your shirt if they cost $101 each to make. Here's where the tool of break-even analysis comes in. (Other tools available for project planning include flowcharts and Gannt charts. See the Appendix.)

Break-Even Analysis—How Many Items Should You Sell to Turn a Profit?

Break-even analysis **is a way of identifying how much revenue is needed to cover the total costs of developing and selling a product.** Let's walk through the computation of a break-even analysis, referring to the illustration. *(See Panel 5.6.)* We assume you are an apparel manufacturer making shirts or blouses. Start in the lower-right corner of the diagram and follow the circled numbers as you read the description on the opposite page.

PANEL 5.6
Break-even analysis

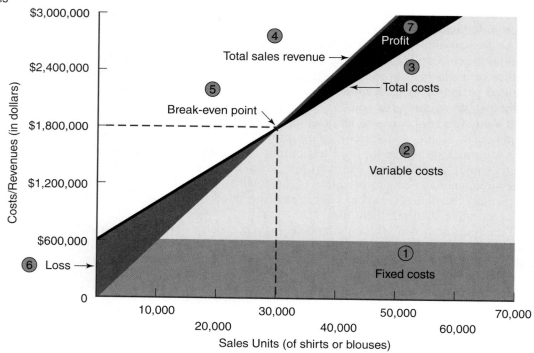

① **Fixed costs (green area):** Once you start up a business, whether you sell anything or not, you'll have expenses that won't vary much, such as rent, insurance, taxes, and perhaps salaries. These are called **fixed costs, expenses that don't change regardless of your sales or output.** Fixed costs are a function of time—they are expenses you have to pay out on a regular basis, such as weekly, monthly, or yearly. Here the chart shows the fixed costs (green area) are $600,000 per year no matter how many sales units (of shirts or blouses) you sell.

② **Variable costs (blue area):** Now suppose you start producing and selling a product, such as blouses or shirts. At this point you'll be paying for materials, supplies, labor, sales commissions, and delivery expenses. These are called **variable costs, expenses that vary directly depending on the numbers of the product that you produce and sell.** (After all, making more shirts will cost you more in cloth, for example.) Variable costs, then, are a function of volume—they go up and down depending on the number of products you make or sell. Here the variable costs (blue area) are relatively small if you sell only a few thousand shirts but they go up tremendously if you sell, say, 70,000 shirts.

③ **Total costs (first right upward-sloping line—green plus blue area added together):** The sum of the fixed costs and the variable costs equals the total costs (the green and blue areas together). This is indicated by the line that slopes upward to the right from $600,000 to $3,000,000.

④ **Total sales revenue (second right upward-sloping line):** This is the total dollars received from the sale of however many units you sell. The sales revenue varies depending on the number of units you sell. Thus, for example, if you sell 30,000 shirts, you'll receive $1,800,000 in revenue. If you sell 40,000 shirts, you'll receive somewhat more than $2,400,000 in revenue.

⑤ **Break-even point (intersection of dashed lines):** Finding this point is the purpose of this whole exercise. **The break-even point is the amount of sales revenue at which there is no profit but also no loss to your company.** On the graph, this occurs where the "Total sales revenues" line crosses the "Total costs" line, as we've indicated here where the dashed lines meet. This means that you must sell 30,000 shirts and receive $1,800,000 in revenue in order to recoup your total costs (fixed plus variable). Important note: Here is where pricing the shirts becomes important. If you raise the price per shirt, you may be able to make the same amount of money (hit your break-even point) by selling fewer of them—but that may be harder to do because customers may resist buying at the higher price.

⑥ **Loss (red area):** If you fail to sell enough shirts at the right price (the break-even point), you will suffer a loss. **Loss means your total costs exceed your total sales revenue.** As the chart shows, here you are literally "in the red"—you've lost money.

⑦ **Profit (black area):** Here you are literally "in the black"—you've made money. All the shirts you sell beyond the break-even point constitute a profit. **Profit is the amount by which total revenue exceeds total costs.** The more shirts you sell, of course, the greater the profit.

The kind of break-even analysis demonstrated here is known as the **graphic method.** The same thing can also be done algebraically.

Example of Break-Even Analysis: Why Do Airfares Vary So Much?

Why do some airlines charge four times more than others for a flight of the same distance?

There are several reasons, but break-even analysis enters into it.

United Airline's average cost for flying a passenger 1 mile in 1998 was 9.24 cents, whereas Southwest's was 7.32 cents. Those are the break-even costs. What they charged beyond that was their profit.

Why the difference? One reason, according to a study by the U.S. Department of Transportation, is that Southwest's expenses are lower (as we discussed earlier in this chapter).[38] United flies more long routes than short ones, so its costs are stretched out over more miles, making its costs for flying shorter routes higher than Southwest's.

Another factor affecting airfares is the type of passengers flying a particular route—whether they are high-fare-paying business travelers or more price-conscious leisure travelers. Business travelers often don't mind paying a lot (they are reimbursed by their companies), and those routes (such as Chicago to Cincinnati) tend to have more first-class seats, which drives up the average price. Flights to vacation spots (such as Las Vegas) usually have more low-price seats because people aren't willing to pay a lot for pleasure travel.

The entry of a discount carrier into a market will usually lower fares on that route by forcing existing major airlines to match the cheaper prices. However, says airline consultant Michael Boyd, it's usually the low-fare carriers that are to blame for setting prices below costs—below the break-even point—and running "themselves out of business."[39]

Benefits   Break-even analysis has two benefits:

- **For doing future "what-if" alternate scenarios of costs, prices, and sales:** This tool allows you to vary the different possible costs, prices, and sales quantities to do rough "what-if" scenarios to determine possible pricing and sales goals. Since the numbers are interrelated, if you change one, the others will change also.

- **For analyzing the profitability of past projects:** While break-even analysis is usually used as a tool for future projects, it can also be used retroactively to find out whether the goal of profitability was really achieved, since costs may well have changed during the course of the project. In addition, you can use it to determine the impact of cutting costs once profits flow.

Limitations   Break-even analysis is not a cure-all.

- **It oversimplifies:** In the real world, things don't happen as neatly as this model implies. For instance, fixed and variable costs are not always so readily distinguishable. Or fixed costs may change as the number of sales units goes up. And not all customers may pay the same price (some may get discounts).

- **The assumptions may be faulty:** On paper, the formula may work perfectly for identifying a product's profitability. But what if customers find the prices too high? Or what if sales figures are outrageously optimistic? In the marketplace, your price and sales forecasts may really be only good guesses.

Click-Along 5.5

Taking Something Practical Away from This Chapter: Motivation Through Goal Setting

Detail Thinkers versus Strategic Thinkers: Are You One or the Other?

When it comes to planning, are you a "big picture" person or a believer that "the importance is in the details"?

"Those with a natural inclination for either detail orientation or strategic thinking often choose jobs that allow them to rely on their preferred skills," says Intel Corp. senior manager Cheryl Shavers, who writes a column for the *San Jose Mercury News*.

Sam Walton. The Wal-Mart founder could see both the big picture ("Everyday low prices") and the small picture (greeters at store entrances, overtime pay for Sunday work, open-door management policy). No wonder Wal-Mart became the largest private employer in the U.S., with 1 million employees.

"It's no coincidence," she continues, "that manufacturing engineers have an ability to pay acute attention to detail—process flow, documentation, data—whereas technology licensing experts are likely to be strategic thinkers, focusing on long-term benefits and ramifications.[40]

So what happens when a person who is good at seeing the forest but not the trees meets up with a person who can see the trees but not the forest?

One reader wrote Shavers that he had been asked to work with a colleague to fix their flawed departmental approval process. However, the coworker was "so process driven" that he was not very open to considering anything but an improved version of the old system, whereas the other wanted to explore a more innovative approach.

While most people with the necessary skills can, with practice, learn to move from detail orientation to strategic thinking (or the reverse), there are those who are inflexible because of fears of "not getting things right" or an inability to deal with ambiguity. Or they may get so wrapped up in a new idea they often fall short on implementation.

When detail and strategic thinkers meet, suggests Shavers, it may help to strike a balance by doing the following:

- **Use a visual to focus the discussion:** Developing a flowchart or other visual can help focus the discussion on how old processes may be stretched before new approaches are introduced.

- **Consider implementation:** The practicalities of implementation should be considered before new solutions are adopted.

- **Have mutual respect:** Both parties should respect the fact that neither approach is right or wrong, only different.

Key Terms Used In This Chapter

Summary

5.1
Planning & Uncertainty

■ Planning is defined as setting goals and deciding how to achieve them. It is also defined as coping with uncertainty by formulating future courses of action to achieve specified results.

■ Two cautions to be aware of are that (1) planning requires you to set aside the time to do it, and (2) you may have to make some decisions without a lot of time to plan.

■ Planning has four benefits. (1) It helps you check your progress. (2) It helps you coordinate activities. (3) It helps you think ahead. (4) Above all, it helps you cope with uncertainty.

■ Uncertainty is of three types. (1) State uncertainty is when the environment is considered unpredictable. (2) Effect uncertainty is when the impacts of environmental changes are unpredictable. (3) Response uncertainty is when the consequences of a decision are uncertain.

■ Organizations respond to uncertainty in one of four ways, becoming defenders, prospectors, analyzers, or reactors. (1) Defenders are expert at producing and selling narrowly defined products or services. (2) Prospectors focus on developing new products or services and in seeking out new markets, rather than

waiting for things to happen. (3) Analyzers let other organizations take the risks of product development and marking and then imitate (or perhaps slightly improve on) what seems to work best. (4) Reactors make adjustments only when finally forced to by environmental pressures.

5.2
Fundamentals of Planning

■ An organization's reason for being is expressed in a mission statement. What the organization wishes to become and where it wants to go strategically—that is, its clear sense of the future and the actions needed to get there—is expressed in a vision statement.

■ From these are derived strategic planning, then tactical planning, then operational planning. In strategic planning, managers determine what the organization's long-term goals should be for the next 1–10 years with the resources they expect to have available. In tactical planning, managers determine what contributions their departments or similar work units can make with their given resources during the next 6 months to 2 years. In operation planning, they determine how to accomplish specific tasks with available resources within the next 1-week to 1-year period.

- Whatever its type—strategic, tactical, or operational—the purpose of planning is to achieve a goal. A goal, also known as an objective, is a specific commitment to achieve a measurable result within a stated period of time. The goal should be followed by an action plan, which defines the course of action needed to achieve the stated goal.

- As with planning, goals are of the same three types—strategic, tactical, and operational. Also, like planning, goals are arranged in a hierarchy known as a means-end chain because in the chain of management (operational, tactical, strategic) the accomplishment of low-level goals are the means leading to the accomplishment of high-level goals or ends.

- Strategic goals are set by and for top management and focus on objectives for the organization as a whole. Tactical goals are set by and for middle managers and focus on the actions needed to achieve strategic goals. Operational goals are set by and for first-line managers and are concerned with short-term matters associated with realizing tactical goals.

- The five characteristics of a good goal are represented by the acronym SMART. A SMART goal is one that is Specific, Measurable, Attainable, Results oriented, and has Target dates. Goals should be stated in specific rather than vague terms. They should be measurable or quantifiable. They should be realistic or attainable. They should be results-oriented—support the organization's vision. They should specify target dates or deadline dates when they are to be attained.

5.3
The Planning/Control Cycle

- Once plans are made, managers must stay in control to ensure they're headed in the right direction. The means for doing so is through the continuous feedback loop known as the planning/control cycle. The planning/control cycle has two planning steps (1 and 2) and two control steps (3 and 4), as follows: (1) Make the plan. (2) Carry out the plan. (3) Control the direction by comparing results with the plan. (4) Control the direction by taking corrective action in two ways—namely, (a) by correcting deviations in the

plan being carried out, or (b) by improving future plans. The planning/control cycle loop exists for each level of planning—strategic, tactical, and operational.

5.4
Promoting Goal Setting: Management by Objectives

- Management by objectives (MBO) is a four-step process in which (1) managers and employees jointly set objectives for the employee, (2) managers develop action plans, (3) managers and employees periodically review the employee's performance, and (4) the manager makes a performance appraisal and rewards the employee according to results. The purpose of MBO is to *motivate* rather than control subordinates.

- For MBO to be successful three things have to happen. (1) The commitment of top management is essential. (2) The program must be applied organizationwide. (3) Objectives must cascade—objectives must be structured in a unified hierarchy, becoming more specific at lower levels of the organization. Top managers set organizational objectives, which are translated into divisional objectives, which are translated in departmental objectives. The hierarchy ends in individual objectives set by each employee.

5.5
Project Planning

- Tasks (work assignments) must be distinguished from programs and from projects. A task is simply something one does. A program is a single-use plan encompassing a range of projects or activities. A project, which appears between a task and a program, is a single-use plan of less scope and complexity than a program; it is a one-time set of events.

- Project planning is becoming the fastest way of getting things done. Project management works outside an organization's usual chain of command. An example of project planning is the skunkworks, the term given to a project team whose members are separated from the normal operation of an organization and asked to produce a new, innovative product.

- A project evolves through a project life cycle involving four stages from start to finish: definition, planning, execution, and closing. (1) In the definition stage, a project manager looks at the big picture, stating the problem, identifying the project's goals and objectives, and determining the budget and schedule. (2) In the planning stage, managers consider the details needed to make the big picture happen, such as identifying equipment, people, and coordination efforts needed. (3) In the execution stage, the actual work stage, managers define the management style and establish the control tools, then ensure the work is being done on time and under budget. (4) In the closing stage, the project is accepted by the client.

- Deadlines are essential to project planning because they become great motivators both for the manager and for subordinates.

5.6
A Project-Planning Tool: Break-Even Analysis

- One tool in the project planner's toolbox is break-even analysis, a way of identifying how much revenue is needed to cover the total costs of developing and selling a product.

- Among the components of break-even analysis are fixed costs, variable costs, total costs, total sales revenue, the break-even point, loss and profit.

- Fixed costs are expenses that don't change regardless of sales or output. Variable costs are expenses that vary directly depending on the numbers of the product that is produced and sold. Total costs are the sum of the fixed costs and the variable costs. Total sales revenue is the total dollars received from the sale of however many units are being sold; sales revenue varies depending on the number of units sold. The break-even point is the amount of sales revenue at which there is no profit but also no loss to the company. Loss means the total costs exceed the total sales revenue. Profit is the amount by which total revenue exceeds total costs.

- Break-even analysis has two benefits. (1) It allows you to do future "what-if" alternate scenarios of costs, prices, and sales. (2) It allows you to analyze the profitability of past projects.

- It also has limitations: (1) Break-even analysis oversimplifies. (2) The assumptions underlying the formula may be faulty.

Management In Action

Mondavi's French Venture Goes Sour

Excerpted from William Echikson, "How Mondavi's French Venture Went Sour," Business Week, *September 3, 2001, p. 60.*

BusinessWeek David Pearson loves wine and France. The San Diego native studied oenology at the University of California and spent a year after graduation working as an intern on French wine estates. So when Robert Mondavi Corp. asked him in 1998 to head up its Vichon Mediterranean subsidiary, the fresh-faced, French-speaking, 39-year-old Pearson crossed the Atlantic and settled in Southern France. In a hard-pressed region best known for producing oceans of cheap wine, he was confident that New World money and technology could produce superb bottles selling for $60 or more.

But [in August 2001], the energetic American packed up his belongings and returned to California. An unlikely coalition of local farmers, ecologists, hunters, and communists had painted him as a capitalist plotter and succeeded in killing his ambitious $7.5 million plan to acquire 120 acres of prime grape-growing land on an untamed Mediterranean hillside. . . .

Pearson spent his first two years conducting geological surveys to locate top-quality wine real estate. He needed a large tract to produce 260,000 bottles a year, the minimum number that made economic sense for a giant such as Mondavi. He finally settled on a swath of hillside above the 2,000-person village of Aniane, about 15 miles northwest of the regional center of Montpellier. . . . In July, 2000, Aniane's town council voted to give Mondavi a 99-year lease.

A violent backlash ensued. Hunters worried that planting vineyards would frighten away the wild boar. Environmentalists railed against razing a forest. Pearson sipped pastis with the locals, reassuring them that the company intended to plant small "islands" of vines and leave much of the natural scrubland untouched. Hunters, he promised, still could roam the the hillside during autumn.

But the American couldn't shake off one far-reaching charge—that the invading Anglo-Saxons would destroy the village's social cohesion and deform traditional winemaking methods, imposing an alien, money-grubbing industrial model. Leading this crusade was Aimé Guibert, a former businessman whose glove factory had been driven into bankruptcy by Asian competition and whose Mas de Daumas Gassac vineyard produces an internationally renowned red. The 76-year-old Guibert eschews pesticides, harvests his grapes by hand, and traces the origins of his vines back to Palestine at the time of Jesus Christ. "The Mondavis will end up destroying our traditional artisans who make wine, just like McDonald's is destroying French gastronomy," Guibert thunders.

In March municipal elections, Aniane's voters threw out the town council and elected as mayor an anti-Mondavi communist, Manuel Diaz. Diaz denounced Mondavi as a menacing multinational similar to Marks & Spencer, which was throwing thousands of French workers out of jobs in order to invest more in its British stores. "When we heard what he was saying, we knew there was no point in staying," Pearson says. In May, Mondavi canceled the vineyard project and is preparing to sell its Vichon brand.

Back in Aniane, winegrowers are suffering. Almost 15% of last year's harvest remains unsold. Mayors of 30 other French villages have written Mondavi seeking investment. But it's too late. "For now, we've decided it is too difficult to make wine in France," Pearson says.

For Discussion

1. If planning is coping with uncertainty, what kind of uncertainty were Mondavi and Pearson dealing with—state, effect, or response?

2. Which adjective best describes Mondavi's approach to uncertainty—defender, prospector, analyzer, or reactor?

3. Would you say that Pearson's goals were SMART goals?

4. In the planning/control cycle, what should Pearson have done to have had a better chance of success?

Take It to the Net

As this chapter described, planning is one of the foundation principles of management. Planning is critical not only for organizations but for you as an individual trying to succeed in an ever-evolving workplace. Futurists say that a great many jobs people will do in the next 20 years don't exist today. But by planning in a general way—gathering knowledge, honing your skills, learning to think critically—you can enhance your effectiveness.

The following online self-assessment from the Brefi Group of the UK helps you evaluate where you are now so you can plan how to improve your personal effectiveness. Go to *http://www.corporate feedback.co.uk/training_needs_analysis.html* Click

on Personal Effectiveness. Log on, take the test, and then submit your answers for analysis. Once you receive the analysis, go back to the questions and use the feedback to think what plans you might now make.

Questions

1. What useful information did you receive from the questionnaire and your results? Explain.

2. Do you think that others might benefit from this type of self-knowledge? Why or why not?

3. How can you improve your personal effectiveness? Explain.

Self-Assessment

Holland Personality Types & You: Matching Your Personality to the Right Work Environment & Occupation*

Objectives

1. To understand the need to plan for your career.
2. To try to match your personality with an occupation.

Introduction: What do you want to be when you grow up? Some people seem to know early in life. Others come to a realization in college. Still others may be forced to such awareness by a crisis in later life, such as being dismissed from a job. Of course, most of us make some sort of plans for our careers. But in doing so we may not always be knowledgeable about how to match our personalities with the choices available.

Instructions: There are four parts to this exercise.

First, you are to select a number from the list of seven personality types.

Second, you are to match that choice with the personality you think that type would have.

Third, you are to select the work environment you think would be best for that personality type and personality.

Fourth, based on the preceding three choices, you are to select which occupation would fit best. (For example, if you selected #1, C, and f, the best fit for an occupation would be artist, musical conductor, and other related occupations.)

Try to connect each of the four parts and then check the key to see if your pairings are correct. After that, go through the list again, identifying what you think your personality type is, what your personality is, the work environment you like or think you would like best, and then the occupation that you would or do like best. See if there is an alignment by using the scoring guidelines and interpretation shown below; if there is such an alignment, this suggests you may be on your way to a successful career.

Personality Type

1. Artistic
2. Conventional
3. Realistic
4. Enterprising
5. Social
6. Investigative

Personality

A. Prefers to work with things; is present oriented, athletic, and mechanical.

B. Is analytical, a problem solver, scientific, and original.

C. Relies on feelings and imagination, is expressive, is intuitive, and values esthetics.

D. Sensitive to needs of others, enjoys interpersonal gatherings, and values educational and social issues.

E. Adventurous, leadership, persuasive, and values political and economic matters.

F. Structured, accurate, detail-oriented, and loyal followers.

Work Environments

a. Technical/mechanical and industrial.

b. Traditional and rewards conformity and dependability.

c. Cooperative and rewards personal growth.

d. Managerial role in organizations and rewards monetary gains and achievements.

e. Rewards high academic achievement and uses technical abilities to complete tasks.

f. Unstructured and allows nonconformity and rewards creativity.

Occupations

7. Chemist/biological scientists, computer analyst, and emergency medical technicians.

8. Lawyers, flight attendants, sales representatives, reporters.

9. Accountants, bank tellers, medical record technicians.

10. Cooks, drywall installers, auto mechanics.

11. Artists/commercial artists, musical directors, architects, writers/editors.

12. Teachers, clergy, nurses, counselors, librarians.

Scoring Guidelines & Interpretation

Scoring is as follows:

1. 1-C-f-11
2. 2-F-b-9
3. 3-A-a-10
4. 4-E-d-8
5. 5-D-c-12
6. 6-B-e-7

The purpose of this type of exercise is to see how personality type, personality, work environment, and occupation can best fit together. When the elements mesh, you will usually feel more competent and more satisfied with your work conditions and occupation. When these elements or factors are mismatched, one can be very frustrated, feel incompetent, or not be good at one's job.

If you wish to know more about career planning, you can avail yourself of a much more in-depth planning process at *http://www.soice.state.nc.us/sociss/planning/jh-types.htm.*

Questions for Discussion

1. Does your assessment suggest that your career choice is best for your personality type? How do you feel about this assessment?

2. What do you think the management challenges are for those who are mismatched in their work? Explain.

3. Can you see and describe yourself more clearly in terms of personality type, personality, work environment and occupation given the results of your scoring? Explain.

*Developed by Anne C. Cowden, Ph.D., based on the information provided by the website *http://www.soice.state.nc.us/sociss/planning/jh-types.htm*

Group Exercise

Trying to Solve an "Electric" Problem in Managerial Planning*

Objectives

1. To assess a specific problem where planning is required.
2. To arrive at a mutual and effective solution as a group, taking into consideration different perspectives and different goals.

Introduction

Increasingly problems are being solved by groups of people, each with a different stake in the outcome. However, for a company to achieve its goals successfully, these problems must be solved without alienating members of the group.

Scenario

The company, a large processing center operating in a highly bureaucratic fashion, was experiencing challenging problems in a major division of its operations. Fifteen months earlier, when an electrical storm caused loss of power in one company building, five of the seven members of the night-shift *service staff* reported strange sensations emanating from their computer terminals causing tingling in their hands. In the following days, other staff members reported similar sensations, as well as numbness, headaches, and nausea. Two weeks later there were almost 100 reports of such "electrical shocks." Union representatives requested immediate action on the problems. The issues of workplace health and safety at the company became a hot topic in the local media. Various health and government agencies began to investigate.

Reports of the shocks continued sporadically for the next nine months, then began to rise significantly. During a 10-week period, there were more than 150 reports, many from people working in other parts of the company. The ensuing uproar produced a walkout lasting three days, costing the company an estimated $1 million in lost revenue. The problem didn't seem to be solvable simply by top managers' exercising their authority and dictating a solution. What could be done to get the company back on the right track?

Instructions

The class should divide into groups of seven people each. Within each group, each person should assume one of the roles described below. Take turns discussing the case from each of the seven perspectives, with each person staying within his or her role, until your group has solved the problem by consensus. The goal of the group is to arrive at a solution that will get the company moving efficiently and effectively again.

Roles: The Perspectives of the Positions Involved

1. **Senior management:** "We don't need this problem. We have to restore normal levels of control and efficiency, based on measured results."

2. **The ergonomists:** "There are some routine ergonomic problems that can be improved through the physical redesign of equipment. But there is no evidence of major health and safety problems."

3. **Labor leaders:** "This mess has got to be cleared up. The health and safety features are critical. Management has to take action, but we don't trust them. We are strong and can apply a lot of pressure if necessary."

4. **The politicians:** "We don't want more media coverage on this one and more charges of mismanagement that consume our time. We don't want the unions asking us to solve their problems."

5. **The services staff:** "We're working with a poor system. We don't want the strain and stress. Management has to sort the situation out. More stress breaks. Safer equipment. Find the 'techies' that are 'zapping us.'"

6. **The human resources people:** "The problem rests with the stressful nature of the work itself. We need to redesign the work process. We also need to deal with the collective stress phenomenon that's emerged."

7. **Line managers:** "The situation has changed on us. We're held accountable, but we don't have the power to deliver. We need to get better informed and to learn new skills for managing in a turbulent world."

Questions for Discussion

1. How did your group resolve the situation? Explain.

2. How did you feel, as you had to stay "in role" and respond from that position's perspective?

3. How difficult do you think it is it for people to see each other's perspectives and manage a situation? Explain.

4. How would you manage people who are in conflict about a situation such as the one presented above? Describe.

* Written by Anne C. Cowden, Ph.D.; adapted from a case in Gareth Morgan, *Imaginization: The Art of Creative Management* (Newbury Park, Calif.: Sage, 1993), Chapter 5.

Ethical Dilemma

Retention Bonuses Are Used for Management Employees at Kmart

Joann S. Lublin, "As Their Companies Crumbled, Some CEOs Got Big-Money Payouts,"
The Wall Street Journal, February 26, 2002, p. B4.

In a clear sign of board dissatisfaction, Kmart Corp. directors dismissed their leader, Charles C. Conaway, as chairman last month [January 2002]. The demotion occurred five days before the Troy, Mich., discount chain filed for bankruptcy protection.

Yet Mr. Conaway still runs Kmart. The company values its CEO so much that it has sought bankruptcy court approval to pay him a bonus of $6.5 million and forgive a $5 million loan it gave him as long as he still works for Kmart on July 31, 2003. Mr. Conaway will receive the same deal if the retailer fires him without cause before then.

It's all part of a proposed stay-put package covering 9,700 management employees. The retention program "is typical of what companies do to keep key talent during bankruptcy," says Jack Ferry, a

Kmart spokesman. The program could cost up to about $200 million, a company filing with the bankruptcy court says.

The planned management-retention rewards outrage many Kmart workers, however. "Retention bonuses need to be going to the (rank-and-file) people who are doing the work," insists Dollene Skanes, a warehouse employee at a Kmart distribution center.

Ms. Skanes heads a local for Unite, a union that has filed objections to the retention plan with the bankruptcy court. Kmart seeks to rush its program through, the filing said, even though "thousands of bargaining units and other employees have been laid off and are sustaining momentous personal or business losses."

Solving the Dilemma

What would you do if you were the presiding judge in the bankruptcy court?

1. Allow the retention bonuses to be paid as proposed by Kmart management.

2. Not allow any retention bonuses because the company is bankrupt.

3. Allow retention bonuses equitably for both managers and rank-and-file employees.

4. Invent other options. Discuss.

CHAPTER 6

Strategic Management
How Star Managers Realize a Grand Design

MAJOR QUESTIONS YOU SHOULD BE ABLE TO ANSWER

6.1 The Dynamics of Strategic Planning

Major Question: Am I really managing if I don't have a strategy?

6.2 The Strategic-Management Process

Major Question: What's the five-step recipe for the strategic-management process?

6.3 Establishing the Grand Strategy

Major Question: How can SWOT and forecasting help me establish my strategy?

6.4 Formulating Strategy

Major Question: How can two techniques—Porter's competitive strategies and the product life cycle—help me formulate strategy?

6.5 Carrying Out & Controlling Strategy

Major Question: How can two techniques—balanced scorecard and measurement management—help me carry out and control strategy?

WHAT DOES THE SUCCESSFUL TOP MANAGER DO TO STAY SUCCESSFUL?

"Management tools are not silver bullets. They are more like chain saws—potentially powerful when applied to the right problems but extraordinarily dangerous in the wrong hands."

So writes Darrell K. Rigby, who should know.[1] A director of Bain & Co., he prepares that consulting firm's annual Management Tools and Techniques survey, a multiyear research project concerning the usage and satisfaction levels of such tools and techniques among managers.

You may have already heard such buzz words as *reengineering, knowledge management,* and *activity-based costing.* But according to Bain & Co.'s 1998 survey of top managers in 15 countries, those three tools, once considered hot, are among "the most dangerous in the wrong hands."

■ **Lesson #1—In an era of management fads, strategic planning is still tops:** The lesson here, as Rigby points out, is that management tools and techniques "are to some extent fashion items," becoming popular or unpopular as intellectual and economic currents change. Today's two most popular tools are *strategic planning,* favored by 90% of the senior managers surveyed, and *mission and vision statements,* favored by 87%. Strategic planning is concerned with developing a comprehensive program for long-term success. Mission statements describe the organization's purpose, and vision statements describe its intended long-term goal.

■ **Lesson #2—A manager's most valuable character trait: be willing to make large, painful decisions to suddenly alter strategy:** But there's another lesson. In a world of rapid and discontinuous change, managers must always be prepared to make large, painful decisions and radically alter their business design—the very basis of how the company makes money. Today, say two consultants with Boston's Mercer Management Consulting, "a static business model is death."[2]

Intel, for example, used to make memory chips. When that began to look like a hypercompetitive commodity business (a commodity is a mass-produced, unspecialized product), Intel switched to making processor chips. When processors were threatened with becoming commodities, it began marketing them as branded consumer products ("Intel Inside!"). When General Electric chairman Jack Welch foresaw that the profitability of aircraft engines and appliances was dropping, he steered the company into financing, serving, and maintaining these products.[3] Because of fast-spreading world conditions such as the threat of products becoming commodities, rapidly increasing productivity, and global overcapacity, managers must be able to make difficult decisions: "exiting businesses, firing people, admitting you were wrong (or at least not omniscient)," as writer Geoffrey Colvin puts it. "So the future will demand ever more people with the golden trait, the fortitude to accept and even seek psychic pain."[4]

Many managers think they can make painful decisions about things that obviously need doing. But, Colvin points out, "those with the far greater courage to make unpleasant decisions based on what they see that *no one else sees*—these people will dominate." These decisions are at the very heart of strategic management.

FORECAST: WHAT'S AHEAD IN THIS CHAPTER

We describe strategic management and strategic planning and why they're important. We go through the five steps in the strategic-management process. Then we show how grand strategy is developed, using two strategic-planning tools—SWOT analysis and forecasting. Next we show how strategy is formulated, using such techniques as Porter's four competitive strategies and product life cycles. Finally, we show how strategy is carried out and controlled.

Am I really managing if I don't have a strategy?

The Big Picture

This section distinguishes among strategy, strategic management, and strategic planning. We describe three reasons why strategic management and strategic planning are important and how they may work for both large and small firms.

Is thinking strategically really necessary?

After all, in the 1970s and 1980s, Japanese companies rarely developed strategic positions. Instead, they pioneered in what is known as *operational effectiveness*, which means they learned to perform *similar* activities *better* than rivals performed them. Through such practices as total quality management and continuous improvement, Japanese manufacturers gained substantial cost and quality advantages, and for many years they appeared unstoppable.

But most Japanese companies try to imitate one another, so that competitors match one another's plant designs, employ the same distribution channels, and offer most of the same product features and varieties. In the 1990s, as the gap narrowed in operational effectiveness, these companies found themselves engaged in mutually destructive battles. Now they are having to learn strategic positioning—that is, to perform activities that are *different* from those of their rivals or similar activities that are performed in *different* ways.[5]

In this section, we do the following:

■ Define strategy and strategic management,

■ Explain why strategic planning is important,

■ Discuss strategic management in large versus small firms.

Operational effectiveness, not strategic effectiveness. Japanese makers of television sets have been more apt to imitate each other than to do strategic planning. When you buy a TV set made in Japan, do you see any difference among those made by Sony, Toshiba, or Panasonic?

Strategy, Strategic Management, & Strategic Planning: What They Are, Why They're Important

Every organization needs to have a "big picture" about where it's going and how to get there. These are matters of strategy, strategic management, and strategic planning.

Strategy A *strategy* **is a large-scale action plan that sets the direction for an organization.** It represents an "educated guess" about what must be done in the long term for the survival or prosperity of the organization or its principal parts.

We hear the word expressed in terms like "Budweiser's ultimate strategy . . ." or "Visa's overseas strategy . . ." or *financial strategy, marketing strategy,* and *human resource strategy.*

An example of a strategy is "Find out what customers want, then provide it to them as cheaply and quickly as possible" (the strategy of Wal-Mart). As we stated in this chapter's introduction, however, strategy is not something that can be decided on just once. Because of fast-changing conditions, it needs to be revisited from time to time, whether every year or every five years.

Strategic Management In the late 1940s, most large U.S. companies were organized around a single idea or product line. By the 1970s, Fortune 500 companies were operating in more than one industry and had expanded overseas.[6] It became apparent that to stay focused and efficient, companies had to begin taking a strategic-management approach.

Strategic management **is a process that involves managers from all parts of the organization in the formulation and the implementation of strategies and strategic goals.** This definition doesn't mean that managers at the top dictate ideas to be followed by people lower down. Indeed, precisely because middle managers are the ones who will be asked to understand and implement the strategies, they should also help to formulate them.[7] The steps in this process are covered in Section 6.2.

Strategic Planning *Strategic planning*, as we stated in Chapter 5, determines not only the organization's long-term goals for the next 1–5 years regarding growth and profits but also the ways the organization should achieve them.

As Bryan W. Barry, author of *Strategic Planning Workbook for Nonprofit Organizations*, states: "Strategic planning is the process of determining what your organization intends to accomplish, and how you will direct the organization and its resources toward accomplishing these goals in the coming months and years."[8]

Why Strategic Management & Strategic Planning Are Important

There are three reasons why an organization should adopt strategic management and strategic planning: They can (1) provide *direction and momentum*, (2) *encourage new ideas*, and above all (3) *develop a sustainable competitive advantage*.[9] Let's consider these three matters.

Rojo intenso. "The style for this fall: intense red," the ad reads. Using strategic management and strategic planning, Ford Motor Co. sells its cars all over the world.

La moda de este otoño: **rojo intenso.**

destaka
Información y prueba **902 442 442** o www.ford.es

ford**ka** collection *Ford*

1 Providing Direction & Momentum "Leaders of some groups become so preoccupied with day-to-day pressures," says Bryan Barry, "that their organizations lose momentum." Strategic planning can help people focus on the most critical problems, choices, and opportunities. If everyone is involved in the process, that can also help create teamwork, promote learning, and build commitment across the organization.

Unless a strategic plan is in place, managers may well focus on just whatever is in front of them, the usual run-of-the-mill problems—until they get an unpleasant jolt when a competitor moves out in front because it has been able to take a long-range view of things and act more quickly. Recently this surprise has been happening over and over as companies have had an attack of Internet anxiety because some upstart online company suddenly emerged as a threat—as Schwab.com did to Merrill Lynch, and Amazon.com did to Barnes & Noble.[10]

But there are many other instances in which a big company didn't take a competitor seriously (as Sears didn't Wal-Mart, IBM didn't Microsoft, and GM didn't Toyota). "We were five years late in recognizing that [microbreweries] were going to take as much market as they did," says August Busch III, CEO of massive brewer Anheuser-Busch, "and five years late in recognizing we should have joined them."[11]

Of course, a poor plan can send an organization in the wrong direction. Bad planning usually results from faulty assumptions about the future, poor assessment of an organization's capabilities, ineffective group dynamics, and information overload.[12]

2 Encouraging New Ideas Some people object that planning can foster rigidity, that it creates blinders that block out peripheral vision and reduces creative thinking and action. "Setting oneself on a predetermined course in unknown waters," says one critic, "is the perfect way to sail straight into an iceberg."[13]

Actually, far from being a straitjacket for new ideas, strategic planning can help encourage them by stressing the importance of innovation in achieving long-range success. Gary Hamel, head of Strategos, an international consulting firm specializing in strategy, says that companies such as Nike have been successful because they have been able to unleash the spirit of "strategy innovation." Strategy innovation, he says, is "the ability to reinvent the basis of competition within existing industries and to invent entirely new industries."

Some successful innovators are companies creating new wealth in the grocery business, where Starbucks Coffee, Trader Joe's, Petco, ConAgra, and Wal-Mart, for example, have developed entirely new product categories and retailing concepts. For instance, says Hamel, Starbucks "took a sleepy supermarket commodity—coffee—and began selling it in infinite varieties in trendy stores, thereby establishing a whole new market."[14]

3 Developing a Sustainable Competitive Advantage Strategic management provides a sustainable *competitive advantage*, which, you'll recall (from Chapter 1), is the ability of an organization to produce goods or services more effectively than its competitors do, thereby outperforming them. Sustainable competitive advantage occurs when an organization is able to get and stay ahead in four areas: (1) in being responsive to customers, (2) in innovating, (3) in quality, and (4) in effectiveness.

Five years late. Not having a strategic plan for taking competitors seriously, big brewer Anheuser–Busch, maker of Budweiser, Busch, and Michelob, was slow to recognize the inroads being made by "boutique" or microbrewery beers, such as those shown here. Now Anheuser-Busch also offers specialty beers, such as Red Wolf Lager and Ziegenboch Amber. Are there any trends that you see that you think are going unnoticed by major companies who could capitalize on them?

Example of Developing Competitive Advantage: Swatch Brings Watch-Making Back to Switzerland

An example of developing competitive advantage is that originated by Nicolas G. Hayek, who brought watch-making back to Switzerland by turning out low-cost plastic Swatch watches that were fashion and art statements as much as timepieces. In addition, Hayek created a product pyramid or "birthday cake," as he calls it, with Brequet, Blancpain, Jaquet Droz, Glashutte-Original/Union, Leon Hatot, and Omega as luxury brands on top; Tixxot, Calvin Klein, Certina, Mido, Balmain, and Hamilton in the middle; and Swatch, Flik Flak, and Endura in the basic layer. "Swatch serves as his 'firewall brand,'" says one account, "making it difficult for competitors to get a toehold and use it to take away potential buyers of his more expensive offerings. That protection was overlooked by Detroit auto makers who ceded the low-end, entry-model car market to the Japanese, who later moved up the product pyramid to capture many luxury-car buyers."[15]

Does Strategic Management Work for Small as Well as Large Firms?

You would expect that a large organization, with its thousands of employees and even larger realm of "stakeholders," would benefit from strategic management and planning. After all, how can a huge company such as Ford Motor Co. run without some sort of grand design?

But what about smaller companies, which account for more than half of total employment and the bulk of employment growth in recent years? One analysis of several studies found that strategic planning was appropriate not just for large firms—companies with fewer than 100 employees could benefit as well, although the improvement in financial performance was small. Nevertheless, the researchers concluded, "it may be that the small improvement in performance is not worth the effort involved in strategic planning unless a firm is in a very competitive industry where small differences in performance may affect the firm's survival potential."[16]

Pierogi makers. From left, brothers Tom, Ted, and Tim Twardzik, whose company, Ateeco Inc., of Shenandoah, Pa., produces Mrs. T's Pierogies, have made a success by going after an ethnic market that food giants such as Kraft and Nestlé have largely ignored. (Pierogies are dumplings filled with cheese, onions, potatoes, sauerkraut, and sometimes roasted garlic or jalapeños.) Founder Ted Twardzik, their father, expanded the company by deemphasizing pierogies' Polish origins and stressing them as "child-friendly food" for fussy eaters. Is this good enough strategic planning?

What's the five-step recipe for the strategic-management process?

The Big Picture

The strategic-management process has five steps: Establish the mission and the vision, establish the grand strategy, formulate the strategic plans, carry out those plans, and maintain strategic control. In addition, all the steps may be affected by feedback that enables the taking of constructive action.

When is a good time to begin the strategic-management process? Often it's touched off by some crisis.

Coca-Cola was compelled to do serious soul searching when in 1985 buyers turned away in droves from its New Coke, one of the worst marketing disasters in history. For Clorox Co., the crisis came in 1988, when it introduced a line of powdered detergents, which was rejected by consumers who not only favored liquid detergents but also identified Clorox with bleach. And the backers of the DVD were confronted by the Divx disk.

Example of a Crisis Leading to the Strategic-Management Process: The Video-Disk War—DVD versus Divx

Every new technology must overcome resistance. And the DVD, short for digital video disk, had some major hurdles.[17]

First, the VCR was perhaps the most popular consumer-electronics product in a generation. The DVD, intended to replace it, not only cost more, it offered few new features. Second, just as the DVD was beginning to sell, in 1997 a rival disk appeared, the Divx, backed by the huge electronics chain of Circuit City Stores (along with a Hollywood law firm). The key idea behind Divx was that it would be a movie-on-a disk that could offer an alternative to renting VCR videotapes. Consumers could buy a disk with a movie on it for the price of a video rental, then have 48 hours in which to view it. After that, they could choose between simply throwing the disk away or paying an extra $15—billed by Divx directly to their credit card. This credit-card fee authorized the company's central computer, through a modem connection to the customer's home computer—to grant outright ownership for unlimited viewing, thereby obviating further rental fees at video stores.

The crisis forced DVD backers, led by Warner Home Video, to reexamine their business design. They were able to take advantage of three external factors. First, only 750 of some 10,000 electronics stores nationwide agreed to carry Divx, most not wishing to boost the revenues of rival Circuit City. Second, only three manufacturers agreed to make Divx players, mainly because they didn't wish to offend the mammoth retailer. Third, video stores realized the Divx would cut their rentals in half, so they started offering DVD rentals.

The DVD strategy for success was based on forming an alliance among Hollywood movie studios, hardware makers, and retailers. Hollywood wanted not only better image and audio quality but also longer playing time and a parental "lockout" feature. As the film studios began making more and more movies available on DVD, Toshiba, Sony, and other DVD hardware manufacturers began slicing prices and pouring millions into promotion, including giving away five DVDs with every player sold.

In June 1999, after losing $375 million, Circuit City announced it was discontinuing Divx.

The next challenge for DVD: how to deal with technology that will deliver rental movies over the Internet.

The Five Steps of the Strategic-Management Process

The strategic-management process has five steps, plus a feedback loop, as shown below. *(See Panel 6.1.)* Let's consider these five steps.

PANEL 6.1
The strategic-management process. The process has five steps.

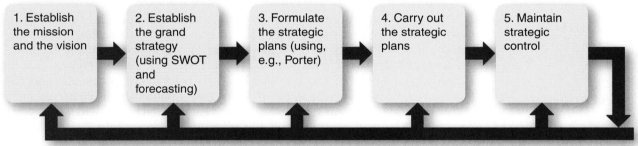

Feedback: Revise actions, if necessary, based on feedback

Step 1 **Establish the Mission & the Vision** We discussed mission and vision in Chapter 5. If you were called on to write a mission statement and a vision statement, how would you go about it?

Characteristics of a Good Mission Statement The *mission*, you'll recall, is the organization's purpose or reason for being, and it is expressed in a *mission statement*. For example, the mission statement of McGraw-Hill, publisher of this book, is

> *To serve the worldwide need for knowledge at a fair profit by gathering, evaluating, producing, and distributing valuable information in a way that benefits our customers, employees, authors, investors, and our society.*

Mission statements answer some or all of the following questions:[18]

1 Who are our customers?

2 What are our major products or services?

3 In what geographical areas do we compete?

4 What is our basic technology?

5 What is our commitment to economic objectives?

6 What are our basic beliefs, values, aspirations, and philosophical priorities?

7 What are our major strengths and competitive advantages?

8 What are our public responsibilities, and what image do we wish to project?

9 What is our attitude toward our employees?

Family business. Do small, family-owned businesses need a vision statement? If yes, what should the one for Branch's Driving School convey? If no, why not?

Characteristics of a Good Vision Statement An organization's vision, you'll recall, is its long-term goal describing what it wants to become. It is expressed in a *vision statement*, which describes its long-term direction and strategic intent. For example, Walt Disney's original vision for Disneyland went in part like this:

Disneyland will be something of a fair, an exhibition, a playground, a community center, a museum of living facts, and a showplace of beauty and magic. It will be filled with the accomplishments, the joys and hopes of the world we live in. And it will remind us and show us how to make those wonders part of our own lives.[19]

A Chicago company that produces artistic architectural woodwork produced a vision statement that stated it wanted "to grow rapidly to become a company that is known nationally as the manufacturer of leading-edge, highly technical, and deeply designed architectural woodwork." The statement continued that the company wanted to become one that Chicago contractors, architects, and customers would automatically think of when they required high-quality architectural woodwork. "We will achieve this," the vision statement elaborated, "by rapidly expanding our markets and our products, continuously improving our process, training our people, and developing long-term relationships with those we serve and who serve us."[20]

A powerful and transforming vision should answer "yes" to the following seven questions, according to Burt Nanus of the University of Southern California's School of Business Administration:[21]

1 Is it appropriate for the organization and for the times?

2 Does it set standards of excellence and reflect high ideals?

3 Does it clarify purpose and direction?

4 Does it inspire enthusiasm and encourage commitment?

5 Is it well articulated and easily understood?

6 Does it reflect the uniqueness of the organization, its distinctive competence, what it stands for, what it's able to achieve?

7 Is it ambitious?

"Visions that have these properties challenge and inspire people in the organization and help align their energies in a common direction," says Nanus. "They prevent people from being overwhelmed by immediate problems because they help distinguish what is truly important from what is merely interesting."

Step 2 **Establish the Grand Strategy** The next step is to translate the broad mission and vision statements into a _**grand strategy**_, **which, after an assessment of current organizational performance, then explains how the organization's mission is to be accomplished.**[22] **Three common grand strategies are growth, stability, and defensive.**

The first part of the process of developing a grand strategy, then, is to make a rigorous analysis of the organization's present situation to determine _where it is presently headed_. The second part is to determine where it _should be headed in the future_.

Let's consider the three common grand strategies.

1 The Growth Strategy A _growth strategy_ is a grand strategy that involves expansion—as in sales revenues, market share, number of employees, or number of customers or (for nonprofits) clients served. A company can implement a growth strategy in several ways:

It can improve an existing product or service to attract more buyers.

It can increase its promotion and marketing efforts to try to expand its market share.

It can expand its operations, as in taking over distribution or manufacturing previously handled by someone else.

It can expand into new products or services.

It can acquire similar or complementary businesses.

It can merge with another company to form a larger company.

2 The Stability Strategy A _stability strategy_ is a grand strategy that involves little or no significant change. A company might decide to go for a no-change or little-change strategy if, for example, it has found that too-fast growth leads to foul-ups with orders and customer complaints. Or if a company has been growing at break-neck speed and feels it needs a period of consolidation.

3 The Defensive Strategy A _defensive strategy_, or a _retrenchment strategy_, is a grand strategy that involves reduction in the organization's efforts. A company can do this in several ways:

It can reduce costs, as by freezing hiring or tightening expenses.

It can sell off (liquidate) assets—land, buildings, inventories, and the like.

It can gradually phase out product lines or services.

It can divest part of its business, as in selling off entire divisions or subsidiaries.

It can declare bankruptcy.

It can attempt a turnaround—do some retrenching, with a view toward restoring profitability.

Growth strategy. Standing on stage at the product roll-out, Apple Computer founder and CEO Steve Jobs unveils a new 15-inch liquid crystal display screen, which attaches by a chrome swivel bar to a white base that holds the computer's system unit.

Click-Along 6.1

Example of Grand Strategy: How One ISP Differentiates Itself from Other Internet Hookups

How do you establish a grand strategy? Among the strategic-planning tools and techniques used are (1) _SWOT analysis_ and (2) _forecasting_, as we describe in Section 6.3.

Step 3 **Formulate Strategic Plans** The grand strategy must then be translated into more specific *strategic plans*, which determine what the organization's long-term goals should be for the next 1–5 years. These should communicate not only the organization's general goals about growth and profits but also information about how these goals will be achieved. Moreover, like all goals, they should be SMART—Specific, Measurable, Attainable, Results-oriented, and specifying Target dates (Chapter 5).

***Strategy formulation* is the process of choosing among different strategies and altering them to best fit the organization's needs.** Because the process is so important, formulating strategic plans is a time-consuming process. Among the techniques used to formulate strategy are *Porter's competitive strategies* and *product life cycles*, which we describe in Section 6.4.

Step 4 **Carry Out the Strategic Plans** Putting strategic plans into effect is *strategy implementation*. Strategic planning isn't effective, of course, unless it can be translated into lower-level plans. This means that top managers need to check on possible roadblocks within the organization's structure and culture and see if the right people and control systems are available to execute the plans.[23]

Often implementation means overcoming resistance by people who feel the plans threaten their influence or livelihood. This is particularly the case when the plans must be implemented rapidly, since delay is the easiest kind of resistance there is (all kinds of excuses are usually available to justify delays). Thus, top managers can't just announce the plans; they have to actively sell them to middle and supervisory managers.

Step 5 **Maintain Strategic Control: The Feedback Loop** *Strategic control* consists of **monitoring the execution of strategy and making adjustments, if necessary.** To keep strategic plans on track, managers need control systems to monitor progress and take corrective action—early and rapidly—when things start to go awry. Corrective action constitutes a feedback loop in which a problem requires that managers return to an earlier step to rethink policies, redo budgets, or revise personnel arrangements. To keep a strategic plan on track, suggests Bryan Barry, you need to do the following:[24]

- **Engage people:** You need to actively engage people in clarifying what your group hopes to accomplish and how you will accomplish it.

- **Keep it simple:** Keep your planning simple, unless there's a good reason to make it more complex.

- **Stay focused:** Stay focused on the important things.

- **Keep moving:** Keep moving toward your vision of the future, adjusting your plans as you learn what works.

Bill Gates. The founder and chairman of Microsoft testifies before the Senate Judiciary Committee in March 1998, which was looking into allegations his company employed monopolistic practices to limit market competition. Gates came under intense questioning as he was asked repeatedly whether his company restricted Internet businesses from promoting products of rival Netscape Communications Corp. Should Microsoft's strategic planning have included the intent to monopolize markets and eliminate competition, as many of its competitors allege? Should any company set a goal of monopoly, and if not, why?

Now let us consider some of the tools used for Step 2, establishing a grand strategy—SWOT and forecasting.

How to Streamline Meetings

"Beware of designing a planning process that requires 40 hours of meetings if your staff or board cannot realistically make the time commitment," advises Bryan W. Barry. "Frustration and failure can result. Effective strategic planning can be done in 10 to 15 hours of meeting time, with good preparation between meetings."[25]

Meetings are a fact of management life—one study of 299 managers found they spent half their time in meetings.[26] If you're not in a position to call meetings but have to attend them regularly, it is frustrating to have to be a victim of a poorly run meeting. As a participant, you can always pull an off-track conversation back by saying, for example, "We were discussing the 2003 budget, but now we seem to be discussing the shortfalls of last year." Or you can try making a summary of a series of comments to prevent others from covering the same ground again. If you're constantly exposed to ineffective meetings, you can also offer your assistance to the meeting leader in creating an agenda, with time frames attached for each item, suggests productivity specialist Odette Pollar. She adds: "Your approach, timing, and tone of voice are important. You must avoid appearing to tell the person what to do."[27]

If you're leading meetings, here are three good ways to streamline them:[28]

Eliminate Unnecessary Meetings & Meeting Attendance Don't call a meeting if the same result can be accomplished in some other way: phone call, e-mail, memo, one-on-one visit, and so on. Invite only people who need to attend, and let them know they need stay for only those

Virtual meeting. Videoconference rooms are operated by many big companies, but users can also rent these sites at Kinko's. Videoconferencing etiquette may take some getting used to: Introduce yourself with a nod or wave. Sit still (rocking in your chair blurs the video). Don't yell (microphones are sensitive). Don't shuffle papers or whisper (everything gets amplified in a video call). Don't doodle, yawn, or eat pizza (everyone can see you).

parts of the meeting that concern them. Hold the meeting in a place where distractions will be minimal. Consider using telephone conferencing or videoconferencing.

Distribute an Action Agenda in Advance Do your homework about the issues. Prepare a list of meeting objectives, topics to be covered and the number of minutes allowed for discussion, and information participants should bring. Organize the topics with the most important ones first. Distribute this agenda a day or more in advance, if possible. For informal meetings, phone conversations, and one-on-one appointments, make a list of items to cover.

Stay in Control of the Meeting Start on time and stay within the time frame of the agenda items. (Coffee breaks, lunchtime, or quitting time provide built-in limits.) Reserve judgments and conclusions until after discussion so that everyone will feel free to give their input. Don't allow a few members to monopolize the discussion. Encourage silent members to participate. Try to reach a decision or make an assignment for every item. Use two note pads or pieces of paper, one for general notes, the other for tasks and assignments. Summarize the highlights at the end of the meeting. Map out a timetable for actions to be taken.

Do Follow-Up After the meeting, type up tasks and assignments for distribution. Set date for follow-up meeting to assess progress.

major question

How can SWOT and forecasting help me establish my strategy?

The Big Picture

To develop a grand strategy, you need to gather data and make projections, using the tools of SWOT analysis and forecasting.

The first part in developing a grand strategy, Step 2 of the five-step strategic management process, is intelligence gathering—internally and externally. The next part is to make some projections.

Two kinds of strategic-planning tools and techniques are (1) *SWOT analysis* and (2) *forecasting*—trend analysis and contingency planning.

SWOT Analysis

The starting point in establishing grand strategy is often a **_SWOT analysis_—also known as *a situational analysis*—which is a search for the Strengths, Weaknesses, Opportunities, and Threats affecting the organization.** A SWOT analysis should provide you with a realistic understanding of your organization in relation to its internal and external environments so you can better formulate strategy in pursuit of its mission. *(See Panel 6.2.)*

PANEL 6.2
SWOT analysis. SWOT stands for Strengths, Weaknesses, Opportunities, Threats.

INSIDE MATTERS—analysis of internal Strengths & Weaknesses

S—Strengths: inside matters
Strengths could be work processes, organization, culture, staff, product quality, production capacity, image, financial resources & requirements, service levels, other internal matters

W—Weaknesses: inside matters
Weaknesses could be in the same categories as stated for Strengths: work processes, organization, culture, etc.

O—Opportunities: outside matters
Opportunities could be market segment analysis, industry & competition analysis, impact of technology on organization, product analysis, governmental impacts, other external matters

T—Threats: outside matters
Threats could be in the same categories as states for Opportunities: market segment analysis, etc.

OUTSIDE MATTERS—analysis of external Opportunities & Threats

The SWOT analysis is divided into two parts: inside matters and outside matters—that is, an analysis of *internal strengths and weaknesses* and an analysis of *external opportunities and threats.*

Inside Matters: Analysis of Internal Strengths & Weaknesses Does your organization have a skilled workforce? a superior reputation? strong financing? These are examples of ***organizational strengths***—the skills and capabilities that give the organization special competencies and competitive advantages in executing strategies in pursuit of its mission.

Or does your organization have obsolete technology? outdated facilities? a shaky marketing operation? These are examples of ***organizational weaknesses***—the drawbacks that hinder an organization in executing strategies in pursuit of its mission.

Outside Matters: Analysis of External Opportunities & Threats Is your organization fortunate to have weak rivals? emerging markets? a booming economy? These are instances of ***organizational opportunities***—environmental factors that the organization may exploit for competitive advantage.

Alternatively, is your organization having to deal with new regulations? a shortage of resources? substitute products? These are some possible ***organizational threats***—environmental factors that hinder an organization's achieving a competitive advantage.

Example of a SWOT Analysis: How Would You Analyze Starbucks Coffee?

If you were presently a manager for Starbucks Corp., what would be the kinds of things you would identify in a SWOT analysis?[29]

First, the internal *Strengths:* No small part of the company's success is based on the loyalty of the staff—most of whom are young (average age: 26) and 85% of whom have some education beyond high school—which Starbucks calls "partners." Because the company offers above-average pay for food service, health insurance for all, stock options, and channels such as e-mail for employee feedback, partners feel quite involved with the company, and turnover is half the industry average. Employees receive painstaking training in the art of making a high-quality cup of coffee, handling coffee beans and equipment, and dealing with customers. Following a McDonald's-like strategy, Starbucks has been breaking into new markets, opening retail stores throughout the country and the world, expanding into different retail channels such as supermarkets, bookstores, and airports. The payoff: Starbucks took in $2.6 billion in the 52 weeks ending September 2001.

Second, the internal *Weaknesses:* To be able to charge $1.40 for a cup instead of 50 cents, Starbucks's focus has been to turn coffee—traditionally an inexpensive commodity-type product—into a premium-placed brand, imitating Coca-Cola's strategy of getting people to think "Coke" versus plain old "cola." But if customers are to continue to pay top dollar for specialty coffee, Starbucks can't slip on quality and service. Thus, complaints about "tepid coffee, gruff employees, long waits" in New York can't be ignored. Nor can press accounts expressing disappointment in the company's new food ventures. In addition, the company can't allow itself to be distracted from its core business. In early 1999, CEO Howard Schultz became infatuated with the Internet and began aggressively pursuing a Web e-commerce strategy; as a result of taking his eye off the ball, the company suffered an earnings shortfall, which caused the price of the stock to drop.

Starbucks in Vienna. The first Starbucks Coffee shop in downtown Vienna, birthplace of the coffeehouse tradition, ever since Turkish invaders left in 1683. After gaining a foothold in Great Britain, American-based Starbucks entered the continental market in 2001 with six shops in Switzerland. In late 2001, it expanded into Austria. "Coffee in Vienna is something that takes time," sniffs one Viennese college student. "Starbucks is just fast food." Would you say Vienna is an Opportunity or a Threat for Starbucks?

Third, the external *Opportunities:* Other chains—Boston Chicken, Rainforest Café, Planet Hollywood—have found the restaurant business tough sledding. But the fact that Starbucks has extremely loyal customers (another Strength) gives the company an Opportunity. Many of the aforementioned theme restaurants were done in because they couldn't get customers to return after the novelty wore off. Moreover, it's been pointed out that coffee is not a fad but rather "the last socially acceptable addiction." Starbucks is also fortunate to have numerous overseas opportunities such as Asia. Indeed, it is even invading Europe, despite Europe's age-old coffee culture.

Fourth, the external *Threats:* Specialty-coffee companies like Starbucks account for only 12% of the coffee roasted in the United States. Most coffee is bought in supermarkets and is dominated by Folgers, Maxwell House, Taster's Choice, and Hills Bros. In years past, they could have turned coffee into either a special beverage, as Starbucks has done, or a drink with mass appeal, like Coke and Pepsi, but they did neither. Instead, they got into price wars with one another, and to cut costs they gradually reduced the quality of coffee. And in fighting one another, they ignored the biggest threat to their industry: soda pop. The result: The coffee industry lost a generation of consumers, who were wooed away by the aggressive marketing of soft drinks. Starbucks is also a victim of its own success, so that in some areas when it moves into a new neighborhood and displaces existing coffee shops it is viewed as a Darth Vader-like corporate giant.

Forecasting: Predicting the Future

Once they've analyzed their organization's Strengths, Weaknesses, Opportunities, and Threats, planners need to do forecasting for making long-term strategy. **A _forecast_ is a vision or projection of the future.**

Lots of people make predictions, of course—and often they are wrong. In the 1950s, the head of IBM, Thomas J. Watson, estimated that the demand for computers would never exceed more than five for the entire world. In the late 1990s, many computer experts predicted power outages, water problems, transportation disruptions, bank shutdowns, and far worse because of computer glitches (the "Y2K bug") associated with the change from year 1999 to 2000.

Of course, the farther into the future one makes a prediction, the more difficult it is to be accurate, especially in matters of technology. Yet forecasting is a necessary part of planning.

Two types of forecasting are trend analysis and contingency planning.

Trend Analysis   A *trend analysis* is a hypothetical extension of a past series of events into the future.[30] The basic assumption is that the picture of the present can be projected into the future. This is not a bad assumption, if you have enough historical data, but it is always subject to surprises. And if your data is unreliable, it will produce erroneous trend projections.

An example of trend analysis is a time-series forecast, which predicts future data based on patterns of historical data. Time-series forecasts are used to predict long-term trends, cyclic patterns (as in the up-and-down nature of the business cycle), and seasonal variations (as in Christmas sales versus summer sales).

In 1999, Merle Gilmore, president of Motorola's Communications Enterprise, figured that, according to projected rates of growth, the trend in numbers of telecommunciations users would be as follows: The number of people in the world using fixed telephone lines, 1 billion, would remain unchanged in 2005. However, the number of Internet users would grow from 200 million to 1 billion, and the number of wireless telephones would go from 300 million to a billion also.[31]

Contingency Planning: Predicting Alternative Futures   *Contingency planning*—also known *as scenario planning* and *scenario analysis*—is the creation of alternative hypothetical but equally likely future conditions.** The scenarios present alternative combinations of different factors—different economic pictures, different strategies by competitors, different budgets, and so on.

Because the scenarios try to peer far into the future—perhaps five or more years—they are necessarily written in rather general terms. Nevertheless, the great value of contingency planning is that it not only equips an organization to prepare for emergencies and uncertainty, it also gets managers thinking strategically.

Example of Contingency Planning: Royal Dutch/Shell Beat Competitors by Preparing for a Price Collapse

Scenarios, said a Royal Dutch/Shell's group planning coordinator, are there "to condition the organization to think." They enable managers in the Anglo-Dutch multinational oil company to be better prepared for "future shocks."[32]

Because the petroleum business is so risky—oil prices can fluctuate tremendously, new supply sources are uncertain, and a country's business conditions may depend on the whims of a dictator—Shell has made dealing with unpredictability a high priority. Top executives study alternative scenarios that look 10 years into the future so that they can formulate strategic plans for handling the unexpected.

In 1984, when oil was $30 a barrel, most Shell managers and outside analysts believed the price would rise to $50 a barrel by 1990. Nevertheless, the planning department prepared a scenario envisioning a drop to $15 a barrel, and Shell managers then drafted contingency plans for handling this occurrence.

Top executives looked at the plans, which included cutbacks on unprofitable stations and increased investment in more efficient refineries, and decided they would help the company become more profitable in any event. With the plans put into effect, therefore, Shell was already prepared when, in fact, oil prices *did* nosedive to $15 a barrel in the mid-1980s. As a result, by 1990, Royal Dutch/Shell had become such an efficient operator in the new world of lower oil prices that it surpassed Exxon to become the largest oil company.[33]

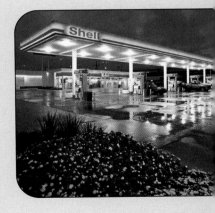

major question

How can two techniques—Porter's competitive strategies and the product life cycle—help me formulate strategy?

The Big Picture

Strategy formulation makes use of several concepts, two examples of which are (1) Porter's four competitive strategies—cost-leadership, differentiation, cost-focus, and focused-differentiation—and (2) the four-stage product life cycle.

After the grand strategy has been determined (Step 2 in the strategic-management process), it's time to turn to strategy formulation (Step 3). Examples of techniques that can be used to formulate strategy are *Porter's four competitive strategies* and the *product life cycle*.

Porter's Four Competitive Strategies

Click-Along 6.2

Two Other Strategy Formulations: Driving Force Analysis & Strategies for New Venture Firms

Harvard Business School professor **Michael Porter** "is the single most important strategist working today, and maybe of all time," raves Kevin Coyne of consulting firm McKinsey & Co.[34]

Is this high praise deserved? Certainly Porter's status as a leading authority on competitive strategy is unchallenged. The Strategic Management Society, for instance, voted him the most influential living strategist.

Porter's reputation stems from work during the 1980s in which he suggested that five forces affect industry competition. They are (1) threats of new entrants, (2) bargaining power of suppliers, (3) bargaining power of buyers, (4) threats of substitute products or services, and (5) rivalry or jockeying for position among industry firms.[35] An organization should do a good SWOT analysis that examines these five competitive forces, Porter felt. Then it was in a position to formulate effective strategy, using what he identified as four competitive strategies.

Porter's four competitive strategies (also called *four generic strategies*) are **(1) cost-leadership, (2) differentiation, (3) cost-focus, and (4) focused-differentiation.**[36] The first two strategies focus on *wide* markets, the last two on *narrow* markets. *(See Panel 6.3.)* AOL Time Warner, which produces lots of media and publications, serves wide markets around the world. Your neighborhood video store serves a narrow market of just local customers.

Let's look at these four strategies.

Strategy	Wide	Narrow
1. Cost-leadership	√	
2. Differentiation	√	
3. Cost focus		√
4. Focused-differentiation		√

Type of market targeted

PANEL 6.3

Porter's four competitive strategies

1 Cost-Leadership Strategy: Keeping Costs & Prices Low for a Wide Market The _cost-leadership strategy_ is to keep the costs, and hence prices, of a product or service below those of competitors and to target a wide market.

This puts the pressure on R&D managers to develop products or services that can be created cheaply, production managers to reduce production costs, and marketing managers to reach a wide variety of customers as inexpensively as possible.

Firms implementing the cost-leadership strategy include car maker Volkswagen, computer maker Dell, watch maker Timex, hardware retailer Home Depot, and pen maker Bic.

2 Differentiation Strategy: Offering Unique & Superior Value for a Wide Market The _differentiation strategy_ is to offer products or services that are of unique and superior value compared to those of competitors but to target a wide market.

Because products are expensive, managers may have to spend more on R&D, marketing, and customer service. This is the strategy followed by the makers of Lexus automobiles and Ritz-Carlton hotels.

The strategy is also pursued by companies trying to create _brands_ to differentiate themselves from competitors. Although Pepsi may cost only cents more than a supermarket's own house brand of cola, Pepsi-Co. spends millions on ads.

3 Cost-Focus Strategy: Keeping Costs & Prices Low for a Narrow Market The _cost-focus strategy_ is to keep the costs, and hence prices, of a product or service below those of competitors and to target a narrow market.

This is a strategy you often see executed with low-end products sold in discount stores, such as low-cost beer or cigarettes, or with regional gas stations, such as the Terrible Herbst or Rotten Robbie chains in parts of the West.

Needless to say, the pressure on managers to keep costs down is even more intense than it is with those in cost-leadership companies.

4 Focused-Differentiation Strategy: Offering Unique & Superior Value for a Narrow Market The _focused-differentiation strategy_ is to offer products or services that are of unique and superior value compared to those of competitors and to target a narrow market.

Some luxury cars are so expensive—Rolls-Royce, Ferrari, Lamborghini—that only a few car buyers can afford them. Other companies following the strategy are jeweler Cartier and shirtmaker Turnbull & Asser. Yet focused-differentiation products need not be expensive. The publisher Chelsea Green has found success with niche books, such as _The Straw Bale House_.

2002 Lamborghini Murcielago, an example of focused differentiation. Only 400 of these Italian cars were made, of which perhaps 100 were sold in the United States. This model was photographed at a Philadelphia car show.

The Product Life Cycle: Different Stages Require Different Strategies

In Chapter 5, we described a *project* life cycle. A *product* life cycle has a similar curve (although the end is usually not quite so abrupt). **A *product life cycle* is a model that graphs the four stages that a product or a service goes through during the "life" of its marketability: (1) introduction, (2) growth, (3) maturity, and (4) decline.** *(See Panel 6.4.)*

| Stage 1: Introduction | Stage 2: Growth | Stage 3: Maturity | Stage 4: Decline |

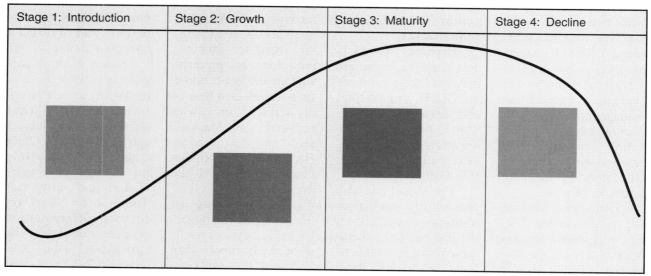

PANEL 6.4

The product life cycle. Managers can use this cycle to create strategies appropriate to each stage.

Some products, such as faddish toys or collectibles (for example, Beanie Babies), may have a life cycle of only months or a year or so. Others, such as a shopping center, may have a life cycle equivalent to a human generation (about 30 years) before they begin to decline and need to be redesigned for fresh appeal and modern sensibilities.

For you as a manager it's useful to know about the concept of product life cycle because different strategies—such as those advanced by Michael Porter—can be used to support different products or services in different stages of the cycle. Let's look at these stages.

What stage in the life cycle? This shopping center clearly has seen better days. Do you think a shopping center could be built that would last 100 years?

Stage 1 Introduction—Getting the Product to Market The _introduction stage_ is the stage in the product life cycle in which a new product is introduced into the marketplace.

This is the stage that is heavy on startup costs for production, marketing, and distribution. Managers have to concentrate on building inventory and staff without loss of quality. With sales usually low during this period, the product is probably losing the company money.

There is also the huge risk that the product may be rejected. Following the smashing reception of the original Apple II (and II-Plus) personal computer, for example, Apple Computer introduced the Lisa—which was a good deal less than a resounding success. Fortunately for Apple, the Lisa evolved into the company's best-selling Macintosh.

During the introduction stage, one should, to use a military analogy, follow a strategy of infiltration. A differentiation or a focus (cost-focus or focused-differentiation) strategy may be appropriate.

Stage 2 Growth—Demand Increases The _growth stage_, which is the most profitable stage, is the period in which customer demand increases, the product's sales grow, and (later) competitors may enter the market.

At the start, the product may have the marketplace to itself and demand for it may be high. Managers need to worry about getting sufficient product into the distribution pipeline, maintaining quality, and expanding the sales and distribution effort.

This phase may go on for years. But all the while, competitors will be scrambling to enter the market. "For 40 years, all we had to do was open restaurants," said McDonald's CEO Jack Greenberg in 1999. "That's not enough anymore."[37] The reason: the competition has become fierce, with other fast-food giants spending millions on promotions.

During the growth stage, managers would advance their attack, probably continuing Stage 1 differentiation or focus strategies.

Stage 3 Maturity—Growth Slows The _maturity stage_ is the period in which the product starts to fall out of favor and sales and profits to fall off.

In this phase, sales start to decline as competition makes inroads. At this point, managers need to concentrate on reducing costs and instituting efficiencies to maintain the product's profitability. Sometimes they can extend the life of the product by tinkering with its various features.

McDonald's CEO Greenberg, for instance, put a lid on domestic growth, opening only 92 new restaurants in 1998 compared to 1,130 in 1995, and he laid off 525 employees. He also introduced a $350 million cooking system that allows food to be served fresher and hotter. And he increased international expansion, so that 90% of the new stores opened in 1999 were outside the U.S.[38]

During the maturity stage, managers would become more defensive, perhaps using a cost-leadership or focus strategy.

Stage 4 Decline—Withdrawing from the Market The _decline stage_ is the period in which the product falls out of favor, and the organization withdraws from the marketplace.

In this stage, the product falls out of favor, and managers sound the bugle for retreat, scaling down relevant inventory, supplies, and personnel.

While this phase may mean withdrawal of support for the old product, it doesn't necessarily mean a complete shutdown for the organization. Much of the same expertise will be required to support new products.

Hismanal was a once-promising prescription antihistamine drug for Johnson & Johnson, but the company announced its discontinuation in 1999. "This was a voluntary decision in response to a marketplace crowded with alternatives," said a company spokesman.

Hismanal was one of the first prescription antihistamines that did not cause drowsiness, but later it was found to produce heart problems when taken with other drugs.[39]

major question

How can two techniques—balanced scorecard and measurement management—help me carry out and control strategy?

The Big Picture

In carrying out the grand strategy, managers need to do strategic control. Two techniques for this are the balanced scorecard, which provides four indicators for progress, and measurement management.

Stage 1 of the strategic-management process was establishing the mission and the vision. Stage 2 was establishing the grand strategy. Stage 3 was formulating the strategic plans. Now we come to the last two stages—4, carry out the strategy, and 5, control the strategy.

Two techniques used here are the *balanced scorecard* and *measurement management*, matters that even new managers will find useful.

The Balanced Scorecard

Robert Kaplan is a professor of accounting at the Harvard Business School. David Norton is founder and president of Renaissance Strategy Group, a Massachusetts consulting firm. Kaplan and Norton developed what they call the **<u>*balanced scorecard*</u>, which gives top managers a fast but comprehensive view of the organization via four indicators: (1) customer satisfaction, (2) internal processes, (3) the organization's innovation and improvement activities, and (4) financial measures.**

"Think of the balanced scorecard as the dials and indicators in an airplane cockpit," write Kaplan and Norton. For a pilot, "Reliance on one instrument can be fatal. Similarly, the complexity of managing an organization today requires that managers be able to view performance in several areas simultaneously."[40] It is not enough, say Kaplan and Norton, to simply measure financial performance, such as sales figures and return on investment. Operational matters, such as customer satisfaction, are equally important.

The balanced scorecard establishes (a) *goals* and (b) *performance measures* according to four "perspectives" or areas—*financial, innovation and learning, customer,* and *internal business. (See Panel 6.5.)*

Southwest Airlines. Performance is measured in several areas. As a passenger, the part you see is Southwest's customer service—arrival times, food and beverage service, lost luggage, and the like. However, the balanced scorecard is concerned with three other measurable keys to company success—measures that passengers don't see.

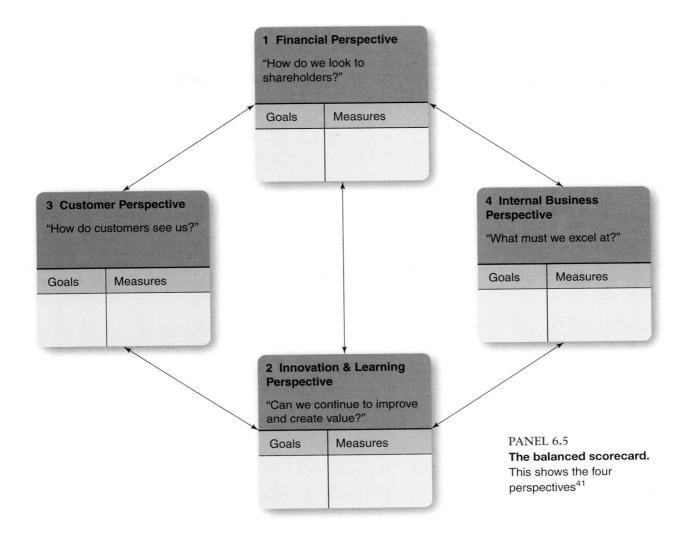

1 Financial Perspective

"How do we look to shareholders?"

Goals	Measures

3 Customer Perspective

"How do customers see us?"

Goals	Measures

4 Internal Business Perspective

"What must we excel at?"

Goals	Measures

2 Innovation & Learning Perspective

"Can we continue to improve and create value?"

Goals	Measures

PANEL 6.5
The balanced scorecard.
This shows the four perspectives[41]

1 Financial Perspective: "How Do We Look to Shareholders?" Typical financial goals have to do with profitability, growth, and shareholder value. Financial measures such as quarterly sales have been criticized as being short-sighted and not reflecting contemporary value-creating activities. Moreover, critics say that traditional financial measures don't improve customer satisfaction, quality, or employee motivation.

However, making improvements in just the other three operational "perspectives" we will discuss won't *necessarily* translate into financial success. Kaplan and Norton mention the case of an electronics company that made considerable improvements in manufacturing capabilities that did not result in increased profitability.

The hard truth is that "if improved [operational] performance fails to be reflected in the bottom line, executives should reexamine the basic assumptions of their strategy and mission," say Kaplan and Norton. "Not all long-term strategies are profitable strategies. . . . A failure to convert improved operational performance, as measured in the scorecard, into improved financial performance should send executives back to their drawing boards to rethink the company's strategy or its implementation plans."[42]

Click-Along 6.3

Example of the Balanced Scorecard: Cigna Healthcare Measures Its success

2 Innovation & Learning Perspective: "Can We Continue to Improve & Create Value?" Because global competition keeps changing the targets for success, companies (1) must make continual improvements to their existing products and processes and (2) must introduce new products. Thus, an organization must measure its research and development efforts and its efficiencies in manufacturing and delivery.

For example, a company might have a time-to-market measure comparing the time taken for introducing a new product with that of the competition. Or it might measure the percentage of products equal to 80% of the company's sales.

3 Customer Perspective: "How Do Customers See Us?" Many organizations make taking care of the customer a high priority. The balanced scorecard translates the mission of customer service into specific measures of concerns that really matter to customers—time between placing an order and taking delivery, quality in terms of defect level, performance and service, and cost.

Examples of customer measures are mean-time response to a service call, customer report cards of price and quality compared to the competition, and third-party surveys (such as the J. D. Powers quality survey of automobiles).

4 Internal Business Perspective: "What Must We Excel At?" This part translates what the company must do internally to meet its customers' expectations. These are business processes such as quality, employee skills, and productivity.

Top management's judgment about key internal processes must be linked to measures of employee actions at the lower levels, such as time to process customer orders, get materials from suppliers, produce products, and deliver them to customers. Computer information systems can help, for example, in identifying late deliveries, tracing the problem to a particular plant.

Measurement Management

Bellhop. The job of the hotel bellman is like many service-industry jobs, in which, unlike manufacturing jobs, productivity is difficult to measure. What other kinds of jobs can you think of in which "measurement management" is difficult to perform?

"You simply can't manage anything you can't measure," says Richard Quinn, vice president of quality at the Sears Merchandising Group.[43]

Is this really true? Measurement concepts such as the balanced scorecard seem like good ideas, but how well do they actually work? John Lingle and William Schiemann, principals in a New Jersey consulting firm specializing in strategic assessment, decided to find out.[44]

In a survey of 203 executives in companies of varying size they identified the organizations as being of two types: *measurement-managed* and *nonmeasurement-managed*. The measurement-managed companies were those in which senior management reportedly agreed on measurable criteria for determining strategic success, and management updated and reviewed semiannual performance measures in three or more of six primary performance areas. The six areas were financial performance, operating efficiency, customer satisfaction, employee performance, innovation/change, and community/environment.

The results, concluded Lingle and Schiemann: "A higher percentage of measurement-managed companies were identified as industry leaders, as being financially in the top third of their industry, and as successfully managing their change effort." (The last indicator suggests that measurement-managed companies tend to anticipate the future and are likely to remain in a leadership position in a rapidly changing environment.) "Forget magic," they say. "Industry leaders we surveyed simply have a greater handle on the world around them."

Joy Chittum makes luggage. What measures matter to small businesses?

Why Measurement-Managed Firms Succeed Why do measurement-managed companies outperform those that are less disciplined? The study's data point to four mechanisms that contribute to these companies' success:

■ **Top executives agree on strategy:** Most top executives in measurement-managed companies agreed on business strategy, whereas most of those in nonmeasurement-managed companies reported disagreement. Translating strategy into measurable objectives helps make them specific.

■ **Communication is clear:** The clear message in turn is translated into good communication, which was characteristic of measurement-managed organizations and not of nonmeasurement-managed ones.

■ **There is better focus and alignments:** Measurement-managed companies reported more frequently that unit (division or department) performance measures were linked to strategic company measures and that individual performance measures were linked to unit measures.

■ **The organizational culture emphasizes teamwork and allows risk taking:** Managers in measurement-managed companies more frequently reported strong teamwork and cooperation among the management team and more willingness to take risks.

The Barriers to Effective Measurement The four most frequent barriers to effective measurement, according to Lingle and Schiemann, are these:

■ **Objectives are fuzzy:** Company objectives are often precise in the financial and operational areas but not in areas of customer satisfaction, employee performance, and rate of change. Managers need to work at making "soft" objectives measurable.

■ **Managers put too much trust in informal feedback systems:** Managers tend to overrate feedback mechanisms such as customer complaints or sales-force criticisms about products. But these mechanisms aren't necessarily accurate.

■ **Employees resist new measurement systems:** Employees want to see how well measures work before they are willing to tie their financial futures to them. Measurement-managed companies tend to involve the workforce in developing measures.

■ **Companies focus too much on measuring activities instead of results:** Too much concern with measurement that is not tied to fine-tuning the organization or spurring it on to achieve results is wasted effort.

Click-Along 6.4

The Feedback Loop

Throughout the five-step process, there is a feedback loop (refer back to Panel 6.1) so that when problems are encountered along the way, managers are directed to return to earlier steps to take corrective action.

Taking Something Practical Away from this Chapter: The Business Plan—Strategic Planning for the Small-Business Entrepreneur

Key Terms Used in This Chapter

Summary

6.1
The Dynamics of Strategic Planning

■ Every organization needs to have a "big picture" about where it's going and how to get there. These are matters of strategy, strategic management, and strategic planning.

■ A strategy is a large-scale action plan that sets the direction for an organization. Strategic management is a process that involves managers from all parts of the organization in the formulation and implementation of strategies and strategic goals. Strategic planning determines not only the organization's long-term goals for the next 1–5 years regarding growth and profits but also the ways the organization should achieve them.

■ There are three reasons why an organization should adopt strategic management and strategic planning. They can (1) provide direction and momentum, (2) encourage new ideas, and above all (3) develop a sustainable competitive advantage. Sustainable competitive advantage occurs when an organization is able to get and stay ahead in four areas: (1) in being responsive to customers, (2) in innovating, (3) in quality, and (4) in effectiveness. Strategic planning is appropriate not just for large firms but also for companies with fewer than 100 employees as well.

6.2
The Strategic Management Process

■ The strategic management process has five steps plus a feedback loop.

■ Step 1 is to establish the mission statement and the vision statement. The mission statement expresses the organization's purpose or reason for being. The vision statement describes the organization's long-term direction and strategic intent.

■ Step 2 is to translate the broad mission and vision statements into a grand strategy, which, after an assessment of current organizational performance, then explains how the organization's mission is to be accomplished. Three common grand strategies are growth, stability, and defensive. (1) A growth strategy is a grand strategy that involves expansion—as in sales revenues, market share, number of employees, or number customers or clients served. (2) A stability strategy is a grand strategy that involves little or no significant change. (3) A defensive strategy, or retrenchment strategy, is a grand strategy that involves reduction in the organization's efforts. Among the strategic planning tools and techniques used are (1) SWOT analysis and (2) forecasting, as described in Section 6.3.

- Step 3 is strategy formulation, the translation of the grand strategy into more specific strategic plans, which determine what the organization's long-term goals should be for the next 1–5 years. Strategy formulation is the process of choosing among different strategies and altering them to best fit the organization's needs. Among the techniques used to formulate strategy are Porter's competitive strategies and product life cycles, as described in Section 6.4.

- Step 4 is strategy implementation—putting strategic plans into effect, which may mean overcoming resistance by people who feel the plans threaten their influence or livelihood.

- Step 5 is strategic control, which consists of monitoring the execution of strategy and making adjustments, if necessary.

- Corrective action constitutes a feedback loop in which a problem requires that managers return to an earlier step to rethink policies, redo budgets, or revise personnel arrangements.

6.3
Establishing the Grand Strategy

- To develop a grand strategy (Step 2 above), you need to gather data and make projections, using the tools of SWOT analysis and forecasting.

- SWOT analysis—also known as situational analysis—is a search for the Strengths, Weaknesses, Opportunities, and Threats affecting the organization. The SWOT analysis is divided into two parts—inside matters and outside matters—that is, an analysis of internal strengths and weaknesses and an analysis of external opportunities and threats. Organizational strengths are the skills and capabilities that give the organization special competencies and competitive advantages in executing strategies in pursuit of its mission. Organizational weaknesses are the drawbacks that hinder an organization in executing strategies in pursuit of its mission. Organizational opportunities are environmental factors that the organization may exploit for competitive advantage. Organizational threats are environmental factors that

hinder an organization's achieving a competitive advantage.

- Forecasting is another tool for developing a grand strategy. A forecast is a vision or projection of the future. Two types of forecasting are trend analysis and contingency planning. A trend analysis is a hypothetical extension of a past series of events into the future. Contingency planning—also known as scenario planning and scenario analysis—is the creation of alternative hypothetical but equally likely future conditions.

6.4
Formulating Strategy

- Strategy formulation (Step 3 in the strategic-management process) makes use of several concepts, two of which are (1) Porter's four competitive strategies and (2) product life cycles.

- Porter's four competitive strategies (also called four generic strategies) are cost-leadership, differentiation, cost-focus, and focused-differentiation. (1) The cost-leadership strategy is to keep the costs, and hence the prices, of a product or service below those of competitors and to target a wide market. (2) The differentiation strategy is to offer products or services that are of unique and superior value compared to those of competitors but to target a wide market. (3) The cost-focus strategy is to keep the costs and hence prices of a product or service below those of competitors and to target a narrow market. (4) The focused-differentiation strategy is to offer products or services that are of unique and superior value compared to those of competitors and to target a narrow market.

- A product life cycle is a model that graphs the four stages that a product or service goes through during the "life" of its marketability: introduction, growth, maturity, and decline. (1) The introduction stage is the stage in which a new product is introduced into the marketplace. This is the stage that is heavy on startup costs for production, marketing, and distribution. (2) The growth stage, which is the most profitable stage, is the period in which customer demand increases, the product's sales grow, and later competitors may enter the market. (3) The maturity stage is the period in which the product starts to fall out of favor and sales and profits fall off. (4) The decline stage is the period in which the product falls out of favor, and the organization withdraws from the marketplace.

6.5
Carrying Out & Controlling Strategy

■ In carrying out the grand strategy (Stage 4) and controlling the strategy (Stage 5), managers can avail themselves of two techniques: (1) the balanced scorecard, and (2) measurement management.

■ The balanced scorecard gives top managers a fast but comprehensive view of the organization via four indicators. The balanced scorecard establishes (a) goals and (b) performance measures according to four "perspectives" or areas—financial, innovation and learning, customer, and internal business. (1) The financial perspective has to do with profitability, growth, and shareholder values. (2) The innovation and learning perspective

has to do with the question of how the organization can continue to improve and create value. (3) The customer perspective is concerned with specific measures of concerns that really matter to customers, such as product defects and costs. (4) The internal business perspective has to do with what the company must do to meet customer expectations, such as quality, employee skills, and productivity.

■ The balanced scorecard is an example of measurement management, in which an organization uses measurable criteria to determine strategic success. Measurement-managed firms succeed because top executives agree on strategy, communication is clear, there is better focus, and the organizational culture emphasizes teamwork and allows risk taking. Four barriers to effective measurement are that the objectives are fuzzy, managers put too much trust in informal feedback systems, employees resist new measurement systems, and companies focus too much on measuring activities instead of results.

Management in Action

Intel Adopts a Many-Pronged Strategy

Excerpted from Cliff Edwards and Ira Sage, "Intel: Can CEO Craig Barrett Reverse the Slide?"
Business Week, *October 15, 2001, pp. 80–90.*

BusinessWeek After launching a bold new strategy three years ago [1998] to move Intel beyond PCs and into such markets as communications, information appliances, and Internet services, the chipmaker is in its worst shape in more than 15 years. Oh sure, there isn't a tech exec on the planet who isn't having a crummy year because of a souring economy and the threat of war in the wake of the terrorist attacks. But Intel's problems run deeper than these events. For the past three years, Intel has seesawed between product shortages and product delays in its core computer-chip business. Piled on top of that have been embarrassing bugs, recalls, and overpriced processors that opened the door for rivals. By year end [of 2001], analysts expect Intel's share of the PC chip market to drop to 78%— nine percentage points below what it had been when Barrett [Craig Barrett is Intel's CEO] took over.

Barrett's invasion into new markets has been even more dismal. So far, some $4 billion of Intel's

more than $10 billion in new investments have produced little. This year, Intel stopped making network servers and routers after some of its biggest chip customers, including Dell Computer Corp. and Cisco Systems Inc., slapped Barrett's hands for competing against them. In February, Barrett shut down a service for broadcasting shareholder meetings and training sessions over the Web. He shuttered iCat, an e-commerce and hosting service for small and midsize businesses. And he has retreated so far in the information-appliance business that Intel now markets its Web-surfing devices only in Spain . . .

What went wrong? Critics say Barrett has been trying to move Intel into too many new markets, fracturing the company's focus on its core business. To execute so many fronts, he has decentralized the organization and delegated a lot of decision-making. But getting a workable structure in place has been a challenge. Barrett has restructured the business groups at least three times in as many years, shuffling execs like cards in a deck. Even in the core microprocessor group, a startling 80% of the unit's staff were given new roles in a March shakeup. "Typically, people moving around a lot are not sure where they are going," says one longtime customer. Adds G. Carl Everett Jr., a former general manager of Intel's Desktop Products group, who left the company in 1996: "They're dabbling in everything and overwhelming nothing."

Now Intel is bracing for its worst financial results since it fled the memory-chip business in 1985 . . . Indeed, Barrett isn't the least chastened by Intel's flagging performance or criticism of his many-pronged strategy. With a temper at times as prickly as the cactus towering over his 9-by-9 cubicle, Barrett says his strategy has not created a company without focus. "Guilty as charged, we had product screwups," he says curtly. "Not guilty as charged that we can't do more than one thing at a time." The product shortages, bugs, and recalls, he says, were "side effects" of pushing forward into many markets at a breakneck pace . . . Barrett says he's not backing off those bets. Three years ago, he vowed to branch out into communications, info appliances, and Internet services. His original vision was not only called for making chips for networking gear, cell phones, and handheld computers but also for churning out Intel hardware-network servers, Web-surfing devices, and routers to guide data over networks. At the same time, Barrett tried to build a services business, with Intel running e-commerce operations for others or dishing up business software to corporate customers over the Net. The full scope of his vision has been far from realized. Intel has retreated from most of the Intel-branded product offerings to rely on what Intel knows best—making chips. Now, his beyond-the-PC plans translate into producing tiny slivers of silicon to go into wireless and other communications products.

Intel's problems, Barrett says, are largely the result of the economic downturn. Still, he maintains, he's turning that to his advantage by plowing gobs of money into research and manufacturing advances—$11.5 billion, a staggering 45% of revenues—at a time when rivals can ill afford such lavish spending. That's classic Intel, a ploy Grove used against cash-strapped microprocessor rivals to widen his lead in the mid 1980s. With a $10 billion cash reserve and a seasoned team, Barrett says Intel is positioning itself to come out of the downturn in better shape than rivals both old and new. The downturn, he argues, is giving Intel time to hone its next-generation products in all markets he has targeted. "We've got the technology, we've got the strategy," he says . . .

In three years, Barrett has pumped more than $10 billion into 34 acquisitions to bolster efforts in new markets, betting that those deals would help such units as the Communications Group and the Wireless Communications & Computing Group grow 50% annually. Revenue did rise sharply, to $6.4 billion last year from $3.9 billion a year earlier, and now amount to nearly one-fifth of Intel's total. But that's mostly thanks to Intel's flash-memory chips, which are used in cellular phones to hold data stored in memory when a device is turned off. Even including the profitable flash-memory operation, Intel's new businesses—everything from Web hosting to processors for phones—have reaped zilch in profits, with losses doubling nearly every year since 1998.

It hasn't helped Intel's cause that Barrett has been shuffling management and reorganizing business units nearly as often as the company trots out new processors. First, Barrett formed a new wireless unit in December 1999, combining Intel's flash-memory business and new acquisitions, such as DSP Communications Inc., a leading supplier of chipsets and software for digital cellular communications. A year later, Barrett combined the manufacturing and development groups working on its core processors into the Architecture Group. This year, Intel's networking and communications businesses were merged into a new unit, and the architecture unit was revamped for a second time in two years. "We reset the whole thing," says Paul Otellini, senior vice-president for the Architecture Group.

Barrett and Grove say the moves were necessary to clean out organizational cobwebs and to reflect the realities of a more segmented marketplace. The reorganizations were designed to make Intel more fleet-footed and to avoid duplication of efforts in various units, such as the networking and communications operations each pitching similar products to customers with no coordination. Barrett explains that in the past three years he has moved four executive vice-presidents into new positions to give them experience in sales, marketing, and operations in preparation for choosing his eventual successor . . . When Barrett moved into the corner office, he vowed to reinvent not only Intel's business but also its culture. He brought in consultants such as Harvard Business School professor Clayton M. Christensen, author of *The Innovator's Dilemma*, to encourage the troops to tear down the old ways. But Barrett has yet to purge Intel of a culture that is used to competing in such markets where it is the only choice. Take Intel's much-hyped broadband effort. In 1998, Intel began publishing a new standard for a speedy, low-cost, digital subscriber line (DSL) chip without phone-company input, says Bob Merritt, director of emerging markets for chip researcher Semico Research Corp. That frustrated phone companies, which then refused to support Intel. In March, Intel quietly admitted it has no plans to ship the chip, and the future of the business is now up in the air. Barrett has worked on improving customer relations, but some say Intel's take-no-prisoners culture remains unchanged. "To be candid, Intel has been Intel," days Duane E. Zitzner, president of HP's computing-systems group. "I haven't observed any difference in the way they do business."

For Discussion

1. As described in this article, does Intel's strategy seem clear or confusing? Explain.

2. How would you describe Intel's grand strategy?

3. Using Panel 6.2 as a framework, conduct a SWOT analysis of Intel. What are your conclusions?

4. Which of Porter's four generic competitive strategies is Intel pursuing? Explain.

5. Using the descriptions in Panel 6.5, describe the driving force behind Intel's strategic decisions.

Take It to the Net

In our fast-paced and sometimes stressful world, each of us is trying to find our way. This is just as true for students entering college as it is for the laid-off or downsized employee who has worked for 30 years or the retired person looking for a new challenge. Each of us needs to balance our short- and long-term plans. The same is true for organizations. In this case, however, organizations rely on strategic planning. The purpose of this exercise is to allow you to bring the concept of strategic planning to life by applying it to your own life.

To assist you in understanding how to use strategic planning for yourself, please go to *http://www.morrisey.com/case4psp.html*. Read the information presented there and add it to the knowledge you have gained from class and reading the chapter. Then formulate a strategic plan for yourself based on this database.

Questions for Discussion

1. How does it feel to be doing strategic planning for real and not as an abstract concept as large companies do? Describe and explain.

2. What do you see in your future, and how can strategic planning help you get there? Illustrate and explain.

3. How important do you think it is to do your own personal strategic planning? Explain.

Self-Assessment

Core Skills Required in Strategic Planning*

Objectives

1. To assess if you have the skills to be in strategic planning.
2. To see what you think are the important core skill areas in strategic planning.

Introduction: Strategic planning became important as a method of managing the increasing velocity of change. The business environment no longer evolves at a manageable pace but increasingly through a process Charles Handy calls "discontinuous change"—change that radically alters how we think, work, and often behave. The computer, for instance, has completely changed how we communicate, research, write, and work. To meet this challenge, companies have strategic planners and others knowledgeable about their organizations, culture, and environment to shape strategy. Individuals must develop knowledge about their own abilities so that they formulate their own kind of strategic planning.

Instructions: To see whether or not you have the required skills needed to be a strategic planner, truthfully and thoughtfully assess your ability level for the following list of 12 skills. Rate each skill by using a five-point scale in which 1 = exceptional, 2 = very high, 3 = high, 4 = low, and 5 = very low.

1. Ability to synthesize	1	2	3	4	5
2. Analytical skills	1	2	3	4	5
3. Computer skills	1	2	3	4	5
4. Decisiveness	1	2	3	4	5
5. Interpersonal skills	1	2	3	4	5
6. Listening skills	1	2	3	4	5
7. Persuasiveness	1	2	3	4	5
8. Problem-solving skills	1	2	3	4	5
9. Research skills	1	2	3	4	5
10. Team skills	1	2	3	4	5
11. Verbal skills	1	2	3	4	5
12. Written skills	1	2	3	4	5

Scoring & Interpretation: According to research conducted at the Ohio State University College of Business (see *http://fisher.osu.edu/fin/jobs/spjobs.htm* for more on strategic planning), the core required skills for the 12 skills above rate as follows:

Ability to synthesize	2
Analytical skills	1
Computer skills	3
Decisiveness	3
Interpersonal skills	1
Listening skills	2
Persuasiveness	2
Problem-solving skills	3
Research skills	3
Team skills	2
Verbal skills	2
Written skills	3

If you scored mostly 4s and 5s, strategic planning is probably not for you.

If you scored near the "perfect" score, it may be a possible career path.

If you scored all 1s and 2s, you might do extremely well at this type of work and might want to look it to it more.

Questions for Discussion

1. Based on your results, do you think you would like to make a career out of strategic planning? Why or why not?

2. What appeals or does not appeal to you about this career? Explain.

3. How might you enhance your strategic skills? Discuss.

*Developed by Anne C. Cowden, Ph.D., from information provided by the above-cited website.

Group Exercise

Strategizing for Real*

Objectives

1. To help you understand the complexity of the strategic planning process.
2. To more completely familiarize yourself with strategic planning.

Introduction

Social psychologist Kurt Lewin argued that there is nothing as useful as a good theory. The important word here is *good* since bad theories can cause a great deal of trouble. An example of a bad theory was the introduction of the New Coke in 1985 by Coca-Cola, one of the world's most successful companies. Management's "theory" was that customers wanted a New Coke. But its introduction was an enormous fiasco and furious customers demanded that traditional Coke be brought back. Companies that effectively use strategic planning can try to avoid these blunders.

To have a sense of what function a strategic plan can have, you must (1) look at the theory (as you have just done through reading the chapter and in the above Internet exercise) and (2) apply those ideas to an actual situation that you know. In this way, you can see if you like doing strategic planning, what it entails in terms of complexity and insight, and whether or not you think it is a career area you might like to pursue. Because of transitions in the world economy, the demand for strategists will likely increase. The purpose of this exercise is to provide you the opportunity to create a strategic plan for your college or university.

Instructions

Students should be divided into groups of five each. One person should go to the website for the New Mexico State University Planning Process at *http://www.nmsu.edu/Strategic/process/fig1.html,* download the chart there, and make copies for everyone. The task of the group is to use this chart as a guide to develop a strategic plan for your college or university. Your first step is to discover if such a document already exists, acquire a copy, and then compare it to your chart, filling in the specifics and trying to improve the process as you go along. This exercise should help make you a better strategic planner of your own education and career.

Questions for Discussion

1. Why is it important for an organization—whether private, public, or not-for-profit—to have a strategic plan? Explain your rationale.
2. Do you think that a strategic plan can ever be totally accurate? Why or why not?
3. Who do you think should be involved in developing and maintaining a strategic plan?
4. How would you grade (A through F) the strategic plan at your college? Explain your rationale.

*Developed by Anne C. Cowden, Ph.D.

Ethical Dilemma

Some American Companies Follow Strategy of Creating Nominal Headquarters in Bermuda to Avoid Paying U.S. Taxes

Excerpted from David Cay Johnston, "Senators Assail Corporate Use of Bermuda as Tax Shelter," New York Times, March 22, 2002, pp. C1, C4.

Senior senators from both parties used blunt language [March 22, 2002] to denounce companies that use Bermuda as a mail drop to reduce their American income taxes by tens of millions of dollars, calling them "greedy" and "unpatriotic" tax evaders whose actions could not be tolerated "in a time of war" [the Bush administration's war against terrorism].

Senator Max Baucas, Democrat of Montana and chairman of the [U.S. Senate] Finance Committee, and Senator Charles E. Grassley of Iowa, the committee's ranking Republican, said they would introduce legislation next month to end the Bermuda tax break. . . .

Companies including Ingersoll-Rand, Accenture, Tyco International, and Seagate Technology reorganized to create a nominal headquarters in Bermuda or the Cayman Islands, which have no corporate income taxes, while maintaining their working headquarters in the United States.

Senator Grassley labeled the Bermuda moves shams and warned executives contemplating such reorganizations that "you should proceed at your own peril."

Mr. Grassley said that Stanley Works, whose shareholders will vote next month on a Bermuda tax move, and Ingersoll-Rand, which became a nominal Bermuda company in December, have about 300 total contracts as government suppliers.

Holding up a Stanley Works saw, he said anyone thinking about buying Stanley Works tools should consider that the company is "evading U.S. taxes and making profits off the taxes of middle-class Americans who are paying their taxes honestly."

"This is corporate greed," Mr. Grassley added. . . .

Gerard J. Gould, a Stanley Works vice president, said . . . [t]he company . . . "feels there is nothing unpatriotic about following existing law and reinvesting the tax savings to grow the company for all its shareholders."

Solving the Dilemma

If you were in charge of corporate strategy for Stanley Works, would you continue to relocate your nominal headquarters to Bermuda?

1. Yes, because the action will make the company more money.

2. No, because the move is bad public relations and might cost the company customer goodwill and government contracts.

3. I'd delay the decision until I see what action the U.S. Senate takes.

4. Other possible options. Discuss.

CHAPTER 7

Individual & Group Decision Making
How Managers Make Things Happen

MAJOR QUESTIONS YOU SHOULD BE ABLE TO ANSWER

7.1 The Nature of Decision Making
Major Question: How do I decide to decide?

7.4 Group Decision Making: How to Work with Others
Major Question: How do I work with others to make things happen?

7.2 Two Kinds of Decision Making: Rational & Nonrational
Major Question: How do people know when they're being logical or illogical?

7.5 How to Overcome Barriers to Decision Making
Major Question: Trying to be rational isn't always easy. What are the barriers?

7.3 Solving Problems & Seizing Opportunities: Making Practical Decisions
Major Question: What are the four steps in practical decision making?

HOW EXCEPTIONAL MANAGERS MAKE DECISIONS

"Failure is a great teacher."

That is one of the life lessons of David Dorman, who at age 45 is the CEO of a $10 billion joint venture between AT&T and British Telecommunications.[1] During his meteoric career, Dorman has had to make many decisions—the subject of this chapter—for which failure is always a possible outcome. But he has learned that that possibility can't stop one from making decisions. And you can probably always learn from the result.

■ **When should you make a decision and when should you delay?** Often you want to stay open-minded before making a decision. But sometimes that can just be a cover for procrastination. (After all, *not* making a decision is in itself a kind of decision.) How do you know when you're keeping an open mind or are procrastinating? Ralph L. Keeney, coauthor of *Smart Choices: A Practical Guide to Making Better Decisions*, offers some questions to consider:[2]

Understanding: Do you have a reasonable grasp of the problem?

Comfort level about outcome: Would you be satisfied if you chose one of the existing alternatives?

Future possible alternatives: Would it be unlikely that you could come up with a better alternative if you had more time?

Seizing the opportunity: Could the best alternatives disappear if you wait?

If you can answer "yes" to those questions, you almost certainly should decide now, not wait.

■ **Making tough choices:** To reach the top, as Dorman has, a manager needs to be able to make tough choices. "On a daily and weekly basis we can be faced with making hundreds of decisions," says management consultant Odette Pollar. "Most of them are small, but the larger ones where more is at stake can be truly painful." Here are some ways she suggests making decision making easier, some of which resemble Keeney's:[3]

Decide in a timely fashion: "Rarely does waiting significantly improve the quality of the decision," says Pollar. In fact, delay can result in greater unpleasantness in loss of money, time, and peace of mind.

Don't agonize over minor decisions: Postponing decisions about small problems can mean that they simply turn into large ones later.

Separate outcome from process: Does a bad outcome mean you made a bad decision? Not necessarily. The main thing is to go through a well-reasoned process of choosing among alternatives, which increases the chances of success. But even then you can't be sure there will always be a positive outcome.

Learn when to stop gathering facts: "Gather enough information to make a sound decision," suggests Pollar, "but not all the possible information." Taking extra time may mean you'll miss a window of opportunity.

When overwhelmed, narrow your choices: Sometimes there are many good alternatives, and you need to simplify decision making by eliminating some options.

FORECAST: WHAT'S AHEAD IN THIS CHAPTER

We describe decision making and types of decisions, and we describe the range of decision-making conditions. Next we distinguish between rational and nonrational decision making, and we describe five nonrational models. We then consider four steps in practical decision making. We follow with a discussion of group decision making, including participative management and group problem-solving techniques. We conclude by considering how individuals respond to decision situations and four common decision-making biases.

How do I decide to decide?

The Big Picture

Decision making, the process of identifying and choosing alternative courses of action, may be programmed or nonprogrammed. The range of decision-making conditions ranges from certainty to risky to uncertainty to confusion.

The Campbell's Soup label became such a beloved icon that pop artist Andy Warhol used it as the subject of a famous silkscreen rendering. But in 1999, faced with flagging soup sales, Campbell decided after 102 years to give its brand a shot in the arm by changing the famous label to better attract time-pressed shoppers.

This decision involves some uncertainty, according to analysts and brand-image experts, because the changes—such as adding photos of the soup inside the can and colored banners with such labels as "classic," "fun favorites," and "98% fat free"—represent only minor tinkering. Although the new design minimized the risk of consumer backlash by retaining crucial elements of the old label, it was described as being "the cosmetic equivalent of highlights instead of a full dye job."[4] The change, image-identity experts said, might not be enough for an aging brand in need of a second wind.

Could the top managers have made better decisions? To be better able to solve both crises and day-to-day problems, we need to know how decision making works.

Decision Making Defined

A *decision* **is a choice made from among available alternatives.** For example, should your college offer computer-based distance learning to better serve students who work odd hours or are home bound and can't easily get to lectures on campus? That question is a decision that the college administrators must make.

Decision making **is the process of identifying and choosing alternative courses of action.** For example, the college could offer distance learning by televising the lectures of a single professor into several classrooms or to community centers off campus. Or it could offer distance learning interactively over the Internet. It could offer distance learning only for certain subjects (business and education, say) or for selected courses in all majors. It could offer distance learning only during the summer or only during the evenings. It could charge extra for such courses. It could offer them for credit to high school students or to students attending other colleges. Identifying and sorting out these alternatives is the process of decision making.

Campbell's updated. Can you tell which label is traditional, which is new?

Click-Along 7.1

Emergency Decision Making: Did Coca-Cola Choose Right?

Distance learning. This student is logged onto the distance-learning website at Camden County (N.J.) College. Today students frequently have the option to take many courses that previously were not available to them. Do you think the addition of distance-learning courses to a college's course offerings gives you more freedom of choice—or simply more headaches? What must it be like for college administrators?

Types of Decisions: Programmed versus Nonprogrammed

In most day-to-day matters, you will automatically know what kind of decision needs to be made and when, who will decide it, who will need to be consulted about it, who should be informed about it. That is, the decisions are *programmed*. However, when you have to stop and think about these matters, then the decisions are *nonprogrammed*.[5]

Let's distinguish further between programmed and nonprogrammed decisions.

Programmed Decisions *Programmed decisions* **are repetitive and routine.** Because they are fairly structured and occur fairly frequently, such decisions tend to follow established rules and so are virtually automatic. This does not mean, however, that the issues are necessarily simple. Even a complicated issue, if its components can be analyzed, may be decided by a programmed decision.

Do you know if you have enough credits or the right courses to graduate? That is a programmed decision that someone in the college registrar's or dean of students' office can help you figure out. Are you the owner of a gun shop trying to decide whether you should sell someone a firearm? State and federal laws spell out whom you can and can't sell to—you need only make a programmed decision.

Lumber wholesaler. In areas where home building is a seasonal industry, do contractors face programmed or nonprogrammed decisions in determining how much lumber to buy?

Nonprogrammed Decisions *Nonprogrammed decisions* **are those that occur under nonroutine, unfamiliar circumstances.** Because they occur in response to unusual, unpredictable opportunities and threats, nonprogrammed decisions are relatively unstructured. Often, too, they tend to involve complex, important situations. The farther you move up the organizational hierarchy, the more important your ability to make nonprogrammed decisions becomes.

Trying to decide what elective courses to take in college or what to major in? Those are both nonprogrammed decisions. Want to decorate an office? Price may be one factor in choosing between stainless steel and wood furniture, but so also may be matters such as appearance to clients, making this a nonprogrammed decision.

General Decision-Making Styles: Directive, Analytical, Conceptual, Behavioral

A _decision-making style_ reflects the combination of how an individual perceives and responds to information. A team of researchers developed a model of decision-making styles based on the idea that styles vary along two different dimensions: value orientation and tolerance for ambiguity.[6]

Value orientation reflects the extent to which a person focuses on either task and technical concerns or people and social concerns when making decisions. Some people, for instance, are very task focused at work and do not pay much attention to people issues, whereas others are just the opposite.

The second dimension pertains to a person's _tolerance for ambiguity_. This individual difference indicates the extent to which a person has a high need for structure or control in his or her life. Some people desire a lot of structure in their lives (a low tolerance for ambiguity) and find ambiguous situations stressful and psychologically uncomfortable. In contrast, others do not have a high need for structure and can thrive in uncertain situations (a high tolerance for ambiguity). Ambiguous situations can energize people with a high tolerance for ambiguity.

When the dimensions of value orientation and tolerance for ambiguity are combined, they form four styles of decision making: _directive, analytical, conceptual,_ and _behavioral. (See Panel 7.1.)_

Who is this, er, man? Herb Kelleher, former CEO of highly successful Southwest Airlines, was much beloved by his employees for his humor, informal management style, and extraordinary people orientation. What kind of decision-making styles do you think his successors would try to follow?

PANEL 7.1
Decision-making conditions

	Task & technical concerns	People & social concerns
High	Analytical	Conceptual
Tolerance for ambiguity		
	Directive	Behavioral
Low		

Value orientation

1 Directive People with a directive style have a low tolerance for ambiguity and are oriented toward task and technical concerns in making decisions. They are efficient, logical, practical, and systematic in their approach to solving problems.

People with this style are action oriented and decisive and like to focus on facts. In their pursuit of speed and results, however, these individuals tend to be autocratic, to exercise power and control, and to focus on the short run.

2 Analytical This style has a much higher tolerance for ambiguity and is characterized by the tendency to overanalyze a situation. People with this style like to consider more information and alternatives than managers following the directive style.

Analytic individuals are careful decision makers who take longer to make decisions but who also respond well to new or uncertain situations.

3 Conceptual People with a conceptual style have a high tolerance for ambiguity and tend to focus on the people or social aspects of a work situation. They take a broad perspective to problem solving and like to consider many options and future possibilities.

Conceptual types adopt a long-term perspective and rely on intuition and discussions with others to acquire information. They also are willing to take risks and are good at finding creative solutions to problems. However, a conceptual style can foster an indecisive approach to decision making.

4 Behavioral This style is the most people oriented of the four styles. People with this style work well with others and enjoy social interactions in which opinions are openly exchanged. Behavioral types are supportive, receptive to suggestions, show warmth, and prefer verbal to written information.

Although they like to hold meetings, people with this style have a tendency to avoid conflict and to be concerned about others. This can lead behavioral types to adopt a wishy-washy approach to decision making and to have a hard time saying no.

Which Style Do You Have? Research shows that very few people have only one dominant decision-making style. Rather, most managers have characteristics that fall into two or three styles. Studies also show that decision-making styles vary across occupations, job level, and countries.[7] There is not a best decision-making style that applies to all situations.

You can use knowledge of decision making styles in three ways:

- Knowledge of styles helps you to understand yourself. Awareness of your style assists you in identifying your strengths and weaknesses as a decision maker and facilitates the potential for self-improvement.

- You can increase your ability to influence others by being aware of styles. For example, if you are dealing with an analytical person, you should provide as much information as possible to support your ideas.

- Knowledge of styles gives you an awareness of how people can take the same information and yet arrive at different decisions by using a variety of decision-making strategies. Different decision-making styles represent one likely source of interpersonal conflict at work.

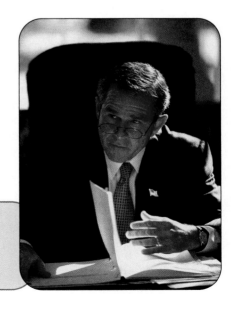

Presidential style. George W. Bush's decision-making style—which supposedly reflects his business-school training—has been admired by some and criticized by others. Which of the four types—directive, analytical, conceptual, or behavioral—would you say best describes his kind of decision making?

major question

How do people know when they're being logical or illogical?

The Big Picture

Decision making may be rational, but often it is nonrational. Five nonrational models are satisficing, incremental, coalitional, garbage can, and intuitional.

Space phone. The caller talks on a 1995 Iridium world-wide telephone while demonstrating a pocket-sized pager. If you had been a Motorola manager, what decisions would you have urged in the development of a phone that could be used anywhere?

Iridium LLC's network of 66 low-orbit satellites was supposed to revolutionize telecommunications by allowing people to make phone calls at any time from anywhere in the world. But nine months after its splashy 1998 launch, the Motorola-led consortium had filed for bankruptcy protection.

What happened? Critics say that Iridium and Motorola became so focused on making the technology work they failed to pay attention to marketing problems. In an era of pocket-size cellphones, the clunky Iridium "space phone" weighed one pound, was the size of a brick, and featured an array of ungainly accessories and adapters. Moreover, because of technology limitations, phone users had to position themselves so nothing blocked the line of sight between the phone's antenna and the satellites overhead. This meant the handset couldn't be used inside buildings, moving cars, or many other locations where the high-powered managers Iridium was targeting tended to make calls. Finally, the phones retailed for $3,000 apiece and calls ran $2–$8 a minute—at a time when competitors were even giving phones away to induce consumers to subscribe to their low-cost calling plans.[8]

Were Iridium's decisions rational? Let us look at the two approaches managers may take to making decisions: They may follow a *rational model* or various kinds of *nonrational models*.

Rational Decision Making: Managers Should Make Logical & Optimum Decisions

The *rational model of decision making*, also called the *classical model*, explains how managers *should* make decisions; it assumes managers will make logical decisions that will be the optimum in furthering the organization's best interests. The rational model is *prescriptive*, describing how managers ought to make decisions. It doesn't describe how managers *actually* make decisions.

Click-Along 7.2

Are People Really Rational?

The rational model makes some highly desirable assumptions:

- **Complete information, no uncertainty:** You should obtain complete, error-free information about all alternative courses of action and the consequences that will follow from each choice.

- **Logical, unemotional analysis:** Having no prejudices or emotional blind spots, you are able to logically evaluate the alternatives, ranking them from best to worst according to your personal preferences.

- **Best decision for the organization:** Confident of the best future course of action, you coolly choose the alternative that you believe will be to the maximum benefit of the organization.

Does this sound like the decision process of anyone you know?

Nonrational Decision Making: Managers Find It Difficult to Make Optimum Decisions

In contrast to models that show how decisions *should* be made are various models of how decisions actually *are* made. <u>*Nonrational models of decision making*</u> **explain how managers do make decisions; they assume that decision making is nearly always uncertain and risky, making it difficult for managers to make optimum decisions.** The nonrational models are *descriptive* rather than prescriptive: They describe how managers *actually* make decisions rather than how they should. Five nonrational models are *satisficing, incremental, coalitional, garbage can,* and *intuitional.*

1 Bounded Rationality & the Satisficing Model: "Satisfactory Is Good Enough" During the 1950s, economist **Herbert Simon**—who later received the Nobel Prize—began to study how managers actually make decisions. From his research he proposed that managers could not act truly logically because their rationality was bounded by so many restrictions.[9] Called <u>*bounded rationality*</u>**, the concept suggests that the ability of decision makers to be rational is limited by numerous constraints,** such as complexity, time and money, and their cognitive capacity, values, skills, habits, and unconscious reflexes. *(See Panel 7.2.)*

Science under glass. Columbia University's Biosphere 2, a huge glass and metal ecological research facility located 20 miles north of Tucson, Ariz., is a three-acre test tube meant to mimic Biosphere 1—planet earth. In this kind of model, would decision makers' rationality be less bounded?

PANEL 7.2
Some hindrances to perfectly rational decision making

- **Complexity:**
The problems that need solving are often exceedingly complex, beyond understanding.

- **Time and money constraints:**
There is not enough time and money to gather all relevant information.

- **Different cognitive capacity, values, skills, habits, and unconscious reflexes:**
Managers aren't all built the same way, of course, and all have personal limitations and biases that affect their judgment.

- **Imperfect information:**
Managers have imperfect, fragmentary information about the alternatives and their consequences.

- **Information overload:**
There is too much information for one person to process.

- **Different priorities:**
Some data is considered more important, so certain facts are ignored.

- **Conflicting goals:**
Other managers, including colleagues, have conflicting goals.

Because of such constraints, managers don't make an exhaustive search for the best alternative. Instead, they follow what Simon calls the *satisficing model*—that is, **managers seek alternatives until they find one that is satisfactory, not optimal.** Iridium's decision to proceed with a clunky one-pound satellite phone instead of waiting to improve the technology is an example of satisficing.

While looking for a solution that is merely "satisficing" might seem to be a weakness, it may well outweigh any advantages gained from delaying making a decision until all information is in and all alternatives weighed. However, making snap decisions can also backfire.

2 The Incremental Model: "The Least That Will Solve the Problem"
Another nonrational decision-making model is the *incremental model*, **in which managers take small, short-term steps to alleviate a problem,** rather than steps that will accomplish a long-term solution. Of course, over time a series of short-term steps may move toward a long-term solution. However, the temporary steps may also impede a beneficial long-term solution.

3 The Coalitional Model: "Let's Negotiate a Solution"
A *coalition* is an informal alliance of people supporting a particular goal. In the *coalitional model* of decision making, **managers band together in groups favoring different alternatives, and the groups bargain, negotiate, and compromise on a particular problem.** Thus, the coalition model is political, with different groups of managers using power to negotiate an outcome.

4 The Garbage-Can Model: "Anything Goes"
Some problems are so complex that they are not well understood. Some problems are also made complex because powerful individuals push their own personal agendas or have pet solutions looking for problems to fix. Some problems are aggravated because of management turnover. Any of these conditions can produce the *garbage-can model* of decision making, **which means managers make virtually random decisions.** While sometimes this model leads to a desirable outcome because a manager stumbles on an opportunity and gives it full attention, this approach can also lead to chaos.

Example of Garbage-Can Decision Making: Novell's Buying Spree

Novell, of Orem, Utah, is the maker of NetWare, a popular network operating system for coordinating microcomputer-based local area networks (LANs) throughout a company or a college campus. LANs allow personal computers to share programs, data files, and printers and other devices.

Novell thrived as corporate data managers realized that networks of PCs could exchange information more cheaply than the previous generation of mainframe and midrange computers. Today the company still has a substantial presence in the corporate network software market, although its market share is down owing to the rise of the Internet and competition from Microsoft. Moreover, during the early 1990s, under the influence of a new CEO, Novell went on a buying spree of consumer software titles (WordPerfect suite, Quattro Pro spreadsheet) in an attempt to turn itself into a rival to Microsoft. This garbage-can decision making distracted the company from changes in the network market beginning in 1994, when the Internet began growing in popularity.[10]

Click-Along 7.3

Example of Incremental Decision Making: Hilton Hotels Offers High-Speed Web Access

Click-Along 7.4

Example of Coalitional Decision Making: ICANN on Internet Governance

5 The Intuition Model: "What Experience Tells Me" The *intuitive model* of decision making consists of a manager's quickly sizing up a situation and making a decision based on his or her experience or practice, though often the judgment is made without conscious thought. The intuition may be nonrational, but it is not irrational because it is based on a manager's years of experience.

When a fire chief senses danger in the living room of a house while the flames are still small and orders the crew to withdraw—moments before the floor collapses—is the chief's insight the result of some psychic sixth sense? Not at all, says psychologist Gary Klein, an expert on this kind of decision making. Intuition is not mysterious. It's simply the recognition of complex patterns based on personal experience "without knowing how we do the recognizing," he says.[11]

Pat Riley, coach for the Miami Heat. One of pro basketball's most successful coaches, Riley led the Los Angeles Lakers to four World Championships and later led the New York Knicks to the team's first NBA finals in more than two decades. Like many good coaches, Riley applies the intuition model.

Example of Intuitive Decision Making: How Much Is Hotmail Worth?

In California, following graduate school at Stanford University, Sabeer Bhatia, then 27, built a startup company from daydream to a $400 million buyout by Microsoft Corp. in just two years. He did so by having not just a hot concept but also a cool head, with an intuition for negotiating based on his cultural experience as a child in India.

The concept was Hotmail, an idea that came from a coworker. The notion was to build a "webmail" system supported by advertising that would offer free e-mail accounts accessible anonymously over the World Wide Web. It was expected to appeal to people working for businesses who wanted to exchange personal messages with friends but didn't want to get in trouble by using their employers' e-mail. A further advantage was that people could log on from anywhere in the world—"from a McDonald's in Czechoslovakia or a café in Taiwan," as writer Po Bronson describes it.[12] Launched July 4, 1996, the company signed up thousands of users.

A year later, when Microsoft expressed interest in acquiring Hotmail, it began by offering a figure that would have put tens of millions of dollars in Bhatia's pocket. He rejected it, and the Microsoft executives stormed out. But they came back next week, and every week after that for a period of two months. Bhatia eventually countered with a price of a half billion dollars. Sputtering expletives, his adversaries shouted that he was crazy, out of his mind. But Bhatia realized these outbursts were only tactical. As a child in Bangalore, Bhatia had watched family servants haggling over groceries at the bazaar, and he had learned the tricks of Indian vendors.

Microsoft's offers continued to rise. Several times the software giant's negotiator pounded the table and stormed out. When Microsoft offered $350 million, everyone on Hotmail's management team except Bhatia voted to accept it. "Saying no to that offer was the scariest thing I ever did," he said later. "Everyone had told me, 'This is on your head if you screw it up.'"

On New Year's Eve, 1997, however, the deal was announced, for a reported $400 million worth of Microsoft stock.

Eight months later, when Hotmail had tripled in size, that figure looked like a bargain.

major question

What are the four steps in practical decision making?

The Big Picture
Four steps in making a decision are (1) identify the problem or opportunity, (2) think up alternative solutions, (3) evaluate alternatives and select a solution, and (4) implement and evaluate the solution chosen.

Whether a decision is programmed or nonprogrammed, rational or nonrational, typically there are four stages associated with making a practical decision. *(See Panel 7.3.)*

PANEL 7.3
The four steps in practical decision making

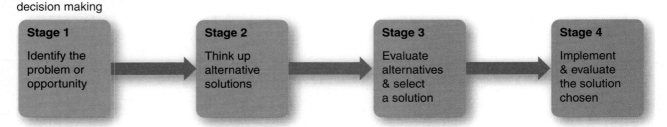

Stage 1	Stage 2	Stage 3	Stage 4
Identify the problem or opportunity	Think up alternative solutions	Evaluate alternatives & select a solution	Implement & evaluate the solution chosen

Stage 1: Identify the Problem or Opportunity— Determining the Actual versus the Desirable

As a manager, you'll probably find no shortage of ***problems*** **or difficulties that inhibit the achievement of goals.** Customer complaints. Supplier breakdowns. Staff turnover. Sales shortfalls. Competitor innovations.

However, you'll also often find ***opportunities***—**situations that present possibilities for exceeding existing goals.** It's the farsighted manager, however, who can look past the steady stream of daily problems and seize the moment to actually do *better* than the goals he or she is expected to achieve. When a competitor's top salesperson unexpectedly quits, that creates an opportunity for your company to hire that person away—or at least to take advantage of the vacuum and promote your product more vigorously in his or her sales territory.

Problems may also be opportunities in disguise. When your top salesperson quits, that may give you the opportunity to reexamine your company culture or system of motivations so that the job can be made more attractive for the next person.

The Commissioner. Bud Selig, the commissioner of Major League Baseball, has had to address the problem of player free agency, which has led to skyrocketing salaries for professional baseball players. Team owners may see this as a problem—they can't afford to meet the ever-escalating salaries. Or some may see it as an opportunity— a quick way to acquire star players and win the World Series, as the Arizona Diamondbacks did in 2001.

Whether you're confronted with a problem or an opportunity, you're dealing with the difference between the present *actual situation* versus the future *desirable situation*. The decision you're called on to make is how to make *improvements*—how to change conditions from the present to the desirable. This is a matter of **_diagnosis_**—**analyzing the underlying causes.**

Click-Along 7.5

How Do You Distinguish
Between Deadlines & Crises?

Example of Making Correct Diagnosis:
NASCAR Pit Crew Chief Wins Races

Former NASCAR race car driver Ray Evernham, now boss of a pit crew for racer Jeff Gordon, heads a crew of seven who change tires and add fuel during pit stops. Using two-way radio communication with the driver, Evernham makes all the decisions as the race proceeds, such as when to make pit stops, how many tires to change, and how much gas to pump. Thus, if a driver says the car is oversteering or understeering, Evernham must determine what kind of repairs must be made at pit stops, such as adjusting weight bolts on tires. By witnessing how other drivers make their pit stops, Evernham plans his, always trying to save a little time.

One day in 1994, for example, Evernham's correct diagnosis shaved crucial seconds off Jeff Gordon's pit stop time, enabling him to overtake Rusty Wallace and win a major race. He watched as Wallace's crew spent 17 seconds changing all four tires. Thus, when Gordon pulled in, Evernham ordered his crew to change just two tires, which took only nine seconds. The eight seconds difference allowed Gordon to win the race by $2^1/_2$ seconds.[13]

Stage 2: Think Up Alternative Solutions—Both the Obvious & the Creative

Employees burning with bright ideas are an employer's greatest competitive resource. "Creativity precedes innovation, which is its physical expression," says *Fortune* magazine writer Alan Farnham. "It's the source of all intellectual property."[14]

After you've identified the problem or opportunity and diagnosed its causes, you need to come up with alternative solutions. For a programmed decision, the alternatives will probably be easy and obvious. For nonprogrammed decisions, the more creative and innovative the alternatives, the better.

Cooking ideas. Home appliances have been Whirlpool Corp.'s main stock in trade, but in the face of a 1999 economic downturn the company called on its 75-member cross-company Innovation Team to come up with new ideas for business growth. The result: Inspired Chef, a new business in which chefs give cooking-class parties in private homes and then offer to sell knives, cutting boards, and Whirlpool products. Can you think of ways of generating creative ideas in an organization?

Stage 3: Evaluate Alternatives & Select a Solution— Ethics, Feasibility, & Effectiveness

In this stage, you need to evaluate each alternative not only according to cost and quality but also according to ethics, feasibility, and effectiveness.

Is It Ethical? No doubt at times a proposed alternative will seem to be right on nearly all counts. However, if it isn't ethical, you shouldn't give it a second look. *(See Panel 7.4.)*

Is It Feasible? A proposed solution may not be feasible for a variety of reasons: The top decision makers or customers won't accept it. Time is short. Costs are high. Technology isn't available. Company policies don't allow it. The action can't be reversed if there's trouble.

Is It Ultimately Effective? Satisficing is opting for a course of action because it is "good enough" rather than because it is optimal. For example, managers themselves may continue to operate a business that has been struck by its workers. This may "satisfice" for a while, but the most effective solution is to have the strikers back at work.

PANEL 7.4
Is it ethical? Here are some tests for business-people worried about whether they're committing fraud.[15]

- **The Smell Test:** Can you look yourself in the eye and tell yourself that the decision you have made is okay? Or does the situation have a bad smell to it?

- **The "What Would Your Parents Say?" Test:** Could you explain to your parents (or family) the basis for the action you are considering?

- **The Deposition Test:** Could you swear in court or in a deposition (testimony taken by lawyers while you're under oath) that the activity you are doing is right?

Stage 4: Implement & Evaluate the Solution Chosen

With programmed decisions, implementation is usually straightforward (though not necessarily easy—firing employees who steal may be an obvious decision but it can still be emotionally draining). With nonprogrammed decisions, implementation can be quite difficult; when one company acquires another, for instance, it may take months to consolidate the departments, accounting systems, inventories, and so on.

Successful Implementation For implementation to be successful, you need to do two things:

- **Plan carefully:** Especially if reversing an action will be difficult, you need to make careful plans for implementation. Nonprogrammed decisions may require written plans.

- **Be sensitive to those affected:** You need to consider how the people affected may feel about the change—inconvenienced, insecure, even fearful, all of which can trigger resistance. This is why it helps to give employees and customers latitude during a changeover in business practices or working arrangements.

Example of Faulty Implementation: Consumer Resentment over "Retirement" of Beanie Babies

In the fall of 1999, word spread that the maker of Beanie Babies, Ty Inc., would retire the collectible toys by the end of the year. Although some customers were simply disappointed that the small stuffed animals might actually be discontinued, others were suspicious that the company was trying to manipulate them by relaunching Beanie Babies out under a different name and raising the toys' high prices even higher.

Yet Ty also filed trademark registration for new names (such as "Bean E Bears"), leading toy industry experts to suggest that the company was trying to bring about a slight name change to drive sales as Beanies began to lose their appeal to youngsters. Consumers, however, were exasperated. "I have a sneaking suspicion that they are trying to clear the shelves all out and they are going to come out with more at the beginning of the year," said one. "I'm tired of being put off by a company that has no care or concern for the consumer," said another. "Could you please work on improving your communication with us, your CUSTOMERS!!" pleaded a frustrated consumer on a Ty Internet chat room.

"There is a great risk here of having the whole thing backfire in Ty's face," said the editor of a trade publication. "If Ty is manipulating what children want, that is going to affect the parents of those children. I think they have a right to feel like they are being manipulated at this point."[16]

Banished Beanie Babies?

Evaluation One "law" in economics is the Law of Unintended Consequences—things happen that weren't foreseen. For this reason, you need to follow up and evaluate the results of the decision.

What should you do if the action is not working? Some possibilities:

- **Give it more time:** You need to make sure employees, customers, and so on have had enough time to get used to the new action.

- **Change it slightly:** Maybe the action was correct, but it just needs "tweaking"—a small change of some sort.

- **Try another alternative:** If Plan A doesn't seem to be working, maybe you want to scrap it for another alternative.

- **Start over:** If no alternative seems workable, you need to go back to the drawing board—to Stage 1 of the decision-making process.

Example of Evaluation: Abercrombie Catches Flak for T-Shirts

Clothing maker Abercrombie & Fitch has had some success selling edgy T-shirts that, says a spokesman, "poke fun at everybody, from . . . football coaches to Irish Americans to snow skiers." In 2002, it began selling T-shirts it thought would appeal to young Asians with a sense of humor. One, for instance, had the slogan "Wong Brothers Laundry Service—Two Wongs Can Make It White." Some Asians were irate. "The stereotypes they depict are more than a century old," said one. "It denigrates Asian men," said another.

Should Abercrombie have given the product more time? After all, not everyone objected. "I think it's a humorous T-shirt, and you should have a sense of humor about these things," said a Vietnamese American accountant. Or should it have tried to change the concept slightly—perhaps removed the 1900s-era caricatured faces of slanted eyes and rice-paddy hats? Or should it have tried an entirely new alternative—and perhaps this time test-marketed the shirts (as it had not the first time)?

In the end, the company decided it was best to yank the shirts, apologize, and start over.[17]

major question

How do I work with others to make things happen?

The Big Picture

Group decision making has five potential advantages and four potential disadvantages. There are a number of characteristics of groups a manager should be aware of, as well as participative management and group problem-solving techniques.

The movies celebrate the lone heroes who, like Clint Eastwood, make their own moves, call their own shots. Most managers, however, work with groups and teams (as we discuss in Chapter 13). Although groups don't make as high-quality decisions as the best individual acting alone, research suggests that groups make better decisions than *most* individuals acting alone.[18] Thus, to be an effective manager, you need to learn about decision making in groups.

Advantages & Disadvantages of Group Decision Making

Because you may often have a choice as to whether to make a decision by yourself or to consult with others, you need to understand the advantages and disadvantages of group-aided decision making. *(See Panel 7.5.)*

PANEL 7.5

Group-aided decision making: potential advantages and disadvantages

Potential advantages	Potential disadvantages
1. Greater pool of knowledge	1. A few people dominate
2. Different perspectives	2. Groupthink
3. Intellectual stimulation	3. Satisficing
4. Better understanding of decision rationale	4. Goal displacement
5. Deeper commitment to the decision	

Different perspectives or groupthink? A diversified team can offer differing points of view, as well as a greater pool of knowledge and intellectual stimulation. Or it can offer groupthink and satisficing. What has been your experience as to the value of decision making in the groups you've been in?

Advantages Using a group to make a decision offers five possible advantages.[19] For these benefits to happen, however, it's important that the group be made up of diverse participants, not just people who all think the same way.

- **Greater pool of knowledge:** When several people are making the decision, there is a greater pool of information on which to draw. If one person doesn't have the pertinent knowledge and experience, someone else might.

- **Different perspectives:** Because different people have different perspectives—marketing, production, legal, and so on—they see the problem from different angles.

- **Intellectual stimulation:** A group of people can brainstorm or otherwise bring greater intellectual stimulation and creativity to the decision-making process than is usually possible with one person acting alone.

- **Better understanding of decision rationale:** If you participate in making a decision, you are more apt to understand the reasoning behind the decision, including the pros and cons leading up to the final step.

- **Deeper commitment to the decision:** If you've been part of the group that has bought into the final decision, you're more apt to be committed to seeing that the course of action is successfully implemented.

Disadvantages The disadvantages of group-aided decision making spring from problems in how members interact.[20]

- **A few people dominate or intimidate:** Sometimes a handful of people will talk the longest and the loudest, and the rest of the group will simply give in. Or one individual, such as a strong leader, will exert disproportional influence, sometimes by intimidation. This cuts down on the variety of ideas.

- **Groupthink:** _Groupthink_ **occurs when group members strive to agree for the sake of unanimity and thus avoid accurately assessing the decision situation.** Here the positive team spirit of the group actually works against sound judgment.

- **Satisficing:** Because most people would just as soon cut short a meeting, the tendency is to seek a decision that is "good enough" rather than to push on in pursuit of other possible solutions. Satisficing can occur because groups have limited time, lack the right kind of information, or are unable to handle large amounts of information.[21]

- **Goal displacement:** Although the primary task of the meeting may be to solve a particular problem, other considerations may rise to the fore, such as rivals trying to win an argument. _Goal displacement_ **occurs when the primary goal is subsumed by a secondary goal.**

Ford Mustang. Highly motivated work teams depend on open communication and self-management. Ford Motor Co. provided such an atmosphere for its Team Mustang work group. The work team, suppliers, and consumers worked together to make the Mustang convertible a winner in the competitive automobile market.

Group Decision Making: How to Work with Others

What Managers Need to Know about Groups & Decision Making

If you're a manager deliberating whether to call a meeting for group input, there are four characteristics of groups to be aware of:

1 They Are Less Efficient Groups take longer to make decisions. Thus, if time is of the essence, you may want to make the decision by yourself. Faced with time pressures or the serious impact of a decision, groups use less information and fewer communication channels, which increases the probability of a bad decision.[22]

2 Their Size Affects Decision Quality The larger the group, the lower the quality of the decision.[23]

3 They May Be Too Confident Groups are more confident about their judgments and choices than individuals are. This, of course, can be a liability because it can lead to groupthink.

4 Knowledge Counts Decision making accuracy is higher when group members know a good deal about the relevant issues. It is also higher when a group leader has the ability to weight members' opinions.[24] Depending on whether group members know or don't know one another, the kind of knowledge also counts. For example, people who are familiar with one another tend to make better decisions when members have a lot of unique information. However, people who aren't familiar with one another tend to make better decisions when the members have common knowledge.[25]

Some guidelines to using groups are presented below. *(See Panel 7.6.)* Remember that individual decisions are not *necessarily* better than group decisions. As we said at the outset, although groups don't make as high-quality decisions as the *best* individual acting alone, groups generally make better decisions than *most* individuals acting alone.

PANEL 7.6

When a group can help in decision making: three practical guidelines.[26] The following guidelines may help you as a manager decide whether to include people in a decision making process and, if so, which people.

1 When it can increase quality: If additional information would increase the quality of the decision, managers should involve those people who can provide the needed information. Thus, if a type of decision occurs frequently, such as deciding on promotions or who qualifies for a loan, groups should be used because they tend to produce more consistent decisions than individuals do.

2 When it can increase acceptance: If acceptance within the organization is important, managers need to involve those individuals whose acceptance and commitment are important.

3 When it can increase development: If people can be developed through their participation, managers may want to involve those whose development is most important.

Participative Management: Involving Employees in Decision Making

"Only the most productive companies are going to win," says former General Electric CEO Jack Welch about competition in the world economy. "If you can't sell a top-quality product at the world's lowest price, you're going to be out of the game. In that environment, 6% annual improvement may not be good enough anymore; you may need 8% to 9%."[27]

One technique that has been touted for meeting this productivity challenge is _participative management (PM)_, **the process of involving employees in (a) setting goals, (b) making decisions, (c) solving problems, and (d) making changes in the organization.**[28] Employees themselves seem to want to participate more in management: In one nationwide survey of 2,408 workers, two thirds expressed the desire for more influence or decision-making power in their jobs.[29] Thus, participative management is predicted to increase motivation, innovation, and performance because it helps employees fulfill three basic needs: autonomy, meaningfulness of work, and interpersonal contact.[30]

Is PM Really Effective? Does participative management really work? Certainly it can increase employee job involvement, organizational commitment, and creativity, and it can lower role conflict and ambiguity.[31] Yet it has been shown that, although participation has a significant effect on job performance and job satisfaction, that effect is small—a finding that calls into question the practicality of using PM at all.[32]

So what's a manager to do? In our opinion, PM is not a quick-fix solution for low productivity and motivation. Yet it can probably be effective in certain situations, assuming that managers and employees interact constructively—that is, have the kind of relationship that fosters cooperation and respect rather than competition and defensiveness.[33]

Welch. The GE CEO was one of the most successful executives in American business history.

Making PM Work Although participative management doesn't work in all situations, it can be effective if the following factors are present:[34]

- **Top management is continually involved:** Implementing PM must be monitored and managed by top management.[35]

- **Middle and supervisory managers are supportive:** These managers tend to resist PM because it reduces their authority. Thus, it's important to gain the support and commitment of managers in these ranks.

- **Employees trust managers:** PM is less likely to succeed when employees don't trust management.

- **Employees are ready:** PM is more effective when employees are properly trained, prepared, and interested in participating.

- **Employees don't work in interdependent jobs:** Interdependent employees generally don't have a broad understanding of the entire production process, so their PM contribution may actually be counterproductive.

- **PM is implemented with TQM:** A study of Fortune 1000 firms during three different years found employee involvement was more effective when it was implemented as part of a broader total quality management (TQM) program.[36] (TQM was discussed in Chapter 1 and is discussed again in Chapter 16.)

Group Problem-Solving Techniques: Reaching for Consensus

Using groups to make decisions generally requires that they reach a *consensus*, **which occurs when members are able to express their opinions and reach agreement to support the final decision.** More specifically, consensus is reached "when all members can say they either agree with the decision or have had their 'day in court' and were unable to convince the others of their viewpoint," says one expert in decision making. "In the final analysis, everyone agrees to support the outcome."[37] This does not mean, however, that group members agree with the decision, only that they are willing to work toward its success.

One management expert offers the following dos and don'ts for achieving consensus.[38]

■ **Dos:** Use active listening skills. Involve as many members as possible. Seek out the reasons behind arguments. Dig for the facts.

■ **Don'ts:** Avoid log rolling and horse trading ("I'll support your pet project if you'll support mine"). Avoid making an agreement simply to keep relations amicable and not rock the boat. Finally, don't try to achieve consensus by putting questions to a vote; this will only split the group into winners and losers, perhaps creating bad feeling among the latter.

Toward consensus. Working to achieve cooperation in a group can tell you a lot about yourself. How well do you handle the negotiation process? What do you do when you're disappointed in a result reached by consensus?

More Group Problem-Solving Techniques

Decision-making experts have developed three group-problem-solving techniques to aid in problem solving: (1) *interacting groups*, (2) *nominal groups*, and (3) *Delphi groups*. These may be assisted with (4) *computer-aided decision making*.

1 The Interacting Group: For Open Discussion The most common decision-making group, the *interacting group* **is a group in which members interact and deliberate with one another to reach a consensus.** No doubt you've been in such a group—discussing, arguing, persuading, agreeing, disagreeing until a consensus was achieved.

2 The Nominal Group: For Generating Ideas Members of a nominal group don't talk to one another—at least in the beginning. Rather, **the purpose of a *nominal group* is to generate ideas and evaluate solutions, which members do so by writing down as many ideas as possible. The ideas are then listed on a blackboard, then discussed, then voted on.**

During the discussion period, there may be a "30-second soapbox" format, in which every participant is allowed 30 seconds to argue for or against any idea listed. After discussion, group members may vote—anonymously—using a weighted voting procedure (for example, first choice = 3 points, second choice = 2 points, third choice = 1 point). The group leader tallies the points to determine the group's choice.[39]

3 The Delphi Group: For Consensus of Experts   The Delphi group technique was originally designed for technological forecasting but now is used as a multi-purpose planning tool.[40] **The _Delphi group_ uses physically dispersed experts who fill out questionnaires to anonymously generate ideas; the judgments are combined and in effect averaged to achieve a consensus of expert opinion.**

The Delphi group technique is useful when face-to-face discussions are impractical. It's also practical when disagreement and conflicts are likely to impair communication, when certain individuals might try to dominate group discussions, and when there is a high risk of groupthink.[41]

4 Computer-Aided Decision Making   As in nearly every other aspect of business life, computers have entered the area of decision making, where they are useful not only in collecting information more quickly but also in reducing roadblocks to group consensus.

The two types of computer-aided decision making systems are *chauffeur driven* and *group driven*, as follows:[42]

■ **Chauffeur-driven systems—for push-button consensus:** So-called *"chauffeur-driven" computer-aided decision-making systems* ask participants to answer predetermined questions on electronic keypads or dials. These have been used as polling devices, for instance, with audiences on live television shows such as "Who Wants to Be a Millionaire," allowing responses to be computer-tabulated almost instantly.

■ **Group-driven systems—for anonymous networking:** A *group-driven computer-aided decision system* involves a meeting within a room of participants who express their ideas anonymously on a computer network. Instead of talking with one another, participants type their comments, reactions, or evaluations on their individual computer keyboards. The input is projected on a large screen at the front of the room for all to see. Because participation is anonymous and no one person is able to dominate the meeting on the basis of status or personality, everyone feels free to participate, and the roadblocks to consensus are accordingly reduced.

Compared to the nominal-group technique or traditional brainstorming, group-driven systems have been shown to produce greater quality and quantity of ideas for large groups of people, although there is no advantage with groups of 4–6 people.[43] The technique also produces more ideas as group size increases from 5 to 10 members.

Computer-aided decision making. This photo shows the kind of arrangement that might be set up for group-driven, anonymous networking. In reality, this is an early-morning flower auction in Alsmeer, Netherlands, in which buyers bid via electronic network on 17 million flowers, which are shipped to shops around the world.

major question

Trying to be rational isn't always easy. What are the barriers?

The Big Picture
Responses to a decision situation may take the form of four ineffective reactions or three effective reactions. Managers should be aware of four common decision-making biases.

Do you make decisions based on how happy or unhappy you think you're going to feel about the outcome? Then here's some interesting news.

It seems that people expect certain life events to have a much greater emotional effect than in fact they do, according to Harvard University psychologist Daniel Gilbert, who has studied individual emotional barometers in decision making. College professors, for example, expect to be quite happy if they are given tenure and quite unhappy if they aren't. However, Gilbert found those who received tenure were happy but not as happy as they themselves had predicted, whereas those denied tenure did not become very unhappy.

The expectation about the level of euphoria or disappointment was also found to be true of big-jackpot lottery winners and of people being tested for H.I.V. infection. That is, people are often right when they describe what outcome will make them feel good or bad, but they are often wrong when asked to predict how strongly they will feel that way and how long the feeling will last. "Even severe life events have a negative impact on people's sense of well-being and satisfaction for no more than three months," says one report, "after which their feelings at least go back to normal."[44]

Perhaps knowing that you have this "immune system" of the mind, which blunts bad feelings and smoothes out euphoric ones, can help make it easier for you to make difficult decisions.

Big decisions. Everything about the events of September 11, 2001, the day terrorist-hijacked jetliners crashed into New York's World Trade Center (remnants of which are shown here, at what became known as Ground Zero), as well as into the Pentagon and in a field in Pennsylvania, created difficult, emotional decisions for millions of people. Among the heroes of that day was Todd Beamer, a 32-year-old businessman who, with other passengers, apparently took action against hijackers aboard United Airlines Flight 93. The terrorists, it is surmised, planned to aim the Boeing 757 at a target in Washington, D.C., such as the White House, but probably because of the efforts of Beamer and other travelers the plane crashed outside Pittsburgh, killing everyone on board. The last words anyone on the ground heard Beamer say, in a phone call to a GTE operator, was to other passengers who had agreed to jump the terrorists: "Let's roll." It's unlikely you would be directly involved in an event of this magnitude during your lifetime, but it could happen. How decisive do you think you would be?

How Do Individuals Respond to a Decision Situation? Ineffective & Effective Responses

What is your typical response when you're suddenly confronted with a challenge in the form of a problem or an opportunity? There are perhaps four ineffective reactions and three effective ones.[45]

Four Ineffective Reactions Four defective problem-recognition and problem-solving approaches that act as barriers when you must make an important decision in a situation of conflict are the following:

1 Relaxed Avoidance—"There's no point in doing anything; nothing bad's going to happen": In *relaxed avoidance*, **a manager decides to take no action in the belief that there will be no great negative consequences.** This condition, then, is a form of complacency: You either don't see or you disregard the signs of danger (or of opportunity).

For example, you might decide to accept a job offer without checking the financial status of your new employer, even though the company is in an industry being whipsawed by technological change. After his first employer went out of business because of poor money management, programmer Bryan Galdrikian began asking prospective employers more about their finances.[46]

2 Relaxed Change—"Why not just take the easiest way out?": In *relaxed change*, **a manager realizes that complete inaction will have negative consequences but opts for the first available alternative that involves low risk.** This is, of course, a form of "satisficing"; the manager avoids exploring a variety of alternatives in order to make the best decision.

For example, if you go to the college career center, sign up for one job interview, and are offered and accept a job based on that single interview, you may have no basis for comparison to know that you made the right choice.

3 Defensive Avoidance—"There's no reason for me to explore other solution alternatives": In *defensive avoidance*, **a manager can't find a good solution and follows by (a) procrastinating, (b) passing the buck, or (c) denying the risk of any** negative consequences. This is a posture of resignation and a denial of responsibility for taking action. By procrastinating, you put off making a decision ("I'll get to this later"). In passing the buck, you let someone else take the consequences of making the decision ("Let George do it"). In denying the risk that there will be any negative consequences, you are engaging in rationalizing ("How bad could it be?").

Global Sports Interactive of King of Prussia, Pa., didn't procrastinate; it offered an applicant for its new engineering director's job the position just eight days after he first responded to an Internet want ad. In the hot world of recruiting job candidates at this level, the quick decision paid off. A rival, a Big Five accounting firm, lost out because it waited until five weeks later to make an offer. If that firm "had been a little quicker," said the 48-year-old applicant, "I probably would have gone the other way."[47]

4 Panic—"This is so stressful, I've got to do something—anything—to get rid of the problem": This reaction is especially apt to occur in crisis situations. **In *panic*, a manager is so frantic to get rid of the problem that he or she can't deal with the situation realistically.** This is the kind of situation in which the manager has completely forgotten the idea of behaving with "grace under pressure," of staying cool and calm. Troubled by anxiety, irritability, sleeplessness, and even physical illness, if you're experiencing this reaction, your judgment may be so clouded that you won't be able to accept help in dealing with the problem or to realistically evaluate the alternatives.

Panic can even be life-threatening. When in 1999 a jetliner skidded off the runway at Little Rock National Airport, passenger Clark Brewster and a flight attendant tried repeatedly to open an exit door that would not budge. "About that time I hear someone say the word 'Fire!'" Brewster said. "The flight attendant bends down and says, 'Please pray with me.'" Fortunately, cooler, quicker-thinking individuals were able to find another way out.[48]

Three Effective Reactions: Deciding to Decide In *deciding to decide*, a manager agrees that he or she must decide what to do about a problem or opportunity and take effective decision-making steps. Three ways to help you decide whether to decide are to evaluate the following:[49]

1 Importance—"How high priority is this situation?": You need to determine how much priority to give the decision situation. If it's a threat, how extensive might prospective losses or damage be? If it's an opportunity, how beneficial might the possible gains be?

2 Credibility—"How believable is the information about the situation?": You need to evaluate how much is known about the possible threat or opportunity. Is the source of the information trustworthy? Is there credible evidence?

3 Urgency—"How quickly must I act on the information about the situation?": Is the threat immediate? Will the window of opportunity stay open long? Can actions to address the situation be done gradually?

Xtreme decisions. The Xtreme Football League was financed by NBC Television and the World Wrestling Federation. After only one season, with the XFL losing money from insufficient advertising and fan support, the owners had to consider whether to cut their losses or give it a second chance at the risk of even greater loss. XFL president Basil DeVito Jr. is shown here making the announcement that the league was folding.

Example of Deciding to Decide: If You Own a Fast Thoroughbred, Should You Even Bother to Race It?

Owning a racehorse, especially one with the potential to win the famed Kentucky Derby, is like owning a million-dollar business. If your objective is to make money, how should you manage such valuable property?

After a horse named Fusaichi Pegasus won the 2000 Kentucky Derby, his owner, Fusao Sekiguchi, had to decide: To make the most money, should he continue to race the horse? Or should he auction it off to a commercial breeder, who would use him to breed with mares to produce a strain of superior thoroughbreds? Because the money involved millions, the answer to his first decision—*Should this be considered a high-priority matter?*—seems obvious.

Sekiguchi decided the facts warranted that he should sell rather than race. The main determinant here was *How believable is the information?* For this decision, research would have shown that the career leader in winning purses, $10 million, was a horse named Cigar, which ran through age 6. Research would also show the stud fees of retired successful race horses ran, per mare, from $5,000 (for Grindstone) to $80,000 (for Charismatic). Finally, recent history showed that breeding had caused horses to be faster but less durable than earlier thoroughbreds, making injury more likely.

The final decision—*How quickly should this information be acted on?*—was affected by the fact that most race horses are finished by age 4, even age 2.

After three more races, Fusaichi Pegasus was sold for $60 million to a stud farm, where he is bred to more than 100 mares a year for a record stud fee of $135,000 a mare.[50]

Four Common Decision-Making Biases: Rules of Thumb, or "Heuristics"

If someone asked you to explain the basis on which you make decisions, could you even say? Perhaps, after some thought, you might come up with some "rules of thumb." Scholars call them _heuristics_ (pronounced "hyur-_ris_-tiks")—**strategies that simplify the process of making decisions.**

Despite the fact that people use such rules of thumb all the time, that doesn't mean they're reliable. Indeed, some are real barriers to high-quality decision making. Among those that tend to bias how decision makers process information are (1) _availability_, (2) _representativeness_, (3) _anchoring and adjustment_, and (4) _escalation of commitment_.[51]

1 The Availability Bias: Using Only the Information Available If you had a perfect on-time work attendance record for nine months but then were late for work four days during the last two months because of traffic, shouldn't your boss take into account your entire attendance history when considering you for a raise? Yet managers tend to give more weight to more recent behavior. This is because of the _availability bias_—**managers use information readily available from memory to make judgments.**

The bias, of course, is that readily available information may not present a complete picture of a situation. The availability bias may be stoked by the news media, which tends to favor news that is unusual or dramatic. Thus, for example, because of the efforts of interest groups or celebrities, more news coverage may be given to AIDS or to breast cancer than to heart disease, leading people to think the former are the bigger killers when in fact the latter is the biggest killer.

2 The Representativeness Bias: Faulty Generalizing from a Small Sample or a Single Event As a form of financial planning, playing state lotteries leaves something to be desired. When, for instance, in a recent year the New York jackpot reached $70 million, a New Yorker's chance of winning was one in 12,913,588.[52] (A person would have a greater chance of being struck by lightning.) Nevertheless, millions of people buy lottery tickets because they read or hear about a handful of fellow citizens who

have been the fortunate recipients of enormous winnings. This is an example of the _representativeness bias_, **the tendency to generalize from a small sample or a single event.**

The bias here is that just because something happens once, that doesn't mean it is representative—that it will happen again or will happen to you. For example, just because you hired an extraordinary sales representative from a particular university, that doesn't mean that same university will provide an equally qualified candidate next time. Yet managers make this kind of hiring decision all the time.

3 The Anchoring & Adjustment Bias: Being Influenced by an Initial Figure Managers will often give their employees a standard percentage raise in salary, basing the decision on whatever the workers made the preceding year. They may do this even though the raise may be completely out of alignment with what other companies are paying for the same skills. This is an instance of the _anchoring and adjustment bias_, **the tendency to make decisions based on an initial figure.**

The bias is that the initial figure may be irrelevant to market realities. This phenomenon is sometimes seen in real estate sales. A homeowner may at first list his or her house at an extremely high (but perhaps randomly chosen) selling price. The seller is then unwilling later to come down substantially to match the kind of buying offers that reflect what the marketplace thinks the house is really worth.

4 The Escalation of Commitment Bias: Feeling Overly Invested in a Decision If you really hate to admit you're wrong, you need to be aware of the *escalation of commitment bias*, **whereby decision makers increase their commitment to a project despite negative information about it.** History is full of examples of heads of state who escalated their commitment to an original decision in the face of overwhelming evidence that it was producing detrimental consequences. A noteworthy example was President Lyndon B. Johnson's pressing on of the Vietnam War despite mounting casualties abroad and political upheavals at home.

The bias is that what was originally made as perhaps a rational decision may continue to be supported for irrational reasons—pride, ego, the spending of enormous sums of money, and being "loss averse." Indeed, scholars have advanced what is known as the *prospect theory*, which suggests that decision makers find the notion of an actual loss more painful than giving up the possibility of a gain.[53] We saw a variant of this when we described the tendency of investors to hold on to their losers but cash in their winners.

Escalation of commitment. Hewlett-Packard Co. CEO Carly Fiorina and Compaq Computer Corp. chief executive Michael Capellas do a friendly bumping of knuckles before an investors meeting. The acquisition of Compaq—a leader in the personal computer revolution in the 1980s and 1990s—by technology leader HP in May 2002 was finally achieved after months of a long and bitter corporate war that threatened to derail the biggest computer merger in history. Many analysts and stockholders were against the merger of these two global corporations—first, because of the enormity of the challenge of integrating the two companies and, second, because of the disastrous track record of past computer-company mergers (as when Compaq acquired DEC). Particularly vociferous in their opposition were the descendants of the Hewlett and Packard families, who objected not only to the incredibly risky business strategy but also to the prospect of 15,000 job cuts in what had been an employee-friendly environment. A lawsuit brought by director Walter Hewlett that accused HP of drawing overly optimistic financial targets and of buying shareholder votes to approve the merger was unsuccessful, and stockholders finally approved the merger in a close vote. Perhaps you're now in a position to judge whether the resulting $87 billion global company fulfilled Fiorina's optimistic predictions. Was there too much of an escalation of commitment bias operating here?

Click-Along 7.6

Taking Something Practical Away from This Chapter— Encouraging Creativity

practical action

Being Aware of Your Possible Biases: How Can Your Judgment Be Distorted?

The four common decision-making biases described in the text may be expressed in more specific distortions of judgment. Here are five types of questions that you might ask yourself next time you're poised to make a decision:

"Am I Being Too Cocky?" The Overconfidence Bias If you're making a decision in an area in which you have considerable experience or expertise, you're less likely to be overconfident. Interestingly, however, you're more apt to be overconfident when dealing with questions on subjects you're unfamiliar with or questions with moderate to extreme difficulty.[54]

In addition, many sorts of managers—especially top managers who worked their way up to the top—have a kind of overconfidence that makes them overestimate their ability to control events (the *illusion-of-control bias*).

Recommendation: When dealing with unfamiliar or difficult matters, think how your impending decision might go wrong. Afterward pay close attention to the consequences of your decision for feedback about your judgment.

"Am I Considering the Actual Evidence, or Am I Wedded to My Prior Beliefs?" The Prior-Hypothesis Bias Do you tend to have strong beliefs? When confronted with a choice, decision makers with strong prior beliefs tend to make their decision based on their beliefs—even if evidence show those beliefs are wrong. This is known as the *prior-hypothesis bias.* In addition, people tend to look for evidence to support their beliefs rather than contradict them.[55]

Recommendation: Although it's always more comforting to look for evidence to support your prior beliefs, you need to be tough-minded and weigh the evidence.

No New Coke. What kind of biases do you think Coca-Cola's managers might have been operating under when, in 1985, they decided to scrap their successful traditional cola formula in favor of New Coke, which became a marketing disaster?

"Are Events Really Connected, or Are They Just Chance?" The Ignoring-Randomness Bias Is a rise in sales in athletic shoes because of your company's advertising campaign or because it's the start of the school year? Many managers don't understand the laws of randomness and believe chance events—even multiple chance events—are connected to one another.

Recommendation: Don't attribute trends or connections to a single, random event.

"Is There Enough Data on Which to Make a Decision?" The Unrepresentative Sample Bias If all the secretaries in your office say they prefer dairy creamer to real cream or milk in their coffee, is that enough data on which to launch an ad campaign trumpeting the superiority of dairy creamer? It might if you polled 3,000 secretaries, but not if you asked only 3 or even 30. This is too small a sample to reflect the sentiments of secretaries everywhere.

Recommendation: You need to be attuned to the importance of the size of your sample when making a decision.

"Looking Back, Did I (or Others) Really Know Enough Then to Have Made a Better Decision?" The 20-20 Hindsight Bias Once managers know what the consequences of a decision are, they may begin to think they could have predicted it ahead of time. They can no longer recall how uncertain the circumstances were at the time they made the decision. Instead, they may remember the facts as being a lot clearer than they actually were.[56]

Recommendation: Try to keep in mind—especially when you're evaluating negative outcomes of decisions made by subordinates—that hindsight does not equal foresight.

Key Terms Used in This Chapter

Summary

7.1
The Nature of Decision Making

- A decision is a choice made from among available alternatives. Decision making is the process of identifying and choosing alternative courses of action.

- Decisions are of two types: programmed and nonprogrammed. Programmed decisions are repetitive and routine. They tend to follow established rules and so are virtually automatic. Nonprogrammed decisions are those that occur under nonroutine, unfamiliar circumstances. Because they occur in response to unusual, unpredictable opportunities and threats, nonprogrammed decisions are relatively unstructured.

- A decision-making style reflects the combination of how an individual perceives and responds to information. Decision-making styles may tend to have a value orientation, which reflects the extent to which a person focuses on either task or technical concerns versus people and social concerns when making decisions. Decision-making styles may also reflect a person's tolerance for ambiguity, the extent to which a person has a high or low need for structure or control in his life.

When the dimensions of value orientation and tolerance for ambiguity are combined, they form four styles of decision making: directive, analytical, conceptual, and behavioral.

- Knowledge of decision-making styles helps you understand yourself, increase your ability to influence others, and give you an awareness of how people arrive at different decisions from the same information.

7.2
Two Kinds of Decision Making: Rational & Nonrational

- Two models managers follow in making decisions that are rational and nonrational.

- The rational model of decision making, also called the classical model, explains how managers should make decisions; it assumes managers will make logical decisions that will be the optimum in furthering the organization's best interests. The rational model is prescriptive, describing how managers ought to make decisions. It doesn't describe how managers actually make decisions. The rational model assumes that managers have complete information and there is no uncertainty, that they can do unemotional analysis, and that they are coolly capable of making the best decision for the organization.

- Nonrational models of decision making explain how managers do make decisions; they assume that decision making is nearly always uncertain and risky, making it difficult for managers to make optimum decisions. The nonrational models are descriptive rather than prescriptive: they describe how managers actually make decisions rather than how they should.

- Five nonrational models are satisficing, incremental, coalitional, garbage can, and intuitional. (1) Satisficing falls under the concept of bounded rationality—that is, that the ability of decision makers to be rational is limited by enormous constraints, such as complexity or time and money. These constraints force managers to make decisions according to the satisficing model—that is, managers seek alternatives until they find one that is satisfactory, not optimal. (2) Another nonrational decision-making model is the incremental model, in which managers take small, short-term steps to alleviate a problem rather than steps that will accomplish a long-term solution. (3) In the coalitional model, managers band together in groups favoring different alternatives, and the groups bargain, negotiate, and compromise on a particular problem. (4) In the garbage-can model of decision making, managers make virtually random decisions. (5) The intuitive model of decision making consists of a manager's quickly sizing up a situation and making a decision based on his or her experience or practice; it is nonrational but not irrational because it is based on a lot of experience.

7.3
Solving Problems & Seizing Opportunities: Making Practical Decisions

- There are four steps in making a decision.

- Stage 1 is identifying the problem or opportunity. A problem is a difficulty that inhibits the achievement of goals. An opportunity is a situation that presents possibilities for exceeding existing goals. Whether you're dealing with a problem or an opportunity, you're dealing with the difference between the present actual situation versus the future desirable situation. The decision you're called upon to make is how to make improvements—to change from the present to the desirable. This is a matter of diagnosis—analyzing the underlying causes.

- Stage 2 is thinking up alternative solutions. For programmed decisions, alternatives will be easy and obvious. For nonprogrammed decisions, the more creative and innovative the alternatives, the better.

- Stage 3 is evaluating the alternatives and selecting a solution. Alternatives should be evaluated not only according to cost and quality but also according to ethics, feasibility, and effectiveness.

- Stage 4 is implementing and evaluating the solution chosen. For implementation to be successful, you need to do two things: plan carefully and be sensitive to those affected. When evaluating the decision made, if the action isn't working, you could give it more time, change it slightly, try another alternative, or start over again with Stage 1.

7.4
Group Decision Making: How to Work with Others

- Most managers work with groups and teams. Groups make better decisions than most individuals acting alone, though not as good as the best individual acting alone.

- Using a group to make a decision offers five possible advantages: (1) a greater pool of knowledge; (2) different perspectives; (3) intellectual stimulation; (4) better understanding of the reasoning behind the decision; and (5) deeper commitment to the decision. It also has four disadvantages: (1) a few people may dominate or intimidate; (2) it will produce groupthink, when group members strive for agreement among themselves for the sake of unanimity and so avoid accurately assessing the decision situation; (3) satisficing; and (4) goal displacement, when the primary goal is subsumed to a secondary goal.

- Some characteristics of groups to be aware of are (1) groups are less efficient, (2) their size affects decision quality, (3) they may be too confident, and (4) knowledge counts—decision-making accuracy is higher when group members know a lot about the issues.

■ Participative management (PM) is the process of involving employees in setting goals, making decisions, solving problems, and making changes in the organization. Although the impact of PM is small, it can increase employee job involvement, organizational commitment, and creativity and can lower role conflict and ambiguity. PM can be effective if top management is continually involved, middle and supervisory managers are supportive, employees trust managers, employees are ready, employees don't work in interdependent jobs, and PM is implement with total quality management (TQM).

■ Using groups to make decisions generally requires that they reach a consensus, which occurs when members are able to express their opinions and reach agreement to support the final decision.

■ Three group-problem solving techniques to aid in problem solving are use of three kinds of groups. (1) In interacting groups, members interact and deliberate with one another to reach a consensus. (2) In nominal groups, members generate ideas and evaluate solutions by writing down as many ideas as possible; the ideas are then listed on a blackboard, then discussed, then voted on. (3) In Delphi groups, physically dispersed experts fill out questionnaires to anonymously generate ideas; the judgments are combined and in effect averaged to achieve consensus of expert opinion. These three groups may be assisted by computer-aided decision making, using either chauffeur-driven systems, which ask participants to answer predetermined questions on electronic keypads or dials, or group-driven systems, in which participants in a room express their ideas anonymously on a computer network.

7.5
How to Overcome Barriers to Decision Making

■ When confronted with a challenge in the form of a problem or an opportunity, individ-

uals may respond in perhaps four ineffective ways and three effective ones.

■ The ineffective reactions are as follows: (1) In relaxed avoidance, a manager decides to take no action in the belief that there will be no great negative consequences. (2) In relaxed change, a manager realizes that complete inaction will have negative consequences but opts for the first available alternative that involves low risk. (3) In defensive avoidance, a manager can't find a good solution and follows by procrastinating, passing the buck, or denying the risk of any negative consequences. (4) In panic, a manager is so frantic to get rid of the problem that he or she can't deal with the situation realistically.

■ The effective reactions consist of deciding to decide—that is, a manager agrees that he or she must decide what to do about a problem or opportunity and take effective decision-making steps. Three ways to help a manager decide whether to decide are to evaluate (1) importance—how high priority the situation is; (2) credibility—how believable the information about the situation is; and (3) urgency—how quickly the manager must act on the information about the situation.

■ Heuristics are rules of thumb or strategies that simplify the process of making decisions. Some heuristics or barriers that tend to bias how decision makers process information are availability, representativeness, anchoring and adjustment, and escalation of commitment. (1) The availability bias means that managers use information readily available from memory to make judgments. (2) The representativeness bias is the tendency to generalize from a small sample or a single event. (3) The anchoring and adjustment bias is the tendency to make decisions based on an initial figure or number. (4) The escalation of commitment bias describes when decision makers increase their commitment to a project despite negative information about it. An example is the prospect theory, which suggests that decision makers find the notion of an actual loss more painful than giving up the possibility of a gain.

Management in Action

Nike's Decision Making Affects Its Revenue and Earnings

Excerpted from Douglas Robson, "Just Do Something: Nike's Insularity and Foot-Dragging
Have It Running in Place," Business Week, *July, 2, 2001, pp. 70–71.*

BusinessWeek In the spring of 2000, Nike's president of outdoor products, Gordon O. McFadden, was on a mission. He was out to persuade Nike's top brass that they should buy North Face Inc., a maker of popular outdoor gear and clothing. Nike had been slow to get in the race for the fast-growing hiking market, though it did eventually manage to build a decent business in "all-conditions" shoes and boots. Buying North Face, with its $240 million in sales, would have catapulted Nike into the top ranks of outdoor-gear makers. "It would have doubled the business overnight and Nike the dominant player," says McFadden.

So McFadden spent months courting North Face and fiercely lobbying for the purchase. But in the end he got shot down. As they had many times before, CEO Phillip H. Knight and his top lieutenants concluded that the company would be better off with a homegrown business than taking on the hassles of integrating another acquisition. Says McFadden, who has since left the company and now works at an apparel company, the Gerry Group: "The decision not to act stemmed from an insecurity of moving outside the Nike domain." . . . The problem? Wall Street analysts, industry rivals, and former Nike executives say the company is in serious need of fresh blood and new ideas. They believe Nike's insular mindset is a major reason for its current troubles. That inward focus has driven off new talent the company recruited to help get it out of its rut, caused it to miss major shifts in consumer tastes, and resulted in botched or forgone acquisitions that could have boosted its prospects. Nike needs to revitalize its core domestic footwear business—about 30% of revenues—and develop new products and brands, critics say. Faye I. Landes, an analyst at Sanford C. Bernstein Co., says that Nike's corporate culture will make that hard to do. "The feeling is 'what we do is special, no outsider can ever understand it,'" says Landes. "That's flawed thinking." . . . Yet Knight's siege mentality seems only to deepen as Nike struggles. The visionary entrepreneur who started the company by selling shoes from the trunk of his car has always done things his own way, critics be damned. Knight pooh-poohed charges of unfair overseas labor prac-

tices for years before addressing the issue. The resulting public-relations damage has yet to abate. And dissatisfied with the company's progress late last year, he pushed aside trusted aide and former Nike president Thomas E. Clarke—only to take the president's title himself. In March, the mercurial Knight once again realigned Nike's top management, this time stacking the corporate suite with a number of 20-year company veterans, including two chief operating officers as head of Nike brand. Few newcomers advanced in the management shuffle. "This was a decision to get the old warriors back in place," says board member John E. Jaqua. . . . Turner [Ellen Turner was the former Chief Marketing Officer], who was lured to Nike from Kinko's Inc. in 1999, left after six months. She says she came to Nike intent on bringing some sophistication to the sales and marketing departments, which she says were run "like a $1 billion company, not a $9 billion company." Turner wanted to create systems that could measure the effectiveness of advertising and bring more customer focus and accountability to Nike's product-design and marketing programs. But her efforts, she says, "died on the vine." Turner says that three weeks after starting her job, she was advised by the head of global human resources, Jeffrey M. Cava, to resist making bold changes and instead "lie low and keep your head down." Cava, who left Nike June 1, says he does not recall that talk. And Knight, Turner says, urged her to "spend a lot more time with oldtimers who know our brand." . . . But Nike underplayed the importance of the shift three years ago from a white-shoe, athletic look to a more urban, brown-shoe trend—largely because of its long-held insistence on performance at the expense of fashion. That blunder left the door open for competitors such as New Balance Athletic Shoe Inc., which came out with a line of shoes that fed off the more muted, trail-look trend. Reebok and such upstarts as And1 and Skechers also have made inroads with flashy, well-priced shoes that trend-setting urban teenagers covet.

Most glaringly, Nike has neglected the crucial "kill-zone," the $60-to-$90-a-pair sneaker segment that analysts say makes up most domestic sales—and 50% to 60% of Nike's U.S. shoe sales. "They put too much emphasis on new technologies like Shox and lost market share in the midpriced arena," says Shawn Neville, president and CEO of Irving (Tex.)-based retailer Footaction USA. The result: a 15% drop in U.S. footwear sales for Nike's most recent quarter while No. 2 shoemaker Reebok International Ltd. saw a 3.4% uptick. Privately held New Balance expects 25% growth in 2001, while analysts are forecasting Nike's domestic footwear business will drop 6%.

For Discussion

1. What examples of programmed and nonprogrammed decisions were made by management?

2. What types of decision-making styles seem to characterize Gordon McFadden and Philip Knight? Explain your rationale.

3. Which of the five nonrational models of decision making best characterizes the decision making at Nike? Explain.

4. Describe the apparent advantages and disadvantages of group decision making among Nike's top management team?

5. How would you describe the decision-making culture at Nike?

Take It to the Net

Decision making involves identifying and choosing among alternative courses of action—for example, choosing among alternative career options. One decision you might need to make: Would you ever want to own and run your own business? This exercise allows you to explore this possibility.

Go to *http://www.monster.com* and click on *First Timers*. Then click on *Career Center, #3*. On the far right side, click on *Career Changers*. Then click on *Self-Assessment*. There are many choices here to choose from, but for now click on *Entrepreneurial Quiz* and take the test and enter your score.

Questions

1. What is your reaction to the test scores? Explain.
2. From the results you received, do you want to explore becoming an entrepreneur? Why or why not?
3. Do you think the results might change in 5 years? Why or why not?

Self-Assessment

What Is Your Decision-Making Style?*

Objectives

1. To assess your decision-making style.
2. To consider the implications of your decision-making style.

Introduction: This chapter discussed a model of decision-making styles. Decision-making styles are thought to vary according to a person's tolerance for ambiguity and value orientation. In turn, the combination of these two dimensions results in four different decision-making styles (see Panel 7.1). This exercise gives you the opportunity to assess your decision-making style.

Instructions: Following are nine items that pertain to decision making. Read each statement and select the option that best represents your feelings about the issue. Remember, there are no right or wrong answers.

1. I enjoy jobs that
   a. are technical and well defined
   b. have considerable variety
   c. allow independent action
   d. involve people
2. In my job, I look for
   a. practical results
   b. the best solutions
   c. new approaches or ideas
   d. good working environment
3. When faced with solving a problem, I
   a. rely on proven approaches
   b. apply careful analysis
   c. look for creative approaches
   d. rely on my feelings
4. When using information, I prefer
   a. specific facts
   b. accurate and complete data
   c. broad coverage of many options
   d. limited data that are easily understood
5. I am especially good at
   a. remembering dates and facts
   b. solving difficult problems
   c. seeing many possibilities
   d. interacting with others
6. When time is important, I
   a. decide and act quickly
   b. follow plans and priorities
   c. refuse to be pressured
   d. seek guidance and support
7. I work well with those who are
   a. energetic and ambitious
   b. self-confident
   c. open-minded
   d. polite and trusting
8. Others consider me
   a. aggressive
   b. disciplined
   c. imaginative
   d. supportive
9. My decisions typically are
   a. realistic and direct
   b. systematic or abstract
   c. broad and flexible
   d. sensitive to the needs of others

Scoring & Interpretation: Score the exercise by giving yourself one point for every time you selected an A, one point for every B, and so on. Add up your scores for each letter. Your highest score represents your dominant decision-making style. If your highest score was A, you have a directive style; B = analytical; C = conceptual; and D = behavioral. See the related material in this chapter for a thorough description of these four styles.

Questions
1. What are your highest and lowest rated styles?
2. Do the results accurately reflect your self-perceptions? Explain.
3. What are the advantages and disadvantages of your style? Discuss.
4. Which of the other decision-making styles is least consistent with your style? How might you work more effectively with someone who has this style? Discuss.

*Adapted from A. J. Rowe, J. D. Boulgaides, and M. R. McGrath, *Managerial Decision Making* (Chicago: SRA, 1984).

Group Exercise

Ethical Decision Making

Objectives

1. To look at the stages in practical decision making.
2. To gain practice in ethical decision making.

Introduction

In this chapter you learned there are four stages in making practical decisions. The third stage involves evaluating alternatives and selecting a solution. Part of this evaluation entails deciding whether or not the solution is ethical. The purpose of this exercise is to examine the stages in practical decision making and consider the issue of ethical decision making.

Instructions

Break into groups of five or six people and read the following case. As a group discuss the decision made by the company and answer the questions for discussion at the end of the case. Before answering questions 6–7, brainstorm alternative decisions the managers at TELECOMPROS could have made. Finally, the entire class can reconvene and discuss the alternative solutions that were generated.

The Case

For large cellular service providers, maintaining their own customer service call center can be very expensive. Many have found they can save money by outsourcing their customer service calls to outside companies.

TELECOMPROS is one such company. It specializes in cellphone customer service, saving large cellular companies money by eliminating overhead costs associated with building a call center, installing additional telephone lines, and so on. Once TELECOMPROS is hired by large cellular service providers, TELECOMPROS employees are trained on the cellular service providers' systems, policies, and procedures. TELECOMPROS derives its income from charging a per-hour fee for each employee.

Six months ago, TELECOMPROS acquired a contract with Cell2U, a large cellular service provider serving the western United States. At the beginning of the contract, Cell2U was very pleased. As a call center, TELECOMPROS has a computer system in place that monitors the number of calls the center receives and how quickly the calls are answered. When Cell2U received its first report, the system showed that TELECOMPROS was a very productive call center and handled the call volume very well. A month later, however, Cell2U launched a nationwide marketing campaign. Suddenly, the call volume increased and TELECOMPROS customer service reps were unable to keep up. The phone-monitoring system showed that some customers were on hold for 45 minutes or longer, and at any given time throughout the day there were as many as 50 customers on hold. It was clear to Cell2U that the original number of customer service reps they had contracted for was not enough. They renegotiated with upper management at TELECOMPROS and hired additional customer service reps. TELECOMPROS managers were pleased because they were now receiving more money from Cell2U for the extra employees, and Cell2U was happy because the call center volume was no longer overwhelming and its customers were happy with the attentive customer service.

Three months later, though, TELECOMPROS customer service supervisors noticed a decrease in the number of customer service calls. It seemed that the reps had done such a good job that Cell2U customers had fewer problems. There were too many people and not enough calls; with little to do, some reps were playing computer games or surfing the Internet while waiting for calls to come in.

Knowing that if Cell2U analyzed its customer service needs it would want to decrease the number of reps to save money, TELECOMPROS upper management made a decision. Rather than decrease its staff and lose the hourly pay from Cell2U, upper management told customer service supervisors to call the customer service line. Supervisors called in and spent enough time on the phone with reps to ensure that the computer registered the call and the time it took to "resolve" the call. They would then hang up and call the call center again. Thus, TELECOMPROS did not have to decrease its customer service reps, and Cell2U continued to pay for the allotted reps until the end of the contract.

Questions for Discussion

1. Was the decision made by TELECOMPROS an ethical one? Why or why not?

2. If you were a supervisor at TELECOMPROS, could you pass the tests listed in Panel 7.4, p. 220. Explain.

3. What stages in the Practical Decision Making Process did TELECOMPROS managers skip? Describe and explain.

4. Which of the Nonrational Models of Decision Making did managers at TELECOMPROS follow? Explain.

5. Which of the hindrances to rational decision making listed in Panel 7.2 explain the decision made by TELECOMPROS managers? Explain.

6. What is your recommended solution? Explain why you selected this alternative.

7. How would you implement your preferred solution? Describe in detail.

Ethical Dilemma

UBS PaineWebber Fires a Broker Who Makes Independent Decision

Excerpted from Richard A. Oppel, Jr., "The Man Who Paid the Price for Sizing Up Enron," New York Times, *March 27, 2002, pp. C1, C4.*

Enron executives pressed UBS PaineWebber to take action against a broker who advised some Enron employees to sell their shares in August and was fired by the brokerage firm within hours of the complaint, according to e-mail messages released [March 26, 2002] by Congressional investigators.

The broker, Charles Wu, of PaineWebber's Houston office, sent a message to clients early on Aug. 21 warning that Enron's "financial situation is deteriorating" and that they should "take some money off the table."

That afternoon, an Enron executive in charge of its stock-option program sent a stern message to PaineWebber executives, including the Houston branch office manager. "Please handle this situation," the newly released message stated. "This is extremely disturbing to me."

PaineWebber fired Mr. Wu less than three hours later.

That evening, the firm retracted Mr. Wu's assessment of Enron's stock—then about $36—by sending his clients an optimistic report that Enron was "likely heading higher than lower from here on out." A few months later, the stock was worthless and [Enron] was in bankruptcy court. . . .

A PaineWebber spokesman declined to elaborate on the matter involving Mr. Wu but pointed to a letter sent to Congress last week.

In that letter, PaineWebber said that Mr. Wu had violated a rule of the National Association of Securities Dealers requiring that sales literature be reviewed by a supervisor before being sent to clients. The firm also said that Mr. Wu's advice was hastily drafted and "raises basic suitability concerns" and pointed to his suggestion that investors who hold the stock or vested options might want to use options to hedge their exposure. . . .

A lawsuit against PaineWebber filed by Enron investors, including some clients of Mr. Wu, argues that PaineWebber "directly lied to its clients for its own pecuniary gain by failing to reveal adverse information which it knew about Enron."

It asserts that other PaineWebber brokers in the Houston office "were selling as much Enron stock as they possibly could for highly placed Enron clients, despite the fact that inside PaineWebber, brokers commonly joked about Enron's stability."

The lawsuit also suggests another reason PaineWebber wanted to keep Enron happy. The brokerage firm had "an exclusive arrangement with Enron that PaineWebber would be the first brokerage company any Enron employee would deal with concerning the Enron employees' stock options and deferred benefits plans."

The suit also says that "getting first crack at these Enron employees paid off for PaineWebber in that about one of every three employees decided to keep their portfolios at PaineWebber."

Solving the Dilemma

What would you do if you were a PaineWebber supervisor aware of the rumors about Enron's stability and received the Enron complaint?

1. Fire Mr. Wu. That is, go along with Enron's request, because they are an important client.

2. Not fire Mr. Wu and let his recommendation to clients stand in order to encourage independent decision making and fiduciary responsibility to all clients. Send a tactful letter to the Enron executive who complained.

3. Buck the whole problem to your own supervisor, even though your being neutral will satisfy no one and may even invite litigation.

4. Invent other options. Discuss.

Video Case

Living Room Café

As the video case opens, partners Jonas Goldberg and Rande Gedaliah exchange greetings. In addition to being business partners, Rande and Jonas are long-time friends. Rande is under increasing stress and doesn't feel that Jonas is "holding up his end" of running the business. Jonas agrees. His spouse is extra busy at work, and he is taking on greater child-care responsibilities. But after all, they always agreed that their families would come first. However, Rande's family life is also affected.

Jonas has missed several meetings. He had "things to do" and felt confident that Rande could handle anything that arose. He twice missed payroll deadlines, delaying salary payments to employees. According to Jonas this is not a significant issue. Jonas feels he can accomplish his normal workload, it just might not be on the tight schedule that Rande is expecting. "It will all get done anyway." However, Rande feels the work is getting done because she is picking up the slack, causing her to be "totally stressed out." Rande senses a lack of concern for both their friendship and the business. She suggests a solution: find a partner to buy Jonas' share of the business. However, at this important juncture Jonas abruptly ends the meeting.

Privately Rande expresses frustration at the tone of the meeting, acknowledging that Jonas is likely frustrated as well. Jonas's goals have changed, and he is no longer taking an active interest in the business. She sees no hope of salvaging the partnership and would rather retain their friendship. Saving both no longer seems possible.

When Rande and Jonas reconvene, Jonas puts forth a proposal. He will "bow out gracefully" and sell his share of the business. For Jonas as well, maintaining their friendship is important. So far, the two partners are in agreement. However, a major point of contention arises. Jonas wants complete control over the choice of buyer, with the intention to sell to the highest bidder. Rande strongly opposes this idea, as the buyer would be her day-to-day partner. She should have total control over that decision and legally has the right of first refusal. Rande has reviewed their contract and consulted with their attorneys, while Jonas is unaware of the legal ramifications. Jonas doesn't want to leave Rande with an undesirable partner but still feels he has the right to sell to whomever he pleases. The discussion becomes heated, and again Jonas must abruptly leave to attend to family business. However, at least the friends have agreed that their partnership can no longer continue.

Privately Rande reflects on Jonas's proposal. With certainty, she states, "we will not be partners." Rande also perceives that the situation has been influenced by their gender differences, and that she has been forced into the mother-like role of disciplinarian. Perhaps a female partner would be a better choice, as they would likely have more similar communication and management styles.

Discussion Questions

1. Are Rande and Jonas experiencing functional or dysfunctional conflict? Support your response with evidence from the case.

2. Critique Rande and Jonas's decision-making process thus far. What might they do to improve this process?

3. Jonas is clearly attempting to maintain a comfortable balance between work and family life. Suggest how he might more successfully maintain this balance.

4. Did gender differences play a role in this situation? Support your answer with evidence from the case.

CHAPTER 8

Organizational Culture, Structure, & Design
Building Blocks of the Organization

MAJOR QUESTIONS YOU SHOULD BE ABLE TO ANSWER

8.1 What Kind of Organizational Culture Will You Be Operating In?

Major Question: How do I find out about an organization's "social glue," its normal way of doing business?

8.4 Basic Types of Organizational Structures

Major Question: How would one describe the eight organizational structures?

8.2 What Is an Organization?

Major Question: How do for-profit, non-profit, and mutual-benefit organizations differ?

8.5 Contingency Design: Factors in Creating the Best Structure

Major Question: What factors affect the design of an organization's structure?

8.3 The Major Elements of an Organization

Major Question: When I join an organization, what seven elements should I look for?

8.6 Toward Building a Learning Organization

Major Question: Why do organizations resist learning, and what is a new way for employees in an organization to view themselves?

MENTORING: THE NEW RULES

Who's going to help you learn the ropes in a new organization? Maybe you need a mentor.

If you can find an experienced employee to mentor you—to be your organizational sponsor and help you understand and navigate the organization's culture and structure—it can be a great asset to your career. Indeed, mentoring may be especially useful for female and minority managers, for whom there may be fewer role models within their particular organizations.

What's the best advice about acquiring a mentor? Here are some of the new rules.[1]

- **Choose anyone you can learn from, not just someone higher up:** It used to be thought that a mentor should be a seasoned manager higher up in the organization. But a mentor can also be a peer—someone at your own level inside in the organization.

- **Choose more than one mentor:** It might be nice to have a single mentor who can give you lots of one-on-one attention. But everyone's busy, so look around and see if there are two or three people who might be helpful to you. "Diversify your mentor portfolio," goes one piece of advice.

- **Pick your mentors, don't wait to be picked:** Don't wait for organizational veterans to select you to be their protégé. It's up to you to make the first move, to be assertive in a nice way.

- **Do a self-assessment:** Before you begin contacting people to be mentors, assess where you want to go and what skills and knowledge you need to get there, so that you'll know the kind of help you need.

- **Look for someone different from you:** It used to be thought the mentor and mentee should have a lot in common, as in personal chemistry or personal style. But someone who is different from you will challenge you and help you be more objective.

- **Investigate your prospects:** Before approaching prospective mentors, call their administrative assistants, explain your plans, and ask what their bosses are like to work with. Find out the best time to approach them.

- **Show your prospective mentor how you can be helpful:** "Mentoring is a two-way street," says Anne Hayden, senior vice president of Metropolitan Life insurance company. "The person being mentored gets help, advice, and coaching, and the person doing the mentoring generally gets extra effort—someone very committed to working on special projects or on assignments that maybe don't fall within the boxes on the organizational chart."[2]

- **Agree on how your mentoring relationship will work:** In your first meeting, set the ground rules for how frequently you will meet and the type of contact, such as whether it will be in the office, over lunch, or at the gym. A minimum of one meeting a month is recommended, and in between the two of you should keep in touch by phone and e-mail.

FORECAST: WHAT'S AHEAD IN THIS CHAPTER

In this chapter, we consider organizational cultures and why they are important. We then consider the three types of organizations and seven basic characteristics of an organization. We next consider eight types of organizational structures. We look at five factors that should be considered when one is designing the structure of an organization. Finally, we describe the characteristics of a learning organization, why people resist learning, and what a manager can do to help build a learning organization.

major question

How do I find out about an organization's "social glue," its normal way of doing business?

The Big Picture

The study of organization, the second of the four functions in the management process, begins with a study of organizational culture, which exists on two levels, invisible and visible. An organizational culture has four functions.

As a newcomer to *Fast Company* magazine, Cheryl Dahl wanted to meet new people but found that the office was far too hectic to allow coworkers to give her the kind of time she was looking for. So, she reported, "I nabbed a few minutes whenever I could—walking to the subway station with fellow editors, or popping my head into their offices to say hello." Dahl also wanted to check in frequently with her boss during her first 60 days. Her problem, however, was "How do you set up a meeting in a place that doesn't believe in meetings?" She learned to corner her boss at the coffee pot whenever she just "happened" to stroll by.[3]

People have different behavioral and psychological characteristics. So do organizations—only they're called "cultures." They consist not only of the slightly quirky features that Dahl encountered but also all of an organization's normal way of doing business.

What Is an Organizational Culture?

Kick what? Scott McNeal is CEO for Sun Microsystems.

According to scholar **Edgar Schein**, *organizational culture*, sometimes called *corporate culture*, **is a system of shared beliefs and values that develops within an organization and guides the behavior of its members.**[4] This is the "social glue" that binds members of the organization together. Just as a human being has a personality—fun-loving, warm, uptight, competitive, or whatever—so an organization has a "personality," too, and that is its culture. At Sun Microsystems in Mountain View, Calif., for instance, the corporate culture follows CEO Scott McNeal's model of "kick butt and have fun."[5] The corporate culture at Houston energy trader Enron was said to be a "a very arrogant place, with a feeling of invincibility," according to whistleblower Sherron Watkins.[6]

Culture can vary considerably, with different organizations having differing emphases on risk taking, treatment of employees, teamwork, rules and regulations, conflict and criticism, and rewards. And the sources of these characteristics also vary. They may represent the strong views of the founders, of the reward systems that have been instituted, of the effects of competitors, and so on.

The Two Levels of Culture: Invisible & Visible

Culture exists on two levels—invisible and visible.

The Invisible Level: The Core Culture The invisible level is the *core culture*, which consists of values, beliefs, and assumptions. These underlying beliefs and values are so widely shared that they are rarely discussed. Considered "the right way to behave," the core culture is followed nearly automatically—indeed, people feel threatened when their assumptions are challenged, often saying, "That's the way it's always been done here."

The invisible culture often has two sources: the vision, assumptions, and biases of the organization's founders, and the outlook that the initial employees learned from their own experiences of the formative years.[7] For example, the founders of technology company Hewlett-Packard stressed a collegial, egalitarian culture that gave as much authority and job security to employees as possible. When a new CEO, Carleton Fiorina, joined the company, employees felt threatened when she began planning a merger with computer maker Compaq that might have led to 15,000 layoffs—a direct challenge to the company's cherished "HP Way" culture.[8]

The Visible Level: The Observable Culture The *visible level* is the *observable culture*, which—besides such obvious manifestations as slogans, office layout, and manner of dress—is expressed in symbols, stories, heroes, and rites and rituals.[9]

H-P founders. David Packard (left) and William Hewlett created a close-knit organizational culture that gave a lot of authority and job security to Hewlett-Packard employees.

- **Symbols: A *symbol* is an object, act, quality, or event that conveys meaning to others.** In an organization, symbols convey its most important values. For instance, 3M has a trophy known as the Gold Step award, which is presented every year to employees whose new products achieve significant revenue levels.

- **Stories: A *story* is a narrative based on true events, which is repeated—and sometimes embellished—to emphasize a particular value.** Stories are oral histories that are told and retold by members about the organization's history.

  An example is the one told at Home Depot about the irate customer who called the Tampa store a couple of days before Christmas to complain that they had delivered a carpet that was way too small. The store delivered the right size of carpet via air freight the next day—which happened to be December 24th—and the installation was completed by midday, just in time for Christmas Eve.[10]

- **Heroes: A *hero* is a person whose accomplishments embody the values of the organization.** The accomplishments of heroes, past and present, are put forth to motivate other employees to do the right thing.

  For instance, famed pro football coach Vince Lombardi took over the losing Green Bay Packers in 1959 and forged a juggernaut team that won five championships in the next nine years. Although he was reputed to be tough, he was also patient, teaching quarterbacks fewer plays than his predecessor had but with more options within each play, which he explained so they would not feel confused or overwhelmed. Along with each play, he presented the logic of it. "They call it coaching, but it is teaching," he said. "You do not just tell them it is so, but you show them the reasons why it is so, and you repeat and repeat until they are convinced, until they know."[11]

Click-Along 8.1

Example of Use of Symbols as Expression of Organizational Culture: Close the GM Executive Dining Room

"Thank you, Mary Kay!" Top-performing salespeople are rewarded with cars (such as this new Cadillac), vacations, and diamonds at three-day rallies of the Mary Kay, Inc. Would these kinds of rewards, along with the emotional rewards of company-wide public recognition, make you want to work for a company with this kind of culture?

■ **Rites and rituals:** *Rites and rituals* are the activities and ceremonies, planned and unplanned, that celebrate important occasions and accomplishments in the organization's life.

Of course, military units have long known the value of rites and rituals, which is why ceremonies awarding decorations and medals are so important. Sports teams, too, recognize the importance of awards ceremonies recognizing winners and "most valuable player." But many companies, too, have rites and rituals.

Mary Kay, Inc., for instance, annually hosts five back-to-back conventions attended by 50,000 independent Beauty Consultants to recognize and reward its top producers for outstanding achievements in sales and recruiting. The founder, the late Mary Kay Ash, would personally present the best salespeople with jewelry, trips, and pink Cadillacs—items still awarded today.[12]

The Importance of Culture

Culture can powerfully shape an organization's long-term success.

"If employees know what their company stands for, if they know what standards they are to uphold, then they are much more likely to make decisions that will support those standards," write management experts Terrence Deal and Alan Kennedy. "They are also more likely to feel as if they are an important part of the organization. They are motivated because life in the company has meaning for them."[13] Much the same thing could be said for employees in non-profit organizations.

An organization's culture has four functions:[14]

1 It Gives Members an Organizational Identity At Southwest Airlines, for instance, top executives constantly reinforce the company's message that workers should be treated like customers and continually celebrate employees whose contributions go beyond the call of duty.[15]

2 It Facilitates Collective Commitment Consider 3M, one of whose corporate values is to be "a company that employees are proud to be part of." This collective commitment results in a turnover rate of less than 3% among salaried personnel. "I'm a 27-year 3Mer because, quite frankly, there's no reason to leave," says one manager. "I've had great opportunities to do different jobs and to grow a career. It's just a great company."[16]

3 It Promotes Social-System Stability The more effectively conflict and change are managed within an organization and the more that employees perceive the work environment to be positive and reinforcing, the more stable the social system within the organization. At 3M, social stability is encouraged by promoting from within, by hiring capable college graduates in a timely manner, and by providing displaced workers six months to find new jobs.

4 It Shapes Behavior by Helping Employees Make Sense of Their Surroundings The culture helps employees understand why the organization does what it does and how it intends to accomplish its long-term goals. 3M sets expectations for innovation, for example, by having an internship and co-op program, which provides 30% of the company's new college hires.

Sometimes culture can be strong enough to take the place of structure—that is, the expectations of the culture replace formal rules and regulations. In these cases, the sense of orderliness and predictability that employees look to for guidance are provided by the culture rather than by a rule book.

Surviving & Thriving in a New Job: The First 60 Days of Fitting into an Organization's Culture

"Probably 95% of firings are the result of failing to fit into a company's culture," suggests Linda Seale, head of an executive coaching firm for clients in such top-rated companies as American Express and Avon Products. "If people don't know you, they can't trust you."[17]

This is why, when you take a new job, it's important to go into it with a sense of urgency and make the first two months count. It's a cliché, but it's true: You never get a second chance to make a first impression. "It's a lot easier to develop a reputation for sloppy work or tardiness than it is to get rid of one," points out a journalist who specializes in career advancement.[18]

Among the things you should do in the first two months in a new job are the following:[19]

Get to Know Some People & Listen to What They Have to Say During the first two weeks, get to know a few people and try to have lunch with them. Find out how the organization works, how people interact with the boss, what the corporate culture encourages and discourages. Your role here is to listen, rather than to slather on the charm. Realize that you have a lot to learn.

Remember the Seven-Second Rule for First Impressions Roger Ailes, CEO of Fox News and former top Republican strategist, points out that seven seconds is all the

Delighted to meet you. When meeting someone new, how much time do you take to start forming an impression in your mind about them? About seven seconds? What kind of cues do you look for?

time people need to start making up their minds about you, so this is the period in which to make a good first impression. "When meeting someone for the first time, concentrate on one thing: your energy level," Ailes says. Amp it up. "If you don't demonstrate energetic attitude on your first day, you're already screwing up."[20] And don't wear a poker face, Ailes advises. Be warm and open, which is generally perceived as being stronger and less afraid.

Make It Easy for Others to Give You Feedback Ask your boss, coworkers, and subordinates to give you feedback about how you're doing. Be prepared to take unpleasant news gracefully. "Don't get defensive," advises Lois P. Frankel, author of *Overcoming Your Strengths*. "It's not other people's job to tell you how to correct your performance."[21] At the end of 30 days, have a "How am I doing meeting?" with your boss. And review how your job differs from the initial job description and what opportunities you might pursue.

Get Something Done Performance reviews for new-hires generally take place at 60–90 days, so be sure to have accomplished enough to show your boss your potential. Pick projects that are neither too complex nor too easy.

major question

How do for-profit, nonprofit, and mutual-benefit organizations differ?

The Big Picture

There are three types of organizations—for-profit, nonprofit, and mutual-benefit—and their organizational structure may be expressed vertically or horizontally on an organization chart.

In 1998, Hewlett-Packard Co., mentioned in the last section, found itself "stuck in one of the deepest funks of its 60-year history," according to *Business Week.*

It was then that up-and-coming star Ann M. Livermore was finally able to break from HP's highly decentralized structure of "warring tribes," as the article called them, to create an E-services division—which included server computers, services, and software—so that the company could compete with IBM and Sun Microsystems in the Internet era. The idea was that, with this enterprise division, corporate customers would outsource computer operations to HP, which would manage complex applications and websites via the Internet for a monthly service fee—which might ultimately come to make up as much as 80% of Hewlett-Packard's enterprise revenues.[22]

Why is it important to know about the differences in structures in organizations, such as centralized versus decentralized? Because, as this example shows, they can affect an organization's effectiveness—and your ability to take advantage of opportunities.

E-services. The computers, software, and communications links required to run a division that manages corporate applications and websites for other companies are all tremendously expensive. So are the people required to staff it. Would it ever make sense for a company such as Hewlett-Packard to decentralize these services—to have several different divisions doing similar functions?

The Organization: Three Types

According to **Chester I. Barnard's** classic definition, an *organization* **is a system of consciously coordinated activities or forces of two or more people.**[23] By this definition, a crew of two coordinating their activities to operate a tuna fishing boat is just as much an organization as the entire StarKist Tuna Co.—assuming the two fishers are catching tuna for a living and not just for fun.

There are three types of organizations classified according to the three different purposes for which they are formed—*for-profit, nonprofit,* and *mutual-benefit.*[24] Clearly, you might have an occupation (such as auditor or police officer) that is equally employable in any one of these three sectors. As a manager, however, you would be required to focus on different goals—making profits, delivering public services, or satisfying member needs—depending on the type of organization.

1 For-Profit Organizations: For Making Money For-profit, or business, organizations are formed to make money, or profits, by offering products or services. When most people think of "management," they think of business organizations, ranging from Allstate to Zenith, from Altavista to Zagat.

2 Nonprofit Organizations: For Offering Services Managers in nonprofit organizations are often known as "administrators." Nonprofit organizations may be either in the public sector, such as the University of California, or in the private sector, such as Stanford University. Either way, their purpose is to offer services to some clients, not make a profit. Examples of such organizations are hospitals, colleges, and social-welfare agencies (The Salvation Army, The Red Cross).

One particular type of nonprofit organization is called the *commonweal organization*. Unlike nonprofit service organizations, which offer services to *some* clients, commonweal organizations offer services to *all* clients within their jurisdictions. Examples are the military services, the U.S. Postal Service, and your local fire and police departments.

3 Mutual-Benefit Organizations: For Aiding Members Mutual-benefit organizations are voluntary collections of members—political parties, farm cooperatives, labor unions, trade associations, and clubs—whose purpose is to advance members' interests.

Example of an Organization That Defies Conventional Wisdom: A For-Profit Cellphone Network Makes Money in a Poor Country

The Asian country of Bangladesh is so poor that the per-capita income is one-hundredth what it is in the United States, "so you need 100 Bangladeshis to provide the buying power of one American," points out Iqbal Z. Quadir, a Bangladesh native who is now a Harvard University professor. Accordingly, when in the early 1990s Quadir was looking for financial backing for his idea for a cellphone network for his homeland, he was turned down by 16 prospective investors, one of whom said, "We're not the Red Cross."

Many Americans have this mindset that only certain kinds of organizations work for certain purposes—that only nonprofit charities can help the poor, that for-profits only work with consumers of a certain affluence. Microsoft's Bill Gates, for instance, has said that places with widespread poverty and unreliable electricity can't support sophisticated technology.

At the end of 2001, however, Quadir had showed how a for-profit venture in a developing country could both provide a service and make a profit. GrameenPhone, the Bangladesh cellphone company he founded, had made $27 million in pretax profits—and after just five years. The company sells phones and air time to urban customers and it enables people in rural areas to take out small loans for cellphones and to buy air time at cost. In fact, GrameenPhone now has more subscribers than Bangladesh's government-owned phone company.[25]

Indeed, throughout the world the mobile phone is affecting people in lower economic levels in dramatic ways, says a Motorola-backed study carried out by Sadie Plant of England's Warwick University. She points out the example of Dubai, a country of great wealth but with many poor workers. Cellphones haven't made a big difference to the rich, she says, "but they have to the porters who work around the harbor or to traders on wooden ships going between East Africa and the Middle East. Traders, for instance, can now find out about shipping news and who's selling what to whom."[26]

The Organization Chart

Whatever the size or type of organization, it can be represented in an organization chart. **An _organization chart_ is a box-and-lines illustration showing the formal lines of authority and the organization's official positions or division of labor.** This is the family-tree-like pattern of boxes and lines posted on workplace walls and given to new hires. *(See Panel 8.1.)*

PANEL 8.1
Organization chart.
Example for a hospital

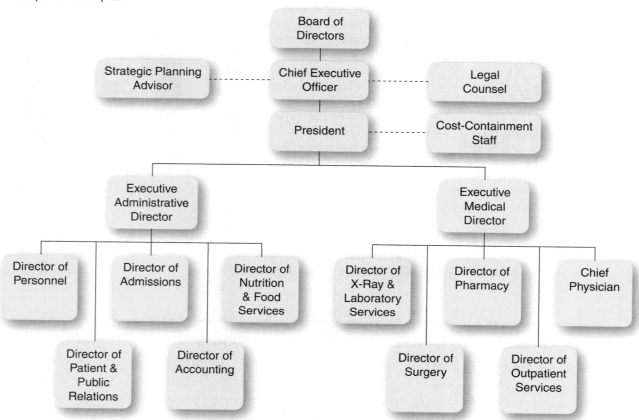

Two kinds of information that organization charts reveal about organizational structure are (1) the *vertical hierarchy of authority*—who reports to whom, and (2) the *horizontal specialization*—who specializes in what work.

The Vertical Hierarchy of Authority: Who Reports to Whom A glance up and down an organization chart shows the *vertical hierarchy*, the chain of command. A formal vertical hierarchy also shows the official communication network—who talks to whom. In a simple two-person organization, the owner might communicate with just a secretary or an assistant. In a complex organization, the president talks principally to the vice-presidents, who in turn talk to the assistant vice-presidents, and so on.

The Horizontal Specialization: Who Specializes in What Work A glance to the left and right on the line of an organization chart shows the *horizontal specialization*, the different jobs or work specialization. The husband-and-wife partners in a two-person desktop-publishing firm might agree that one is the "outside person," handling sales, client relations, and finances, and the other is the "inside person," handling production and research. A large firm might have vice-presidents for each task—marketing, finance, and so on.

practical action

When Should You Delegate & When Not? Using Your Authority Wisely

Failure to delegate can happen even with high-powered executives, including those you might least suspect—such as the president of Harvard University. Dr. Neil L. Rudenstine, who became president of Harvard in 1991, initially became so exhausted from overwork that he had to stay home for two weeks to recover. The incident sent a message that his future survival would depend on his ability to set priorities and delegate responsibility.[27]

There are many reasons why managers fail to delegate.[28] An excessive need for perfection. A belief that only they should handle "special," "difficult," or "unusual" problems or clients. A wish to keep the parts of a job that are fun. A fear that others will think them lazy. A reluctance to let employees lower down in the hierarchy take risks. A worry that subordinates won't deliver. A concern that the subordinates will do a better job and show them up.

Delegation. For delegation to be effective, workers must be able to function independently. Scientists running experiments often depend on assistants doing independent—and careful—work, as this lab technician is doing here.

If you find yourself often behind, always taking work home, doing your subordinates' work for them, and constantly having employees seeking your approval before they can act, you're clearly not delegating well. "To do more in a day, you must do less—not do everything faster," says productivity expert Odette Pollar.

How do you decide when to delegate and when not to? Here are some guidelines:[29]

Delegate Routine & Technical Matters Always try to delegate routine tasks and routine paperwork. When there are technical matters, let the experts handle them.

Delegate Tasks That Help Your Subordinates Grow Let your employees solve their own problems whenever possible. Let them try new things so they will grow in their jobs.

Don't Delegate Confidential & Personnel Matters Any tasks that are confidential or that involve the evaluation, discipline, or counseling of subordinates should never be handed off to someone else.

Don't Delegate Emergencies By definition, an emergency is a crisis for which there is little time for solution, and you may have to handle this yourself.

Don't Delegate Special Tasks That Your Boss Asked You to Do—Unless You Have His or Her Permission If your supervisor entrusts you with a special assignment, such as attending a particular meeting, don't delegate it unless you have permission to do so.

Match the Tasks Delegated to Your Subordinates' Skills & Abilities While recognizing that delegation involves some risk, make your assignments appropriate to the training, talent, skills, and motivation of your employees.

Finally, be prepared to live with a less than perfect result.

major question

When I join an organization, what seven elements should I look for?

The Big Picture

Seven basic elements or features of an organization are described in this section.

Whether for-profit, nonprofit, or mutual-benefit, organizations have four elements, according to organizational psychologist **Edgar Schein:** (1) *common purpose*, (2) *coordinated effort*, (3) *division of labor*, and (4) *hierarchy of authority*.[30] To these we should add three other elements that most authorities agree on: (5) *span of control*; (6) *authority, responsibility, and delegation*; and (7) *centralization versus decentralization of authority*.

1 Common Purpose: The Means for Unifying Members

An organization without purpose soon begins to drift and become disorganized. **The _common purpose_ unifies employees or members and gives everyone an understanding of the organization's reason for being.**

2 Coordinated Effort: Working Together for Common Purpose

The common purpose is realized through **_coordinated effort_, the coordination of individual efforts into a group or organizational-wide effort.** Although it's true that individuals can make a difference, they cannot do everything by themselves.

3 Division of Labor: Work Specialization for Greater Efficiency

Division of labor, also known as *work specialization*, is the arrangement of having discrete parts of a task done by different people. Even a two-person crew operating a fishing boat probably has some work specialization—one steers the boat, the other works the nets. With division of labor, an organization can parcel out the entire complex work effort to be performed by specialists, resulting in greater efficiency.

4 Hierarchy of Authority: The Chain of Command

The _hierarchy of authority_, or *chain of command*, is a control mechanism for making sure the right people do the right things at the right time. If coordinated effort is to be achieved, some people—namely, managers—need to have more authority, or the right to direct the work of others. Even in member-owned organizations, some people have more authority than others, although their peers may have granted them it.

In addition, authority is most effective when arranged in a hierarchy. Without tiers or ranks of authority, a lone manager would have to confer with everyone in his or her domain, making it difficult to get things done. Even in newer organizations that flatten the hierarchy, there still exists more than one level of management.

5   Span of Control: Narrow (or Tall) versus Wide (or Flat)

The *span of control*, or *span of management*, refers to the number of people reporting directly to a given manager.[31] There are two kinds of spans of control, narrow (or tall) and wide (or flat). *(See Panel 8.2.)*

PANEL 8.2
Spans of control. Narrow versus wide

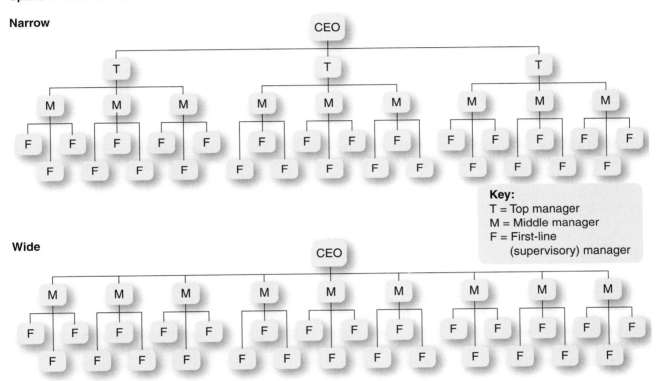

Narrow

Wide

Key:
T = Top manager
M = Middle manager
F = First-line
(supervisory) manager

Narrow Span of Control This means a manager has a limited number of people reporting—two vice-presidents reporting to a president, for example, instead of nine vice-presidents. An organization is said to be *tall* when there are many levels with narrow spans of control.

Wide Span of Control This means a manager has several people reporting—a first-line supervisor may have 40 or more subordinates, if little hands-on supervision is required, as is the case in some assembly-line workplaces. An organization is said to be *flat* when there are only a few levels with wide spans of control.

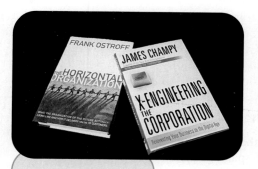

Reengineering. Books frequently appear discussing ways to reengineer or redesign organizational structures and processes in order to be more competitive and achieve dramatic improvements.

Historically, spans of five or seven subordinates were considered best, but there is no consensus as to what is ideal. In general, when managers must be closely involved with their subordinates, as when the management duties are complex, they are advised to have a narrow span of control. This is why presidents tend to have only a handful of vice-presidents reporting to them. By contrast, first-line supervisors directing subordinates with similar work tasks may have a wide span of control.

The recent emphasis on lean management staffs and more efficiency has meant that spans of control need to be as wide as possible while still providing adequate supervision. Wider spans also fit in with the trend toward allowing workers greater autonomy in decision making.

6 Authority, Responsibility, & Delegation: Line versus Staff Positions

Male sea lions have to battle other males to attain authority over the herd. In human organizations, however, authority is related to the management authority in the organization; it has nothing to do with the manager's fighting ability or personal characteristics. With authority goes *accountability*, *responsibility*, and the ability to *delegate* one's authority.

Accountability *Authority* **refers to the rights inherent in a managerial position to make decisions, give orders, and utilize resources.** In the military, of course, orders are given with the expectation that they will be obeyed, disobedience making one liable to a dishonorable discharge or imprisonment. In civilian organizations, disobeying orders may lead to less dire consequences (demotion or firing), but subordinates are still expected to accept that a higher-level manager has a legitimate right to issue orders.

Authority means *accountability*—**managers must report and justify work results to the managers above them.** Being accountable means you have the responsibility for performing assigned tasks.

Responsibility With more authority comes more responsibility. *Responsibility* **is the obligation you have to perform the tasks assigned to you.** A car assembly-line worker has little authority but also little responsibility: Just install those windshields over and over. A manager, however, has greater responsibilities.

It is a sign of faulty job design when managers are given too much authority and not enough responsibility, in which case they may become abusive to subordinates and capricious in exerting authority.[32] The reverse is also true: Managers may not be given enough authority to accomplish their responsibilities, in which case the job becomes difficult, though with luck still perhaps doable.

Delegation *Delegation* **is the process of assigning managerial authority and responsibility to managers and employees lower in the hierarchy.** To be more efficient, most managers are expected to delegate as much of their work as possible. However, a business entrepreneur may fall into the common trap of perfection, believing, as one writer puts it, that "you are the only person who can handle a given situation, work with a special client, design a program."[33] But a surprising number of managers fail to realize that delegation is an important part of their job.

Regarding authority and responsibility, the organization chart distinguishes between two positions, *line* and *staff*. (See Panel 8.3.)

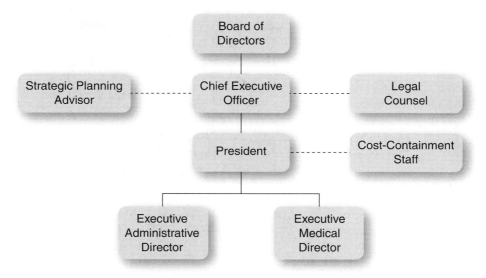

PANEL 8.3
Line and staff. Line have solid lines, staff have dotted lines.

Line Position *Line managers* **have authority to make decisions and usually have people reporting to them.** Examples: the president, the vice-presidents, the director of personnel, and the head of accounting. Line positions are indicated on the organization chart by a *solid line* (usually a vertical line).

Staff Position *Staff personnel* **have authority functions; they provide advice, recommendations, and research to line managers.** Examples: specialists such as legal counsels and special advisors for mergers and acquisitions or strategic planning. Staff positions are indicated on the organization chart by a *dotted line* (usually a horizontal line).

7 Centralization versus Decentralization of Authority

Who makes the important decisions in an organization? That is what the question of centralization versus decentralization of authority is concerned with.

Centralized Authority With *centralized authority*, **important decisions are made by higher-level managers.** Very small companies tend to be the most centralized, although nearly all organizations have at least some authority concentrated at the top of the hierarchy. Kmart and McDonald's are examples of companies using this kind of authority.

An advantage in using centralized authority is that there is less duplication of work, because fewer employees perform the same task; rather, the task is often performed by a department of specialists. Another advantage of centralization is that procedures are uniform and thus easier to control; all purchasing, for example, may have to be put out to competitive bids.

Decentralized Authority With *decentralized authority*, **important decisions are made by middle-level and supervisory-level managers.** Here, obviously, power has been delegated throughout the organization. Among the companies using decentralized authority are General Motors and Sears, Roebuck.

An advantage in having decentralized authority is that managers are encouraged to solve their own problems rather than to buck the decision to a higher level. In addition, decisions are made more quickly, which increases the organization's flexibility and efficiency.

major question

How would one describe the eight organizational structures?

The Big Picture

Eight types of organizational structures are simple, functional, divisional, conglomerate, hybrid, matrix, team-based, and network.

Culture and structure are often intertwined. When in 1997 the Federal Railroad Administration (FRA) sent inspectors to Union Pacific's headquarters in Omaha, Neb., to examine why the railroad had had a series of fatal accidents, they learned that the company had a top-down, military-style hierarchy and culture that seemed to discourage teamwork and communication. The antiquated style of management had its roots in the days when railroads' executive ranks were filled with combat-hardened former Civil War officers. "When something happened," said a railroad vice-president explaining the attitude of leading by fear, "you pulled out your gun and shot the guy in charge of the territory." Said the head of the FRA of Union Pacific's dysfunctional working arrangements, "They were separated from each other in a way that almost guaranteed problems."[34]

We may categorize the arrangements of organizations into eight types of structures: (1) *simple*, (2) *functional*, (3) *divisional*, (4) *conglomerate*, (5) *hybrid*, (6) *matrix*, (7) *team-based*, and (8) *network*.

Small firm. What type of organizational structure is best suited to a company this size? Should the number of employees influence the decision?

1   The Simple Structure: For the Small Firm

The first organizational form is the simple structure. This is the form often found in a firm's very early, entrepreneurial stages, when the organization is apt to reflect the desires and personality of the owner or founder. **An organization with a _simple structure_ has authority centralized in a single person, a flat hierarchy, few rules, and low work specialization.** *(See Panel 8.4.)*

PANEL 8.4

Simple structure: an example.
There is only one hierarchical level of management beneath the owner.

There are hundreds of thousands of organizations that are arranged according to a simple structure—for instance, small mom 'n' pop firms running landscaping, construction, insurance sales, and similar businesses. Some of these firms, of course, grow into larger organizations with different kinds of structures. Both Hewlett-Packard and Apple Computer began as two-man garage startups that later became large.

2 The Functional Structure: Grouping by Similar Work Specialties

The second organizational form is the functional structure. **In a _functional structure_, people with similar occupational specialties are put together in formal groups.** This is a quite commonplace structure, seen in all kinds of organizations, for-profit and nonprofit. *(See Panel 8.5.)*

PANEL 8.5

Functional structure: two examples. This shows the functional structure for a business and for a hospital.

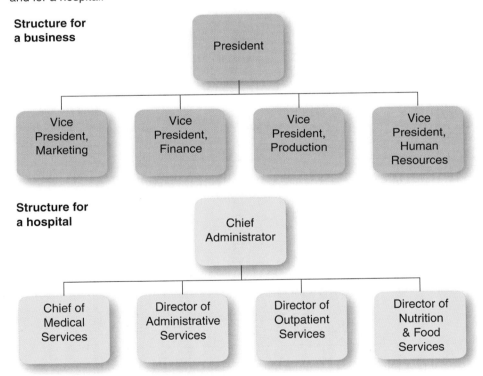

Big Apple. When founded in a garage in the late 1970s, Apple Computer was a two-man enterprise consisting of Steve Jobs—shown here in 2001 introducing the latest Macintosh—and Stephen Wozniak. Do you think the era of garage-based startups in the computer industry is over in the United States?

A manufacturing firm, for example, will often group people with similar work skills in a Marketing Department, others in a Production Department, others in Finance, and so on. A nonprofit educational institution might group employees according to work specialty under Faculty, Admissions, Maintenance, and so forth.

3 The Divisional Structure: Grouping by Similarity of Purpose

The third organizational form is the divisional structure. **In a _divisional struc-_
ture, people with diverse occupational specialties are put together in formal
groups by similar products or services, customers or clients, or geographic
regions.** _(See Panel 8.6.)_

PANEL 8.6

Divisional structure: three examples.

This shows product, customer, and geographic divisions.

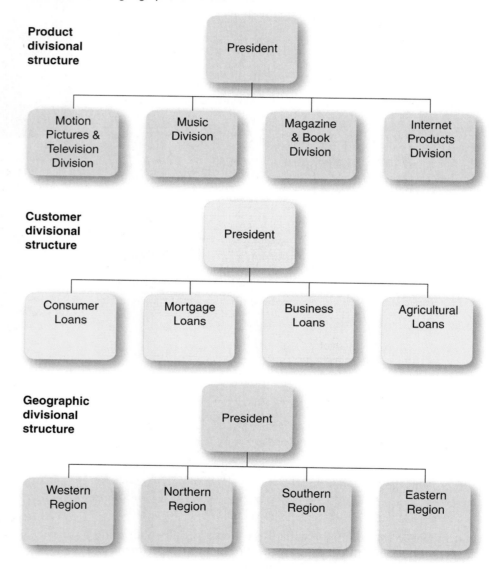

**Product
divisional
structure**

President

Motion
Pictures &
Television
Division

Music
Division

Magazine
& Book
Division

Internet
Products
Division

**Customer
divisional
structure**

President

Consumer
Loans

Mortgage
Loans

Business
Loans

Agricultural
Loans

**Geographic
divisional
structure**

President

Western
Region

Northern
Region

Southern
Region

Eastern
Region

How many divisions does Home Depot have? The leading retailer in the home improvement industry, Atlanta-based Home Depot operates 1,103 Home Depot stores, which sell building materials and home-improvement and lawn and garden products for do-it-yourself customers. The company also operates 26 EXPO Design Center stores, aimed at professional customers (contractors) interested in interior design and renovation projects. The Maintenance Warehouse subsidiary is a direct marketer of products serving the multi-family housing and lodging facilities management market. The National Blinds & Wallpaper subsidiary is a telephone mail order service for wallpaper and custom window treatments. The company has also experimented with Villager's Hardware test stores, which offer products for home enhancement and small projects, and The Home Depot Flooring Store, which sells only flooring products.

Product Divisions: Grouping by Similar Products or Services *Product divisions* **group activities around similar products or services.** For instance, the media giant AOL Time Warner has different divisions for magazines, movies, recordings, cable television, and so on. The $10 billion Warner Bros. part of the empire alone has divisions spanning movies and television, a broadcast network, retail stores, theaters, amusement parks, and music.[35]

Customer Divisions: Grouping by Common Customers or Clients *Customer divisions* **tend to group activities around common customers or clients.** For instance, Ford Motor Co. has separate divisions for passenger-car dealers, for large trucking customers, and for farm products customers. A savings and loan might be structured with divisions for making consumer loans, mortgage loans, business loans, and agricultural loans.

Geographic Divisions: Grouping by Regional Location *Geographic divisions* **group activities around defined regional locations.** This arrangement is frequently used by government agencies. The Federal Reserve Bank, for instance, has twelve separate districts around the United States. The Internal Revenue Service also has several districts.

4 The Conglomerate Structure: Grouping by Industry

A large-scale variant on the divisional structure is the conglomerate structure. A *conglomerate* is a large company that is doing business in different, quite unrelated areas. For example, General Electric has lighting products, appliances, aircraft engines, plastics, financial services, and broadcasting. **The *conglomerate structure* groups divisions around similar businesses or industries.** *(See Panel 8.7.)*

PANEL 8.7
Conglomerate structure.
This resembles the structure of General Electric.

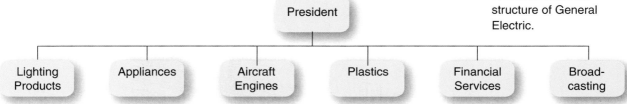

5   The Hybrid Structure: Functional & Divisional Used within the Same Organization

The fifth organizational form is the hybrid structure. **In a _hybrid structure_, an organization uses functional and divisional structures in different parts of the same organization.** *(See Panel 8.8.)*

PANEL 8.8

Hybrid structure. Hypothetical example of General Motors

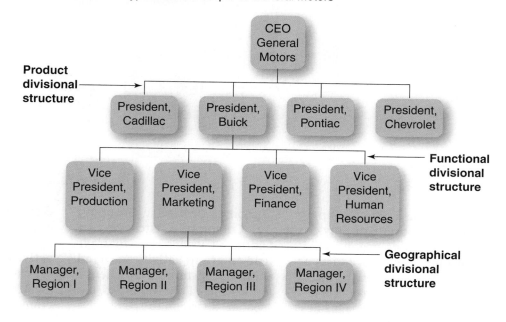

Many different kinds of possible hybrid structures exist. One example is General Motors, which at the top rung of the hierarchy could be organized into product (or customer) divisions: Cadillac, Buick, Pontiac, Chevrolet. (Oldsmobile was recently discontinued.) Within each product division, there could be a functional division according to type of work. Thus, Buick would be organized into Production, Marketing, Finance, Human Resources. Each functional division in turn is organized into a geographical division. Thus, Marketing would be organized into Region I, Region II, Region III, and Region IV.

General Motors' many divisions. Some GM dealers carry all of General Motors' brands, but some carry only a few.

6 The Matrix Structure: A Grid of Functional & Divisional for Two Chains of Command

The sixth organizational form is the matrix structure. **In a _matrix structure_, an organization combines functional and divisional chains of commands in a grid so that there are two command structures—vertical and horizontal.** The functional structure usually doesn't change—it is the organization's normal departments or divisions, such as Finance, Marketing, Production, and Research & Development. The divisional structure may vary—as by product, brand, customer, or geographic region. _(See Panel 8.9.)_

PANEL 8.9
Matrix structure. An example of an arrangement that Ford might use

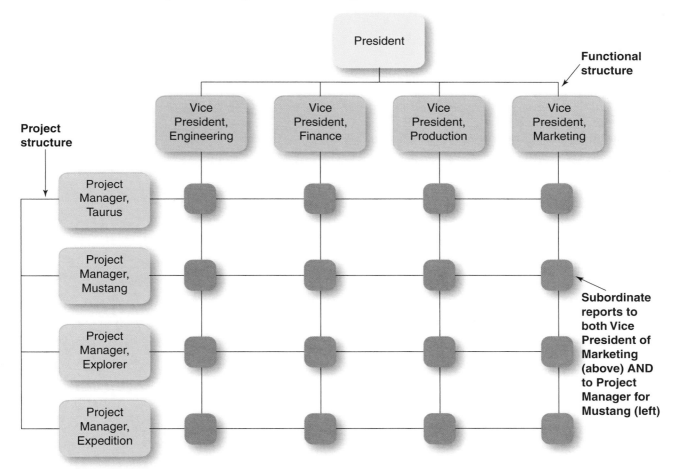

For example, the functional structure might be the departments of Engineering, Finance, Production, and Marketing, each headed by a vice president. Thus, the reporting arrangement is vertical. The divisional structure might be by product (the new models of Taurus, Mustang, Explorer, and Expedition, for example), each headed by a project manager. This reporting arrangement is horizontal. Thus, a marketing person, say, would report to _both_ the Vice President of Marketing _and_ to the Project Manager for the Ford Mustang. Indeed, Ford Motor Co. used the matrix approach to create the Taurus and a newer version of the Mustang.

7 The Team-Based Structure: Eliminating Functional Barriers to Solve Problems

The seventh organizational form is the team-based structure. **In a _team-based structure_, teams or workgroups, either temporary or permanent, are used to improve horizontal relations and solve problems throughout the organization.**[36] When managers from different functional divisions are brought together in teams—known as cross-functional teams—to solve particular problems, the barriers between the divisions break down. The focus on narrow divisional interests yields to a common interest in solving the problems that brought them together. Yet team members still have their full-time functional work responsibilities and still formally report to their own managers above them in the functional-division hierarchy. *(See Panel 8.10.)*

Click-Along 8.2

Example of Use of Team-Based Structure: Designing the Boeing 777

PANEL 8.10
Team-based structure. This shows a mix of functional and team arrangements

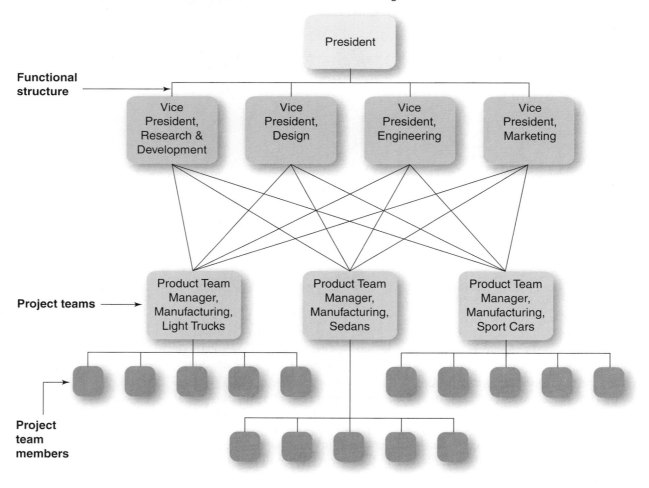

8 The Network Structure: Connecting a Central Core to Outside Firms by Computer Connections

The eighth organizational form is the network structure. **In a _network structure_, the organization has a central core that is linked to outside independent firms by computer connections, which are used to operate as if all were a single organization.** Corporations using this structure are sometimes called *virtual corporations.*[37] *(See Panel 8.11.)*

PANEL 8.11
Network structure. This is an example of a personal computer company

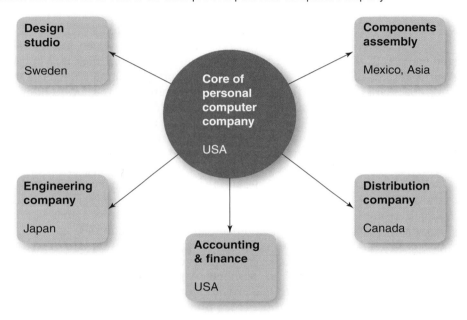

"The notion of where a corporation starts and stops is going to be very different in the future," said a Hewlett-Packard chief information officer and vice president. "Your expertise might be harvesting timber or processing lumber, but you also need to move your product to the construction industry. Traditionally, we brought all those steps together in a soup-to-nuts operation. Now, given [network structures], someone else can run your truck fleet, but it will still operate like your own fleet."[38]

With a network structure, an organization can operate with extensive, even worldwide operations, yet its basic core can remain small, thus keeping payrolls and overhead down. The glue that holds everything together is information technology, along with strategic alliances and contractual arrangements with supplier companies. Thus, telephones, computer networks, fax machines, overnight delivery services, and contract lawyers become important in linking all the network participants.

Click-Along 8.3

Example of Network Structure: How Wayerhaeuser Makes Doors

What factors affect the design of an organization's structure?

The Big Picture

Five factors affecting an organization's structure are whether its environment is mechanistic or organic, whether its environment stresses differentiation or integration, and size, technology, and life cycle.

What is the optimum size for an organization? How big is too big?

"The real growth and innovation in this country," says famed management consultant Peter F. Drucker, "has been in medium-size companies that employ between 200 and 4,000 workers." Despite the informality, smaller than 200 is not necessarily better. "If you are in a small company, you are running all out," says Drucker. "You have neither the time nor the energy to devote to anything but yesterday's crisis." A medium-size company, by contrast, "has the resources to devote to new products and markets, and it's still small enough to be flexible and to move fast. And these companies now have what they once lacked—they've learned how to manage."[39]

When managers are considering what organizational arrangements to choose from, size is one of several factors, or *contingencies*, to consider. Recall from Chapter 2 that the *contingency approach* to management emphasizes that a manager's approach should vary according to—that is, be contingent on—the individual and environmental situation. Thus, the manager following the contingency approach simply asks, "What method is the best to use under these particular circumstances?" **The process of fitting the organization to its environment is called _contingency design_.**

Managers taking a contingency approach must consider the following factors in designing the best kind of structure for their particular organization at that particular time:

1. *Environment—mechanistic versus organic*
2. *Environment—differentiation versus integration*
3. *Size*
4. *Technology*
5. *Life cycle.*

JetBlue CEO David Neeleman. "You don't have to do something grand to be a great company," says the founder of one of the U.S.'s newest airlines, which became profitable only six months after its February 2000 launch. "The ability to focus on customer service is something that applies to every single business you're in." Good customer service also stems from taking good care of employees, who from the first day at JetBlue are given benefits, profit sharing, and double-time overtime pay for hourly workers. The result is a culture in which employees are used to pitching in and helping. "When the plane lands," Neeleman says, "every employee on the plane, be it the CEO or someone from sales, pitches in and helps get the airplane ready. The pilots even come back and do it." What kind of factors affecting JetBlue's structure do you think figure in the company's success?

1 The Environment: Mechanistic versus Organic Organizations—the Burns & Stalker Model

"Here every job is broken down into the smallest of steps, and the whole process is automated," wrote *Business Week* correspondent Kathleen Deveny, reporting about a day she spent working in a McDonald's restaurant. "Anyone could do this, I think."[40]

Actually, Deveny found that she fell behind in, say, bagging French fries, but it was certainly the intention of McDonald's founder Ray Kroc that, in fact, nearly anyone *should* be able to do this—and that a Big Mac should taste the same anywhere. Thus, for example, procedure dictates that a hamburger is always dressed the same way: first the mustard, then the ketchup, then two pickles.

McDonald's is a hugely successful example of what British behavioral scientists **Tom Burns** and **G. M. Stalker** call a *mechanistic organization,* as opposed to an *organic organization.*[41] *(See Panel 8.12.)*

Could anyone do this? McDonald's follows the model of a mechanistic organization.

PANEL 8.12
Mechanistic versus organic organizations

Mechanistic organizations	Organic organizations
Centralized hierarchy of authority	Decentralized hierarchy of authority
Many rules and procedures	Few rules and procedures
Specialized tasks	Shared tasks
Formalized communication	Informal communication
Few teams or task forces	Many teams or task forces
Narrow span of control, taller structures	Wider span of control, flatter structures

Mechanistic Organizations: When Rigidity & Uniformity Work Best In a *mechanistic organization,* authority is centralized, tasks and rules are clearly specified, and employees are closely supervised. Mechanistic organizations, then, are bureaucratic, with rigid rules and top-down communication. This kind of structure is effective at McDonald's because the market demands uniform product quality, cleanliness, and fast service.

In general, mechanistic design works best when an organization is operating in a stable environment. Yet new companies that have gone through a rough-and-tumble startup period may decide to change their structures so that they are more mechanistic, with clear lines of authority.

Organic Organizations: When Looseness & Flexibility Work Best In an *organic organization,* authority is decentralized, there are fewer rules and procedures, and networks of employees are encouraged to cooperate and respond quickly to unexpected tasks. Tom Peters and Robert Waterman called this kind of organization a "loose" structure.[42]

Organic organizations are sometimes termed "adhoc-racies" because they operate on an ad hoc basis, improvising as they go along. As you might expect, information-technology companies like Motorola favor the organic arrangement because they constantly have to adjust to technological change. Yet so also do companies that need to respond to fast-changing consumer tastes, such as clothing retailer The Limited.

2 The Environment: Differentiation versus Integration—the Lawrence & Lorsch Model

Burns and Stalker's ideas were extended in the United States by Harvard University researchers **Paul R. Lawrence** and **Jay W. Lorsch**.[43] Instead of a *mechanistic-organic dimension*, however, they proposed a *differentiation-integration* dimension—forces that impelled the parts of an organization to move apart or to come together. The stability of the environment confronting the parts of the organization, according to Lawrence and Lorsch, determines the degree of differentiation or integration that is appropriate.

Differentiation: When Forces Push the Organization Apart *Differentiation* **is the tendency of the parts of an organization to disperse and fragment.** The more subunits into which an organization breaks down, the more highly differentiated it is.

This impulse toward dispersal arises because of technical specialization and division of labor. As a result, specialists behave in specific, delimited ways, without coordinating with other parts of the organization. For example, a company producing dental floss, deodorants, and other personal-care products might have different product divisions each with its own production facility and sales staff—a quite differentiated organization.

Integration: When Forces Pull the Organization Together *Integration* **is the tendency of the parts of an organization to draw together to achieve a common purpose.** In a highly integrated organization, the specialists work together to achieve a common goal. The means for achieving this are a formal chain of command, standardization of rules and procedures, and use of cross-functional teams and computer networks so that there is frequent communication and coordination of the parts.

Gather your gladiators. In 1992, John Dooner, president and CEO of McCann-Erickson Advertising Worldwide, watched as the Coca-Cola Co.—his company's major client since the 1950s—gradually handed over nearly all of its advertising business to rival agencies. Instead of pounding on Coke's door and asking to be let back in, Dooner vowed to win back the account by changing everything about his company. Although advertising is staffed by creative geniuses who prefer to work alone, Dooner initiated a strategy of collaboration based on the movie *Gladiator,* in which the preservation-minded gladiators band together. "He tore apart and rebuilt McCann-Erickson into a broad-based shop with blue-chip credentials and a solid creative reputation," says a *Fast Company* account. "He bought 114 agencies that could offer everything from database research to the most cutting-edge video." As a result of the strategic blend, Mc-Cann began to attract a number of important clients, such as MasterCard and Microsoft. By the late 1990s, Coke found itself with too many agencies creating too many tag lines and too many treatments for a single brand. When Dooner approached Coke management, it decided to go with Mc-Cann's parent group, InterPublic Group of Cos., in order to ensure that the basic messages about Coca-Cola would "have a foundation of consistency." How does this story fit the Lawrence & Lorsch model of differentiation versus integration?

3 Size: The Larger the Organization, the More Mechanistic

Organizational size **is usually measured by the number of full-time employees.** In general, research shows that larger organizations—those with 2,000 or more full-time employees (or the equivalent workload in a mix of full- and part-timers)— tend to have more rules, regulations, and procedures and more job specialization, as well as greater decentralization. That is, larger firms tend to be more mechanistic.[44] Small organizations tend to be more informal, to have fewer rules and regulations, and to have less work specialization. In other words, small firms tend to be more organic.

Mitsubishi headquarters in Tokyo. What do you think the company could do about its size to become more efficient?

Economists have long extolled the virtues of economies of scale, suggesting that "bigger is better" because the per-unit cost of production decreases as the organization grows. Opponents, however, contend that "small is beautiful," because large organizations tend to breed apathy, alienation, absenteeism, and turnover. Indeed, bigger is not always better: The world's largest company, Japan's Mitsubishi, with revenues of $176 billion (bigger than those of AT&T, Du Pont, CitiCorp, and Procter & Gamble combined) in a recent year had a puny profit margin of just 0.12%.[45] But the inefficiencies may be related to complexity rather than size.

According to Tom Peters and Robert Waterman, most top-performing organizations keep their division size between $50 million and $100 million, "with a maximum of 1,000 or so employees each. Moreover, they grant their divisions extraordinary independence—and give them the functions and resources to exploit."[46] Cleveland industrial valve and automobile parts maker Parker Hannifin, for example, has nearly 80 autonomous divisions, with 159 plants worldwide, each division operating only a few plants each in order to keep the company nonunion and the managers close to their customers. "Whenever we get more than 200 people in a plant," says chairman Patrick Parker, "we like to move 50 miles down the road and start another."[47]

4 Technology: Small-Batch, Large-Batch, or Continuous-Process—Woodward's Model

Technology has an important influence on organizational design. _Technology_ **consists of all the tools and ideas for transforming materials, data, or labor (inputs) into goods or services (outputs).** A hand-cranked ice-cream-making machine, for instance, is the technology that, with your muscle power, transforms cream, ice, sugar, and flavoring into ice cream. This book, the classroom, the blackboard, the instructor's lectures, and so on are the technologies that deliver an education about management.

In a study of 100 manufacturing firms in England, **Joan Woodward** classified firms according to three forms of technology in increasing levels of complexity: _small-batch, large-batch_, and _continuous process_.[48]

Small-Batch Technology: Custom-Made Products Made by Organic Organizations In *small-batch technology*, often the least complex technology, goods are custom-made to customer specifications in small quantities. The one-of-kind portrait painting, the Saville Row bespoke suit, the *Columbia* space shuttle, the personal stationary you had designed and printed just for you are all examples.

Small-batch organizations, Woodward found, tend to be informal and flexible—that is, organic.

Large-Batch Technology: Mass-Produced Products Made by Mechanized Organizations So-called *large-batch technology* is mass-production, assembly-line technology. Large volumes of finished products are made by combining easily available component parts. The clothes you buy at Macy's, Kenmore washers and dryers, Toyota automobiles, and most of the products we purchase on a daily basis fall into this category.

Large-batch organizations tend to have a higher level of specialization and to be more bureaucratic, according to Woodward.

Continuous Process: Highly Routinized Products Made by Organic Organizations *Continuous-process technology* is highly routinized technology in which machines do all of the work. Examples of this kind of technology are found in petroleum refineries, vodka distilleries, nuclear power plants, and steel mills, in which human operators mainly read dials and repair machine breakdowns.

Successful continuous-process organizations, Woodward found, tend to be more organic than mechanistic—less rigid and formal.

5 Life Cycle: Four Stages in the Life of an Organization

Like the four stages of a *project* life cycle (described in Chapter 5) and of a *product* life cycle (Chapter 6), organizations, too, have a life cycle. **The four-stage *organizational life cycle* has a natural sequence of stages: birth, youth, midlife, and maturity.** In general, as an organization moves through these stages, it becomes not only larger but also more mechanistic, specialized, decentralized, and bureaucratic. Each stage offers different managerial challenges and different organizational design issues.[49]

Pretzel progress. Millions of Auntie Anne's soft pretzels—Glazin' Raisin, Almond, Cinnamon Sugar, and others—are consumed every year by snack-crazed customers throughout the world. The business began in 1988 when Anne Beiler, a housewife in Lancaster, Pa., borrowed $6,000 from her father-in-law to purchase a soft pretzel stand at a local farmer's market. In December 2001, the company opened its 700th store, located in Hicksville, N.Y. Auntie Anne's, Inc. supports stores in 43 states and 11 international territories. It also has expanded into cookies with Cookie Farm in 1999 and into frozen custard with Auntie Anne's Cre-ámo Classic Cones in 2001. Where would you place Auntie Anne's, Inc. in the four-stage organizational life cycle?

Stage 1 The Birth Stage—Nonbureaucratic The *birth stage* is the nonbureaucratic stage, the stage in which the organization is created. Here there are no written rules and little if any supporting staff beyond perhaps a secretary.

The founder may be a lone entrepreneur, such as Michael Dell, who began Dell Computers by selling microcomputers out of his University of Texas college dorm room. Or the founders may be pals who got together, as did Apple Computer founders Steven Jobs and Stephen Wozniak, who built the first computer in Wozniak's parents' Palo Alto, Calif., garage, using the proceeds from the sale of an old Volkswagen.

Stage 2 The Youth Stage—Prebureaucratic In the *youth stage*, the organization is in a prebureaucratic stage, a stage of growth and expansion.

Now the company has a product that is making headway in the marketplace, people are being added to the payroll (most clerical rather than professional), and some division of labor and setting of rules is being instituted.

For Apple Computer, this stage occurred during the years 1978–1981, with the establishment of the Apple II product line.

Stage 3 The Midlife Stage—Bureaucratic In the *midlife stage*, the organization becomes bureaucratic, a period of growth evolving into stability.

Now the organization has a formalized bureaucratic structure, staffs of specialists, decentralization of functional divisions, and many rules.

In the 1980s, Apple Computer became a large company with many of these attributes. In 1983, Pepsi-Cola marketer John Scully was hired as a professional manager. Jobs became chairman; Wozniak left.

Stage 4 The Maturity Stage—Very Bureaucratic In the *maturity stage*, the organization becomes very bureaucratic, large, and mechanistic. The danger at this point is lack of flexibility and innovation.

After Jobs was fired in a boardroom struggle in 1985, Apple entered a period in which it seemed to lose its way, having trouble developing successful products and getting them to market. Scully, who emphasized the wrong technology (a "personal data assistant" called Newton, which failed to establish a following) was followed by two more CEOs who were unable to arrest the company's declining market share.

In 1997, Jobs was brought back as a "temporary" chairman, and Apple's fortunes began to revive.

Krispy Kreme. North Carolina-based Krispy Kreme was launched in 1937 by an entrepreneur named Vernon Rudolph with a secret French doughnut recipe. The company kept a low profile for decades until in the mid-1990s it began to expand by selling franchises. By mid-2002 the chain boasted 217 stores in operation. This is still not a lot compared with Dunkin' Donuts' 5,500 stores; however, business is so popular at Krispy Kreme that locations open at least 18 months have sales up nearly 13%, an impressive statistic in any business. Some stores take in a *profit* of $700,000 a year. As a result, the company has a long list of people—500 a week—trying to apply for a franchise, even though each one costs on average $2 million (compared to up to $750,000 for a McDonald's franchise). Judging where you think Krispy Kreme is in the four stages of an organization's development, would you bet on acquiring a franchise today for $2 million (and sharing a good chunk of your profits with the parent company)?

Employees who were present during birth and youth stages may long for the good old days of informality and fewer rules as the organization moves toward more formalized and bureaucratic structures. Whereas clearly some organizations jump the gun and institute such structures before they are appropriate, some expanding companies in effect never grow up, holding on to the prebureaucratic way of life for too long, hindering their ability to deliver goods or services efficiently in relation to their size.

Why do organizations resist learning, and what is a new way for employees in an organization to view themselves?

The Big Picture

Learning organizations are able to modify their behavior to reflect new knowledge. There are three reasons why organizations resist learning. A way to encourage learning is for all employees to view themselves as collaborators, not competitors

The film *Gorillas in the Mist*, which was being shot in the middle of a jungle in Rwanda and was to use more than 200 animals, had turned into a nightmare, says Peter Guber, who was the producer. In large part, he reports, this was because "the screenplay required the gorillas to do what we wrote—in other words, to 'act.' If they couldn't or wouldn't, we'd have to fall back on a formula that the studio had seen fail before: using dwarfs in gorilla suits on a sound stage."

During an emergency meeting, a young intern had asked, "What if you let the gorillas write the story? . . . . What if you sent a really good cinematographer into the jungle with a ton of film to shoot the gorillas? Then you could write a story around what the gorillas did on the film."

Everyone had laughed and wondered what the intern was doing in a meeting with experienced filmmakers. But ultimately they did exactly what she suggested, and the cinematographer "came back with phenomenal footage that practically wrote the story for us," Guber says. "We shot the film for $20 million—half of the original budget." The moral: The woman's inexperience enabled her to see opportunities where others saw problems."[50]

Guber adopted ideas appropriate to what is known as a *learning organization*. As we said in Chapter 2, a learning organization is an organization that actively creates, acquires, and transfers knowledge within itself and is able to modify its behavior to reflect new knowledge.[51] Learning organizations, says MIT professor **Peter Senge,** who coined the term, are places "where people continually expand their capacity to create the results they truly desire, where new and expansive patterns of thinking are nurtured, where collective aspiration is set free, and where people are continually learning how to learn together."[52]

Peter Guber. The director (left), shown here on the set of *Les Miserables* (1997) with actor Liam Neeson, learned from a novice a new way to put together a movie, *Gorillas in the Mist.*

Why Organizations Might Resist Learning

Like people, organizations must continually learn new things or face obsolescence. A key challenge for managers in today's competitive environment, therefore, is to establish a culture that will enhance their employees' ability to learn. Organizations, like the people in them, do not *consciously* resist learning. But resistance arises anyway, for three reasons.[53] (We discuss resistance further in Chapter 10.)

1 People Believe Competition Is Always Better than Collaboration Most of us live by certain _paradigms_, generally accepted ways of viewing the world. One of the most important in American society and business is the paradigm ("*pare-uh-dime*") that competition is superior to collaboration. This paradigm can lead employees within an organization to battle each other when success depends on their cooperation.

Overemphasis on competition also makes people—particularly leaders—more concerned about "looking good rather than doing good," hampering learning because they are reluctant to admit ignorance or mistakes. It also makes people hesitate to do tasks they worry they won't perform well. Finally, it makes everyone more concerned about short-term measurable results rather than long-term solutions to root causes of problems.

2 Fragmentation Leads to Specialized Fiefdoms That Resist Learning Today most people are specialists, trained to work in specific areas. This fragmented, piecemeal approach solves some kinds of problems but not those of great significance to society, such as lack of health-care coverage. Nor does it help solve organizationwide problems, such as the effect of new technology on the nature of the enterprise. To address these matters, we need people who have an understanding of systems, who view the world as a whole consisting of interrelated parts.

In organizations, fragmentation not only creates specialists working in functional areas, it also erects walls between them, with workers battling each other for power and resources. Left behind on the battlefield are important ideas such as sharing and collaboration and, as a consequence, learning as well.

3 Unless Encouraged, People Won't Take Risks, the Basis for Learning Do you resist learning a new word-processing program because you've gotten along just fine with the one you've used so far? Most of us tend to resist change, choosing to stay within our comfort zones, because change can be frustrating, even stressful. However, you no doubt have some areas of great personal interest (video games? cooking? motorcycles?) that inspire your curiosity, imagination, and experimentation—that is, that fuel the drive to learn and take chances.

Learning requires taking some risks, as in making mistakes or in revealing your ignorance for all to see. But if our natural tendency to want others' approval is coupled with an organizational climate that favors management by fear and intimidation, people will resist taking risks, and so little learning will take place.

The New Paradigm: "We're All Stakeholders"

Many traditional organizational behaviors have outlived their usefulness, and you need to seriously challenge them if you want to create a learning organization. A principal challenge is to create a climate in which managers and employees stop thinking of in terms of "us" versus "them" and start thinking of themselves as mutual stakeholders in the same enterprise.

"This is a company of owners, of partners, of businesspeople," reads one company's mission statement. "We are in business together. . . . No one in this company is just an employee. People have different jobs, make different salaries, have different levels of authority. But all workers will see the same basic information and will have a voice in matters affecting them. And it will be everyone's responsibility to understand how the business operates, to keep track of its results, and to make decisions that contribute to its success in the marketplace."[54]

There could be no better statement of the new managerial paradigm.

Click-Along 8.4

Taking Something Practical Away from This Chapter— More about Corporate Culture: The Toxic Organization

Key Terms Used in This Chapter

accountability, 256

authority, 256

birth stage, 271

centralized authority, 257

common purpose, 254

conglomerate structure, 261

contingency design, 266

continuous-process
technology, 270

coordinated effort, 254

customer divisions, 261

decentralized authority, 257

delegation, 256

differentiation, 268

division of labor, 254

divisional structure, 260

functional structure, 259

geographic divisions, 261

hero, 247

hierarchy of authority, 254

hybrid structure, 262

integration, 268

large-batch technology, 270

line managers, 257

matrix structure, 263

maturity stage, 271

mechanistic organization, 267

midlife stage, 271

network structure, 265

organic organization, 267

organization, 250

organization chart, 252

organizational culture, 246

organizational life cycle, 270

organizational size, 269

paradigms, 273

product divisions, 261

responsibility, 256

rites and rituals, 248

simple structure, 258

small-batch technology, 270

span of control, 255

staff personnel, 257

story, 247

symbol, 247

team-based structure, 264

technology, 269

youth stage, 271

Summary

8.1
What Kind of Organizational Culture Will You Be Operating In?

■ Organizational culture, sometimes called corporate culture, is a system of shared beliefs and values that develops within an organization and guides the behavior of its members.

■ Culture exists on two levels—invisible and visible. (1) The invisible level is the core culture, which consists of values, beliefs, and assumptions—beliefs and values so widely shared that they are rarely discussed. (2) The visible level is the observable culture, which is expressed in symbols, stories, heroes, and rites and rituals. A symbol is an object, act, quality, or event that conveys meaning to others. A story is a narrative based on true events, which is repeated—and sometimes embellished on—to emphasize a particular value. A hero is a person whose accomplishments embody the values of the organization. Rites and rituals are the activities and ceremonies, planned and unplanned, that celebrate important occasions and accomplishments in the organization's life.

■ Culture, which can powerfully shape an organization's success over the long term, has four functions. (1) It gives members an organizational identity. (2) It facilitates collective commitment. (3) It promotes social-system stability. (4) It shapes behavior by helping employees make sense of their surroundings.

8.2
What Is an Organization?

■ An organization is a system of consciously coordinated activities or forces of two or more people. There are three types of organizations classified according to the three different purposes for which they are formed. (1) For-profit organizations are formed to make money by offering products or services. (2) Nonprofit organizations offer services to some, but not to make a profit. Commonweal organizations offer services to all clients within their jurisdiction. (3) Mutual-benefit organizations are voluntary collections of members created to advance members' interests.

■ Whatever the size of organization, it can be represented in an organization chart, a boxes-

and-lines illustration showing the formal lines of authority and the organization's official positions or division of labor. Two kinds of information that organizations reveal about organizational structure are (1) the vertical hierarchy of authority—who reports to whom, and (2) the horizontal specialization—who specializes in what work.

8.3
The Major Elements of an Organization

■ Organizations have seven elements: (1) Common purpose, which unifies employees or members and gives everyone an understanding of the organization's reason for being. (2) Coordinated effort, the coordination of individual efforts into a group or organizational-wide effort. (3) Division of labor, also known as work specialization, which the arrangement of having discrete parts of a task done by different people. (4) Hierarchy of authority, or chain of command, which is a control mechanism for making sure the right people do the right things at the right time. (5) Span of control, or span of management, which refers to the number of people reporting directly to a given manager. A narrow span of control means a manager has a limited number of people reporting; a wide span of control means that several people are reporting. (6) Authority and accountability, responsibility, and delegation. Authority refers to the rights inherent in a managerial position to make decisions, give orders, and utilize resources. Accountability means that managers must report and justify work results to the managers above them. Responsibility is the obligation you have to perform the tasks assigned to you. Delegation is the process of assigning managerial authority and responsibility to managers and employees lower in the hierarchy. Regarding authority and responsibility, the organization chart distinguishes between two positions, line and staff. Line managers have authority to make decisions and usually have people reporting to them. Staff personnel have advisory functions; they provide advice, recommendations, and research to line managers. (7) Centralization versus decentralization of authority. With centralized authority, important decisions are made by higher-level managers. With decentralized authority, important decisions are made by middle-level and supervisory-level managers.

8.4
Basic Types of Organizational Structure

■ Organizations may be arranged into eight types of structures: (1) A simple structure has authority centralized in a single person, a flat hierarchy, few rules, and low work specialization. (2) In a functional structure, people with similar occupational specialties are put together in formal groups. (3) In a divisional structure, people with diverse occupational specialties are put together in formal groups by similar products or services, customers or clients, or geographic regions. Product divisions group activities around similar products or services. Customer divisions group activities around common customers or clients. Geographic divisions group activities around defined regional locations. (4) The conglomerate structure groups divisions around similar businesses or industries. (5) In a hybrid structure, an organization uses functional and divisional structures in different parts of the same organization. (6) In a matrix structure, an organization combines functional and divisional chains of commands in grids so that there are two command structures—vertical and horizontal. (7) In a team-based structure, teams or workgroups, either temporary or permanent, are used to improve horizontal relations and solve problems throughout the organization. (8) In a network structure, the organization has a central core that is linked to outside independent firms by computer connections, which are used to operate as if all were a single organization.

8.5
Contingency Design: Factors to Consider in Creating the Best Structure

■ The process of fitting the organization to its environment is called contingency design. Managers taking a contingency approach must consider five factors in designing the best kind of structure for their organization at that particular time.

■ (1) An organization may be either mechanistic or organic. In a mechanistic organization, authority is centralized, tasks and rules are clearly specified, and employees are closely supervised. In an organic organization, authority is decentralized, there are fewer rules and procedures, and networks of employees are encouraged to cooperate and respond quickly to unexpected tasks.

(2) An organization may also be characterized by differentiation or integration. Differentiation is the tendency of the parts of an organization to disperse and fragment. Integration is the tendency of the parts of an organization to draw together to achieve a common purpose.

(3) Organizational size is usually measured by the number of full-time employees. Larger organizations tend to have more rules, regulations, job specialization, and decentralization. Smaller organizations tend to be more informal, have fewer rules, and have less work specialization.

(4) Technology consists of all the tools and ideas for transforming materials, data or labor (inputs) into goods or services (outputs). Firms may be classified according to three forms of technology in increasing levels of complexity. In small-batch technology, often the least complex technology, goods are custom-made to customer specifications in small quantities. Large-batch technology is mass-production, assembly-line technology. Continuous-process technology is highly routinized technology in which machines do all the work.

(5) The four-stage organizational life cycle has a natural sequence of stages: birth, youth, midlife, and maturity. The birth stage is the nonbureaucratic stage, the stage in which the organization is created. The youth stage is the prebureaucratic stage, a stage of growth and expansion. In the midlife stage, the organization becomes bureaucratic, a period of growth evolving into stability. In the maturity stage, the organization becomes very bureaucratic, large, and mechanistic. The danger at this point is lack of flexibility and innovation.

8.6
Toward Building a Learning Organization

Learning organizations are able to modify their behavior to reflect new knowledge. There are three reasons why organizations resist learning. (1) People believe that competition is always better than collaboration—this is an important paradigm, or generally accepted way of viewing the world, that is important in American society. (2) Fragmentation leads to specialized fiefdoms that resist learning. (3) Unless encouraged, people won't take risks, the basis for learning.

A way to encourage learning is a new paradigm—namely, for all employees to view themselves as collaborators, not competitors.

Management in Action

How Accounting Firm Arthur Andersen Changed Its Culture

Excerpted from Ken Brown and Jonathan Weil, "How Andersen's Embrace of Consulting Altered the Culture of the Auditing Firm," The Wall Street Journal, *March 12, 2002, pp. C1, C16.*

The cover of Arthur Andersen's 2000 "highlights report" speaks volumes about how the accounting firm has evolved. It features partner Alberto Pelizzaro in a black leather jacket and buzz cut astride a red Ducati motorcycle. Mr. Pelizzaro had helped Ducati, the Italian motorcycle maker, design a new website—he hadn't audited its books. Nowhere in the flashy report is there an image of an accountant poring over a ledger. There are scant references to auditing or clean financial statements.

Andersen realized long ago that no one was going to get rich doing just audits. So for partners to share in hundreds of dollars of firm profits each year, Andersen would have to boost its lucrative consulting business. That quest for revenue is how the

firm lost sight of its obligation to cast a critical eye on its clients' accounting practices, some critics say.

Andersen partners embraced consulting, says Barbara Ley Toffler, a Columbia Business School professor and former Andersen partner. "Now they had an opportunity to be part of much more glitzy firms, and equity partners started making enormous amounts of money," she said. "What became available became seductive."

. . . Former Federal Reserve Chairman Paul A. Volcker, who has been hired by Andersen to help overhaul the firm, issued recommendations that included splitting accounting and consulting services. He said there should be no revenue-sharing arrangements between the two groups, and he called for banning the practice of tying part of the auditors' pay to "solicitation and marketing of nonaudit-related services."

In interview on CNBC-TV, Mr. Volcker said there has been a tendency in accounting, "certainly in Andersen, to lose their way by preoccupation with consulting businesses." . . .

There is at least one irony in Andersen's focus on its consulting business. For most of the 20th century, an Andersen audit opinion was viewed as the gold standard for the [accounting] industry. But fees for audits began to fall in the mid-1980s as firms began to outbid one another aggressively for audit engagements. This gave incentive for partners to attract nonaudit business from their clients. "You have to remember that these accounting-firm partners have one client," said Jay Nisberg, an accounting-industry consultant based in Ridgefield, Conn. "Their income is derived from their ability to generate fees from that client." . . .

The problems with focusing on consulting are evident in Andersen's biggest accounting blowups. Consider Waste Management Inc., which generated millions of dollars in consulting fees for Andersen.

[In 2001] securities regulators alleged that Andersen bent the accounting rules so far the firm committed fraud. Time and again, starting in 1988 up through 1997, when Waste Management announced what at the time was the biggest financial restatement in U.S. history, Andersen auditors knew the company was violating generally accepted accounting principles, the Securities and Exchange Commission said in a settled complaint filed in a Washington, D.C., federal court.

For Discussion

1. How would you describe the "core culture" of Arthur Andersen?

2. Would you say there was more than one culture, and were they in conflict?

3. What kind of a divisional structure does the company seem to have had?

4. Was Andersen characterized by differentiation or integration, according to the Lawrence and Lorsch model?

Self-Assessment

Is Your Organization a Learning Organization?

Objectives

1. To gain familiarity with the characteristics of learning organizations.
2. To identify if your organization is a learning organization.

Introduction: As we learned in this chapter, a learning organization is one that actively creates, acquires, and transfers new knowledge. Learning organizations are places in which new ideas and patterns of thinking are are nurtured and in which people are allowed to continually expand their abilities to achieve desired results. Most importantly, a learning organization is a place in which the organization and individuals in it are continually learning in order to achieve its goals. The purpose of this exercise is to identify whether or not the organization in which you work is a learning organization.

Instructions: The following survey was created to assess the extent to which an organization follows the principles of a learning organization. If you are currently working, you should answer the questions in regard to this organization. If you are not currently working but have worked in the past, use a past job in completing the survey. If you have never had a job, you can use your school as a reference or use an organization you might be familiar with. For example, you might interview your parents to determine the extent to which the organization they work for follows the principles of a learning organization. Read each statement and use the following scale to indicate which answer most closely matches your response: 1 = strongly disagree; 2 = disagree; 3 = neither agree nor disagree; 4 = agree; 5 = strongly agree.

1. Management uses rewards, praise, and recognition to get what they want done.

   1   2   3   4   5

2. The company promotes teamwork.

   1   2   3   4   5

3. People are recognized and rewarded on the basis of what they do rather than *who* they know.	1	2	3	4	5
4. I see more examples of optimistic attitudes/behaviors rather than negative and cynical ones.	1	2	3	4	5
5. I have a clear picture of the organization's vision and my role in helping to accomplish it.	1	2	3	4	5
6. This organization relies more on team-based solutions than individual ones.	1	2	3	4	5
7. This organization tends to look at the big picture rather than analyzing problem from a narrow perspective.	1	2	3	4	5
8. People have an open mind when working with others.	1	2	3	4	5
9. This company looks for the root cause of a problem rather than a "quick fix."	1	2	3	4	5
10. I have the skills and knowledge to continuously improve the way I do my job.	1	2	3	4	5

Total _____

Scoring

To get your score, add up the numbers that correspond to your responses. The range will be from 10 to 50. Comparative norms for learning organizations are as follows:

Total score of 10–23 = low learning organization

Total score of 24–36 = moderate learning organization

Total score of 37–50 = high learning organization

Group Exercise

Designing Your Own Organization

Objectives

1. To learn more about organizational structures.
2. To consider the relationship between organizational culture and structure.

Introduction

As we learned in this chapter, an organization's culture consists of a system of shared beliefs and values that develops within the organization and guides the behavior of its members. An organization's culture and its structure are closely intertwined. The purpose of this exercise is to examine the relationship between an organization's culture and its structure. To accomplish this, you will design your own company.

Instructions

Break into groups of five or six people. Your first task is to start your own organization. Your organization can be anything from a baseball team to a car company to a bank. Once you have determined what type of organization your group wants to create, the group needs to establish the organizational values that will underlie your organization's culture. Once the values are established, we want you to propose two different organizational structures. Begin by examining the eight types of organizational structures covered in the text. Your first organizational chart should represent your proposed structure at the beginning of your organization's inception. The second organization chart should represent the structure of your organization once it has 300 or more employees.

Questions for Discussion

1. What are your organization's values? Explain why they were chosen.
2. How do the values and culture of your organization correspond to its structure? Explain.
3. How did your organization chart change once your company reached 300 employees? What type of structure does this chart represent? Explain.
4. Do you believe your organization is more mechanistic or organic? Explain.

Take It to the Net

What values are important in your life? What are your pet peeves? How do your friends describe you? Do they note little quirks and behaviors that make you unique? Just as you have your own unique personality, organizations too have a "personality." As we learned in this chapter, this is the organization's "social glue," its culture. The purpose of this exercise is to gain familiarity with different aspects of culture and to identify an organization's culture.

Go to *www.microsoft.com*. Go to *About Microsoft* along the top of the screen and go to the section for *Mission and Values*. Read the sections and look for elements of Microsoft's organizational culture. Also look over the Jobs section—read the sections that cover diversity and benefits.

Questions for Discussion

1. What values make up Microsoft's organizational culture? Describe your reaction to them.

2. To what extent do Microsoft's organizational values match your own? What are the implications of this match or mismatch? Explain.

3. Do you feel Microsoft's organizational culture promotes a common purpose? Why or why not?

Ethical Dilemma

Enron's Organizational Culture & Reward System Contribute to Its Problems

Excerpted from John A. Byrne, Mike France, and Wendy Zellner, "The Environment Was Ripe for Abuse,"
Business Week, February 25, 2002, pp. 118-120.

BusinessWeek [Houston energy trader] Enron didn't fail just because of its entrepreneurial culture—the very reason Enron attracted so much attention and acclaim. The unrelenting emphasis on earnings growth and individual initiative, coupled with a shocking absence of the usual corporate checks and balances, tipped the culture from one that rewarded aggressive strategy to one that increasingly relied on unethical corner-cutting. . . .

Central to forging a new Enron culture was an unusual performance review system that [former CEO Jeffrey] Skilling adapted from his days at McKinsey. Under this peer-review process, a select group of 20 people were named to a performance review committee (PRC) to rank more than 400 vice presidents, then all the directors, and finally all of Enron's managers. The stakes were high because all the rewards were linked to ranking decisions by the PRC, which had to unanimously agree on each person. Managers judged "superior"—the top 5%—got bonuses 66% higher than those who got an "excellent" rating, the next 30%. They also got much larger stock option grants. . . .

In practice, the system bred a culture in which people were afraid to get crossways with someone who could screw up their reviews. How did managers ensure they passed muster? "You don't object to anything," says one former Enron executive. "The whole culture at the vice-president level and above just became a yes-man culture."

Several former and current Enron execs say that Andrew S. Fastow, the ex-chief financial officer who is at the center of Enron's partnership controversy, had a reputation for exploiting the review system to get back at people who expressed disagreement or criticism.

Solving the Dilemma

What would you do to the performance evaluation system?

1. Leave it alone because it rewards individual achievement.

2. Keep the basic ranking process, but drop the requirement that the PRC must unanimously agree on each person's evaluation. The company might use an average ranking across all raters as the final rating.

3. Drop the entire ranking process because it is too subjective.

4. Invent other options. Discuss

CHAPTER 9

Human Resource Management
Getting the Right People for Managerial Success

MAJOR QUESTIONS YOU SHOULD BE ABLE TO ANSWER

9.1 Strategic Human Resource Management

Major Question: How do star managers view the role of people in their organization's success?

9.2 The Legal Requirements of Human Resource Management

Major Question: To avoid exposure to legal liabilities, what areas of the law do I need to be aware of?

9.3 Recruitment & Selection: Putting the Right People into the Right Jobs

Major Question: How can I reduce mistakes in hiring and find great people who might work for me?

9.4 Orientation, Training, & Development

Major Question: Once people are hired, what's the best way to see that they do what they're supposed to do?

9.5 Performance Appraisal

Major Question: How can I assess employees' performance more accurately and give more effective feedback?

9.6 Managing an Effective Workforce: Compensation & Benefits

Major Question: What are the various forms of compensation?

9.7 Other Concerns in Managing an Effective Workforce

Major Question: How do I manage contemporary workplace problems such as drug abuse and sexual harassment?

KEEPING EMPLOYEES INVESTED IN THEIR JOBS

"*Get a life!*" everyone says. But what, exactly, is a "life," anyway?

As more and more people have begun asking this question, it has spilled over into organizational life. The result has been a new category of work rewards and incentives called *work-life benefits*.

As one definition has it, work-life benefits are programs "used by employers to increase productivity and commitment by removing certain barriers that make it hard for people to strike a balance between their work and personal lives."[1] Examples are nonsalary incentives such as flexible work arrangements, tuition assistance, and paid time off for education and community service.

Managing human resources, the subject of this chapter, focuses on managing people. You need to be thinking about employees not as "human capital" or "capital assets" but as people who are *investors:* They are investing their time, energy, and intelligence—their lives—in your organization, for which they deserve a return that makes sense to them.[2]

To keep your employees invested in their jobs and performing well for the company, it helps for you to know what the Gallup Organization discovered in surveying 80,000 managers and 1 million workers over 25 years.[3] Gallup found that in the best workplaces employees gave strong "Yes" answers to the following 12 questions:

1. Do I know what's expected of me?
2. Do I have the right materials and equipment I need to do my work right?
3. Do I have the opportunity to do what I do best every day?
4. In the last seven days, have I received recognition or praise for good work?
5. Does my supervisor, or someone at work, seem to care about me as a person?
6. Is there someone at work who encourages my development?
7. Does my opinion seem to count?
8. Does the mission of my company make me feel like my work is important?
9. Are my coworkers committed to doing quality work?
10. Do I have a best friend at work?
11. In the last six months, have I talked with someone about my progress?
12. Have I had opportunities to learn and grow?

The best managers, Gallup says, meet with workers individually at least every three months, not just once or twice a year. In doing so, they not only discuss performance but also try to find out what employees want to accomplish and how the manager can help. In addition, good managers focus on strengths, rather than weaknesses, allowing employees to devote time to what they do best.

Since *Fortune* magazine began publishing its annual list of "The 100 Best Companies to Work For," managers have been concerned about trying to take better care of their employees. The best organizations, according to a project leader who helps with the *Fortune* list, keep their employees an average of 6 years, as opposed to the nationwide average of 3.6 years. They accomplish this by pushing for employees at all levels to feel involved in the company's success.[4]

FORECAST: WHAT'S AHEAD IN THIS CHAPTER

This chapter considers human resource (HR) management—planning for, attracting, developing, and retaining an effective workforce. We consider how this subject fits in with the overall company strategy, how to evaluate current and future employee needs, and how to recruit and select qualified people. We discuss orientation, training, and development; how to assess employee performance and give feedback; and what HR laws managers should be aware of. Finally, we consider how to manage compensation and benefits, promotions and discipline, and workplace performance problems.

major question

How do star managers view the role of people in their organization's success?

The Big Picture

Human resource management consists of the activities managers perform to plan for, attract, develop, and retain an effective workforce. Planning the human resources needed consists of understanding current employee needs and predicting future employee needs.

SAS child-care center. If the U.S. Senate can fund itself a child-care center (recently only one Senator, John Edwards, had a child young enough to use it), shouldn't every company have one? Considering how often the working parents of school-age children have to scramble to make special arrangements for their offspring during school closures, wouldn't you find a day-care center at work a special inducement to stay with—and perform well for—a company?

One company that has appeared on *Fortune*'s "The 100 Best Companies to Work For" list (#2 in 2001, #3 in 2002) is SAS Institute, a developer of statistical software located on the outskirts of Raleigh, N.C. SAS (pronounced "Sass") "is the closest thing to a workers' utopia in America: on-site child care, health center with physicians and dentists, massage therapist, wooded campus, and profit sharing."[5] At least that's according to Robert Levering and Milton Moskowitz, authors of the Best Companies list. SAS also offers flexible work schedules and fills jars all around the company with M&M candies—22.5 tons a year.[6] As a result, SAS has had the lowest employee turnover rate of any company on the list—4%, compared with a software industry average of 17%.

The software has made a billionaire of cofounder James H. Goodnight, whose mansion is on the grounds of the privately held company's country club–like campus. "I like happy people," he says, to explain the perks he lavishes on his employees. The software industry is notorious for inflicting brutal 60- to 80-hour weeks, but SAS workers—more than half of whom are women, drawn to its family-flexible policies—normally work 35 hours a week. Besides providing the free health clinic, two day-care centers, an elder-care program, private offices for everyone, and a pianist in the subsidized cafeteria, SAS gives employees an extra week of vacation between Christmas and New Year's, along with a year-end bonus and profit-sharing. Employees also get discounts on memberships in a local country club and tuition breaks for their children at a private school founded by Goodnight.

Too good to be true? SAS can do all these things because it is a privately held company, although it has entertained the idea of going public. (But investors in a public company might ask Goodnight to justify the M&M expense.) However, perhaps the catch, if any, is this: SAS offers benefits that cement employee loyalty while avoiding those that promote autonomy, such as commissions for salespeople, stock options, and tuition reimbursement for further training.[7]

Human Resource Management: Managing an Organization's Most Important Resource

**Human resource (HR) management** **consists of the activities managers perform to plan for, attract, develop, and retain an effective workforce.** Whether it's McKenzie looking for entry-level business consultants, the U.S. Navy trying to fill its ranks, or churches trying to reverse the declining number of priests and ministers, all organizations must deal with staffing.

The fact that the old Personnel Department is now called the Human Resources Department is not just a cosmetic change. It is intended to suggest the importance of staffing to a company's success. Although talking about people as "resources" might seem to downgrade them to the same level as financial resources and material resources, in fact people are an organization's most important resource. Indeed, companies such as box retailer The Container Store (#1 on _Fortune_ magazine's Best Companies list two years running, #2 in 2002), Cisco Systems, Southwest Airlines, and Charles Schwab have discovered that putting employees first has been the foundation for their success. "If you're not thinking all the time about making every person valuable, you don't have a chance," said General Electric head Jack Welch. "What's the alternative? Wasted minds? Uninvolved people? A labor force that's angry or bored? That doesn't make sense!"[8]

At many companies human resources has become part of the strategic-planning process, so that HR departments deal not only with employee paperwork and legal accountability—a very important area, as we describe in Section 9.2—but also with helping the company maintain a competitive advantage. At clothing retailer Liz Claiborne, says its HR vice president, Kathryn Connors, human resources is "part of policy development, line extension planning, and the merger and acquisition processes."[9] As a result, she says, little is done in the company that doesn't involve the human resources department. The purpose of the strategic human resource management process, then—shown in the blue-gray shaded boxes at right—is to get the optimum work performance that will help realize the company's mission and vision.[10] _(See Panel 9.1.)_

PANEL 9.1
The strategic human resource management process

 Establish the mission & the vision

 Establish the grand strategy

 Formulate the strategic plans

 Plan human resources needed

 Recruit & select people

 Orient, train, & develop

 Perform appraisals of people

Purpose: Get optimum work performance to help realize company's mission & vision

The Container Store. Considered the #1 _Fortune_ magazine Best Company two years in a row, this chain of 22 stores selling storage and organizing products is growing at 20% per year. "One greater person is equal to three good people," says the store's president. "If you truly believe that, then you can afford to pay that great person twice what someone else might. Then everybody wins." What do you think The Container Store is doing right? How can you find out? (Hint: Use an Internet search engine.)

Planning the Human Resources Needed

When a building contractor, looking to hire someone for a few hours to dig ditches, drives by a group of idle day laborers standing on a street corner, is that a form of HR planning? Certainly it shows the contractor's awareness that a pool of laborers usually can be found in that spot. But what if the builder needs a lot of people with specialized training—to give him or her the competitive advantage that the strategic planning process demands?

Here we are concerned with something more than simply hiring people on an "as needed" basis. *Strategic human resource planning* **consists of developing a systematic, comprehensive strategy for (a) understanding current employee needs and (b) predicting future employee needs.** Let's consider these two parts.

Understanding Current Employee Needs   To plan for the future, you must understand the present—what today's staffing picture looks like. This requires that you (or a trained specialist) do, first, a *job analysis* and from that write a *job description* and a *job specification*.[11]

United Parcel Service. A UPS driver's problems of driving in a big city—traffic, double parking, addressees not at home—are different from those of driving in rural areas, where there may be long stretches of boredom. Specialists in job analysis can interview drivers about their problems in order to write job descriptions that allow for varying circumstances.

■ **Job analysis:** The purpose of *job analysis* **is to determine, by observation and analysis, the basic elements of a job.** Specialists who do this interview job occupants about what they do, observe the flow of work, and learn how results are accomplished. For example, United Parcel Service has specialists who ride with the couriers and time how long it takes to deliver a load of packages and what problems are encountered (traffic jams, vicious dogs, recipients not home, and so on).

■ **Job description and job specification:** Once the fundamentals of a job are understood, then you can write a *job description*, **which summarizes what the holder of the job does and how and why he or she does it.** Next you can write a *job specification*, **which describes the minimum qualifications a person must have to perform the job successfully.**

This process can produce some surprises. Jobs that might seem to require a college degree, for example, might not after all. Thus, the process of writing job analyses, descriptions, and specifications can help you avoid hiring people who are overqualified (and presumably more expensive) or underqualified (and thus not as productive) for a particular job.

In addition, by entering a job description and specification with their attendant characteristics into a database, an organization can do computer-searching for candidates by matching keywords (nouns) on their résumés with the keywords describing the job. A position in desktop publishing, for instance, might be described by the kinds of software programs with which applicants should be familiar: *Adobe Illustrator, Adobe PageMaker, Adobe Photoshop, Quark, Adobe Acrobat.*

Predicting Future Employee Needs   Job descriptions change, of course: Auto mechanics, for instance, now have to know how computer chips work in cars. And new jobs are created: Who could have visualized the position of "e-commerce accountant" 10 years ago, for example?

As you might expect, predicting future employee needs means you have to become knowledgeable about the *staffing the organization might need* and the *likely sources for that staffing*:

The staffing the organization might need:
You can assume your organization won't change much. In that case, you can fairly easily predict that jobs will periodically become unoccupied (because of retirement, resignations, and so on) and that you'll need to pay the same salaries and meet the same criteria about minority hiring to fill them.

Better, however, to assume the organization will change. Thus, you need to understand the organization's vision and strategic plan so that the proper people can be hired to meet the future strategies and work.

The likely sources for staffing: You can recruit employees either from inside or outside the organization. In looking at those inside, you need to consider which employees are motivated, trainable, and promotable and what kind of training your organization might have to do.

In looking outside, you need to consider the availability of talent in your industry's and geographical area's labor pool, the training of people graduating from various schools, and such factors as what kind of people are moving into your area. The U.S. Bureau of Labor Statistics and the U.S. Census Bureau issue reports on such matters.

Click-Along 9.1

Sources of Staffing in Prosperous Times: Women, Immigrants, & Older People

Outside staffing. What kind of person does First Union/Wachovia, the financial services firm, look for when it goes outside for staffing? Does this ad suggest the firm is expanding or that it needs to bring in more talent than it currently has?

major question

To avoid exposure to legal liabilities, what areas of the law do I need to be aware of?

The Big Picture

Four areas of human resource law any manager needs to be aware of are labor relations, compensation and benefits, health and safety, and equal employment opportunity.

Click-Along 9.2

Expanded Table: Major U.S. Federal Laws Protecting Employees

Whatever your organization's human resource strategy, in the United States (and in U.S. divisions overseas) it has to operate within the environment of American law. Four areas you need to be aware of are as follows. Some important laws are summarized in the table opposite. *(See Panel 9.2.)*

1 Labor Relations

The earliest laws affecting employee welfare had to do with unions, and they can still have important effects. Legislation passed in 1935 (the Wagner Act) resulted in the ***National Labor Relations Board***, **which enforces procedures whereby employees may vote to have a union and for collective bargaining.** *Collective bargaining* **consists of negotiations between management and employees about disputes over compensation, benefits, working conditions, and job security.**

A 1947 law (the Taft-Hartley Act) allows the President of the United States to prevent or end a strike that threatens national security.

2 Compensation & Benefits

The Social Security Act in 1935 established the U.S. retirement system. The passage of the Fair Labor Standards Act three years later established a minimum wage and required overtime pay for employees working more than 40 hours a week. Salaried executive, administrative, and professional employees are exempt from overtime rules. (We discuss compensation further in Section 9.6.)

3 Health & Safety

From miners risking tunnel cave-ins to cotton mill workers breathing lint, industry has always had dirty, dangerous jobs. Beginning with the Occupational Safety and Health Act (OSHA) of 1970, there has grown a body of law requiring organizations to provide employees with nonhazardous working conditions. Later laws extended health coverage for employees.

4 Equal Employment Opportunity

The effort to reduce discrimination in employment based on racial, ethnic, and religious bigotry and gender stereotypes began with the Civil Rights Act of 1964. This established the ***Equal Employment Opportunity (EEO) Commission***, **whose job it is to enforce anti-discrimination and other employment-related laws.** Later laws prevented discrimination against older workers and people with physical and mental disabilities.

Two important concepts covered by EEO laws are *discrimination* and *affirmative action*.

PANEL 9.2 Some important recent U.S. federal laws and regulations protecting employees

Year	Law or regulation	Provisions
1963	Equal Pay Act	Requires men and women be paid equally for performing equal work
1964	Civil Rights Act, Title VII	Prohibits discrimination on basis of race, color, religion, national origin, or sex
1967, amended 1978 and 1986	Age Discrimination in Employment Act (ADEA)	Prohibits discrimination in employees over 40 years old; restricts mandatory retirement
1970	Occupational Safety & Health Act (OSHA)	Establishes minimum health and safety standards in organizations
1974	Employee Retirement Income Security Act (ERISA)	Sets rules for managing pension plans; provides federal insurance to cover bankrupt plans
1978	Pregnancy Discrimination Act	Broadens discrimination to cover pregnancy, childbirth, and related medical conditions; protects job security during maternity leave
1978	Mandatory Retirement Act	Prohibits forced retirement of employees under 70
1986	Consolidated Omnibus Budget Reconciliation Act (COBRA)	Requires an extension of health insurance benefits after termination
1986	Immigration Reform & Control Act	Prohibits unlawful employment of aliens and unfair immigration-related employment practices
1988	Worker Adjustment and Retraining Notification Act	Requires organizations with 100 or more employees to give 60 days notice for mass layoffs or plant closings
1990	Americans with Disabilities Act (ADA)	Prohibits discrimination against qualified employees with physical or mental disabilities or chronic illness; requires "reasonable accommodation" be provided so they can perform duties
1991	Civil Rights Act	Amends and clarifies Title VII, ADA, and other laws; permits suits against employers for punitive damages in cases of intentional discrimination
1993	Family & Medical Leave Act	Requires employers to provide 12 weeks of unpaid leave for medical and family reasons, including for childbirth, adoption, or family emergency

Discrimination *Discrimination* **occurs when people are hired or promoted—or denied hiring or promotion—for reasons not relevant to the job,** such as skin color or eye shape, gender, religion, national origin, and the like. When an organization is found to have been practicing discrimination, the people discriminated against may sue for back pay and punitive damages.

Affirmative Action *Affirmative action* **focuses on achieving equality of opportunity within an organization.** It tries to make up for past discrimination in employment by actively finding, hiring, and developing the talents of people from groups traditionally discriminated against. Steps include active recruitment, elimination of prejudicial questions in interviews, and establishment of minority hiring goals. It's important to note that EEO laws *do not* allow use of hiring quotas.

major question

How can I reduce mistakes in hiring and find great people who might work for me?

The Big Picture

Qualified applicants for jobs may be recruited from inside or outside the organization. The task of choosing the best person is enhanced by such tools as reviewing candidates' application forms, résumés, and references; doing interviews, either structured or unstructured; and screening with ability, personality, performance, and other kinds of employment tests.

"Digital résumés, digital employment advertising, digital résumé searches—it's a rebuilding of the [employment] infrastructure," says former Intel chairman Andy Grove.[12]

Companies are marrying the public Internet with their own internal intranets to revolutionize their human resource departments, going online for everything from listing job openings to conducting new employee orientations.[13] Recruitment efforts have migrated from simple online classified-ad–like postings of jobs available to websites that try to attract candidates by downloading video and audio feeds. For instance, at the New York office of DVC Worldwide, a provider of Internet solutions, a webcam broadcasts live to the world videos of employees working. "We had to differentiate ourselves," says Haim Ariav, whose movements—a wave, pen chewing, typing—are broadcast online. "It's been phenomenal. We've hired a lot of people through it, and we're still getting e-mail."[14]

Recruitment: How to Attract Qualified Applicants

DVC's recruitment methods may be unusual, but at some time nearly every organization has to think about how to find the right kind of people. ___Recruiting is the process of locating and attracting qualified applicants for jobs open in the organization.___ The word "qualified" is important: You want to find people whose skills, abilities, and characteristics are best suited to your organization. Recruiting is of two types: *internal* and *external*.

1 Internal Recruiting: Hiring from the Inside ___Internal recruiting___ **means making people already employed by the organization aware of job openings.** Indeed, most vacant positions in organizations are filled through internal recruitment.[15] The principal means of letting employees know of job openings is through ___job posting___, **placing information about job vacancies and qualifications on bulletin boards, in newsletters, and on the organization's intranet.**

DVC webcam used for recruitment. Would you mind having a video camera record you working and sending your images over the World Wide Web? Would it depend on how much you liked or disliked your job?

Internal recruitment has both advantages and disadvantages:

■ **Advantages:** There are three advantages: (1) Employees tend to be inspired to greater effort and loyalty. Morale is enhanced because they realize that working hard and staying put can result in more opportunities. (2) The whole process of advertising, interviewing, and so on is cheaper. (3) There are fewer risks. Internal candidates are already known and are familiar with the organization.

■ **Disadvantages:** There are three disadvantages: (1) Internal recruitment restricts the competition for positions and limits the pool of fresh talent and fresh viewpoints. (2) It may encourage employees to assume that longevity and seniority will automatically result in promotion. (3) Whenever a job is filled, it creates a vacancy elsewhere in the organization.

2 External Recruiting: Hiring from the Outside   *External recruiting* means attracting job applicants from outside the organization.

Notices of job vacancies are placed through newspapers, employment agencies, executive recruiting firms, union hiring halls, college job-placement offices, technical training schools, and word of mouth through professional associations. Many organizations—and not just high-technology companies—are advertising job openings on the Internet.

■ **Advantages:** Two advantages of recruiting from outside the organization are that applicants may have (1) specialized knowledge and experience and (2) fresh viewpoints.

■ **Disadvantages:** Two disadvantages are (1) the recruitment process is more expensive and takes longer, and (2) the risks are higher, because the persons hired are less well known.

Which External Recruiting Methods Work Best?   Both as a manager trying

to hire good candidates and as a job seeker yourself, you'll benefit from knowing which external recruiting sources are most effective in producing superior employees, although these techniques vary by job. (Note: At the time of this research, use of the Internet as a recruiting device had not been evaluated. It's clear, however, that it is now a major recruiting and screening device. Indeed, there are now some 2,500 sites that promise to match job candidates with employers.[16])

■ **Above-average sources:** The most effective sources are employee referrals, say human resource professionals.[17] The reasons: (1) To protect their own reputations, employees are fairly careful about whom they recommend. (2) They know the qualifications of both the job and the prospective employee.

    HR professionals also consider college recruiters and executive search firms above-average sources.

■ **Average sources:** HR professionals ranked professional associations as a slightly above-average source for job candidates. Newspaper ads were also considered slightly above average (although they may also produce numerous unqualified applicants).

■ **Below-average sources:** HR executives rated direct applications and private employment agencies as below-average sources of candidates. Public employment agencies and unions were considered the least satisfactory sources for finding qualified applicants.

Salisbury State University is a four-year college located on the Eastern Shore of Maryland. Should a student's choice of college be affected by the extent of job recruiting activity done on campus and the kinds of companies doing it?

Realistic Job Previews Often an organization will put on its best face to try to attract the best outside candidates—and then wonder why the new hires leave when the job doesn't turn out to be as rosy as promised.

A better approach is to present what's known as a _realistic job preview_, **which gives a candidate a picture of both positive and negative features of the job and organization before he or she is hired.**[18] People with realistic expectations tend to quit less frequently and be more satisfied than those with unrealistic expectations. Realistic job previews are a must for people who will be living or working outside their home companies.

Selection: How to Choose the Best Person for the Job

Whether the recruitment process turns up a handful of job applicants or thousands, now you turn to the _selection process_, **the screening of job applicants to hire the best candidate.** Essentially this becomes an exercise in _prediction_: How well will the candidate perform the job and how long will he or she stay?

Three types of selection tools are _background information, interviewing_, and _employment tests_.

1 Background Information: Application Forms, Résumés, & Reference Checks Application forms and résumés provide basic background information about job applicants, such as citizenship, education, work history, and certifications.

Unfortunately, a lot of résumé information consists of mild puffery or even outrageous fairy tales. Lying on job applications has been around since Adam was expelled from the Garden of Eden for biting into the apple, goes an old business joke, when he then put down "quality control supervisor, Eden Produce" on his résumé. The American Psychological Association reports that 67% of all job seekers fabricate or embellish their managerial or supervisory duties on their résumés. The head of the Certified Reference Checking Co. of St. Louis says 36% of résumés contain some untruth, as in past job titles, salary history, and length of employment.[19] Lying about education is most prevalent (such as pretending to hold a college degree). Other common fabrications, according to one account, "include inflating salary history, puffing up job titles, plugging gaps in employment histories, and embellishing achievements on projects."[20]

Companies now routinely check résumés or hire companies that do so, such as Illinois-based Credentials LLC, which signs contracts with most major universities to tap into their databases to glean basic information about their students. Unfor-

tunately, many employers don't give honest assessments of former employees, for two reasons: They fear that if they say anything negative, they can be sued by the former employee. And they fear that if they say anything positive and the job candidate doesn't pan out, they can be sued by the new employer.

In addition, some companies now resort to computer prescreening, which job seekers must pass before obtaining an in-person interview. Macy's, for instance, requires applicants to undergo an 8- or 10-minute screening, using a phone's keypad to answer multiple-choice questions (such as "If a customer complained to you about the selection of merchandise in a store, what would you do?").[21] Information services firm EDS has an entire website for screening candidates.[22]

Because honest references are so hard to get, candidates are now being scrutinized more carefully for character and candor during the interview process. Indeed, a survey by Robert Half International, a big staffing services firm, found that nearly one-third of executives polled rated honesty and integrity as the most critical qualities in a candidate. "Without such attributes as trustworthiness and integrity, even the most highly skilled and articulate job seeker or employee will have limited success," says Max Messmer, head of Robert Half.[23]

2 Interviewing: Unstructured, Situational, & Behavioral-Description Interviewing, the most commonly used employee-selection technique, may take place face to face, by videoconferencing, or—as is increasingly the case—via the

Internet.[24] To help eliminate bias, interviews can be designed, conducted, and evaluated by a committee of three or more people. The most commonly used employee-selection technique, interviewing, takes three forms:

■ **Unstructured interview:** Like an ordinary conversation, an *unstructured interview* **involves asking probing questions to find out what the applicant is like.** There is no fixed set of questions asked of all applicants and no systematic scoring procedure. As a result, the unstructured interview has been criticized as being overly subjective and apt to be influenced by the biases of the interviewer. Equally important, nowadays it is susceptible to legal attack, because some questions may infringe on non-job-related matters such as privacy, diversity, or disability.[25]

■ **Structured interview type 1—the situational interview:** The *structured interview* **involves asking each applicant the same questions and comparing their responses to a standardized set of answers.**

In one type of structured interview, the *situational interview*, **the interviewer focuses on hypothetical situations.** Example: "What would you do if you saw two of your people arguing loudly in the work area?" The idea here is to find out if the applicant can handle difficult situations that may arise on the job.

■ **Structured interview type 2—the behavioral-description interview:** In the second type of structured interview, the *behavioral-description interview*, **the interviewer explores what applicants have actually done in the past.** Example: "What was the best idea you ever sold to a supervisor, teacher, peer, or subordinate?" This question (asked by the U.S. Army of college students applying for its officer training program) is designed to assess the applicant's ability to influence others.

practical action

The Right Way to Conduct an Interview

Because hiring people who later have to be let go is such an expensive proposition, companies are now putting a great deal of emphasis on effective interviewing. Although this is a subject worth exploring further, here are some minimal suggestions:[26]

Before the Interview: Define Your Needs & Review Applicant's Résumé Write out what skills, traits, and qualities the job requires. "Looking to hire somebody is like going to the supermarket," says one HR manager. "You need to have a list and know what you need."[27]

Look at the applicant's résumé or application form to determine relevant experience, gaps, and discrepancies.

Write Out Interview Questions You should ask each candidate the same set of questions, so that you can compare their answers. (This helps keep you out of legal trouble, too.) In general, the questions should be designed to elicit the following types of information:

■ **Does the applicant have the knowledge to do the job?** Examples: "Give an example where you came up with a creative solution." "How do you do research on the Internet?"

■ **Can the applicant handle difficult situations?** Examples: "Tell me about a time when you dealt with an irate customer. How did you handle the situation and what was the outcome?"

■ **Is the applicant willing to cope with the job's demands?** Examples: "How do you feel about making unpopular decisions?" "Are you willing to travel 30% of the time?"

■ **Will the applicant fit in with the organization's culture?** Examples: "How would your last supervisor describe you?" "How much leeway did they give you in your previous job in charging travel expenses?"

(continued)

Follow a Three-Scene Interview Scenario The interview itself may follow a three-scene script.

- **Scene 1: The first 3 minutes—small talk and "compatibility" test:** The first scene is really a "compatibility test." It takes about 3 minutes and consists of exchanging small talk, giving you a chance to establish rapport and judge how well the candidate makes a first impression.

- **Scene 2: The next 15–60 minutes—asking questions and listening to the applicant's "story":** In the next scene, you ask the questions you wrote out (and answer those the candidate directs to you). Allow the interviewee to do 70%–80% of the talking.

Take notes to remember important points. Don't ignore your "gut feelings." Intuition plays a role in hiring decisions.

- **Scene 3: The final 1–2 minutes—closing the interview and setting up the next steps:** In the final minute, you listen to see whether the candidate expresses interest in taking the job.

After the Interview Write a short report making some sort of quantitative score of the candidate's qualifications. Indicate your reasons for your decision.

Check the applicant's references before inviting him or her to a second interview.

3 Employment Tests: Ability, Personality, Performance, & Others It used to be that employment selection tests consisted of paper-and-pencil, performance, and physical-ability tests. Now, however, *employment tests* **are legally considered to consist of any procedure used in the employment selection decision process.** Thus, even application forms, interviews, and educational and experience requirements are now considered tests.[28]

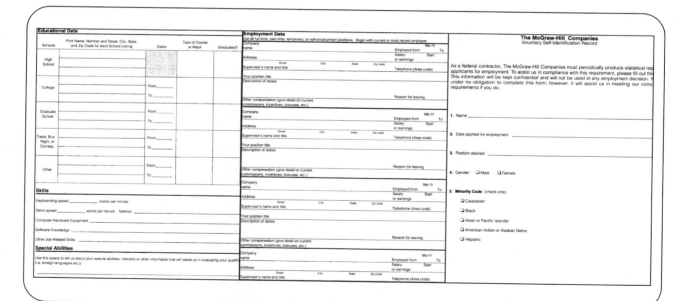

Application form. This is for McGraw-Hill, publisher of this book. Note that it asks for educational and employment history, which is usually subject to verification, since these are areas where applicants may try to stretch the truth. The form also asks if applicants wish to disclose their racial/ethnic background, which would help the company, as a federal contractor, report on the diversity of its employees.

Probably the three most common employment tests are the following.

- **Ability tests:** *Ability tests* measure physical abilities, strength and stamina, mechanical ability, mental abilities, and clerical abilities. Telephone operators, for instance, need to be tested for hearing. Assembly-line workers are tested for manual dexterity.

- **Personality tests:** *Personality tests* measure such personality traits as adjustment, energy, sociability, independence, and need for achievement. Such tests should be used with caution because of the difficulty of measuring personality characteristics and of making a legal defense if the results are challenged.[29]

- **Performance tests:** *Performance tests* measure performance on actual job tasks, as when secretarial applicants take a typing test or middle managers work on a small project. Some companies have an ___assessment center___, **in which management candidates participate in activities for a few days while being assessed by evaluators.**

Example of a Personality Test: A Cosmetics Company Uses the Predictive Index to Guide Hiring

Steve DiAntonio, head of a cosmetics company called Color Me Beautiful in Chantilly, Va., decided to adopt a short personality test called the Predictive Index (PI) to help him with hiring decisions. In the course of building his company, he had discovered he had hired the wrong kind of people to be salespeople. Some of his 15 account managers were too shy to pitch the line to department stores and beauty salons. Others were intimidated by the rough-and-tumble world of retail and lost counter space to competitors. Despite training programs and cash and travel incentives, nothing had seemed to work.

In desperation, he turned to PI, which asks job applicants to choose from a list of 86 adjectives those that they think best describe themselves—"selfish," "obstinate," "dutiful," "fussy," "brave," "talkative," and so on. Taking only 10 minutes to administer, the PI is inexpensive and easy for someone without a Ph.D. to evaluate. It is available in 58 languages, from Laotian to Latvian. Some 3,000 organizations, ranging from car-rental firms to college sports teams, use it to hire and manage workers.

Although some academics are skeptical of the test because its maker, Praendex in Wellesley Hills, Mass., has never submitted results for rigorous validity testing, companies like Color Me Beautiful swear by it. Using PI, DiAntonio was able to rebuild his sales force. Sales rebounded, new accounts poured in, and revenues soared.

- **Other tests:** The list of employment testing techniques has grown to include—in appropriate cases—drug testing, polygraph (lie detectors), genetic screening, and even (a questionable technique) handwriting analysis.

However, with any kind of test, an important legal consideration is the test's *validity*. That is, with any test used to make decisions about people (for performance appraisal), the law says that the test has to be valid. A valid test is one that measures what it purports to measure, and it must be free of bias. Using an invalid test to hire people can lead to poor selection decisions. It also can create legal problems if the test is ever challenged in a court of law.

Polygraph test. Defense contractors and other security-minded companies are apt to require this test. Would the idea of taking a polygraph deter you from applying to certain companies even if the income and career were attractive?

major question

Once people are hired, what's the best way to see that they do what they're supposed to do?

The Big Picture

Three ways newcomers are helped to perform their jobs are through *orientation*, to fit them into the job and organization; *training*, to upgrade the skills of technical and operational employees; and *development*, to upgrade the skills of professionals and managers.

In muckraker Upton Sinclair's 1906 novel *The Jungle*, "employers barely paused when a worker swooned from overwork or fell into a rendering tank," writes columnist Sue Shellenbarger. "They just got another warm body to replace him."[30]

That's hardly the case anymore. Now the emphasis is on "human capital." Only a third to half of most companies' stock-market value is accounted for by hard assets such as property, plant, and equipment, according to a Brookings Institution report. Most of a firm's value is in such attributes as patents, processes, and—important to this discussion—employee or customer satisfaction.[31] The means for helping employees perform their jobs are orientation, training, and development.

FedEx employee going through initial training. Such employees get an average of 12 weeks of training. Have you ever encountered a FedEx worker you thought was poorly trained or uncertain about the job responsibilities?

Orientation: Helping Newcomers Learn the Ropes

The finalist candidate is offered the job, has accepted it, and has started work. Now he or she must begin, in that old sailor's phrase, to "learn the ropes." This is the start of **_orientation_**, **helping the newcomer fit smoothly into the job and the organization.**

Helping New Employees Get Comfortable: The First Six Months
"How well will I get along with other employees?" "What if I screw up on a project?" Coming into a new job can produce a lot of uncertainty and anxiety. In part this is because, depending on the job, a new hire can accomplish only 60% as much in the first three months as an experienced worker, according to MCI Communications.[32]

The first six months on a job can be critical to how one performs over the long haul, because that's when the psychological patterns are established. Thus, employers have discovered that it's far better to give newcomers a helping hand than to let them learn possibly inappropriate behavior that will be hard to undo later.[33]

The Desirable Characteristics of Orientation Like Orientation Week for new college students, the initial socialization period is designed to give new employees the information they need to be effective. In a large organization, orientation may be a formal, established process. In a small organization, it may be so informal that employees find themselves having to make most of the effort themselves.

Following orientation, the employee should emerge with information about three matters (much of which he or she may have acquired during the job-application process):

■ **The job routine:** At minimum, the new employee needs to have learned what is required in the job for which he or she was hired, how the work will be evaluated, and who the immediate coworkers and managers are. This is basic.

■ **The organization's mission and operations:** Certainly all managers need to know what the organization is about—its purpose, products or services, operations, and history. And it's now understood that low-level employees perform better if they, too, have this knowledge.

■ **The organization's work rules and employee benefits:** A public utility's HR department may have a brochure explaining formalized work rules, overtime requirements, grievance procedures, and elaborate employee benefits. A technology startup may be so fluid that many of these matters will have not been established yet. Even so, there are matters of law (such as those pertaining to sexual harassment) affecting work operations that every employee should be made aware of.

Casino worker. Card dealers must go through an extensive orientation program at many gambling casinos. What would you guess are the principal concerns of casino management?

Training & Development: Helping People Perform Better

Which business strategy offers the highest returns: (1) downsizing; (2) total quality management, which focuses on work methods and process control; or (3) employee involvement, which focuses on upgrading workers' skills and knowledge? According to a study of 216 big firms, the winner is employee involvement, which had an average return on investment of 19.1% (versus 15.4% for downsizing and 15% for TQM).[34]

In hiring, you always try to get people whose qualifications match the requirements of the job. Quite often, however, there are gaps in what new employees need to know. These gaps are filled by training. The training process involves five steps, as shown below. *(See Panel 9.3.)*

PANEL 9.3
Five steps in the training process

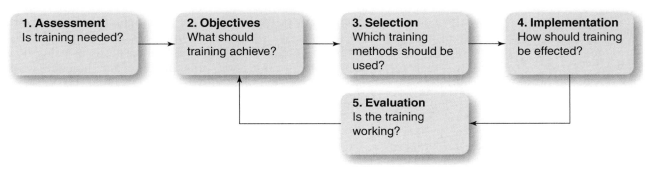

1. Assessment Is training needed? → **2. Objectives** What should training achieve? → **3. Selection** Which training methods should be used? → **4. Implementation** How should training be effected?

5. Evaluation Is the training working?

HR professionals distinguish between *training* and *development*.

■ **Training—upgrading skills of technical and operational employees:** Electronics technicians, word processors, computer network administrators, and X-ray technicians, among many others, need to be schooled in new knowledge as the requirements of their fields change. *Training*, then, refers to educating technical and operational employees in how to better do their current jobs.

■ **Development—upgrading skills of professionals and managers:** Accountants, nurses, lawyers, and managers of all levels need to be continually educated in how to do their jobs better not just today but also tomorrow. *Development* refers to educating professionals and managers in the skills they need to do their jobs in the future.

The top 15 areas for which training and development is given, according to a 1996 survey of 2,833 U.S. companies with 100 or more employees, are shown in the following chart.[35] *(See Panel 9.4.)*

PANEL 9.4

Top 15 areas in which training and development are given

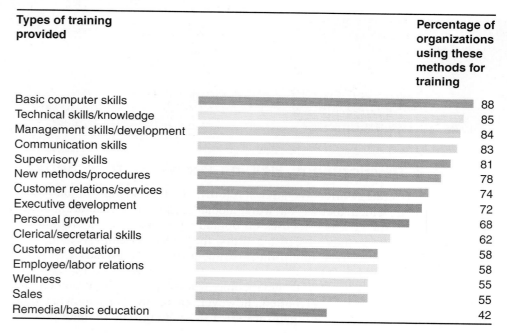

Types of training provided	Percentage of organizations using these methods for training
Basic computer skills	88
Technical skills/knowledge	85
Management skills/development	84
Communication skills	83
Supervisory skills	81
New methods/procedures	78
Customer relations/services	74
Executive development	72
Personal growth	68
Clerical/secretarial skills	62
Customer education	58
Employee/labor relations	58
Wellness	55
Sales	55
Remedial/basic education	42

The Different Types of Training or Development   There are all kinds of training and development methods, and their effectiveness depends on whether what is being taught are facts or skills. If people are to learn *facts*—such as work rules or legal matters—lectures, videotapes, and workbooks are effective. If people are to learn *skills*—such as improving interpersonal relations or using new tools—then techniques such as discussion, role playing, and practice work better.

Another way to categorize training methods is to distinguish on-the-job methods from off-the-job methods.

■ **On-the-job training methods:** On-the-job training takes place in the work setting while employees are performing job-related tasks Four major techniques are as follows:

(1) In *coaching*, a subordinate is taken under the wing of an experienced employee who points out what's required in the new job.

(2) In *training positions*, trainees are given positions as assistants to experienced managers.

(3) In *job rotation*, employees are given lateral transfers to allow them to work at different jobs.

(4) In *planned work activities*, trainees are given important work assignments (such as heading a task force) to develop their experience.

Small company training. How would you expect training in a small company to differ from training in a large company?

■ **Off-the-job training methods:** The most frequently used kinds of off-the-job instruction, in one survey, are these:

(1) classroom programs (used by 91% of the 2,833 companies surveyed),

(2) videotapes (79%),

(3) workbooks or manuals (77%),

(4) overhead/opaque transparencies (56%),

(5) business books (55%),

(6) role playing (55%).[36]

Other methods are audiotapes, self-testing instruments, case studies, and slides. Lots of off-the-job training also consists of ***computer-assisted instruction (CAI)*,** **in which computers are used to provide additional help or to reduce instructional time.**

Example of Off-the-Job Training: Practical Courses Through Distance Learning

A college degree isn't the end of the educational road. Between 40 million and 45 million people are taking short-term, practical courses related to their careers, mostly at business schools and continuing-education institutions around the country.[37] Even top managers are brushing up. John Klotsche, 56, chairman of Baker & McKenzie, a global law firm, decided he and his 550 partners didn't know enough about managing a business in today's fast-changing marketplace, so all attorneys in his firm took a two-week executive-education course at Northwestern University.

But while most students are taking classes on campuses, the fastest-growing method of continuing education is via distance learning from videotapes, satellite lectures, or courses offered on the World Wide Web. On the Internet alone, a reported 26,000 courses are being taught to 750,000 students.[38]

The benefits of a virtual education are that no transportation is needed and you can follow a flexible schedule and often work at your own pace. But because of the lack of classroom interaction between students and teachers, the online model of education means that both must assume more responsibility. "If students do not receive adequate teacher feedback and reinforcement," points out one writer, "they will not always know whether they possess an accurate knowledge of the subject matter."[39]

major question

How can I assess employees' performance more accurately and give more effective feedback?

The Big Picture

Performance appraisal, assessing employee performance and providing them feedback, may be objective or subjective. Appraisals may be by peers, subordinates, customers, oneself. Feedback may be formal or informal.

Feedback for Starbucks. An important part of performance appraisal, feedback on employee performance may come in the form of a manager's comments or, as here, through customer comments. If you worked in a service industry, do you think it would be possible to have bad feedback from your customers and good feedback from your managers?

"Ask most managers the most difficult part of their job, and they'll likely answer having to fire someone," writes Carol Hymowitz in *The Wall Street Journal.* "Ask what they endlessly put off doing, and they'll say advising weak employees that they must improve or risk losing their jobs."[40]

Clearly, it's unfair to underperforming employees to assume that time alone will enable them to shape up. And it's unfair to the organization to allow those employees to continue to stumble along without direction. It's part of your job as a manager to give the people who work for you honest appraisals.

Defining Performance Appraisal

Performance appraisal **consists of (1) assessing an employee's performance and (2) providing him or her with feedback.** Thus, this management task has two purposes: First, performance appraisal helps employees understand how they are doing in relation to objectives and standards; here you must *judge* the employee. Second, it helps in their training and personal development; here you must *counsel* the employee.[41]

Appraisals are of two general types—objective and subjective:

1 Objective Appraisals *Objective appraisals,* **also called** *results appraisals,* **are based on facts and are often numerical.** In these kinds of appraisals, you would keep track of such matters as the numbers of products the employee sold in a month, customer complaints filed against an employee, miles of freight hauled, and the like. The good thing about objective appraisals is that they measure results. It doesn't matter if two appliance sales people have completely different personal traits (one is formal, reserved, and patient, the other informal, gregarious, and impatient) if each sells the same number of washers and dryers.

We discussed an objective approach in Chapter 5 under *management by objectives,* which can encourage employees to feel empowered to adopt behavior that will produce specific results. MBO, you'll recall, is a four-step process in which (1) managers and employees jointly set objectives for the employee, (2) managers develop action plans, (3) managers and employees periodically review the employee's performance, and (4) the manager makes a performance appraisal and rewards the employee according to results. For example, an objective for a copier service technician might be to increase the number of service calls 15% during the next three months.

Click-Along 9.3

Six Criteria of Legally Defensible Performance Appraisal Systems

2 Subjective Appraisals   Few employees can be adequately measured just by objective appraisals—hence the need for ___subjective appraisals___, **which are based on a manager's perceptions of an employee's (1) traits or (2) behaviors.**

■ **Trait appraisals:** *Trait appraisals* are ratings of such subjective attributes as "attitude," "initiative," and "leadership." Trait evaluations may be easy to create and use, but their validity is questionable because the evaluator's personal bias can affect the ratings.

■ **Behavioral appraisals:** Behavioral appraisals measure specific, observable aspects of performance—being on time for work, for instance—although making the evaluation is still somewhat subjective. An example is the ___behaviorally anchored rating scale (BARS)___, **which rates employee gradations in performance according to scales of specific behaviors.** For example, a five-point BARS rating scale about attendance might go from "Always early for work and has equipment ready to fully assume duties" to "Frequently late and often does not have equipment ready for going to work," with gradations in between.

How'm I doing? One of the most important tasks of being a manager is giving employees accurate information about their work performance. Which would you be more comfortable giving—objective appraisals or subjective appraisals?

Who Should Make Performance Appraisals?

As you might expect, most performance appraisals are done by managers. However, to add different perspectives, sometimes appraisal information is provided by other people knowledgeable about particular employees.

Peers, Subordinates, Customers, & Self   Among additional sources of information are coworkers and subordinates, customers and clients, and the employees themselves.

■ **Peers and subordinates:** Coworkers, colleagues, and subordinates may well see different aspects of your performance. Such information can be useful for development, although it probably shouldn't be used for evaluation. (Many managers will resist soliciting such information about themselves, of course, fearing negative appraisals.)

■ **Customers and clients:** Some organizations, such as restaurants and hotels, ask customers and clients for their appraisals of employees. Publishers ask authors to judge how well they are doing by them in handling the editing, production, and marketing of their books. Automobile dealerships may send follow-up questionnaires to car buyers.

■ **Self-appraisals:** How would you rate your own performance in a job, knowing that it would go into your personnel file? Probably the bias would be toward the favorable. Nevertheless, *self-appraisals* help employees become involved in the whole evaluation process and may make them more receptive to feedback about areas needing improvement.

Example of Self-Appraisal: Workers Review Themselves at International Paper Co.

Passing judgment on everything done by every subordinate is an impossible task, contends P. J. Smoot, learning and development leader in International Paper Co.'s Memphis, Tenn., office. The real job of a manager, she suggests, is to listen and learn from employees and then, by asking questions, guide them to a mutually agreed-on performance plan for the coming year.

"Listen for understanding," Smoot advises managers. "And then react honestly and constructively. Focus on the business goals, not on the personality." A manager should then use questions—"What about this?" "Would this be more effective?"—to guide the employee to mutual understanding.

Employees should be asked to describe not what they did during the past review period but what they did that made a difference. In addition, they should be guided to describe something that didn't go right and what they learned from it. This, Smoot suggests, gets across the idea to employees that it's okay not to be perfect.

In addition, Smooth recommends that employees identify other people they work with. Then at review time, the manager can solicit their evaluation of the employee as well.[42]

Click-Along 9.4

Example of 360-Degree Assessment: Hewlett-Packard

360-Degree Assessment We said performance appraisals may be done by peers, subordinates, customers, and oneself. Sometimes all these may be used, in a technique called 360-degree assessment.

In a "theater in the round," the actors in a dramatic play are watched by an audience on all sides of them—360 degrees. Similarly, as a worker, you have many people watching you from all sides. Thus has arisen the idea of the _**360-degree assessment**_, or _**360-degree feedback appraisal**_, **in which employees are appraised not only by their managerial superiors but also by peers, subordinates, and sometimes clients,** thus providing several perspectives.

Typically, an employee chooses between six and 12 other people to make evaluations, who then fill out anonymous forms, the results of which are tabulated by computer. The employee then goes over the results with his or her manager and together they put into place a long-term plan for performance goals.

Evidence as to the effectiveness of 360-degree feedback is scarce. One study of 48 managers in a large public utility company found that the group as a whole developed its skills as a result of the feedback, "but there was substantial variability among individuals in how much change occurred."[43]

Customer service. Julie Bowers (left), director of the Austin station for Austin Express, a small commuter airline, and customer service representative Jayson Haile help customer Missy Hacker of San Antonio, who was buying a ticket to East Texas. Aren't there times when you've been an airline customer and would have wished airline management would call on you to take part in a 360-degree assessment of one of their employees? Isn't this a technique companies should use more often?

Effective Performance Feedback

The whole point of performance appraisal, of course, is to stimulate better job performance. To gather information to feed back to the employee, a manager can use two kinds of appraisals—formal and informal.

1 Formal Appraisals *Formal appraisals* **are conducted at specific times throughout the year and are based on performance measures that have been established in advance.** An emergency medical technician might be evaluated twice a year by his or her manager, using objective performance measures such as work attendance time sheets and more subjective measures such as a BARS to indicate the employee's willingness to follow emergency procedures and doctors' and nurses' orders.

As part of the appraisal, the manager should give the employee feedback, describing how he or she is performing well and not so well and giving examples. Managers are sometimes advised to keep diaries about specific incidents so they won't have to rely on their memories (and so that their evaluations will be more lawsuit-resistant).

Facts should always be used rather than impressions. For example, a newspaper-delivery driver might be told "There were only three complaints last month from people who didn't receive their paper compared with five the month before." This is preferable to "You seem to have become more motivated about your work in the last few weeks."

2 Informal Appraisals Formal appraisals are the equivalent of a student receiving a grade on a midterm test and a grade on a final test—weeks may go by in which you are unaware of how well you're doing in the course. Informal appraisals are the equivalent of occasional unscheduled pop quizzes and short papers or drop-in visits to the professor's office to talk about your work—you have more frequent feedback about your performance. *Informal appraisals* **are conducted on an unscheduled basis and consist of less rigorous indications of employee performance.**

You may not feel comfortable about critiquing your employees' performance, especially when you have to convey criticism rather than praise. Nevertheless, giving performance feedback is one of the most important parts of the manager's job. One way to handle it is to think of yourself as a *coach*, as though you were managing a basketball team. Your purpose is not to give criticism and find fault, which may only undermine your players' confidence and demotivate them. Rather, your purpose is to show them how to improve.

Some suggestions for improvement appear below. *(See Panel 9.5.)*

PANEL 9.5 How to give performance feedback to employees. Think of yourself as a coach, as though you were managing a team of athletes.

■ *Take a problem-solving approach, avoid criticism, and treat employees with respect:* Recall the worst boss you ever worked for. How did you react to his or her method of giving feedback? Avoid criticism that might be taken personally.

Example: Don't say "You're picking up that bag of cement wrong" (which criticizes by using the word "wrong"). Say "Instead of bending at the waist, a good way to pick up something heavy is to bend your knees. That'll help save your back."

■ *Be specific in describing the employee's present performance and in the improvement you desire:* Describe your subordinate's current performance in specific terms and concentrate on outcomes that are within his or her ability to improve.

Example: Don't say "You're always late turning in your sales reports." Say "Instead of making calls on Thursday afternoon, why don't you take some of the time to do your sales reports so they'll be ready on Friday along with those of the other sales reps."

■ *Get the employee's input:* In determining causes for a problem, listen to the employee and get his or her help in crafting a solution.

Example: Don't say "You've got to learn to get here at 9:00 every day." Say "What changes do you think could be made so that your station is covered when people start calling at 9:00?"

What are the various forms of compensation?

The Big Picture

Managers must manage for compensation—which includes wages or salaries, incentives, and benefits.

Do we work only for a paycheck? Many people do, of course. But money is only one form of compensation.

Compensation **has three parts: (1) wages or salaries, (2) incentives, and (3) benefits.** In different organizations one part may take on more importance than another. For instance, in some nonprofit organizations (education, government), salaries may not be large, but health and retirement benefits may outweigh that fact. In a high-technology startup, the salary and benefits may actually be somewhat humble, but the promise of a large payoff in incentives, such as stock options or bonuses, may be quite attractive. Let's consider these three parts briefly. (We expand on them in Chapter 12 when we discuss ways to motivate employees.)

Wages or Salaries

Base pay **consists of the basic wage or salary paid employees in exchange for doing their jobs.** The basic compensation is determined by all kinds of economic factors: the prevailing pay levels in a particular industry and location, what competitors are paying, whether the jobs are unionized, if the jobs are hazardous, what the individual's level is in the organization, and how much experience he or she has.

Incentives

To induce employees to be more productive or to attract and retain top performers, many organizations offer incentives, such as commissions, bonuses, profit-sharing plans, and stock options. We discuss these in detail in Chapter 12.

Benefits

Benefits, **or** *fringe benefits,* **are additional nonmonetary forms of compensation** designed to enrich the lives of all employees in the organization, which are paid all or in part by the organization.

Stock options. Companies like to offer favored employees stock options rather than higher salaries as benefits. Not only do employees place a high value on options, but companies can issue as many as they want without hurting corporate profits because, under present accounting rules, they don't have to count the options' value as an expense.

Examples are many: health insurance, dental insurance, life insurance, disability protection, retirement plans, holidays off, accumulated sick days and vacation days, recreation options, country club or health club memberships, family leave, discounts on company merchandise, counseling, credit unions, legal advice, and education reimbursement. For top executives, there may be "golden parachutes," generous severance pay for those who might be let go in the event the company is taken over by another company.

Benefits are no small part of an organization's costs. One survey of American manufacturing firms found that benefits constituted 37.7% of the organizations' payroll.[44]

practical action

How to Make Incentive Pay Plans Meet Company Goals: Communicate Them to Employees[45]

There are many incentive compensation plans, ranging from cash awards and gifts to profit sharing and stock ownership, as we discuss in detail in Chapter 12.

Here let's ask the question: Do they work?

A 1998 survey of 139 companies, more than a third of them in the Fortune 500, found that 72% had variable pay plans. But only 22% said their plans had helped them achieve all their business objectives, and 28% said their plans had achieved none of them.

What explains the difference? Good plan design is important but so is good communication and oversight.

According to Ken Abosch, a consultant at Chicago-based Hewett Associates, which conducted the survey, often plans fail to deliver on their intended goals because employees aren't told enough about them and aren't kept up to date on the progress of the plans. Eighty-nine percent of companies that regularly

Communication is everything. The questions human resource managers need to keep in mind are: What good does it do a company to have attractive incentive plans if employees don't understand them? Will an employee exert the extra effort in pursuit of rewards if he or she doesn't know what the rewards are?

communicated with their employees said their incentive plans met their goals, compared with only 57% of companies that did not discuss them with their employees.

Five keys to a successful incentive-pay plan are the following, according to Abosch:

■ **Simplicity:** Does the plan pass the simplicity test? As Abosch puts it, "Can you explain it on an elevator ride?"

■ **Clear goals:** Are the goals clear? Are the goals fully supported by management?

■ **Realistic goals:** Are the goals realistic—that is, neither too difficult nor too easy to achieve?

■ **Consistency with present goals:** Is the plan in line with the organization's present goals? Company goals change. "There are very few organizations that have the same business objective for five to seven years," points out Abosch.

■ **Regular communication:** Do managers regularly communicate with employees about the plan? "People want a scorecard," Abosch says.

How do I manage contemporary workplace problems such as drug abuse and sexual harassment?

The Big Picture

Managers must also manage for promotions, transfers, discipline problems, and dismissals, as well as for workplace problems such as drug abuse and sexual harassment.

American society, points out George Washington University sociologist Amitai Etzioni, can be depicted by the terms "pluralism within unity." Unlike Europeans, who have great difficulty accepting the idea of diversity—of Turkish-Germans, Algerian-Frenchmen, or Romanian-Austrians, for example—in the United States we pretty much take it for granted that hyphenated Americans can be good workers and citizens.[46]

Indeed, our sense of inclusiveness seems to be gradually growing to embrace not only ethnic and racial diversity but also both genders and different ages, religions, sexual orientation, and physical and mental abilities. And there's more, as roles continue to change. Now more men seek paternity leaves, working parents want flexible hours, employees want to telecommute from home, and questions of "work-life balance" are receiving greater priority.

What this shows is that as a manager you may have quite a complex workforce. Let us see what matters you'll have to deal with.

Managing Promotions, Transfers, Disciplining, & Dismissals

Among the major—and most difficult—decisions you will make as a manager are those about employee movement within an organization: Whom should you promote? transfer? discipline? fire? All these matters go under the heading of *employee replacement*. And, incidentally, any time you need to deal with replacing an employee in a job, that's a time to reconsider the job description to see how it might be made more effective for the next person to occupy it.

You'll have to deal with replacement whenever an employee quits, retires, becomes seriously ill, or dies. Or you may initiate the replacement action by promoting, transferring, demoting, laying off, or firing.

1 Promotion *Promotion*—moving an employee to a higher-level position—is the most obvious way to recognize that person's superior performance (apart from giving raises and bonuses). Three concerns are these:

- ■ **Fairness:** It's important that promotion be *fair*. The step upward must be deserved. It shouldn't be for reasons of nepotism, cronyism, or other kind of favoritism.

- ■ **Nondiscrimination:** The promotion cannot discriminate on the basis of race, ethnicity, gender, age, or physical ability.

- ■ **Others' resentments:** If someone is promoted, someone else may be resentful about being passed over. As a manager, you may need to counsel the people left behind about their performance and their opportunities in the future.

2 Transfer Transfer is movement of an employee to a different job with *similar responsibility*. It may or may not mean a change in geographical location (which might be part of a promotion as well).

There are four reasons why employees might be transferred.

- **Solve organizational problems:** An organization may order an employee to transfer because it needs his or her skills in solving a particular problem. If you're working as a manager in a hotel chain, for instance, and have built a reputation as a good problem solver, the company may ask you to relocate to take over management of a hotel that's having trouble.

- **Broaden managers' experience:** If you are being groomed for a management career in the hotel industry, you may be transferred to positions with an equal level of responsibility and salary in several departments—in charge of reservations and the front desk, catering, convention sales, and so on—to widen your experience.

- **Retain managers' interest and motivation:** Talented managers may feel stultified and bored if they are stuck in one job. A hotel and resort company might move you from managing a hotel in Fresno, Calif., to one in St. Louis, Mo., then to one in the American Virgin Islands.

- **Solve some employee problems:** Sometimes employees who are unhappy with their current jobs or have personal differences with their bosses will request a job transfer. Or managers may shift poor-performing employees when they can't or are reluctant to demote or fire them.

3 Disciplining & Demotion Poor-performing employees may be given a warning or reprimand and then disciplined. That is, they may be temporarily removed from their jobs, as when a police officer is placed on suspension or administrative leave—removed from his or her regular job in the field and perhaps given a paperwork job or told to stay away from work.

Alternatively, an employee may be demoted—that is, have his or her current responsibilities, pay, and perquisites taken away, as when a middle manager is demoted to a first-line manager. (Sometimes this may occur when a company is downsized, resulting in fewer higher-level management positions.)

4 Dismissal *Dismissals* are of three sorts:

- **Layoffs:** The phrase being *laid off* tends to suggest that a person has been dismissed *temporarily*—as when a car maker doesn't have enough orders to justify keeping its production employees—and may be recalled later when economic conditions improve.

- **Downsizings:** A *downsizing* is a *permanent* dismissal; there is no rehiring later. An auto maker discontinuing a line of cars or on the path to bankruptcy might permanently let go of its production employees.

- **Firings:** The phrase being *fired,* with all its euphemisms and synonyms—being "terminated," "separated," "let go," "canned"—tends to mean that a person was dismissed *permanently "for cause":* absenteeism, sloppy work habits, failure to perform satisfactorily, breaking the law, and the like.

It used to be that managers could use their discretion about dismissals. Today, however, because of the changing legal climate, steps must be taken to avoid employees suing for "wrongful termination." That is, an employer has to carefully *document* the reasons for dismissals.

The Practical Action box on the next page offers some suggestions for handling dismissals.

So long, Enron. Dismissed employees wait on the sidewalk in front of the Houston headquarters after the energy trader filed for bankruptcy. From an emotional point of view, would you feel any different whether you were laid off, downsized, or fired?

practical action

The Right Way to Handle a Dismissal

"Employment at will" is the governing principle of employment in the great majority of states, which means that anyone can be dismissed at any time for any reason at all—or for no reason. Exceptions are whistleblowers and people with employment contracts. Civil-rights laws also prohibit organizations' dismissing people for their gender, skin color, or physical or mental disability.[47]

The following are four suggestions for handling a dismissal.

Give the Employee a Chance First If you're dealing with someone who has a problem with absenteeism, alcohol/drug dependency, or the like, articulate to that employee what's wrong with his or her performance, then set up a plan for improvement (which might include counseling). Or if you're dealing with an employee who has a bad cultural or personality fit with the company—a buttoned-down, by-the-book style, say, that's at odds with your flexible, fast-moving organization—have a conversation and give the employee time to find a job elsewhere.[48]

Don't Delay the Dismissal, & Make Sure It's Completely Defensible If improvements aren't forthcoming, don't carry the employee along because you feel sorry for him or her. Your first duty is to the performance of the organization. Make sure, however, that you've *documented* all the steps taken in advance of the dismissal. Also be sure that they follow the law and all important organizational policies.

Be Aware How Devastating a Dismissal Can Be—Both to the Individual & to Those Remaining To the person being let go, the event can be as much of a blow as a divorce or a death in the family. Dismissals can also adversely affect those remaining with the company. This is what psychiatrist Manfred Kets de Vries calls *layoff survivor sickness*, which is characterized by anger, depression, fear, guilt, risk aversion, distrust, vulnerability, powerlessness, and loss of motivation. Indeed, a five-year study by Cigna and the American Management Association found an enormous increase in medical claims, particularly for stress-related illnesses, not only among those dismissed but among continuing employees as well.[49]

Offer Assistance in Finding Another Job Dismissing a long-standing employee with only a few weeks of severance pay not only hurts the person let go but will also hurt the organization itself, as word gets back to the employees who remain. Knowledgeable employers offer assistance in finding another job.

"The best demonstration that a company's values are real," says management scholar Rosabeth Moss Kanter, "is to act on them today even for people who will not be around tomorrow. A company, like a society, can be judged by how it treats its most vulnerable. . . . Bad treatment of departing employees can destroy the commitment of those who stay."[50]

Maintaining Effective Relationships with Employees

Dealing with compensation, promotion, and similar matters would seem to be straightforward if sometimes difficult requirements of the manager's job. But there are other, less straightforward matters as well. We discussed the need to deal with a diversified workforce in Chapter 2 and an international workforce in Chapter 3. There are many, many other sensitive topics that we could discuss (and do so later), but here let us consider just two: (1) alcohol and other drug abuse and (2) sexual harassment.

Alcohol & Other Drug Abuse   Have an employee who's often late? Who frequently calls in sick on Mondays? Whose work is somewhat sloppy? Maybe he or she is afflicted with *alcoholism*, a chronic, progressive, and potentially fatal disease characterized by a growing compulsion to drink. Alcoholics come from every social class, from students to college professors to priests to airline pilots. Alcoholism may not interfere with a person's job in an obvious way until it shows up in absenteeism, accidents, slipshod work, or significant use of a company's medical benefits.

Alcohol is the most common drug of abuse, but the misuse of others may also affect a person's productivity—legal drugs such as tranquilizers or illegal drugs such as marijuana, ecstasy, cocaine, or heroin. It is estimated that productivity losses caused by alcohol problems amount to $86 billion a year and by drug problems to $54 billion a year.[51]

If you as a manager think you might be dealing with an employee with a substance-abuse problem, it's suggested you not try to make accusations but firmly point out that productivity is suffering and that it's up to the subordinate to do something about it. While not doing any counseling yourself, you can try steering the employee to the Human Resources Department, which may have an employee assistance program that may help employees overcome personal problems affecting their job performance.

Sexual Harassment *Sexual harassment* **consists of unwanted sexual attention that creates an adverse work environment.** This means suggestive remarks, unwanted touching, sexual advances, requests for sexual favors, sexually oriented posters and graffiti, and similar verbal or physical actions of a sexual nature. The harassment may be by a man of a woman, by a woman of a man, by a member of the same sex, by a manager of an employee, by a coworker of a coworker, or an outsider of an employee. If the harasser is a manager or an agent of the organization, the organization itself can be sued, even if it had no knowledge of the situation.[52]

There are two types of sexual harassment, according to the U.S. Supreme Court and the Equal Opportunity Employment Commission:

- **Quid pro quo—tangible economic injury:** In the *quid pro quo* type, the person to whom the unwanted sexual attention is directed is put in the position of jeopardizing being hired for a job or obtaining job benefits or opportunities unless he or she implicitly or explicitly acquiesces.

- **Hostile environment—offensive work environment:** In the *hostile environment* type, the person being sexually harassed doesn't risk economic harm but experiences an offensive or intimidating work environment, as might be the case when one has to put up with lewd jokes or sexually oriented graffiti.

The box below shows some guidelines for preventing sexual harassment.[53] *(See Panel 9.6.)*

PANEL 9.6
Guidelines for preventing sexual harassment

- Don't make unwanted sexual demands or advances.
- Don't touch a person who doesn't want to be touched.
- Do not make sexually demeaning remarks, gestures, or jokes about others.
- Don't laugh at others' sexually harassing words or behaviors.
- Remember to put yourself in the other person's shoes. How would it feel?

Click-Along 9.5

Taking Something Practical Away from This Chapter: Online Job Hunting, Résumés, & Interviewing

Key Terms Used In This Chapter

360-degree assessment, 300

affirmative action, 287

assessment center, 293

base pay, 302

behavioral-description
   interview, 291

behaviorally anchored rating
   scale (BARS), 299

benefits, 302

collective bargaining, 286

compensation, 302

computer-assisted instruction
   (CAI), 297

development, 296

discrimination, 287

employment tests, 292

Equal Employment
   Opportunity (EEO)
   Commission, 286

external recruiting, 289

formal appraisals, 301

human resource (HR)
   management, 283

informal appraisals, 301

internal recruiting, 288

job analysis, 284

job description, 284

job posting, 288

job specification, 284

National Labor Relations
   Board, 286

objective appraisals, 298

orientation, 294

performance appraisal, 298

realistic job preview, 290

recruiting, 288

selection process, 290

sexual harassment, 307

situational interview, 291

strategic human resource
   planning, 284

structured interview, 291

subjective appraisels, 299

training, 296

unstructured interview, 291

Summary

9.1
Strategic Human Resource Management

■ Human resource management consists of the activities managers perform to plan for, attract, develop, and retain an effective workforce. The purpose of the strategic human resource management process is to get the optimum work performance that will help realize the company's mission and vision.

■ Strategic human resource planning consists of developing a systematic, comprehensive strategy for (a) understanding current employee needs and (b) predicting future employee needs.

■ Understanding current employee needs requires first doing a job analysis and then writing a job description and job specification. The purpose of job analysis is to determine, by observation and analysis, the basic elements of a job. Once the fundamentals of a job are understood, a job description can be written, which summarizes what the holder of the job does and how and why he or she does it. Next comes the job specification, which de-

scribes the minimum qualifications a person must have to perform the job successfully.

■ Predicting employee needs means a manager needs to become knowledgeable about the staffing an organization might need and the likely sources of staffing.

9.2
The Legal Requirements of Human Resource Management

■ Four areas of human resource law that any manager needs to be aware of are labor relations, compensation and benefits, health and safety, and equal employment opportunity. (1) Labor relations are dictated in part by the National Labor Relations Board, which enforces procedures whereby employees may vote to have a union and for collective bargaining. Collective bargaining consists of negotiations between management and employees about disputes over compensation, benefits, working conditions, and job security. (2) Compensation and benefits are covered by the Social Security Act of 1935 and the Fair Labor Standards Act, which established minimum wage and overtime pay regulations. (3) Health and safety are covered by the Occupational Safety and Health Act of 1970, among other laws. (4) Equal employment opportunity is covered by the Equal Employment Opportunity (EEO) Commission, whose job it is to enforce antidiscrimination and other employment-related laws. Two important concepts covered by EEO are (a) discrimination, which occurs when people are hired or promoted—or denied hiring or promotion—for reasons not relevant to the job, such as skin color or national origin, and (b) affirmative action, which focuses on achieving equality of opportunity within an organization.

9.3
Recruitment & Selection: Putting the Right People into the Right Jobs

■ Recruiting is the process of locating and attracting qualified applicants for jobs open in the organization. Recruiting is of two types: internal and external. (1) Internal recruiting means making people already employed by the organization aware of job openings. The principal means of doing this is through job postings, placing information about job vacancies and qualifications on bulletin boards, in newsletters, and on the organization's intranet. (2) External recruiting means attracting job applicants from outside the organization. The most effective sources are employee referrals, then college recruiters and executive search firms, followed by professional associations and newspaper ads. A useful approach with external recruitment is the realistic job preview, which gives a candidate a picture of both positive and negative features of the job and organizations before he or she is hired; this can reduce new hires leaving.

■ The selection process is the screening of job applicants to hire the best candidates. Three types of selection tools are background information, interviewing, and employment tests. (1) Background information is ascertained through application forms, resumes, and reference checks. (2) Interviewing takes three forms. (a) The unstructured interview involves asking probing questions to find out what the applicant is like. (b) The structured interview involves asking each applicant the same questions and comparing their responses to a standardized set of answers. The first type of structured interview is the situational interview, in which the interview focuses on hypothetical situations. (c) The second type of structured interview is the behavioral-description interview, in which the interviewer explores what applicants have actually done in the past. (3) Employment tests are legally considered to consist of any procedure used in the employment selection decision process, but the three most common tests are ability tests, personality tests, and performance tests. Some companies have assessment centers, in which management candidates participate in activities for a few days while being assessed in performance tests by evaluators. Other tests include drug testing, polygraphs, and genetic screening.

9.4
Orientation, Training, & Development

■ Three ways in which newcomers are helped to perform their jobs are through orientation, training, and development.

■ Orientation consists of helping the newcomer fit smoothly into the job and organization. Following orientation, the employee should emerge with information about the job routine, the organization's mission and operations, and the organization's work rules and employees benefits.

■ Training must be distinguished from development. Training refers to educating technical and operational employees in how to better do their current jobs.

■ Development is the term describing educating professionals and managers in the skills they need to do their jobs in the future.

■ Both training and development may be effected through on-the-job training methods and off-the-job training methods.

9.5
Performance Appraisal

■ Performance appraisal consists of assessing an employee's performance and providing him or her with feedback. Appraisals are of two general types—objective and subjective. (1) Objective appraisals, also called results appraisals, are based on facts and are often numerical. An example is management by objectives. (2) Subjective appraisals are based on a manager's perceptions of an employee's traits or behaviors. Trait appraisals are ratings of subjective attributes such as attitude and leadership. Behavioral appraisals measure specific, observable aspects of performance. An example is the behaviorally anchored rating scale (BARS), which rates employee gradations in performance according to scales of specific behaviors.

■ Most performance appraisals are made by managers, but they must also be made by coworkers and subordinates, customers and clients, and employees themselves (self-appraisals). Sometimes all of these may be used, in a technique called the 360-degree assessment, or 360-degree feedback appraisal, in which employees are appraised not only by their managerial superiors but also by their peers, subordinates, and sometimes clients.

■ Effective performance feedback can be effected in two ways: formal and informal. Formal appraisals are conducted at specific times throughout the year and are based on performance measures that have been established in advance. Informal appraisals are conducted on an unscheduled basis and consist of less rigorous indications of employee performance.

9.6
Managing an Effective Workforce: Compensation & Benefits

■ Compensation has three parts: wages or salaries, incentives, and benefits. (1) In the category of wages or salaries, the concept of base pay consists of the basic wage or salary paid employees in exchange for doing their jobs. (2) Incentives include commissions, bonuses, profit-sharing plans, and stock op-

tions. (3) Benefits, or fringe benefits, are additional nonmonetary forms of compensation, such as health insurance, retirement plans, and family leave.

9.7
Other Concerns in Managing an Effective Workforce

■ Managers must manage promotions, transfers, disciplining, and dismissals. (1) In considering promotions, managers must be concerned about fairness, nondiscrimination, and other employees' resentment. (2) Transfers, or moving employees to a different job with similar responsibility, may take place in order to solve organizational problems, broaden managers' experience, retain managers' interest and motivation, and solve some employee problems. (3) Poor-performing employees may need to be disciplined or demoted. (4) Dismissals may consist of layoffs, downsizings, or firings.

■ Managers must also deal with such sensitive matters as dealing with a diversified workforce or international workforce. A third matter is alcohol and drug abuse, which may be helped by referring employees with substance-abuse problems to the Human Resources Department, which may have an employee assistance program that may help employees overcome personal problems affecting their job performance. A fourth matter is sexual harassment, which consists of unwanted sexual attention that creates an adverse work environment and which may be of two types—the quid pro quo type, which may cause direct economic injury, and the hostile environment type, in which the person being harassed experiences an offensive work environment.

Management in Action

Workforce Shifts to Big Companies

Excerpted from Jim Hopkins, "Workforce Shifts to Big Companies,"
USA Today, *March 19, 2002, p. 1A.*

For the first time, big businesses appear to employ more U.S. workers than small businesses. Big companies employed 49.7% of the 111 million U.S. workers in 1999—up from 45.5% in 1988, the lat-est U.S. Small Business Administration Data show [reported March 2002]. The share of the workforce employed by big companies probably passed 50% in 2000, the SBA says.

The SBA defines big firms as those with 500 or more workers. Experts say the shift toward big companies is likely to continue as the U.S. economy matures and consolidates. "The general trends are in place," says economist Mark Zandi at Economy.com.

The shift will have a big impact on employees. As more people work for large companies, more will have health insurance. About 82% of big employers offer it, versus 68% of small firms, says the Employee Benefit Research Institute.

Also, 46% of employees at small companies have retirement plans, versus 79% of employees at bigger companies, EBRI says. As more people work for larger companies, more are likely to have those plans.

The shift also could affect productivity. Workers at bigger companies are more removed from top management—and in some cases are less loyal, says John Challenger, CEO of outplacement firm Challenger Gray & Christmas. That can lead to higher turnover, which hurts productivity, he says.

Small business is woven into the fabric of U.S. history. Legendary American patriots included small-businessmen Paul Revere and Benjamin Franklin. The United States was a nation of small firms until the late 1800s, which brought the first corporate goliaths—railroads and the Standard Oil Trust. And entrepreneurship is highly valued in the U.S. psyche.

Certainly small firms still have clout. They create 75% of new jobs. They are among the most powerful political lobbies in Washington. About 89% of the nation's 5.6 million employers have fewer than 20 workers.

But big firms are moving up as industries consolidate—even though 60% of employees polled in October 2000 by Gallup say mergers are bad for them. Nearly 17,000 large companies account for about 55 million employees.

The retail sector consolidated more than any other in the 1990s. A big gainer: Wal-Mart, which began 40 years ago as a small five-and-dime. [In 2001] it became the nation's biggest company based on revenue. Its 1 million U.S. employees make it the largest private-sector employer in the USA. . . .

For Discussion

1. How could the shift to large companies affect the purpose of the strategic human resource management process?

2. If you were the human resources director for a large company, would company size make it actually easier to predict future employee needs than if you worked for a small company?

3. If your company had to quickly slash its workforce because of an economic downturn, what kinds of matters would you have to take into consideration when contemplating layoffs?

4. Suppose you had to hire a number of skilled workers very quickly in hot competition with other employers. What parts of the selection process would you feel you could drop yet still ensure reliable, qualified workers?

5. Research suggests that shares of companies that spend the most on employee training and development outperform those that spend the least. What kinds of employee education do you think is best?

Take It to the Net

As we learned in this chapter, part of a career in HR management involves looking for the brightest and the best to work for an organization. Whether the organization is recruiting internally or externally, the selection process involves trying to determine how well the employee will perform in the job and how long he or she will stay. An essential screening tool is the interview. Here the HR professional can determine if the applicant has the knowledge to do the job, cope with its demands, or fit within the organization's culture.

In pursuing a career, do you think you could you make it through a standard HR screening process?

Could you make it through the interview? Do you know the right things to say? Do you know what is expected of you?

The purpose of this exercise is to give you practice answering questions in a real interview scenario. Go to *http://interview.monster.com/virtualinterview/campus/* Read each hypothetical interview question and answer honestly. Submitting your answer provides feedback on whether you gave the best answer possible or if there is an alternative. If you like, you can go back and try the question again if you think you have a better answer. There are 30 questions and the test takes approximately 15–20 minutes to complete.

After you have received your feedback, you should read the "tips and advice" section to further prepare you for an interview. You can come back and take this quiz as often as you like; the questions change regularly.

Questions for Discussion

1. Were you surprised at some of the feedback? Describe and explain.

2. To what extent did you feel confident answering these interview questions? Explain.

3. Which type of question did you find the hardest to answer? Explain.

Self-Assessment

HR 101: An Overview*

Objectives

1. To learn that there is more to HR than recruitment and hiring.
2. To assess your skills and determine if a career in HR is right for you.

Introduction: Your chosen career should optimally be based on your interests. The HR field, for example, offers many different career paths that require many different skills. The purpose of this exercise is to help you become familiar with the different career paths available to an HR professional and to see which path best fits your interests. This experience may help you decide if an HR career is right for you.

Among the professionals in the HR field are the following:

The HR generalist: HR generalists take on many different roles, whether negotiating a company's employee benefits package or interviewing a candidate for a director-level position. An HR generalist is supposed to be flexible and able to change gears at a moment's notice.

Compensation professional: Compensation professionals, who are very much in demand, design reward systems that attract, retain, and motivate employees. The job requires not only good technical skills but good people skills as well, a rare combination. It also requires a great deal of number crunching, creativity, and ingenuity, because a compensation package that might work for one employee might not work for another.

HRIS professional: HRIS stands for Human Resource Information Systems. With technology now such a key part of human resources, HRIS products help companies manage their personnel. Because the information systems are now so sophisticated, there is now great demand for experienced HRIS professionals, who must be very detail oriented and, of course, enjoy working with computers. Such professionals are involved in product selection, systems customization, implementation, and ongoing administration.

Benefits professional: This individual is responsible for designing and implementing benefits plans. The job requires strong technical and communication skills.

Training and development professional: This individual is responsible for building environments that foster learning and management and leadership development. People in this field may be involved in distance learning programs as well as on-site, computer-based training programs.

Organizational development professional: Organizational development professionals work with top management to make sure that the organizational design sticks to the company's mission, vision, and goals. Besides doing some training and development, an OD professional must be able to embrace change and work long hours.

Instructions: Ask yourself the following questions and circle whether or not the statement applies to you. Once you have answered all of the questions, use the interpretation guidelines to analyze your responses and determine if a career in HR is right for you.

1. Do I enjoy changing gears on a moment's notice?		**Yes**	**No**
2. Am I open to learning about areas in which I currently have no expertise?		**Yes**	**No**
3. Am I comfortable leaving a project unfinished to handle emergency situations?		**Yes**	**No**
4. Do I consider myself fairly flexible?		**Yes**	**No**
5. Am I good at creatively solving problems when resources and instructions are scarce?		**Yes**	**No**
6. Do I have an aptitude for numbers?		**Yes**	**No**
7. Am I comfortable seeing other people's salaries?		**Yes**	**No**
8. Do I have strong communication skills?		**Yes**	**No**
9. Do I have strong computer skills?		**Yes**	**No**
10. Am I comfortable working at a computer all day?		**Yes**	**No**
11. Am I well organized?		**Yes**	**No**
12. Am I detail-oriented?		**Yes**	**No**
13. Am I comfortable constantly reworking projects I thought were already done?		**Yes**	**No**
14. Am I willing to pay for and donate my free time to professional certifications?		**Yes**	**No**
15. Am I good at taking complex ideas and making them understandable to the average person?		**Yes**	**No**
16. Am I good at expressing my ideas and getting people to go along with them?		**Yes**	**No**
17. Am I creative person with strong computer skills?		**Yes**	**No**
18. Am I comfortable in front of an audience?		**Yes**	**No**
19. Am I comfortable working one very long project instead of lots of small projects?		**Yes**	**No**
20. Am I passionate about learning and about teaching others?		**Yes**	**No**
21. Can I handle change? Can I handle it well?		**Yes**	**No**
22. Do I enjoy pulling together pieces of a puzzle?		**Yes**	**No**
23. Do I perform well in times of stress?		**Yes**	**No**
24. Am I a big-picture person?		**Yes**	**No**

Interpretation: If you answered "yes" to three or more of questions 1–4 (which apply to the HR generalist), three or more of questions 5–8 (compensation professional), three or more of questions 9–12 (HRIS professional), three or more of questions 13–16 (benefits professional), three or more of 17–20 (training and development professional), and three or more of questions 21–24 (organizational development professional), then you are well suited for the field of HR.

If you answered "no" to most of the previous 24 questions, the field of HR may not be right for you. (However, since this is only a small sampling of the many aspects of this field, there may still be a place for you in HR.)

Questions for Discussion

1. To what extent did the results fit your interests? Explain.

2. Look at the top two areas of HR for which you tested as being best suited. Look over the descriptions of these fields. What skills do you need to have to be successful? Describe.

3. Even if you do not pursue a career in HR, which skills do you feel you should continue to develop? Explain.

*Adapted from R.C. Matuson, "HR 101: An Overview, Parts I and II," *Monster HR: www.monster.com*, June 2002.

Group Exercise

Choosing the Best Person for the Job*

Objectives

1. To gain further knowledge of the selection process.

2. To practice looking for the skills that help HR professionals find the best person for a job.

Introduction

As you learned from this chapter, the recruitment process may turn up a handful of applicants or it may turn up thousands. During the selection process, how do hiring managers make their decisions? What can an applicant do to stand out in the crowd? It is important for applicants to be able to highlight the skills that make them unique. Skills can be looked at in three ways: (1) those gained from past experience, (2) those that can carry through to any job (portable skills), and (3) personal skills. The purpose of this exercise is to enable you to practice looking for skills that help HR professionals find the best person for the job.

Instructions

Break into groups of five to six people. Read the following case about Gina, who has applied for a job at a high-technology company. The company has its own ideas about the ideal applicant, but it hasn't given out much information about them. You are going to try to help Gina get the job. (Remember, she's not the only applicant, so she needs to stand out.) After reading the case, do the following:

1. Take a piece of paper and divide it into three columns—the first headed "Past experience," the second "Portable skills" (skills that will carry to any job), and the third "Personality skills." Your group is to identify what skills you think Gina should have based on "Past experience," "Portable skills," and "Personality skills."

2. Using these skills as a guide, brainstorm which of these skills you think Gina has. Make sure you put them in the correct column.

3. Then examine Gina's case again and come up with as many different skills as you can that go *beyond* what the company is looking for. Think about what past skills Gina has besides marketing experience that would make her the perfect candidate.

The Case

After five years, Gina was laid off as a marketing manager for a high-tech company. "Gina hates not having a job," her roommate says. "She always has to have something to do. If not, she'll jump up and start cleaning just to be productive. She's also very organized. For instance, she files all her CDs in alphabetical order."

At her old job, Gina was in charge of marketing the company over the World Wide Web and so she spent a lot of time at the computer. Since being laid off, she has been using the computer to look for another job, as well as searching the Web for art projects to do in her spare time. Her friends describe her as being not only fiercely independent but also very creative. In college, they say, she was always writing. "She used to write short stories," her roommate recalls, "and also worked part time on the college newspaper."

Her friends also say Gina's sense of humor keeps her from feeling unbearably depressed about the layoff, and they believe she will find a new job quickly. Her mother agrees. "Gina is the oldest child," she says, "and she has always been a very good team leader. She's very organized and ever since she was a little girl she's been good at coordinating things." Her father says his daughter has a great head for numbers, and he hoped she would follow in his tracks and become an accountant.

Gina's supervisor at her old job says they hated to see her go. "She was so good at dealing with our customers," he says. "She was also one of the few marketing managers who had a close business relationship with our vendors. In addition, she was very goal oriented: We would tell her what we wanted to achieve and she would dive in head first." Her direct reports state that Gina had a good attitude, a great sense of humor, excellent follow-through, and a superior ability to solve problems. Her colleagues and supervisor all comment on Gina's creativity and her ability to learn things quickly. One coworker noted that Gina was "very flexible" and "always showed good judgment."

Questions for Discussion

1. If you were the HR professional at this high-tech company, would you hire Gina? Do you feel she has the appropriate skills? Why or why not?

2. Are there any skills Gina does not exhibit that you feel she should develop in order to be a more appealing candidate? Discuss.

3. What are some things Gina can do to improve her skills for her future job in marketing? Explain.

*Adapted from "Assessing Your Skills: What Makes you Different from All the Others?" *http://interview.monster.com/rehearsal/assessing*, June 2002.

Ethical Dilemma

More Companies Want the FBI to Screen Employees for Terrorist Connections

Excerpted from Ana Davis, "Companies Want the FBI to Screen Employees for Suspected Terrorists," The Wall Street Journal, February 6, 2002, pp. B1, B4.

A wide range of industry groups, from trucking associations to sporting-event organizers, are trying to gain access to the FBI's closely guarded data on suspected terrorists and criminals in an effort to screen their own employees.

The American Trucking Association, for one, is lobbying Congress to give it authority to go directly to the Federal Bureau of Investigation with names and fingerprints of drivers, loading-dock workers, and job applicants of its member companies. . . .

Fueling this push is the supposition that, next time around, terrorists may attack something besides an airplane. But allowing companies to tap into FBI intelligence banks opens a can of worms both for the government and civil liberties advocates. Unions protest that employers could use the system to find old skeletons in people's closets and use them as a pretext for dismissal. . . .

Giving an industry access to the FBI lists typically requires an act of Congress or a new federal regulation. Some industries, such as banking, airlines, and nuclear power plants, already have such access. . .

Of particular interest to this latest round of companies are the FBI's watch lists of suspected terrorists, including people who may have infiltrated the American workplace years ago as "sleeper" agents. One of these lists, from the State Department, contains 64,000 names from around the world. The FBI keeps its own list and won't say how many people are on it. . . .

Although terrorists typically are trained to avoid detection, at least a few of the Sept. 11 hijackers were on watchlists because their names had popped up in connection with prior attacks: Mohamed Atta had been flagged by the Customs Service, and Khalid al-Midhar was on a CIA list.

FBI background checks should turn up anybody with, among other things, an arrest record, criminal conviction, or protective order filed against them. Not all this information is readily accessible to those outside the agency, and companies are concerned about missing such information in a check on their own. . .

But truckers and others who want FBI background checks say the pros outweigh the cons. Tony Chrestman, president of the trucking unit of Ruan Transportation Management Systems, says: "Previously, I would never have thought about anyone taking one of our loads of propane and running it into a building. There's got to be improvements to background checks."

Solving the Dilemma

What would you do if you were evaluating the trucking industry's desire for FBI background checks?

1. Allow the trucking industry to obtain FBI background checks.

2. Not allow the trucking industry access to FBI records because such information might adversely affect employment conditions for potential and existing employees.

3. Allow the trucking industry to obtain limited information (that is, only information pertaining to terrorism) about people.

4. Invent other options. (Explain.)

CHAPTER 10

Organizational Change & Innovation
Life-Long Challenges for the Exceptional Manager

MANAGING FOR INNOVATION & CHANGE TAKES A CAREFUL HAND

"What I try to do is go out and grab lightning every day."

That's the way Terry Fadem, head of business development at DuPont Co., describes the company's never-ending search for tomorrow's breakthroughs.[1]

Managing for innovation and change takes a careful hand. "Even when their jobs depend on adopting and inventing new maneuvers," says columnist Carol Hymowitz, "most workers hold fast to old ones. The majority either are overwhelmed when asked to do things differently or become entrenched, clinging harder to the past. . . ."[2]

Because the revolution in technology is inflicting what Tom Peters calls Discontinuous Times, or "a brawl with no rules," dealing with change is an ongoing challenge for every manager.[3] "The one constant factor in business today is we live in a perpetual hurricane season," says Mellon Bank Corp. vice chairman Martin McGuinn. "A leader's job is less about getting through the current storm and more about enabling people to navigate the ongoing series of storms."[4]

Some ways to deal with change and innovation:[5]

- **Allow room for failure:** McGuinn won over many Mellon employees when he told them "If everything we try works, we aren't trying enough. And if something isn't working, it is okay to say so."

- **Give one consistent explanation for the change:** When a company is undergoing change, myriad rumors will fly and employees will be uneasy; you and the managers who report to you need to give one

consistent explanation. In McGuinn's case, the explanation for overhauling Mellon Bank's retail division was "We want to be the best retailer in financial services."

- **Look for opportunities in unconventional ways:** Most "new" products and services are really knock-offs or marginal variations of the things already on the market and hence are doomed to failure, says Robert Cooper, professor of marketing at Ontario's McMaster University. This doesn't mean, of course, that there isn't room for leveraging existing products with utterly unoriginal ideas. But most people are blinded by the limits of conventional wisdom and their own experience and fail to see huge potential markets in unconventional concepts.

- **Have the courage to follow your ideas:** This may be the hardest job of all—trying to convince others that your ideas for change are feasible, especially if the ideas are radical. This may mean working to gain allies within the organization, standing up to intimidating competitors inside and out, and perhaps being prepared to follow a lonely course for a long time.

- **Allow grieving, then move on:** Managers overseeing change need to give long-term employees a chance to grieve over the loss of the old ways, says McGuinn, who found that staffers were more willing to change after they had a chance to vent their fears.

FORECAST: WHAT'S AHEAD IN THIS CHAPTER

In this chapter, we consider the nature of change in organizations, including the two types of change—reactive and proactive—and the forces for change originating outside and inside the organization. We describe the four areas in which change is often needed: people, technology, structure, and strategy. We then explore the threat of change and how you can manage employee fear and resistance. We next discuss organization development, a set of techniques for implementing planned change. Finally, we discuss how to promote innovation within an organization.

major question

Since change is always with us, what should I understand about it?

The Big Picture

Two types of change are reactive and proactive. Forces for change may consist of forces outside the organization—demographic characteristics, market changes, technological advancements, and social and political pressures. Or they may be forces inside the organization—employee problems and managers' behavior. Four areas in which change is often needed are people, technology, structure, and strategy.

E-learning. IBM's Lotus LearningSpace is a Web-based learning environment for training employees. The technology offers collaborative electronic learning with self-paced content supplemented by online discussions, one-to-one messaging, and virtual classrooms. E-learning can help us learn the "hows" of adapting to change.

People are generally uncomfortable about change, even change in apparently minor matters. Philosopher Eric Hoffer told how as a younger man he spent a good part of one year as an agricultural worker picking peas, starting in southern California in January and working his way northward. He picked the last of the peas in June, then moved to another area where, for the first time, he was required to pick string beans. "I still remember," he wrote, "how hesitant I was that first morning as I was about to address myself to the string bean vines. Would I be able to pick string beans? Even the change from peas to string beans had in it elements of fear."

If small changes can cause uneasiness, large changes can cause considerable stress. And as a manager, you will no doubt have to deal with both.

Fundamental Change: What Will You Be Called On to Deal With?

"It is hard to predict, especially the future," physicist Niels Bohr is supposed to have quipped.

But it is possible to identify and prepare for *the future that has already happened*, in the words of management theorist Peter Drucker, by looking at some fundamental changes that are happening now. Declining population in developed countries. More diversity in the workforce. The ascent of knowledge work. Further globalization. The rise of business-to-business (B2B) technology. Digital long-distance networks. The increase in data storage. The capturing of customer-specific information. The customization of mass goods. Sales in the form of auctions instead of fixed prices.[6] All these trends suggest that organizations should prepare for change.

Clearly, we are all in for an interesting ride.

Two Types of Change: Reactive versus Proactive

As a manager, you will typically have to deal with two types of change: *reactive* and *proactive*.

1 Reactive Change: Responding to Unanticipated Problems & Opportunities When managers talk about "putting out fires," they are talking about ___reactive change___, **making changes in response to problems or opportunities as they arise.** When you have to respond to surprises, there is usually less time to get all the information and resources you need to adequately manage the change, and serious mistakes may be made. Nevertheless, some of the best stories in business concern the intelligent management of unanticipated calamities.

2 Proactive Change: Managing Anticipated Problems & Opportunities In contrast to reactive change, ___proactive change___ or planned change involves making carefully thought-out changes in anticipation of possible or expected problems or opportunities.[7]

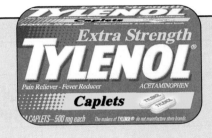

Example of Reactive Change: Johnson & Johnson Faces the Tylenol-Contamination Crisis

Many companies do not handle crises well. Among the instances: Exxon's handling of the 1989 *Exxon Valdez* oil spill in the Gulf of Alaska, Jack In The Box's management of the 1993 botulism crisis in Washington, TWA's actions on the 1996 crash of Flight 800 off Long Island, and Coca-Cola's reactions to the 1999 illnesses in Europe attributed to bottlers in Belgium and France.

All had had plenty of opportunity to learn from a famous crisis faced down by Johnson & Johnson in 1982. At that time, Extra-Strength Tylenol was the best-selling over-the-counter drug in the United States, netting J&J $400 million a year and a symbol of the company's reputation for quality health care. In Chicago, however, someone added cyanide to Tylenol packages on store shelves, as a result of which seven people died. Although the problem seemed to be confined to the Chicago area, an opinion poll showed that 61% of consumers nationally intended to stop buying the pain reliever.

The Food and Drug Administration and the FBI advised Johnson & Johnson not to take any drastic action. Nevertheless, that's exactly what the company did. Despite the pressures, J&J managers opened themselves up to national media coverage, taking pains to keep the public informed. They also took the unprecedented step of recalling 31 million unsold Tylenol bottles from store shelves at a cost of $100 million. Shortly afterward, they reintroduced the product in a triple-sealed package that would resist tampering. They created a consumer crisis hotline. They launched an advertising campaign offering a refund to consumers who had bought the drug before the crisis. The company's chairman appeared on *Donahue*, a well-known talk show.

The result of these efforts: Three months after the crisis, a poll showed that 93% of the public felt that the company had done a good job handling itself.[8]

Click-Along 10.1

The Tylenol Contamination Crisis Continued

Example of Proactive Change: Ford Pushes Onto the Web

Anticipating that the Internet will change everything, Ford Motor Co. is trying to reinvent car manufacturing and selling. "We're going to turn the old ways on their ears," said former chief executive Jacques A. Nasser.

This is not easy. Cars can contain some 10,000 parts and across Ford's entire line some 1 million possible variations. Yet Ford is attempting to enter the made-to-order automobile business in the same way that Dell Computer Corp. custom-assembles personal computers for customers. Moreover, it hopes to "turn the family car into a Web portal on four wheels," in the words of one executive, wiring future vehicles for e-mail, news, voice-recognition systems, and satellite phone systems. Rival General Motors Corp. launched e-GM in 1999, an initiative to link suppliers and dealers to forge Internet ties to consumers. But Ford wants to do this plus wire up its entire workforce, as was shown when it offered every one of its 350,000 far-flung employees a personal computer and Net access for only $5 a month.

In the end, Ford is trying to change car building from a "push" to a "pull" model. In the old "push" model, cars are built, then shipped to dealers who rely on rebates or super-salespeople to move cars that customers don't want. In the "pull" model, customers decide what they want built, and delivery time is drastically reduced.[9]

The Forces for Change: Outside & Inside the Organization

How do managers know when their organizations need to change? The answers aren't clear-cut, but you can get clues by monitoring the forces for change—both outside and inside the organization. *(See Panel 10.1, opposite.)*

Forces Originating Outside the Organization External forces consist of four types, as follows.

1 Demographic Characteristics Earlier we discussed the demographic changes occurring in the U.S. workforce. We've pointed out that the workforce is now more diverse, and organizations need to effectively manage this diversity if they are to receive the maximum contribution and commitment of their employees.

2 Market Changes As discussed in Chapter 4, the global economy is forcing companies to change the way they do business, with U.S. companies forging new partnerships and alliances with employees, suppliers, and competitors. The merger of AOL and Time Warner beginning in 2000 is one indicator of the changing landscape.

3 Technological Advancements Information technology may be one of the greatest forces for productivity in our lifetime. But it can also create headaches. For instance, as computers change, data stored on older machines may become "just as useless as music stored on a 1970s eight-track tape," as one writer puts it.[10]

4 Social & Political Pressures Social events can create great pressures. Changing drinking habits, for example, have led to a rise in wine sales and a decline in whiskey sales. Political events can also create substantial change. The collapse of communism in Europe beginning in 1989 led to new business opportunities.

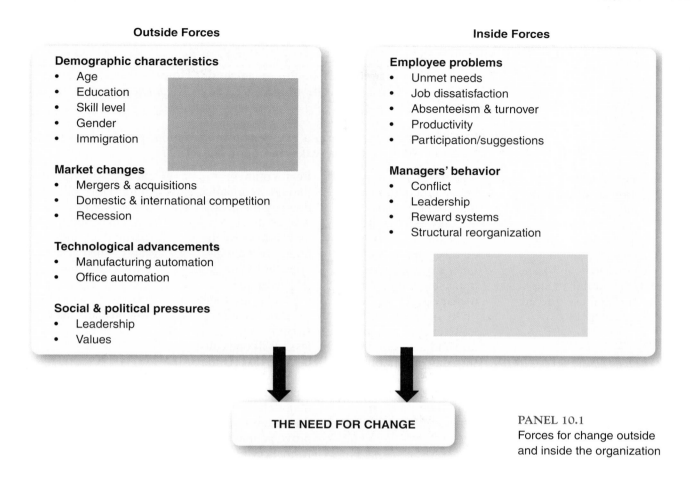

Outside Forces

Demographic characteristics
- Age
- Education
- Skill level
- Gender
- Immigration

Market changes
- Mergers & acquisitions
- Domestic & international competition
- Recession

Technological advancements
- Manufacturing automation
- Office automation

Social & political pressures
- Leadership
- Values

Inside Forces

Employee problems
- Unmet needs
- Job dissatisfaction
- Absenteeism & turnover
- Productivity
- Participation/suggestions

Managers' behavior
- Conflict
- Leadership
- Reward systems
- Structural reorganization

THE NEED FOR CHANGE

PANEL 10.1
Forces for change outside and inside the organization

Forces Originating Inside the Organization Internal forces affecting organizations may be subtle, such as low job satisfaction, or more dramatic, such as constant labor-management conflict. Internal forces may be of two types:

1 Employee Problems Is there a gap between the employees' needs and desires and the organization's needs and desires? Job dissatisfaction—as expressed through high absenteeism and turnover—can be a major signal of the need for change. Organizations may respond by addressing job design, reducing employees' role conflicts, and dealing with work overload, to mention a few matters.

For instance, when Marin McGuinn was reorganizing the retail division of Mellon Bank, many of the employees who were upset over expanded banking hours were appeased when they were given more freedom to arrange their own schedules.

2 Managers' Behavior Excessive conflict between managers and employees may be another indicator that change is needed. Perhaps there is a personality conflict, so that an employee transfer may be needed. Or perhaps some interpersonal training is required.

Phil Dusenberry, chairman of ad agency BBDO, says that he used to have a gentle way of letting people down because he didn't want to hurt their feelings. Often, however, this would simply confuse people. "They'd go off thinking that I liked their work even if I didn't," he says. "Over time I realized that dealing in terms of black and white wasn't a bad thing. I became much more direct."[11]

Areas in Which Change Is Often Needed: People, Technology, Structure, & Strategy

Change can involve any part of the organization. However, the four areas in which change is most apt to be needed are *people, technology, structure*, and *strategy.*

1 Changing People Even in a two-person organization, people changes may be required. The changes may take the following forms:

■ **Perceptions:** Employees might feel they are underpaid for what they do. Managers might be able to show that pay and benefits are comparable or superior to those offered by competitors.

■ **Attitudes:** In old-line manufacturing industries, employees may feel that it is the nature of things that they should be in an adversarial relationship with their managers. It may be up to management to try to change the culture and the attitudes by using educational techniques to show why the old labor wars should become a thing of the past.

■ **Performance:** Should an organization pay the people who contract to wash its windows by the hour? by the window? or by the total job? Will one method cause them to work fast and sloppily but cost less? Will one cause them to do pristine windows but cost too much? It's often a major challenge to find incentives to improve people's performance.

■ **Skills:** Altering or improving skill levels is often an ongoing challenge, particularly these days, when new forms of technology can change an organization's way of doing business, as we describe next.

2 Changing Technology Technology is a major area of change for many organizations. **_Technology_ is not just computer technology; it is any machine or process that enables an organization to gain a competitive advantage in changing materials used to produce a finished product.** Breweries, for example, used to make beer by letting malted cereal grain flavored with hops brew slowly by fermentation; nowadays, the process is often speeded up by the direct injection of carbonation (from carbon dioxide) into the process.

Touch-screen technology. Using touch-screen computer terminals to record beverage and food orders has made the restaurant industry more efficient. Not all computer technology improves productivity, however. "For all their power," says an economics writer, "computers may be costing U.S. companies tens of billions of dollars a year in downtime, maintenance and training costs, useless game playing, and information overload." One study in the 1990s estimated microcomputer users wasted 5 billion hours a year waiting for programs to run, checking computer output for accuracy, helping coworkers use their applications, organizing cluttered disk storage, and calling for technical support. What problems have you encountered with computers that have actually reduced, rather than increased, your productivity?

Example of Changing Technology: Digital Books

The Internet is already changing the book business in terms of sales and distributions, as shown by Amazon.com. There are also e-books such as the Gemstar REB 1200 from RCA, the Palm m515, and the Compaq iPaq 3335, handheld gadgets called "readers" into which you can download files of novels or nonfiction for portable, paper-free reading. Finally, there are web clearinghouses for distributing books in electronic form, such as iUniverse.com.

But there's more coming: Under development is electronic paper that aims to display electronic text on thin, flexible sheets that look and feel like paper. Electronic paper is different from electronic books, which generally work like laptop computer screens. The sheets of e-paper are filled with millions of microscopic capsules that show either dark or light images in response to electrical charges. As envisioned, the electronic paper can be bound together in book or newspaper form, and content can be downloaded onto the pages through wireless technology. Thus, for example, you could have a daily e-newspaper or book beamed in each morning.

What will this do to the traditional type-and-paper publishing industries?[12]

3 Changing Structure   When one organization acquires another, the structure often changes—perhaps from a divisional structure, say, to a matrix structure. The recent trend is toward "flattening the hierarchy," eliminating several middle layers of management, and to using work teams linked by electronic networks.

4 Changing Strategy   Shifts in the marketplace often may lead organizations to have to change their strategy. As a result of the sudden rise in popularity of the Netscape Navigator Web browser, Microsoft Corp. found itself having to shift from a PC-based strategy to an Internet strategy.

Changing structure. AT&T CEO Michael Armstrong (left) shakes hands with Comcast Corp.'s CEO Ralph Roberts and president Brian Roberts on the merger of AT&T Broadband with Comcast in December 2001. Would you have approved of such a merger? Many companies try to grow by making big acquisitions, but it often doesn't work. For instance, WorldCom tried to become the world's biggest telecommunications company by making about five dozen acquisitions, but it ended with the stock dropping 95%. The merger of Hewlett-Packard and Compaq was expected to result in the layoff of 15,000 employees. Mergers change the structure of the merged companies, but do they result in higher productivity and profitability?

major question

How are employees threatened by change, and how can I help them adjust?

The Big Picture

This section discusses the degree to which employees fear change, from least threatening to most threatening. It also describes Lewin's three-stage change model: unfreezing, changing, and refreezing. Finally, it describes Kotter's eight steps for leading organizational change, which correspond to Lewin's three stages.

As a manager, particularly one working for an American organization, you may be pressured to provide short-term, quick-fix solutions. But when applied to organizational problems, this approach usually doesn't work: Quick-fix solutions have little staying power.

What, then, are effective ways to manage organization change and employees' fear and resistance to it? In this section, we discuss the following:

■ The extent to which employees fear change

■ Lewin's change model

■ Kotter's eight stages for leading organizational change

The Degree to Which Employees Fear Change: From Least Threatening to Most Threatening

Whether organizational change is administrative or technological, the degree to which employees feel threatened by it in general depends on whether the change is *adaptive, innovative,* or *radically innovative.*[13]

Turnaround artist. New IBM CEO Samuel Palmisano (left), with predecessor Lou Gerstner, IBM's CEO from 1993 to 2002, who succeeded in returning the company to its former status as industry leader. As discussed in the Management in Action case study at the end of this chapter, Gerstner believes strategy and corporate culture are linked. "You can't talk a culture into changing," he says. "You can't just exhort people to be different. You've got to point to fundamental strategic changes you're going to implement in a company and then drive the execution of that strategy. And it is in the execution of the strategy that the culture begins to change." If you had been an IBM employee in 1993, how do you think you would have reacted to Gerstner?

Least Threatening: Adaptive Change *Adaptive change* is reintroduction of a familiar practice—the implementation of a kind of change that has already been experienced within the same organization. This form of change is lowest in complexity, cost, and uncertainty. Because it is familiar, it is the least threatening to employees and thus will create the least resistance.

For example, during annual inventory week, a department store may ask its employees to work 12 hours a day instead of the usual 8. During tax-preparation time, the store's accounting department may imitate this same change in work hours. Although accounting employees are in a different department from stockroom and sales employees, it's expected they wouldn't be terribly upset by the temporary change in hours since they've seen it in effect elsewhere in the store.

Somewhat Threatening: Innovative Change   *Innovative change* is the introduction of a practice that is new to the organization. This form of change involves moderate complexity, cost, and uncertainty. It is therefore apt to trigger some fear and resistance among employees.

For example, should a department store decide to adopt a new practice of competitors by staying open 24 hours a day, requiring employees to work flexible schedules, it may be felt as moderately threatening.

Very Threatening: Radically Innovative Change   *Radically innovative change* involves introducing a practice that is new to the industry. Because it is the most complex, costly, and uncertain, it will be felt as extremely threatening to managers' confidence and employees' job security and may well tear at the fabric of the organization.[14]

For example, a department store converting some of its operations to e-commerce—selling its goods on the Internet—may encounter anxiety among its staff, especially those fearing being left behind.

Example of Radically Innovative Change: Merrill Lynch Confronts Online Trading

The title of the book is *The Innovator's Dilemma: When New Technologies Cause Great Firms to Fail.* In it author Clayton M. Christensen, a Harvard Business School professor, argues that when successful companies are confronted with a giant technological leap that transforms their markets, all choices are bad ones.

Before the advent of online trading, for instance, full-service stock brokerage firms such as Merrill Lynch & Co. justified their high commissions on the basis of all the advice and handholding they provided clients. Then along came the e-brokers such as E*Trade, Ameritrade, and Charles Schwab, which offered individuals the chance to trade for a flat fee of as little as $14.95 per trade. That permitted the start of the craze known as day trading.

Was Merrill Lynch supposed to give up its old way of doing business—or its 14,800 brokers? In 1999, the firm decided to launch a new account that would include online trading, at $29.95 per trade, taking their stated pricing down more than 80%. But its real thrust was to offer clients a full range of Merrill services, such as access to an actual broker, financial planning advice, and a Visa card, in return for an annual fee based on a percentage of client assets. This strategy also had the benefit of being least threatening to its existing workforce of brokers.

Will it work? A Schwab executive says that Merrill's plan to match them on the flat per-trade fee suggests that Merrill believes "there's no difference in service that makes Merrill worthy of a higher price. We agree with that." But Merrill is not convinced that bare-bones trading is really what customers want. It believes that the majority of investors want a human being to provide advice and assistance.

For Christensen, Merrill has chosen the middle path, which may mean getting the worst of both worlds, since it keeps the high cost structure of a big company while incurring the expenses of a startup. Christensen thinks it's very difficult for an existing successful company to take full advantage of a technological breakthrough such as the Internet, what he calls a "disruptive innovation." Instead, he argues that such a company should set up an entirely separate organization that can operate much like a startup.[15]

Lewin's Change Model: Unfreezing, Changing, & Refreezing

Most theories of organizational change originated with the landmark work of social psychologist **Kurt Lewin.** Lewin developed a model with three stages—*unfreezing, changing*, and *refreezing*—to explain how to initiate, manage, and stabilize planned change.[16]

1 "Unfreezing": Creating the Motivation to Change In the *unfreezing stage*, managers try to instill in employees the motivation to change, encouraging them to let go of attitudes and behaviors that are resistant to innovation. For this "unfreezing" to take place, employees need to become dissatisfied with the old way of doing things. Managers also need to reduce the barriers to change during this stage.

2 "Changing": Learning New Ways of Doing Things In the *changing stage*, employees need to be given the tools for change: new information, new perspectives, new models of behavior. Managers can help here by providing benchmarking results, role models, mentors, experts, and training. It's advisable, experts say, to convey the idea that change is a continuous learning process, not just a one-time event.[17]

3 "Refreezing": Making the New Ways Normal: In the *refreezing stage*, employees need to be helped to integrate the changed attitudes and behavior into their normal ways of doing things. Managers can assist by encouraging employees to exhibit the new change and then, through additional coaching and modeling, by reinforcing the employees in the desired change.

One technique used in Stage 1, to help unfreeze organizations, is **_benchmarking_, a process by which a company compares its performance with that of high-performing organizations.**[18] Professional sports teams do this all the time, but so do other kinds of organizations, including nonprofit ones.

For example, one company discovered that their costs to develop a computer system were twice as high as those of the best companies in their industry. They also learned that the time it took to get a new product to market was four times longer than the benchmarked organizations. This data was ultimately used to unfreeze employees' attitudes and motivate people to change the organization's internal processes in order to remain competitive.[19]

Lookalikes. One key to the success of Southwest Airlines is that all the planes in its fleet have been the same type, Boeing 737s, which saves on maintenance and training costs. Southwest established its reputation and profitability by being a short-haul, low-fare carrier. In late 2002, the airline decided to enter the long-haul business—nonstop, coast-to-coast flights between Baltimore/Washington International and Los Angeles—invading the domain of bigger airlines such as United. To do so, it is adding new-generation 737s, which can travel longer distances than the older planes. Southwest will still offer no-frills service—no seat assignments, and snacks instead of meals—and will compete principally on fare price. In expanding from short routes to long ones, would you expect the company to have to undergo any of the steps in Lewin's change model—unfreezing, changing, and refreezing?

Kotter's Eight Steps for Leading Organizational Change

An expert in leadership and change management, **John Kotter** believes that, to be successful, organizational change needs to follow eight steps to avoid the eight common errors senior management usually commits.[20] These correspond with Lewin's unfreezing-changing-refreezing stages.

Unfreezing   The first four of Kotter's steps represent unfreezing.

1 Establish a Sense of Urgency Top managers often fail to establish a sense of urgency about the need for change. The first step should be to "unfreeze" the organization by showing a compelling reason why change is needed.

2 Create the Guiding Coalition Senior management needs to create a powerful enough guiding coalition—a group that spans both the functions and the levels of the organization—with the authority to lead the change.

3 Develop a Vision & a Strategy Top management must create a *vision* and a *strategic plan* to guide the change process.

4 Communicate the Change Vision Senior management must create and implement a communication strategy that consistently *communicates* the new vision and strategic plan.

Changing   The next three steps represent the changing stage.

5 Empower Broad-Based Action Managers must eliminate barriers to change, and they must encourage risk taking and creative problem solving. They must identify the components of an organization that may be changed, known as the *target elements of change*.

6 Generate Short-Term Wins "Short-term wins" represent the achievement of important results or goals. It's important for managers to recognize and reward people who contribute to the wins.

7 Consolidate Gains & Produce More Change Sometimes managers declare victory too soon, derailing the long-term changes needed. Managers can use the credibility achieved by short-term wins to create more change. For example, more people may be brought in as change cascades throughout the organization.

Refreezing   Kotter's last step corresponds to Lewin's refreezing stage.

8 Anchor New Approaches in the Culture   It takes years for long-term changes to become embedded in the organization's culture. To achieve this, managers must reinforce changes by highlighting connections between new behaviors and processes and organizational success. Managers must also develop methods for developing change leaders and their successors.

Now let us turn to organization development, which is a systematic way of instituting planned change.

Click-Along 10.2

Examples of Kotter's Steps

major question

What are the uses of OD, and how effective is it?

The Big Picture

Organization development (OD) is a set of techniques for implementing change, such as managing conflict, revitalizing organizations, and adapting to mergers. Three characteristics of OD are that it aims for fundamental change; it is process-oriented, not content-oriented; and it is value-loaded. OD has three steps: diagnosis, intervention, and evaluation. Five factors have been found to make OD programs effective.

If you're a bookstore owner, a car dealer, a travel agent, or a stockbroker and aren't worried about the future of your business, you probably haven't been paying attention. The increasing importance of the Internet as a sales and distribution tool gives buyers and sellers the opportunity to link up directly; the middleman is becoming less necessary. Maybe, then, you need to start thinking about how to redesign your business—and soon. Maybe, therefore, you're a candidate for organization development.

__Organization development (OD)__ **is a set of techniques for implementing planned change to make people and organizations more effective.** Note the inclusion of people in this definition. OD focuses specifically on people in the change process. Often OD is put into practice by a person known as a *__change agent__*, **a consultant with a background in behavioral sciences who can be a catalyst in helping organizations deal with old problems in new ways.**

The techniques of OD apply to each of the change models discussed in the preceding section. For example, OD is used during each of Lewin's stages of "unfreezing," "change," and "refreezing."

Is small beautiful? With airlines cutting commissions and more travelers ordering tickets off websites, how can a small travel agent compete? In other industries, many large corporations aren't structured to take advantage of the Web because they view it as a mass-marketing medium. However, says the owner of a San Diego Web design firm, "It's very easy for a small business to go out and control an entire niche market. Maybe it's only six to 10,000 users, but that can be enough." Adds the chief strategy officer for a Florida-based online jeweler, "Big companies think they can adapt their environments to them, not adapt to their environments." Whether you work for a big company or small one, do you think you could use OD techniques to help your organization "adapt to its environment"?

What Can OD Be Used For?

OD can be used to address the following:

1 Managing Conflict Conflict is inherent in most organizations. Sometimes an OD expert in the guise of an executive coach will be brought in to help advise an executive on how to improve relationships with others in the organization.

For instance, David Hitz and Michael Malcolm, two cofounders of Network Appliance, a data-storage firm in Sunnyvale, Calif., were feuding with each other. The problem: Malcolm couldn't stick to his decisions, which drove Hitz crazy. An organization behavior specialist began working with the warring executives in separate sessions to solve the problem.[21]

2 Revitalizing Organizations Information technology is wreaking such change that nearly all organizations these days are placed in the position of having to adapt new behaviors in order to resist decline. OD can help by opening communication, fostering innovation, and dealing with stress.

3 Adapting to Mergers Mergers and acquisitions are associated with increased anxiety, stress, absenteeism, and turnover and decreased productivity.[22] What is the organizational fit between two disparate organizations, such as AOL and Time Warner? OD experts can help integrate two firms with varying cultures, products, and procedures.

AOL + Time Warner. Steve Case (left), CEO of New Economy company America Online, shakes hands with Gerald Levin, CEO of Old Economy media company Time Warner, which was acquired by AOL in January 2000. For a while this seemed to be a good deal. But then old AOL shareholders saw their stock plummet 75% and Time Warner holders found the AOL stock they got down 58% from the presale price. Why do you think this happened? Was the problem in the organizational fit, which might have been solved by OD? Or was it the fault of people's boom-time expectations in 2000 for Internet companies?

Characteristics of OD

Three identifying characteristics of OD are as follows:[23]

1 OD Aims for Fundamental Change Managers and consultants using OD aren't looking for temporary improvements. They generally want deep, long-lasting, *fundamental* change. "By fundamental change, as opposed to fixing a problem or improving a procedure," says OD consultant Warner Burke, "I mean that some significant aspect of an organization's culture will never be the same."[24] The emphasis is on changing an organization's *culture*, which, of course, involves people.

2 OD Is Process-Oriented, Not Content-Oriented You might not understand much of a conversation between product design engineers and marketing managers discussing a new computer chip. But that's all right. The important thing is to focus on the *process*—to coach the two parties to better communicate. In dealing with processes, OD consultants concentrate on such matters as conflict handling, trust, problem solving, power sharing, decision making, and career development.

3 OD Is Value-Loaded OD consultants prefer cooperation over conflict, self-control over institutional control, and participative management over autocratic management. Thus, OD carries certain values, or biases, rooted in humanistic psychology.[25]

How OD Works

Like physicians, OD managers and consultants follow a medical-like model. They approach the organization as if it were a sick patient, using *diagnosis, intervention*, and *evaluation*—"diagnosing" its ills, "prescribing" treatment or intervention, and "monitoring" or evaluating progress.[26] *(See Panel 10.2.)*

PANEL 10.2
The OD process

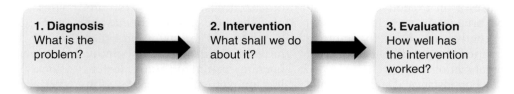

1. Diagnosis
What is the problem?

2. Intervention
What shall we do about it?

3. Evaluation
How well has the intervention worked?

1 Diagnosis: What Is the Problem? To carry out the diagnosis, OD consultants or managers use some combination of questionnaires, surveys, interviews, meetings, records, and direct observation to ascertain people's attitudes and to identify problem areas.

2 Intervention: What Shall We Do about It? "Treatment" or *intervention* **is the attempt to correct the diagnosed problems.** Often this is done using the services of an OD consultant who works in conjunction with management teams. Some OD activities for implementing planned change are shown in the box below. *(See Panel 10.3.)*

3 Evaluation: How Well Has the Intervention Worked? An OD program needs objective evaluation to see if it has done any good. Answers may lie in hard data about absenteeism, turnover, grievances, and profitability, which should be compared with earlier statistics. The change agent can use questionnaires, surveys, interviews, and the like to assess changes in employee attitudes.

PANEL 10.3
Some OD activities for implementing change

■ **Survey feedback:** A questionnaire is distributed to employees to ascertain their perceptions and attitudes. The results are then shared with them. The questionnaire may ask about such matters as group cohesion, job satisfaction, and managerial leadership. Once the survey is done, meaningful results can be communicated with employees so that they can then engage in problem solving and constructive changes.[27]

■ **Process consultation:** An OD consultant observes the communication process—interpersonal-relations, decision-making, and conflict-handling patterns—occurring in work groups and provides feedback to the members involved. In consulting with employees (particularly managers) about these processes, the change agent hopes to give them the skills to identify and improve group dynamics on their own.

■ **Team building:** Work groups are made to become more effective by helping members learn to function as a team. For example, members of a group might be interviewed independently by the OD change agent to establish how they feel about the group, then a meeting may be held away from their usual workplace to discuss the issues. To enhance team cohesiveness, the OD consultant may have members work together on a project such as rock climbing, with the consultant helping with communication and conflict resolution.[28] The objective is for members to see how they can individually contribute to the group's goals and efforts.

■ **Intergroup development:** Intergroup development resembles team building in many of its efforts. However, intergroup development attempts to achieve better cohesiveness among several work groups, not just one. During the process, the change agent tries to elicit misperceptions and stereotypes that the groups have for each other so that they can be discussed, leading to better coordination among them.

■ **Technostructural activities:** Technostructural activities are interventions concerned with improving the work technology or organizational design with people on the job. An intervention involving a work-technology change might be the introduction of e-mail to improve employee communication. An intervention involving an organizational-design change might be making a company less centralized in its decision making.

The Effectiveness of OD

Among organizations that have practiced organization development are American Airlines, B.F. Goodrich, General Electric, Honeywell, ITT, Polaroid, Procter & Gamble, Prudential, Texas Instruments, and Westinghouse Canada. Were the OD projects successful? Not always. Moreover, the link between OD interventions and increased productivity has not really been established, although there is a link between interventions and improvement in employee attitudes.[29] Some of the successes may actually result from good luck, improved economic conditions, and so on.[30]

What makes OD successful? A survey of 245 OD consultants taken in the early 1980s found that just 53% of projects were considered to be successful; the rest were unsuccessful.[31] Five factors that made programs work, they said, included the following:

1 Readiness for Change Consultants said that conditions in the organization had reached the point that people were ready to change. Management should not engage in organizational change for the sake of change. Change efforts should produce positive results.[32]

2 Management Support Top managers gave the OD program their full support, and the OD consultant's principal contact was a powerful member. Employee satisfaction with change was higher when top management was highly committed to the change effort.[33]

3 Expectations & Awareness The expectations of top managers for change were not unrealistic. In addition, managers were informed about alternative OD techniques.

4 Access & Collaboration The OD consultants had a high degree of access to the organization's resources, such as records and people, and there was a high degree of collaboration between consultant and client.

5 Multiple Interventions OD success stories tended to use multiple interventions. Indeed, one analysis found that combined interventions worked better than single interventions in improving employee attitudes and satisfaction.[34]

Team building. One technique for implementing change is team building. Teams are often diverse in gender, age, ethnicity, and educational background and experience. Would you prefer to work with a highly diverse team of people?

major question

What do I need to know to encourage innovation?

The Big Picture

Innovation may be a product innovation or a process innovation, an incremental innovation or a radical innovation. Four characteristics of innovation are that it is uncertain, people closest to it know the most about it, it may be controversial, and it may be complex. Three ways to encourage innovation are by providing the organizational culture, the resources, and the reward system. To make innovation happen, you need to recognize problems and opportunities, gain allies, and overcome employee resistance.

Innovation can happen by design or by accident, and it need not come about because of a for-profit orientation. For instance, the computer operating system Linux was written by Finnish programmer Linus Torvalds, who then put his work in the public domain. It is now a free operating system created by hundreds of programmers around the world, who contribute to its "source code," its underlying instructions, which are available to anyone. Indeed, unlike the Microsoft Windows or Macintosh operating systems, Linux is protected by a sort of reverse copyright, called a "copyleft," which prohibits programmers who work on it from taking their versions out of the public domain. "Geeks love Linux because they can lift up the hood of their software and mess around inside, customizing and fixing up what they want," says one report. "The constant tinkering by thousands of coders [programmers] also improves the code, making it ever more sophisticated and crash proof."[35]

As we've said earlier in the book, innovation is the activity of creating new ideas and converting them into useful applications—specifically new goods and services. The spirit of innovation is essential to keeping an organization vital and in maintaining a competitive advantage. Otherwise, the innovation will come from your competitors, forcing you to scramble to catch up—if you can.

Types of Innovation: Product or Process, Incremental or Radical

Innovations may be of the following types.

Product versus Process Innovations As a manager, you may need to improve your organization's product or service itself; this is generally a technological innovation. Or you may need to improve the process by which the product or service is created, manufactured, or distributed; this is generally a managerial innovation.

Linus Torvalds. In 1991, computer programmer Torvalds, then a graduate student in Finland, posted his free Linux operating system on the Internet. Linux is a free version of Unix, and its continual improvements result from the efforts of tens of thousands of volunteer programmers. Can you think of any other innovations that occurred that did not come about because of a for-profit orientation?

More formally, a **_product innovation_** is a change in the appearance or the performance of a product or a service or the creation of a new one. A **_process innovation_** is a change in the way a product or service is conceived, manufactured, or disseminated.

Incremental versus Radical Innovations An innovation may be small or large. The difference is in modifying versus replacing existing products or services. That is, you might have **_incremental innovations_**—the creation of products, services, or technologies that modify existing ones. Or you might have **_radical innovations_**—the creation of products, services, or technologies that replace existing ones.

Click-Along 10.3

Example of Radical Process Innovation: Commander Taco Invents Slashdot

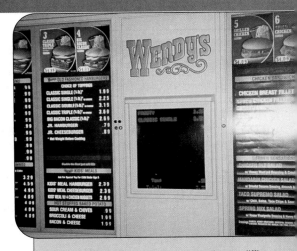

No, *no* fries with that! Ever experience difficulty with your order at a fast-food drive-thru? Wendy's and its competitors are trying to solve this problem with display screens that show your order and its price. What type of innovation is this?

practical action

What Makes a Startup?

Lots of books are written about creativity and innovation in organizational life. In general, the message is the same: "Fire up your companywide brainpower to hatch ideas," as one *Business Week* writer put it, "and make sure the ideas reach the people who can implement them." But it's difficult to come up with a formula for turning companies into prodigious idea factories.[36] As Gina O'Connor, a marketing professor at Rensselaer Polytechnic Institute, points out: "American companies are doing a great job of developing better products. But there's been very little improvement in radical, or 'discontinuous,' innovation."[37]

Interestingly, though, many start-ups don't begin with radical ideas. According to Amar V. Bhidé, author of *The Origin and Evolution of New Businesses*, successful entrepreneurs start out by making "a small modification in what somebody else is doing."[38] One has only to think of how the notion of disposability has been extended to so many products—phone cards, DVDs, even cellphones.[39]

Most entrepreneurs, he explains, see a small niche opportunity—one in which the company he or she is working for is already involved, or a supplier or customer is involved. "And the person jumps in with very little preparation and analysis," he says, "but with direct firsthand knowledge of the profitability of that opportunity—and pretty much does what somebody else is already doing, but does it better and faster."

And "better and faster" seems to be the main difference. Such entrepreneurs don't have anything in the way of technology or concept that differentiates them from other businesses. "They just work harder, hustle for customers, and know that the opportunity may not last for more than six or eight months," says Bhidé. "But they expect to make a reasonable return on those six to eight months. And along the way they'll figure out something else that will keep the business going."

Another quality of entrepreneurs is "a tolerance for ambiguity," Bhidé says. They are willing to jump into things when it's hard to even imagine what the possible outcomes will be, going ahead in the absence of information, very much capital—or even a very novel idea.

An example of a startup fitting these criteria is Netflix, which rents DVD movies by mail to customers ordering online. This concept does not seem very innovative. The wrinkle, however, which struck founder Reed Hastings when he was charged $40 for returning a movie late to a video rental outfit, is that for $15 a month, customers can keep two movies at once for as long as they like—no late fees. Another differentiating feature: When you rate the movie you rented, Netflix will recommend other movies you might enjoy that you might never have heard of.[40]

Four Characteristics of Innovation

According to Harvard management scholar Rosabeth Moss Kanter, innovation has four characteristics:[41]

1 Innovating Is an Uncertain Business   Being an innovator means being like the first driver in a line of cars in a snowstorm: You're dealing with the unknown while the less adventurous souls behind you may be carping about your performance. When you're innovating, progress is difficult to predict, and the ultimate success of your endeavor is always somewhat in doubt.

2 People Closest to the Innovation Know the Most About It, at Least Initially   Innovation is knowledge-intensive. The people closest to the development of the idea know the most about it, at least in the early stages. Consequently, it is often difficult for outsiders—such as coworkers or managers who are removed from the process—to understand and appreciate it. This leads to characteristic #3.

3 Innovation May Be Controversial   Whoever is doing the innovating is using the organization's people and funds for that purpose. Since there is always competition for resources, others in the organization may take issue with the way they are being used here—especially since the innovation has not yet shown positive results.

4 Innovation Can Be Complex Because It May Cross Organizational Boundaries   An innovation may involve more than one department or business unit. This, of course, increases the complexity of the process. Thus, you as a manager need to understand not only how the process of innovation works in general but also how it requires special handling to make it successful within different parts of the organization. Shepherding an innovation, therefore, may require you to draw on your finest communication skills—especially because of characteristic #2 above.

COOL

YOUR CUSTOMERS BUY AT WEB SPEED.

WAY COOL

UPS NOW HELPS YOU HANDLE E-RETURNS JUST AS FAST.

REASON FOR RETURN

✔ Please Select

Changed My Mind

Want Another Color

Want A Different Item

Want A Different Size

Announcing point-and-click returns. UPS now offers the quickest, simplest way to handle your e-returns. A new, customizable solution that allows your customers to print return labels directly from their PC—shrinking the process from five days to five minutes. In addition, you'll be able to route your returns to the right vendor and rapidly restock your inventory, with full visibility tracking throughout. It all adds up to fewer customer inquiries, lower operating costs, and much happier returns. How cool is that? To find out more, visit us at ec.ups.com

ups

MOVING at the SPEED of BUSINESS®

E-returns. Ever had to return a product you ordered from Amazon.com or another website retailer because it wasn't right or you changed your mind? Returns are the bane of many e-commerce retailers. This ad from United Parcel Service offers an innovation to help solve the problem.

Celebrating Failure: Cultural & Other Factors Encouraging Innovation

Innovation doesn't happen as a matter of course. Organizations have to develop ways to make it happen—over and over. Three ways to do so are by providing (1) the right organizational *culture*, (2) the appropriate *resources*, and (3) the correct *reward system*.

1 Culture: Is Innovation Viewed as a Benefit or a Boondoggle?

Although much of American culture seems oriented toward punishing failure, an organizational culture that doesn't just allow but *celebrates* failure is vital toward fostering innovation.[42] Most new ideas will fail. Only a few will be successful. But if an organization doesn't encourage this kind of risk taking—if people tend to view experimentation as a boondoggle—that organization won't become a superstar in innovation.

An organizational culture, as we said in Chapter 8, is the "social glue," or system of shared beliefs and values, that binds members together. Among the companies with cultures that strongly encourage innovation are Apple Computer, Corning, Hewlett-Packard, Johnson & Johnson, Merck, Monsanto, Texas Instruments, and 3M (*see example, next page*).

2 Resources: Do Managers Put Money Where Their Mouths Are?

An organization's managers may say they encourage innovation, but if they balk at the expense, they aren't putting their money where their mouths are. Innovation doesn't come cheap. Its costs can be measured in all kinds of ways: dollars, time, energy, and focus. For instance, an organization's research and development (R&D) department may need to hire top scientists, whose salaries may be high.

Of course, because there is always competition within an organization for resources, innovation may simply be given short shrift because other concerns seem so urgent—even within a company with a culture encouraging experimentation. But the risk of downgrading innovation in favor of more immediate concerns is that a company may "miss the next wave"—the next big trend, whatever that is.

3 Rewards: Is Experimentation Reinforced in Ways That Matter?

Top-performing salespeople are often rewarded with all kinds of incentives, such as commissions, bonuses, and perks. Are R&D people rewarded the same way? Every year Monsanto Corp., for instance, presents a $50,000 award to the scientist or scientists who developed the largest commercial breakthrough.

The converse is also important: People should not be punished when their attempts to innovate don't work out, or else they won't attempt new things in the future. By the nature of experimentation, the end result can't be foreseen. Top managers at 3M, for instance, recognize that three-fifths of the new ideas suggested each year fail in the marketplace. Only when people attempting an innovation are acting half-heartedly, sloppily, or otherwise incompetently should sanctions be used such as the withholding of raises and promotions.

The culture of innovation. Salespeople are rarely charged with responsibility for innovations in products or services, even though they typically have frequent interaction with customers. Should they be given such a role?

Example of Achieving Success by Celebrating Failure: 3M's Culture of Innovation

In Chapter 3 we mentioned 3M's Art Fry, inventor of Post-it Notes, as an example of an intrapreneur. But 3M is also famous for having a culture of innovation that celebrates taking chances—which means achieving success by celebrating failure.

A story told around 3M is about an outside inventor, Francis Okie, who in the 1920s wrote 3M for samples of various sandpaper grit. Okie had an idea for a waterproof sandpaper, which he thought might have use in shaving and would reduce the cuts inflicted by razor blades. That idea turned out to be a failure. However, 3M was still interested in the sandpaper, later named Wetordry, and Okie sold them his idea after the company agreed to help bring the product to market. The result was a hugely successful product that became widely used in the automotive market, where previously dry sanding had created clouds of dust and lead-based paint that made people sick. Okie joined 3M in 1921 and became the company's first real inventor.

Only with 20-20 hindsight can people see that a policy of celebrating failure can lead to success. No one can know, when setting out on a new course, whether the effort will yield positive results, and usually, in fact, most such experiments *are* failures. But the *attempts* must be encouraged, or innovation will never happen.

3M builds innovation into its culture. Mistakes are allowed, destructive criticism is forbidden, experimentation is encouraged, and divisions and individuals are allowed to operate with a good deal of autonomy. 3M sets goals decreeing that 25%–30% of annual sales must come from products that are only five years old or less. Investment in research and development is almost double the rate of that of the average American company. In addition, 3M employees are permitted to spend 15% of their time pursuing personal research interests that are not related to current company projects, knowing that if their ideas aren't successful, they will be encouraged to pursue other paths.[43]

How You Can Foster Innovation: Three Steps

If you're going to not just survive but *prevail* as a manager, you need to know how to make innovation happen within an organization. Here we offer three steps for doing so.[44] *(See Panel 10.4.)*

PANEL 10.4
Three steps for fostering innovation

1 Recognize Problems & Opportunities & Devise Solutions Change may be needed because you recognize a *problem* or recognize an *opportunity*.

- **Recognizing a problem— find a "better way":** Problems, whether competitive threat or employee turnover, tend to seize our attention.

  Sometimes problems lead to new business ideas. When John Decker of Maui, Hawaii, took up classical guitar, he discovered Hawaii's tropical climate was hard on wooden instruments. This led to his forming a company to turn out high-quality classical guitars made of synthetic materials known for their stiffness and durability.[45]

- **Recognizing an opportunity:** Recognition of opportunities may come from long-term employees who regularly expose themselves to new ideas ("technological gate-keepers" in one phrase).[46] Ideas originating at the grass-roots level of an organization may be a particularly fruitful source of innovation.[47]

2 Gain Allies by Communicating Your Vision Once you've decided how you're going to handle the problem or opportunity, you need to start developing and communicating your vision. You need to create a picture of the future and paint in broad strokes how your innovation will be of benefit. That is, you need to start persuading others inside—and perhaps outside—the organization to support you. Having hard data helps. Others will be more persuaded, for example, if you can demonstrate that a similar idea has been successful in another industry. Or if you can take current trends (such as sales or demographics) and project them into the future.

But a great deal of innovation comes about precisely because the future has no resemblance to the past. Thus, you may have to use your imagination to paint the brightest picture you can of the possible payoffs of your innovation.

3 Overcome Employee Resistance, & Empower & Reward Them to Achieve Progress Once you've persuaded and got the blessing of your managerial superiors, then you need to do the same with the people reporting to you. It's possible, of course, that the idea for innovation came from them and that you already have their support.

Alternatively, you may have to overcome their resistance. Then you'll need to remove obstacles that limit them in executing the vision, such as having to get management to sign off on all aspects of a project. Finally, you'll need to hand out periodic rewards—recognition, celebrations, bonuses—for tasks accomplished. And the rewards should not be withheld until the end of the project, which may be many months away, but given out for the successful accomplishment of short-term phases in order to provide constant encouragement.

Click-Along 10.4

Taking Something Practical Away from This Chapter: More About Resistance to Change

Recognizing problems—and opportunities. Carl Caspers, CEO and co-founder of TEC Interface Systems in Waite Park, Minn., understands the limits of most prosthetic limbs because he is an amputee himself. TEC's Harmony System is a breakthrough product that may well change standards for measuring mobility and control. The difference is that the TEC prosthesis has a built-in vacuum pump, which prevents the limb from shrinking throughout the day and becoming a looser fit with the prosthesis, a recurring, painful problem for amputees using traditional devices.

Key Terms Used in This Chapter

benchmarking, 326

change agent, 328

incremental innovations, 333

intervention, 330

organization development, 328

proactive change, 319

process innovation, 333

product innovation, 333

radical innovations, 333

reactive change, 319

technology, 322

Summary

10.1
The Nature of Change in Organizations

■ Two types of change are reactive and proactive. Reactive change is making changes in response to problems or opportunities as they arise. Proactive change, or planned change, involves making carefully thought-out changes in anticipation of possible or expected problems or opportunities.

■ Forces for change may consist of forces outside the organization or inside it. (1) External forces consist of four types: demographic characteristics, market changes, technological advancements, and social and political pressures. (2) Internal forces may be of two types: employee problems and managers' behavior.

■ Four areas in which change is most apt to be needed are people, technology, structure, and strategy. (1) People changes may require changes in perceptions, attitudes, performance, or skills. (2) Technology is not just computer technology; it is any machine or process that enables an organization to gain a competitive advantage in changing materials used to produce a finished product. (3) Changing structure may happen when one organization acquires another. (4) Changing strategy may occur because of changes in the marketplace.

10.2
The Threat of Change: Managing Employee Fear & Resistance

■ The degree to which employees feel threatened by change depends on whether the change is adaptive, innovative, or radically innovative. Adaptive change, the least threatening, is reintroduction of a familiar practice. Innovative change is the introduction of a practice that is new to the organization. Radically innovative change, the most threatening, involves introducing a practice that is new to the industry.

■ Kurt Lewin's change model has three stages—unfreezing, changing, and refreezing—to explain how to initiate, manage, and stabilize planned change. (1) In the unfreezing stage, managers try to instill in employees the motivation to change. One technique used is benchmarking, a process by which a company compares its performance with that of high-performing organizations. (2) In the changing stage, employees need to be given the tools for change, such as new information. (3) In the refreezing stage, employees need to be helped to integrate the changed attitudes and behavior into their normal behavior.

■ In a model corresponding with Lewin's, John Kotter's suggests an organization needs to follow eight steps to avoid the eight common errors senior management usually commits. The first four represent unfreezing: establish a sense of urgency, create the guiding coalition, develop a vision and strategy, and communicate the change vision. The next three steps represent the changing stage: empower broad-based action, generate short-term wins, and consolidate gains and produce more change. The last step, corresponding to refreezing, is to anchor new approaches in the organization's culture.

10.3
Organization Development: What It Is, What It Can Do

■ Organizational development (OD) is a set of techniques for implementing planned change to make people and organizations more effective. Often OD is put into practice by a change agent, a consultant with a background in behavioral sciences who can be a catalyst in helping organizations deal with old problems in new ways. OD can be used to manage conflict, revitalize organizations, and adapt to mergers.

■ OD has three identifying characteristics: it aims for fundamental change; it is process-oriented, not content-oriented; and it is value-loaded, preferring cooperation over conflict. The OD process follows a three-step process: (1) Diagnosis attempts to ascertain the problem. (2) Intervention is the attempt to correct the diagnosed problems. (3) Evaluation attempts to find out how well the intervention worked.

■ Five factors that make OD work successfully are (1) when the organization has reached the point where people are ready to change, (2) top managers give the OD program their support, (3) top managers' expectations for change are not unrealistic, (4) the OD consultants have access to the organization's resources and collaboration with the client, and (5) multiple interventions are used.

10.4
Promoting Innovation within the Organization

■ Innovations may be a product innovation or a process innovation. A product innovation is a change in the appearance or performance of a product or service or the creation of a new one. A process innovation is a change in the way a product or service is conceived, manufactured, or disseminated. Innovations may also be an incremental innovation or a radical innovation. An incremental innovation is the creation of a product, service, or technology that modifies an existing one. A radical innovation is the creation of a product, service, or technology that replaces an existing one.

■ Four characteristics of innovation are that (1) it is an uncertain business; (2) people closest to the innovation know the most about it, at least initially; (3) it may be controversial; and (4) it can be complex because it may cross organizational boundaries.

■ Innovation doesn't happen as a matter of course. Three ways to make it happen are to provide the right organizational culture, so that it is viewed as a benefit rather than as a boondoggle; to provide the resources; and to provide the rewards, so that experimentation is reinforced in ways that matter. Three steps for fostering innovation are as follows. (1) Recognize problems and opportunities and devise solutions. (2) Gain allies by communicating your vision. (3) Overcome employee resistance and empower and reward them to achieve progress.

Management in Action

A Man with No Experience in the Computer Industry Turns IBM Around

From Steve Lohr, "He Loves to Win. At IBM, He Did," New York Times, *March 10, 2002, sec. 3, pp. 1, 11.*

The revival of IBM over the last nine years is most tellingly measured not in numbers but by its return to pre-eminence as the industry leader. Once again, IBM is the model others follow. . . .

In 1993, when Louis V. Gerstner Jr. became chairman and chief executive, the question asked about IBM was whether it would survive. And in choosing him, the IBM board had taken a historic gamble on a professional manager with no experience in the computer industry. . . .

[Reading IBM strategic documents] left him enlightened—and appalled. IBM, he said, was filled with smart people who had recognized the industry's major technological and economic shifts. Yet IBM had repeatedly failed to respond. "Part of the culture was a tendency to debate and argue and raise every issue to the highest level of abstraction," Mr. Gerstner said. . . .

So, a few months after arriving at IBM, when he said the last thing it needed was a vision, he was declaring a break with the old culture of introspection and foot-dragging. Had he spoken of vision at IBM, he said, he knew it would have started "a yearlong debate."

"And we didn't need the vision," he added. "We needed to save the company economically."

Instead he gave marching orders to the IBM troops. "We were going to build this company from the customer back, not from the company out," he said. "That was the big message from my first six months in the company, that the company was going to be driven from the marketplace."

Mr. Gerstner argues that strategy and corporate culture are intimately linked. "You can't talk a culture into changing," he said. "You can't just exhort people to be different. You've got to point to fundamental strategic changes you're going to implement in a company and then drive the execution of that strategy. And it is in the execution of the strategy that the culture begins to change."

The first major decision Mr. Gerstner made was to decide to keep the company together, not split it up into thirteen loosely linked "Baby Blues." Under that [federation] plan, put forward by his predecessor, . . . some would be spun off as separate companies . . .

In theory, the federation plan addressed IBM's fundamental trouble—that as an integrated company it was not quick and nimble. . . .

Mr. Gerstner, an IBM customer at [previous companies he'd been with], liked the concept of "integrated solutions"—that IBM could distill the complexity of computing to solve business problems for companies. In his early travels for IBM, he heard similar sentiments from customers. . . .

Looking back, Mr. Gerstner pointed to three strategic decisions that were "the fundamental underpinnings of building an integrated company." First, he created a broad computer services unit that sold bundles of hardware, software, consulting, and maintenance to manage business processes like manufacturing, purchasing, or marketing. . . .

To be a real computer services company, Mr. Gerstner noted, "it had to be product agnostic."

"The customer would not accept a services company if all it did was flog IBM products," he said.

His decision to move into services set off "an incredible bomb in the company," Mr. Gerstner recalled. . . .

His second crucial decision struck at another IBM heritage, that of relying almost exclusively on its own homegrown technology. . . .

His third decision, made in 1995, was to fully embrace the Internet. . . .

At the conclusion of Mr. Gerstner's tenure, his three strategic pillars have come together in what could be mistaken for the very word he avoided, a vision. And that strategy shift, actually executed, insured a real change in the corporate culture.

For Discussion

1. How does this case show the interrelationship between strategy, culture, innovation, and leadership?

2. Would you say Gerstner's approach represented reactive change or proactive change?

3. Do you see Lewin's change model exemplified in Gerstner's approach?

4. How does Gerstner's approach exemplify the OD process?

5. Would you say making IBM a "product-agnostic" computer-services company represented a product innovation or a process innovation?

Take It to the Net

Can you imagine a world without sandpaper? Scotch® tape? Post-it® notes? These innovative products were the work of 3M Worldwide. As discussed in this chapter, innovation involves the creation of new ideas and converting them into useful applications. 3M Worldwide has been innovating useful products for 100 years. The purpose of this exercise is to show different types of innovation and how innovation can be encouraged.

Go to *www.3m.com*. Click on *About 3M*, then go to *Innovation at 3M*. Browse through each of the three sections. Pay special attention to the historical list of innovations. You may be surprised at just how many products you use on a regular basis would not be here if it weren't for 3M's innovation.

Questions for Discussion

1. What are some *product* innovations at 3M? What are some *process* innovations at 3M?

2. Would you say that 3M has been responsible more for *incremental* innovations or for *radical* innovations, or do you see evidence for both? Discuss in detail.

3. What are some ways 3M fosters innovation? Explain.

Self-Assessment

How Adaptable Am I?*

Objectives

1. To assess your adaptability.
2. To examine how being adaptable can help you cope with organizational change.

Introduction: Ultimately all organizational change passes through an organization's people. People who adapt more easily are better suited to cope with organizational changes and so they clearly are important assets to any organization. The purpose of this exercise is to determine your adaptability.

Instructions: Read the following statements. Using the scale provided, circle the number that indicates the extent to which you agree or disagree with each statement:

1 = strongly disagree

2 = disagree

3 = neither agree nor disagree

4 = agree

5 = strongly agree

1. In emergency situations, I react with clear, focused thinking and maintain emotional control in order to step up to the necessary actions.	1	2	3	4	5
2. In stressful circumstances, I don't overreact to unexpected news. I keep calm, focused, and manage frustration well.	1	2	3	4	5
3. I solve problems creatively by turning them inside out and upside down looking for new approaches to solving them that others may have missed.	1	2	3	4	5
4. I easily change gears in response to uncertain or unexpected events, effectively adjusting my priorities, plans, goals, and actions.	1	2	3	4	5
5. I enjoy learning new ways to do my work and I do what is necessary to keep my knowledge and skills current.	1	2	3	4	5
6. I adjust easily to changes in my workplace by participating in assignments or training that prepares me for these changes.	1	2	3	4	5
7. I am flexible and open-minded with others. I listen and consider others' viewpoints, adjusting my own when necessary.	1	2	3	4	5

8. I am open to both negative and positive feedback. I work well in teams.		1	2	3	4	5
9. I take action to learn and understand the values of other groups, organizations, or cultures. I adjust my own behavior to show respect for different customs.		1	2	3	4	5
10. I adjust easily to differing environmental states such as extreme heat, humidity, cold, or dirtiness.		1	2	3	4	5
11. I frequently push myself to complete strenuous or demanding tasks.		1	2	3	4	5

Total _____

Interpretation: When you are done, add up your responses to get your total score to see how adaptable you are. Arbitrary norms for adaptability:

11–24 = Low adaptability

25–39 = Moderate adaptability

40–55 = High adaptability

Questions for Discussion

1. Were you surprised by your results? Why or why not?

2. Look at the areas where your score was the lowest. What are some skills you can work on or gain to increase your adaptability? Describe and explain.

3. What are some ways being adaptable can improve the way you handle change? Discuss.

*Adapted from S. Arad, M. A. Donovan, K. E. Plamondon, and E. D. Pulakos, "Adaptability in the Workplace: Development of Taxonomy of Adaptive Performance," *Journal of Applied Psychology*, August 2000, pp. 612–624.

Group Exercise

Understanding Resistance to Change*

Objectives

1. To examine reasons why employees resist change.

2. To practice using ways to overcome resistance to change.

Introduction

Managers who need to implement planned change find that success depends on how much their employees accept the change. If errors are made in the ways changes are introduced, employee resistance is likely to increase. The purpose of this exercise is to examine ways managers can overcome employee resistance to change.

Instructions

Break into groups of five to six people. Read the following case of the Canadian Furniture Corp. (CFC). Discuss the case with your group and brainstorm, using Lewin's Change Model, and Kotter's Eight Steps for Organizational Change, to find errors in the way managers at CFC implemented change. After your group has identified the errors, compare your notes with other groups. As a class, discuss some managerial strategies that would prevent errors such as the ones at CFC from occurring.

The Case

The Canadian Furniture Corp. is a manufacturer of household furniture located in southern Ontario. It has been in business since the early 1950s and has always experienced steady growth, even in periods of economic downturn. . . . At present, CFC has an assembly plant in 8 of the 10 Canadian provinces. Because of Canada's geography, the unique provincial differences in consumer preferences, and early transportation problems, CFC has traditionally given local assembly plants considerable freedom of action in all aspects of the business. This is especially true in purchasing.

The business was purchased by Centrex, a manufacturer of office furniture headquartered in

Toronto, that wanted to expand into household furniture. Shortly after the takeover, Mr. Benton, president of Centrex, decided that CFC's operations should be brought more in line with those of Centrex. These included introducing a new position at CFC—Vice President of Purchasing. To fill this position, Benton selected John Speedman, who had been with Centrex for seven years. Benton assured Speedman that he had authority to make whatever changes he wanted, to bring the CFC operations into line with Centrex. . . . In addition, Benton assigned Bob Hestent as Speedman's assistant. Hestent had been with CFC purchasing group since 1984 and was familiar with the assembly plant managers. The new Purchasing Department was to be located at CFC's Toronto home office.

Speedman decided there was no reason to delay efforts to restructure CFC. As far as he was concerned, this was what Benton and the board of directors at Centrex wanted and that's what they would get. His first move was to centralize the purchasing practices of CFC. All assembly plant purchases over $50,000 would be made through the Toronto office. Speedman thought the coordination of assembly plant purchases would ensure a standard quality of furniture and allow the company to obtain quantity discounts when purchasing high-demand items. He presented his plan to Benton and the Board, and they gave it their complete backing.

At the time Speedman enacted his changes, CFC experienced a major increase in demand for furniture. This was likely to have a major impact on future purchases. Nevertheless, Speedman prepared this letter to be sent to assembly plant managers in order to explain his position:

Dear _____:

The home office has recently authorized a change in the way CFC obtains its resources. Starting immediately, all purchases over $50,000 will be sent first to my office for approval. This should be done well before the material is actually needed so that quantity purchases can be made where possible. I am sure that you will agree that such a move will improve the quality of CFC's product and help CFC save money. By accomplishing both these objectives, CFC will be better able to compete in what appears to be a very aggressive industry.

Sincerely yours,

(signed) John Speedman

Before mailing the letters, Speedman asked Hestent (his assistant) for his opinion. Hestent thought the letter was good and clearly made its point. However, he suggested that Speedman first meet with some of the assembly plant managers. Speedman was quick to say no because he was too busy, and, as Hestent said, the letter was clear and to the point. There would be no wasteful field trips.

In the weeks that followed, Speedman's office received positive replies from all assembly plant managers. The following is one such response:

Dear Mr. Speedman:

In response to your letter of the 13th, I see no problems in meeting your request. We at South Shore will do our best to inform you of all purchases over $50,000 and will give you the required lead time.

Although the anticipated increase in sales did occur over the next four months and reports from the field indicated a high level of activity, Speedman's office did not receive any purchase information from the assembly plant managers.

Questions for Discussion

1. Which steps in Lewin's Change Model did Speedman ignore? Describe and explain.

2. How could Speedman have used these steps to overcome the employees' resistance to change? Discuss in detail.

3. How could Speedman have used Kotter's eight steps to more successfully implement change? Explain.

4. Using Panels 10.2 and 10.3 as a guide, describe how Speedman could have used organizational development to implement change. Explain in detail.

*Excerpted from L. W. Mealia and G. P. Latham, "CFC Case Analysis: Understanding Resistance to Change," *Skills for Managerial Success: Theory, Experience, and Practice* (Burr Ridge, IL: Irwin, 1996), pp. 486–488.

Ethical Dilemma

Is This Innovation for Real? Sample of Disposable Cellphone Actually Seems to Be a Modified Nokia

Excerpted from Todd Wallack, "Sample 'New' Cell Phone Really Just Modified Nokia,"
San Francisco Chronicle, *March 29, 2002, p. B-1*

Hop-On.com's new disposable cellphone, touted everywhere from *Time* magazine to CNNfn as a landmark innovation, may be less original than it seems.

In news releases and interviews, the publicly traded California company says it has developed and manufactured an "innovative, technologically advanced" phone so cheap that customers can toss it away when they are done. Hop-On says the phone will retail for $30, including 60 minutes of calls.

But after cracking open several samples with Hop-On's name and kangaroo logo, *The [San Francisco] Chronicle* found the "revolutionary" device appeared to be little more than a jury-rigged Nokia [cellphone] in a new plastic shell.

Underneath the red plastic casing, one sample was clearly labeled inside as a "Nokia 8260."

Another Hop-On cellphone contained a part with Cingular Wireless' name and logo. Cingular spokeswoman Monica Mears said the part, called a SIM card, came from a batch of 100 Nokia 8290s it sold Hop-On last year. A white rechargeable battery in the phone also looks identical to one used in Nokias, though the name has been etched off. Only the circled R, denoting a registered trademark, remains.

"All the components that make it work are ours," said Nokia spokesman Keith Nowak. Nokia, which examined the samples at *The Chronicle*'s request, said it is considering whether to take action against Hop-On.

Hop-On Chief Executive Officer Peter Michaels was initially evasive when asked why the phones appeared to be modified Nokias. "Hop-On technology is proprietary," he said in a faxed reply.

But after *The Chronicle* explained its findings in greater detail, Michaels said the repackaged Nokias were "promotional samples only. They are not Hop-On production phones."

Michaels explained that the Garden Grove (Orange County) company was forced to use Nokias to produce the samples because of glitches with its own invention. "We had to scratch one of our designs," he said. Michaels, however, insists Hop-On is working out the bugs. "We are light years ahead of everyone," he said.

Still, even if Hop-On used the modified Nokias only to show off its concept, an industry analyst said Hop-On should have clearly disclosed that fact.

"I think (to call it) misleading would be putting it lightly," said Allen Nogee, a wireless components analyst. . . .

Moreover, the disclosure raises questions about whether Hop-On will be able to launch an ultra-cheap wireless phone anytime soon.

Hop-On says it hopes to sell its phones in stores for $30 each. But the Nokia models used for the samples carry a wholesale price of $220 to $250, not including talk time, estimates Lance Frey of LetsTalk.com, a San Francisco wireless reseller.

Solving the Dilemma

If you, as the Hop-On CEO, had encountered "glitches" in making your disposable cellphone yet felt you had to have samples available for promotional purposes, what would you do?

1. Postpone the samples until you could make authentic versions—no matter what the pressure on you by your investors and the marketplace.

2. Make samples out of Nokia components and hope no one would notice.

3. Make samples out of Nokia components but attach a sticker reading "Simulated version for promotional purposes"—even though this might generate skepticism about whether you could really make a $30 disposable phone.

4. Invent other options. Discuss.

Saber Union Insurance

As the video opens, Senior Manager Ralph Ramos and Claims Investigator Angela Zanoni meet to discuss Angela's recent performance. Angela has recently started telecommuting and was unaware of a change in an important project deadline. Since she started working from home, Angela feels "out of sight, out of mind." Both she and Ralph realize better communication is necessary. More specifically, Ralph sees two important issues: (1) finding the source of the current miscommunication, and (2) finding ways to keep such misunderstandings from happening in the future. Ralph realizes that Angela is strongly dissatisfied with the way he is managing the telecommuting process. Angela wants to be "part of the team" but feels she's not receiving the appropriate managerial attention. Ralph and Angela set another meeting when they have time to better prepare for this issue.

Privately, Ralph explains that he was unprepared for the issues Angela raised. Perhaps working two or three days in the office and the remainder at home would be a preferable schedule. When critical claims and deadlines arise, Angela could spend all her time in the office. He's still concerned about their communication issues and her future in the organization. Unbeknownst to Ralph, Angela is job hunting and avoiding business calls. She canceled their scheduled meeting and missed another deadline. When they finally meet, Angela again stresses that, because she's working from home, she isn't receiving the same consideration as other employees. She feels forgotten.

Ralph has serious concerns regarding Angela's performance. Although the first missed deadline was due to miscommunication, he suspects the second was intentional since Angela felt she wasn't being treated fairly. Ralph is looking for ways to resolve the issue, but Angela is ready to immediately resign. The situation becomes heated, and

Ralph tries to diffuse the tension. Angela is a valued employee, and they try to find a solution to this dilemma. For the next two weeks, Angela will continue working from home and Ralph will contact her daily via telephone. If their communication problems remain unresolved, Angela will return to the office for two weeks. If at the end of that time Angela is still dissatisfied they will revisit the possibility of resignation.

Privately, Ralph expresses his views. He knows Angela was ready to immediately resign. Listening to her and making it clear she is a valued and important employee diffused the situation. Ralph is not an advocate of telecommuting but feels the key to success is to establish clear expectations and goals in writing, which are agreed upon and signed by both parties. He feels that telecommuting doesn't allow for a personal connection with employees. Managers must instead rely on telephone or e-mail. Another critical issue is the time management skills of telecommuting employees. Regardless of whether employees work at the office or home, all should work under the same performance expectations.

Discussion Questions

1. Miscommunication caused Angela to miss an important deadline. List at least three ways Ralph and Angela can prevent future miscommunication.

2. How can Ralph make Angela feel as though she is still "part of the team"?

3. Are certain jobs more suited to telecommuting than others? Provide examples. What skills are important to be a successful telecommuter?

4. Is Ralph correct? Does telecommuting preclude a close working relationship between manager and employee? Be able to justify your response.

CHAPTER

Managing Individual Differences & Behavior

11.1 Values, Attitudes, & Behavior

Major Question: How do the hidden aspects of individuals—their values and attitudes—affect employee behavior?

11.4 Perception & Individual Behavior

Major Question: What are the distortions in perception that can cloud one's judgment?

11.2 Work-Related Attitudes & Behavior Managers Need to Deal With

Major Question: Is it important for managers to pay attention to employee attitudes?

11.5 Understanding Stress & Individual Behavior

Major Question: What causes workplace stress, and how can it be reduced?

11.3 Personality & Individual Behavior

Major Question: In the hiring process, do employers care about one's personality and individual traits?

LEADING YOUNGER WORKERS IN ATTAINING JOB SATISFACTION

"Younger employees want success now, and on their own terms, but paying dues is often a foreign concept. They are less trusting of organizations, institutions, and authority in general."

So writes one management consultant about younger workers. Is it possible for them to find satisfaction in the workplace?

A survey by the Gallup Organization suggests that supposedly discontented twentysomethings may fit into the workplace better than employers previously thought. But managers need to know how to manage for individual and generational differences.[1]

Young people today are much more apt to have had both parents working, or to come from a single-parent family, and are more likely to have been latch-key kids compared to those in previous generations. As a result, they have been left alone to make their own decisions and have had to assume greater responsibility. They are also used to television as entertainment and to a faster pace of life. In the workplace, these translate into a skepticism about rules, policies, and procedures; a requirement for more autonomy; and a need for constant stimulation.[2]

If you're going to be a leader, what should you know about managing this group? Following are some suggestions, some of which may benefit employees of all ages.[3]

■ **Make training an obsession:** Just waiting to move up the organizational ladder is no longer good enough. Employer-sponsored training and education is a major attraction for young workers. In the Gallup survey, 84% of those who received at least six days of training within the previous year said they were satisfied. (Only 70% of those who received no training said they were satisfied.) Fifty-eight percent of workers 32 years old and younger said training was useful in preparing them for higher-level jobs. (Among those older, only 42% had the same opinion.)

■ **Allow them independent learning while creating bonds with mentors:** The best kind of training for younger workers is not classroom training but forms of independent learning such as internships, work-study programs, and independent study. At the same time, they should be given the chance to create long-term bonds with teaching managers and mentors.

■ **Teach people by showing them their results:** Younger workers need to see the daily tangible results of their work. Managers can help by carving a job up into bite-size chunks—as in dividing a sales job into categories such as making cold calls, making second-round calls, meeting in person with hot leads, and so on. A daily checklist helps workers see their results.

■ **Provide frequent feedback:** Six-month and 12-month reviews are not as effective with young workers. More important is frequent, timely, and specific feedback each time a task is completed, with concrete suggestions for improvement.

■ **Provide frequent rewards for great performance:** Incentives need not always be financial. Such rewards as praise, flex time, telecommuting, and extra responsibility are also recommended. Twentysomethings are likely to want to acquire learning and training opportunities that will make them more marketable, since they have decided to rely on their own abilities, rather than the organization, for security.

FORECAST: WHAT'S AHEAD IN THIS CHAPTER

This first of five chapters on leadership discusses how to manage for individual differences and behaviors. We describe values, attitudes, and behavior, personality dimensions and traits, and specific work-related attitudes and behaviors managers need to be aware of. We next discuss distortions in perception, which can affect managerial judgment. Finally we consider what stress does to individuals.

major question

How do the hidden aspects of individuals—their values and attitudes—affect employee behavior?

The Big Picture

Organizational behavior (OB) considers how to better understand and manage people at work. In this section, we discuss individual values and attitudes and how they affect people's actions and judgments.

If you look at a company's annual report or at a brochure from its corporate communications department, you are apt to be given a picture of its *formal aspects*: Goals. Policies. Hierarchy. Structure.

Could you exert effective leadership—the subject of this and the next four chapters—if the formal aspects were all you knew about the company? What about the *informal aspects*? Values. Attitudes. Personalities. Perceptions. Conflicts. Culture. Clearly, you need to know about these hidden, "messy" characteristics as well. *(See Panel 11.1.)*

PANEL 11.1
Formal and informal aspects of an organization

Formal
Goals
Policies
Hierarchy
Structure

The Organization

Informal
Values
Attitudes
Personalities
Perceptions
Conflicts
Culture

Organizational Behavior: Trying to Explain & Predict Workplace Behavior

The informal aspects are the focus of the interdisciplinary field known as **_organizational behavior (OB)_, which is dedicated to better understanding and management of people at work.** In particular, OB tries to help managers not only *explain* workplace behavior but also to *predict* it, so that they can better lead and motivate their employees to perform productively. OB looks at two areas:

■ **Individual behavior:** This is the subject of this chapter. We discuss such individual attributes as values, attitudes, personality, perception, and learning.

■ **Group behavior:** This is the subject of later chapters, particularly Chapter 13, where we discuss norms, roles, and teams.

Let us begin by considering individual values, attitudes, and behavior.

Values: What Are Your Consistent Beliefs & Feelings about *All* Things?

Values are abstract ideals that guide one's thinking and behavior across all situations.[4] Lifelong behavior patterns are dictated by values that are fairly well set by the time people are in their early teens. After that, however, one's values can be reshaped by significant life-altering events, such as having a child, undergoing a business failure, or surviving the death of a loved one, a war, or a serious health threat.

From a manager's point of view, it's helpful to know that values are those concepts, principles, things, people, or activities for which a person is willing to work hard—even make sacrifices for. Compensation, recognition, and status are common values in the workplace.[5] Younger people, however, may hold the value that it's best to have balance between work and life. According to the Families and Work Institute, 60% of men and women under the age of 25 with children are willing to make significant sacrifices in money and career to spend more time with families.[6] With these employees, it helps managers to know there are limits to the inducements they can offer.

Family time. A question that probably every reader of this book will have to consider: How much money and career opportunity would you be willing to give up to spend more time with your family?

Attitudes: What Are Your Consistent Beliefs & Feelings about *Specific* Things?

Values are abstract ideals—global beliefs and feelings—that are directed toward all objects, people, or events.[7] Values tend to be consistent both over time and over related situations. By contrast, attitudes are beliefs and feelings that are directed toward *specific* objects, people, or events. More formally, an ***attitude* is defined as a learned predisposition toward a given object.**[8]

Example: If you dislike your present job, will you be happier if you change to a different job? Not necessarily. It depends on your attitude. In one study, researchers found that the attitudes of 5,000 middle-aged male employees toward their jobs were very stable over a five-year period. Men with positive attitudes tended to stay positive, those with negative attitudes tended to stay negative. More revealingly, even those who changed jobs or occupations generally expressed the same attitudes they had previously.[9]

The Three Components of Attitudes: Affective, Cognitive, & Behavioral Attitudes have three components:[10]

- **The affective component—"I feel":** The *affective component of an attitude* consists of the feelings or emotions one has about a situation.

    Examples: "I hate people who talk on cellphones in restaurants." "I hate putting on a suit for work." "I really like working from home." "I like commuting by train because I have time to myself." "I don't like working in office cubicles because they don't have doors and so there's no privacy." All these are expressions of the affective component of an attitude.

- **The cognitive component—"I believe":** The *cognitive component of an attitude* consists of the beliefs and knowledge one has about a situation.

    Examples: "I can't appoint Herschel because creative people don't make good administrators." "The tallest building in the world is in Chicago." Such expressions of the cognitive component reflect a person's perceptions, which differ among individuals and objectively may or may not be true. (The world's tallest building is in Kuala Lumpur, by the way.)

- **The behavioral component—"I intend":** The *behavioral component of an attitude*, also known as the *intentional component,* refers to how one intends or expects to behave toward a situation.

    Examples: "I intend to fill out my expense report tomorrow." "I'm going to turn over a new leaf at New Year's and stop eating junk food." "I'm going to try to avoid Al because he's a Democrat." "I'm never going to talk to George because he's a Republican."

All three components are often manifested at any given time. For example, if you call a corporation and get one of those telephone-tree menus ("For customer service, press 1 . . .") that never seems to connect you to a human being, you might be so irritated that you would say:

"I hate being given the run-around." [*affective component—your feelings*]

"That company doesn't know how to take care of customers. [*cognitive component—your perceptions*]

"I'll never call them again." [*behavioral component—your intentions*]

When Attitudes & Reality Collide: Consistency & Cognitive Dissonance

One of the last things you want, probably, is to be accused of hypocrisy—to be criticized for saying one thing and doing another. Like most people, you no doubt want to maintain consistency between your attitudes and your behavior.

But what if a strongly held attitude bumps up against a harsh reality that contradicts it? Suppose you're extremely concerned about getting AIDS, which you believe you might get from contact with body fluids, including blood. Then you're in a life-threatening auto accident in a third-world country and require surgery and blood transfusions—including transfusions of blood from (possibly AIDS-infected) strangers in a blood bank. Do you reject the blood to remain consistent with your beliefs about getting AIDS?

In 1957, social psychologist **Leon Festinger** proposed the term *cognitive dissonance* **to describe the psychological discomfort a person experiences between his or her cognitive attitude and incompatible behavior.**[11] Because people are uncomfortable with inconsistency, Festinger theorized, they will seek to reduce the "dissonance" or tension of the inconsistency. How they deal with the discomfort, he suggested, depends on three factors:

■ **Importance:** How important are the elements creating the dissonance? Most people can put up with some ambiguities in life. For example, many drivers don't think obeying speed limits is very important, even though they profess to be law-abiding citizens. People eat greasy foods even though they know that ultimately they may contribute to heart disease.

■ **Control:** How much control does one have over the matters that create dissonance? A juror may not like the idea of voting the death penalty but feel that he or she has no choice but to follow the law in the case. A taxpayer may object to his taxes being spent on, say, special-interest corporate welfare for a particular company but not feel he or she can withhold taxes.

■ **Rewards:** What rewards are at stake in the dissonance? You're apt to cling to old ideas in the face of new evidence if you have a lot invested emotionally or financially in those ideas. If you're a police officer who worked 20 years to prove a particular suspect guilty of murder, you're not apt to be very accepting of contradictory evidence after all that time.

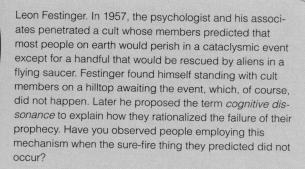

Leon Festinger. In 1957, the psychologist and his associates penetrated a cult whose members predicted that most people on earth would perish in a cataclysmic event except for a handful that would be rescued by aliens in a flying saucer. Festinger found himself standing with cult members on a hilltop awaiting the event, which, of course, did not happen. Later he proposed the term *cognitive dissonance* to explain how they rationalized the failure of their prophecy. Have you observed people employing this mechanism when the sure-fire thing they predicted did not occur?

Among the main ways to reduce cognitive dissonance are the following:

■ **Change your attitude and/or behavior:** This would seem to be the most obvious, even rational, response to take when confronted with cognitive dissonance.

Example: Gregory Withrow once belonged to the White Aryan Resistance and other racist groups. He preached hatred and bashed Japanese tourists in San Francisco. Then he met Sylvia, who rejected his white-supremacist ideas. As he grew to love her, he found himself caught between his ideas and her disapproval. To decrease this cognitive dissonance, he renounced his old racist beliefs and changed his behavior, even becoming a spokesperson for the anti-racist Anti-Defamation League.[12]

■ **Belittle the importance of the inconsistent behavior:** This happens all the time.

Example: All cigarette smokers are repeatedly exposed to information that smoking is hazardous to health. But many belittle the habit as not being as risky as the antismoking messages suggest. ("My grandmother smokes, and she's in her eighties.")

■ **Find consonant elements that outweigh the dissonant ones:** This, too, happens frequently.

Example: According to Sissela Bok, professor of ethics at Brandeis University and author of the book *Lying*, students may justify cheating on an exam by saying "I don't usually do this, but here I really have to do it."[13] Or they may feel everyone does it. As one graduate student said, students see cheating take place and "feel they have to. People get used to it, even though they know it's not right."[14]

This kind of rationalizing goes on quite often in organizations as well, when employees are confronted with ethical dilemmas but fear losing their jobs.

Behavior: How Values & Attitudes Affect People's Actions & Judgments

Values (global) and attitudes (specific) are generally in harmony, but not always. For example, a manager may put a positive *value* on helpful behavior (global) yet may have a negative *attitude* toward helping an unethical coworker (specific). Together, however, values and attitudes influence people's workplace **_behavior_—their actions and judgments.**

Example of How Values & Attitudes Affect Behavior: "If It Ain't Broke, Don't Fix It"?

As a manager, would you think most employees would agree that innovation is beneficial—that the original Silicon Valley technology firms prospered because they were constantly creating new products and services? Employees may have the *value*, then, that innovation is good—that it leads to productivity and profitability.

However, for a particularly successful product within your company, your employees might have the *attitude* that innovation is bad. If the product is so successful, they may say, why mess with it? In other words, "if it ain't broke, don't fix it."

All the while, of course, your competitors may be stealing a march, innovating improvements. As business consultant Ian Jacobsen points out, "One of the challenges of leadership is getting people to take action *before* a situation becomes a problem.[15]

major question

Is it important for managers to pay attention to employee attitudes?

The Big Picture

Attitudes are important because they affect behavior. Managers need to be alert to work-related attitudes having to do with job satisfaction, job involvement, and organizational commitment. Among the types of employee behavior they should attend to are their on-the-job performance and productivity as well as their absenteeism and turnover.

"Keep the employees happy."

It's true that attitudes are important, the reason being that *attitudes affect behavior*. But is keeping employees happy all that managers need to know to get results? We discuss motivation for performance in the next chapter. Here let us consider what managers need to know about work-related attitudes and behaviors.

Work-Related Attitudes: Job Satisfaction, Job Involvement, & Organizational Commitment

Employees will gripe about almost anything. About working in cubicles instead of offices. About not having enough help. About the mediocre cafeteria food. About managers "who don't know anything." They may also say some good things. About the great retirement plan. About flex time. About a product beating competing products. About how cool Manager X is.

Three types of attitudes managers are particularly interested in are (1) *job satisfaction*, (2) *job involvement*, and (3) *organizational commitment*.

1 Job Satisfaction: How Much Do You Like or Dislike Your Job? *Job satisfaction* **is the extent to which you feel positively or negatively about various aspects of your work.** Most people don't like everything about their jobs. Their overall satisfaction depends on how they feel about several components, such as *work, pay, promotions, coworkers,* and *supervision*.[16] Among the key correlates of job satisfaction are stronger motivation, job involvement, organizational commitment, and life satisfaction and less absenteeism, tardiness, turnover, and perceived stress.[17] Job performance seems to be positively correlated with job satisfaction.[18]

2 Job Involvement: How Much Do You Identify with Your Work? *Job involvement* **is the extent to which you identify or are personally involved with your job.** Many people, of course, work simply to put bread on the table; they have no interest in excelling at their jobs. More fortunate are those who actively participate in their jobs and consider their work performance important to their self-worth.

Analysis of nearly 28,000 individuals from 87 different studies demonstrates that job involvement is moderately correlated with job satisfaction.[19] Thus, managers are encouraged to foster satisfying work environments to fuel employees' job involvement.

3 Organizational Commitment *Organizational commitment* **reflects the extent to which an employee identifies with an organization and is committed to its goals.** Research shows a strong relationship between organizational commitment and job satisfaction.[20] Thus, managers are advised to increase job satisfaction to elicit higher levels of commitment. In turn, higher commitment can facilitate higher performance.[21]

Important Workplace Behaviors

Click-Along 11.1

A Third Important Workplace Behavior: Organizational Citizenship

Why, as a manager, do you need to learn how to manage individual differences? The answer, as you might expect, is so that you can influence employees to do their best work. Among the types of behavior are (1) performance and productivity and (2) absenteeism and turnover.

Evaluating Behavior When Employees Are Working: Performance & Productivity Every job has certain expectations, but in some jobs performance and productivity are easier to define than others. How many contacts should a telemarketing sales rep make in a day? How many sales should he or she close? Often a job of this nature will have a history of accomplishments (from what previous job holders have attained) so that it is possible to quantify performance behavior.

However, an advertising agency account executive handling major clients such as a car maker or a beverage manufacturer may go months before landing this kind of big account. Or a researcher in a pharmaceutical company may take years to develop a promising new prescription drug.

In short, the method of evaluating performance must match the job being done.

Evaluating Behavior When Employees Are Not Working: Absenteeism & Turnover Should you be suspicious of every instance of *absenteeism*—**when an employee doesn't show up for work?** Of course, some absences—illness, death in the family, or jury duty, for example—are legitimate. Such no-show behavior is to be expected from time to time, although it may be inconvenient. However, some excuses may be lies to cover hangovers, visits to the ballpark, or just low morale, although you may not be able to tell unless the individual is repeatedly absent.

You need to make allowances for the employee who is on call all the time, such as a computer network administrator who has to wear a pager and be responsible for keeping the network going in off-hours. Or for a lawyer who puts in evenings and weekends after office hours in order to prepare for trial. Such individuals may be given the flexibility to take "comp time" (compensatory time off) whenever their workload eases.

Absenteeism may be a precursor to *turnover*, **when employees leave their jobs.** Every organization experiences some turnover, as employees leave for reasons of family, better job prospects, or retirement. However, except in low-skill industries, a continual revolving door of new employees is usually not a good sign, since replacement and training is expensive. (One study found it costs nearly $108,000 to replace a key worker or manager.[22]) In such cases, you need to see what the causes of turnover are.

Performance monitors. These British Airways customer service reps are being monitored by software that keeps track not only of ticket sales and customer-complaint resolutions but also of amount of time spent on breaks and personal phone calls. In tracking employee effectiveness, the technology can count incentive dollars tied to performance and immediately direct them into their nearest paychecks. Do you think these incentive calculators are justified or do you think they intrude too much on employee privacy?

major question

In the hiring process, do employers care about one's personality and individual traits?

The Big Picture

Personality consists of stable psychological and behavioral attributes that give you your identity. We describe five personality dimensions and four personality traits that managers need to be aware of to understand workplace behavior.

How would you describe yourself? Are you outgoing? aggressive? sociable? tense? passive? lazy? quiet? Whatever the combination of traits, which result from the interaction of your genes and your environment, they constitute your personality.

More formally, **_personality_ consists of the stable psychological traits and behavioral attributes that give a person his or her identity.**[23] As a manager, you need to understand personality attributes because they affect how people perceive and act within the organization.

The Big Five Personality Dimensions

In recent years, the many personality dimensions have been distilled into a list of factors known as the Big Five.[24] The **_Big Five personality dimensions_ are (1) extroversion, (2) agreeableness, (3) conscientiousness, (4) emotional stability, and (5) openness to experience.**

- **Extroversion:** How outgoing, talkative, sociable, and assertive a person is.

- **Agreeableness:** How trusting, good-natured, cooperative, and soft-hearted one is.

- **Conscientiousness:** How dependable, responsible, achievement-oriented, and persistent one is.

- **Emotional stability:** How relaxed, secure, and unworried one is.

- **Openness to experience:** How intellectual, imaginative, curious, and broad-minded one is.

Standardized personality tests are used to score people on each dimension to draw a person's personality profile that is supposedly as unique as his or her fingerprints. For example, if you scored low on the first trait, extroversion, you would presumably be prone to shy and withdrawn behavior. If you scored low on emotional stability, you supposedly would be nervous, tense, angry, and worried.

Assertive and sociable. Does it take a certain kind of personality to be a good door-to-door salesperson? Have you ever known people who were quiet, unassuming, even shy but who were nevertheless very persistent and persuasive—that is, good salespeople?

Do Personality Tests Work for the Workplace? As a manager, you would want to know if the Big Five model in particular and personality testing in general can help predict behavior in the workplace. Is a personality test helpful in predicting a match between personality and job performance? Two findings:

■ **Extroversion—the outgoing personality:** As might be expected, extroversion (an outgoing personality) has been associated with success for managers and salespeople. Also, extroversion is a stronger predictor of job performance than agreeableness, across all professions, according to researchers. "It appears that being courteous, trusting, straightforward, and soft-hearted [that is, agreeableness] has a smaller impact on job performance," conclude the researchers, "than being talkative, active, and assertive [that is, extroversion]."[25]

■ **Conscientiousness—the dependable personality:** Conscientiousness (strong work ethic) has been found to have the strongest positive correlation with job performance and training performance. According to researchers, "those individuals who exhibit traits associated with a strong sense of purpose, obligation, and persistence generally perform better than those who do not."[26]

The box below presents tips to help managers avoid abuses and discrimination lawsuits when using personality and psychological testing for employment decisions.[27] *(See Panel 11.2.)*

Work ethic? This woman could be writing a letter about the wonderful time she's having on vacation. Or she could be using her own personal time off to take care of pressing business, such as replying to an important client. Do you see yourself as having this kind of conscientiousness?

PANEL 11.2
Cautions about using personality tests in the workplace

■ *Use professionals:* Rely on reputable, licensed psychologists for selecting and overseeing the administration, scoring, and interpretation of personality and psychological tests. This is particularly important, since not every psychologist is expert at these kinds of tests.

■ *Don't hire on the basis of personality test results alone:* Supplement any personality test data with information from reference checks, personal interviews, ability tests, and job performance records. Also avoid hiring people on the basis of specified personality profiles. As a case in point, there is no distinct "managerial personality."

■ *Be alert for gender, racial, and ethnic bias:* Regularly assess any possible adverse impact of personality tests on the hiring of women and minorities. This is truly a matter of great importance, since you don't want to find your company (or yourself) embroiled in a lawsuit at some point downstream.

■ *Graphology tests don't work, but integrity tests do:* Personality traits and aptitudes cannot be inferred from samples of people's penmanship, as proponents of graphology tests claim. However, dishonest job applicants can often be screened by integrity tests, since dishonest people are reportedly unable to fake conscientiousness, even on a paper-and-pencil test.

Four Traits Important in Organizations

Four of the most important personality traits that managers need to be aware of to understand workplace behavior are (1) *locus of control*, (2) *self-efficacy*, (3) *self-esteem*, and (4) *self-monitoring*.

1 Locus of Control: "I Am/Am Not the Captain of My Fate"   As we discussed briefly in Chapter 3, *locus of control* **indicates how much people believe they control their fate through their own efforts.** If you have an *internal locus of control*, you believe you control your own destiny. If you have an *external locus of control*, you believe external forces control you.

Research shows internals and externals have important workplace differences. Internals exhibit less anxiety, greater work motivation, and stronger expectations that effort leads to performance. They also obtain higher salaries.[28]

These findings have two important implications for managers:

■ **Different degrees of structure and compliance for each type:** Employees with internal locus of control will probably resist close managerial supervision. Hence, they should probably be placed in jobs requiring high initiative and lower compliance. By contrast, employees with external locus of control might do better in highly structured jobs requiring greater compliance.

■ **Different reward systems for each type:** Since internals seem to have a greater belief that their actions have a direct impact on the consequences of that action, internals likely would prefer and respond more productively to incentives such as merit pay or sales commissions. (We discuss incentive compensation systems in Chapter 12.)

2 Self-Efficacy: "I Can/Can't Do This Task"   A related trait is *self-efficacy*, **belief in one's personal ability to do a task.** Unlike locus of control, this isn't about how much the fates control events (as in believing whether getting a high grade in a course is determined by you or by outside factors, such as the grade curve or trick questions). Rather, it's about your personal belief that you have what it takes to succeed (such as if you study, you'll get a high grade).

Have you noticed that those who are confident about their ability tend to succeed, whereas those preoccupied with failure tend not to? Indeed, high expectations of self-efficacy have been linked with all kinds of positives: not only success in varied physical and mental tasks but also reduced anxiety and increased tolerance for pain.[29] One study found that the sales performance of life-insurance agents was much better among those with high self-efficacy.[30] Low self-efficacy is associated with *learned helplessness*, **the debilitating lack of faith in one's ability to control one's environment.**[31]

Among the implications for managers:

■ **Job assignments:** Complex, challenging, and autonomous jobs tend to enhance people's perceptions of their self-efficacy. Boring, tedious jobs generally do the opposite.

■ **Developing self-efficacy:** Self-efficacy is a quality that can be nurtured. Employees with low self-efficacy need lots of constructive pointers and positive feedback.[32] Goal difficulty needs to match individuals' perceived self-efficacy, but goals can be made more challenging as performance improves.[33] Small successes need to be rewarded. Employees' expectations can be improved through guided experiences, mentoring, and role modeling.[34]

Closing the deal. What personality traits should successful sales managers possess and how likely are they to hire salespeople with these same traits? Why?

3 Self-Esteem: "I Like/Dislike Myself" How worthwhile, capable, and acceptable do you think you are? The answer to this question is an indicator of your _self-esteem_, **the extent to which people like or dislike themselves.**[35] Of interest to managers is a variant called _organization-based self-esteem (OBSE),_ defined as the "self-perceived value that individuals have of themselves as organization members acting within an organizational context."[36] Those scoring high on OBSE tend to view themselves as important, worthwhile, effectual, and meaningful within their organization.

Among the implications for managers are the following:

- **Enhancement of OBSE can produce greater task innovation:** Organization-based self-esteem tends to increase when employees believe their supervisors have a genuine concern for employees' welfare. Flexible, organic organization structures generate higher OBSE than do rigid bureaucratic structures. Complex, challenging jobs foster higher OBSE than do simple, repetitive, boring jobs. These same factors also are associated with greater task innovation.[37]

- **Self-esteem can be improved:** According to one study, "Low self-esteem can be raised more by having the person think of _desirable_ characteristics _possessed_ rather than of undesirable characteristics from which he or she is free."[38]

   Among ways you as a manager can build employee self-esteem: (1) Be supportive by showing concern for employee problems, interests, status, and contributions. (2) Offer work involving variety, autonomy, and challenges that suit the employee's values, skills, and abilities. (3) Strive for management-employee cohesiveness and build trust. (4) Have faith in each employee's self-management ability, and reward successes.[39]

4 Self-Monitoring: "I'm Fairly Able/Unable to Adapt My Behavior to Others" As you're rushing to an important meeting, you are stopped by a coworker, who starts to discuss a personal problem. You need to break away, so you glance at your watch.

(a) Does your coworker Get It? Seeing you look at your watch, he says, "Sorry, I see you're busy. Catch you later." Or (b) does he Not Get It? He keeps talking, until you say "I'm late for a big meeting" and start walking away.

The two scenarios show the difference between a high self-monitor and a low self-monitor. _Self-monitoring_ **is the extent to which people are able to observe their own behavior and adapt it to external situations.** Of course, we would all like to think we are high in self-monitoring—able to regulate our "expressive self-presentation for the sake of desired public appearances," as some experts write, "and thus be highly responsive to social and interpersonal cues" of others.[40] But whereas some high self-monitors are criticized for being chameleons, always able to adapt their self-presentation to their surroundings, low self-monitors are often criticized for being on their own planet and insensitive to others. Instead, their behavior may reflect their own inner states, including their attitudes and feelings.

It might be expected that people in top management are more apt to be high self-monitors able to play different roles—even contradictory roles—to suit different situations. Research shows a positive relationship between high self-monitoring and career success. Among 139 MBA graduates who were tracked for five years, high self-monitors enjoyed more internal and external promotions than did their low self-monitoring classmates.[41] Other research has found that managerial success (in terms of speed of promotions) was tied to political savvy (knowing how to socialize, network, and engage in organizational politics).[42]

Adapting to others. Successful managers are apt to be high self-monitors, able to observe their own behavior in relation to others and to adapt it to the environments in which they find themselves. Probably, like most people, you think you're a high self-monitor. Are you really?

major question

What are the distortions in perception that can cloud one's judgment?

The Big Picture

Perception, a four-step process, can be skewed by three types of distortion: selective perception, stereotyping, and the halo effect. We also consider the self-fulfilling prophecy and causal attribution, which can affect our judgment.

Marilyn Merlot. Would you be apt to notice—to perceive—this bottle among all the others on a wine-shop shelf? The idea grew out of a home winemaking operation near St. Helena, Calif. The first production, in 1983, under the brand name "Maneater," was a wine labeled "Cannibal Sauvignon." As for the merlot ("mer-*loh*") red wine, what began as a light-hearted appeal to Marilyn Monroe fans is now seriously sought out by wine fanciers.

Which envelope would you most likely respond to? One with a bright yellow circle (like a happy-face button) enclosing white letters that say, "Count me in!" Or one with a black-bordered rectangle surrounding bold, black letters warning, "YOUR RESPONSE IS REQUIRED BY LAW."

That was a decision the U.S. Census Bureau was wrestling with, before making its year 2000 population count, to try to improve the response rate to mailed census forms (whose return rate had declined to 65% in 1990).[43] The bureau, in other words, was trying to decide how *perception* would influence behavior.

The Four Steps in the Perceptual Process

<u>*Perception*</u> is the process of interpreting and understanding one's environment. The process of perception is complex, but it can be boiled down to four steps. *(See Panel 11.3.)*

In this book, we are less concerned about the theoretical steps in perception than in how perception is distorted, since this has considerable bearing on the manager's judgment and job. In any one of the four stages of the perception process there is the possibility for misunderstandings or errors in judgment. Perceptual errors can lead to mistakes that can be damaging to yourself, other people, and your organization.

Click-Along 11.2

More about the Four Steps in the Perceptual Process

PANEL 11.3   The four steps in the perceptual process

1. Selective attention "Did I notice something?"	2. Interpretation & evaluation "What was it I noticed & what does it mean?"	3. Storing in memory "Remember it as an event, concept, person, or all three?"	4. Retrieving from memory to make judgments & decisions "What do I recall about that?"

Three Distortions in Perception

Although there are other types of distortion in perception, we will describe the following: (1) *selective perception*, (2) *stereotyping*, and (3) the *halo effect*.

1 Selective Perception: "I Don't Want to Hear about That"   Are there topics that you find especially uncomfortable—your own death, say, or child molestation, or cheating in college—so that you tune out these subjects when people bring them up? For example, many people avoid making a will because they find it too awful to think about their future nonexistence. *Selective perception* **is the tendency to filter out information that is discomforting, that seems irrelevant, or that contradicts one's beliefs.**

One 1958 study found that when executives were asked to determine the key problem in a complex business case, they identified the problem as falling within their particular functional areas of work—they evidently filtered out information about other areas. That is, human resource managers said the principal problem was a people issue, marketing executives said it was a sales issue, and production people said it was a manufacturing issue.[44] This shows how managers can distort problem solving through selective perception.

2 Stereotyping: "Those Sorts of People Are Pretty Much the Same"   If you're a tall black man, do people make remarks about basketball players? If you're of Irish descent, do people believe you drink a lot? If you're Jewish, do people think you're money-oriented? If you're a woman, do people think you're automatically nurturing? All these are stereotypes. *Stereotyping* **is the tendency to attribute to an individual the characteristics one believes are typical of the group to which that individual belongs.**

Female executive. Women make up 46% of the workforce, but among the Fortune 1000 companies—the nation's largest companies—only 11 are headed by female CEOs. The percentage of females holding board seats in Fortune 500 companies is only 12.4%. Avon CEO Andrea Jung made $7.7 million in 2001, making her the highest-paid female chief executive, but that "seems paltry beside Douglas Daft's $55 million bonanza from Coca-Cola," notes *U.S. News & World Report*. Between 1995 and 2000, female managers in seven of the 10 leading industries that employ 71% of women actually saw the wage gap widen; for example, in 1995, a woman in communications management made 86 cents for every dollar earned by a male manager, but by 2000 she made only 73 cents. Still, there is some good news. The number of women-owned companies grew 15% in the years 1997–2002, twice as fast as all firms. Women now own 26% of the 21 million companies in the United States; although most are tiny ventures, about 100,000 have $1 million or more in annual revenue, according to the Census Bureau.

Principal areas of stereotyping that should be of concern to you as a manager are (1) *sex-role stereotypes*, (2) *age stereotypes*, and (3) *race stereotypes*.

■ **Sex-role stereotypes:** A *sex-role stereotype* is the belief that differing traits and abilities make males and females particularly well suited to different roles.

A classic 1972 study found that women were viewed "as relatively less competent, less independent, less objective, and less logical then men; men are perceived as lacking interpersonal sensitivity, warmth, and expressiveness in comparison to women." Moreover, the study found, "stereotypically masculine traits are more often perceived to be desirable than are stereotypically feminine characteristics."[45]

Although research shows that men and women do not differ in such a stereotypical manner, the stereotypes still persist.[46] And, unfortunately, promotional decisions may still be affected by sex-role stereotyping. A study of a multinational Fortune 500 company, for example, revealed that men received more favorable evaluations than women in spite of controlling for age, education, organizational tenure, salary grade, and type of job.[47]

■ **Age stereotypes:** *Age stereotypes* tend to depict older workers as less involved in their work, less satisfied, less motivated, and less committed than younger workers. But in fact research shows that as employees' age increases, so does their job involvement and satisfaction, work motivation, and organizational commitment.[48]

Stereotypes also depict older workers as being less productive; however, this is not borne out.[49] Finally, the stereotype that older workers have higher absenteeism is not supported by the research; if anything, managers should focus more attention on absenteeism among younger rather than older workers.[50]

■ **Race stereotypes:** *Race stereotypes* don't bear repeating here, but it is noteworthy that there are not a lot of African-American, Hispanic, and Asian managers in the United States. For instance, the Labor Department estimates that women and minorities hold only 5% of senior-level positions—and the majority of those are held by women rather than minorities.[51]

Women's work? Is Wall Street a place where women can find equal opportunity in business? Not according to Nancy Thomas, shown here handing out leaflets protesting unfair hiring, pay, and promotion practices for females at Merrill Lynch. The financial services industry, of course, is not the only area with sexual discrimination. What kinds of businesses do you think are the worst offenders? Which are relatively enlightened?

3 The Halo Effect: "One Trait Tells Me All I Need to Know"

Do you think physically attractive people have more desirable traits than unattractive people—that they are happier, kinder, more successful, more socially skilled, more sensitive, more interesting, independent, exciting, sexually warm, even smarter and nicer? All of these traits have been attributed to attractive people.[52] This situation is an example of the _halo effect_, **in which we form an impression of an individual based on a single trait.** (The phenomenon is also called the _horn-and-halo effect_, because not only can a single positive trait be generalized into an array of positive traits but the reverse is also true.)

As if we needed additional proof that life is unfair, it has been shown that attractive people generally are treated better than unattractive people. Teachers have higher expectations of them in terms of academic achievement.[53] Potential employers are more apt to view them favorably.[54] Attractive employees are generally paid higher salaries than unattractive ones are.[55] Clearly, however, if a manager fails to look at all an individual's traits, he or she has no right to complain if that employee doesn't work out.

The Self-Fulfilling Prophecy, or Pygmalion Effect

The _self-fulfilling prophecy_, **also known as the** _Pygmalion_ (pig-_mail_-yun) _effect_, **describes the phenomenon in which people's expectations of themselves or others leads them to behave in ways that make those expectations come true.**

Expectations are important. An example is a waiter who expects some poorly dressed customers to be stingy tippers, who therefore gives them poor service and so gets the result he or she expected—a much lower tip than usual. Research has shown that by raising managers' expectations for individuals performing a wide variety of tasks, higher levels of achievement and productivity can be achieved.[56] The lesson for you as a manager is that when you expect employees to perform badly, they probably will, and when you expect them to perform well, they probably will. (In the G. B. Shaw play _Pygmalion_, a speech coach bets he can get a lower-class girl to change her accent so that she can pass herself off as a duchess. In six months, she successfully "passes" in high society, having become a woman of sensitivity and taste.)

Handsomely compensated. Attractive employees are generally paid better than unattractive ones are. Why do you think that is? Do you think it's inevitable?

practical action

How Can Managers Harness the Pygmalion Effect to Lead Employees?

Does the self-fulfilling prophecy really work?

At Microsoft Corp., employees routinely put in 75-hour weeks, especially when trying to meet shipping deadlines for new products. Because Microsoft prides itself on trying to meet its deadlines, positive group-level expectations help create and reinforce an organizational culture of high expectancy for success. This process then excites people about working for the organization, thereby reducing turnover.[57]

This shows the Pygmalion effect at work—that is, managerial expectations powerfully influence employee behavior and performance. Managers can harness this effect by building a hierarchical framework that reinforces

positive performance expectations throughout the organization. The foundation of this framework is employee self-expectations. In turn, positive self-expectations improve interpersonal expectations by encouraging people to work toward common goals. This cooperation enhances group-level productivity and promotes positive performance expectations within the work group.

How to Create a Pygmalion Effect

Because positive self-expectations are the foundation for creating an organizationwide Pygmalion effect, let us consider how managers can create positive performance expectations. This task may be accomplished using various combinations of the following: _(continued)_

1. Recognize that everyone has the potential to increase his or her performance.
2. Instill confidence in your staff.
3. Set high performance goals.
4. Positively reinforce employees for a job well done.
5. Provide constructive feedback when necessary.
6. Help employees advance through the organization.
7. Introduce new employees as if they have outstanding potential.
8. Become aware of your personal prejudices and non-verbal messages that may discourage others.
9. Encourage employees to visualize the successful execution of tasks.
10. Help employees master key skills and tasks.[58]

Causal Attributions

___Causal attribution___ **is the activity of inferring causes for observed behavior.** Rightly or wrongly, we constantly formulate cause-and-effect explanations for our own and others' behavior. Attributional statements such as the following are common: "Joe drinks too much because has no willpower; but I need a few drinks after work because I'm under a lot of pressure."

Even though our causal attributions tend to be self-serving and are often invalid, it's important to understand how people formulate attributions because they profoundly affect organizational behavior. For example, a supervisor who attributes an employee's poor performance to a lack of effort might reprimand that person. However, training might be deemed necessary if the supervisor attributes the poor performance to a low skill level.

Why are these people drinking? People tend to equate drinking with relaxation, good times, and fellowship. But some people drink to ease pain and problems. If the people shown here drink more than a couple of drinks, is that necessarily bad, in your opinion? (You should be aware that *binge drinking* is defined as consuming five, for men, or four, for women, or more drinks in a row one or more times in a two-week period.) No doubt you will come up with some explanation—some cause-and-effect reason—as to why particular people drink too much after work. Maybe, you may think, it's because they have no willpower. As for yourself, you may think you need "a few drinks to wind down" at the end of the day because you have such a high-pressure job and need to find some relief. Inferring causes for observed behavior, whether correct or not, is known as causal attribution. We all do it, but it's important to know how it works.

One model of attribution (Kelley's model) proposes that people make causal attributions after they gather information about three dimensions of behavior: *consensus, consistency,* and *distinctiveness.*[59]

- **Consensus—"How does Joe's present behavior compare with others'?"** In *consensus*, you compare an individual's behavior with that of his or her peers. You look to see how much other people in the same situation behave the same way.

   Example: As a restaurant manager on duty during an extremely busy Saturday night, you receive three complaints from customers that Joe, a long-time waiter, was rude to them. There were no complaints about other wait-staffers. (Thus, Joe's behavior had *low consensus* because it varied a lot from the others' performance.)

- **Consistency—"How does Joe's present behavior compare with his past behavior?"** In *consistency*, you look to see whether an individual behaves the same way at different times.

   Example: You might recall that Joe often becomes tense and surly during busy evenings. During the 5 years that you've been his supervisor, his manner has provoked a customer complaint or two on those occasions. (Thus, Joe's performance has *high consistency* because he performs the task the same way time after time.)

- **Distinctiveness—"How does Joe's present behavior compare with his behavior in other situations?"** In *distinctiveness*, you look to see whether an individual behaves the same way in other situations.

   Example: Is Joe sometimes surly and rude when the restaurant is not busy? Or when you're catering special events, such as weddings? Or when he's asked to vacuum the restaurant before it opens? Alas, it does seem to be the case. (Thus, Joe's performance has *low distinctiveness* because he performs the same way on other tasks and under other conditions.)

It's been suggested that people attribute behavior to *personal factors* when they perceive low consensus, high consistency, and low distinctiveness (as with Joe). They attribute behavior to *environmental factors* when they perceive high consensus, low consistency, and high distinctiveness.

As a manager, you need to be alert to two attributional tendencies that can distort one's interpretation of observed behavior—the *fundamental attribution bias* and the *self-serving bias*.

- **Fundamental attribution bias:** In the **_fundamental attribution_ bias, people attribute another person's behavior to his or her personal characteristics rather than to situational factors.**

   Example: A study of manufacturing employees found that top managers attributed the cause of industrial back pain to individuals, whereas workers attributed it to the environment.[60]

- **Self-serving bias:** In the **_self-serving bias_, people tend to take more personal responsibility for success than for failure.**

   Example: The way students typically analyze their performance on exams shows self-serving bias, with "A" students likely to

Is this waiter often surly? As his manager, you might use three kinds of clues—consensus, consistency, and distinctiveness—to make this kind of judgment.

attribute their grade to high ability or hard work and "D" students blaming factors such as bad luck, unclear lectures, and unfair testing.[61]

major question

What causes workplace stress, and how can it be reduced?

The Big Picture
Stress is what people feel when enduring extraordinary demands or opportunities and are not sure how to handle them. Sources of stress are five demands: individual task, individual role, group, organizational, and nonwork. We describe three consequences of stress and three ways to reduce it in the organization.

Although most workers are satisfied with their jobs, 24% say their work is "very stressful," and 43% say it is "moderately stressful."[62] A study by one health plan of 46,000 people working for six large employers found that the employers paid nearly 8% a year of total health care for treatment of what employees characterized as out-of-control stress. Such workers, who suffered from a variety of stress-related illnesses, such as migraines, back pain, and gastrointestinal disorders, had 46% higher health costs.[63]

Work stress can also, as you might guess, put managers at risk. Researchers who interviewed 800 hospital heart-attack patients over a five-year period found that managers run twice the normal risk of heart attack the week after they have had to fire someone or face a high-pressure deadline.[64]

Trading frenzy. Many jobs are stressful, but some are more stressful than others, such as those of traders on the floor of the New York Stock Exchange. What occupations do you think are the most stress-inducing?

What Is Stress?

Stress is the tension people feel when they are facing or enduring extraordinary demands, constraints, or opportunities and are uncertain about their ability to handle them effectively.[65] Stress is the feeling of tension and pressure; the source of stress is called a _stressor_.

Stress has both physical and emotional components. Physically, according to Canadian researcher Hans Selye, considered the father of the modern concept of stress, stress is "the nonspecific response of the body to any demand made upon it."[66] Emotionally, stress has been defined as the feeling of being overwhelmed, "the perception that events or circumstances have challenged, or exceeded, a person's ability to cope."[67]

Stressors can be _hassles_, or simple irritants, such as misplacing or losing things, concerns about one's physical appearance, and having too many things to do.[68] Or they can be _crises_, such as sudden occasions of overwhelming terror—a horrible auto accident, an incident of childhood abuse. Or they can be _strong stressors_, which can dramatically strain a person's ability to adapt—extreme physical discomfort, such as chronic severe back pain.

Stressors can be both _negative and positive_. Selye writes: "It is immaterial whether the agent or situation we face is pleasant or unpleasant; all that counts is the intensity of the demand for adjustment and adaptation."[69]

The Sources of Job-Related Stress: Individual Tasks & Roles, Groups, Organizations, & Nonwork Factors

There are five sources of stress on the job: *individual tasks, individual roles, groups, organizations*, and *nonwork factors*. *(See Panel 11.4.)*

PANEL 11.4
Five sources of stress

1 Individual Task Demands: The Stress Created by the Job Itself Some occupations are more stressful than others. Directing a play is more stressful than selling tickets. Doing brain surgery is more stressful than processing medical claims. Managing employees is more stressful than being a receptionist (usually).

Nevertheless, low-level jobs can be more stressful than high-level jobs because employees often have less control over their lives and thus have less work satisfaction. Being a high-speed word processor or doing telemarketing phone sales, for instance, can be quite stressful.

There is also considerable stress caused by worries over the prospective loss of a job. Recent surveys indicate that employees frequently worry about being laid off.[70] Job security is an important stressor to manage because it can result in reduced job satisfaction, organizational commitment, and performance.[71]

2 Individual Role Demands: The Stress Created by Others' Expectations of You *Roles* are sets of behaviors that people expect of occupants of a position.[72] Stress may come about because of *role overload, role conflict*, and *role ambiguity*.

Individual task demands: stress created by the job itself

Individual role demands: role overload, conflict, & ambiguity

Group demands: stress created by coworkers & managers

STRESS!

Organizational demands: stress created by the environment & culture

Nonwork demands: Stresses created by forces outside the organization

Some days. . . You will probably never be able to completely escape stress. The real question is: How are you going to handle it?

■ **Role overload:** Role overload occurs when others' expectations exceed one's ability.

Example: If you as a student are carrying a full course load plus working two-thirds time plus trying to have a social life, you know what role overload is—and what stress is. Similar things happen to managers and workers.

■ **Role conflict:** Role conflict occurs when one feels torn by the different expectations of important people in one's life.

Example: Your supervisor says the company needs you to stay late to meet an important deadline, but your family expects you to be present for your child's birthday party.

■ **Role ambiguity:** Role ambiguity occurs when others' expectations are unknown.

Example: You find your job description and the criteria for promotion vague, a complaint often voiced by newcomers to an organization.

3 Group Demands: The Stress Created by Coworkers & Managers Even if you don't particularly care for the work you do but like the people you work with, that can be a great source of satisfaction and prevent stress. When people don't get along, that can be a great stressor.

In addition, managers can create stress for employees in a number of ways: Exhibiting inconsistent behaviors. Failing to provide support. Showing lack of concern. Providing inadequate direction. Creating a demanding, high-productivity environment. Focusing on negatives while ignoring good performance.[73] People who have bad managers are five times more likely to have stress-induced headaches, upset stomachs, and loss of sleep.[74]

Lunch time. Do you think being a deli worker during a hectic lunch hour would be more or less stressful than being a high-powered manager in a white-collar job with hundreds of employees reporting to you?

4 Organizational Demands: The Stress Created by the Environment & Culture The physical environments of some jobs are great sources of stress: poultry processing, asbestos removal, coal mining, fire fighting, police work, ambulance driving, and so on. Even white-collar work can take place in a stressful environment, with poor lighting, too much noise, improper placement of furniture, and no privacy.[75] An organizational culture that promotes high-pressure work demands on employees will fuel the stress response.[76] Research shows preliminary support for the idea that organizational stress can be reduced by participatory management.[77]

5 Nonwork Demands: The Stresses Created by Forces Outside the Organization As anyone knows who has had to cope with money problems, divorce, support of elderly relatives, or other serious nonwork concerns, the stresses outside one's work life can have a significant effect on work. And people with lower incomes, education level, and work status are particularly apt to have higher stress.[78] But even people with ordinary lives can find the stress of coping with family life rugged going.

Click-Along 11.3

Example of Nonwork Demands: Two-Income Families Battle for a Balanced Life

The Consequences of Stress

Positive stress is constructive and can energize you, increasing your effort, creativity, and performance. Negative stress is destructive, resulting in poorer-quality work, dissatisfaction, errors, absenteeism, and turnover.

Negative stress reveals itself in three kinds of symptoms:

■ **Physiological signs:** Lesser physiological signs are sweaty palms, restlessness, backaches, headaches, upset stomach, and nausea. More serious signs are hypertension and heart attacks.

■ **Psychological signs:** Psychological symptoms include boredom, irritability, nervousness, anger, anxiety, hostility, and depression.

■ **Behavioral signs:** Symptoms include sleeplessness, changes in eating habits, and increased smoking/alcohol/drug abuse. Stress may be revealed through reduced performance and job satisfaction.

De-stressing. Experts say exercise can be a tremendous stress reliever. Wonder whether this corporate physical-fitness center found a lot of use? The photo was taken at the headquarters of Houston energy trader Enron—after the firm filed for bankruptcy protection and laid off thousands of employees.

Over time, stress may lead to **_burnout_, or a state of emotional, mental, and even physical exhaustion,** expressed as listlessness, indifference, or frustration Clearly, the greatest consequence of negative stress for the organization is reduced productivity. Overstressed employees are apt to call in sick, miss deadlines, take longer lunch breaks, and show indifference to performance. However, some may put in great numbers of hours at work without getting as much accomplished as previously. Mental health experts estimate that 10% of the workforce suffers from depression or high levels of stress that may ultimately affect job performance.[79] In addition, researchers estimate that in a recent year stress caused 11% of all cases of employee absenteeism.[80]

Click-Along 11.4

Ten Signs of Burnout

Reducing Stressors in the Organization

There are all kinds of **_buffers_, or administrative changes, that managers can make to reduce the stressors that lead to employee burnout.** Examples: Extra staff or equipment at peak periods. Increased freedom to make decisions. Recognition for accomplishments. Time off for rest or personal development. Assignment to a new position.[81] Three- to five-day employee retreats at offsite locations for relaxation and team-building activities. Sabbatical leave programs to replenish employees' energy and desire to work.[82]

Some general organizational strategies for reducing unhealthy stressors are the following:[83]

Click-Along 11.5

Taking Something Practical Away from This Chapter: How to Reduce Stress

- ■ **Create a supportive organizational climate:** Job stress often results because organizations have evolved into large, informal, and inflexible bureaucracies. Wherever possible, it's better to try to keep the organizational environment less formal, more impersonal, and more supportive of employees.

- ■ **Make jobs interesting:** Stress also results when jobs are routinized and boring. Better to try to structure jobs so that they allow employees some freedom.

- ■ **Make career counseling available:** Companies such as IBM make career planning available, which reduces the stress that comes when employees don't know what their career options are and where they're headed.

Key Terms Used In This Chapter

Summary

11.1
Values, Attitudes, & Behavior

■ Organizational behavior (OB) is dedicated to better understanding and managing people at work. OB looks at two areas: individual behavior (discussed in this chapter) and group behavior (discussed in later chapters).

■ Values must be distinguished from attitudes and from behavior.

(1) Values are abstract ideals that guide one's thinking and behavior across all situations.

(2) Attitudes are defined as learned predisposition toward a given object. Attitudes have three components. The affective component consists of the feelings or emotions one has about a situation. The cognitive component consists of the beliefs and knowledge one has about a situation. The behavioral component, or intentional component, refers to how one intends or expects to behave toward a situation. When attitudes and reality collide, the result may be cognitive dissonance, the psychological discomfort a person experiences between his or her cognitive attitude and incompatible behavior. Cognitive dissonance depends on three factors: importance, control, and rewards. The ways to reduce cognitive

dissonance are to change your attitude and/or your behavior, belittle the importance of the inconsistent behavior, or find consonant elements that outweigh the dissonant ones.

(3) Together, values and attitudes influence people's workplace behavior—their actions and judgments.

11.2
Work-Related Attitudes & Behaviors Managers Need to Deal With

■ Attitudes are important because they affect behavior. Managers need to be alert to work-related attitudes having to do with job satisfaction, job involvement, and organizational commitment. (1) Job satisfaction is the extent to which you feel positively or negatively about various aspects of your work. (2) Job involvement is the extent to which you identify or are personally involved with your job. (3) Organizational commitment reflects the extent to which an employee identifies with an organization and is committed to its goals.

■ Among the types of behavior that managers need to influence are (1) performance and productivity and (2) absenteeism, when an employee doesn't show up for work, and turnover, when employees leave their jobs.

11.3
Personality & Individual Behavior

■ Personality consists of the stable psychological traits and behavioral attributes that give a person his or her identity. There are five personality dimensions and four personality traits that managers need to be aware of to understand workplace behavior.

■ The Big Five personality dimensions are extroversion, agreeableness, conscientiousness, emotional stability, and openness to experience. Extroversion, an outgoing personality, is associated with success for managers and salespeople. Conscientiousness, or a dependable personality, is correlated with successful job performance.

■ There are four personality traits that managers need to be aware of in order to understand workplace behavior. (1) Locus of control indicates how much people believe they control their fate through their own efforts. (2) Self-efficacy is the belief in one's personal ability to do a task. Low self-efficacy is associated with learned helplessness, the debilitating lack of faith in one's ability to control one's environment. (3) Self-esteem is the extent to which people like or dislike themselves. (4) Self-monitoring is the extent to which people are able to observe their own behavior and adapt it to external situations.

11.4
Perception & Individual Behavior

■ Perception is the process of interpreting and understanding one's environment. The process can be boiled down to four steps: selective attention, interpretation and evaluation, storing in memory, and retrieving from memory to make judgments and decisions. Perceptual errors can lead to mistakes that affect management.

■ Three types of distortion in perception are selective perception, stereotyping, and the halo effect. (1) Selective perception is the tendency to filter out information that is discomforting, that seems irrelevant, or that contradicts one's beliefs. (2) Stereotyping is the tendency to attribute to an individual the characteristics one believes are typical of the group to which that individual belongs. Principal areas of stereotyping that should be of concern are sex-role, age, and race stereotypes. (3) The halo effect

is the name for when we form an impression of an individual based on a single trait.

■ The self-fulfilling prophecy, also known as the Pygmalion effect, describes the phenomenon in which people's expectations of themselves or others leads them to behave in ways that make those expectations come true.

■ Causal attribution is the activity of inferring causes for observed behavior, which may be correct or incorrect. People may make causal attributions after they gather information about three dimensions of behavior: consensus, in which you compare a person's behavior with peer behavior; consistency, in which you look to see if a person behaves the same way at different times; and distinctiveness, in which you look to see if a person behaves the same way in other situations.

■ As a manager, you need to be alert to two attributional tendencies that can distort your interpretation of observed behavior. (1) In the fundamental attribution bias, people attribute another person's behavior to his or her personal characteristics rather than to situational factors. (2) In the self-serving bias, people tend to take more personal responsibility for success than for failure.

11.5
Understanding Stress & Individual Behavior

■ Stress is the tension people feel when they are facing or enduring extraordinary demands, constraints, or opportunities and are uncertain about their ability to handle them effectively. Stress is the feeling of tension and pressure; the source of stress is called a stressor.

■ There are five sources of stress on the job: individual tasks, individual roles, groups, organizations, and nonwork factors. (1) Individual task demands are the stresses created by the job itself. (2) Individual role demands are the stresses created by other people's expectations of you. Roles are sets of behaviors that people expect of occupants of a position. Stress may come about because of role overload, role conflict, or role ambiguity. (3) Group demands are the stresses created by coworkers and managers. (4) Organizational demands are the stresses created by the environment and culture of the organization. (5) Nonwork demands are the stresses created by forces outside the organization, such as money problems or divorce.

- Positive stress can be constructive. Negative stress can result in poor-quality work; such stress is revealed through physiological, psychological, or behavioral signs such as burnout, a state of emotional, mental, and even physical exhaustion.

- There are buffers, or administrative changes, that managers can make to reduce the stressors that lead to employee burnout, such as adding extra staff or giving employees more power to make decisions. Some general organizational strategies for reducing unhealthy stressors are to create a supportive organizational climate, make jobs interesting, and make career counseling available.

Management in Action

Having Friends at Work

From Sue Shellenbarger, "Along with Benefits and Pay, Employees Seek Friends on the Job,"
The Wall Street Journal, *February 20, 2002, p. B1.*

Like hundreds of thousands of U.S. workers, a friend, an administrative manager for a New York brokerage firm, has just gone through a corporate reorganization. Now, she's trying to figure out how to regain something she lost.

She kept her job, paycheck, benefits, and title when her company moved her function to a different department. That's not the problem.

What's missing, she says, is her old network of friends. Over several years, the office mates and field reps she worked with shared a wealth of memories and experiences, from the fun of rafting trips to the fear of being stranded together on September 11 [when terrorists struck the Pentagon and New York's World Trade Center] at an off-site meeting halfway across the continent. "It works like families," she says of the closeness.

Now, she is feeling sadness. "You lose people who know who you are when you let your hair down, when you're not putting on a business face," my friend says. She expects her output to drop—not because she's not trying, but because she doesn't know her new coworkers well enough to push them for extra help. It takes at least a year to develop such bonds, she says. . . .

The value of human connections at work was underscored by the harrowing workplace stories of September 11. Just weeks later, a random national survey of 1,000 workers by Aon Consulting's Loyalty Institute, Ann Arbor, Mich., found employees' commitment, or desire to stay with the same employer, had rocketed to a five-year high from a five-year low in March 2001. The third most powerful factor driving that commitment is workers' sense of affiliation, or connectedness on the job, Aon says, behind safety and security, and pay and perks. . . .

While friendships don't appear on balance sheets, they're showing up in research on the underpinnings of productivity. In 28 studies of a total of more than 105,000 employees, the Gallup Organization found that, surprisingly, "having a best friend at work" was one of the 13 employee circumstances most likely to signal a highly productive workplace—right up there with "knowing what's expected of me" and "having the materials and equipment I need." . . .

More important, these workplace ties have human value. People by nature crave deep bonds with others near them, a yen rooted in the tribal communities of our ancestors, says Kent Bailey, a professor emeritus of psychology at Virginia Commonwealth University, Richmond, Va.

Today, by necessity, more people forge these bonds with nonrelatives, says Dr. Bailey, co-author with Susan Ahern of a book on the topic, *Family-by-Choice.* As people spend more time at work, more find these "psychological kin" there. . . .

If you're trying to keep a coworker network alive, don't assume you can do it by e-mail, Ms. Ahern cautions. To find time to meet, she recommends keeping a time log for a week, to see whether there are some activities you could toss, such as TV-watching, in favor of friends. It's worth it, she adds. Such bonds are as important to mental health as exercise is to physical health. They're one way of infusing life with meaning.

For Discussion

1. How does knowing whether one of your employees has a close friend at work help you understand that person as a worker?

2. Which important workplace behaviors would having a best friend at work affect?

3. Do you think having office friends reflects any of the Big Five personality dimensions?

4. Does this case suggest ways to boost OBSE?

5. If you know what the personality of the best friend of one of your long-time employees is, will that tell you anything of work-related importance about your employee?

Take It to the Net

In this chapter we discussed a variety of individual differences that affect employee attitudes and behavior. The Big Five Personality characteristics are one example. Recall that the Big Five—extroversion, agreeableness, conscientiousness, emotional stability, and openness to experience—represent the dominant approach for classifying personality. The purpose of this exercise is to expand your understanding regarding your personality by having you complete a survey assessing the Big Five.

Go to *http://www.outofservice.com/bigfive*. There are 52 questions and the quiz should take approximately 5–10 minutes. Use the given scale of 1–7 to indicate how closely you identify with each statement. Once you have completed the assessment, submit your answers and feel free to print out the results.

Your results reveal the extent to which you display the various Big Five Personality dimensions. The reported percentile score shows you relative to the Big Five score of other people who took the test online—that is, the percentage of people who scored less than you did on each dimension. For example, if your Extroversion percentile is 25, it indicates 25% of the people who took the test online are less extroverted than you, meaning you are rather introverted.

Questions for Discussion

1. To what extent do you agree with the assessment? Explain.

2. How do you think your personality may affect your career? Explain.

Self-Assessment

What Is My Emotional Intelligence Score?*

Objectives

1. To help you assess your emotional intelligence.

2. To expand your knowledge of the new interpretations of intelligence.

Introduction: Employers have long been guided by one dimension of our personality, our intelligence quotient (IQ). However, a number of researchers and observers of human behavior have been examining components of intelligence that include emotions. Your Emotional Intelligence (EI) includes your abilities to motivate yourself and persist even when you are frustrated, to control your impulses and delay gratification, to regulate your mood and keep distress from overwhelming your thinking ability, to empathize with others, and to hope. The recognition of the emotional dimension to intelligence is vital today in a world of constant change and increased stress. Having a sense of your own EI is fundamental to being successful. The purpose of this exercise is to determine your own EI.

Instructions: Use this scale to indicate the extent to which you agree or disagree with each statement below:

    1 = strongly disagree
    2 = disagree
    3 = neither agree nor disagree
    4 = agree
    5 = strongly agree

1. I am usually aware—from moment to moment—of my feelings as they change.	1	2	3	4	5
2. I think before I act.	1	2	3	4	5
3. I am impatient when I want something.	1	2	3	4	5
4. I bounce back quickly from life's setbacks.	1	2	3	4	5
5. I can pick up subtle social cues that indicate others' needs or wants.	1	2	3	4	5
6. I'm very good at handling myself in social situations.	1	2	3	4	5
7. I'm persistent in going after the things I want.	1	2	3	4	5
8. When people share their problems with me, I'm good at putting myself in their shoes.	1	2	3	4	5
9. When I'm in a bad mood, I make a strong effort to get out of it.	1	2	3	4	5
10. I can find common ground and build rapport with people from all walks of life.	1	2	3	4	5

Scoring & Interpretation: This questionnaire taps the five basic dimensions of EI: self-awareness (items 1 and 9), self-management (2, 4), self-motivation (3, 7), empathy (5, 8), and social skills (6, 10). Compute your total EI score by adding your responses to all 10 statements.

Your total score will fall between 10 and 50. While no definite cutoff scores are available, scores of 40 or higher indicate a high EI. Scores of 20 or less suggest a relatively low EI.

Emotional intelligence is a collection of abilities and competencies that have an effect on a person's capacity to succeed in dealing with demands and pressures. People with high EI have the capacity to correctly perceive, evaluate, articulate, and manage emotions and feelings.

EI may be most predictive of performance in jobs such as sales or management, where achievement is based as much on interpersonal skills as on technical ability. EI can also be relevant in selecting members of teams. People with low EI are likely to have trouble managing others, making successful sales presentations, and functioning on teams.

Questions for Discussion

1. Did the results surprise you? Why or why not?

2. Look at the three items on which your score was lowest. What are some skills or attitudes you can work on to improve your EI? Explain.

3. Do you think your EI would help or hinder you when working in a team?

*Based on D. Goleman, *Emotional Intelligence: Why It Can Matter More Than IQ* (New York: Bantam, 1995).

Identifying Important Values in a Classroom Setting*

Objectives

1. To identify values important to you in the classroom.

2. To gain knowledge of others' values in the classroom.

Values are abstract ideals that guide one's thinking and behavior across all situations. Your behavior is dictated by values that were instilled in you by the time you were a teenager. As a student, you probably believe that getting a good grade is a very important value. How hard are you willing to work and what sacrifices are you willing to make to get that grade? From a manager's point of view, it's helpful to know what values—concepts, principles, things, people, or activities—employees will work hard for, even make sacrifices for.

The purpose of this exercise is to help you think about what values are important to you in the classroom. Because values differ from person to person, it's beneficial to know which values people are willing to work hard to maintain and which values others feel are less important.

Instructions

Below are 10 different values from the Rokeach Value Survey. Read the list and then rank each value according to which ones you feel are important in the classroom. Rank the values from 1 to 10, with 1 being equal to "most important" and 10 being equal to "least important." Mark your results in the first column.

Once you rank the values, break into teams of five to six people. As a group, compare each of your individual results and discuss them. What do you notice about the differences in rankings? Were the group members' rankings similar to yours or was there argument as to which values were important? As a team take the average ranking for each value or devise some other method to reach a consensus on which values are important or not important. Mark those results in the second column, again using the scale from 1 to 10, with 1 being equal to "most important" and 10 being equal to "least important." Compare your team's results to the results from the rest of the class.

	My Ranking	Group's Ranking
Broadminded (open-minded)		
Capable (competent, effective)		
Honest (sincere, thoughtful)		
Responsible (dependable, reliable)		
Polite (courteous, well-mannered)		
Sense of accomplishment (lasting contribution)		
Equality (brotherhood, equal opportunity)		
Self-respect (self-esteem)		
Social recognition (respect, admiration)		
True friendship (close companionship)		

Questions for Discussion

1. Were you surprised at how your results differed from the group's? Or were you surprised at how closely your results matched? Why or why not?

2. Imagine you are teaching this course and that your class presented the results of their survey. What are some things you can do to encourage

a learning environment that reflects the values your students feel are important? What changes would have to be made? Explain.

3. To what extent do you feel knowing your classmates' values will help you work more effectively with them in teams? Explain.

*The ten values in this exercise were taken from the 36 values listed in the Rokeach Value Survey, 1967, 1982 by M. Rokeach. Reprinted by permission of HALGREN TESTS, NW 1145 Clifford, Pullman, WA 99163; (509) 334-5636.

Ethical Dilemma

Enron Employees Create a Positive Impression for Wall Street Analysts

From Jason Leopold, "En-Ruse? Workers at Enron Say They Posed as Busy Traders to Impress Visitng Analysts," The Wall Street Journal, *February 17, 2002, p. C1.*

Some current and former employees of Enron's retail-energy unit say the company asked them to pose as busy electricity and natural-gas sales representatives one day in 1998 so the unit could impress Wall Street analysts visiting its Houston headquarters.

Enron rushed 75 employees of Enron Energy Services—including secretaries and actual sales representatives—to an empty trading floor and told them to act as if they were trying to sell energy contracts to businesses over the phone, the current and former employees say.

"When we went down to the sixth floor, I remember we had to take the stairs so the analysts wouldn't see us," said Kim Garcia, who at the time was an administrative assistant for Enron Energy Services and was laid off in December [of 2001].

"We brought some of our personal stuff, like pictures, to make it look like the area was lived in," Ms. Garcia said in an interview. "There were a bunch of trading desks on the sixth floor, but the desks were totally empty. Some of the computers didn't even work, so we worked off of our laptops. When the analysts arrived, we had to make believe we were on the phone buying and selling electricity and natural gas. The whole thing took like 10 minutes."

Penny Marksberry—who also worked as an Enron Energy Services administrative assistant in 1998 and was laid off in December—and two employees who still work at the unit also say they were told to act as if they were trying to sell contracts.

"They actually brought in computers and phones, and they told us to act like we were typing or talking on the phone when the analysts were walking through," Ms. Marksberry said. "They told us it was very important for us to make a good impression, and if the analysts saw that the operation was disorganized, they wouldn't give the company a good rating."

Solving the Dilemma

What would you do if you were asked to act busy in front of the analysts?

1. Follow the company's instructions by going to the sixth floor and pretending to be busy for the analysts.

2. Explain to your manager that this behavior is inconsistent with your personal values and that you will not participate.

3. Go to the sixth floor in support of the company's request but not act busy or bring personal artifacts to create a false impression.

4. Invent other options. (Explain.)

CHAPTER 12

Motivating Employees
Achieving Superior Performance in the Workplace

MANAGING FOR MOTIVATION: THE FLEXIBLE WORKPLACE

Can a company slice and dice the 24 hours in a day, the seven days a week, in ways that can better motivate employees?

With the parents of so many two-paycheck families, single parents, and other diverse kinds of employees in the workforce, employers have begun to recognize the idea of a so-called *flexible workplace* as a way of recruiting, retaining, and motivating employees. Among the types of alternative work schedules available:

■ **Part-time work—less than 40 hours:** Part-time work is any work done on a schedule less than the standard 40-hour workweek. Some part-time workers—so-called temporary workers or contingency workers—do want to work 40 hours or more but can't find full-time jobs. Others, however, work part time by choice. Today an organization can hire not only part-time clerical help, for instance, but also part-time programmers, market researchers, lawyers, even part-time top executives.

■ **Flextime—flexible working hours:** Flextime, or flexible time, consists of flexible working hours or any schedule that gives one some choices in working hours. If, for example, an organization's normal working hours are 9 A.M. to 5 P.M., a flextime worker might be allowed to start and finish an hour earlier or an hour later—for instance, to work from 8 A.M. to 4 P.M. The main requirement is that the employee be at work during certain "core" hours, so as to be available for meetings, consultations, and so on. By offering flextime hours, organizations can attract and keep employees with special requirements such as the need to take care of children or elderly parents. It also benefits employees who wish to avoid commuting during rush hour.

■ **Compressed workweek—40 hours in four days:** In a compressed workweek, employees perform a full-time job in less than five days of standard eight- (or nine-) hour shifts. The most common variation is a 40-hour week performed in four days of 10 hours each, which gives employees three (instead of two) consecutive days off. The benefits are that organizations can offer employees more leisure time and reduced wear and tear and expense from commuting. The disadvantages are possible scheduling problems, unavailability of an employee to coworkers and customers, and fatigue from long workdays.

■ **Job sharing—two people split the same job:** In job sharing, two people divide one full-time job. Usually, each person works a half day, although there can be other arrangements (working alternate days or alternate weeks, for example). As with a compressed workweek, job sharing provides employees with more personal or leisure time. The disadvantage is that it can result in communication problems with coworkers or customers.

■ **Telecommuting & other work—at-home schedules:** There have always been some employees who have had special full-time or part-time arrangements whereby they are allowed to work at home, keeping in touch with their employers and coworkers by mail and phone. The fax machine, the personal computer, the Internet, and overnight-delivery services have now made work-at-home arrangements much more feasible.

Working at home with telecommunications between office and home is called *telecommuting*. The advantage to employers is increased productivity because telecommuters experience less distraction at home and can work flexible hours.

FORECAST: WHAT'S AHEAD IN THIS CHAPTER

This chapter discusses how to motivate people to perform well. We consider motivation from three perspectives: need-based (covering theories by Maslow, Herzberg, and McClelland); process (covering expectancy, equity, and goal-setting theories); and reinforcement. We also consider how to motivate employees through job design. Finally, we discuss using compensation and other rewards to motivate performance.

What's the motivation for studying motivation?

The Big Picture
Motivation is defined as the psychological processes that arouse and direct people's goal-directed behavior. The model of how it works is that people have certain needs that motivate them to perform specific behaviors for which they receive rewards, both extrinsic and intrinsic, that feed back and satisfy the original need. The three major perspectives on motivation are need-based, process, and reinforcement.

What would make you rise a half hour early to ensure you got to work on time— and to perform your best once there?

A new leased car? Help with college tuition? Bringing your dog to work? Onsite laundry, gym, or childcare? Free lunch? Really nice bosses?

Believe it or not, these are among the perks available to some lucky employees—and not just high-level managers.[1] Especially when employment rates are high, as they were in the late 1990s, companies are desperate to attract, retain, and motivate key people.

Motivation: What It Is, Why It's Important

Why do people do the things they do? The answer is this: They are mainly motivated to fulfill their wants, their needs.

Office colleague. Would it affect your feelings about your job if you could bring your dog to work? (What would the office be like if everyone did it?) In trying to keep key workers motivated, some companies will go to such extra efforts. What kind of unusual employee benefit would make a big difference to you?

What Is Motivation & How Does It Work? *Motivation* **may be defined as the psychological processes that arouse and direct goal-directed behavior.** Motivation is difficult to understand because you can't actually see it or know it in another person; it must be *inferred* from one's behavior. Nevertheless, it's imperative that you as a manager understand the process of motivation if you are to guide employees in accomplishing your organization's objectives.

The way motivation works actually is complex. However, in a simple model of motivation, people have certain *needs* that *motivate* them to perform specific *behaviors* for which they receive *rewards* that *feed back* and satisfy the original need. *(See Panel 12.1.)*

For example, you find you are hungry (need), which impels you to seek food (motive). You make a sandwich and eat it (behavior), which provides satisfaction (reward) and informs you (feedback loop) that sandwiches will reduce hunger and so should be used in the future. Or as an hourly worker you desire more money (need), which impels you (motivates you) to work more hours (behavior), which provides you with more money (reward) and informs you (feedback loop) that working more hours will fulfill your need for more money in the future.

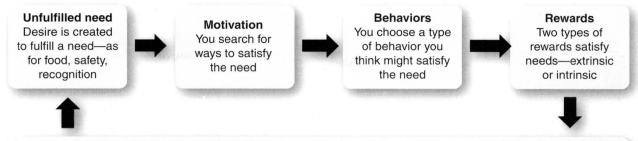

| Unfulfilled need
Desire is created to fulfill a need—as for food, safety, recognition | → | Motivation
You search for ways to satisfy the need | → | Behaviors
You choose a type of behavior you think might satisfy the need | → | Rewards
Two types of rewards satisfy needs—extrinsic or intrinsic |

Feedback Reward informs you whether behavior worked and should be used again

PANEL 12.1
A simple model of motivation

Rewards (as well as motivation itself) are of two types—*extrinsic* and *intrinsic*. Managers can use both to encourage better work performance.

■ **Extrinsic rewards—satisfaction in the payoff from others: An _extrinsic reward_ is the payoff, such as money, a person receives from others for performing a particular task.** An extrinsic reward is an external reward; the payoff comes from pleasing others.

Example: In performing your job as a maker of custom sailboats, you get your principal satisfaction from receiving the great amount of money buyers pay you for a boat—an extrinsic reward.

■ **Intrinsic rewards—satisfaction in performing the task itself: An _intrinsic reward_ is the satisfaction, such as a feeling of accomplishment, a person receives from performing the particular task itself.** An intrinsic reward is an internal reward; the payoff comes from pleasing yourself.

Example: In making custom sailboats, you derive satisfaction—warm feelings of accomplishment and heightened self-esteem—from the process of building a sailboat.

Why Is Motivation Important? It seems obvious that organizations would want to motivate their employees to be more productive. Actually, though, there are five reasons why you as a manager will find knowledge of motivation important.[2]

In order of importance, you want to motivate people to . . .

1 Join Your Organization You need to instill in talented prospective workers the desire to come to work for you.

2 Stay with Your Organization Whether you are in good economic times or bad, you always want to be able to retain good people.

3 Show Up for Work at Your Organization In many organizations, absenteeism and lack of punctuality are tremendous problems.[3]

4 Perform Better for Your Organization: Some employees do just enough to avoid being fired.[4] But what you really want is employees who will give you high productivity.

5 Do Extra for Your Organization You hope your employees will perform extra tasks above and beyond the call of duty (be organizational "good citizens").

The Three Major Perspectives on Motivation: Overview

There is no theory accepted by everyone as to what motivates people. In this chapter, therefore, we present the three principal perspectives. From these, you may be able to select what ideas seem most workable for you. The three perspectives on motivation are (1) *need-based*, (2) *process*, and (3) *reinforcement*, as described in the following three main sections.

Click-Along 12.1

Summary of Three Perspectives on Motivation

major question

What kinds of needs motivate employees?

The Big Picture

Need-based perspectives are theories emphasizing the needs that motivate people. Needs are defined as physiological or psychological deficiencies that arouse behavior. The needs-based perspective includes three theories: Maslow's hierarchy of needs, Herzberg's two-factor theory, and McClelland's acquired needs theory.

Need-based perspectives, also known as *content perspectives*, **are theories that emphasize the needs that motivate people.** Needs theorists ask, "What kind of needs motivate employees in the workplace?" *Needs* **are defined as physiological or psychological deficiencies that arouse behavior.** They can be strong or weak, and, because they are influenced by environmental factors, they can vary over time and from place to place.

In addition to McGregor's Theory X/Theory Y (see Chapter 2), needs-based perspectives include three theories:

1 Maslow's hierarchy of needs theory

2 Herzberg's two-factor theory

3 McClelland's acquired needs theory.

Maslow's Hierarchy of Needs Theory: Five Levels of Human Needs

In 1943, Brandeis University psychology professor **Abraham Maslow,** one of the first researchers to study motivation, put forth his *hierarchy of needs theory*, **which proposes that people are motivated by five levels of needs: (1) physiological, (2) safety, (3) belongingness, (4) esteem, and (5) self-actualization.**[5]

The Five Levels of Needs In proposing this hierarchy of five needs, ranging from basic to highest level, Maslow suggested that needs are never completely satisfied. That is, our actions are aimed at fulfilling the "deprived" needs, the needs that remain unsatisfied at any point in time. Thus, for example, once you have achieved security, which is the second most basic need, you will then seek to fulfill the third most basic need—belongingness.

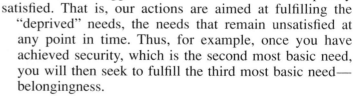

Self-actualization. No one *has* to learn to play the banjo. But for some people, according to Maslow's theory, it represents the kind of realization of the best that life has to offer—after other needs are satisfied. If "you only go around once," as the saying goes, what activity or experience within your lifetime would represent self-fulfillment for you—the best that would realize your potential?

In order of ascendance, from bottom to top, the five levels of needs are as follows. *(See Panel 12.2.)*

1 Physiological Needs These are the most basic human physical needs, in which one is concerned with having food, clothing, shelter, and comfort and with self-preservation. In the workplace, these needs take the form of having enough air, heat, and pay to make one reasonably satisfied.

2 Safety Needs These needs are concerned with physical safety and emotional security, so that a person is concerned with avoiding violence and threats. In organizational life, these take the form of being free from the threat of physical danger, of losing one's job, of losing health benefits.

3 Belongingness Needs Once basic needs and security are taken care of, people look for love, friendship, and affection. In the workplace, belongingness needs are often expressed in the quest to be accepted by coworkers and supervisors and to participate in the work group.

4 Esteem Needs After they meet their social needs, people focus on such matters as self-respect, status, reputation, recognition, and self-confidence. In organizations, esteem is often expressed in the need for recognition for accomplishments and for higher status as a reward for more responsibility.

5 Self-Actualization Needs The highest level of need, self-actualization is self-fulfillment—the need to develop one's fullest potential, to become the best one is capable of being. In the workplace, this need is met by organizations' improving employee skills, helping them be creative, and enabling them to have control over their jobs.

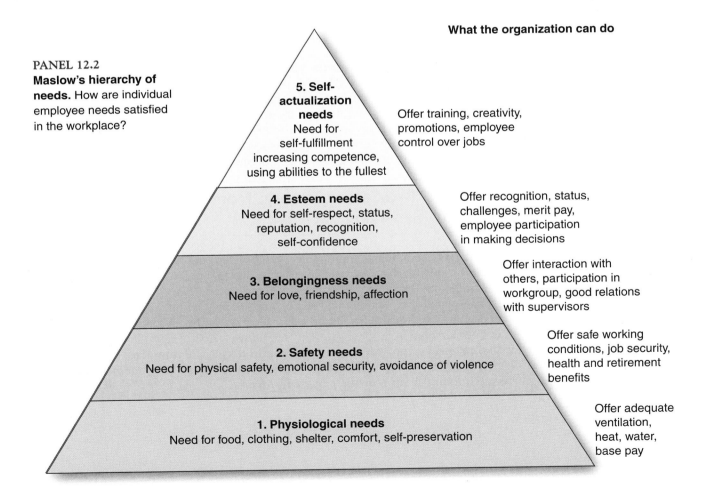

What the organization can do

PANEL 12.2
Maslow's hierarchy of needs. How are individual employee needs satisfied in the workplace?

5. Self-actualization needs
Need for self-fulfillment increasing competence, using abilities to the fullest

Offer training, creativity, promotions, employee control over jobs

4. Esteem needs
Need for self-respect, status, reputation, recognition, self-confidence

Offer recognition, status, challenges, merit pay, employee participation in making decisions

3. Belongingness needs
Need for love, friendship, affection

Offer interaction with others, participation in workgroup, good relations with supervisors

2. Safety needs
Need for physical safety, emotional security, avoidance of violence

Offer safe working conditions, job security, health and retirement benefits

1. Physiological needs
Need for food, clothing, shelter, comfort, self-preservation

Offer adequate ventilation, heat, water, base pay

Example of Higher-Level Needs: "Tempered Radicals" Strike a Balance between Safety & Higher-Level Needs

Peter Grant is a black executive who for years has worked quietly behind the scenes to recruit thousands of minorities—3,500 at one large financial institution alone. Through the years he asked every person he hired to promise to bring other minorities along. With this strategy of "quiet resistance," he achieved his goal of hiring more people of color without making this a huge issue within his company.

Grant is an example of what Debra Meyerson calls a "tempered radical." In her book *Tempered Radicals: How People Use Difference to Inspire Change at Work*, Meyerson writes that "Tempered radicals want to fit in *and* they want to retain what makes them different. They want to rock the boat, and they want to stay in it."[6]

Tempered radicals, in other words, work to strike a balance between what they believe in and what the system expects. In this way, they fulfill both their safety needs while also striving to fulfill their self-actualization needs.

Research does not clearly support Maslow's theory, although it remains popular among managers. "There are still very few studies that can legitimately confirm (or refute) it," one scholar writes. "It may be that the dynamics implied by Maslow's theory of needs are too complex to be operationalized and confirmed by scientific research."[7]

Using the Hierarchy of Needs Theory to Motivate Employees For managers, the importance of Maslow's contribution is that he showed that workers have needs beyond that of just earning a paycheck. To the extent the organization permits, managers should first try to meet employees' level 1 and level 2 needs, of course, so that employees won't be preoccupied with them. Then, however, they need to give employees a chance to fulfill their higher-level needs in ways that also advance the goals of the organization.

Herzberg's Two-Factor Theory: From Dissatisfying Factors to Satisfying Factors

Frederick Herzberg arrived at his needs-based theory as a result of a landmark study of 203 accountants and engineers, who were interviewed to determine the factors responsible for job satisfaction and dissatisfaction.[8] Job satisfaction was more frequently associated with achievement, recognition, characteristics of the work, responsibility, and advancement. Job dissatisfaction was more often associated with working conditions, pay and security, company policies, supervisors, and interpersonal relationships. The result was Herzberg's *__two-factor theory__*, **which proposed that work satisfaction and dissatisfaction arise from two different factors—work satisfaction from so-called** *motivating factors* **and work dissatisfaction from so-called** *hygiene factors*.

Hygiene Factors versus Motivating Factors   In Herzberg's theory, the hygiene factors are the lower-level needs, the motivating factors are the higher-level needs. The two areas are separated by a zone in which employees are neither satisfied nor dissatisfied. *(See Panel 12.3.)*

PANEL 12.3
Herzberg's two-factor theory: satisfaction versus dissatisfaction

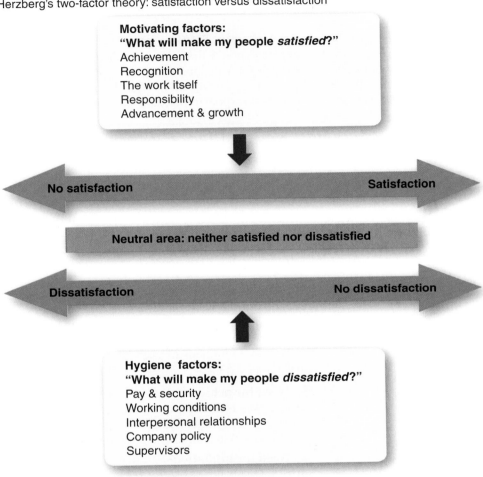

- **Hygiene factors—"Why are my people dissatisfied?"** The lower-level needs, *hygiene factors*, are factors associated with job *dissatisfaction*—such as salary, working conditions, interpersonal relationships, and company policy—all of which affect the job *context* in which people work.

  An example of a hygiene factor is the temperature in a factory that's not air-conditioned during the summer. Installing air-conditioning will remove a cause of job dissatisfaction. It will not, however, spur factory workers' motivation and make them greatly satisfied in their work. Because motivating factors are absent, workers become, in Herzberg's view, merely neutral in their attitudes toward work—neither dissatisfied nor satisfied.

- **Motivating factors—"What will make my people satisfied?"** The higher-level needs, *motivating factors*, or simply *motivators*, are factors associated with job *satisfaction*—such as achievement, recognition, responsibility, and advancement—all of which affect the job content or the

rewards of work performance. Motivating factors—challenges, opportunities, recognition—must be instituted, Herzberg believed, to spur superior work performance.

An example of a motivating factor would be to give factory workers more control over their work. For example, instead of repeating a single task over and over, a worker might join with other workers in a team in which each one does several tasks. This is the approach that Swedish automaker Volvo has taken in building cars.

Using Two-Factor Theory to Motivate Employees The basic lesson of Herzberg's research is that managers should first eliminate dissatisfaction, making sure that working conditions, pay levels, and company policies are reasonable. They should then concentrate on spurring motivation by providing opportunities for achievement, recognition, responsibility, and personal growth.

left
Click-Along 12.2

Using Herzberg's Theory: A Stockbroker Flies Fighter Jets to Forget His Job

McClelland's Acquired Needs Theory: Achievement, Affiliation, & Power

David McClelland, a well-known psychologist, investigated the needs for affiliation and power and as a consequence proposed the *acquired needs theory*, **which states that three needs—achievement, affiliation, and power—are major motives determining people's behavior in the workplace.**[9] McClelland believes that we are not born with our needs; rather we learn them from the culture—from our life experiences.

PANEL 12.4
McClelland's three needs

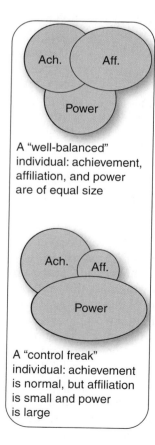

A "well-balanced" individual: achievement, affiliation, and power are of equal size

A "control freak" individual: achievement is normal, but affiliation is small and power is large

The Three Needs Managers are encouraged to recognize three needs in themselves and others and to attempt to create work environments that are responsive to them. The three needs, one of which tends to be dominant in each of us, are as follows. *(See Panel 12.4.)*

■ **Need for achievement—"I need to excel at tasks":** This is the desire to excel, to do something better or more efficiently, to solve problems, to achieve excellence in challenging tasks.

■ **Need for affiliation—"I need close relationships":** This is the desire for friendly and warm relations with other people.

■ **Need for power—"I need to control others":** This is the desire to be responsible for other people, to influence their behavior or to control them.[10]

McClelland identifies two forms of the need for power.

The negative kind is the need for *personal power*, as expressed in the desire to dominate others, and involves manipulating people for one's own gratification.

The positive kind, characteristic of top managers and leaders, is the desire for *institutional power*, as expressed in the need to solve problems that further organizational goals.

The three needs theorists are compared below. *(See Panel 12.5.)*

PANEL 12.5

A comparison of needs theories: Maslow, Herzberg, and McClelland. McClelland has no classification for lower-level needs.

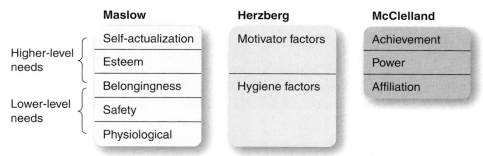

Using Acquired Needs Theory to Motivate Employees McClelland associates the three needs with different sets of work preferences, as follows:[11]

- **Need for achievement:** If you (or an employee) are happy with accomplishment of a task being its own reward, don't mind or even prefer working alone, and are willing to take moderate risks, then you probably have a *high need for achievement.* That being the case, you (or your employee) would probably prefer doing the kind of work that offers feedback on performance, challenging but achievable goals, and individual responsibility for results. People high in need for achievement tend to advance in technical fields requiring creativity and individual skills.

- **Need for power:** If you, like most effective managers, have a *high need for power,* that means you enjoy being in control of people and events and being recognized for this responsibility. Accordingly, your preference would probably be for work that allows you to control or have an impact on people and be publicly recognized for your accomplishments.

- **Need for affiliation:** If you tend to seek social approval and satisfying personal relationships, you may have a *high need for affiliation.* In that case, you may not be the most efficient manager because at times you will have to make decisions that will make people resent you. Instead, you will tend to prefer work, such as sales, that provides for personal relationships and social approval.

Example of Acquired Needs Theory: The Need for Achievement of a Die Engineer at Monroe Auto Equipment

You don't have to be a celebrity or high-powered executive to display the McClelland feature of high need for achievement (which overlaps with Maslow's higher-order needs of esteem and self-actualization). Consider automotive die engineer Bob Stadler.

When, at age 18, Stadler joined Monroe Auto Equipment, a family-owned company in Monroe, Mich., his one great ambition was to be the best tool and die maker in the world. Throughout his career, Monroe has continued to be his only employer, and he has risen to the position of senior staff engineer. Not widely known outside the company, he is greatly admired within the two-story headquarters of Monroe Auto, where his word is final on whether a product is manufacturable.

"He is the best die engineer I have ever seen in my life," says president Jack Thompson, whose late father also worked with Stadler. "No one [else] even comes close."[12]

Is a good reward good enough? How do other factors affect motivation?

The Big Picture
Process perspectives, which are concerned with the thought processes by which people decide how to act, have three viewpoints: expectancy theory, equity theory, and goal-setting theory.

Process perspectives **are concerned with the thought processes by which people decide how to act**—how employees choose behavior to meet their needs. Whereas need-based perspectives simply try to understand employee needs, process perspectives go further and try to understand why employees have different needs, what behaviors they select to satisfy them, and how they decide if their choices were successful.

In this section we discuss three process perspectives on motivation:

1 Expectancy theory

2 Equity theory

3 Goal-setting theory.

Expectancy Theory: How Much Do You Want & How Likely Are You to Get It?

Introduced by **Victor Vroom,** *expectancy theory* **suggests that people are motivated by two things: (1) how much they want something and (2) how likely they think they are to get it.**[13] In other words, assuming they have choices, people will make the choice that promises them the greatest reward if they think they can get it.

The Three Elements of Motivation Theory: Expectancy, Instrumentality, Valence What determines how willing you (or an employee) are to work hard at tasks important to the success of the organization? The answer, says Vroom, is: You will do what you *can* do when you *want* to.

Your motivation, according to expectancy theory, involves the relationship between your *effort*, your *performance*, and the desirability of the *outcomes* (such as pay or recognition) of your performance. These relationships, which are shown in the accompanying drawing, are affected by the three elements of *expectancy*, *instrumentality*, and *valence*. *(See Panel 12.6.)*

How much do you want? Would a well-appointed office represent the tangible realization of managerial success for you? How likely do you think you are to get it? The answers to these questions represent your important motivations, according to expectancy theory.

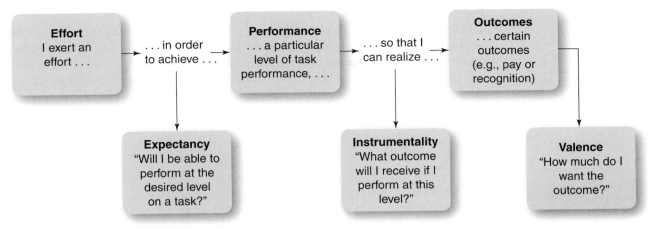

PANEL 12.6
Expectancy theory: The major elements

1 Expectancy—"Will I be able to perform at the desired level on a task?" *Expectancy* **is the belief that a particular level of effort will lead to a particular level of performance.** This is called the *effort-to-performance expectancy.*

Example: If you believe that putting in more hours working at Circuit City selling videogame machines will result in higher sales, then you have high effort-to-performance expectancy. That is, you believe that your efforts will matter. You think you have the ability, the product knowledge, and so on so that putting in extra hours of selling can probably raise your sales of videogame machines.

2 Instrumentality—"What outcome will I receive if I perform at this level?" *Instrumentality* **is the expectation that successful performance of the task will lead to the outcome desired.** This is called the *performance-to-reward expectancy.*

Example: If you believe that making higher sales will cause Circuit City to give you a bonus, then you have high performance-to-reward expectancy. You believe *if* you can achieve your goals, the outcome will be worthwhile. This element is independent of the previous one—you might decide you don't have the ability to make the extra sales, but if you did, you'll be rewarded.

3 Valence—"How much do I want the outcome?" *Valence* **is value, the importance a worker assigns to the possible outcome or reward.**

Example: If you assign a lot of importance or a high value to Circuit City's prospective bonus or pay raise, then your valence is said to be high.

Does my performance matter? If you were a salesperson at Circuit City, one important consideration, according to expectancy theory, is how much you believe your efforts really matter when it comes to achieving rewards. The same feelings apply, incidentally, to your beliefs about studying—that is, do you believe that studying hard will lead to higher grades?

For your motivation to be high, you must be high on all three elements—expectancy, instrumentality, and valence. If any element is low, you will not be motivated. Your effort-to-performance expectancy might be low, for instance, because you doubt making an effort will make a difference (because retail selling has too much competition from Internet sellers). Or your performance-to-reward expectancy might be low because you don't think Circuit City is going to give you a bonus for being a star at selling. Or your valence might be low because you don't think the bonus or raise is going to be high enough to justify working evenings and weekends.

Using Expectancy Theory to Motivate Employees The principal problem with expectancy theory is that it is complex. Even so, the underlying logic is understandable. When attempting to motivate employees, managers should ask the following questions:

- **What rewards do your employees value?** As a manager, you need to get to know your employees and determine what rewards (outcomes) they value, such as pay raises or recognition.

- **What are the job objectives and the performance level you desire?** You need to clearly define the performance objectives and determine what performance level or behavior you want so that you can tell your employees what they need to do to attain the rewards.

- **Are the rewards linked to performance?** You want to reward high performance, of course. If high-performing employees aren't rewarded, they may leave or slow down and affect the performance of other employees. Thus, employees must be aware that X level of performance within Y period of time will result in Z kinds of rewards.

- **Do employees believe you will deliver the right rewards for the right performance?** Your credibility is on the line here. Your employees must believe that you have the power, the ability, and the will to give them the rewards you promise for the performance you are requesting.

Going for the gold. Athletes at the Salt Lake City 2002 Winter Olympics knew what kinds of performance they had to put forth to earn winners' medallions. Do you think the objectives, performance levels, and rewards can be as clear-cut in the business world?

Equity Theory: How Fairly Do You Think You're Being Treated in Relation to Others?

Fairness—or, perhaps equally important, the *perception* of fairness—can be a big issue in organizations. For example, if you received a 10% bonus from Circuit City for doubling your sales, would that be enough? What if other Circuit City salespeople received 15%?

Equity theory focuses on employee perceptions as to how fairly they think they are being treated compared to others. Developed by psychologist **J. Stacy Adams**, equity theory is based on the idea that employees are motivated to see fairness in the rewards they expect for task performance.[14] Clearly, this is an important matter. Experts believe that employee theft, for example, which costs American business about $120 billion a year, represents employees' attempts to even the score when they feel that they haven't been treated fairly by their organizations.[15]

The Elements of Equity Theory: Comparing Your Inputs & Outputs with Those of Others The key elements in equity theory are *inputs, outputs* (*rewards*), and *comparisons. (See Panel 12.7.)*

PANEL 12.7
Equity theory. How people perceive they are being fairly or unfairly rewarded

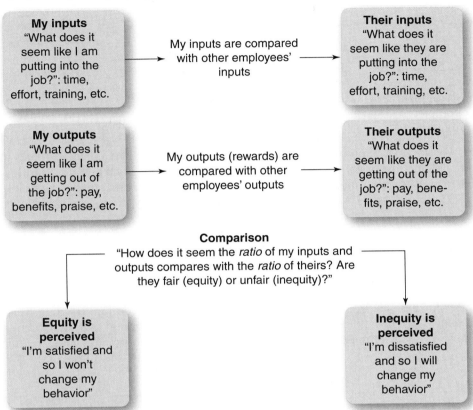

- **Inputs—"What do you think you're putting in to the job?"** The inputs that people perceive they give to an organization are their time, effort, training, experience, intelligence, creativity, seniority, status, and so on.

- **Outputs or rewards—"What do you think you're getting out of the job?"** The outputs are the rewards that people receive from an organization: pay, benefits, praise, recognition, bonuses, promotions, status perquisites (corner office with a view, say, or private parking space), and so on.

- **Comparison—"How do you think your ratio of inputs and rewards compares with those of others?"** Equity theory suggests that people compare the *ratio* of their own outcomes to inputs against the *ratio* of someone else's outcomes to inputs. When employees compare the ratio of their inputs and outputs (rewards) with those of others—whether coworkers within the organization or even other people in similar jobs outside it—they then make a judgment about fairness. Either they perceive there is *equity*—they are satisfied with the ratio and so they don't change their behavior. Or they perceive there is *inequity*—they feel resentful and act to change the inequity.

Using Equity Theory to Motivate Employees Adams suggests that employees who feel they are being underrewarded will respond to the perceived inequity in one or more of the following ways:

- **They will reduce their inputs:** They will do less work, take long breaks, call in "sick" on Mondays, leave early on Fridays, and so on.

- **They will try to change the outputs or rewards they receive:** They will lobby the boss for a raise, for example. Or they will pilfer company equipment.

- **They will distort the inequity:** They will exaggerate how hard they work so they can complain they're not paid what they're worth.

- **They will change the object of comparison:** They may compare themselves to another person instead of the original one.

- **They will leave the situation:** They will quit, transfer, or shift to another reference group.

By contrast, employees who think they are treated fairly are more likely to support organizational change, more apt to cooperate in group settings, and less apt to turn to arbitration and the courts to remedy real or imagined wrongs.

Three practical lessons that can be drawn from equity theory are as follows:

1 Employee Perceptions Are What Count Probably the most important result of research on equity theory is this: no matter how fair managers think the organization's policies, procedures, and reward system are, each employee's *perception* of those factors is what counts.

2 Employee Participation Helps Managers benefit by allowing employees to participate in important decisions. For example, employees are more satisfied with their performance appraisal when they have a "voice" during their appraisal review.[16]

3 Having an Appeal Process Helps When employees are able to appeal decisions affecting their welfare, it promotes the belief that management treats them fairly. Perceptions of fair treatment promote job satisfaction and commitment and reduce absenteeism and turnover.

Goal-Setting Theory: Objectives Should Be Specific & Challenging but Achievable

Goal-setting theory suggests that employees can be motivated by goals that are specific and challenging but achievable. According to psychologists **Edwin Locke** and **Gary Latham**, who developed the theory, it is natural for people to set and strive for goals; however, the goal-setting process is useful only if people *understand* and *accept* the goals. Thus, the best way to motivate performance is to set the right objectives in the right ways.[17]

The benefits of setting goals is that a manager can tailor rewards to the needs of individual employees, clarify what is expected of them, provide regular reinforcement, and maintain equity.

Small business. Do employees in small businesses, such as this worker in a florist's shop, need the same kind of motivational goals as employees in large corporations? Is setting goals in small businesses, where there's apt to be less specialization, more or less difficult than in large organizations?

Three Elements of Goal-Setting Theory A *goal* is defined as an objective that a person is trying to accomplish through his or her efforts. To result in high motivation and performance, according to goal-setting theory, goals must be *specific, challenging*, and *achievable*.

1 Goals Should Be Specific

Goals such as "Sell as many cars as you can" or "Be nicer to customers" are too vague and therefore have no effect on motivation. Instead, goals need to be specific—usually meaning *quantitative*. As a manager, for example, you may be asked to boost the revenues of your unit by 25% and to cut absenteeism by 10%, all specific targets.

2 Goals Should Be Challenging

Goal theory suggests you not set goals that a lot of people can reach, since this is not very motivational. Rather you should set goals that are challenging, which will impel people to focus their attention in the right place and to apply more effort or inputs toward their jobs—in other words, motivate them toward higher performance.

3 Goals Should Be Achievable

Goals can't be unattainable, of course. You might ask data-entry clerks to enter 25% more names and addresses an hour into a database, but if they don't have touch-typing skills, that goal won't be attainable. Thus, managers need to make sure employees have additional training, if necessary, to achieve difficult goals.

Using Goal-Setting Theory to Motivate Employees When developing employee goals, make sure the goals not only are specific, challenging, and achievable but also are as follows:

1. Set jointly with the employee
2. Are measurable
3. Have a target date for attainment.

Finally, make sure that you give feedback so that employees know of their progress—and don't forget to reward people for doing what they set out to do.

Click-Along 12.3

The Porter-Lawler Theory: Integrating Approaches

Exceptional yogurt. The managers at Yoplait Yogurt, shown here savoring their product, grew their business by setting ambitious goals for themselves—goals that were actually higher than those set by Yoplait's parent company, General Mills. Was it worth it? On achieving their targets, they were rewarded with bonuses that amounted to almost half their annual salaries. How does this example relate to the elements of goal-setting theory?

major question

What are the types of incentives I might use to influence employee behavior?

The Big Picture

Reinforcement theory suggests behavior will be repeated if it has positive consequences and won't be if it has negative consequences. There are four types of reinforcement: positive reinforcement, negative reinforcement, extinction, and punishment. This section also describes how to use some reinforcement techniques to modify employee behavior.

Reinforcement evades the issue of people's needs and thinking processes in relation to motivation, as we described under the need-based and process perspectives. Instead, the reinforcement perspective, which was pioneered by **Edward L. Thorndike** and **B. F. Skinner**, is concerned with how the consequences of a certain behavior affect that behavior in the future.[18]

Skinner was the father of *operant conditioning*, the process of controlling behavior by manipulating its consequences. Operant conditioning rests on Thorndike's *law of effect*, which states that behavior that results in a pleasant outcome is likely to be repeated and behavior that results in unpleasant outcomes is not likely to be repeated.

From these underpinnings has come ___reinforcement theory___, **which attempts to explain behavior change by suggesting that behavior with positive consequences tends to be repeated whereas behavior with negative consequences tends not to be repeated.** The use of reinforcement theory to change human behavior is called *behavior modification*.

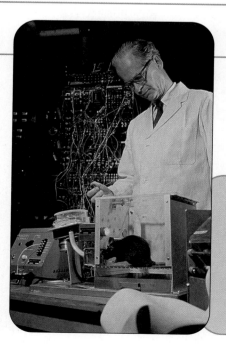

The Four Types of Reinforcement: Positive, Negative, Extinction, & Punishment

___Reinforcement___ **is anything that causes a given behavior to be repeated or inhibited,** whether praising a child for cleaning his or her room or scolding a child for leaving a tricycle in the driveway. There are four types of reinforcement: (1) *positive reinforcement*, (2) *negative reinforcement*, (3) *extinction*, and (4) *punishment*. (*See Panel 12.8.*)

B.F. Skinner and subject. The psychologist known as the father of operant conditioning is shown here in his Harvard University laboratory with a rat in a so-called Skinner box. Besides a lever and food cup, the box contains devices to record every time the animal presses the lever and food pellets are delivered. The goal of the experiment is to condition the rat to press the lever, training it to do so by rewarding it with food every time it does so. A key to operant conditioning is that the reinforcer should immediately follow the desired behavior. Could you use this kind of knowledge to "condition" an employee who is habitually late to show up on time?

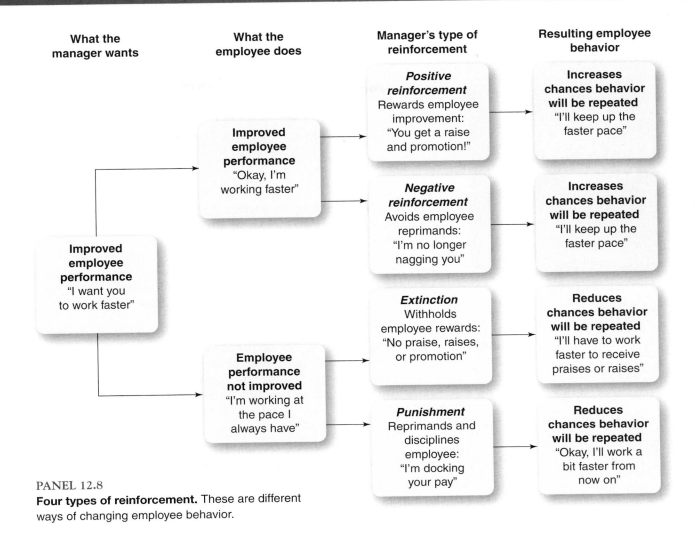

What the manager wants	What the employee does	Manager's type of reinforcement	Resulting employee behavior
		Positive reinforcement Rewards employee improvement: "You get a raise and promotion!"	**Increases chances behavior will be repeated** "I'll keep up the faster pace"
	Improved employee performance "Okay, I'm working faster"	**Negative reinforcement** Avoids employee reprimands: "I'm no longer nagging you"	**Increases chances behavior will be repeated** "I'll keep up the faster pace"
Improved employee performance "I want you to work faster"		**Extinction** Withholds employee rewards: "No praise, raises, or promotion"	**Reduces chances behavior will be repeated** "I'll have to work faster to receive praises or raises"
	Employee performance not improved "I'm working at the pace I always have"	**Punishment** Reprimands and disciplines employee: "I'm docking your pay"	**Reduces chances behavior will be repeated** "Okay, I'll work a bit faster from now on"

PANEL 12.8

Four types of reinforcement. These are different ways of changing employee behavior.

Positive Reinforcement: Giving Rewards *Positive reinforcement* **is the use of positive consequences to encourage desirable behavior.**

Example: A supervisor who's asked an insurance salesperson to sell more policies might reward successful performance by saying, "It's great that you exceeded your quota, and you'll get a bonus for it. Maybe next time you'll sell even more and will become a member of the Circle of 100 Top Sellers and win a trip to Paris as well." Note the rewards: praise, more money, recognition, awards. Presumably this will *strengthen* the behavior and the sales rep will work even harder in the coming months.

Negative Reinforcement: Avoiding Unpleasantness *Negative reinforcement* **is the removal of unpleasant consequences following a desired behavior.**

Example: A supervisor who has been nagging a salesperson might say, "Well, so you exceeded your quota" and stop the nagging. Note the neutral statement; there is no praise but also no longer any negative statements. This could cause the sales rep to *maintain* his or her existing behavior.

Oh, no! Does getting a wallet-busting traffic ticket (as for parking in a bus zone) change your behavior? What if it happens several times? Looking at the four different kinds of reinforcement, which type is being employed here? Yet consider also other, presumably stronger forms of punishment that are supposed to act as deterrents to bad behavior. Does the existence of the death penalty really deter homicides? Why or why not?

Extinction: Withholding Rewards *Extinction* **is the withholding or withdrawal of positive rewards for desirable behavior, so that the behavior is less likely to occur in the future.**

Example: A supervisor might tell a successful salesperson, "I know you exceeded your quota, but now that our company has been taken over by another firm, we're not giving out bonuses any more."

Presumably this will *weaken* the salesperson's efforts to perform better in the future.

Punishment: Applying Negative Consequences *Punishment* **is the application of negative consequences to stop or change undesirable behavior.**

Example: A supervisor might tell an unsuccessful salesperson who's been lazy about making calls to clients and so didn't make quota, "Well, if this keeps up, you'll probably be let go." This could *inhibit* the salesperson from being so lackadaisical about making calls to clients.

Using Reinforcement to Motivate Employees

The following are some guidelines for using two types of reinforcement—positive reinforcement and punishment.

Positive Reinforcement There are several aspects of positive reinforcement, which should definitely be part of your toolkit of managerial skills:

- **Reward only desirable behavior:** You should give rewards to your employees only when they show *desirable* behavior. Thus, for example, you should give praise to employees not for showing up for work on time (an expected part of any job) but for showing up early.

- **Give rewards as soon as possible:** You should give a reward as soon as possible after the desirable behavior appears. Thus, you should give praise to an early-arriving employee as soon as he or she arrives, not later in the week.

- **Be clear about what behavior is desired:** Clear communication is everything. You should tell employees exactly what kinds of work behaviors are desirable and you should tell everyone exactly what they must do to earn rewards.

- **Have different rewards and recognize individual differences:** Recognizing that different people respond to different kinds of rewards, you should have different rewards available. Thus, you might give a word of praise verbally to one person, shoot a line or two by e-mail to another person, or send a hand-scrawled note to another.

Punishment Unquestionably there will be times when you'll need to threaten or administer an unpleasant consequence to stop an employee's undesirable behavior. Sometimes it's best to address a problem by combining punishment with positive reinforcement. Some suggestions for using punishment are as follows:

- **Punish only undesirable behavior:** You should give punishment only when employees show frequent *undesirable* behavior. Otherwise, employees may come to view you negatively as a tyrannical boss. Thus, for example, you should reprimand employees who show up, say, a half hour late for work but not 5 or 10 minutes late.

- **Give reprimands or disciplinary actions as soon as possible:** You should mete out punishment as soon as possible after the undesirable behavior occurs. Thus, you should give a reprimand to a late-arriving employee as soon as he or she arrives.

Enron revisited. Sherron Watkins, a vice president of Enron, testifies in a hearing before the U.S. Congress, as former CEO Jeffrey Skilling looks on. Watkins testified about her attempts to warn top managers of her fears that the company would "implode" because of irregular financial practices—fears that proved correct. Do you think Enron's managers considered her warnings as undesirable behavior? How common is it for employees to successfully criticize their superiors to other managers?

- **Be clear about what behavior is undesirable:** Tell employees exactly what kinds of work behaviors are undesirable and make any disciplinary action or reprimand match the behavior. A manager should not, for example, dock an hourly employee's pay if he or she is only 5 or 10 minutes late for work.

- **Administer punishment in private:** You would hate to have your boss chew you out in front of your subordinates, and the people who report to you also shouldn't be reprimanded in public, which would lead only to resentments that may have nothing to do with an employee's infractions.

- **Combine punishment and positive reinforcement:** If you're reprimanding an employee, be sure to also say what he or she is doing right and state what rewards the employee might be eligible for. For example, while reprimanding someone for being late, say that a perfect attendance record over the next few months will put that employee in line for a raise or promotion.

major question

What's the best way to design jobs—adapt people to work or work to people?

The Big Picture

Job design, the division of an organization's work among employees, applies motivational theories to jobs to increase performance and satisfaction. The traditional approach to job design is to fit people to the jobs; the modern way is to fit the jobs to the people, using job enlargement and enrichment. The job characteristics model offers five job attributes for better work outcomes.

Job design is (1) the division of an organization's work among its employees and (2) the application of motivational theories to jobs to increase satisfaction and performance. There are two different approaches to job design, one traditional, one modern, that can be taken in deciding how to design jobs. The traditional way is _fitting people to jobs_; the modern way is _fitting jobs to people_.

Fitting people to jobs is based on the assumption that people will gradually adapt to any work situation. Even so, jobs must still be tailored so that nearly anyone can do them. This is the approach often taken with assembly-line jobs and jobs involving routine tasks. For managers the main challenge becomes _"How can we make the worker most compatible with the work?"_

One technique is **_job simplification_, the process of reducing the number of tasks a worker performs.** When a job is stripped down to its simplest elements, it enables a worker to focus on doing more of the same task, thus increasing employee efficiency and productivity. This may be especially useful, for instance, in designing jobs for mentally disadvantaged workers, such as those run by Goodwill Industries. However, research shows that simplified, repetitive jobs lead to job dissatisfaction, poor mental health, and a low sense of accomplishment and personal growth.[19]

Fitting Jobs to People

Creating Goodwill. Collecting donated clothing and household goods to sell in its 1,900 stores, Goodwill Industries International provides job training and employment services for people with workplace disadvantages and disabilities. The 100-year-old, $1.8 billion nonprofit international organization is a network of 209 community-based member organizations in 24 countries. What kinds of jobs would you guess they provide training for?

Fitting jobs to people is based on the assumption that people are underutilized at work and that they want more variety, challenges, and responsibility. This philosophy, an outgrowth of Herzberg's theory, is one of the reasons for the popularity of work teams in the United States. The main challenge for managers is _"How can we make the work most compatible with the worker so as to produce both high performance and high job satisfaction?"_ Two techniques for this type of job design include (1) _job enlargement_ and (2) _job enrichment_.

Job Enlargement: Putting More Variety into a Job The opposite of job simplification, _job enlargement_ **consists of increasing the number of tasks in a job to increase variety and motivation.** For instance, the job of installing television picture tubes could be enlarged to include installation of the circuit boards.

Although proponents claim job enlargement can improve employee satisfaction, motivation, and quality of production, research suggests job enlargement by itself won't have a significant and lasting positive impact on job performance. After all, working at two boring tasks instead of one doesn't add up to a challenging job. Instead, job enlargement is just one tool of many that should be considered in job design.[20]

Job Enrichment: Putting More Responsibility & Other Motivating Factors into a Job Job enrichment is the practical application of Frederick Herzberg's two-factor motivator-hygiene theory of job satisfaction. Specifically, _job enrichment_ **consists of building into a job such motivating factors as responsibility, achievement, recognition, stimulating work, and advancement.**

However, instead of the job-enlargement technique of simply giving employees additional tasks of similar difficulty (known as _horizontal loading_), with job enrichment employees are given more responsibility (known as _vertical loading_). Thus, employees take on chores that would normally be performed by their supervisors. For example, one department store authorized thousands of its sales clerks to handle functions normally reserved for store managers, such as handling merchandise-return problems and approving customers' checks.[21]

The Job Characteristics Model: Five Job Attributes for Better Work Outcomes

Developed by researchers **J. Richard Hackman** and **Greg Oldham**, the job characteristics model of design is an outgrowth of job enrichment.[22] The _job characteristics model_ **consists of (a) five core job characteristics that affect (b) three critical psychological states of an employee that in turn affect (c) work outcomes—the employee's motivation, performance, and satisfaction.** The model is illustrated on the next page. _(See Panel 12.9, top of page 398.)_

Skill variety. Flying a commercial airliner requires a greater number of skills than, say, driving a truck. Do highly skilled employees typically make good managers? What skills do airline pilots have that would make them effective managers in other industries?

Five Job Characteristics The five core job characteristics are as follows:

1 Skill Variety—"How many different skills does your job require?" _Skill variety_ describes the extent to which a job requires a person to use a wide range of different skills and abilities.

Example: The skill variety required by a rocket scientist is higher than that for a short-order cook.

2 Task Identity—"How Many Different Tasks Are Required to Complete the Work?" _Task identity_ describes the extent to which a job requires a worker to perform all the tasks needed to complete the job from beginning to end.

Example: The task identity for a craftsperson who goes through all the steps to build a hand-made acoustic guitar is higher than it is for an assembly-line worker who just installs windshields on cars.

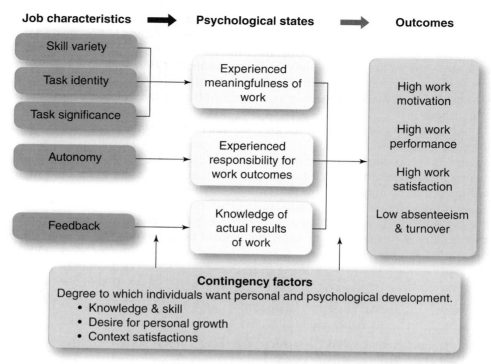

Job characteristics ➡ **Psychological states** ➡ **Outcomes**

- Skill variety
- Task identity
- Task significance

→ Experienced meaningfulness of work

- Autonomy

→ Experienced responsibility for work outcomes

- Feedback

→ Knowledge of actual results of work

High work motivation

High work performance

High work satisfaction

Low absenteeism & turnover

Contingency factors
Degree to which individuals want personal and psychological development.
- Knowledge & skill
- Desire for personal growth
- Context satisfactions

PANEL 12.9
The job characteristics model[23]

3 Task Significance—"How Many Other People Are Affected by Your Job?" *Task significance* describes the extent to which a job affects the lives of other people, whether inside or outside the organization.

Example: A technician who is responsible for keeping a hospital's electronic equipment in working order has higher task significance than a person wiping down cars in a carwash.

4 Autonomy—"How Much Discretion Does Your Job Give You?" *Autonomy* describes the extent to which a job allows an employee to make choices about scheduling different tasks and deciding how to perform them.

Example: College-textbook salespeople have lots of leeway in planning which campuses and professors to call on. Thus, they have higher autonomy than do toll-takers on a bridge, whose actions are determined by the flow of vehicles.

5 Feedback—"How Much Do You Find Out How Well You're Doing?" *Feedback* describes the extent to which workers receive clear, direct information about how well they are performing the job.

Examples: Professional basketball players receive immediate feedback on how many of their shots are going into the basket. Engineers working on new weapons systems may go years before learning how effective their performance has been.

Feedback. This Wal-Mart employee in Temple, Texas, is receiving an award for high productivity. Getting this kind of recognition is one of the five core characteristics of the job characteristics model. Do you think some jobs can be done well without any of these characteristics?

How the Model Works According to the job characteristics model, these five core characteristics affect a worker's motivation because they affect three critical psychological states: *meaningfulness of work, responsibility for results*, and *knowledge of results. (Refer to Panel 12.9 again.)* That is, the more that workers (1) feel that they are doing meaningful work, (2) feel they are responsible for outcomes of the work, and (3) have knowledge of the actual results of the work and how they affect others, then the more likely they are to have favorable work outcomes: *high motivation, high performance, high satisfaction*, and *low absenteeism and turnover*.

One other element—shown at the bottom of Panel 12.9—needs to be discussed: *contingency factors*. This refers to the degree to which a person wants personal and psychological development. Job enrichment will be more successful for employees with high growth-need strength. Not everyone will respond well to enriched jobs. To be motivated, they must have three attributes: (1) necessary knowledge and skill, (2) desire for personal growth, and (3) context satisfactions—that is, the right physical working conditions, pay, and supervision.

High performance. Firefighters represent one profession that clearly manifests both the psychological states and the outcomes of the job characteristics model. For instance, they certainly need to practice a variety of skills, each emergency call has its own task identity and task significance, the job allows a fair amount of autonomy or discretion, and firefighters receive generally immediate feedback on how well they are performing.

Applying the Job Characteristics Model There are three major steps to follow when applying the model.

■ **Diagnose the work environment to see if a problem exists:** Hackman and Oldham developed a self-report instrument for managers to use called the *job diagnostic survey*. This will indicate whether an individual's so-called *motivating potential score (MPS)*—the amount of internal work motivation associated with a specific job—is high or low.

■ **Determine whether job redesign is appropriate:** If a person's MPS score is low, an attempt should be made to determine which of the core job characteristics is causing the problem. You should next decide whether job redesign is appropriate for a given group of employees. Job design is most likely to work in a participative environment in which employees have the necessary knowledge and skills.

■ **Consider how to redesign the job:** Here you try to increase those core job characteristics that are lower than national norms.

Example: At one time, the 470 workers at Alexander Doll Co. individually produced parts for dolls. Based on input from the workers, owners organized employees into seven- or eight-person teams, each responsible for completing about 300 doll or wardrobe assemblies a day. The result: orders can now be filled in one or two weeks instead of eight.[24]

major question

How can I use compensation and other rewards to motivate people?

The Big Picture

Compensation, the main motivator of performance, includes pay for performance, bonuses, profit sharing, gain sharing, and stock options, and pay for knowledge. Other nonmonetary incentives address needs that aren't being met, such as work-life balance, growth in skills, and commitment.

Perhaps the first thing that comes to mind when you think about motivating performance is compensation—how much money you or your employees can make. But consider how motivation works with Mary Morse, a software engineer with a computer-aided design company, Autodesk, in San Rafael, Calif. Every few weeks, another Silicon Valley company tries to lure her away. At least one of them offered a compensation and options package that could have made her rich. So far, Morse has turned them down. The reason: She likes her bosses.[25]

Morse demonstrates the truth of a Gallup Organization poll that found that most workers rate having a caring boss higher than they value monetary benefits.[26] Clearly, then, motivating doesn't just involve dollars.

Motivation & Compensation

Most people are paid an hourly wage or a weekly or monthly salary. Both of these are easy for organizations to administer, of course. But by itself a wage or a salary gives an employee little incentive to work hard. Incentive compensation plans try to do so, although no single plan will boost the performance of all employees.

Characteristics of the Best Incentive Compensation Plans In accordance with most of the theories of motivation we described earlier, for incentive plans to work, certain criteria are advisable, as follows. (1) Rewards must be linked to performance and be measurable. (2) The rewards must satisfy individual needs. (3) The rewards must be agreed upon by manager and employees. (4) The rewards must be perceived as being equitable, believable, and achievable by employees.

Small-business owner. Ernestina Galindo heads an Austin-based company, El Galindo, that specializes in traditional tortillas, chips, salsas, jellies, and other authentic Mexican and Tex-Mex foods. For some people, like Ms. Galindo, the only way to merge motivation and compensation is to own and manage their own business. What factors or incentives motivate you to work hard?

Popular Incentive Compensation Plans How would you like to be rewarded for your efforts? Some of the most well-known incentive compensation plans are *pay for performance, bonuses, profit sharing, gainsharing, stock options*, and *pay for knowledge*.

- **Pay for performance:** Also known as *merit pay*, **_pay for performance_ bases pay on one's results.** Thus, different salaried employees might get different pay raises and other rewards (such as promotions) depending on their overall job performance.

  Examples: One standard pay-for-performance plan, already mentioned, is payment according to a **_piece rate_, in which employees are paid according to how much output they produce,** as is often used with farmworkers picking fruit and vegetables. Another is the **_sales commission_, in which sales representatives are paid a percentage of the earnings the company made from their sales,** so that the more they sell, the more they are paid.

- **Bonuses:** **_Bonuses_ are cash awards given to employees who achieve specific performance objectives.**

  Example: Nieman Marcus, the department store, pays its salespeople a percentage of the earnings from the goods they sell.

- **Profit sharing:** **_Profit sharing_ is the distribution to employees of a percentage of the company's profits.**

  Example: In one T-shirt and sweatshirt manufacturing company, 10% of pretax profits are distributed to employees every month, and more is given out at the end of the year. Distributions are apportioned according to such criteria as performance, attendance, and lateness for individual employees.

- **Gainsharing:** **_Gainsharing_ is the distribution of savings or "gains" to groups of employees who reduced costs and increased measurable productivity.**

  Example: There are different types of gainsharing plans, but in one known as the *Scanlon plan*, developed in the 1920s by a steel-industry union leader named Joseph Scanlon, a portion of any cost savings, usually 75%, are distributed back to employees; the company keeps the other 25%.[27]

- **Stock options:** With **_stock options_, certain employees are given the right to buy stock at a future date for a discounted price.** The motivator here is that employees holding stock options will supposedly work hard to make the company's stock rise so that they can obtain it at a cheaper price. By giving stock options to all its employees, Starbucks Corp. has been able to hold its annual turnover rate to 55%—in an industry (fast food and restaurants) in which 300% is not unheard of.[28]

- **Pay for knowledge:** Also known as *skill-based pay*, **_pay for knowledge_ ties employee pay to the number of job-relevant skills or academic degrees they earn.**

  Example: The teaching profession is a time-honored instance of this incentive, in which elementary and secondary teachers are encouraged to increase their salaries by earning further college credit. However, firms such as Federal Express also have pay-for-knowledge plans.

Click-Along 12.4

Example of Use of Stock Options: Starbucks Offers Them to Rank-&-File Workers

Pay-for-knowledge plan. Teachers are encouraged to increase their knowledge by earning extra college credits, and their efforts are rewarded with pay raises. Readers of this book who are in college might also consider that they are participating in their own pay-for-knowledge plan—since college graduates have higher lifetime earnings than high school graduates do—but of course the rewards aren't immediate. Is immediacy an important part of incentives?

Nonmonetary Ways of Motivating Employees

Employees who can behave autonomously, solve problems, and take the initiative are apt to be the very ones who will leave if they find their own needs aren't being met—namely:[29]

■ **The need for work-life balance:** A Pricewaterhouse-Coopers survey of 2,500 university students in 11 countries found that 57% named as their primary career goal "attaining a balance between personal life and career."[30]

■ **The need to expand skills:** Having watched their parents undergo downsizing, younger workers in particular are apt to view a job as a way of gaining skills that will enable them to earn a decent living in the future.

■ **The need to matter:** Workers now want to be with an organization that allows them to feel they matter. They want to commit to their profession or fellow team members rather than have to profess a blind loyalty to the corporation.

There is a whole class of nonmonetary incentives to attract, retain, and motivate employees. The foremost example is the *flexible workplace*—including part-time work, flextime, compressed workweek, job sharing, and telecommuting. Other incentives can be expressed simply as: *treat employees well*, some examples of which follow.

Click-Along 12.5

Two Examples of Flexible Scheduling

Thoughtfulness: The Value of Being Nice A study by Walker Information, an Indianapolis-based research firm, found that employers spend too little time showing workers they matter, as manifested in lack of communication and lack of interest in new ideas and contributions.[31] A majority of employees feel underappreciated, according to a 1999 survey. Forty percent of employees who rated their boss's performance as poor said they were likely to look for a new job; only 11% of those who rated it excellent said they would.[32] "Being nice" to employees means, for example, reducing criticism, becoming more effusive in your praise, and writing thank-you notes to employees for exceptional performance.

The No. 1 reason people quit their jobs, it's believed, is their dissatisfaction with their supervisors, not their paychecks. Thus, industrial psychologist B. Lynn Ware suggests that if you learn valued employees are disgruntled, you should discuss it with them.[33] "It's extraordinary how often it is the small and often banal gestures that are the most meaningful," says another expert. "People will often say things like, 'I'm not really happy, but not yet prepared to jump ship because my boss was really good to me when my mother was sick.'"[34] Employers can promote personal relationships, which most employees are concerned about on the job, by offering breaks or other opportunities in which people can mix and socialize.

Show me the money. The Principal Financial Group specializes in designing customized benefits packages intended to build employee loyalty. Monetary benefits are far more likely to influence a prospective employee's initially working for a company, but nonmonetary factors are important in building commitment.

Work-Life Benefits Work-life benefits, according to Kathie Lingle, are programs "used by employers to increase productivity and commitment by removing certain barriers that make it hard for people to strike a balance between their work and personal lives."[35]

Lingle, who is national work-life director for KPMG, an accounting and consulting firm, emphasizes that work-life benefits "are not a reward, but a way of getting work done." After all, some employees are low performers simply because of a lack of life-work balance, with great demands at home. "If you only give these 'rewards' to existing high performers," says Lingle, "you're cutting people off who could, with some support, be high performers."

Besides alternative scheduling, work-life benefits include helping employees with daycare costs or even establishing on-site centers; domestic-partner benefits; job-protected leave for new parents; and provision of technology such as mobile phones and laptops to enable parents to work at home.[36]

Surroundings The cubicle, according to new research, is stifling the creativity and morale of many workers, and the bias of modern-day office designers for open spaces and neutral colors is leading to employee complaints that their workplaces are too noisy or too bland.

"There is no such thing as something that works for everybody," says Alan Hedge, a professor of environmental analysis at Cornell University.[37] An 8-foot-by-8-foot cubicle may not be a good visual trigger for human brains, and companies wanting to improve creativity and productivity may need to think about giving office employees better things to look at.

Cubicle culture. It might be too difficult to design a setup in which everyone has an office with a view. But would it be possible to design a layout in which everyone has a private office? Do you think it would motivate employees better?

Skill-Building & Educational Opportunities Learning opportunities can take two forms. Managers can see that workers are matched with coworkers that they can learn from, allowing them, for instance, to "shadow" workers in other jobs or be in interdepartmental task forces. There can also be tuition reimbursement for part-time study at a college or university.

Sabbaticals Intel and Apple understand that in a climate of 80-hour weeks people need to recharge themselves. But even McDonald's offers sabbaticals to long-time employees, giving a month to a year of paid time off in which to travel, learn, and pursue personal projects. The aim, of course, is to enable employees to recharge themselves but also, it is hoped, to cement their loyalty to the organization.[38]

Click-Along 12.6

Taking Something Practical Away from This Chapter— How to Treat Employees Well & Keep Top Performers

Key Terms Used in This Chapter

acquired needs theory, 384

bonuses, 401

equity theory, 388

expectancy, 387

expectancy theory, 386

extinction, 394

extrinsic reward, 379

gainsharing, 401

goal-setting theory, 390

hierarchy of needs theory, 380

hygiene factors, 383

instrumentality, 387

intrinsic reward, 379

job characteristics model, 397

job design, 396

job enlargement, 397

job enrichment, 397

job simplification, 396

motivating factors, 383

motivation, 378

need-based perspectives, 380

needs, 380

negative reinforcement, 393

pay for knowledge, 401

pay for performance, 401

piece rate, 401

positive reinforcement, 393

process perspectives, 386

profit sharing, 401

punishment, 394

reinforcement, 392

reinforcement theory, 392

sales commission, 401

stock options, 401

two-factor theory, 382

valence, 387

Summary

12.1
Motivating for Performance

■ Motivation is defined as the psychological processes that arouse and direct goal-directed behavior. In a simple model of motivation, people have certain needs that motivate them to perform specific behaviors for which they receive rewards that feed back and satisfy the original need. Rewards are of two types: extrinsic and intrinsic. An extrinsic reward is the payoff, such as money, a person receives from others for performing a particular task. An intrinsic reward is the satisfaction, such as a feeling of accomplishment, that a person receives from performing the particular task itself.

■ As a manager, you want to motivate people to do things that will benefit your organization—join it, stay with it, show up for work at it, perform better for it, and do extra for it.

■ Three major perspectives on motivation are (1) need-based, (2) process, and (3) reinforcement.

12.2
Need-Based Perspectives on Employee Motivation

■ Need-based perspectives, or content perspectives, are theories that emphasize the needs that motivate people. Needs are defined as physiological or psychological deficiencies that arouse behavior. Besides the McGregor Theory X/Theory Y (Chapter 1), need-based perspectives include (1) the hierarchy of needs theory, (2) the two-factor theory, and (3) the acquired needs theory.

■ The hierarchy of needs theory proposes that people are motivated by five levels of need: physiological, safety, belongingness, esteem, and self-actualization needs.

■ The two-factor theory proposes that work satisfaction and dissatisfaction arise from two different factors—work satisfaction from so-called motivating factors, and work dissatisfaction from so-called hygiene factors. Hygiene factors, the lower-level needs, are factors associated with job dissatisfaction—such as salary and working conditions—which affect the environment in which people work. Motivating factors, the higher-level needs, are factors associated with job satisfaction—such as achievement and advancement—which affect the rewards of work performance.

■ The acquired-needs theory states that three needs—achievement, affiliation, and power—are major motives determining people's behavior in the workplace.

12.3
Process Perspectives on Employee Motivation

■ Process perspectives are concerned with the thought processes by which people decide how to act. Three process perspectives on motivation are (1) expectancy theory, (2) equity theory, and (3) goal-setting theory.

■ Expectancy theory suggests that people are motivated by how much they want something and how likely they think they are to get it. The three elements affecting motivation are expectancy, instrumentality and valence. (1) Expectancy is the belief that a particular level of effort will lead to a particular level of performance. (2) Instrumentality is the expectation that successful performance of the task will lead to the outcome desired. (3) Valence is the value, the importance a worker assigns to the possible outcome or reward. When attempting to motivate employees, according to the logic of expectancy theory, managers should ascertain what rewards employees value, what job objectives and performance level they desire, whether there are rewards linked to performance, and whether employees believe managers will deliver the right rewards for the right performance.

■ Equity theory focuses on employee perceptions as to how fairly they think they are being treated compared to others. The key elements in equity theory are inputs, outputs (rewards), and comparisons. (1) With inputs, employees consider what they are putting into the job in time, effort, and so on. (2) With outputs or rewards, employees consider what they think they're getting out of the job in terms of pay, praise, and so on. (3) With comparison, employees compare the ratio of their own outcomes to inputs against the ratio of someone else's outcomes to inputs. Three

practical lessons of equity theory are that employee perceptions are what count, employee participation helps, and having an appeal process helps.

■ Goal-setting theory suggests that employees can be motivated by goals that are specific and challenging but achievable. Three elements of this theory are that goals must be specific, challenging, and achievable. In addition, the theory suggests that goals should be set jointly with the employee, be measurable, and have a target date for accomplishment and that employees should receive feedback and rewards.

12.4
Reinforcement Perspectives on Motivation

■ Reinforcement theory attempts to explain behavior change by suggesting that behavior with positive consequences tends to be repeated whereas behavior with negative consequences tends not to be repeated. Reinforcement is anything that causes a given behavior to be repeated or inhibited.

■ There are four types of reinforcement. (1) Positive reinforcement is the use of positive consequences to encourage desirable behavior. (2) Negative reinforcement is the removal of unpleasant consequences followed by a desired behavior. (3) Extinction is the withholding or withdrawal of positive rewards for desirable behavior, so that the behavior is less likely to occur in the future. (4) Punishment is the application of negative consequences to stop or change undesirable behavior.

■ In using positive reinforcement to motivate employees, managers should reward only desirable behavior, give rewards as soon as possible, be clear about what behavior is desired, and have different rewards and recognize individual differences. In using punishment, managers should punish only undesirable behavior, give reprimands or disciplinary actions as soon as possible, be clear about what behavior is undesirable, administer punishment in private, and combine punishment and positive reinforcement.

12.5
Motivation Through Job Design

■ Job design is, first, the division of an organization's work among its employees and, second, the application of motivational theories to jobs to increase satisfaction and performance. Two approaches to job design are fitting people to jobs (the traditional approach) and fitting jobs to people.

■ Fitting jobs to people assumes people are underutilized and want more variety. Two techniques for this type of job design include job enlargement and job enrichment. Job enlargement consists of increasing the number of tasks in a job to increase variety and motivation. Job enrichment consists of building into a job such motivating factors as responsibility, achievement, recognition, stimulating work, and advancement.

■ An outgrowth of job enrichment is the job characteristics model, which consists of (a) five core job characteristics that affect (b) three critical psychological states of an employee that in turn affect (c) work outcomes—the employee's motivation, performance, and satisfaction. The five core job characteristics are (1) skill variety—how many different skills does a job require; (2) task identity—how many different tasks are required to complete the work; (3) task significance—how many other people are affected by the job; (4) autonomy—how much discretion does the job allow the worker; and (5) feedback—how much do employees find out how well they're doing. These five characteristics affect three critical psychological states: meaningfulness of work, responsibility for results, and knowledge of results. Three major steps to follow when applying the job characteristics model are (1) diagnose the work environment to see if a problem exists, (2) determine whether job redesign is appropriate, and (3) consider how to redesign the job.

12.6
Using Compensation & Other Rewards to Motivate

■ Compensation is only one form of motivator. For incentive compensation plans for work, rewards must be linked to performance and be measurable; they must satisfy individual needs; they must be agreed on by manager and employee; and they must be perceived as being equitable, believable, and achievable by employees.

■ Popular incentive compensation plans are the following: (1) Pay for performance bases pay on one's results. One kind is payment according to piece rate, in which employees are paid according to how much output they produce. Another is the sales commission, in which sales representatives are paid a percentage of the earnings the company made from their sales. (2) Bonuses are cash awards given to employees who achieve specific performance objectives. (3) Profit sharing is the distribution to employees of a percentage of the company's profits. (4) Gainsharing is the distribution of savings or "gains" to groups of employees who reduced costs and increased measurable productivity. (5) Stock options allow certain employees to buy stock at a future date for a discounted price. (6) Pay for knowledge ties employee pay to the number of job-relevant skills or academic degrees they earn.

■ There are also nonmonetary ways of compensating employees. Some employees will leave because they feel the need for work-life balance, the need to expand their skills, and the need to matter. To retain such employees, nonmonetary incentives have been introduced, such as the flexible workplace. Other incentives that keep employees from leaving are thoughtfulness by employees' managers, work-life benefits such as daycare, attractive surroundings, skill-building and educational opportunities, and work sabbaticals.

Technology Professionals Corp. Personalizes Its Recognition & Rewards Programs

Excerpted from L. Buchanan, "Managing One-to-One," Inc., October 2001, pp. 84, 87.

Linda Connor is a high-school yearbook editor at heart. The vice-president of corporate culture at Technology Professionals Corp. (TPC), a $6.6-million technology staffing and services company in Grand Rapids, Mich., is constantly amassing and recording lively tidbits about the organization's almost 90 employees. She then takes that information, runs it through her imagination, and pulls out ingenious—occasionally audacious—ideas for customized rewards.

"I sit down at employees' 30-day reviews and ask specific questions about hobbies and interests for each member of their families," says Connor, who has, among other things, arranged for a staffer to fly on an F17 bomber. "I ask about the spouse, children, and even pets, so that if an event occurs that I know has been a drain on the family I can do something special just for the spouse or kids." Connor updates her profiles over time with information and insights gleaned from routine interaction, "so we are prepared to do things that are very timely for their current interests or needs," she explains. "Every time I meet an employee or I hear about a meeting someone else has had, I take mental notes." . . .

Collecting information about individuals and transforming it into tailored offerings is the stuff of one-to-one marketing, . . . the mighty oak of customer-relationship management (CRM). But in a new twist, TPC and companies like it are taking that concept and focusing it on their own employees. . . .

TPC's Connor doesn't need a good memory—she simply consults her extensive notes about employees' peeves and preferences. Connor's entry about consultant Phil Mayrose, for example, reveals that he loves college football, oldies music, and—above all else—golf. "Loves to try different courses. Send him out with either his wife, teammates, or a friend and he's in heaven," reads Connor's Mayrose entry. Last year she used that infor-

mation to reward the hardworking Mayrose with a weekend getaway at a dude ranch that included several rounds of golf.

Connor doesn't focus exclusively on rewards. She also wants to understand employees' personal lives so that she can help when things spin out of balance. Her comments about one employee read more like a page torn from a therapist's notebook than something from a human-resources file: "During stressful periods [she] loses confidence in her ability as a mom, housekeeper, sister, daughter, friend, and aunt," Connor observes. "Ideas during high-stress times: lawn-mowing service, housekeeping, hot meals, day away with her son."

Connor's dedicated chronicling of employees' passions manifests the philosophy of TPC's founder and CEO, Steven Lassig, whose own ballooning workload makes it impossible for him to keep up with every member of his fast-growing staff. . . . Lassig no longer has the time to meet every new hire, so he schedules informal lunches several times a month with groups of no more than six employees, just to chat. "Eventually, everyone attends," says Lassig. "It helps me to get to know them and gives me ideas on how to reward them when they do something well."

For Discussion

1. How are Linda Connor and Steven Lassig using need theory to motivate their employees?

2. To what extent is TPC using principles derived from Herzberg's two-factor theory? Explain.

3. Does TPC's reward and recognition program apply any principles from expectancy theory? Discuss.

4. What are the pros and cons of using the concept of managing one-to-one to motivate employees? Explain.

Take It to the Net

When you apply for a job, one of the first things you probably think is "how much money will I make?" As you learned in this chapter, compensation is certainly part of motivation—a hefty salary and great stock options would factor in if you decided to leave your current job to go to another. But there are also nonmonetary motivators as well.

The purpose of this exercise is to make you aware of how companies might use both monetary and nonmonetary rewards to motivate employees. To accomplish this, we want you to examine the motivational approaches used at Southwest Airlines. Go to *www.iflyswa.com*. Click on the section on *Careers*. Go to the section for *Benefits* and read the information.

Questions for Discussion

1. If you were considering a career with Southwest Airlines, would the company's monetary rewards motivate you? Explain.

2. To what extent do you feel Southwest Airlines fills its employees' need for work-life balance? Explain.

3. Judging from the benefits offered at Southwest Airlines, do you feel the company is trying to satisfy a variety of employee needs?

Self-Assessment

What Is Your Reaction to Equity Differences?*

Objectives

1. Assess your reaction to equity differences.
2. Gain more insight into yourself.

Introduction: Have you ever noticed that certain people scream "No fair!" whenever they perceive something as unequal? Have you also noticed that other people don't seem bothered by inequity at all? According to researchers, when given the same amount of inequity, people respond differently depending on their individual equity sensitivity. There are varying degrees of equity sensitivity:

Benevolents are individuals who prefer their outcome/input ratios to be less than the others being compared. These are people who don't mind being underrewarded.

Equity Sensitives are individuals who prefer outcome/input ratios to be equal. These people are concerned with obtaining rewards that they perceive to be fair in relation to what others are receiving.

Entitleds are individuals who prefer their outcome/input ratios go above those of the others being compared. These people aren't worried by inequities and actually prefer situations in which they see themselves as overrewarded.

The purpose of this exercise is to assess your equity sensitivity.

Instructions: The five statements below ask what you would like your relationship to be within any organization. For each question, *divide* 10 points between the two answers (A and B) *by giving the most points to the answer that is most like you and the fewest points to the answer least like you.* You can give an equal number of points to A and B. You can make use of zeros if you like. Just be sure to use all 10 points on each question. (For instance, if statement A is completely appropriate and B is not at all appropriate, give A 10 points, and B zero points. If A is somewhat appropriate and B is not completely appropriate, give A 7 points and B 3 points.) Place your points next to each letter.

In any organization where I might work:

1. It would be more important for me to:
   A. Get from the organization   ___
   B. Give to the organization   ___

2. It would be more important for me to:
   A. Help others   ___
   B. Watch out for my own good   ___

3. I would be more concerned about:
   A. What I received from the organization   ___
   B. What I contributed to the organization   ___

4. The hard work I would do should:
   A. Benefit the organization   ___
   B. Benefit me   ___

5. My personal philosophy in dealing with the organization would be:
   A. If you don't look out for yourself, nobody else will   ___
   B. It's better to give than to receive   ___

Calculate your total score by adding the points you allocated to the following items: 1B, 2A, 3B, 4A, and 5B. Total score = _____

Analysis & Interpretation: Your total will be between 0 and 50. If you scored less than 29, you are an Entitled; if your score was between 29 and 32, you are Equity Sensitive; and if your score was above 32, you are a Benevolent. If your score was above 32, you are a Benevolent; if your score was between 39 and 32, you are Equity Sensitive; if your score was less than 29, you are an Entitled.

Questions for Discussion

1. To what extent are the results consistent with your self-perception? Explain.
2. Using the survey items as a foundation, how should managers try to motivate Benevolents, Equity Sensitives, and Entitleds? Discuss in detail.

*R. C. Huseman, J. D. Hatfield, and E. W. Miles, "Test for Individual Perceptions of Job Equity: Some Preliminary Findings," *Perceptual and Motor Skills*, vol. 62, 1985, pp. 1055–1064.

Group Exercise

Managing for Motivation

Objectives

1. To apply aspects from motivation theories covered in this chapter.
2. To design a motivation plan.

Introduction

As a student, you've probably found times in your academic career when you just can't seem to get it together: You miss deadlines, you skip class, your work is of poor quality, you procrastinate, and you just don't put in adequate effort to get your assignments done. Have you ever considered why your performance is problematic? Perhaps you don't feel motivated enough by the assignments. Perhaps your attention and motivation are directed elsewhere: packing for spring break, say, or planning for a weekend party.

Managers frequently encounter performance problems as well. Employees miss deadlines, produce poor-quality work, put in inadequate levels of performance, take excessive time off, display negative attitudes and behaviors, and don't cooperate with their team members. Motivation is part of these performance problems, and managers must learn how to motivate employees to improve their performance. The purpose of this exercise is to give you practice at diagnosing the causes of a performance problem and to propose managerial solutions to fix the problem.

Instructions

Break into groups of five or six people. Read the following case study of Mary Martin. First consider how Herzberg's two-factor theory affects Mary's motivation. Brainstorm with the group to come up with some Hygiene factors that may be affecting Mary's motivation. Next consider Motivating factors—what can Mary's manager do to make her *satisfied*? You can also consider McClelland's Acquired Needs Theory in your discussion. Which of the three needs is Mary most concerned with?

After your group has completed its brainstorming, use the information and solutions you came up with to design a motivation plan for Mary's manager.

The Case*

Mary Martin, 30, received her baccalaureate degree in computer science from a reputable state school in the Midwest, graduating with above-average grades. Mary is currently working in the computer support/analysis department as a programmer for a nationally based firm.

During the past year, Mary has missed 10 days of work. She seems unmotivated and rarely has her assignments completed on time. Usually she is given the harder programs to work on.

Recently, the company turned all hourly positions into salary positions. Some employees have complained that they made more money when they were hourly employees because they were paid for overtime. Mary's pay structure was based on an hourly wage, and she would often work long hours and overtime.

Past records indicate that Mary completes programs classified as "routine" in about 45 hours on average, whereas her coworkers take on average 32 hours for such programs. She finishes programs considered "major problems" on average in about 115 hours, compared with about 100 hours on average for her coworkers.

The company has decided to create a more team-based environment. Many of the programmers who once worked on projects alone are now being given projects to tackle as a team. When Mary has worked in programming teams, her peer perfor-

mance reviews are generally average or negative. Her male peers say that she is not creative in attacking problems and that she is difficult to work with.

Last year, the company expanded its office and hired 250 new employees. The company moved its offices from a small to a larger building; some employees who worked for the company before the expansion expressed concern that there were not enough resources and tools to go around. Many of the tenured employees also complained to supervisors that new employees were not adequately trained and that it was slowing down production.

Some of the tenured employees expressed concern when some of the newer employees were promoted to supervisory positions; according to e-mail sent to supervisors, many felt that they were overlooked. Others even felt that the criteria for promotion were not based on experience and performance with the company; instead they suspected the supervisors were playing favorites and promoting their friends to supervisory positions.

Along with new employees came new programming demands. However, employees reported to supervisors that they did not feel they had adequate time to learn how to use new software that would make designing new programs easier and more efficient.

The computer department recently sent a questionnaire to all users of its services to evaluate the usefulness and accuracy of data received. The results indicate many departments are not using computer output because they cannot understand the reports. It was also determined that users of output generated from Mary's programs found the output chaotic and not useful for managerial decision making.

Questions for Discussion

1. What are some Hygiene factors associated with Mary's motivation? Describe.

2. How would you correct these Hygiene factors? Discuss.

3. As Mary's manager, how can you use expectancy theory to motivate Mary? Explain the details.

4. If you were Mary's manager, what additional changes would you implement to increase the employees' performance?

*Adapted from R. Kreitner and A. Kinicki, *Organizational Behavior*, 5th ed. (Burr Ridge, IL: McGraw-Hill, 2001), p. 220.

Would You Fire Someone When You Knew It Might Lead to Divorce as Well as Loss of Income?

From Margaret Popper, "Lost Job, Lost Spouse: Being Fired Can Lead to Divorce,"
Business Week, December 17, 2001, p. 26.

Everyone knows that financial stress can help break up a marriage. But a new study from the National Bureau of Economic Research Inc. shows that some financial problems are more likely than others to lead to divorce.

In particular, the authors of the study, Kerwin Kofi Charles of University of Michigan and Melvin Stephens Jr. of Carnegie Mellon University, find that being fired from a job significantly raises the probability of getting divorced. Married men who are fired have an 18% higher chance of being divorced within the next three years, while women have a 13% higher chance.

But someone losing his or her job because of disability doesn't mean a significantly increased probability of seeing the marriage break up. Similarly, a plant closing that affects a group of people doesn't raise the odds of divorce.

By way of explanation, Charles and Stephens suggest that the character traits that cause a person to be laid off could also make him or her a bad mate. "For example, if a wife can conclude that a husband lost his job because of his repeated irresponsibility or bad temper," they write, "she should conclude both that he is likely to face employment troubles in the future *and* that he may not be a good person with whom to raise children."

By contrast, a plant closing or a sudden disability is viewed as bad luck rather than a deserved punishment for a bad personality. These events are less likely to spark a divorce even though, in the case of disability, the income loss to the couple is generally greater.

Solving the Dilemma

You're supervising an employee, the sole support of his wife and five children, who barely manages to get his work done. Your attempts at using motivational techniques fail to improve his performance. What would you do?

1. Keep him on without expecting too much. After all, everyone has the right to earn a living, and the work does get done.

2. After giving several warnings, fire him, knowing it could lead to considerable hardship in his family. After all, you have to show your bosses you're a productive manager.

3. Fire him, but give him a long time to his termination date and help him with outplacement services, although his continued presence will make you uncomfortable.

4. Invent other options. Discuss.

Groups & Teams
From Conflict to Cooperation

DEALING WITH DISAGREEMENTS

Even if you're at the top of your game as a manager, working with groups and teams of people—the subject of this chapter—will now and then put you in the middle of disagreements, sometimes even destructive conflict. How can you deal with it?

There are five conflict-handling styles, or techniques, a manager can use for handling disagreements with individuals, as follows:[1]

- **Avoiding—"Maybe the problem will go away":** *Avoiding* involves ignoring or suppressing a conflict. Avoidance is appropriate for trivial issues, when emotions are high and a cooling-off period is needed, or when the cost of confrontation outweighs the benefits of resolving the conflict. It is not appropriate for difficult or worsening problems.

  The benefit of this approach is that it buys time in unfolding and ambiguous situations. The weakness is that it provides only a temporary fix and sidesteps the underlying problem.

- **Accommodating—"Let's do it your way":** An accommodating manager is also known as a "smoothing" or "obliging" manager. *Accommodating* is allowing the desires of the other party to prevail. As one writer describes it, "An obliging [accommodating] person neglects his or her own concern to satisfy the concern of the other party."[2] Accommodating may be an appropriate conflict-handling strategy when it's possible to eventually get something in return or when the issue isn't important to you. It's not appropriate for complex or worsening problems.

  The advantage of accommodating is that it encourages cooperation. The weakness is that once again it's only a temporary fix that fails to confront the underlying problem.

- **Forcing—"You have to do it my way":** Also known as "dominating," *forcing* is simply ordering an outcome, when a manager relies on his or her formal authority and power to resolve a conflict. Forcing is appropriate when an unpopular solution must be implemented and when it's not important that others be committed to your viewpoint.

  The advantage of forcing is speed: It can get results quickly. The disadvantage is that in the end it doesn't resolve personal conflict—if anything, it aggravates it by breeding hurt feelings and resentments.

- **Compromising—"Let's split the difference":** In *compromising*, both parties give up something in order to gain something. Compromise is appropriate when both sides have opposite goals or possess equal power. But compromise isn't workable when it is used so often that it doesn't achieve results—for example, continual failure to meet production deadlines.

  The benefit of compromise is that it is a democratic process that seems to have no losers. However, since so many people approach compromise situations with a win-lose attitude, they may be disappointed and feel cheated.

- **Collaborating—"Let's cooperate to reach a win-win solution that benefits both of us":** *Collaborating* strives to devise solutions that benefit both parties. Collaboration is appropriate for complex issues plagued by misunderstanding. It is inappropriate for resolving conflicts rooted in opposing value systems.

  The strength of collaborating is its longer lasting impact because it deals with the underlying problem, not just its symptoms. Its weakness is that it's very time-consuming. Nevertheless, collaboration is the best approach for dealing with groups and teams of people.

Click-Along 13.1

Dealing with Disagreements among Subordinates in a Group

FORECAST: WHAT'S AHEAD IN THIS CHAPTER

In this chapter, we consider the nature of conflict, both bad and good. We also consider cooperation, as expressed through teamwork. We distinguish groups from teams and discuss different kinds of teams. We discuss how groups evolve into teams, and we describe how managers can build effective teams.

major question

Since conflict is a part of life, what should a manager know about it in order to deal successfully with it?

The Big Picture
Conflict, an enduring feature of the workplace, is a process in which one party perceives that its interests are being opposed or negatively affected by another party. Conflict can be negative (bad) or functional (good). Indeed, either too much or too little conflict can affect performance. This section identifies seven sources of conflict in organizations and also describes four ways to stimulate constructive conflict.

"I've fired many employees through the years," writes a manager to an advice columnist, "but right now I've got a guy who scares me. Maybe there's been one too many postal shootings, but I'm afraid this guy could turn violent."[3]

Firings, of course, generate strong emotions and can easily trigger outbursts, though dismissed workers seldom "go postal"—become violent and start shooting people. (About 15 American workers are murdered on the job every week, but few are by enraged coworkers; around 80% of workplace homicides occur during robberies or other crimes.[4]) Nevertheless, employee dismissals—along with increased workloads, pressure-cooker deadlines, demands for higher productivity, and other kinds of stress—are among the sources of that enduring feature of the workplace: conflict.

The Nature of Conflict: Disagreement Is Normal

Mention the term *conflict* and many people envision shouting and fighting. But as a manager, during a typical workday you will encounter more subtle, nonviolent types of conflict: opposition, criticism, arguments. Thus, a definition of conflict seems fairly mild: ___Conflict___ **is a process in which one party perceives that its interests are being opposed or negatively affected by another party.**[5] Conflict is simply disagreement, a perfectly normal state of affairs. Conflicts may take many forms: between individuals, between an individual and a group, between groups, and between an organization and its environment.

While all of us might wish to live lives free of conflict, it is now recognized that certain kinds of conflict can actually be beneficial.[6] Let us therefore distinguish between *negative conflict* (bad) and *constructive conflict* (good).

- **Negative conflict—bad for organizations:** From the standpoint of the organization, ___negative conflict___ **is conflict that hinders the organization's performance or threaten its interests.** As a manager, you need to do what you can to remove negative conflict, sometimes called *dysfunctional conflict*.

- **Constructive conflict—good for organizations:** The good kind of conflict is ___constructive conflict,___ **which benefits the main purposes of the organization and serves its interests.**[7] There are some situations in which this kind of conflict—also called *functional conflict* or *cooperative conflict*—is considered advantageous.

Can Too Little or Too Much Conflict Affect Performance?

It's tempting to think that a conflict-free work group is a happy work group, as
indeed it may be. But is it a productive group? In the 1970s, social scientists
specializing in organizational behavior introduced the revolutionary idea that
organizations could suffer from *too little* conflict.

■ **Too little conflict—indolence:** Work groups,
departments, or organizations that experience
too little conflict tend to be plagued by apathy,
lack of creativity, indecision, and missed deadlines. The result is that organizational performance suffers.

■ **Too much conflict—warfare:** Excessive conflict, on the other hand, can erode organizational
performance because of political infighting, dissatisfaction, lack of teamwork, and turnover.
Workplace aggression and violence are manifestations of excessive conflict.[10]

"Scab!" Striking mem-
bers of the Communica-
tion Workers of America,
a union picketing Veri-
zon, shout at nonstriking
workers passing on the
other side of police bar-
riers. What kinds of mat-
ters lead to too much
conflict in the workplace?

Thus, it seems that a moderate level of conflict can induce creativity and initiative, thereby raising performance, as shown in the diagram below. *(See Panel 13.1.)* As might be expected, however, the idea as to what constitutes "moderate" will vary among managers.

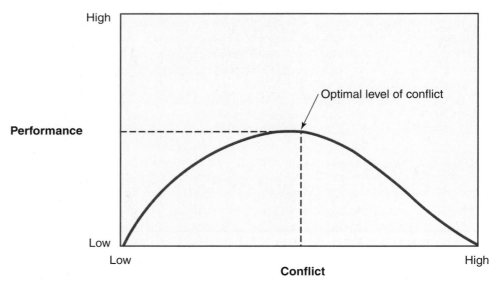

PANEL 13.1
The relationship between level of conflict and level of performance. Too little conflict or too much conflict causes performance to suffer.

Seven Causes of Conflict

There are a variety of sources of conflict—so-called *conflict triggers*. Seven of the principal ones are listed below. *(See Panel 13.2.)* By understanding these, you'll be better able to take charge and manage the conflicts rather than letting the conflicts take you by surprise and manage you.

PANEL 13.2
Seven sources of conflict in organizations

1. Competition for scarce resources	When two parties need the same things
2. Time pressure	When people believe there aren't enough hours to do the work
3. Inconsistent goals or reward systems	When people pursue different objectives
4. Ambiguous jurisdictions	When job boundaries are unclear
5. Status differences	When there are inconsistencies in power & influence
6. Personality clashes	When individual differences can't be resolved
7. Communication failures	When people misperceive & misunderstand

1 Competition for Scarce Resources: When Two Parties Need the Same Things Within organizations there is often a scarcity of needed resources—for example, funds, office space, equipment, employees, and money for raises. When resources are scarce, being a manager becomes more difficult and conflict more likely.[11]

Example: There are lots of computer software glitches but not enough programmers to fix them.

2 Time Pressure: When People Believe There Aren't Enough Hours to Do the Work Setting a deadline is a useful way of inducing people to perform. Or it can be a source of resentment, rage, and conflict if employees think their manager has unrealistic expectations.

Example: If you're in the business of marketing Christmas items to department stores and gift shops, it's imperative that you have your product ready for those important trade shows at which store buyers will appear. But the product-ready deadline for Marketing may be completely unworkable for your company's Production Department, leading to angry conflict.

3 Inconsistent Goals or Reward Systems: When People Pursue Different Objectives It's natural for people in functional organizations to be pursuing different objectives and to be rewarded accordingly, but this means that conflict is practically built in to the system.

Example: The sales manager for a college textbook publisher may be rewarded for achieving exceptional sales of newly introduced titles. But individual salespeople are rewarded for how many books they sell overall, which means they may promote the old tried and true books they know.

4 Ambiguous Jurisdictions: When Job Boundaries Are Unclear "That's not my job and those aren't my responsibilities." "Those resources belong to me because I need them as part of my job." When task responsibilities are unclear, that can often lead to conflict.

Examples: Is the bartender or the waiter supposed to put the lime in the gin tonic and the celery in the Bloody Mary? Is management or the union in charge of certain work rules? Is Marketing or Research & Development supposed to be setting up focus groups to explore ideas for new products?

5 Status Differences: When There Are Inconsistencies in Power & Influence. It can happen that people who are lower in status according to the organization chart actually have disproportionate power over those theoretically above them, which can lead to conflicts.

Examples: If a restaurant patron complains his or her steak is not rare enough, the chef is the one who cooked it, but the waiter—who is usually lower in status—is the one who gave the chef the order. Airlines could not hold their schedules without flight crews and ground crews working a certain amount of overtime. But during labor disputes, pilots, flight attendants, and mechanics may simply refuse managers' requests to work overtime.

6 Personality Clashes: When Individual Differences Can't Be Resolved Personality, values, attitudes, and experience can be so disparate that sometimes the only way to resolve individual differences—personality clashes—is to separate two people.

Example: Are you easy-going, but she's tense and driven? Does he always shade the facts, while you're a stickler for the truth? If you're basically Ms. Straight Arrow and he's Mr. Slippery, do you think you could adapt your personality to fit his? Maybe you should ask for a transfer.

7 Communication Failures: When People Misperceive & Misunderstand The need for clear communication is a never-ending, ongoing process. Even under the best of circumstances, people misunderstand others, leading to conflict.

Example: Hewlett-Packard hired a consulting firm to explore acquisition of the computer maker Compaq, and at a crucial directors' meeting the consultant gave H-P board members a document about the two companies to discuss. However, an important board member, Walter Hewlett, son of one of the founders, wasn't there. He was playing his cello somewhere—at an annual event he had appeared in for the past three years—and had assumed the board would accommodate him, as it had in the past. But the board plowed ahead, believing Hewlett wouldn't miss such an important session. This turned out to be a crucial misstep for H-P management.[12] The miscommunication ultimately led to a major battle between Hewlett and top H-P officers, including CEO Carleton Fiorina. Heirs of the company's founders, which owned 18% of the stock, were upset at the personal tone Fiorina took in painting Hewlett as a musician and academic who flip-flopped over board decisions.

How to Stimulate Constructive Conflict

As a manager you are being paid not just to manage conflict but even to create some, where it's constructive and appropriate, in order to stimulate performance. Constructive conflict, if carefully monitored, can be very productive under a number of circumstances: When your work group seems afflicted with inertia and apathy, resulting in low performance. When there's a lack of new ideas and resistance to change. When there seem to be a lot of yes-men and yes-women (expressing so-called *groupthink*, described later) in the work unit. When there's high employee turnover. When managers seem unduly concerned with peace, cooperation, compromise, consensus, and their own popularity rather than in achieving work objectives.

Four devices used to stimulate constructive conflict are as follows:

1 Spur Competition among Employees Competition is, of course, a form of conflict, but competition is often healthy in spurring people to produce higher results. Thus, a company will often put its salespeople in competition with each other by offering bonuses and awards for achievement—a trip to a Caribbean resort, say, for the top performer of the year.

2 Change the Organization's Culture & Procedures. Competition may also be established by making deliberate and highly publicized moves to change the corporate culture—by announcing to employees that the organization is now going to be more innovative and reward original thinking and unorthodox ideas. Procedures, such as paperwork sign-off processes, can also be revamped. Results can be reinforced in visible ways through announcements of bonuses, raises, and promotions.

3 Bring in Outsiders for New Perspectives Without "new blood," organizations can become inbred and resistant to change. This is why managers will often bring in outsiders—people from a different unit of the organization, new hires from competing companies, or consultants. With their different backgrounds, attitudes, or management styles, these outsiders can bring a new perspective and can shake things up.

4 Use Programmed Conflict: Devil's Advocacy & the Dialectic Method *Programmed conflict* is designed to elicit different opinions without inciting people's personal feelings.[13]

Sometimes decision-making groups become so bogged down in details and procedures that nothing of substance gets done. The idea here is to get people, through role playing, to defend or criticize ideas based on relevant facts rather than on personal feelings and preferences.

The method for getting people to engage in this debate of ideas is to do disciplined role playing, for which two proven methods are available: *devil's advocacy* and the *dialectic method*.

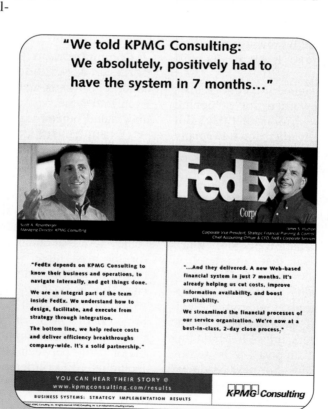

"We told KPMG Consulting: We absolutely, positively had to have the system in 7 months..."

"FedEx depends on KPMG Consulting to know their business and operations, to navigate internally, and get things done.

We are an integral part of the team inside FedEx. We understand how to design, facilitate, and execute from strategy through integration.

The bottom line, we help reduce costs and deliver efficiency breakthroughs company-wide. It's a solid partnership."

"...And they delivered. A new Web-based financial system in just 7 months. It's already helping us cut costs, improve information availability, and boost profitability.

We streamlined the financial processes of our service organization. We're now at a best-in-class, 2-day close process."

YOU CAN HEAR THEIR STORY @
www.kpmgconsulting.com/results
BUSINESS SYSTEMS: STRATEGY IMPLEMENTATION RESULTS

KPMG Consulting

The outsider. Sometimes organizations need a new perspective. Evidently FedEx felt it did when it hired management consultant KPMG Consulting, according to this ad.

The devil's in the details. Gatorade is owned by Quaker Oats. At one time, Coca-Cola Co. CEO Doug Daft entered into negotiations to buy Quaker and Gatorade—without first informing Coke's board of directors. When he then proposed the acquisition during a board meeting, the directors, resentful over being ignored, embarrassed Daft by turning it down. What Daft had done, in other words, was to force his board members into the role of playing devil's advocate against the acquisition. And since they had the power to punish him for his secret initiative, they did so—probably unwisely, as it turned out, because eventually Quaker and the coveted brand of Gatorade were acquired by Coke's major rival, Pepsico.

These two methods work as follows:

- **Devil's advocacy—role-playing criticism to test whether a proposal is workable:** *Devil's advocacy* **is the process of assigning someone to play the role of critic** to voice possible objections to a proposal and thereby generate critical thinking and reality testing.[14]

  Periodically role-playing devil's advocate has a beneficial side effect in that it is good training for developing analytical and communicative skills. However, it's a good idea to rotate the job so no one person develops a negative reputation.

- **The dialectic method—role-playing two sides of a proposal to test whether it is workable:** Requiring a bit more skill training than devil's advocacy does, the *dialectic method* **is the process of having two people or groups play opposing roles in a debate in order to better understand a proposal.** After the structured debate, managers are better able to make a decision.[15]

Example of the Use of the Dialectic Method: How Anheuser-Busch Debates Important Moves

When the corporate policy committee of Anheuser-Busch is considering a major move—such as whether to make a big capital expenditure or get into or out of a business—it sometimes assigns two, even three, groups of people to make the case for each side of the question. Each team is knowledgeable about the subject, and each has the same information. Sometimes an opponent of the project is asked to argue for it—and vice versa.

The exercise may produce a final decision that represents a synthesis of the opposing views. "We end up with decisions and alternatives we hadn't thought of," says Pat Stokes, who heads the company's beer empire. "You become a lot more anticipatory, better able to see what might happen, because you have thought through the process."[16]

Whatever kind of organization you work for, you'll always benefit from knowing how to manage conflict. Now let's consider how to advance from conflict to cooperation—by studying how to manage groups and teams.

major question

If the best managers are usually independent of the herd, why should they cultivate teamwork skills?

The Big Picture

Teamwork promises to be a cornerstone of future management. The claims made for teamwork is that it increases productivity, increases speed, reduces costs, improves quality, reduces destructive internal competition, and improves workplace cohesiveness.

"We have this mythology in America about the lone genius," says Tom Kelley, general manager of Ideo, an industrial design company in Palo Alto, Calif., that helped create the Apple mouse and the Palm V handheld computer. "We love to personify things. But Michelangelo didn't paint the Sistine Chapel alone, and Edison didn't invent the light bulb alone."[17]

At Ideo, teamwork is the name of the game—several people "each doing a part but all subordinating personal prominence to the efficiency of the whole," as the dictionary defines it. And the key element of effective teamwork is a commitment to a common purpose.[18]

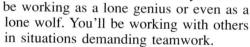

More Teamwork: The Change Today's Employees Need to Make

The use of teamwork is having substantial impacts on organizations and individuals, and it promises to be a cornerstone of progressive management. According to management guru Peter Drucker, tomorrow's organizations will not only be flatter and information-based but also organized around teamwork.[19] This opinion is bolstered by a survey of human resource executives in which 44% called for *more teamwork* as a change that employees need to make to achieve today's business goals.[20]

When you take a job in an organization, therefore, the chances are you won't be working as a lone genius or even as a lone wolf. You'll be working with others in situations demanding teamwork.

A self-managed team. Employees of Published Image, Inc., a full-service newsletter management group in Boston, work together on the layout of a publication. Teamwork helps the work get done quickly and efficiently. Not all companies allow employees the necessary independence and responsibility that makes effective teams possible.

Why Teamwork Matters

What are the results that teamwork can achieve? Some of the claims are as follows:

Increased Productivity At General Electric's Puerto Rico factory for manufacturing arresters (surge protectors to guard power stations and transmission lines against lightning strikes), use of teamwork resulted in a work force that was 20% more productive than comparable work units elsewhere in the company.[21] Hourly workers were rotated through different work areas every six months to learn how their jobs affected other workers in the plant.

Increased Speed Guidant Corp. in Santa Clara, Calif., which makes devices for life-saving medical procedures, used teamwork to create new products and get them to market more quickly—halving the time it took previously.[22] In four years, it also doubled its sales. Finally, it reduced its technical workforce turnover to only 2%–10% annually in an area where typical employee attrition is 20% a year.

Reduced Costs Boeing used teamwork to develop its latest commercial jetliner, the 777, at costs that were far less than would have been the case with its traditional management techniques.[23]

Improved Quality Westinghouse used teamwork in its truck and trailer division and within its electronic components division to improve quality performance. In addition, its nuclear fuel division earned one of the first Malcolm Baldrige Quality Awards.

Reduced Destructive Internal Competition Clothing-store chain Men's Wearhouse actually fired one of its most successful "wardrobe consultants" because he wasn't sharing walk-in customer traffic with other salespeople. After the self-centered salesman was let go, none of his colleagues matched his sales record. But total sales volume for the store nevertheless increased significantly.[24]

Improved Workplace Cohesiveness At Microsoft Corp., the organization of the software development group into an R&D teamwork system helped members become more motivated and satisfied and to coordinate their efforts.[25]

The basis of teamwork is, as you might guess, an entity called the team. Let us see what this is.

Plane teamwork. In creating the 777 jetliner, Boeing used new approaches to design and build it. All kinds of specialties—designers, manufacturing representatives, tooling, engineers, finance, suppliers, customers, and others—worked jointly to create the airplane's parts and systems. Design/build teams—238 in all—were linked by mainframe computers in a system that used three-dimensional software allowing designers to see parts as solid images and then simulate the assembly of those parts on screen. As a result of this system, the 777 program exceeded its goal of reducing changes, errors, and rework by 50%. The first 777 aircraft was just .023 of an inch—about the width of a playing card—away from perfect alignment; most airplanes line up to within a half inch.

How is one collection of workers different from any other?

The Big Picture

A group typically is management-directed, a team self-directed. Groups may be formal, created to do productive work, or informal, created for friendship. Work teams, which engage in collective work requiring coordinated effort, may be organized according to four basic purposes: advice, production, project, and action. Two types of teams are quality circles and self-managed teams.

Martin Jack Rosenblum is a bearded long-hair who likes to wear snakeskin boots and cowboy shirts to his job as archivist at the Milwaukee headquarters for Harley-Davidson motorcycles. At one time, Rosenblum was an English professor at the University of Wisconsin, but he hated the academic politics and backstabbing. Now, he says, "For the first time in my life, I feel like I'm part of a community. Harley is the University I've always been looking for."[26] The reason: In Harley's team-oriented and more open, goal-directed environment, he found more camaraderie and a sense of accomplishment.

Groups & Teams: How Do They Differ?

Aren't a group of people and a team of people the same thing? By and large, no. One is a collection of people, the other a powerful unit of collective performance. One is typically management-directed, the other self-directed.

Consider the differences.

What a Group Is: Collections of People Performing as Individuals A *group* is defined as two or more freely interacting individuals who share collective norms, share collective goals, and have a common identity.[27] A group is different from a crowd, a transitory collection of people who don't interact with each other, such as a crowd gathering on a sidewalk to watch a fire. And it is different from an organization, such as a labor union, which is so large that members also don't interact.[28]

An example of a work group would be a collection of, say, 10 employees meeting to exchange information about various companies' policies on wages and hours.

What a Team Is: Collections of People with Common Commitment McKinsey & Company management consultants Jon R. Katzenbach and Douglas K. Smith say it is a mistake to use the terms group and team interchangeably. Successful teams, they say, tend to take on a life of their own. Thus, a *team* is defined as a small group of people with complementary skills who are committed to a common purpose, performance goals, and approach for which they hold themselves **mutually accountable.**[29] "The essence of a team is common commitment," say Katzenbach and Smith. "Without it, groups perform as individuals; with it, they become a powerful unit of collective performance."[30]

An example of a team would be a collection of 2–10 employees who are studying industry pay scales with the goal of making recommendations for adjusting pay grades within their own company.

Click-Along 13.2

How Groups & Teams Differ:
A Summary

Formal versus Informal Groups

Groups may be either formal or informal.

■ **Formal groups—created to do productive work: A** *formal group* **is a group established to do something productive for the organization and is headed by a leader.** A formal group may be a division, a department, a work group, or a committee. It may be permanent or temporary. In general, people are assigned to them according to their skills and the organization's requirements.

■ **Informal groups—created for friendship: An** *informal group* **is a group formed by people seeking friendship and has no officially appointed leader, although a leader may emerge from the membership.** An informal group may be simply a collection of friends who hang out with one another, such as those who take coffee breaks together, or it may be as organized as a prayer breakfast, a bowling team, a service club, or other voluntary organization.

What's important for you as a manager to know is that informal groups can advance or undercut the plans of formal groups. The formal organization may make efforts, say, to speed up the plant assembly line or to institute workplace reforms. But these attempts may be sabotaged through the informal networks of workers who meet and gossip over lunch pails and after-work beers.[31]

However, interestingly, informal groups can also be highly productive—even more so than formal groups.

Example of How Informal Groups Can Be Productive: A Siemens Plant Finds Worker Chitchat "Is Not Goofing Off, It's Training"

To a manager, it may look like goofing off—those quick visits between coworkers, the brief exchanges near the coffeepot. But a two-year $1.6 million study by the Center for Workplace Development showed something more interesting: Workers learn most of what they know on the fly, and often from one another.

Though companies now spend up to $50 billion a year on formal training programs, up to 70% of workplace learning is informal, according to the study, which examined such companies as Motorola, Boeing Commercial Airplane Group, and Siemens Power Transmission and Distribution.[32]

At the Siemens plant in Wendell, N.C., for example, managers had been wondering how to stop workers from gathering so often in the company cafeteria. "The assumption was made that this was chitchat, talking about their golf game," said Barry Blystone, director of training. "But there was a whole lot of work activity."

Following the study, Siemens managers placed overhead projectors and empty pads of paper in the lunchroom to facilitate informal meetings. They also alerted supervisors about the unofficial gatherings. "We tell them, 'Keep an open mind, allow it to go on, and don't get in the way,'" said Blystone.

Work Teams for Four Purposes: Advice, Production, Project, & Action

The names given to different kinds of teams can be bewildering. We have identified some important ones below. *(See Panel 13.3.)*

PANEL 13.3

Various types of teams. These teams are not mutually exclusive. Work teams, for instance, may also be self-managed, cross-functional, or virtual.

Cross-functional team	Members composed of people from different departments, such as sales and production, pursuing a common objective
Problem-solving team	Knowledgeable workers who meet as a temporary team to solve a specific problem and then disband
Quality circle	Volunteers of workers and supervisors who meet intermittently to discuss workplace and quality-related problems
Self-managed team	Workers are trained to do all or most of the jobs in a work unit, have no direct supervisor, and do their own day-to-day supervision
Top-management team	Members consist of the CEO, president, and top department heads and work to help organization achieve its mission and goals
Virtual team	Members interact by computer network to collaborate on projects
Work team	Members engage in collective work requiring coordinated effort; purpose of team is advice, production, project, or action *(see text discussion)*.

You will probably benefit most by understanding the various types of work teams distinguished according to their purpose. Work teams, which engage in collective work requiring coordinated effort, are of four types, which may be identified according to their basic purpose:[33]

1 Advice Teams
Advice teams are created to broaden the information base for managerial decisions. Examples are committees, review panels, advisory councils, employee involvement groups, and quality circles (as we'll discuss).

2 Production Teams
Production teams are responsible for performing day-to-day operations. Examples are mining teams, flight-attendant crews, maintenance crews, assembly teams, data processing groups, and manufacturing crews.

3 Project Teams
Project teams work to do creative problem solving, often by applying the specialized knowledge of members of a ***cross-functional team*, which is staffed with specialists pursuing a common objective.** Examples are task forces, research groups, planning teams, architect teams, engineering teams, and development teams.

4 Action Teams
Action teams work to accomplish tasks that require people with (1) specialized training and (2) a high degree of coordination, as on a baseball team, with specialized athletes acting in coordination. Examples are hospital surgery teams, airline cockpit crews, mountain-climbing expeditions, police SWAT teams, and labor contract negotiating teams.

Two Types of Teams in Action: Quality Circles Compared with Self-Managed Teams

To give you an idea of how teams work, consider two approaches, one of which may evolve into the other: quality circles and self-managed teams. Their differences are summarized below. *(See Panel 13.4.)*

PANEL 13.4
Quality circles and self-managed teams compared

Quality circles	Self-managed teams
Advice teams	Production, project, or action teams
Consultation—limited empowerment	Delegation—high empowerment
Voluntary membership	Assigned membership
Outside normal channels of organization's structure	Integrated within organization's structure
Influence low-level operations	Influence possibly all organizational levels

Quality Circles: Organizational Effectiveness through Employee Involvement *Quality circles*, **or** *quality-control circles*, **consist of small groups of volunteers or workers and supervisors who meet intermittently to discuss workplace and quality-related problems.** Typically a group of 10–12 people will meet for 60–90 minutes once or twice a month, with management listening to presentations and the important payoff for members usually being the chance for meaningful participation and skills training.

The movement began when American quality-control experts introduced quality circles to Japanese industry after World War II, then returned to the United States during the 1970s. At its zenith in the 1980s, the quality-circle movement included millions of employee participants and hundreds of U.S. companies and government agencies hoping to duplicate Japan's industrial success, although early enthusiasm frequently gave way to disappointment.[34] Still, quality circles can be more than a management fad. As one pair of researchers state, "quality circles can be an important first step toward organizational effectiveness through employee involvement."[35]

The lifeblood of quality circles is the fact that they are made up of *volunteers*. Thus, management's first hurdle is to sell the idea to suspicious and mistrusting employees as well as to supervisors who may view employee participation as a threat to their authority. Besides training, honesty, and patience, monetary rewards can help, such as a gainsharing formula that will let everyone participate in the benefits of performance improvement.[36]

A quality circle. Employees of Square D, a Palatine, Ill., supplier of electrical industrial controls and automation systems, gather in a circle to discuss workplace and quality-related problems. To be effective, quality circles must be made up of volunteers, people who can see the benefits—both for themselves and for the company—of participating in these monthly or bimonthly events.

Self-Managed Teams: Workers with Own Administrative Oversight   In Malaysia, the quality circles at the Texas Instruments electronics factory near Kuala Lumpur have evolved into a system made up almost entirely of self-managed teams, with routine activities formerly performed by supervisors now performed by team members. "Self-managed" does not, however, mean simply turning workers loose to do their own thing. ___Self-managed teams___ **are defined as groups of workers who are given administrative oversight for their task domains.** Administrative oversight involves delegated activities such as planning, scheduling, monitoring, and staffing.

Self-managed teams are an outgrowth of a blend of behavioral science and management practice.[37] The goal has been to increase productivity and employee quality of work life. The traditional clear-cut distinction between manager and managed is being blurred as nonmanagerial employees are delegated greater authority and granted increased autonomy.

In creating self-managed teams, both technical and organizational redesign are necessary. Self-managed teams may require special technology. Volvo's team-based auto assembly plant, for example, relies on portable assembly platforms rather than traditional assembly lines. Structural redesign of the organization must take place because self-managed teams are an integral part of the organization, not patched onto it, as is the case with quality circles. Personnel and reward systems need to be adapted to encourage teamwork. Staffing decisions may shift from management to team members who hire their own coworkers. Individual bonuses must give way to team bonuses. Supervisory development workshops are needed to teach managers to be facilitators rather than order givers.[38] Finally, extensive team training is required to help team members learn more about technical details, the business as a whole, and how to be team players.

A Volvo plant. This team-based Volvo assembly plant in Torslanda, Sweden, makes cars by using portable assembly platforms rather than a single constantly moving assembly line. Volvo puts the names of team members on every engine they build to instill pride in their work. Although teams have been used since the Egyptians built the pyramids, the idea didn't really gain currency in the workplace until it was promoted by management theorists such as Frederick Taylor and Douglas McGregor. In the 1930s, teams were adopted in factories to streamline manufacturing. In the 1960s, teams gained popularity as ways to improve worker satisfaction. Ironically, Volvo was acquired in 1999 by the company that was instrumental in using the assembly-line concept in manufacturing—Ford Motor Co. Despite Volvo's reputation for building the world's safest cars, it had not been selling well enough to generate the cash needed to develop new models. As an affordable European car, Volvo fits well in Ford's product mix, which includes Mazda, Jaguar, and Aston Martin as well as Ford, Lincoln, and Mercury.

The Challenge of Managing Virtual Teams: Reaching Across Time & Space

Once upon a time, managers subscribed to the so-called Fifty-Foot Rule—namely, "If people are more than 50 feet apart, they are not likely to collaborate." That is no longer true in today's era of virtual teams. Virtual teams are groups of people who use information technology—computers and telecommunications—to collaborate across space, time, and organizational boundaries.

Teams are generally defined as consisting of 2–16 people. But virtual collaborations may be even larger. For instance, NCR Corp. created a virtual "team" (group) of more than 1,000 people working at 17 locations to develop a next-generation computer system. Using a high-bandwidth audio-video-data telecommunications network, members completed the project on budget and ahead of schedule.[39] And Hong Kong-based Cathay Pacific Airlines designed a network, called GalaCXy, appropriate for a company where employees are never in one place for very long but need to be able to communicate intelligently wherever they go. "GalaCXy users can set up meetings with each other without calling to check one another's schedules," says one account. "They can access one another's schedules to see when they're available and then suggest a time by e-mail."[40]

As technology has made it easier for workers to function from remote places, it has posed challenges for managers. Following are some suggestions from *Business Week* for managing virtual workers, especially those working at home:[41]

PeopleSoft Human Resources Management
PeopleSoft 8 HRMS has arrived, and it revolutionizes the way people work. Now, for the first time, employees have instant access to information anytime, anywhere to make quick, informed decisions—all from a web browser. Recruit prospective employees all over the world and use intelligent tools to retain the right talent. Know that your employees can work and get paid in their own currency, no matter where they are. All with a single global solution that saves you money and puts human capital management in the hands of the humans. To set your people free, call 1-888-773-8277.

Instant • Intelligent • Global

CUSTOMERS · EMPLOYEES · SUPPLIERS

People power the internet.

■ **Take baby steps:** When trying out virtual arrangements with new employees, take it slow. Let them show they can handle the challenge.

■ **State expectations:** Nip problems in the bud by letting virtual workers know what you expect from them. With home-based workers, for example, go over the terms of your virtual arrangement—whether, for example, you want them to carry an office cellphone—and tell them if there are specific ways you want the job done.

■ **Write it down:** Record directions, project changes, and updates in writing, by sending an e-mail or fax or using Web-based services that allow for sharing calendars and tracking projects.

■ **Communicate:** Whether your virtual workers take an occasional day away or work from home full-time, make sure they're reachable during business hours. Phone call, e-mail, fax, and chat all work well—but they have to be able to reach you, too.

■ **Manage by results:** Focus on what's accomplished, not whether your employee is working from her patio or at 10 P.M. Set interim deadlines on projects and stick to them.

■ **Meet regularly:** Human contact still matters. When possible, schedule periodic and regular meetings where all team members can discuss current projects and telecommuters can catch up on office gossip. Fly out-of-towners in at least quarterly, so they can develop working friendships with your in-office staff.

major question

How does a group evolve into a team?

The Big Picture
Groups may evolve into teams by going through five stages of development: forming, storming, norming, performing, and adjourning.

Elsewhere in this book we have described how products and organizations will go through stages of development. Groups and teams go through the same thing. One theory proposes five stages of development: *forming, storming, norming, performing, adjourning.*[42] *(See Panel 13.5, opposite page.)* Let us consider these stages in which groups may evolve into teams—bearing in mind that the stages aren't necessarily of the same duration or intensity.

Stage 1: Forming—"Why Are We Here?"

The first stage, **_forming_, is the process of getting oriented and getting acquainted.** This stage is characterized by a high degree of uncertainty as members try to break the ice and figure out who is in charge and what the group's goals are. For example, if you were to become part of a team that is to work on a class project, the question for you as an individual would be "How do I fit in here?" For the group, the question is "Why are we here?"

At this point, mutual trust is low, and there is a good deal of holding back to see who takes charge and how. If the formal leader (such as the class instructor or a supervisor) does not assert his or her authority, an emergent leader will eventually step in to fill the group's need for leadership and direction.

What the Leader Should Do Leaders typically mistake this honeymoon period as a mandate for permanent control, but later problems may force a leadership change. During this stage, leaders should allow time for people to become acquainted and socialize.

Stage 2: Storming—"Why Are We Fighting Over Who Does What & Who's in Charge?"

The second stage, **_storming_, is characterized by the emergence of individual personalities and roles and conflicts within the group.** For you as an individual, the question is "What's my role here?" For the group, the issue is "Why are we fighting over who does what and who's in charge?" This stage may be of short duration or painfully long, depending on the goal clarity and the commitment and maturity of the members.

This is a time of testing. Individuals test the leader's policies and assumptions as they try to determine how they fit into the power structure.[43] Subgroups take shape, and subtle forms of rebellion, such as procrastination, occur. Many groups stall in stage 2 because power politics may erupt into open rebellion.

What the Leader Should Do In this stage, the leader should encourage members to suggest ideas, voice disagreements, and work through their conflicts about tasks and goals.

PANEL 13.5
Five stages of group and team development

Stage 3: Norming—"Can We Agree on Roles & Work as a Team?"

In the third stage, _**norming**_, **conflicts are resolved, close relationships develop, and unity and harmony emerge.** For individuals, the main issue is "What do the others expect me to do?" For the group, the issue is "Can we agree on roles and work as a team?" Note, then, that the _group_ may now evolve into a _team._

Teams set guidelines related to what members will do together and how they will do it. The teams consider such matters as attendance at meetings, being late, and missing assignments as well as how members treat one another.

Groups that make it through stage 2 generally do so because a respected member other than the leader challenges the group to resolve its power struggles so something can be accomplished. Questions about authority are resolved through unemotional, matter-of-fact group discussion. A feeling of team spirit is experienced because members believe they have found their proper roles. _**Group cohesiveness**_, **a "we feeling" binding group members together,** is the principal by-product of stage 3. (We discuss cohesiveness next, in Section 13.5.)

What the Leader Should Do   This stage generally does not last long. Here the leader should emphasize unity and help identify team goals and values.

Stage 4: Performing—"Can We Do the Job Properly?"

In _**performing**_, **members concentrate on solving problems and completing the assigned task.** For individuals, the question here is "How can I best perform my role?" For the group/team, the issue is "Can we do the job properly?"

What the Leader Should Do   During this stage, the leader should allow members the empowerment they need to work on tasks.

Stage 5: Adjourning—"Can We Help Members Transition Out?"

In the final stage, _**adjourning**_, **members prepare for disbandment.** Having worked so hard to get along and get something done, many members feel a compelling sense of loss. For the individual, the question now is "What's next?" For the team, the issue is "Can we help members transition out?"

What the Leader Should Do   The leader can help ease the transition by rituals celebrating "the end" and "new beginnings." Parties, award ceremonies, graduations, or mock funerals can provide the needed punctuation at the end of a significant teamwork project. The leader can emphasize valuable lessons learned in group dynamics to prepare everyone for future group and team efforts.

How can I as a manager build an effective team?

The Big Picture

Two types of change are reactive and proactive. Forces for change may consist of forces outside the organization—demographic characteristics, market changes, technological advancements, and social and political pressures. Or they may be forces inside the organization—employee problems and managers' behavior.

Within an organization, you may hear managers loosely (and incorrectly) use the word *team* to describe any collection of people that have been pulled together. But because traditional managers are often reluctant to give up control, no thought is given to providing the "team" (really just a group) with training and support. That is, no attempt is made to sharpen communication skills, reward innovation, or encourage independence without group members running away and losing control.[44]

Thus, as a manager, the first thing you have to realize is that building a high-performance team is going to require some work. But the payoff will be a stronger, better-performing work unit.

The considerations in building a group into an effective team are (1) *performance goals and feedback*, (2) *motivation through mutual accountability*, (3) *size*, (4) *roles*, (5) *norms*, (6) *cohesiveness*, and (7) *groupthink*.

1 Performance Goals & Feedback

As an individual, you no doubt prefer to have measurable goals and to have feedback about your performance. The same is true with teams. Teams are not just collections of individuals. They are individuals organized for a collective purpose. That purpose needs to be defined in terms of specific, measurable performance goals with continual feedback to tell team members how well they are doing.

An obvious example are the teams you see on television at Indianapolis or Daytona Beach during automobile racing. When the driver guides the race car off the track to make a pit stop, a team of people swarm over the wall and quickly jack up the car to change tires, refuel the tank, and clean the windshield—all operating in a matter of seconds. The performance goals are to have the car back on the track as quickly as possible. The number of seconds of elapsed time—and the driver's place among competitors once back in the race—tells them how well they are doing.

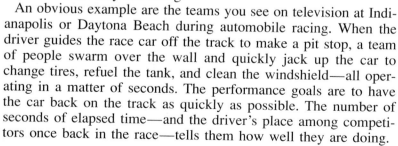

Every second counts. Each team member of this race-car pit crew knows exactly what to do when the car comes off the track. One manufacturing company that wanted to significantly reduce its production-cycle times studied the teamwork and preparation of a NASCAR pit crew and now has one of the lowest cycle times in its industry.

2 Motivation through Mutual Accountability

Do you work harder when you're alone or when you're in a group? When clear performance goals exist, when the work is considered meaningful, when members believe their efforts matter, and when they don't feel they are being exploited by others, this kind of culture supports teamwork.[45] Being mutually accountable to other members of the team rather than to a supervisor makes members feel mutual trust and commitment—a key part in motivating members for team effort. To bring about this team culture, managers often allow teams to do the hiring of new members.

3 Size: Small Teams or Large Teams?

Size, which is often determined by the team's purpose, can be important in affecting members' commitment and performance. Whereas in some flat-organization structures, groups may consist of 30 or more employees, teams seem to range in size from 2 to 16 people, with those of 5 to 12 generally being the most workable. A survey of 400 workplace team members in the United States found that the average team consisted of 10 members, with 8 being the most common size.[46]

Small and large teams have different characteristics, although the number of members is, to be sure, somewhat arbitrary.[47]

Small Teams: 2–9 Members for Better Interaction & Morale   Teams with 9 or fewer members have two advantages:

- **Better interaction:** Members are better able to interact, share information, ask questions of one another, and coordinate activities than those in larger teams. In particular, teams with five or fewer offer more opportunity for personal discussion and participation.

- **Better morale:** They are better able to see the worth of their individual contributions and thus are more highly committed and satisfied. Members are less apt to feel inhibited in participating. Team leaders are subject to fewer demands and are able to be more informal.[48]

However, small teams also have some disadvantages:

- **Fewer resources:** With fewer hands, there will be fewer resources—less knowledge, experience, skills, and abilities to apply to the team's tasks.

- **Possibly less innovation:** A group that's too small may show less creativity and boldness because of the effect of peer pressure.

- **Unfair work distribution:** Because of fewer resources and less specialization, there may be an uneven distribution of the work among members.

Example of Team Sizes: What's the Optimum Number for a Team?

Various companies have had various ideal sizes for the number of members on a team: Titeflex, 6–10; EDS, 8–12; Johnsonville Foods, 12; DEC, 14–15; Volvo, 20. The general rule is: Small teams make members feel like large contributors. Thus, managers are advised to keep teams small but large enough to accomplish the work needed.

At Microsoft Corp., Nathan Myhrvold, senior vice president for advanced technology, found that the optimum size of a software-development team was 8. Besides keeping members motivated and committed, this number enables programmers and software engineers to better see the importance of their contributions, interact with one another, share information, and coordinate their efforts.[49]

Large Teams: 10–16 Members for More Resources & Division of Labor

Teams with 10–16 members have different advantages over small teams. (Again, the numbers are somewhat arbitrary.)

■ **More resources:** Larger teams have more resources to draw on: more knowledge, experience, skills, abilities, and perhaps time. These will give them more leverage to help them realize the team's goals.

■ **Division of labor:** In addition, a large team can take advantage of **_division of labor_, in which the work is divided into particular tasks that are assigned to particular workers.**

Yet bigness has its disadvantages:

■ **Less interaction:** With more members, there is less interaction, sharing of information, and coordinating of activities. Leaders may be more formal and autocratic, since members in teams this size are apt to be more tolerant of autocratic leadership. The larger size may also lead to the formation of cliques.

■ **Lower morale:** Because people are less able to see the worth of their individual contributions, they show less commitment and satisfaction and more turnover and absenteeism. They also express more disagreements and turf struggles and make more demands on leaders.

■ **Social loafing:** The larger the size, the more likely performance is to drop, owing to the phenomenon known as **_social loafing_, the tendency of people to exert less effort when working in groups than when working alone.**[50]

---

4 Roles: How Team Members Are Expected to Behave

A _role_ is a socially determined expectation of how an individual should behave in a specific position. As a team member, your role is to play a part in helping the team reach its goals. Members develop their roles based on the expectations of the team, of the organization, and of themselves, and they may do different things. You, for instance, might be a team leader. Others might do some of the work tasks. Still others might communicate with other teams.

The Saturn cheer. This group of Saturn Corp. employees, builders of the General Motors car, is winding up a team-building exercise, which ends with everyone arranged in a so-called Commitment Circle for closing ceremonies. As a last activity, everyone engages in the Saturn "I Say" cheer: "I say, I say, I say . . . Saturn!" (Some of the Saturn dealers got the idea to do the same cheer for their customers upon buying a car.)

Two types of team roles are task and maintenance.[51]

Task Roles: Getting the Work Done A *task role*, or *task-oriented role*, consists of behavior that concentrates on getting the team's tasks done. Task roles keep the team on track and get the work done. If you stand up in a team meeting and say, "What is the real issue here? We don't seem to be getting anywhere," you are performing a task role.

Examples: Coordinators, who pull together ideas and suggestions; orienters, who keep teams headed toward their stated goals; initiators, who suggest new goals or ideas; and energizers, who prod people to move along or accomplish more are all playing task roles.

Maintenance Roles: Keeping the Team Together A *maintenance role*, or *relationship-oriented role*, consists of behavior that fosters constructive relationships among team members. Maintenance roles focus on keeping team members. If someone at a team meeting says, "Let's hear from those who oppose this plan," he or she is playing a maintenance role.

Examples: Encouragers, who foster group solidarity by praising various viewpoints; standard setters, who evaluate the quality of group processes; harmonizers, who mediate conflict through reconciliation or humor; and compromisers, who help resolve conflict by meeting others "halfway."

Task or maintenance? If you were to guess, what role would you say the man in the center is playing?

Click-Along 13.3

When Major Role Disruptions Occur: Overload, Conflict, & Ambiguity

5 Norms: Unwritten Rules for Team Members

Norms are more encompassing than roles. **_Norms_ are general guidelines or rules of behavior that most group or team members follow.** Norms point up the boundaries between acceptable and unacceptable behavior.[52] Although norms are typically unwritten and seldom discussed openly, they have a powerful influence on group and organizational behavior.[53]

Texas Instruments in Malaysia. The Dallas-based technology company makes several products overseas—such as the computer chips used in all kinds of devices. Would you expect an American company to take a close look at typical group norms before deciding to invest heavily in plants overseas?

Example of Team Norms: At Westinghouse, Peer Pressure "Makes Sure You Get the Job Done"

A good example of the use of team norms (and cohesiveness, discussed next page) is Westinghouse's highly automated military radar electronics plant in College Station, Texas. Compared with their counterparts at a traditional factory in Baltimore, each of the Texas plant's 500 employees produces *eight times* more—at half the per-unit cost.

The key? It's not the factory robots used in the manufacturing operation. It's the people, who work in teams of 8–12 members. "Members devise their own solutions to problems," says a *Business Week* account. "Teams measure daily how each person's performance compares with that of other members and how the team's performance compares with the plant's."[54]

Employee morale is way up. At his previous hourly factory job, says Joseph L. Johnson, a robotics technician, he cared only about "picking up my paycheck." Here, he says, peer pressure "makes sure you get the job done."

Why Norms Are Enforced: Four Reasons

Norms tend to be enforced by group or team members for four reasons:[55]

■ **To help the group survive—"Don't do anything that will hurt us":** Norms are enforced to help the group, team, or organization survive.

Example: The manager of your team or group might compliment you because you've made sure it has the right emergency equipment.

■ **To clarify role expectations—"You have to go along to get along":** Norms are also enforced to help clarify or simplify role expectations.

Example: At one time, new members of Congress wanting to buck the system by which important committee appointments were given to those with the most seniority were advised to "go along to get along"—go along with the rules in order to get along in their Congressional careers.

■ **To help individuals avoid embarrassing situations—"Don't call attention to yourself":** Norms are enforced to help group or team members avoid embarrassing themselves.

Examples: You might be ridiculed by fellow team members for dominating the discussion during a report to top management ("Be a team player, not a show-off"). Or you might be told not to discuss religion or politics with customers, whose views might differ from yours.

■ **To emphasize the group's important values and identity—"We're known for being special":** Finally, norms are enforced to emphasize the group, team, or organization's central values or to enhance its unique identity.

Examples: Nordstrom's department store chain emphasizes the great lengths to which it goes in customer service. Every year a college gives an award to the instructor whom students vote best teacher.

Special norms. Nordstrom gets high marks from shoppers because its employees are instructed to put the customer before the profit line. A customer may return a purchase for any reason, with minimal hassle. As one writer states, "It is hard to find a [non-Nordstrom department] store that actually values the people who keep them in business."

6 Cohesiveness: The Importance of Togetherness

Another important characteristic of teams is _**cohesiveness,**_ **the tendency of a group or team to stick together.** This is the familiar sense of togetherness or "we-ness" you feel, for example, when you're a member of a volleyball team, a fraternity or sorority, or a company's sales force. (We gave an example of cohesiveness in the Westinghouse example in the box opposite.)

Managers can stimulate cohesiveness by allowing people on work teams to pick their own teammates, allowing off-the-job social events, and urging team members to recognize and appreciate each other's contributions to the team goal.[56] Cohesiveness is also achieved by keeping teams small, making sure performance standards are clear and accepted, and following the tips in the following table. *(See Panel 13.6.)*

Click-Along 13.4

The Two Types of Cohesiveness

PANEL 13.6
What managers can do to enhance team cohesiveness

- Keep the team relatively small

- Strive for a favorable public image to increase the status and prestige of belonging

- Encourage interaction and cooperation

- Emphasize members' common characteristics and interests

- Point out environmental threats—e.g., competitors' achievements—to rally the team

- Regularly update and clarify the team's goals

- Give every group member a vital "piece of the action"

- Channel each team member's special talents toward the common goals

- Recognize and equitably reinforce each member's contributions

- Frequently remind group members they need each other to get the job done

7 Groupthink: When Peer Pressure Discourages "Thinking Outside the Box"

Cohesiveness isn't always good. An undesirable byproduct that may occur, according to psychologist **Irvin Janis**, is _**groupthink**_—**a cohesive group's blind unwillingness to consider alternatives.** In this phenomenon, group or team members are friendly and tight-knit, but they are unable to think "outside the box." Their "strivings for unanimity override their motivation to realistically appraise alternative courses of action," says Janis.[57]

Bankrupted by groupthink? In early 2002, the entire system of U.S. corporate governance came under fire, when several huge companies filed for bankruptcy. Before the bankruptcy of Worldcom, the largest in history was Enron, but telecommunications giant Global Crossing was fourth largest. Critics charged that their boards of directors were mere lackeys to their CEOs and failed their oversight roles.

Example of Groupthink: When Corporate Directors Hate to Be "the Skunk at the Garden Party"

Groupthink can happen anywhere within an organization. Thus, even when the management of a company is performing badly, members of the board of directors—supposedly the top overseers—may be unwilling to take a tough line or rock the boat.

"No one likes to be the skunk at the garden party," says management consultant Victor Palmieri. "One does not make friends and influence people in the boardroom or elsewhere by raising hard questions that create embarrassment or discomfort for management."[58]

By contrast, Kenneth A. Macke, chairman and CEO of Dayton Hudson Corp., the department store giant, created a groupthink-resistant board by making 12 of its 14 directors outsiders, with one chosen to act as special liaison between the board and Macke. The result was a board of directors so independent that in one year it felt strong enough to withhold CEO Macke's bonus, which was nearly $600,000 the year before.[59]

Symptoms of Groupthink How do you know that you're in a group or team that is suffering from groupthink? Some symptoms:[60]

■ **Invulnerability, inherent morality, and stereotyping of opposition:** Because of feelings of invulnerability, group members have the illusion that nothing can go wrong, breeding excessive optimism and risk taking. Members may also be so assured of the rightness of their actions that they ignore the ethical implications of their decisions. These beliefs are helped along by stereotyped views of the opposition, which leads the group to underestimate its opponents.

■ **Rationalization and self-censorship:** Rationalizing protects the pet assumptions underlying the group's decisions from critical questions. Self-censorship also stifles critical debate. It is especially hard to argue with success, of course. But if enough key people, such as outside analysts, had challenged the energy giant Enron when it seemed to be flying high, it might not have led to the largest bankruptcy in corporate history.

■ **Illusion of unanimity, peer pressure, and mindguards:** The illusion of unanimity is another way of saying that silence by a member is interpreted to mean consent. But if people do disagree, peer pressure leads other members to question the loyalty of the dissenters. In addition, in a groupthink situation there may exist people who might be called *mindguards*—self-appointed protectors against adverse information.

The Results of Groupthink: Decision-Making Defects Groups with a moderate amount of cohesiveness tend to produce better decisions than groups with low or high cohesiveness. Members of highly cohesive groups victimized by groupthink make the poorest decisions—even though they show they express great confidence in those decisions.[61]

Walking papers. An employee leaves Enron's Houston headquarters. Why did the company go bust? "Start with arrogance," suggested *Fortune* magazine. "Add greed, deceit, and financial chicanery. What do you get? A company that was never what it was cracked up to be." Would you have felt strong enough to try to turn the tide in a culture like this?

Among the decision-making defects that can arise from groupthink are the following:

■ **Reduction in alternative ideas:** The principal casualty of groupthink is a shrinking universe of ideas. Decisions are made based on few alternatives. Once preferred alternatives are decided upon, they are not reexamined and, of course, rejected alternatives are not reexamined.

■ **Limiting of other information:** When a groupthink group has made its decision, others' opinions, even those of experts, are rejected. If new information is considered at all, it is biased toward ideas that fit the group's preconceptions. Thus, no contingency plans are made in case the decision turns out to be faulty.

Preventing Groupthink: Making Criticism & Other Perspectives Permissible

Janis believes it is easier to prevent groupthink than to cure it. As preventive measures, he suggests the following:

■ **Allow criticism:** Each member of a team or group should be told to be a critical evaluator, able to actively voice objections and doubts. Subgroups within the group should be allowed to discuss and debate ideas. Once a consensus has been reached, everyone should be encouraged to rethink their position to check for flaws.

■ **Allow other perspectives:** Outside experts should be used to introduce fresh perspectives. Different groups with different leaders should explore the same policy questions. Top-level executives should not use policy committees to rubber-stamp decisions that have already been made. When major alternatives are discussed, someone should be made devil's advocate to try to uncover all negative factors.

Click Along 13.5

Taking Something Practical Away from This Chapter— Becoming an Effective Negotiator: Winning Tactics

The jolt to Janus. This impressive building is the Denver headquarters of Janus, the mutual-fund company. In the early 2000s, virtually all of Janus's growth funds were loaded with technology stocks, and many of them overlapped, investing in the same Internet, computer, and telecommunications companies. Thus, when the so-called "Internet bubble" burst beginning in early 2001, the Janus funds collectively tanked. What kind of warning does this convey to investors about mutual-fund managers and groupthink?

Key Terms Used in This Chapter

adjourning, 429

cohesiveness, 435

conflict, 414

constructive conflict, 414

cross-functional team, 424

devil's advocacy, 419

dialectic method, 419

division of labor, 432

formal group, 423

forming, 428

group, 422

group cohesivenss, 429

groupthink, 435

informal group, 423

maintenance role, 433

negative conflict, 414

norms, 433

norming, 429

performing, 429

programmed conflict, 418

quality circles, 425

role, 432

self-managed teams, 426

social loafing, 432

storming, 428

task role, 433

team, 422

Summary

13.1
Managing Conflict

■ Conflict, an enduring feature of the work-place, is a process in which one party perceives that its interests are being opposed or negatively affected by another party. Conflict can be negative. However, constructive, or functional, conflict benefits the main purposes of the organization and serves its interests. Too little conflict can lead to indolence; too much conflict can lead to warfare. Either way, both affect the organization negatively.

■ Seven causes of conflict, or conflict triggers, are (1) competition for scarce resources, (2) time pressure, (3) inconsistent goals or reward systems, (4) ambiguous jurisdictions, (5) status differences, (6) personality clashes, and (7) communication failures.

■ Four devices for stimulating constructive conflict are (1) spurring competition among employees, (2) changing the organization's culture and procedures, (3) bringing in outsiders for new perspectives, and (4) using programmed conflict to elicit different opinions without inciting people's personal feelings. Two methods used in programmed conflict are devil's advocacy, in which someone is assigned to play the role of critic to voice possible objections to a proposal, and (2) the dialectic method, in which two people or groups play opposing roles in a debate in order to better understand a proposal.

13.2
Teamwork: Cornerstone of Progressive Management

■ Teamwork promises to be a cornerstone of future management. The claims made for teamwork is that it increases productivity, increases speed, reduces costs, improves quality, reduces destructive internal competition, and improves workplace cohesiveness.

13.3
Groups versus Teams

■ Groups and teams are different—a group is typically management-directed, a team self-directed. A group is defined as two or more freely interacting individuals who share collective norms, share collective goals, and have a common identity. A team is defined as a small group of people with complementary skills who are committed to a common purpose, performance goals, and approach for which they hold themselves mutually accountable.

■ Groups may be either formal or informal. A formal group is a group established to do something productive for the organization and is headed by a leader. An informal group is a group formed by people seeking friendship and has no officially appointed leader, although a leader may emerge from the membership.

Teams are of various types, but one of the most important is the work team, which engages in collective work requiring coordinated effort. Work teams may be of four types, which may be identified according to their basic purpose: advice teams, production teams, project teams, and action teams. A project team may also be a cross-functional skill, which is staffed with specialists pursuing a common objective.

Two types of teams worth knowing about are quality circles and self-managed teams. Quality circles, or quality-control circles, consist of small groups of volunteers or workers and supervisors who meet intermittently to discuss workplace and quality-related problems. Self-managed teams are defined as groups of workers who are given administrative oversight for their task domains.

13.4
Stages of Group & Team Development

A group may evolve into a team, according to one theory, through five stages of development. (1) Forming is the process of getting oriented and getting acquainted. (2) Storming is characterized by the emergence of individual personalities and roles and conflicts within the group. (3) In norming, conflicts are resolved, close relationships develop, and unity and harmony emerge. (4) In performing, members concentrate on solving problems and completing the assigned task. (5) In adjourning, members prepare for disbandment.

13.5
Building Effective Teams

There are seven considerations managers must take into account in building a group into an effective team.
(1) They must establish measurable goals and have feedback about members' performance.
(2) They must motivate members by making them mutually accountable to each other.
(3) They must consider what size is optimum. Teams with nine or fewer members have bet-

ter interaction and morale, yet they also have fewer resources, are possibly less innovative, and may have work unevenly distributed among members. Teams of 10–16 members have more resources and can take advantage of division of labor—dividing work into particular tasks that are assigned to particular workers—yet they may be characterized by less interaction, lower morale, and what is known as social loafing, the tendency of people to exert less effort when working in groups than when working alone.
(4) They must consider the role each team member must play. A role is defined as the socially determined expectation of how an individual should behave in a specific position. Two types of team roles are task and maintenance. A task role, or task-oriented role, consists of behavior that concentrates on getting the team's tasks done. A maintenance role, or relationship-oriented role, consists of behavior that fosters constructive relationships among team members.
(5) They must consider team norms, the general guidelines or rules of behavior that most group or team members follow. Norms tend to be enforced by group or team members for four reasons: to help the group survive, to clarify role expectations, to help individuals avoid embarrassing situations, and to emphasize the group's important values and identity.
(6) They must consider the team's cohesiveness, the tendency of a group or team to stick together.
(7) They must be aware of groupthink, a cohesive group's blind unwillingness to consider alternatives. Symptoms of groupthink are feelings of invulnerability, certainty of the rightness of their actions, and stereotyped views of the opposition; rationalization and self-censorship; and illusion of unanimity, peer pressure, and the appearance of mindguards or self-appointed protectors against adverse information. The results of groupthink can be reduction in alternative ideas and limiting of other information. Two ways to prevent groupthink are to allow criticism and to allow other perspectives.

Management in Action

Virtual Teamwork: Using Web-Software Collaboration Tools to Work with Partners

Excerpted from Faith Keenan and Spencer E. Ante, "The New Teamwork,"
Business Week e.biz, February 18, 2002, pp. EB12–EB16.

BusinessWeek Mark the time and place: October 26, 2001, Lockheed Martin Aeronautics Co. in Fort Worth. On that day, the defense contractor won the first piece of the biggest manufacturing contract ever—$200 billion to build a new family of supersonic stealth fighter planes for the Defense Department. That Friday also marks the kickoff of a new technology era, one that could transform the basic workings of every major corporation.

Lockheed's mega-win will require some intricate teamwork. More than 80 suppliers will be working at 187 locations to design and build components of the Joint Strike Fighter. It's up to the 75-member tech group at Lockheed's Aeronautics division to link them all together, as well as let the U.S. Air Force, Navy and Marines, Britain's Defense Ministry, and eight other U.S. allies track progress and make changes midstream if necessary. All told, people sitting at more than 40,000 computers will be collaborating to get the first plane in the air in just four years—the same amount of time it took to get the much simpler F-16 from contract to delivery in the 1970s.

A project this enormous requires a feat of computing to keep all its moving parts in sync. Lockheed and its partners will be using a system of 90 Web software tools to share designs, track the exchange of documents, and keep an eye on progress against goals. Major partners such as Northrop Grumman Corp. already are hooked up. In about six months, the rest will be on board. "We're getting the best people, applying the best designs, from wherever we need them," says Mark Peden, vice-president for information systems at Lockheed Martin Aeronautics. "It's the true virtual connection."

Management experts have long talked about the so-called virtual corporation: A company that focuses on what it does best and farms out the rest to specialists who can do it better. Now, a new generation of Net-collaboration technologies is making it easier for companies to work hand-in-hand with their partners to bring new products to the market in record time—and on penny-pinching budgets. . . .

These Web tools let people separated by oceans interact with one another as if there were not even a wall between them. They can talk via their computers while looking at shared documents, carry on e-mail chats, and use electronic white boards—where two or more people can draw pictures or charts, in real time, as the others watch and respond. . . .

Tighter relationships between companies also could spur innovation as they tap the best talent from anywhere in the world. Workers might end up identifying less with their company than with their cross-company team—and get bonuses based on the team's performance. . . .

One of the most effective uses of the new collaboration technologies is in the area of product development—everything from designing cars to developing new prescription drugs. This kind of teamwork not only increases efficiency but boosts innovation—the holy grail of companies hoping to produce the Next Big Thing in their industry. General Motors, for one, has chalked up big wins since setting up a collaborative engineering system in 1999 that allows GM employees and external auto parts suppliers to share product design information. . . .

GM's collaboration system serves as a centralized clearinghouse for all the design data. More than 16,000 designers and other workers use the new Web system from Electronic Data Systems Corp. to share 3-D designs and keep track of parts and subassemblies. The system automatically updates the master design when changes are finalized so everyone is on the same page. The result: GM has slashed the time it takes to complete a full mock-up of a car from 12 weeks to two.

For Discussion

1. What kind of work teams would you think are operating here?

2. Do you see a place for self-managed teams in this arrangement?

3. If you never meet your virtual collaborators in the flesh, how do you suppose the stages of group and team development (Section 13.4) take place?

4. How do you think the considerations in building an effective team (Section 13.5) are altered by this Web-based system?

Take It to the Net

We learned in this chapter that teamwork substantially affects organizations. Teamwork increases productivity and speed, reduces costs, improves quality, reduces destructive internal competition, and improves workplace cohesiveness. It is likely that you will have to work in situations requiring teamwork. The purpose of this exercise is to determine your orientation toward teamwork.

Go to *http://content.monster.com/tools/quizzes/teamplayer/* and answer the ten questions in the quiz. After you complete the quiz, you'll receive feedback on whether or not you are a team player and a question-by-question analysis of your answers.

Questions for Discussion

1. Were you surprised by your results? Why or why not? Explain.

2. Use the question-by-question analysis and pick three questions where you scored the lowest. What are some skills you can work on to improve your score and your ability to be a team player? Describe.

Self-Assessment

What Is Your Conflict-Management Style?*

Objectives

1. To assess your conflict-management style.
2. To gain insight on how you manage conflict.

Introduction: Have you ever had a professor whose viewpoints were in conflict with your own? Have you worked in a group with someone who seems to disagree just to cause conflict? How did you react in that situation? In this chapter, you learned that there are five different ways of handling conflict: (1) *avoiding*—this approach is seen in people who wish to suppress conflict or back down from it all together; (2) *accommodating*—this approach is seen in people who place the other party's interests above their own; (3) *forcing*—this approach is seen when people rely on their authority to solve conflict; (4) *compromising*—this approach is seen in people who are willing to give up something in order to reach a solution; and (5) *collaboration*—this approach is seen in people who desire a win-win situation, striving to address concerns and desires of all the parties involved in the conflict. The purpose of this exercise is to determine your conflict handling style.

Instructions: Read each of the statements below and use the following scale to indicate how often you rely on each tactic:

1 = very rarely
2 = rarely
3 = sometimes
4 = fairly often
5 = very often

1. I work to come out victorious no matter what.	1	2	3	4	5
2. I try to put the needs of others above my own.	1	2	3	4	5
3. I look for a mutually satisfactory solution.	1	2	3	4	5
4. I try to get involved in conflicts.	1	2	3	4	5
5. I strive to investigate and understand the issues involved in the conflict.	1	2	3	4	5

6. I never back away from a good argument.	1	2	3	4	5	
7. I strive to foster harmony.	1	2	3	4	5	
8. I negotiate to get a portion of what I propose.	1	2	3	4	5	
9. I avoid open discussion of controversial subjects.	1	2	3	4	5	
10. When I am trying to resolve disagreements, I openly share information.	1	2	3	4	5	
11. I would rather win than compromise.	1	2	3	4	5	
12. I work through conflict by accepting suggestions of others.	1	2	3	4	5	
13. I look for a middle ground to resolve disagreements.	1	2	3	4	5	
14. I keep my true opinions to myself to avoid hard feelings.	1	2	3	4	5	
15. I encourage the open sharing of concerns and issues.	1	2	3	4	5	
16. I am reluctant to admit I am wrong.	1	2	3	4	5	
17. I try to save others from embarrassment in a disagreement.	1	2	3	4	5	
18. I stress the advantages of give and take.	1	2	3	4	5	
19. I give in early on rather than argue about a point.	1	2	3	4	5	
20. I state my position and stress that it is the only correct point of view.	1	2	3	4	5	

Scoring & Interpretation: Enter your responses, item by item, in the five categories below. Add your responses to get your total for each of the five conflict handling styles. Your primary conflict-handling style will be the area where you scored the highest. Your back-up conflict-handling style will be your second highest score.

Avoiding		Accommodating		Forcing		Compromising		Collaborating	
Item	Score	Item	Score	Item	Score	Item	Score	Item	Score
4.	_____	2.	_____	1.	_____	3.	_____	5.	_____
9.	_____	7.	_____	6.	_____	8.	_____	10.	_____
14.	_____	12.	_____	11.	_____	13.	_____	15.	_____
19.	_____	17.	_____	16.	_____	18.	_____	20.	_____
Total =	_____	Total =	_____	Total =	_____	Total =	_____	Total =	_____

Questions for Discussion

1. Were you surprised by the results? Why or why not? Explain.
2. Were the scores for your primary and back-up conflict-handling styles relatively similar, or was there a large gap? What does this imply? Discuss.
3. Is your conflict-handling style one that can be used in many different conflict scenarios? Explain.
4. What are some skills you can work on to become more effective at handling conflict? Describe and explain.

*The survey was developed using conflict-handling styles defined by K. W. Thomas, "Conflict and Conflict Management," in M. Dunnette (ed.), *Handbook of Industrial and Organizational Psychology* (Chicago: Rand McNally, 1976), pp. 889–935.

Managing Conflict

Objectives

1. To examine workplace conflict.
2. To assess ways in which third parties manage conflict.

Introduction

As you learned in this chapter, conflict is not only a way of life but is sometimes necessary to generate new ideas. Conflict can be constructive or dysfunctional. Managers stimulate conflict by spurring competition among employees, changing the organization's culture and procedures, bringing in outsiders for a fresh perspective and sometimes playing devil's advocate, using programmed conflict. However, if there is too much conflict in an organization, it can be very destructive, leading to warfare. The purpose of this exercise is to examine a situation and consider alternative solutions for resolving the conflict.

Instructions

Break into groups of five to six people and read the following case study. Once you have read the case, discuss it with your group by brainstorming ways you could handle the situation if you were senior vice-president of operations at the furniture company. Use the questions for discussion at the end of the case to aid in your discussion.

The Case

Jack Smith is the senior vice-president of operations at a major producer of muscle-car performance accessories. His close personal friend Joe Black reports to him as vice-president and general manager of his largest engine-parts assembly plant. Joe has been with the company for nearly 40 years and will retire soon. Joe worked his way up from the assembly line to his current position and has successfully operated the division for 5 years. Joe is a hard worker and very professional; his staff, however, is rumored to be only somewhat competent. Jack always felt that Joe purposely hired only moderately competent people. He agrees with another manager that Joe is threatened by talented assistants.

Last week, Jack went to lunch with another friend, Charles Williams, who happens to be Joe's second in command. Jack has been concerned about Joe's replacement for some time, and Charles seemed to be a good candidate. He is bright and well liked and a business-school graduate. Jack, who has known Charles for some time, also knows that Charles loves muscle cars and spends his free

time restoring them. He shows a huge amount of enthusiasm for the company and its operations. At Jack's insistence, Joe hired him at the plant. Jack was relieved because there were would finally be someone in the plant with talent and competence.

As Jack ate his lunch, however, he soon learned that Charles and Joe seemed to be engaged in some sort of feud. Jack was disappointed that Joe had not taken to Charles as he had hoped. It seems that Joe is in the process of developing a 5-year plan for his plant. The plan will lead to some major reinvestment and reorganization decisions that will be proposed to Jack and the rest of senior management. However, Joe has not included Charles at all in developing the plan. Because he did not feel like he was part of the team, Charles complained to Jack that he was no longer enthused about his job. Charles told Jack that his dissatisfaction was affecting his performance and that he was not putting forth any effort at managing the plant team. He told Jack he was considering a transfer to another plant or a transfer to a rising competitor's company.

Jack left the restaurant very worried and upset. He did not know the details of Joe's plan; he knew only what he had heard from Charles, but it worried him that Jack was making arbitrary decisions without including the rest of his staff. If Charles did stay at the company, Jack knew that once Joe retired, then Charles would have to live with Joe's plan. Jack was also frustrated because Joe's support is necessary if Charles is to develop as a leader. Jack also felt that Joe ran a good ship and he did not want to undermine his authority or upset him. Despite some of his hiring choices, Joe had shown really good judgment and the plant was one of the most successful in the company. Jack didn't know if Joe had a good reason for excluding Charles.

Questions for Discussion

1. Look at Panel 13.2. Does this situation fit into one or more of the Seven Sources of Conflict? Which ones? Discuss your rationale.
2. If you were Jack, what would you do to ease the rising conflict between Joe and Charles? Would you intervene? Explain.
3. Why would you take this action? Discuss.
4. If you were Charles, which conflict-handling style would work best to get Joe to include you in developing the plan? Discuss your rationale.

Ethical Dilemma

Virtual Morality: A New Workplace Quandary

From Michael J. McCarthy, "Virtual Morality: A New Workplace Quandary," The Wall Street Journal, *October 21, 1999, pp. B1, B4.*

The explosion of the Internet into the workplace has empowered millions of employees, in a matter of keystrokes, to quietly commandeer company property for personal use. And ethical questions are mushrooming well beyond the propriety of workers frittering away a morning shopping online or secretly viewing pornographic Web sites. . . .

This is a new spin on the old nuisance of employees making personal phone calls at work, but with greatly magnified possibilities. For one thing, the Web can be extremely seductive, lulling users to click screen after screen for hours at a time. Productivity can indeed suffer when dozens or hundreds of workers succumb to the temptation. . . .

Boeing Co. . . . seems to accept the inevitable with a policy specifically allowing employees to use faxes, e-mail, and the Internet for personal reasons. But the aerospace and aircraft company also sets guidelines. Use has to be of "reasonable duration and frequency" and can't cause "embarrassment to the company." And chain letters, obscenity, and political and religious solicitation are strictly barred.

Other companies are more permissive, but make it abundantly clear that employees can't expect privacy. Saying it recognizes that employees may occasionally need to use the Web or e-mail for personal reasons, Columbia/HCA Healthcare Corp. issues this warning in its "electronic communication" policy: "It is sometimes necessary for authorized personnel to access and monitor their contents." . . .

But even if a manager is within legal rights to peek at employee e-mail, does that make any kind of digital fishing expedition ethical? What's an employer to do, for example, if such a search of an employee's e-mail reveals that he has an undisclosed drug problem or is looking for another job? . . .

Some companies and government agencies are trying to cling to "zero tolerance" policies, prohibiting the personal use of company equipment. One is Ameritech Corp., whose business code of conduct specifically states that computers and other company equipment "are to be used only to provide service to customers and for other business purposes," says a spokeswoman for the telecommunications company.

Solving the Dilemma

In the new world of virtual teamwork, companies will probably continually have to address the matter of how much to allow employees to use computers for personal use. How would you handle this?

1. I would handle matters on a case-by-case basis, firing employees I caught viewing online pornography but just warning employees doing online shopping during business hours.

2. I would institute a no-exceptions policy in which employees first would be warned and then dismissed for going online for any kind of personal use.

3. In the interests of keeping my employees happy and productive, I would tell them I expected them to use work hours mainly for work, but that using company computers for personal uses was acceptable "if kept within reason" (whatever that might mean).

4. Invent other options. Discuss.

CHAPTER 14

Power, Influence, & Leadership
From Becoming a Manager to Becoming a Leader

MAJOR QUESTIONS YOU SHOULD BE ABLE TO ANSWER

14.1 The Nature of Leadership: Wielding Influence

Major Question: I don't want to be just a manager; I want to be a leader. What's the difference between the two?

14.4 Contingency Approaches: Does Leadership Vary with the Situation?

Major Question: How might effective leadership vary according to the situation at hand?

14.2 Trait Approaches: Do Leaders Have Distinctive Personality Characteristics?

Major Question: What does it take to be a successful leader?

14.5 Emerging Approaches to Help Develop Your Leadership Skills

Major Question: How can I become a leader rather than a manager?

14.3 Behavioral Approaches: Do Leaders Show Distinctive Patterns of Behavior?

Major Question: Do effective leaders behave in similar ways?

HOW TO BECOME A STAR IN THE WORKPLACE

People who are stars at work "are made, not born," says Carnegie Mellon professor Robert E. Kelley. "They have a fundamentally different conception of what work is."

Here are nine "star strategies" Kelly has identified, which average performers can adopt to become star performers—even leaders, the subject of this chapter.[1]

Initiative: Initiative, says Kelley, is doing something outside your regular job that makes a difference to the company's core mission—doing something beyond your job description that helps other people. Initiative means you need to see the activity through to the end and you may need to take some risks.

Networking: Star performers use networking to multiply their productivity, to do their current jobs better. "Average performers wait until they need some information, then cold-call someone to get it," Kelley says. "Stars know that you can't get work done today without a knowledge network and that you've got to put it in place beforehand."

Self-management: Stars know how to get ahead of the game instead of waiting for the game to come to them. They look at the big picture and think about managing their whole life at work. They understand who they are and how they work best.

Perspective: Average performers tend to see things just from their own points of view, says Kelley. Star performers try to think how things look through the eyes of their boss, coworkers, clients, and competitors. That depth of perspective can lead to better solutions.

Followership: Stars know not only how to stand out but also how to help out—to be a follower as well as a leader. The idea is that if you help out others, they will later look out for you.

Leadership: Star performers lead by understanding other people's interests and by using persuasion to bring out the best in people. People want leaders who are knowledgeable, who bring energy to a project and create energy in other people, and who pay close attention to the needs of everyone involved in the project.

Teamwork: Stars join only workplace teams in which they think they will make a difference, and they become very good participants. They "make sure, once the team is put together, that it actually gets the job done," says Kelley.

Organizational savvy: Average performers think of office politics as being dirty. Stars avoid getting needlessly involved in office melodramas, but they learn how to manage competing interests to achieve their work goals. They learn that not just one perspective is right, but that there are different perspectives.

Show and tell: In both formal and informal meetings, stars learn how to craft their messages and to time them so that people pay attention. To excel at "show and tell," they learn to match the language of their communication to the language that people speak, then deliver the message in a way that works for them.

The good news is that these nine strategies can be learned. Like improving yourself in a sport, you identify the areas in which you need to improve and then practice those improvements every day. Take a look at yourself, then at the star performers you know. Then become a student of the stars—do what they do.

FORECAST: WHAT'S AHEAD IN THIS CHAPTER

Are there differences between managers and leaders? This chapter considers this question. We discuss the sources of a leader's power and how leaders use persuasion to influence people. We then consider four approaches or perspectives on leadership: trait, behavioral, contingency, and contemporary.

I don't want to be just a manager; I want to be a leader. What's the difference between the two?

The Big Picture

Being a manager and being a leader are not the same. A leader is able to influence employees to voluntarily pursue the organization's goals. Leadership is needed for organizational change. We describe five sources of power leaders may draw on. Leaders use the power of persuasion or influence to get others to follow them. Four theories of leadership are described in the next four sections.

Leadership. What is it? Is it a skill anyone can develop?

Leadership is the ability to influence employees to voluntarily pursue organizational goals. In an effective organization, leadership is present at all levels, say Tom Peters and Nancy Austin in *A Passion for Excellence*, and it represents the sum of many things. Leadership, they say, "means vision, cheerleading, enthusiasm, love, trust, verve, passion, obsession, consistency, the use of symbols, paying attention as illustrated by the content of one's calendar, out-and-out drama (and the management thereof), creating heroes at all levels, coaching, effectively wandering around, and numerous other things."[2]

Managers & Leaders: Not Always the Same

You see the words "manager" and "leader" used interchangeably all the time. However, as one leadership expert has said, "leaders manage and managers lead, but the two activities are not synonymous."[3]

Retired Harvard Business School professor **John Kotter** suggests that one is not better than the other, that in fact they are complementary systems of action. The difference is that . . .

- *Management* is about coping with *complexity*,

- *Leadership* is about coping with *change*.[4]

Let's consider these differences.

Manager or leader? Steve Spurrier became head coach of the Washington Redskins football team in 2001. Earlier he coached the University of Florida football team to its first conference championship in 56 years and captured four conference titles. Are successful coaches great managers, great leaders, or both? Could someone like Spurrier be successful as the CEO of a Fortune 500 company?

Being a Manager: Coping with Complexity
Management is necessary because complex organizations, especially the large ones that so much dominate the economic landscape, tend to become chaotic unless there is good management.

According to Kotter, companies manage complexity in three ways:

- **What needs to be done—planning and budgeting:** Companies manage complexity first by *planning and budgeting*—setting targets or goals for the future, establishing steps for achieving them, and allocating resources to accomplish them.

- **Creating arrangements of people to accomplish an agenda—organizing and staffing:** Management achieves its plan by *organizing and staffing*, Kotter says—creating the organizational structure and hiring qualified individuals to fill the necessary jobs, then devising systems of implementation.

- **Ensuring people do their jobs—controlling and problem solving:** Management ensures the plan is accomplished by *controlling and problem solving*, says Kotter. That is, managers monitor results versus the plan in some detail by means of reports, meetings, and other tools. They then plan and organize to solve problems as they arise.

Being a Leader: Coping with Change As the business world has become more competitive and volatile, doing things the same way as last year (or doing it 5% better) is no longer a formula for success. More changes are required for survival—hence the need for leadership.

Leadership copes with change in three ways:

- **What needs to be done—setting a direction:** Instead of dealing with complexity through planning and budgeting, leaders strive for constructive change by *setting a direction*. That is, they develop a vision for the future, along with strategies for realizing the changes.

- **Creating arrangements of people to accomplish an agenda—aligning people:** Instead of organizing and staffing, leaders are concerned with *aligning people*, Kotter says. That is, they communicate the new direction to people in the company who can understand the vision and build coalitions that will realize it.

- **Ensuring people do their jobs—motivating and inspiring:** Instead of controlling and problem solving, leaders try to achieve their vision by *motivating and inspiring*. That is, they appeal to "basic but often untapped human needs, values, and emotions," says Kotter, to keep people moving in the right direction, despite obstacles to change.

Do Kotter's ideas describe real leaders in the real business world? Certainly many participants in a September 2001 seminar convened by *Harvard Business Review* appeared to agree. "The primary task of leadership is to communicate the vision and the values of an organization," Frederick Smith, chairman and CEO of FedEx, told the group. "Second, leaders must win support for the vision and values they articulate. And third, leaders have to reinforce the vision and the values."[5]

Managers have legitimate power (as we'll describe) that derives from the formal authority of the positions to which they have been appointed. This power allows managers to hire and fire, reward and punish. Managers plan, organize, and control, but they don't necessarily have the characteristics to be leaders.

Whereas management is a process that lots of people are able to learn, leadership is more visionary. As we've said, leaders inspire others, provide emotional support, and try to get employees to rally around a common goal. Leaders also play a role in creating a vision and strategic plan for an organization, which managers are then charged with implementing.[6]

Kotter's crew. Home Depot's chairman Bernie Marcus (blue shirt, center), CEO Arthur Blank (white shirt, center), and cofounder Ken Langone (other white shirt) celebrate their 1000th store by ringing the bell at the New York Stock Exchange. They have done nearly everything Kotter prescribes.

Five Sources of Power

To really understand leadership, we need to understand the concept of power and authority. _**Authority**_ **is the right to perform or command;** it comes with the job. In contrast, _**power**_ **is the extent to which a person is able to influence others so they respond to orders.**

People who pursue _**personalized power**_—**power directed at helping oneself**—as a way of enhancing their own selfish ends may give the word power a bad name. However, there is another kind of power, _**socialized power**_—**power directed at helping others.**[7] This is the kind of power you hear in expressions such as "My goal is to have a powerful impact on my community."

Within organizations there are typically five sources of power leaders may draw on: _legitimate, reward, coercive, expert_, and _referent_.

1 Legitimate Power: Influencing Behavior Because of One's Formal Position _Legitimate power_, **which all managers have, is power that results from managers' formal positions within the organization.** All managers have legitimate power over their employees, deriving from their position, whether it's a construction supervisor, ad account supervisor, sales manager, or CEO. This power may be exerted both positively or negatively—as praise or as criticism, for example.

2 Reward Power: Influencing Behavior by Promising or Giving Rewards _Reward power_, **which all managers have, is power that results from managers' authority to reward their subordinates.** Rewards can range from praise to pay raises, from recognition to promotions.

Example: Lloyd D. Ward, former CEO of Maytag and among the highest-ranking African-Americans in corporate America, skillfully uses praise to reward positive behavior both on and off the job. For instance, while teaching karate moves during a workout with a reporter, he used such phrases as "You got it. Cool!" and "Outstanding! . . . Go! Go, David!"[8]

3 Coercive Power: Influencing Behavior by Threatening or Giving Punishment _Coercive power_, **which all managers have, results from managers' authority to punish their subordinates.** Punishment can range from verbal or written reprimands to demotions to terminations. In some lines of work, fines and suspensions may be used. Coercive power has to be used judiciously, of course, since a manager who is seen as being constantly negative will produce a lot of resentments among employees.

4 Expert Power: Influencing Behavior Because of One's Expertise _Expert power_ **is power resulting from one's specialized information or expertise.** Expertise, or special knowledge, can be mundane, such as knowing the work schedules and assignments of the people who report to you. Or it can be sophisticated, such as having computer or medical knowledge. Secretaries may have expert power because, for example, they have been in a job a long time and know all the necessary contacts. CEOs may have expert power because they have strategic knowledge not shared by many others.

"Can we change the world?" asks Rupert Murdoch. "No, but hell, we can all try." Now an American citizen, the Australian-born Murdoch inherited a small newspaper from his father, which he transformed into a major success. Today he is chairman and CEO of the $5.3 billion News Corporation, a media empire that owns newspapers (_The New York Post_, _The Times_ of London), movie studios (20th Century Fox), and television networks (Fox TV), as well as the Los Angeles Dodgers baseball team. Widely criticized for lowering the quality of everything he has ever worked on, Murdoch believes the criticism is mainly because he is a "catalyst for change." How would you describe his sources of power?

5 Referent Power: Influencing Behavior Because of One's Personal Attraction

Referent power is power deriving from one's personal attraction. As we will see later in this chapter (under the discussion of charisma), this kind of power characterizes strong, visionary leaders who are able to persuade their followers by dint of their personality, attitudes, or background. Referent power may be associated with managers, but it is more likely to be characteristic of leaders.

Example of a Strong Leader: Jack Welch, Former CEO of General Electric

When John F. (Jack) Welch retired in late 2001, the CEO of General Electric signaled the end of an era. Under Welch, GE went from being a manufacturer with $25 billion in annual sales in 1981 to a $170 billion broad-based conglomerate, with businesses ranging from light bulbs to plastics to aircraft engines to medical-imaging equipment to insurance to financial services. Known as The House That Jack Built, GE is the ninth-biggest and second-most profitable company in the world. And superCEO Welch became one of the most legendary and widely imitated business leaders of all time.[9]

Jack Welch (left), with his successor as GE chairman and CEO, Jeffrey R. Immelt.

GE's success stems from two strategies. First, Welch encouraged diversity in businesses, rather than adherence to a "core" business. Second, he reduced bureaucratic obstructionism by encouraging quick thinking and entrepreneurial action. One tool, for instance, is the Work-Out, a GE-trademarked term, which are meetings that can be called by anyone to address any problem, with no supervisor in the room. When the participants have a plan, they take it to the boss, who must say yes or no on the spot. Says Welch, "Getting a company to be informal is a huge deal, and no one ever talks about it." But the informal just-do-it culture is a key to GE success.

How was Welch's leadership manifested? First was his mastery in motivating people. He personally reviewed the performance of the company's top 3,000 managers every year and personally handed out hundreds of bonuses for good work. In addition, he was a prolific writer of notes to managers and employees, thanking them, suggesting changes, making note of family crises. He also taught at GE's training center, lecturing, cajoling, and listening to the audience of elite managers. Second, he insisted on candor, demanding it from executives and returning it. When managers met goals, Welch showered them with gratitude and monetary rewards. Bad performance, however, was severely punished, often with dismissals. The Welch technique is to use both the carrot and the stick and to insist on a steady flow of information. In an era of management fads, says _Business Week_, the lesson from GE is: personality still counts.[10]

Being a successful leader also depends on having a fair amount of good luck. Welch had hoped to continue GE's success through his carefully chosen successor as chairman and CEO, Jeffrey R. Immelt. However, Immelt's taking the helm was as tumultuous as any leader could have experienced. On his second day on the job, terrorists attacked the World Trade Center, killing two GE employees and inflicting a $600 million hit to the company's insurance business and a slowdown in its aircraft engine operations. That was followed by anthrax attacks at NBC, which is owned by GE. Accounting scandals following in the wake of Enron Corp's. bankruptcy, which diminished stockholders' faith in the financial transparency of American corporations, including that of GE, resulting in a declining stock price. Immelt was to observe, "even Jack's schtick wouldn't work in this environment."

Leadership & Influence: Using Persuasion to Get Your Way at Work

What would you do if you discovered your car stolen from the parking lot? Here's what Doug Dusenberg, a Houston, Texas, businessman, did on noticing his Jeep Cherokee missing. He telephoned the number of his car phone, and when one of the pair of young joyriders answered, he talked them into returning the car in exchange for keeping $20 that was in the glove compartment.[11]

Dusenberg probably would be considered to have leadership skills because of his powers of persuasion, or *influence*. Influence is the ability to get others to follow your wishes. There are eight general tactics for trying to influence others, but some work better than others. In one pair of studies, employees were asked in effect, "How do you get your boss, coworker, or subordinate to do something you want?" The eight answers—ranked from most used to least used tactics—were as follows.[12]

1 Consultation Getting others to participate in a decision or change.

Example: "Wonder if I could get your thoughts about this matter."

2 Rational Persuasion Trying to convince someone by using reason, logic, or facts.

Example: "You know, all the cutting-edge companies use this approach."

3 Inspirational Appeals Trying to build enthusiasm or confidence by appealing to others' emotions, ideals, or values.

Example: "If we do this as a goodwill gesture, customers will love us."

4 Ingratiating Tactics Acting humble or friendly or making someone feel good or feel important before making a request.

Example: "I hate to impose on your time, knowing how busy you are, but you're the only one who can help me."

5 Coalition Tactics Getting others to support your effort to persuade someone.

Example: "Everyone in the department thinks this is a great idea."

6 Pressure Tactics Using demands, threats, or intimidation to gain compliance.

Example: "If this doesn't happen, you'd better think about cleaning out your desk."

7 Upward Appeals Trying to persuade someone by citing the express or implied support of superiors.

Example: "This has been green-lighted at the highest levels."

8 Exchange Tactics Reminding someone of past favors or offering to trade favors.

Example: "Since I backed you at last month's meeting, maybe you could help me this time around."

These influence tactics are considered *generic* because they are applied in all directions—up, down, and sideways within the organization. Note that consultation, rational persuasion, and inspirational appeals are the most favored tactics. Pressure tactics, upward appeals, and exchange tactics are the least favored. As it happens, research shows that of the three possible responses to an influence tactic—enthusiastic commitment, grudging compliance, and outright resistance—commitment is most apt to result when the tactics used are consultation, strong rational persuasion, and inspirational appeals.[13]

Knowing this, do you think you have what it takes to be a leader? To answer this, you need to understand what factors produce people of leadership character. We consider these in the rest of the chapter.

Fashion leader Ralph Lauren. Born Ralph Lifshitz in the Bronx, N.Y., where he shared a bedroom with two brothers, today Lauren has a $1 billion net worth, a classic car collection, a ranch in Colorado, and homes in New York and Jamaica. Following college, two years in the army, and marriage, Lauren worked for a glove maker and a tie manufacturer, then used a $50,000 loan to found Polo Fashions. The company has become a $900 million clothing and home-furnishings business by selling a lifestyle image of sophistication and taste. With his strong design sense, business acumen, perseverance, and innovative mind, Lauren is the kind of visionary leader who has been able to triumph over several business failures and achieve great success. Could you?

Four Approaches to Leadership

The next four sections describe four principal approaches or perspectives on leadership, which have been refined by research. They are (1) *trait*, (2) *behavioral*, (3) *contingency*, and (4) *emerging*. (See Panel 14.1.)

PANEL 14.1
Four approaches to leadership

Theories	Characteristics
Trait	■ Kouzes & Posner's five traits—honest, competent, forward-looking, inspiring, intelligent. ■ Bossidy—ability to execute, career runway, team orientation, multiple experiences ■ Goleman emotional intelligence—self-awareness, self-management, social awareness, relationship management ■ Gender studies—motivating others, fostering communication, producing high-quality work, etc.
Behavioral	■ Michigan model—two leadership styles: job-centered & employee-centered ■ Ohio State model—two dimensions: initiating-structure behavior & consideration behavior ■ Blake & Mouton's managerial/leadership grid—concern for production or concern for people
Contingency	■ Fiedler's contingency model—task-oriented style and relationship-oriented style—and three dimensions of control: leader-member, task structure, position power ■ House's path–goal leadership model—clarifying paths for subordinates' goals—and four leadership styles: directive, supportive, participative, achievement-oriented ■ Hersey & Blanchard's situational leadership model—adjusting leadership style to employee readiness
Emerging	■ Transactional—rewarding subordinates for performing as expected ■ Charismatic—challenging subordinates to superior achievement—four ingredients: vision, communication, inspire trust, positive self-regard ■ Greenleaf's servant leadership model—providing service to others, not oneself ■ Reichheld's six principles—preach what practice, play win-win, be picky, keep it simple, reward right results, listen hard & talk straight

What does it take to be a successful leader?

The Big Picture

Trait approaches attempt to identify distinctive characteristics that account for the effectiveness of leaders. Four representatives of this approach described here are Kouzes and Posner, (2) Bossidy, (3) Goleman, and (4) gender studies.

Consider two high-powered leaders. Each "personifies the word 'stubborn,'" says a *Fortune* magazine account. Both "are piercingly analytical thinkers who combine hands-on technical smarts with take-no-prisoners business savvy. Both absolutely hate to lose."[14]

Who they are? They are two of the most successful former CEOs in American business—Bill Gates of Microsoft and Andy Grove of Intel. Do they have distinctive personality traits that might teach us something about leadership? Perhaps they do. They would seem to embody the traits of (1) dominance, (2) intelligence, (3) self-confidence, (4) high energy, and (5) task-relevant knowledge.

These are the five traits that researcher **Ralph Stogdill** in 1948 concluded were typical of successful leaders.[15] Stogdill is one of many contributors to *__trait approaches to leadership__*, **which attempt to identify distinctive characteristics that account for the effectiveness of leaders.** Indeed, over the past 70 years, over 300 trait studies have been done.[16]

Trait theory is the successor to what used to be thought of as the "great man" approach to leadership, which held that leaders such as Napoleon Bonaparte and Abraham Lincoln were supposed to have some inborn ability to lead. Trait theorists believed that leadership skills were not innate, that they could be acquired through learning and experience. Today traits still often play a central role in how we perceive leaders, and organizations may find it beneficial to consider selected leadership traits when choosing among candidates for leadership positions. Gender, race, and ethnicity should not be used as any of these traits.

Unfortunately, researchers do not agree on a universal set of traits possessed by leaders. This is partly due to difficulties associated with measuring the multitude of possible traits and partly due to a chicken-and-egg problem: Is Bill Gates a good leader because he has self-confidence, or does he have self-confidence because he was put into a leadership role within Microsoft at an early age? Despite controversies regarding the existence of one clear set of leadership traits, examining trait profiles provides a useful framework for understanding what it takes to be an effective leader.

Click-Along 14.1

Other Trait Research: Ghiselli's Research on Supervisory Ability as the Top Leadership Trait

Kouzes & Posner's Research: Is Honesty the Top Leadership Trait?

During the 1980s, **James Kouzes** and **Barry Posner** surveyed more than 7,500 managers throughout the United States as to what personal traits they looked for and admired in their superiors.[17] The respondents suggested that a credible leader should have five traits. He or she should be (1) honest, (2) competent, (3) forward-looking, (4) inspiring, and (5) intelligent. (*See Panel 14.2.*)

Five traits identified by Kouzes and Posner

1. *Honest:* Are you honest? This trait was selected by 87% of the respondents, suggesting that people want their leaders to be ethical.

2. *Competent:* Are you effective? Can you get the job done? This trait was important to 74% of respondents.

3. *Forward-looking:* Do you have vision and a sense of direction? This characteristic was identified by 67%.

4. *Inspiring:* Can you motivate people to achieve work goals? Sixty-one percent chose this trait. (As Jack Welch has said: "If you can't energize others, you can't be a leader.")

5. *Intelligent:* Do you think you have the requisite brain power to be a leader? No doubt it helps to be smart. But this trait was seen as being not as important as others, being selected by only 46% of the 7,500 respondents.

Although this research has been unable to predict which people might be successful leaders, it does reveal those traits preferred by employees. We now go beyond studies to present some current thinking about leader traits.

Bossidy's Observations: A Working CEO Tells How to Find & Develop Great Leaders

Larry Bossidy became CEO of AlliedSignal in 1991, when the company was suffering from low everything—morale, stock price, operating margins, and return on equity. Based on his previous experience of 34 years at General Electric, he realized that AlliedSignal's "inattention to leadership was a major problem."[18] He thereupon began a two-year program of devoting up to 40% of his time to the task of hiring and developing leaders, a successful effort to which he attributes the company's turnaround.

You probably won't find Bossidy's ideas discussed in the scholarly literature about management. Nevertheless, he is worth including because his approach represents the kinds of judgments that working top managers have to practice when they go about the empirical job of finding people who can be groomed into future leaders. The four qualities he looks for when interviewing and evaluating job candidates are (1) the ability to execute, (2) a career runway, (3) a team orientation, and (4) multiple experiences. *(See Panel 14.3.)* Brossidy claims a 70% success rate in hiring leaders, and his approach contributed to a ninefold return for AlliedSignal shareholders from 1991 to 1999.

PANEL 14.3
The leadership traits Brossidy looks for in job candidates

1. *Ability to execute:* Look for a demonstrated history of real accomplishment and execution. Are you honest?

2. *A career runway:* Leaders have "plenty of runway" left in their careers, with the perspective to go beyond the present job.

3. *A team orientation:* Someone able to work with other people has better potential than someone who's an individual contributor.

4. *Multiple experiences:* People with significant responsibility in two or three different industries or companies have a range of good experience.

Goleman's Concepts of "Emotional Intelligence": Do Moods Make a Leader?

Daniel Goleman, cochairman of the Consortium for Research on Emotional Intelligence in Organizations at Rutgers University, is the author of the popular 1995 book *Emotional Intelligence*. In 1998, he made a contribution to trait theory in an article that argued that the most important attribute in a leader is ___emotional intelligence___, **the ability to cope, empathize with others, and be self-motivated.**[19] "When I compared star performers with average ones in senior leadership positions," Goleman wrote, "nearly 90% of the difference in their profiles was attributable to emotional intelligence factors rather than cognitive abilities."[20] The traits of emotional intelligence are (1) self-awareness, (2) self-management, (3) social awareness, and (4) relationship management. *(See Panel 14.4.)*

PANEL 14.4
The traits of emotional intelligence[21]

1. *Self-awareness:* The most essential trait. This is the ability to read your own emotions and gauge your moods accurately, so you know how you're affecting others.

2. *Self-management:* This is the ability to control your emotions and act with honesty and integrity in reliable and adaptable ways. You can leave occasional bad moods outside the office.

3. *Social awareness:* This includes empathy, allowing you to show others that you care, and organizational intuition, so you keenly understand how your emotions and actions affect others.

4. *Relationship management:* This is the ability to communicate clearly and convincingly, disarm conflicts, and build strong personal bonds.

Emotional intelligence. Daniel Goleman has been instrumental in publicizing the notion of emotional intelligence. Do you think you have a high "E.Q." as it's sometimes called (to contrast it with "I.Q.," the standard Intelligence Quotient type of intelligence)?

Later Goleman and colleagues expanded on the importance of emotional intelligence in leadership by suggesting that a leader's *mood* plays a key role. "The leader's mood and behaviors drive the behaviors of everyone else," they wrote. "A cranky and ruthless boss creates a toxic organization filled with negative underachievers who ignore opportunities; an inspirational, inclusive leader spawns acolytes for whom any challenge is surmountable."[22]

Good moods can inspire good performance. Still, leaders shouldn't display cheerfulness when sales are down. Indeed, the article suggests, the most effective executives display moods and behaviors that match the situation at hand, with a healthy dose of optimism mixed in. "They respect how other people are feeling—even if it is glum or defeated—but they also model what it looks like to move forward with hope and humor."

Are Goleman's ideas accurate? Preliminary evidence suggests that high emotional intelligence can land you a job. A simulated interview process indicated that interviewers' assessments of an applicant's emotional intelligence were positively associated with their impression of the applicant.[23] However, given the difficulty of measuring emotional intelligence, further research is needed on this leadership trait.[24]

Gender Studies: Do Women Have Traits That Make Them Better Leaders?

AS LEADERS, WOMEN RULE shouts a headline in a November 2000 issue of *Business Week*. "Management gurus," says the story below it, "now know how to boost the odds of getting a great executive: Hire a female."[25]

Is there anything to this? Do women have traits that make them better managers—indeed, better leaders—than men?

Business Week summarized conclusions from a number of management studies conducted in the United States for companies ranging from high-tech to manufacturing to consumer services. By and large, says the article, the studies showed that "women executives, when rated by their peers, underlings, and bosses, score higher than their male counterparts on a wide variety of measures—from producing high-quality work to goal-setting to mentoring employees." Researchers accidentally stumbled on these findings about gender differences while compiling hundreds of routine performance evaluations and analyzing the results. In one study of 425 high-level executives, women won higher ratings on 42 of the 52 skills measured.[26]

What are the desirable traits in which women excel? Among those traits mentioned are teamwork and partnering, being more collaborative, seeking less personal glory, being motivated less by self-interest than in what they can do for the company, being more stable, and being less turf-conscious. Women were also found to be better at producing quality work, recognizing trends, and generating new ideas and acting on them. A gender comparison of skills is summarized below. *(See Panel 14.5.)*

PANEL 14.5

Where female executives do better: a scorecard. The check mark denotes which group scored higher on the respective studies. The asterisk indicates that in one study women's and men's scores in these categories were statistically even.[27]

Skill	Men	Women
Motivating others		√√√√
Fostering communication		√√√*
Producing high-quality work		√√√√
Strategic planning	√√	√√*
Listening to others		√√√√
Analyzing issues	√√	√√*

Why, then, aren't more women in positions of leadership? Males and females disagree about this issue. A team of researchers asked this question of 461 executive women holding titles of vice president or higher in Fortune 100 companies and all the male Fortune 100 CEOs. CEOs believed that women are not in senior leadership positions because (1) they lack significant general management experience and (2) women have not been in the executive talent pool long enough to get selected. Women, by contrast, believed that (1) male stereotyping and (2) exclusion from important informal networks are the biggest barriers to promotability.[28]

major question

Do effective leaders behave in similar ways?

The Big Picture

Behavioral leadership approaches try to determine the distinctive styles used by effective leaders. Three models we describe are the University of Michigan model, the Ohio State model, and the Blake and Moulton Managerial/Leadership Grid.®

Maybe what's important to know about leaders is not their *personality traits* but rather their *patterns of behavior* or *leadership styles*. This is the line of thought pursued by those interested in ***behavioral leadership approaches*, which attempts to determine the distinctive styles used by effective leaders.** By *leadership styles*, we mean the combination of traits, skills, and behaviors that leaders use when interacting with others.

The important models of leadership behavior that we will describe are (1) *the University of Michigan model* and *the Ohio State University model* and (2) the *Blake and Moulton Managerial/Leadership Grid.*®

The University of Michigan Leadership Model & the Ohio State Leadership Model

What all models of leadership behavior have in common is the consideration of *task orientation versus people orientation*. Two classic studies came out of the universities of Michigan and Ohio State.

The University of Michigan Leadership Model In the late 1940s, researchers at the University of Michigan came up with what came to be known as the **University of Michigan Leadership Model.** A team led by **Rensis Likert** began studying the effects of leader behavior on job performance, interviewing numerous managers and subordinates.[29] The investigators identified two forms of leadership styles: *job-centered* and *employee-centered*.

Assembly line. Which kind of leadership behavior is appropriate for directing assembly-line workers?

Click-Along 14.2

Early Research: The Iowa Studies

■ **Job-centered behavior—"I'm concerned more with the needs of the job":** In *job-centered behavior*, managers paid more attention to the job and work procedures. Thus, their principal concerns were with achieving production efficiency, keeping costs down, and meeting schedules.

■ **Employee-centered behavior—"I'm concerned more with the needs of employees":** In *employee-centered behavior*, managers paid more attention to employee satisfaction and making work groups cohesive. By concentrating on subordinates' needs they hoped to build effective work groups with high-performance goals.

The Ohio State Leadership Model   A second approach to leadership research was begun in 1945 at Ohio State University under **Ralph Stogdill** (mentioned in the last section). Hundreds of dimensions of leadership behavior were studied, resulting in what came to be known as the **Ohio State Leadership Model.**[30] From surveys of leadership behavior, two major dimensions of leader behavior were identified, as follows.

- **Initiating structure—"What do I do to get the job done?"** *Initiating structure* is leadership behavior that organizes and defines what group members should be doing. It consists of the efforts the leader makes to get things organized and get the job done. This is much the same as Likert's "job-centered behavior."

- **Consideration—"What do I do to show consideration for my employees?"** *Consideration* is leadership behavior that expresses concern for employees by establishing a warm, friendly, supportive climate. This behavior, which resembles Likert's "employee-centered behavior," is sensitive to subordinates' ideas and feelings and establishes mutual trust.

All in all, one management expert concluded from the Michigan and Ohio studies that effective leaders (1) tend to have supportive or employee-centered relationships with employees, (2) use group rather than individual methods of supervision, and (3) set high performance goals.[31]

Click-Along 14.3

More on the Ohio & Michigan Leadership Models

practical action

Transition Problems on Your Way Up: How to Avoid the Pitfalls

Before you can become a good leader you need to become a good manager. Making the leap from individual contributor to a manager of several employees "is one of the most difficult in peoples' careers," suggests *Wall Street Journal* columnist Hal Lancaster.

Although corporations and managements may make noises about training and mentoring support, newly promoted managers may not see any of this and may simply be expected to know what to do. And, as managers move up the ladder, they may encounter other problems that they have not anticipated. How can you avoid some pitfalls as you make your ascent? Some suggestions:[32]

- **Have realistic expectations:** New managers often focus on the rights and privileges of their new jobs and underestimate the duties and obligations.

- **Don't forget to manage upward and sideways as well as downward:** You not only need to manage your subordinates but also the perceptions of your peers and your own managers above you.

- **Stay in touch with managers in other departments:** In addition, you need to have good relationships with managers in other departments—and be perceptive about their needs and priorities—since

they have the resources you need to get your job done. Don't make the mistake of thinking your own department is the center of the universe.

- **Think about what kind of manager or leader you want to be:** Make a list of all your previous bosses and their good and bad attributes. This may produce a list of dos and don'ts that can serve you well.

- **Get guidance from other managers:** You may not get advice on how to manage from your own manager, who may have promoted you to help reduce his or her workload, not add to it by expecting some coaching. If this is the case, don't be shy about consulting other managers as well as people in professional organizations.

- **Resist isolation:** If you're promoted beyond supervisor of a small team and you have to manage hundreds rather than dozens, or thousands rather than hundreds, you may find the biggest surprise is isolation. The way to stay in touch is to talk daily with your senior managers, perhaps have "town meetings" with staffers several times a year, and employ "management by walking around"—bringing teams together to talk.

Blake & Mouton's Managerial/Leadership Grid® Model: Concern for Both Production & People

The Michigan and Ohio State studies gave rise to the notion that the ideal leader was both performance-oriented and people-oriented. Perhaps the best-known leadership training model was one devised at the University of Texas by **Robert Blake** and **Jane Mouton** that was first known as the Managerial Grid® and later, when **Anne Adams McCanse** replaced Moulton, as the Leadership Grid®. **The _leadership grid model_ identifies the ideal leadership style as having a high concern for (1) production, the job aspects of subordinates' behavior, and (2) people, the human aspects of their behavior.**

Five Major Leadership Styles Using a questionnaire to measure both these concerns on a scale of from 1 to 9, the developers identified five major styles, as expressed in the extreme corners and in the middle of the grid, an adaptation of which is shown below.[33] _(See Panel 14.6.)_

PANEL 14.6

Leadership grid model. This adaptation of the Leadership Grid® identifies the location of the five principal management styles.

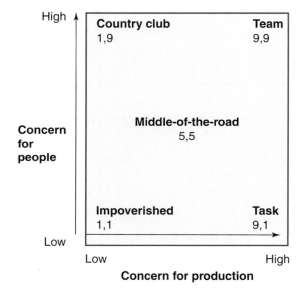

One kind of work. With white-collar workers, such as those shown here, would you be more inclined to be a people-oriented manager?

- **(1,1) Impoverished management—"I just want to exert minimal effort":** The impoverished leader, who shows low concern for both people and production, exerts the minimum effort required to stay employed.

- **(9,1) Task management—"I'm mainly focused on getting the job done":** The task-management (or authority-compliance) leader, with high concern for production but low concern for people, is mainly concerned with getting the work done with a minimum of involvement with human elements.

- **(1,9) Country-club management—"I'm mainly focused on keeping my people happy":** The country-club leader is the reverse of the task-management leader. With a low concern for production but a high concern for people, this leader mainly wants to keep people happy in their jobs.

- **(5,5) Middle-of-the-road management—"I want to do the minimum to keep everything balanced":** This leader has balanced concerns for both people and production, but these concerns rank only in the middle of the scale. In other words, this kind of leader is concerned with doing just enough to maintain satisfactory morale to achieve satisfactory production.

- **(9,9) Team management—"I want maximum performance and maximum employee satisfaction":** The team manager is considered most effective because he or she gets the utmost from employees along both dimensions—production and satisfaction.

Which Style Is Most Effective? As you might expect, behavioral theorists believed that the team-management style would be the most effective. In this style, work is accomplished by having committed people who are linked by having a common stake in the organization's purpose, which in turn generates relationships of trust and respect.

These are high-minded ideas. Unfortunately, the behavioral approach has failed to identify any consistent set of behaviors that leaders should use. Rather, the research shows that effective leaders display different types of behavior in different situations.[34] This conclusion has fueled interest in the contingency approach, to which we turn next.

Another kind of work. With blue-collar workers, such as these fast-food workers, would you be more inclined to be a production- or task-oriented manager?

How might effective leadership vary according to the situation at hand?

The Big Picture

Effective leadership behavior depends on the situation at hand, say believers in the three contingency approaches: Fiedler's contingency leadership model, House's path-goal leadership model, and Hersey and Blanchard's situational leadership model.

Perhaps leadership is not characterized by universally important traits or behaviors. Perhaps there is no one best style that will work in all situations. This is the point of view of proponents of the ***contingency approach*** to leadership, who **believe that effective leadership behavior depends on the situation at hand.** That is, as situations change, different styles become appropriate.

Let's consider three contingency approaches: (1) the *contingency leadership model* by Fiedler, (2) the *path-goal leadership model* by House, and (3) the *situational leadership model* by Hersey and Blanchard.

1 The Contingency Leadership Model: Fiedler's Approach

The oldest model of the contingency approach to leadership was developed by **Fred Fiedler** and his associates in 1951.[35] The ***contingency leadership model*** **determines if a leader's style is (1) task-oriented or (2) relationship-oriented and if that style is effective for the situation at hand.** Fiedler's work was based on 80 studies conducted over 30 years.

Two Leadership Orientations: Tasks versus Relationships Are you task-oriented or relationship-oriented? That is, are you more concerned with task accomplishment or with people?

To find out, you or your employees would fill out a questionnaire (known as the least preferred coworker, or LPC, scale), in which you think of the coworker you least enjoyed working with and rate him or her according to an eight-point scale of 16 pairs of opposite characteristics (such as friendly/unfriendly, tense/relaxed, efficient/inefficient).

The higher the score, the more the relationship-oriented the respondent; the lower the score, the more task-oriented.

Tile style. Do successful entrepreneurs or small-business managers need to be task-oriented, relationship-oriented, or both? What style of leadership model would best suit a small tile manufacturing business in which employees need to work with a great deal of independence?

The Three Dimensions of Situational Control Once the leadership orientation is known, then you determine *situational control*—how much control and influence a leader has in the immediate work environment.

There are three dimensions of situational control: *leader-member relations, task structure*, and *position power*.

■ **Leader-member relations—"Do my subordinates accept me as a leader?"** This dimension, the most important component of situational control, reflects the extent to which a leader has or doesn't have the support, loyalty, and trust of the work group.

■ **Task structure—"Do my subordinates perform unambiguous, easily understood tasks?"** This dimension refers to the extent to which tasks are routine, unambiguous, and easily understood. The more structured the jobs, the more influence a leader has.

■ **Position power—"Do I have power to reward and punish, hire and fire?"** This dimension refers to how much power a leader has to make work assignments, give raises and promotions, reward and punish, hire and fire. More power equals more control and influence.

For each dimension, the amount of control can be *high*—the leader's decisions will produce predictable results because he or she has the ability to influence work outcomes. Or it can be *low*—he or she doesn't have that kind of predictability or influence. By combining the three different dimensions with different high/low ratings, we have eight different leadership situations.

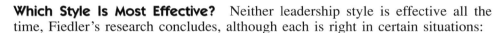

Click-Along 14.4

Eight Leadership Situations Resulting from Contingency Leadership Theory

Which Style Is Most Effective? Neither leadership style is effective all the time, Fiedler's research concludes, although each is right in certain situations:

■ **When task-oriented style is best:** The task-oriented style works best in either *high-control* or *low-control* situations.

Example of *high-control* situation (leader decisions produce predictable results because he or she can influence work outcomes): Suppose you were supervising parking-control officers ticketing cars parked illegally in expired meter zones, bus zones, and the like. You have (1) high leader-member relations because your subordinates are highly supportive of you and (2) high task structure because their jobs are clearly defined. (3) You have high position control because you have complete authority to evaluate their performance and dole out punishment and rewards. Thus, a task-oriented style would be best.

Example of *low-control* situation (leader decisions can't produce predictable results because he or she can't really influence outcomes): Suppose you were a high school principal trying to clean up graffiti on your private-school campus, helped only by whatever students you can find after school. You might have (1) low leader-member relations because many people might not see the need for the goal. (2) The task structure might also be low because people might see many different ways to achieve the goal. And (3) your position power would be low because the committee is voluntary and people are free to leave. In this low-control situation, a task-oriented style would also be best.

Task-oriented job. What type or level of task structure is involved in managing this employee? Does dealing with people whose main job is to feed cable into underground utilities involve trying to form special relationships?

■ **When relationship-oriented style is best:** The relationship-oriented style works best in situations of *moderate control*.

Example: Suppose you were working in a government job supervising a group of firefighters fighting wildfires. You might have (1) low leader-member relations if you were promoted over others in the group but (2) high task structure, because the job is fairly well defined. (3) You might have low position power, because the rigidity of the civil-service job prohibits you from doing much in the way of rewarding and punishing. Thus, in this moderate-control situation, relationship-oriented leadership would be most effective.

What do you do if your leadership orientation does not match the situation? Then, says Fiedler, it's better to try to move leaders into suitable situations rather than try to alter their personalities to fit the situations.

In the line of fire. Fighting wildfires is still a fairly low-tech, high-effort job, despite use of satellite imagery and flame retardants. What management style is best suited to motivating firefighters?

2 The Path-Goal Leadership Model: House's Approach

A second contingency approach, advanced by **Robert House**, is the ___path-goal leadership model___, **which holds that the effective leader clarifies paths through which subordinates can achieve *goals*, both organizational and personal.** A successful leader helps followers progress along these paths by (1) clarifying the paths, (2) removing barriers, and (3) increasing opportunities for personal satisfaction, so as to increase "the number and kinds of personal payoffs to subordinates for work-goal attainment."[36]

Four Leadership Styles to Increase Employee Motivation Personal characteristics, demands, and environmental pressures will vary depending on the situation, according to House. Thus, he says, there are *four leadership styles* that may be used contingently to increase subordinates' motivation:[37]

■ **Directive leadership—"Here's what's expected of you and here's how to do it":** The directive leader tells people what's expected of them, gives specific guidance, schedules work, and maintains standards of performance.

■ **Supportive leadership—"I want things to be pleasant, since everyone's about equal here":** The supportive leader shows concern for the well-being and needs of subordinates, is friendly and approachable, and treats employees as equals.

■ **Participative leadership—"I want your suggestions in order to help me make decisions":** The participative leader consults with employees and seriously considers their ideas when making his or her decisions.

■ **Achievement-oriented leadership—"I'm confident you can accomplish the following great things":** The achievement-oriented leader encourages employees to perform at their highest level by emphasizing challenging goals, excellence, and confidence in their abilities.

Which Style Is Most Effective?   Unlike Fiedler, who felt that managers could not change their basic leadership styles, House suggests that managers can (and do) shift their styles, depending upon the situation. Examples:[38]

■ **Directive style:** This order-giving style seems effective with employees working on *ambiguous* tasks and not effective with employees working on *clearly defined* tasks.

Example: Common laborers on a construction site you're managing might be more satisfied and effective if given specific goals and guidance. Specialists, such as carpet or dry-wall installers, might not react as well to this style.

■ **Supportive style:** This kind of hand-holding style seems to be effective in elevating the satisfaction of employees working on *dissatisfying, stressful,* or *frustrating* tasks.

Example: The manager of a crew having to search for victims of an airliner that has crashed into a mountainside or passengers of a ship lost at sea might find this style effective.

■ **Participative style:** This kind of consultative style seems to work well with subordinates engaged in *intellectually or emotionally involving, nonrepetitive* tasks.

Example: If you were the chief scientist directing a team of researchers investigating the causes of different diseases, you would probably get farther using this kind of leadership.

■ **Achievement-oriented style:** This is the skilled-facilitator kind of style. It can positively affect confidence among subordinates working on *ambiguous and nonrepetitive* tasks so that their efforts will lead to effective performance.

Example: Highly educated, self-motivated employees in the telecommunications or computer industry will probably find this style most successful.

Cranium's grand poo-bah and chief noodler. Richard Tait (left), responsible for business operations and marketing for the 14-person, Seattle-based game company Cranium, takes the unorthodox title of grand poo-bah. Whit Alexander, who focuses on product development, editorial content, and manufacturing, is called chief noodler. In devising the board game Cranium, the two entrepreneurs decided to adopt the acronym CHIFF—for "clever, high quality, innovative, friendly, and fun"— as the criterion by which all decisions would be guided. "Our survival and success will come from optimizing fun, focus, passion, and profits," says Tait. Which one of the four path-goal leadership styles would you expect to find dominating this organization?

3 The Situational Leadership Theory Model: Hersey & Blanchard's Approach

A third contingency approach has been proposed by management writers **Paul Hersey** and **Kenneth Blanchard.**[39] **In their _situational leadership theory_, leadership behavior reflects how leaders should adjust their leadership style according to the readiness of the followers.** The model suggests that managers should be flexible in choosing a leadership behavior style and be sensitive to the readiness level of their employees. _Readiness_ **is defined as the extent to which a follower possesses the ability and willingness to complete a task.** Subordinates with high readiness (with high ability, skills, and willingness to work) require a different leadership style than do those with low readiness (low ability, training, and willingness)

The appropriate leadership style is found by cross-referencing follower readiness (low–high) with one of four leaderships styles. (See Panel 14.7.)

PANEL 14.7
Hersey and Blanchard's situational leadership model

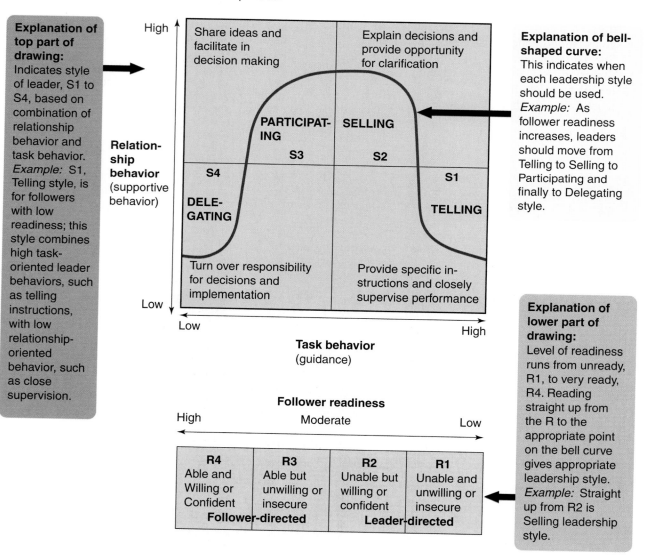

Explanation of top part of drawing:
Indicates style of leader, S1 to S4, based on combination of relationship behavior and task behavior. _Example:_ S1, Telling style, is for followers with low readiness; this style combines high task-oriented leader behaviors, such as telling instructions, with low relationship-oriented behavior, such as close supervision.

Explanation of bell-shaped curve:
This indicates when each leadership style should be used. _Example:_ As follower readiness increases, leaders should move from Telling to Selling to Participating and finally to Delegating style.

Explanation of lower part of drawing:
Level of readiness runs from unready, R1, to very ready, R4. Reading straight up from the R to the appropriate point on the bell curve gives appropriate leadership style. _Example:_ Straight up from R2 is Selling leadership style.

How the Situational Leadership Model Works Let's see what the illustration means.

- **Leadership styles—relationship behavior plus task behavior:** The upper part of the drawing shows the leadership style, which is based on the combination of relationship behavior (vertical axis) and task behavior (horizontal axis).

  Relationship behavior is the extent to which leaders maintain personal relationships with their followers, as in providing support and keeping communication open.

  Task behavior is the extent to which leaders organize and explain the role of their followers, which is achieved by explaining what subordinates are to do and how tasks are to be accomplished.

- **Four leadership styles—telling, selling, participating, delegating:** The bell-shaped curve indicates when each of the four leadership styles—telling (S1), selling (S2), participating (S3), and delegating (S4)—should be used.

- **When a leadership style should be used—depends on the readiness of the followers:** How do you know which leadership style to employ? You need to have an understanding of the *readiness* of your followers, as represented by the scale at the bottom of the drawing, where R4 represents high readiness and R1 represents low readiness.

  Let's consider which leadership style to apply when.

  Telling is providing instructions and close supervision of performance. This leadership style works best for followers with a low level of readiness—that is, subordinates are neither willing nor able to take responsibility.

  Selling is explaining decisions and allowing opportunity for clarification. Because it offers both direction and support, this leadership style is most suitable for followers who are unable but willing to assume task responsibility.

  Participating is sharing of ideas and having communication with subordinates to reinforce them in the skills they have acquired. Because it shares decision making, this leadership style encourages subordinates in performing tasks. Thus, it is most appropriate for followers whose readiness is in the moderate to high range.

  Delegating is providing subordinates with little support or direction. This leadership style is best for followers who have a high level of readiness, both able and willing to perform tasks.

Does the Hersey-Blanchard Model Work? The situational leadership model is widely used as a training tool, but it is not strongly supported by scientific research. For instance, a study of 459 salespeople found that leadership effectiveness was not attributable to the predicted interaction between follower readiness and leadership style.[40] Researchers also have concluded that the self-assessment instrument used to measure leadership style and follower readiness is inaccurate.[41] In sum, managers should exercise discretion when using prescriptions from this model.

Click-Along 14.5

Another Contingency Model: Vroom-Yetton-Jago's Leader-Participation Model

major question

How can I become a leader rather than a manager?

The Big Picture

This section considers transactional, charismatic, and servant approaches to leadership. Transactional leaders motivate people to perform what's expected of them. Charismatic leaders move beyond transactional leaders to motivate people to perform beyond what's expected. Servant leaders focus on providing increased service to others, meeting the goals of both followers and organization. We also describe "loyalty leaders."

We have considered the major traditional approaches to understanding leadership—the trait, behavioral, and contingency approaches. But newer approaches seem to offer something more by trying to determine what factors inspire and motivate people to perform beyond their normal levels.

Let us now describe some newer perspectives, which are relevant to anyone wanting to become a true leader. We begin by comparing (1) *transactional leadership*, an older approach, with (2) *charismatic leadership*; then we describe (3) *servant leadership*.

Moving Beyond the Transactional Leader: Motivating People to Perform What's Expected

As a manager, your power stems from your ability to provide rewards (and threaten reprimands) in exchange for your subordinates' doing the work. When you do this, you are performing as a ***transactional leader*, focusing on the interpersonal transactions between managers and employees.** In the *transaction*, your people give their labor, and in exchange you give them their rewards. The two underlying characteristics of transactional leadership are (1) leaders use contingent rewards to motivate employees, and (2) leaders exert corrective action only when subordinates fail to achieve performance goals.

Clearly, a "transactional leader" is pretty much the same thing as what we have been calling a manager—someone who while competent is not visionary. Of course, you could be a very good transactional leader—efficient, organized, considerate, fair-minded, tolerant, hardworking, committed to the goals of the organization and the needs of your subordinates. But the transactional orientation of your leadership may cause you to focus principally on the nonpeople aspects of your work unit, such as plans, budgets, and schedules.

Plans, budgets, schedules. Would you expect management in the construction field to focus more on the nonpeople aspects of work?

The Charismatic Leader: Motivating People to Perform Above & Beyond What's Expected

We shouldn't think of a transactional leader as being a mediocre leader—indeed, competent transactional leaders are badly needed. But transactional leaders are best in stable situations. What's needed in rapidly changing situations, as is often the case in many organizations today, is a different kind of leader—a charismatic leader, as was GE's Jack Welch.

Charismatic ("kare-riz-*mat*-ik") *leaders* **are visionaries who challenge people to perform above and beyond what's expected of them—to pursue organizational goals over self-interests.** Whereas transactional leaders try to get their people to do *ordinary* things, charismatic leaders encourage their people to do *exceptional* things—exceptionally high levels of motivation, performance, and morality.[42] Whereas transactional leaders are dispassionate, charismatic leaders excite passion, inspiring and empowering—in a word, *transforming*—people to look beyond their own interests to the interests of the organization.

Four Qualities That Contribute to Charismatic Leadership   There are at least four ingredients of charismatic leadership:[43]

1 Vision Charismatic leaders have an agenda, a grand design, an ultimate goal—in short a *vision*—that stimulates notice and makes people pay attention.

Examples: Civil rights leader Martin Luther King Jr. had a vision—a "dream," as he put it—of racial equality. United Farm Workers leader Cesar Chavez had a vision of better working conditions and pay for agricultural workers. Candy Lightner, founder of Mothers Against Drunk Driving (MADD), had a vision of getting rid of alcohol-related car crashes. Apple Computer's Steve Jobs had a vision of developing an "insanely great" desktop computer. Microsoft's Bill Gates had a vision of "a computer on every desktop and in every home."

2 Ability to Communicate Many people have grand schemes, but charismatic leaders are able to *communicate* their goals in dramatic ways: through words, actions, symbolism—or all three.

Examples: Martin Luther King Jr. was able to express his vision of racial equality in inspiring speeches such as his "I have a dream" speech. Ben Cohen, co-founder of Ben & Jerry's, was able to communicate his vision that making ice cream shouldn't be just about profits but also about using some profits for good works. Anita Roddick of The Body Shop cosmetics company has been able to communicate her visionary beliefs in fair trade, environmental awareness, animal protection, and respect for human rights.

3 Ability to Inspire Trust Charismatic leaders are able *to inspire trust* in their followers because they express their integrity by being consistent, single-minded, and persistent in the pursuit of their goal.

Examples: In 1982, when seven people died consuming cyanide-laced Tylenol capsules, Johnson & Johnson CEO James Burke retained consumer confidence by his actions in taking the drug off the market.

Curt "Curre" Lindström as head coach of the Finnish national ice hockey team was able to be the caring, fatherly figure to his athletes that enabled them to trust his leadership—and to go from gloomy failure to world championship victory in 1995.

4 Positive Self-Regard Charismatic leaders are usually self-confident. They know about their strengths but work on overcoming their weaknesses. They take risks rather than try to avoid failure.

Example: The Body Shop's Anita Roddick began in 1976 with no business experience. Roddick believes that people can fulfill all their values (such as social activism) in the workplace. "If I had learned more about business ahead of time, I would have been shaped into believing that it was only about finances and quality management," she says, showing her self-confidence. "But by not knowing any of that, I had an amazing freedom." Today her business empire consists of 1,700 stores serving customers in 24 different languages.

There are three ways in which such leaders go about transforming followers and three ways in which followers are transformed, as we discuss next.[44]

How Charismatic Leaders Transform Their Followers Charismatic leaders cause excitement among followers in these ways:

1 They Are Visionary and Inspirational—"Let me share a vision that transcends us all." In the United States, we have had "larger than life" figures—visionary and inspirational figures—in civil rights leader Martin Luther King Jr., labor leader Cesar Chavez, and presidents Franklin D. Roosevelt, John F. Kennedy, and Ronald Reagan. In business life, we have had such leaders in IBM's Thomas Watson, Chrysler's Lee Iacooca, Apple's Steve Jobs, Walt Disney's Michael Eisner, Microsoft's Bill Gates, as well as GE's Welch. This kind of leader has the vision, confidence, and communication ability to arouse a sense of excitement and adventure in subordinates and inspire them to transcend their expected performance.

Clearly, *charisma* ("ka-*riz*-muh") is a somewhat elusive concept, but in essence it means that leaders who have it are able to inspire trust, confidence, affection, admiration, emotional involvement, and—important for management purposes—exceptional performance. Using superior communication or story-telling skills, charismatic leaders are able to communicate a lofty vision of the future that subordinates can identify with.

2 They Are Intellectually Stimulating—"Let me describe the great challenges we can conquer together." These leaders are so gifted at communicating the organization's strengths, weaknesses, opportunities, and threats that subordinates develop a new sense of purpose. They become less apt to view problems as insurmountable or "that's not my department." Instead, they come to view them as personal challenges that they are responsible for overcoming.

3 They Support and Encourage Subordinates—"You have the opportunity here to grow and excel." Charismatic leaders don't just express concern for subordinates' well being. They actively encourage them to grow and to excel by giving them challenging work, more responsibility, and one-on-one mentoring.

Sir Branson. One of today's most flamboyant businessmen, Britain's Richard Branson (right) is shown here in 1999 with Singapore Airlines CEO Cheong Choon Kong announcing a global partnership. Branson left school at 16 to start a 1960s counterculture magazine. By 2002 he was heading a $5 billion empire—the Virgin Group—that included airlines (Virgin Atlantic), entertainment companies (Virgin Records, Virgin Radio), car dealerships, railroads, bridal gowns, soft drinks, and financial services. Knighted in 2000—which entitles him to be called "Sir"—he has been accused of relying too heavily on marketing gimmicks (such as driving a tank through Manhattan to publicize Virgin Cola) as an approach to business problems. Indeed, some critics believe his mostly privately held companies make aggressive financial projections that are rarely achieved. Supporters, however, say that whereas the vast majority of new businesses fail, Branson's businesses at least survive. In any case, Branson, who is dyslexic, says he is not one for scrutinizing spreadsheets and plotting strategies based on estimates of market share. "In the end," he says, "it is your own gut and your own experience of running businesses." Do you think charismatic business leaders like Sir Richard are able to be more successful than more conventional and conservative managers?

How Followers of Charismatic Leaders Are Transformed The proof that leadership is really charismatic is in the effects on subordinates. There are three ways by which employees may be transformed or changed:

1 They Realize Their Jobs and Performance Matter—"I know what I do here counts for something." This is the opposite of the uninvolved, indifferent, or disgruntled worker. A charismatic leader succeeds in convincing subordinates that what they do and how well they do it has an important effect on the organization—whether they are cafeteria workers or vice presidents. As a result, such employees come to realize their jobs and performance matter because what they do counts for something.

2 They Become Aware of Their Own Growth Needs—"I want to realize my full potential." At heart, most of us want to "be all that you can be," in that U.S. Army slogan. Under charismatic leadership, subordinates become awakened to their own needs for personal development and accomplishment and how the organization may help them achieve them. This awareness may come about, for example, as the result of belonging to self-managed work teams or of company empowerment, training, or career-fast-track programs.

3 They Want to Work for the Good of the Organization, Not Just for Themselves—"I want to be a part of something bigger than myself." Professional football players don't work for just their paychecks (large though they may be). Ultimately, they want something bigger—the division championship, the league pennant, the Super Bowl ring. It's the same with employees in other organizations: They want to work for some greater good. A charismatic leader can give them this kind of vision.

Servant Leadership: Meeting the Goals of Followers & the Organization, Not of Oneself

The term *servant leadership*, coined in 1970 by **Robert Greenleaf**, reflects not only his one-time background as a management researcher for AT&T but also his views as a life-long philosopher and devout Quaker.[45] *Servant leaders* **focus on providing increased service to others—meeting the goals of both followers and the organization—rather than to themselves.**

Former UCLA coach John Wooden, described as "a humble, giving person who wants nothing in return but to see other people succeed," is one such example. Wooden led the university's men's basketball teams to ten national championships.[46] Wal-Mart's Sam Walton believed that leadership consisted in providing employees with the products, training, and support needed to serve customers and then standing back and letting them do their jobs.[47]

Servant leadership is not a quick fix approach to leadership. Rather, it is a long-term, transformational approach to life and work. Ten characteristics of the servant leader are shown at right. *(See Panel 14.8.)* One can hardly go wrong by trying to adopt these characteristics.

1. Focus on listening.

2. Ability to empathize with others' feelings.

3. Focus on healing suffering.

4. Self-awareness of strengths and weaknesses.

5. Use of persuasion rather than positional authority to influence others.

6. Broad-based conceptual thinking.

7. Ability to foresee future outcomes.

8. Belief they are stewards of their employees and resources.

9. Commitment to the growth of people.

10. Drive to build community within and outside the organization.

PANEL 14.8
Ten characteristics of the servant leader

Leading for Loyalty: Six Principles for Generating Faithful Employees, Customers, & Investors

Frederick F. Reichheld, former director of Bain & Company in Boston, is the author of two books on loyalty, the latest being *Loyalty Rules! How Today's Leaders Build Lasting Relationships*.[48] After a decade of research, he has concluded that companies that are most successful in winning and retaining the allegiance of employees, customers, and investors are those that inspire loyalty. And outstanding loyalty, he suggests, "is the direct result of the words and deeds—the decisions and practices—of committed top executives who have personal integrity."[49]

Loyalty leader companies are quite diverse, ranging from Enterprise Rent-A-Car to Harley-Davidson to Northwestern Mutual. But what all have in common, says Reichheld, are six principles designed to engender and retain loyalty—principles that begin with executives at the top of the organization and affect all the relationships within it. Let's consider them.

1 Preach What You Practice "Many business leaders are vaguely embarrassed by the idea of trumpeting their deepest values," says Reichheld. They feel that their actions should speak louder than their words.

Loyalty leaders realize that more is required—that they need to constantly preach the importance of loyalty in clear, powerful terms to fight beliefs that today loyalty is irrelevant to success. Scott Cook, CEO of personal-finance software maker Intuit, constantly delivers the message to employees that the company's mission is to treat customers right.

2 Play to Win-Win "In building loyalty, it's not enough that your competitors lose," says Reichheld. "Your partners must win." It is not a good strategy, he suggests, to browbeat employees, unions, and suppliers to make concession after concession or to tolerate dealers who abuse customers, as U.S. carmakers do. By treating employees right, loyalty leaders inspire them to deliver superior value to their customers.

Harley-Davidson, for example, has respectful dealings with its unions, and both labor and management have such good relations with customers that many even tattoo the company's logo on their bodies.

3 Be Picky "Arrogance is thinking your company can be all things to all customers," says Reichheld. "A truly humble company knows it can satisfy only certain customers, and it goes all out to keep them happy." Enterprise Rent-A-Car has become successful by satisfying its existing customer base, not chasing after frequent travelers in every air terminal.

Loyalty leaders are also picky about their employees. Not everyone can get a job with Southwest Airlines, which accepts only 4% of its applicants. As a result, Southwest is known for both service and customer loyalty.

Example of Being Picky about Employees: An Aircraft Cleaner Helps Passengers

Phoenix native Skip Tobey, 36, doesn't work for Southwest but for Arizona-based America West. Even so, he's the kind of employee any airline would wish to hire. "I'm not just an aircraft cleaner," he says. "That's my title, but that's not the end of my job."

Tobey says he looks for ways to help passengers, as in assisting elderly travelers in boarding or in helping young families pushing strollers to negotiate the narrow aircraft aisles. "My satisfaction is tied into quality, helping the passengers," he says. "No matter what it takes, if it means going to the furthest extreme, I'll do it."[50]

Tobey's behavior is not only inspirational, it may show that he is even leadership material himself. Leadership expert Warren Bennis has characterized managers as people who do things right and leaders as individuals who do the "right" things. Tobey is clearly doing the "right" things to help America West provide excellent customer service.

4 Keep It Simple In a complex world, people need simple rules to guide their decision making, and they work better in small teams that simplify responsibility and accountability. Simplicity also helps companies deal with fast-changing business demands. And small teams help keep customers from getting lost in a faceless bureaucracy.

Northwestern Mutual CEO Jim Ericson piloted the insurance company through a "brutally complex business," Reichheld says, "by keeping his company on one simple rule: Do whatever is in the customer's best interest."

5 Reward the Right Results Many companies reward the wrong customer or employee, Reichheld points out. For example, they may reward employees who work for short-term profits rather than for long-term value and customer loyalty.

Enterprise Rent-A-Car CEO Andy Taylor devised a pay system that balanced profit inducements with incentives for building long-term employee and customer loyalty, as reflected in a survey measuring customer satisfaction and repeat business.

6 Listen Hard, Talk Straight "Long-term relationships require honest, two-way communication and learning," writes Reichheld. "True communication promotes trust, which in turn engenders loyalty. Communication also enables businesses to clarify their priorities and coordinate responses to problems and opportunities as they develop."

Dell Computer, for instance, posts all costs on a website, so customers are never confused about prices. It also grades its vendors on a publicly posted online supplier report card, so that suppliers can see how their performance measures against other vendors.

Example of a Strong Loyalty Leader: Pat Croce & Customer Service

Pat Croce is best known as part owner of the Philadelphia 76ers basketball team, but before that he owned a company called Sports Physical Therapists (SPT)—which he eventually sold for a reported $40 million.

SPT was when his obsession with taking care of the customer really began. When asked later whether he was a marketing or customer-service person, he responded they were both one and the same. "If you want to be a great marketer, you have to fulfill what you're selling with customer service." Acting on an intuition about "how to make people feel great," Croce extended this idea to everyone. "I truly would put myself in the other person's shoes, be it an employee, a customer, a physician, or a season-ticket holder. The vendors, the TV people—I made sure we made it easy for them to do what they do."

Among Croce's Ten Commandments: "Every customer gets a hello and a goodbye." "Listen, listen, listen." "Communicate clearly." "Extend compliments."[51]

Communicating clearly. Croce (right) scaled a bridge in Philadelphia to hang a banner honoring the 76ers as 2001 Eastern Conference champions.

The High Road "Low-road" companies can survive for some time—maybe even generate impressive financial returns in the short-run—by taking advantage of customers, employees, and vendors when they are vulnerable. Ultimately, however, such companies fail to anticipate market shifts or are blindsided by competitors.

Leaders of "high-road" companies realize that high standards of decency and consideration don't diminish profitability. Rather they enable it. Loyalty leaders, says Reichheld, show "they believe that business is not a zero-sum game, that an organization thrives when its partners and customers thrive."

Click-Along 14.6

Taking Something Practical Away from This Chapter: Women in Top Management

Key Terms Used in This Chapter

Summary

14.1
The Nature of Leadership: Wielding Influence

■ Leadership is the ability to influence employees to voluntarily pursue organizational goals. Being a manager and being a leader are not the same. Management is about coping with complexity, whereas leadership is about coping with change. Companies manage complexity by planning and budgeting, organizing and staffing, and controlling and problem solving. Leadership copes with change by setting a direction, aligning people to accomplish an agenda, and motivating and inspiring people.

■ To understand leadership, we must understand authority and power. Authority is the right to perform or command; it comes with the manager's job. Power is the extent to which a person is able to influence others so they respond to orders. People may pursue personalized power, power directed at helping oneself, or, better, they may pursue socialized power, power directed at helping others.

■ Within an organization there are typically five sources of power leaders may draw on. (1) Legitimate power, which all managers have, is power that results from managers' formal positions within the organization. (2) Reward power, which all managers also

have, is power that results from managers' authority to reward their subordinates. (3) Coercive power, which all managers have, results from managers' authority to punish their subordinates. (4) Expert power is power resulting from one's specialized information or expertise. (5) Referent power is power deriving from one's personal attraction; it may be associated with managers but is more likely to be characteristic of leaders.

■ There are eight influence tactics for trying to get others to do something you want, ranging from most used to least used tactics as follows: consultation, rational persuasion, inspirational appeals, ingratiating tactics, coalition tactics, pressure tactics, upward appeals, and exchange tactics.

■ Four principal approaches or perspectives on leadership, as discussed in the rest of the chapter, are (1) trait, (2) behavioral, (3) contingency, and (4) emerging.

14.2
Trait Approaches: Do Leaders Have Distinctive Personality Characteristics?

■ Trait approaches to leadership attempt to identify distinctive characteristics that account for the effectiveness of leaders. Representatives of this approach are Kouzes and Posner, Bossidy, Goleman, and gender studies.

(1) Kouzes and Posner identified five traits of leaders. A leader should be honest, competent, forward-looking, inspiring, and intelligent. (2) Bossidy, a working CEO, identifies four qualities he looks for when assessing prospective leaders: ability to execute, a career runway (ability to go beyond present job), a team orientation, and multiple experiences. (3) Goleman contributed to trait theory by arguing that the most important attribute in a leader is emotional intelligence, the ability to cope, empathize with others, and be self-motivated. The traits of emotional intelligence are self-awareness, self-management, social awareness, and relationship management. Goleman also suggests a leader's mood plays a key role. (4) Some studies suggest that women rate higher than men on several measures, from producing high-quality work to goal-setting to mentoring employees. Women excel in such traits as teamwork and partnering, being more collaborative, seeking less personal glory, being motivated less by self-interest than company interest, being more stable, and being less turf-conscious.

14.3
Behavioral Approaches: Do Leaders Show Distinctive Patterns of Behavior?

■ Behavioral leadership approaches try to determine the distinctive styles used by effective leaders. Leadership styles means the combination of traits, skills, and behaviors that leaders use when interacting with others. Two important models of leadership behavior are (1) the University of Michigan and Ohio State University models and (2) the Blake and Moulton Managerial/Leadership Grid.

■ In the University of Michigan Leadership Model, researchers identified two forms of leadership styles: job-centered and employee-centered. In job-centered behavior, managers paid more attention to the job and work procedures. In employee-centered behavior, managers paid more attention to employee satisfaction and making work groups cohesive. In the Ohio State Leadership Model, researchers identified two major dimensions of leader behavior: initiating structure and consideration. Initiating structure organizes and defines what group members should be doing. Consideration is leadership behavior that expresses concern for employees by establishing a supportive climate. One expert concludes from the Michigan and Ohio studies that effective leaders tend to have supportive relationships with employees, use group rather than individual methods of supervision, and set high performance goals.

■ The Blake and Moulton (and McCanse) Leadership Grid model identifies the ideal leadership style as having a high concern for production (the job aspects of subordinates' behavior) and people (the human aspects). Five principal management styles were identified: impoverished management, task management, country club management, middle-of-the-road management, and team management. Team management, which gets the utmost from employees along both production and people dimensions, was deemed most effective.

14.4
Contingency Approaches: Does Leadership Vary with the Situation?

■ Proponents of the contingency approach to leadership believe that effective leadership behavior depends on the situation at hand—that as situations change, different styles become effective. Three contingency approaches are (1) the contingency leadership model by Fiedler, (2) the path-goal leadership model by House, and (3) the situational leadership model by Hersey and Blanchard.

■ The Fiedler contingency leadership model determines if a leader's style is task-oriented or relationship-oriented and if that style is effective for the situation at hand. Once it is determined whether a leader is more oriented toward tasks or toward people, then it's necessary to determine how much control and influence a leader has in the immediate work environment. The three dimensions of situational control are leader-member relations, which reflects the extent to which a leader has the support of the work group; the task structure, which reflects the extent to which tasks are routine and easily understood; and position power, which reflects how much power a leader has to reward and punish and make work assignments. For each dimension, the leader's control may be high or low. A task-oriented style has been found to work best in either high-control or low-control situations; the relationship-oriented style best in situations of moderate control.

■ The House path-goal leadership model holds that the effective leader clarifies paths through which subordinates can achieve goals, both organizational and personal. House says there are four leadership styles that may be used contingently to increase subordinates' motivation: directive leadership, which gives specific guidance; supportive leadership, which shows concern for employee well-being; participative leadership, which consults with employees; and achievement-oriented leadership, which emphasizes challenges and expresses confidence in employees. House suggests managers shift their styles depending on the situation.

■ Hersey and Blanchard's situational leadership theory suggests that leadership behavior reflects how leaders should adjust their leadership style according to the readiness of the followers. Readiness is defined as the extent to which a follower possesses the ability and willingness to complete a task. The appropriate leadership style is found by cross-referencing follower readiness (low to high) with one of four leadership styles: telling, selling, participating, delegating.

14.5
Emerging Approaches to Help Develop Your Leadership Skills

■ Newer leadership perspectives we consider are (1) transactional leadership, (2) charismatic leadership, and (3) servant leadership. We conclude the chapter with (4) six principles for generating faithful employees, customers, and investors.

■ Transactional leadership focuses on the interpersonal transactions between managers and employees—in the transaction, employees give their labor and the managers give rewards. In transactional leadership, leaders use contingent rewards to motivate employees and leaders exert corrective action only when subordinates fail to achieve performance goals. A transactional leader is essentially the same thing as a manager—someone who is competent but not visionary.

■ Charismatic leaders are visionaries who challenge people to perform above and beyond what's expected of them—to pursue organizational goals over self-interests. Transactional leaders try to get their people to do ordinary things, but charismatic leaders encourage people to do exceptional things; that is, such leaders are transforming. Four qualities that contribute to charismatic leadership are vision, ability to communicate, ability to inspire trust, and positive self-regard. Three ways in which charismatic leaders transform their followers are: they are visionary and inspirational, they are intellectually stimulating, and they support and encourage subordinates. Followers of charismatic leaders are transformed because they realize their jobs and performance matter, they become aware of their own growth needs, and they want to work for the good of the organization and not just for themselves.

■ Servant leaders focus on providing increased service to others—meeting the goals of both followers and the organization—rather than to themselves.

■ Six principles suggested by Frederick Reichheld for generating faithful employees, customers, and investors are preach what you practice, play to win-win, be picky, keep it simple, reward the right results, and listen hard and talk straight.

The New Xerox Chief Shakes Up the Culture

Excerpted from Pamela L. Moore, "She's Here to Fix the Xerox," Business Week, *August 6, 2001, pp. 47–48.*

BusinessWeek If Anne M. Mulcahy ever does manage to save Xerox Corp., then surely June 14 [2001] will look like a turning point. Mulcahy, president and CEO-in-waiting [she was promoted to CEO January 2002], flew from headquarters in Stamford, Conn., to Rochester, N.Y., the home of Xerox' big operations, to deliver devastating news. The company was killing its entire line of desktop inkjet printers—a one-year-old business that employed 1,500 people worldwide and had been championed by Mulcahy herself. The division would not turn a profit for at least two years, though, and Xerox needed cash now. "In a year of tough decisions, this one was toughest," Mulcahy says.

Tough hardly does justice to the year. . . . The company was close to foundering after years of weak sales and high costs; employees were as disgruntled as customers. . . .

Skeptics say Mulcahy belongs to the old guard herself, a veteran Xeroid who started 25 years ago selling copiers. They regard her as part of a past that weighs heavily on Xerox: a culture paralyzed by politics and earlier success. . . . Mulcahy, though, says she's ready to shake up the entire culture: "There needs to be far more innovation and receptivity to new ideas. I have very little time for endless debate and consensus." . . .

As president, Mulcahy has been chief cheerleader in a company where executives usually keep to themselves. During her first three months, she crisscrossed the country, holding nearly two dozen meetings with employees. She even promised to fly anywhere, anytime to help salespeople close tough deals. Then, when Xerox' financial situation worsened last September, the company was forced to take drastic action. . . . Mulcahy focused on operations, promising to slash $1 billion from Xerox' annual costs. She's more than halfway there. Some 8,600 middle managers and factory workers have been let go; she tries to make the announcements in person. And she said she'll reduce high manufacturing costs, which have put Xerox at a decided disadvantage to competitors. . . .

Meanwhile, Mulcahy spreads her message with a regular memo called "Turnaround Talk," which alternates between enthusiasm ("Together We Can Do It!") and pragmatism ("When we shut off the bottled water, it's not because we want to be mean-spirited. It's because all these little expenses . . . can spell the difference between losing money and turning a profit").

Mulcahy has raised the energy level at Xerox. A big Bruce Springsteen fan, she's also a real gym rat. Mulcahy grew up in a Long Island (N.Y.) household with four brothers; her father was an editor in a publishing firm, and her mother took care of the kids. Now her mom looks after her teenage sons when she is away, which is often, since Mulcahy is usually on the road three days a week. She doesn't mind traveling, even to hear criticism from employees. But they better be prepared to hear some back. "She doesn't sugar-coat," says a [Xerox manager].

Today the company bills Mulcahy as "the future of Xerox." To her, at least, that means a Xerox that looks more like IBM, offering services to help businesses manage their vast cache of documents. . . .

So maybe it will take a Xeroid to dispose of the toxic parts of the company's culture that have made it so resistant to change. "There's an all-out battle going on between boxes and solutions," says James W. Lundy, a Gartner Group Inc. consultant and ex-Xeroid. Mulcahy is blunt about wanting her salespeople to learn to sell services, too. "It's the ability to walk and chew gum," she says. "We can't be [just] the giant copier company." Ditto that.

For Discussion

1. How many of the five sources of power that leaders draw on do you see depicted here?

2. Which of the eight influence techniques that leaders employ does Mulcahy seem to use?

3. Does Mulcahy show any of the leadership traits that were discussed in Section 14.2?

4. Can you tell from this case whether Mulcahy seems to be more relationship-oriented or task-oriented?

5. Would you say Mulcahy is a charismatic leader?

Take It to the Net

What does it take to lead a troop of Girl Scouts? To lead a country? To lead a baseball team to a World Series victory? As you learned in this chapter, there is a difference between managing others and leading others. There are also several different approaches to leadership: Do great leaders have distinctive personality traits? Different patterns of behavior? Or does leadership vary from situation to situation? Regardless of which approach is "correct," there will always be certain people that come to mind when we think of great leaders. Something about them sets them apart and gets their names in the history books. They motivate us to go beyond what is expected of us. They challenge us to change the world. They are visionaries with a great deal of charisma.

The purpose of this exercise is to examine what makes a charismatic leader. Go to *http://gi.grolier. com/presidents/ea/bios/35pkenn.html*. Read the biographical information about John F. Kennedy. Once you are finished, answer the questions below.

Questions for Discussion

1. Which qualities that contribute to charismatic leadership did Kennedy possess? Describe and explain.

2. In what ways did Kennedy cause excitement among his followers? Explain in detail.

3. How were Kennedy's followers transformed? Explain in detail.

Self-Assessment

Do You Have What It Takes to Be a Leader?*

Objectives

1. To learn more about the skills required for being a leader.
2. To assess your own leadership ability.

Introduction: Managers cope with complexity: They look at what needs to be done (planning and budgeting), pull together the people needed to get the job done together (organizing and staffing), and ensure that people do their jobs (controlling and problem solving). Leaders, on the other hand, cope with change: They look at what needs to be done by setting a direction rather than planning and budgeting, pull people together to do the job through alignment rather than organizing and staffing, and ensure people do their jobs through motivation and inspiration instead of controlling and problem solving. The purpose of this exercise is to assess your skills and determine if you have what it takes to be a leader.

Instructions: Read each of the following statements, and circle the number that best represents your self-perceptions, where 1 = strongly disagree, 2 = disagree, 3 = neither agree nor disagree, 4 = agree, 5 = strongly agree. There is no right or wrong answer.

1. I can separate my personal life from work/school.	1	2	3	4	5
2. I'm honest with myself.	1	2	3	4	5
3. I communicate my ideas clearly.	1	2	3	4	5
4. I regularly prioritize what I need to get done.	1	2	3	4	5
5. I am on time for meetings/classes.	1	2	3	4	5
6. I am positive and upbeat.	1	2	3	4	5
7. I am solution oriented rather than problem oriented.	1	2	3	4	5
8. I take responsibility for my actions.	1	2	3	4	5
9. I do not blame others for my mistakes.	1	2	3	4	5
10. When working in a group, I work with members to solve and prevent problems.	1	2	3	4	5
11. I don't have to redo things because my work is thorough and complete.	1	2	3	4	5

12. I do not procrastinate on projects/tasks.	1	2	3	4	5
13. I do not get distracted when working on projects/tasks.	1	2	3	4	5
14. I work well in a group.	1	2	3	4	5
15. I am people oriented, not just results oriented.	1	2	3	4	5
16. I listen to others beyond just the words being spoken.	1	2	3	4	5
17. When working in a group, I am more concerned with the group's success than my own.	1	2	3	4	5
18. I adjust well to different communication styles.	1	2	3	4	5
19. I praise others when they are doing a good job.	1	2	3	4	5
20. I work at getting ahead, but within appropriate boundaries.	1	2	3	4	5

Total _____

Scoring & Interpretation: Compute your score by adding the responses for all 20 items. The questions in this survey were designed to give you feedback on your skills in the following areas: (1) personal stability, (2) productivity, (3) self-management, (4) communication, (5) boundary setting, (6) work quality, (7) teamwork. All of these skills are found in good managers, and they represent necessary skills for leaders.

Arbitrary norms for leadership skills:

Excellent leadership skills (95–100)

Good leadership skills (85–90)

Moderate leadership skills (75–80)

Low leadership skills (65–70)

Poor leadership skills (60 and below)

Questions for Discussion

1. Were you surprised by your results? Why or why not?
2. Look at the five questions where you scored the lowest. What can you do to improve or develop your skills represented by these items? Explain.
3. Does the content in the five lowest areas relate to Panels 14.2–14.4? If it does, can you identify additional ways you can improve these skills? Describe and explain.

*Questions for this survey were adapted from Interlink Training and Coaching, "The Leadership Assessment Tool," *http://www.interlinktc.com/assessment.html*. Interlink Training and Coaching, 3655 W. Anthem Way, Box 315, Anthem, AZ 85086.

Group Exercise

How Do They Do It? Examining the Skills of Famous Leaders

Objectives

1. To examine the leadership skills of famous leaders.
2. To further explore different approaches to leadership.

Introduction

In this chapter you learned four different approaches to explaining leadership. We know that leaders possess traits and skills that make them successful. They are effective communicators. They are guided by a vision that is shared by others. They are skillful planners. They are champions for their cause. They are successful at motivating people to voluntarily pursue goals. Leaders can be villains or heroes, trailblazers and visionaries, revolutionaries or college students. The purpose of this exercise is to examine the skills displayed by famous leaders and to determine how you might use this knowledge to improve your leadership skills.

Instructions

Break into groups of five to six people. First, brainstorm a list of famous leaders—CEOs, presidents, politicians, monarchs, or whoever, as long as the group knows something about their skills as leaders. Next, the group needs to pick two leaders to compare and contrast. Try to pick leaders that seem vastly different from one another—for example, Joan of Arc and Mother Teresa. Once you have decided on the two leaders, use the following survey to profile them in terms of their skills and traits. Use the panels and additional material in this chapter to help guide your discussion. Answer the questions for discussion after completing the survey.

Profile Survey

	Leader A Name:		Leader B Name:	
In terms of power: This person uses/used which sources of power?	Personalized power	_____	Personalized power	_____
	Socialized power	_____	Socialized power	_____
	Legitimate power	_____	Legitimate power	_____
	Reward power	_____	Reward power	_____
	Coercive power	_____	Coercive power	_____
	Expert power	_____	Expert power	_____
	Referent power	_____	Referent power	_____
In terms of influence: What influence tactics does/did this person use?	Consultation	_____	Consultation	_____
	Rational persuasion	_____	Rational persuasion	_____
	Inspirational appeals	_____	Inspirational appeals	_____
	Ingratiating tactics	_____	Ingratiating tactics	_____
	Coalition tactics	_____	Coalition tactics	_____
	Pressure tactics	_____	Pressure tactics	_____
	Upward appeals	_____	Upward appeals	_____
	Exchange tactics	_____	Exchange tactics	_____
In terms of the trait approach to leadership: Which traits does/did this person exhibit?	Honest	_____	Honest	_____
	Competent	_____	Competent	_____
	Forward-looking	_____	Forward-looking	_____
	Inspiring	_____	Inspiring	_____
	Intelligent	_____	Intelligent	_____
	Self awareness	_____	Self awareness	_____
	Self-management	_____	Self-management	_____
	Social awareness	_____	Social awareness	_____
	Relationship management	_____	Relationship management	_____
In terms of behavioral approaches to leadership: Which leadership behaviors did/does this person exhibit?	**U of Michigan Model**		**U of Michigan Model**	
	Job-centered behavior	_____	Job-centered behavior	_____
	Employee-centered behavior	_____	Employee-centered behavior	_____
	Ohio State Model		**Ohio State Model**	
	Initiating structure	_____	Initiating structure	_____
	Consideration	_____	Consideration	_____
	Leadership Grid Model		**Leadership Grid Model**	
	Impoverished leader	_____	Impoverished leader	_____

continued

	Task leader	_____	Task leader	_____
	Country-club leader	_____	Country-club leader	_____
	Middle-of-the-road leader	_____	Middle-of-the-road leader	_____
	Team leader	_____	Team leader	_____
In terms of transactional and charismatic leadership: What general type of leader is/was this person?	Transactional leader	_____	Transactional leader	_____
	Charismatic leader	_____	Charismatic leader	_____
	Servant leader	_____	Servant leader	_____

Questions for Discussion

1. What criteria did your group use to determine which two leaders you would profile? Describe.

2. In what ways are the leadership styles of these leaders similar? In what ways are they different? Explain.

3. After completing this survey, were you surprised at the similarity or dissimilarity between these leaders? Discuss.

4. Which one of these leaders would you want to work for? Explain your rationale.

Ethical Dilemma

Cashing in on Expense Accounts

Excerpted from Mary McNamara and Martin Miller, "Brothel or Wedding Gown: Putting It on Company Tab," Los Angeles Times, *March 5, 2002, pp. E1, E4.*

Padding expense reports is as time-honored as cheating on taxes. . . .

While few modern-day toilers admit to doing it themselves, almost everyone knows of "this one guy" who was absolutely fearless when it comes to toting up those Travel and Entertainment columns. . . . A former financial officer said he saw reimbursement requests for "customer entertainment" that included $500 for an outing to a strip club and $2,500 for Super Bowl tickets. A mid-level investment-firm executive remembered weekend fishing getaways with clients that ran $10,000. A salesman for an East Coast tech company knew a supervisor who organized a spur-of-the-moment gambling trip to Bermuda that set the company back $25,000.

Though such expenses are far from routine, people submit them because they usually get away with it. When challenged about costs, the supervisor who led the Bermuda excursion righteously defended his decision. "I just brought in $5 million in business," he said. . . .

In many cases, there's a good reason for lavish expense accounts—clients like to be wooed, stellar employees like to be rewarded, and wooing and rewarding doesn't come cheap. But according to fraud investigators, most padding is not about a desire to achieve. It's about greed. . . .

Employees at all levels also see expense reports as an opportunity to even the scales. . . . Someone didn't get the raise she wanted so she takes it out in mileage or in really nice dinners.

"You'd be surprised how many executives, I mean top executives, think they are special and that they are only taking back what is owed them," said [fraud investigator Craig] Greene, who has written extensively for accounting journals about falsified expense reports.

Solving the Dilemma

You closed a $5 million deal for your company, but no promotion, bonus, or raise has been forthcoming. Your frequent travel, however, gives you an opportunity to pad your expense accounts. Would you?

1. No, it's dishonest. And as a manager myself, I'd be setting a bad example for my employees.

2. I might be tempted to do some small stuff—trade in first-class plane tickets for coach and pocket the difference, say.

3. I'd in effect take my "commission" for the $5 million deal however I could—altering receipts, using blank receipts, expensing lavish meals. I'd do that until I could find a job with a company that recognized my true worth.

4. Invent other options. Discuss.

CHAPTER 15

Interpersonal & Organizational Communication

15.1 The Communication Process: What It Is, How It Works

Major Question: What do I need to know about the communication process to be an effective communicator?

15.4 Communication in the Information Age

Major Question: How do contemporary managers use information technology to communicate more effectively?

15.2 Barriers to Communication

Major Question: What are the important barriers I need to be aware of, so I can improve my communication skills?

15.5 Improving Communication Effectiveness

Major Question: How can I be a better listener, reader, writer, and speaker?

15.3 How Managers Fit into the Communication Process

Major Question: How can I use the different channels and patterns of communication to my advantage?

the manager's toolbox

BECOMING A BETTER COMMUNICATOR: BEING TELEPHONE-SAVVY

Some communication doesn't matter much (such as small talk with the latte server). Some matters a lot, as when you're using the phone to try to get a job interview. Indeed, despite e-mail, the phone is still the most used business tool, so you need to become skilled at it.

Ever feel that someone you called (whether a prospective date or prospective employer) is ignoring you because they never call back? Maybe the reason is inadequate telephone skills. Following are some suggestions for becoming phone-savvy, which will give you a practical introduction to the subject of communication.[1]

■ **Consider the impression you make on the phone:** Watch out for self-defeating telephone behavior. Talking too fast, for instance, makes what you say seem unimportant. Talking too slowly makes you sound tired or uninterested. Talking too softly makes you hard to understand. Talking too loudly grates on others' ears. Talking too much— giving more details than your listener wants— makes people impatient.

■ **When you call someone:** When you make a call to someone you don't know, do you speak briefly and above all *clearly*? When leaving a message, do you *slowly* give your name, organization, and phone number (*twice*)? Do you give the date and time you called? If you want a call back, do you specify a *time when you'll be available*? (Don't say: "Uh, I'll be around maybe later.")

■ **When someone calls you:** Do you give a favorable first impression, showing the caller that you're helpful and confident? Do you identify yourself? Do you repeat (and *jot down*) the caller's name? (Don't say: "Um, what'd you say your name was again?")

■ **Being courteous:** Do you keep your voice interested, attentive, and friendly? Do you say "please" and "thank you"? Do you ask callers if it's okay to put them on hold or if you should call back in a few minutes? Do you say "Thank you for waiting" when you come back on? Do you let the caller hang up first? (Of course, as a time-starved manager you'll sometimes have to politely terminate the conversation first.)

■ **Making difficult calls:** When you have to make a difficult telephone call, as when you're angling for a job interview, are you prepared? Do you have a script written out beforehand on which you've practiced? Do you get to the point right away? (Attention spans are shorter on the phone.) Do you repeat the other person's name once in a while to make the conversation more personal?

■ **Dealing with phone tag:** You phone. Your caller isn't in. That person calls you back. You're not in. That's "phone tag." To deal with it, you need to be aware of the following tricks. (1) Persistence is important. Four or five calls are fine. More than that and the other person may consider you a pest. (2) Don't just use the other person's answering machine or voice mail. If he or she has a secretary or administrative assistant, leave messages with that person as well. (And get to know that person by name and become allies.) (3) Describe your schedule and your availability. (4) If the other person calls back, note the time, which may be when he or she is always at a desk making calls. (5) When you leave a message, make it clear and complete but not overly long.

FORECAST: WHAT'S AHEAD IN THIS CHAPTER

This chapter describes the process of transferring information and understanding from one person to another. It also describes three communications barriers—physical, semantic, and personal. It shows how you can use different channels and patterns of communication, both formal and informal, to your advantage. It discusses how star managers use information technology to communicate more effectively. Finally, we talk about how to be a better listener, talker, writer, and reader.

What do I need to know about the communication process to be an effective communicator?

The Big Picture

Communication is the transfer of information and understanding from one person to another. The process involves sender, message, and receiver; encoding and decoding; the medium; feedback; and dealing with "noise," or interference. Managers need to tailor their communication to the appropriate medium (rich or lean) for the appropriate situation.

"Good writing is one of two key abilities I focus on when hiring," says Richard Todd at the Federal Reserve Bank of Minneapolis; "the other is the ability to read critically. I can train people to do almost anything else, but I don't have time to teach this."[2]

Because many students have not had sufficient training of this sort and because today's work environment is so fast-paced, faulty communication has become a real problem in the workplace. According to one survey, executives say 14% of each 40-hour workweek is wasted because of poor communication between staff and managers.[3] That's the equivalent of seven workweeks of lost productivity a year. Thus, there's a hard-headed argument for better communication: It can save money.

Communication Defined: The Transfer of Information & Understanding

Communication—**the transfer of information and understanding from one person to another**—is an activity that you as a manager will have to do a lot of. Indeed, one study found that 81% of a manager's time in a typical work day is spent communicating.[4]

The fact that managers do a lot of communicating doesn't mean they're necessarily good at it—that is, that they are efficient or effective. You are an _efficient communicator_ when you can transmit your message accurately in the least time. You are an _effective communicator_ when your intended message is accurately understood by the other person. Thus, you may well be efficient in sending a group of people a reprimand by e-mail. But it may not be effective if it makes them angry so that they can't absorb its meaning.

From this, you can see why it's important to have an understanding of the communication process.

Improve or else. How would you like to be reprimanded by your boss? By an e-mail message? Harshly in person? Gently in person?

How the Communication Process Works

Communication has been said to be a process consisting of "a sender transmitting a message through media to a receiver who responds."[5] Let's look at these and other parts of the process.

Sender, Message, & Receiver The _sender_ is the person wanting to share information—called a _message_—and the _receiver_ is the person for whom the message is intended, **as follows.**

Sender → Message → Receiver

Encoding & Decoding Of course, the process isn't as simple as just sender/message/receiver. If you were sending the message over a telegraph line, you would first have to encode the message, and the receiver would have to decode it. But the same is true if you are sending the message by voice to another person in the same room, when you have to decide what language to speak in and what terms to use.

Encoding **is translating a message into understandable symbols or language.** _Decoding_ **is interpreting and trying to make sense of the message.** Thus, the communication process is now

Sender **[Encoding]** → Message → **[Decoding]** Receiver

The Medium The means by which you as a communicator send a message is important, whether it is by typing an e-mail traveling over the Internet, by voice over a telephone line, or by hand-scrawled note. This is the _medium_, **the pathway by which a message travels:**

Sender [Encoding] → Message **[Medium]** Message → [Decoding] Receiver

Feedback "Flight 123, do you copy?" In the movies, that's what you hear the flight controller say when radioing the pilot of a troubled aircraft to see if he or she received ("copied") the previous message. And the pilot may radio back, "Roger, Houston, I copy." This is an example of _feedback_—**the receiver expresses his or her reaction to the sender's message.**

Sender [Encoding] → Message [Medium] Message → [Decoding] Receiver

[Feedback]   Message

I hear you. Today some people can work almost anywhere. This man is sitting in an outdoor café and using his cellphone and laptop computer to conduct business. Do you think our ability to work outside traditional offices because of today's technology will negatively affect the communication process and employee camaraderie?

Say again? London traffic is only one cause of noise.

Noise Unfortunately, the entire communication process can be disrupted at several different points by what is called **_noise_**—**any disturbance that interferes with the transmission of a message.** The noise can occur in the medium, of course, as when you have static in a radio transmission or fade-out on a cellphone or when there's loud music when you're trying to talk in a noisy restaurant. Or it can occur in the encoding or decoding, as when a pharmacist can't read a prescription because of a doctor's poor handwriting.

Noise also occurs in *nonverbal communication* (discussed in Chapter 4 and again later in this chapter), as when our physical movements send a message that is different from the one we are speaking, or in *cross-cultural communication* (discussed in Chapter 4), as when we make assumptions about other people's messages based on our own culture instead of theirs. We discuss noise further in the next section.)

The communication process is shown below. *(See Panel 15.1.)*

PANEL 15.1

The communication process. "Noise" is not just noise or loud background sounds but any disturbance that interferes with transmission—static, fadeout, distracting facial expressions, uncomfortable meeting site, competing voices, and so on.

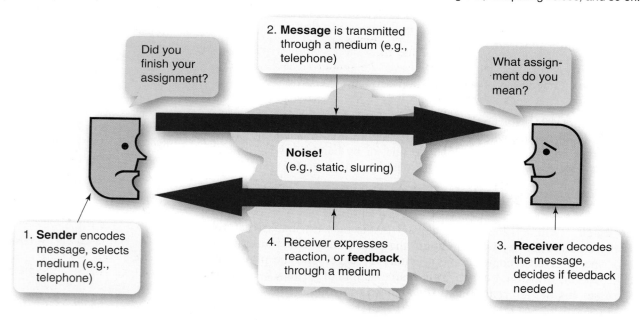

Selecting the Right Medium for Effective Communication

There are all kinds of communications tools available to managers, ranging from one-to-one face-to-face conversation all the way to use of the mass media. However, managers need to know how to use the right tool for the right condition—when to use e-mail, when to meet face to face, for example. Should you praise an employee by voicing a compliment, sending an e-mail, posting an announcement near the office coffee machine—or all three? How about when carrying out a reprimand?

Is a Medium Rich or Lean in Information? As a manager, you will have many media to choose from: conversations, meetings, speeches, the telephone, e-mail, memos, letters, bulletin boards, PowerPoint presentations, videoconferencing, printed publications, videos, and so on. Beyond these are the sophisticated communications possibilities of the mass media: public relations, advertising, news reports via print, radio-TV, the Internet.

Media richness **indicates how well a particular medium conveys information and promotes learning.** That is, the "richer" a medium is, the better it is at conveying information. The term *media richness* was proposed by respected organizational theorists Richard Daft and Robert Lengel as part of their contingency model for media selection.[6]

Ranging from high media richness to low media richness, types of media may be positioned along a continuum as follows:

High media richness
(Best for nonroutine, ambiguous situations)

Low media richness
(Best for routine, clear situations)

Face-to-face presence	Video-conferencing	Telephone	Personal written media (e-mail, memos, letters)	Impersonal written media (newsletters, fliers, general reports)

Face-to-face communication, also the most personal form of communication, is the richest. It allows the receiver of the message to observe multiple cues, such as body language and tone of voice. It allows the sender to get immediate feedback, to see how well the receiver comprehended the message. At the other end of the media richness scale, impersonal written media is just the reverse—only one cue and no feedback—making it low in richness.

Matching the Appropriate Medium to the Appropriate Situation In general, the rule for effective communication is this:

■ **Rich medium—best for nonroutine situations and to avoid oversimplification:** A *rich* medium is more effective with nonroutine situations.

Examples: In what way would you like to learn the facts from your boss of a nonroutine situation such as a major company reorganization, which might affect your job? Via a memo tacked on the bulletin board (a lean medium)? Or via face-to-face meeting or phone call (rich medium)?

The danger of using a rich medium for routine matters (such as monthly sales reports) is that it results in information *overloading*—more information than necessary.

■ **Lean medium—best for routine situations and to avoid overloading:** A *lean* medium is more effective with routine situations.

Examples: In what manner would you as a sales manager like to get routine monthly sales reports from your 50 sales reps? Via time-consuming phone calls (somewhat rich medium)? Or via written memos or e-mails (somewhat lean medium)? The danger of using a lean medium for nonroutine manners (such as a company reorganization) is that it results in information *oversimplification*—it doesn't provide enough of the information the receiver needs and wants.

Click-Along 15.1

Example of Using Wrong Medium: Westinghouse CEO Confesses "Very Poor Job of Communicating"

major question

What are the important barriers I need to be aware of, so I can improve my communication skills?

The Big Picture

We describe three barriers to communication. Physical barriers include sound, time, and space. Semantic barriers include unclear use of words and jargon. Personal barriers include variations in communication skills, trustworthiness and credibility, stereotypes and prejudices, and faulty listening skills.

Stand up and give a speech to a group of coworkers? Connecticut businessman Robert Suhoza would prefer to be trampled by elephants, says a news story. "Make small talk at a cocktail party?" it goes on. "Just go ahead and shoot him. Introduce himself to a room full of strangers? Maybe he'll just come back some other time. . . . Even answering the phone seemed at times an insurmountable task: He knew he should pick up the receiver, but he was paralyzed by not knowing who was on the other end, or what the caller wanted."[7]

Suhoza is 53 years old, but all his life he has suffered from social phobia or social anxiety disorder. In this he has plenty of company: One in every eight Americans apparently meet the diagnostic criteria for social anxiety disorder at some point in their lives, making it the third most common psychiatric condition. More women suffer from it than men, although men are more likely to seek treatment.[8]

Social anxiety disorder is an example (though an extreme one) of a communication *barrier*—a barrier being anything interfering with accurate communication between two people. Some barriers may be thought of as happening within the communication process itself, as the panel opposite shows. *(See Panel 15.2.)* It's more practical, however, to think of barriers as being of three types: (1) *physical barriers*, (2) *semantic barriers*, and (3) *personal barriers*.

Without walls. Supposedly businesses that have open floor plans with cubicles instead of private offices function better because people can more easily talk across the shoulder-high partitions. But do you think the absence of floor-to-ceiling physical barriers might, in fact, lead to other kinds of barriers—such as others' talking making it hard to hear on the phone?

1 Physical Barriers: Sound, Time, Space, & So On

Try shouting at someone on the far side of a construction site—at a distance of several yards over the roar of earth-moving machinery—and you know what physical barriers are. Other such barriers are time-zone differences, telephone-line static, and crashed computers. Office walls can be physical barriers, too, which is one reason for the trend toward open floor plans with cubicles instead of offices in many workplace settings.

PANEL 15.2

Some barriers that happen within the communication process. All it takes is one blocked step in the communication process described in the text for communication to fail. Consider the following.

■ *Sender barrier—no message gets sent:* Have you ever had an idea but were afraid to voice it because (like Robert Suhoza) you feared criticism? Then obviously no message got sent.

But the barrier need not be for psychological reasons. Suppose as a new manager you simply didn't realize (because you weren't told) that supervising your subordinates' expense accounts was part of your responsibility. In that case, it may be understandable why you never call them to task about fudging their expense reports—why, in other words, no message got sent.

■ *Encoding barrier—the message is not expressed correctly:* No doubt you've sometimes had difficulty trying to think of the correct word to express how you feel about something. If English is not your first language, perhaps, then you may have difficulty expressing to a supervisor, coworker, or subordinate what it is you mean to say.

■ *Medium barrier—the communication channel is blocked:* You never get through to someone because his or her phone always has a busy signal. The computer network is down and the e-mail message you sent doesn't go through. These are

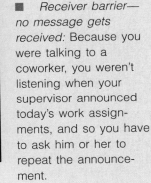

instances of the communication medium being blocked.

■ *Decoding barrier—the recipient doesn't understand the message:* Your boss tells you to "lighten up" or "buckle down," but because English is not your first language, you don't understand what the messages mean. Or perhaps you're afraid to show your ignorance when someone is throwing computer terms at you and says that your computer connection has "a bandwidth problem."

■ *Receiver barrier—no message gets received:* Because you were talking to a coworker, you weren't listening when your supervisor announced today's work assignments, and so you have to ask him or her to repeat the announcement.

■ *Feedback barrier—the recipient doesn't respond enough:* No doubt you've had the experience of giving someone street directions, but since they only nod their heads and don't repeat the directions back to you, you don't really know whether you were understood. The same thing can happen in many workplace circumstances.

2 Semantic Barriers: When Words Matter

When a supervisor tells you, "We need to get this done right away," what does it mean? Does "We" mean just you? You and your coworkers? Or you, your coworkers, and the boss? Does "right away" mean today, tomorrow, or next week? These are examples of semantic barriers. *Semantics* **is the study of the meaning of words.**

practical action

Minding Your Manners: Workplace Etiquette Can Be Crucial to Your Career

Even when you're not talking, you're often communicating—nonverbally (as we discuss elsewhere in this chapter). Manners are a big part of this.

Consider: While at lunch with your business clients, do you eat your soup by swiping the spoon from 12 o'clock to 6 o'clock in the bowl? (It should be the reverse.) Do you order a glass of wine with your meal? (Best not to drink alcohol on someone else's clock.) Do you squeeze lemon into your ice tea with a client across the table? (Best not—you might squirt him or her in the eye.) Do you scratch your back with your fork?

We are talking about a form of communication known as *etiquette* or *manners*. Despite the informality (including not just dress-down Fridays but dress-down everydays) of many offices, managers need to learn business etiquette—manners, politeness, appropriate behavior—if they are to achieve career success. Etiquette is more than table manners; it is the expression of being considerate. If you have to take clients out to dinner a couple times a week, you'll be glad if you know which fork to use. MBA candidates at Daniels College of Business at the University of Denver are required to attend an etiquette dinner, and the Massachusetts Institute of Technology also runs a not-for-credit charm school. These and similar courses provide lessons in dining etiquette, pager protocol, cellphone politeness, and the like. "In climbing the slippery ladder of success," says the founder of an etiquette training firm, "people have to recognize that they will never get promoted if their bosses and customers don't see them as looking and acting the part."

Some matters to be aware of:[9]

■ **Handshakes:** The proper manner is to clasp firmly at an angle, then give two or three pumps.

Such a simple act. Handshakes are an everyday occurrence, but the clasp should be neither too strong nor too weak. After all, first impressions are important.

■ **Introductions:** When your boss is meeting your client, you should start with the person you want to honor—the client. ("Mr. Smith, I'd like you to meet my boss, Janet Jones. Jan, this is Horatio Smith, vice-president of Associated Success Inc.") Also, you should give some information about each person in order to get a conversation started. ("Jan is head of our Far West Division, and she just got back from a rock-climbing vacation.")

■ **Thank-you notes:** When someone prepares an all-day or all-week program in which you've participated, send him or her a thank-you note. When the boss entertains you on her boat, send her a thank-you note. When a client gives you a plant tour, send him a note. And ALWAYS send a thank-you note after a job interview.

■ **Dining tips and table manners:** Don't order the most expensive item. Don't start eating before your host. Avoid ordering food you think you might have difficulty handling properly because of splattering (such as soup or pasta). Know what to do with your bread. (Take the bread or roll, hold it over your plate—it's the plate on the left—break off a piece of it, and then put butter on it. If you drop a roll on the floor, don't pick it up; point it out to the waiter.) Don't kick your shoes off under the table. Turn off your cellphone so it won't beep. When you leave the table and plan to return, leave your napkin on your chair; when you're leaving for good, leave it on the table. In the U.S., you should keep your elbows off the table, and it's okay to keep your hands beneath it. In European countries, however, the reverse is considered polite.

We may encounter semantic difficulties when dealing with other cultures (as discussed in Chapter 4). In addition, as our society becomes more technically oriented, semantic meaning becomes a problem because jargon develops. ***Jargon* is terminology specific to a particular profession or group.** (Example: "The HR VP wants the RFP to go out ASAP." Translation: "The Vice President of Human Resources wants the Request For Proposal to go out as soon as possible.") As a manager in a specialized field, you need to remember that what are ordinary terms for you may be mysteries to outsiders.

3 Personal Barriers: Individual Attributes That Hinder Communication

"Is it them or is it me?"

How often have you wondered, when someone has shown a surprising response to something you said, how the miscommunication happened? Let's examine nine personal barriers that contribute to miscommunication.[10]

> You mean an ordinary person is supposed to understand this? Why, would you guess, do professional tax preparers do such a brisk business in the months of March and April?

Variable Skills in Communicating Effectively As we all know, some people are simply better communicators than others. They have the speaking skills, the vocabulary, the facial expressions, the eye contact, the dramatic ability, the "gift of gab" to express themselves in a superior way. Conversely, other people don't have this quality. But better communication skills can be learned.

Variations in How Information Is Processed & Interpreted Are you from a working-class or privileged background? Are you from a particular ethnic group? Are you better at math or at language? Are you from a chaotic household filled with alcoholism and fighting, which distracts you at work?

Because people use different frames of reference and experiences to interpret the world around them, they are selective about what things have meaning to them and what don't. All told, these differences affect what we say and what we think we hear.

Variations in Trustworthiness & Credibility Without trust between you and the other person, communication is apt to be flawed. Instead of communicating, both of you will be concentrating on defensive tactics, not the meaning of the message being exchanged.[11] How will subordinates react to you as a manager if your predecessors in your job

lied to them? They may give you the benefit of a doubt, but they may be waiting for the first opportunity to be confirmed in the belief that you will break their trust.

Oversized Egos Our egos—our pride, our self-esteem, even arrogance—are a fifth barrier. Egos can cause political battles, turf wars, and the passionate pursuit of power, credit, and resources. Egos influence how we treat each other as well as how receptive we are to being influenced by others. Ever had someone take credit for an idea that was yours? Then you know how powerful ego feelings can be.

Faulty Listening Skills When you go to a party, do people ever ask questions of you and about who you are and what you're doing? Or are they too ready to talk about themselves? And do they seem to be waiting for you to finish talking so that they can then resume saying what they want to say? (But here's a test: Do you actually *listen* when they're talking?)

Tendency to Judge Others' Messages Suppose another student in this class sees you reading this text and says, "I like the book we're reading." You might say, "I agree." Or you might say, "I disagree—it's boring." The point is that we all have a natural tendency, according to psychologist Carl Rogers, to judge others' statements from our own point of view (especially if we have strong feelings about the issue).[12]

Inability to Listen with Understanding

To really listen with understanding, you have to imagine yourself in the other person's shoes. Or, as Rogers and his coauthor put it, you have to "see the expressed idea and attitude from the other person's point of view, to sense how it feels to him, to achieve his frame of reference in regard to the thing he is talking about."[13] When you listen with understanding, it makes you feel less defensive (even if the message is criticism) and improves your accuracy in perceiving the message.

Stereotypes & Prejudices

A *stereotype* consists of oversimplified beliefs about a certain group of people. There are, for instance, common stereotypes about old people, young people, males, and females. Wouldn't you hate to be categorized according to just a couple of exaggerated attributes—by your age and gender, for example? ("Young men are reckless." "Old women are scolds." Yes, *some* young men and *some* old women are this way, but it's unrealistic and unfair to tar every individual in these groups with the same brush.)

We consider matters of gender communication further in another two pages.

Nonverbal Communication

Do your gestures and facial expressions contradict your words? This is the sort of nonverbal communication that you may not even be aware of. We discuss this subject in more detail next.

Nonverbal Communication

You're listening to a sales pitch from the representative of a printing firm who would like to sell your organization a lot of printing business. What do you find yourself responding to? The words? Or the twitching fingers, lack of eye contact, and flat tone of voice?

As we stated in Chapter 4, *nonverbal communication* consists of messages sent outside the written or spoken word. Researchers estimate that 65%–95% of face-to-face communication is interpreted through body language.[14] Given the prevalence of nonverbal communication and its impact on organizational behavior (such as hiring decisions, perceptions of others, and getting one's ideas accepted by others), it is important that you become familiar with the various sources of nonverbal communication.[15] Let us consider some ways in which your nonverbal communication is expressed by your body language, setting, and use of time.[16]

Body language. Who's paying attention and who isn't? If you were a manager speaking at this meeting and you noticed the man at the end of the row looking out the window as you talked, would you continue to speak to those who seem attentive? Or would you try to adjust your remarks—and your own body language—to try to reach the man who is tuning you out?

Body Language—Facial Expression, Tone of Voice, Touch, and So On

Body language includes posture, facial expressions, gestures, vocal quality, and touch. What does it mean, for instance, when your listeners cross their arms? Frown? Scratch their heads? Yawn excessively? Speak too quickly? In the culture of the United States, at least, it means that you as the speaker should realize your message is not being received well. *(See Panel 15.3.)*

PANEL 15.3

Toward better nonverbal communication skills.[17] You can practice these skills by watching TV with the sound off and interpreting people's emotions and interactions.

Do	Don't
Maintain eye contact	Look away from the speaker
Lean toward the speaker	Turn away from the speaker
Speak at a moderate rate	Speak too quickly or slowly
Speak in a quiet, reassuring tone	Speak in an unpleasant tone
Smile and show animation	Yawn excessively
Occasionally nod head in agreement	Close your eyes

Setting—Arrangement of the Meeting Space   How do you feel when you visit someone who sits behind a big desk and is backlit by a window so her face is obscured? What does it say when someone comes out from behind his desk and invites you to sit with him on his office couch? The location of an office (such as corner office with window versus interior office with no window), its size, and the choice of furniture often express the accessibility of the person in it.

Time—Using Appropriately to Show Interest   When your boss keeps you waiting 45 minutes for an appointment with him, how do you feel? When she simply grunts or makes one-syllable responses to your comments, what does this say about her interest in your concerns? As a manager yourself, you should always give the people who work for you adequate time. You should also talk with them frequently during the meeting so they will understand your interest.

A long day, or . . . ? People's behavior doesn't always reflect what's going on around them. It may reflect what's going on *inside* of them. Perhaps this man was up late the night before with a sick child or has been burning the midnight oil for several days to make a project deadline. Even so, when speaking, you need to watch your audience for their reactions. Judging by the looks of the other three in this photo, do you think the speaker is boring?

Gender-Related Communication Differences

Some possible general differences in communication between genders are summarized below. *(See Panel 15.4.)* Note, however, that these don't apply in all cases, which would constitute stereotyping. How useful do you think these specific styles are in a managerial context? (Recall the discussion of men and women with reference to leadership in Chapter 14.)

PANEL 15.4

Communication differences. How do men and women differ?[18]

Linguistic characteristic	Men	Women
Taking credit	Greater use of "I" statements (e.g., "I did this" and "I did that"); more likely to boast about their achievements	Greater use of "We" statements (e.g., "We did this" and "We did that"); less likely to boast about their achievements
Displaying confidence	Less likely to indicate that they are uncertain about an issue	More likely to indicate a lack of certainty about an issue
Asking questions	Less likely to ask questions (e.g., asking for directions)	More likely to ask questions
Conversation rituals	Avoid making apologies because it puts them in a one-down position	More frequently say "I'm sorry"
Giving feedback	More direct and blunt	More tactful; tend to temper criticism with praise
Giving compliments	Stingy with praise	Pay more compliments than men
Indirectness	Indirect when it comes to admitting fault or when they don't know something	Indirect when telling others what to do

Author Judith Tingley suggests that women and men should learn to "genderflex"—temporarily use communication behaviors typical of the other gender to increase the potential for influence.[19] For example, a female manager might use sports analogies to motivate a group of males.

Deborah Tannen, by contrast, recommends that everyone become aware of how differing linguistic styles affect our perceptions and judgments. For example, in a meeting, regardless of gender, "those who are comfortable speaking up in groups, who need little or no silence before raising their hands, or who speak out easily without waiting to be recognized are more apt to be heard," she says. "Those who refrain from talking until it's clear that the previous speaker is finished, who wait to be recognized, and who are inclined to link their comments to those of others will do fine at a meeting where everyone else is following the same rules but will have a hard time getting heard in a meeting with people whose styles are more like the first pattern."[20]

Example of How Female Leaders Often Communicate: Sharing Rather Than Controlling Information

Women, says *Business Week*, are more apt than men "to disregard as a useless power trip [one] long-held management bugaboo: keeping information tightly controlled."

A representative of this viewpoint is Anu Shukla, who sold her Internet marketing-software company, Rubric Inc., in 2000 for $390 million—and made 65 of her 85 employees millionaires.

"It's better to overcommunicate," says Shukla. As an example, she made it her policy to share information with all of her employees, rather than impart it to selected employees on a need-to-know basis. In addition, she created what she called the "CEO lunch," in which she invited six to eight employees at a time to discuss the business with her.

No wonder that various studies have found that women consistently outscore men on communication skills.[21]

Anu Shukla, formerly of Rubric Inc. If forced to choose between equally qualified male and female candidates for a top-level job, she says, "I would rather hire a woman." This is not because of affirmative action but because, like other executives, she thinks a woman will usually do a better job. "I know I'm going to get a certain quality of work," she says. "I know I'm going to get a certain dedication." She adds that she realizes that not all women executives excel. Do you think the essential difference is that women communicate better than men?

By now most male students and managers know they should avoid the use of masculine wording for jobs or roles that are occupied by both genders, using *police officer* instead of *policeman; supervisor* rather than *foreman*. (Conversely, secretaries, nurses, and babysitters should no longer be referred to as "she.") If you stay alert, it's fairly easy to avoid sentence constructions that are demeaning to women. (Instead of saying "he is," say "he or she is" or "they are.")

But, of course, there's more to effective managerial communication than that. Indeed, there are executive-training programs designed to teach men the value of emotion in relationships—the use of "soft skills" to communicate, build teams, and develop flexibility. "The nature of modern business requires what's more typical to the female mold of building consensus as opposed to the top-down male military model," says Millington F. McCoy, managing director of a New York executive search firm. One program given by London-based James R. Traeger helps participants break down the stereotype of the aggressive, controlling man who always wants to take charge and solve problems and to learn to listen and work in harmony.[22]

Interestingly, although men hold 94% of the top corporate jobs, when they want the advice of an executive coach—a trained listener to help them with their goals and personal problems—they usually turn to a woman. And, in fact, females always want another female as a coach. As a result, 7 out of 10 graduates of Coach U, the largest training school for executive coaches, are women. Because good coaches, says Coach U's CEO Sandy Vilas (who is male), are intuitive communicators and have done a lot of personal development work, "that profile tends to fit women better." Says Susan Bloch, who heads an executive coaching practice, "When a man is asked to coach another, they have a tendency to compete. Man to man, they have to show each other how great they are."[23]

major question

How can I use the different channels and patterns of communication to my advantage?

The Big Picture

Formal communication channels follow the chain of command, which is of three types—vertical, horizontal, and external. Informal communication channels develop outside the organization's formal structure. One type is gossip and rumor. Another is management by wandering around, in which a manager talks to people across all lines of authority.

If you've ever had a low-level job in nearly any kind of organization, you know that there is generally a hierarchy of management between you and the organization's president, director, or CEO. If you had a suggestion you wanted him or her to hear, you doubtless had to go up through management channels. That's formal communication.

However, you may have run into that top manager in the elevator. Or in the restroom. Or in a line at the bank. You could have voiced your suggestion casually then. That's informal communication.

Each type of communication requires different kinds of skills. Let's consider how they work.

Formal Communication Channels: Up, Down, Sideways, & Outward

Formal communication channels follow the chain of command and are recognized as official. The organization chart we described in Chapter 8 indicates how official communications—memos, letters, reports, announcements—are supposed to be routed.

Formal communication is of three types: (1) *vertical*—meaning upward and downward, (2) *horizontal*—meaning laterally (sideways), and (3) *external*—meaning outside the organization.

1 Vertical Communication: Up & Down the Chain of Command Vertical communication is the flow of messages up and down the hierarchy within the organization: bosses communicating with subordinates, subordinates communicating with bosses. As you might expect, the more management levels through which a message passes, the more it is prone to distortion.

How do you communicate with a manager two or three levels above you in the organization's hierarchy? You can send a memo through channels. Or you can watch for when that manager goes to the water cooler or the coffee pot.

- **Downward communication—from top to bottom:** *Downward communication* **flows from a higher level to a lower level (or levels).** Most downward communication involves one of the following kinds of information:[24]

    (1) Instructions related to particular job tasks. Example (supervisor to subordinate): "The store will close Monday for inventory. All employees are expected to participate."

    (2) Explanations about the relationship between two or more tasks. Example: "While taking inventory, employees need to see what things are missing. Most of that might be attributable to shoplifting."

    (3) Explanations of the organization's procedures and practices. Example: "Start counting things on the high shelves and work your way down."

    (4) A manager's feedback about a subordinate's performance: Example: "It's best not to try to count too fast."

    (5) Attempts to encourage a sense of mission and dedication to the organization's goals. Example: "By keeping tabs on our inventory, we can keep our prices down and maintain our reputation of giving good value."

    In small organizations, top-down communication may be delivered face to face. In larger organizations, it's delivered via meetings, e-mail, official memos, and company publications.

- **Upward communication—from bottom to top:** *Upward communication* **flows from lower levels to higher level (or levels).** Often this type of communication is from a subordinate to his or her immediate manager, who in turn will relay it up to the next level, if necessary. Most upward communication involves the following kinds of information:[25]

    (1) Reports of progress on current projects. Example: "We shut down the store yesterday to take inventory."

    (2) Reports of unsolved problems requiring help from people higher up. Example: "We can't make our merchandise count jibe with the stock reports."

    (3) New developments affecting the work unit. Example: "Getting help from the other stores really speeded things up this year."

    (4) Suggestions for improvements. Example: "The stores should loan each other staff every time they take inventory."

    (5) Reports on employee attitudes and efficiency. Example: "The staff likes it when they go to another store and sometimes they pick up some new ways of doing things."

    Effective upward communication depends on an atmosphere of trust. No subordinate is going to want to be the bearer of bad news to a manager who is always negative and bad-tempered.

Example of Upward Communication: How Anonymous Phone Calls Improved Communication at Pillsbury

At Pillsbury, the baking-products company, which is now part of General Mills, managers were encouraged to foster two-way communication among all employees. But if this didn't seem to be working, there was another way: anonymous phone calls.

The way this worked is that employees who seemed unable to bring themselves to communicate with higher management could telephone a third party anonymously. By giving people the opportunity to make an end run around the hierarchical chain of command, the system helped to expose inefficiencies and put out brush fires. Every word of such a call was transcribed, and the transcript went to Pillsbury's chief executive officer. Because employees knew this, they kept calling.

This arrangement helped to change how Pillsbury did business. "This is not some warm and fuzzy human-resource program," said the Pillsbury company's chief. "People know it gets read, and they know it will get action."[26]

2 Horizontal Communication: Within & Between Work Units

Horizontal communication **flows within and between work units; its main purpose is coordination.** As a manager, you will spend perhaps as much as a third of your time in this form of communication—consulting with colleagues and coworkers at the same level as you within the organization. In this kind of sideways communication, you will be sharing information, coordinating tasks, solving problems, resolving conflicts, and getting the support of your peers. Horizontal communication is encouraged through the use of committees, task forces, and matrix structures.

Horizontal communication can be impeded in three ways: (1) by specialization that makes people focus just on their jobs alone; (2) by rivalry between workers or work units, which prevents sharing of information; and (3) by lack of encouragement from management.[27]

3 External Communication: Outside the Organization

External communication **flows between people inside and outside the organization.** These are other stakeholders: customers, suppliers, shareholders or other owners, and so on. Companies have given this kind of communication heightened importance, especially with customers or clients, who are the lifeblood of any company.

Feedback about food. In 1979, Tim and Nina Zagat, two lawyers well acquainted with New York fine dining, collected the opinions of 200 friends into a self-published rating system of local restaurants. Today their consumer-driven evaluations covering restaurants in 45 cities, hotels, resorts, and spas have become bestsellers. Indeed, you can access the results of their surveys through your computer, Palm Pilot, or certain cellphones. Have you ever completed one of Zagat's surveys?

Informal Communication Channels

Informal communication channels **develop outside the formal structure and do not follow the chain of command**—they skip management levels and cut across lines of authority.

There are two aspects of informal channels that are important to know about: (1) the *grapevine*, and (2) *management by wandering around.*

Click-Along 15.2

Formal & Informal Channels of Communication Illustrated

1 The Grapevine: Informal Communication through Gossip & Rumor

The *grapevine* **is the unofficial communication system of the informal organization,** a network of gossip and rumor of what is called "employee language." One survey found that employees used the grapevine (a term from the Civil War practice of stringing battlefield telegraph lines between trees, resembling hanging grape vines) as their most frequent source of information.[28] Indeed, research shows, (1) the grapevine is faster than formal channels; (2) it is about 75% accurate; (3) people rely on it when they are insecure or faced with organizational changes; and (4) employees use the grapevine to acquire the majority of their on-the-job information.[29]

Two grapevine patterns predominate. In the *gossip chain*, one person seeks out and communicates with several others. In the *cluster pattern*, one person tells the message to three (or more) other people, and then each of them tells three others.[30]

Click-Along 15.3

Two Most Typical Grapevine Patterns Illustrated

Some gossips are beneficial, consistently passing along important grapevine information to others. Often they are friendly, outgoing people whose jobs allow them to cross departmental lines. Some secretaries, for example, are able to communicate with all kinds of people up and down the hierarchy, from janitor to top executive.[31] Others, called *moles*, use the grapevine to obtain information, often negative, to enhance their power and status. They secretly report their perceptions about other employees' difficulties or failures to managers in power.[32] Moles can sow conflict, destroy teamwork, and impair productivity.

Since gossip and rumor can't be extinguished, the practical course for managers is to try to *monitor* and *influence* the grapevine by selectively sending information along it. They can talk with individuals important in the gossip chain to make sure information gets spread to people who tend to ignore the formal communications system. They can openly share relevant news, as in providing advance notice of organizational changes.

2 Management by Wandering Around: Informal Communication through Spontaneous Conversations Can executives manage by staying in their offices? No doubt many do. But many managers—even top executives of, for example, soft-drink maker PepsiCo, oil company ARCO, and hotel chain Marriott—find that getting out from behind the desk helps them get a better feel for their operations.

This kind of informal communication is called ***management by wandering around (MBWA)*—a manager literally wanders around his or her organization and talks with people across all lines of authority.**[33] Management by wandering around helps to reduce the problems of distortion that inevitably occur with formal communication flowing up a hierarchy. As telecommunications head Brian Thompson of LCI International puts it, "The problem with being a CEO is that everybody between you and them wants to tell you what you want to hear. So it's really being visible to people, walking around . . ."[34]

MBWA allows managers to listen to employees and learn about their problems. It also enables managers to express to employees what values and goals are important to them. Needless to say, however, if the wandering-around executive is looking for problems for the purpose of disciplining people, the technique won't work.

At Detroit Diesel, which manufactures truck diesel engines, the general manager tours the plant and talks to various employees, listening to them express their concerns. One result is that the company increased its market share significantly as employees were able to voice their suggestions for improvement in quality.[35]

MBWA. Management by wandering around is sort of the reverse of employees exchanging informal views with top managers at the water cooler. That is, by wandering around the organization, top managers can stop and talk to nearly anyone—and thus perhaps learn things that might be screened out by the formal up-the-organization reporting process. If top managers can do MBWA, do you think mid-level managers can as well?

How do contemporary managers use information technology to communicate more effectively?

The Big Picture

We discuss five communications tools of information technology: (1) the Internet and its associated intranets and extranets, (2) e-mail, (3) videoconferencing, (4) collaborative computing, and (5) telecommuting. We also discuss how to deal with information overload.

Sun designed the first intranet back when people thought intranet was a typo.

"I'm dangerous," jokes Gregory Summe between downhill runs at a Utah ski resort, as he pulls out his tiny cellphone and his electronic organizer with its 12,000-name contact list. With this kind of portable information technology, Summe, 42, CEO of EG&G Inc., is able to work anywhere and contact anyone. "There's an expectation for CEOs to be much more in touch with customers, employees, and investors than in the past," he says. "A big part of the reason may be [portable information] technology."[36]

Communications Tools of Information Technology: Offspring of the Internet

Here let us explore some of the more important aspects of information technology: (1) the Internet along with intranets and extranets, (2) e-mail, (3) videoconferencing, (4) collaborative computing, and (5) telecommuting.

1 The Internet, Intranets, & Extranets The Internet, or more simply "the Net," is more than a computer network. It is a network of computer networks. **The _Internet_ is a global network of independently operating but interconnected computers, linking hundreds of thousands of smaller networks around the world.** The Internet connects everything from personal computers to supercomputers in organizations of all kinds.

Two private uses of the Internet are as intranets and extranets.

■ **Intranets: An _intranet_ is nothing more than an organization's private Internet.** Intranets also have _firewalls_ that block outside Internet users from accessing internal information. This is done to protect the privacy and confidentiality of company documents. According to one source, more than half of companies with more than 500 employees have corporate intranets.[37]

■ **Extranets: An _extranet_ is an extended intranet in that it connects internal employees with selected customers, suppliers, and other strategic partners.** Ford Motor Co., for instance, has an extranet that connects its dealers worldwide. Ford's extranet was set up to help support the sales and servicing of cars and to enhance customer satisfaction.

2 E-mail *E-mail,* for *electronic mail,* **uses the Internet to send computer-generated text and documents between people.** A recent study found that 73% of the executives responding felt that e-mail would be the leading form of business communication for employees by 2005.[38]

E-mail has become a major communication medium because of four key benefits.[39]

■ **Reduced cost of distributing information:** E-mail reduces the cost of distributing information to a large number of employees. Software developer MicroBiz in Mahway, N.J., found its phone bill dropped by more than half after it mandated that its dealers and Micro-Biz employees use e-mail rather than the telephone.[40]

■ **Increased teamwork:** E-mail increases teamwork because it enables workers to quickly send messages to colleagues anywhere—another floor, building, or country. In one study, managers indicated three reasons for using e-mail: (1) to keep others informed; (2) to follow up on an earlier communication; and (3) to communicate the same thing to many people.[41]

■ **Reduced paper costs:** E-mail reduces the costs and time associated with print duplication and paper distribution.

■ **Increased flexibility:** E-mail fosters flexibility, as in enabling employees with portable computers to log on from anywhere anytime.

Free e-mail. Yahoo! offers free e-mail service, as do Hot-mail and Planet-Save.com.

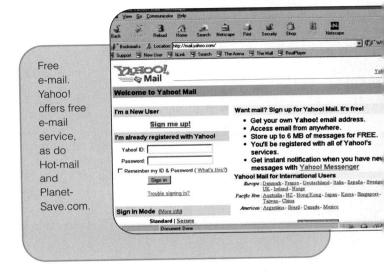

However, there are three drawbacks to e-mail:

■ **Wasted time:** Sending and receiving e-mail can lead to a lot of wasted time and effort, or it can distract employees from completing critical job duties. One survey found that e-mail users at work average nearly an hour a day managing their e-mail.[42] Astronomer Seth Shostak, for instance, receives about 50 electronic messages a day. "If I spend five minutes considering and composing a response to each correspondence," he complains, "then two hours of my day are busied with e-mail, even when I don't initiate a single one."[43]

■ **Information overload:** E-mail users tend to send and receive more messages. Some of this is *spam*—**unsolicited jokes and junk mail.** Some of it is simply "cc's" ("carbon copies") of correspondence to other people. The result is information overload. "You come into the office in the morning," says a sales and marketing vice-president, "and you have 120 [e-mail] messages in your box. And maybe only 10 of them include worthwhile information, but you still have to sift through the whole 120 to get to those 10."[44]

■ **Neglect of other media:** People may use e-mail to communicate when they should be using other media. For example, a four-year study in one university found that increased use of e-mail was associated with decreased face-to-face interactions and with a drop in the overall amount of organizational communication. Employees also said they felt less connected and less cohesive as a department as the amount of e-mails increased.[45]

3 Videoconferencing Also known as *teleconferencing*, *videoconferencing* uses video and audio links along with computers to enable people located at different locations to see, hear, and talk with one another. This enables people from many locations to conduct a meeting without having to travel. Videoconferencing can thus significantly reduce an organization's travel expenses.

Many organizations set up special videoconferencing rooms or booths with specially equipped television cameras. More recent equipment enables people to attach small cameras and microphones to their desks or computer monitors. This enables employees to conduct long-distance meetings and training classes without leaving their office or cubicle.

4 Collaborative Computing *Collaborative computing* entails using state-of-the-art computer software and hardware to help people work better together. Collaborative systems enable people to share information without the constraints of time and space. This is accomplished using computer networks to link people across a room or across the globe. Collaborative applications include messaging and e-mail systems, calendar management, videoconferencing, and electronic whiteboards.

Organizations that use full-fledged collaborative systems have the ability to create virtual teams (described in Chapter 13), which tend to use Internet or intranet systems, collaborative software, and videoconferencing to communicate with team members at any time.

5 Telecommuting *Telecommuting* involves doing work that is generally performed in the office away from the office, using a variety of information technologies. Employees typically receive and send work from home via phone and fax or by using a modem to link a home computer to an office computer. Among the benefits are (1) reduction of capital costs, because employees work at home; (2) increased flexibility and autonomy for workers; (3) competitive edge in recruiting hard-to-get employees; (4) increased job satisfaction and lower turnover; (5) increased productivity; and (6) ability to tap nontraditional labor pools (such as prison inmates and homebound disabled people).[46]

Telecommuting is more common for jobs that involve computer work, writing, and phone or brain work that requires concentration and limited interruptions. There were an estimated 32 million telecommuters in the United States in 2001, and the number is expected to increase.[47]

Although telecommuting represents an attempt to accommodate employee needs and desires, it requires adjustments and is not for everybody. People who enjoy the social camaraderie of the office setting, for instance, probably won't like it. Others lack the self-motivation needed to work at home.

Videoconferencing. In this arrangement three people in different locations can computer-conference— view and interact with each other— while studying a document on screen. Videoconferencing offers considerable savings in time and money over the cost of travel. Do you think you would feel inhibited working with people in this way?

Dealing with Information Overload

The primary benefit of the Internet and its variants is that they can enhance employees' ability to find, create, manage, and distribute information. How well they work, however, depends on how well employees know how to deal with the enormous repository of data that the Internet offers. Moreover, the Internet is not the only source of information. According to one study (probably not very reliable, however), the average U.S. employee in 1999 was found to receive 201 messages a day of all kinds.[48] Over half were phone calls and e-mail and voice-mail messages.

Clearly, then, dealing with information overload becomes a critical skill. ***Information overload*** **occurs when the amount of information received exceeds a person's ability to handle or process it.** Chapter 1 offered some suggestions for helping you deal with information overload. Here let us consider a greater information-management strategy: (1) reducing your information load, and (2) increasing your information-processing capacity.[49]

Reducing Your Information Load There are three ways to reduce the amount of information coming your way:

- **Preview and ignore messages:** The first thing you need to do is learn which messages to ignore. When going through your e-mail, for example, quickly glance at the subject line and immediately delete anything that looks like spam or (if you can) messages from people you don't know. You can do the same with voice mail or phone slips, just as you probably already do now with postal junk mail.

- **Filter messages:** One executive puts all "cc" e-mails in a special file and rarely reads them. Many e-mail programs have message filtering, so that an urgent message from your boss, for example, will go to the top of your e-mail queue. Spam-killer software is available to help you eliminate junk mail. Top executives, of course, have assistants to screen their messages and summarize the important ones.

- **Organize your e-mail inbox:** Set up a folder for e-mails you want to keep. Don't use your e-mail inbox for general storage, otherwise you'll have to sort through last week's messages every time you check your e-mail.

Increasing Your Information-Processing Capacity The best way to increase your information-processing ability is to learn to manage your time better (as discussed in Chapter 1). Some other tips:

- **Use discipline:** Handle every message only once. When an e-mail message arrives, for instance, read it and then either respond to it, delete it, or file it away in a folder. But deal with it immediately.

- **Get a unified messaging site:** It's possible to get one unified messaging site to which all your faxes, e-mails, and voice mails are delivered. Voice mails arrive as audio files that you can listen to, while e-mails are read to you over the phone by a virtual (robot) assistant.

How can I be a better listener, reader, writer, and speaker?

The Big Picture

We describe how you can be a more effective listener, as in learning to concentrate on the content of a message. We also describe how to be an effective reader. We offer four tips for becoming a more effective writer. Finally, we discuss how to be an effective speaker, through three steps.

The principal activities that managers spend their time doing have to do with communication—listening, reading, writing, and speaking.[50] Listening and speaking often take place in meetings (see the Practical Action box in Chapter 5, "How to Streamline Meetings"), although they are not the only occasions. Regardless of the environment, let's see how you can be more effective at these four essential communication skills.

Being an Effective Listener

Is listening something you're good at? Then you're the exception. Generally, people comprehend only about 25% of a typical verbal message, experts say.[51] Interestingly, the average speaker communicates 125 words per minute, while we can process 500 words per minute. Poor listeners use this information-processing gap to daydream. They think about other things, thus missing the important parts of what's being communicated.[52] Good listeners know how to use these gaps effectively, mentally summarizing the speaker's remarks, weighing the evidence, and listening between the lines.

Understand me. What's the recipe for effective listening—for really finding out what someone has to say? Probably it is *listen, watch, write, think, question*. What do you do to fight flagging concentration if you're tired or bored? You suppress negative thoughts, ignore distractions about the speaker's style of delivery or body language, and encourage the speaker with eye contact, an interested expression, and an attentive posture. This will make you more involved and interested in the subject matter.

How do you become the kind of manager who others say is a good listener? Here are some suggestions (you can practice them in your college lectures and seminars):[53]

Concentrate on the Content of the Message   Don't think about what you're going to say until the other person has finished talking.

- **Judge content, not delivery:** Don't tune out someone because of his or her accent, clothing, mannerisms, personality, or speaking style.

- **Ask questions, summarize remarks:** Good listening is hard work. Ask questions to make sure you understand. Recap what the speaker said.

- **Listen for ideas:** Don't get diverted by the details; try to concentrate on the main ideas.

- **Resist distractions, show interest:** Don't get distracted by things other people are doing, paperwork on your desk, things happening outside the window, television or radio, and the like. Show the speaker you're listening, periodically restating in your own words what you've heard.

- **Give a fair hearing:** Don't shut out unfavorable information just because you hear a term—"Republican," "Democrat," "union," "big business," "affirmative action"—that suggests ideas you're not comfortable with. Try to correct for your biases.

Asking questions. One of the most effective ways to concentrate on a message is to ask the speaker questions. In fact, learning experts recommend that students do this kind of participation in class. Participation helps people memorize because it obliges them to become actively engaged and to organize the speaker's material in their minds.

practical action

Communication by Listening

Often the reason that people act subversively against their employers is that they can't or are afraid to communicate with their managers.

Resistance may take the form of "malicious compliance" (following supervisors' instructions to the letter while ignoring the real goal), withholding crucial data, or sabotaging projects that reflect directly on the manager.

One bookstore employee sabotaged his nonlistening, always-angry boss by going through the store and discreetly pocketing any pens, pencils, even crayons, then

(continued)

hiding them in a backroom cabinet. "My already preternaturally enraged boss," he reported later, "reached glorious heights of apoplexy."[54]

As we discuss in the text, effective communication begins with listening. There is a technique for doing this. "To begin with, listen to people as if you don't know the answer," suggests Meg Price, a Reno, Nev., human resource professional. "This means that you will ask more questions to try to understand the situation from the other person's perspective. When you think you've got it, make a statement to the speaker summarizing what you believe they have told you. Only when they agree that indeed you do 'get it' should you begin to offer potential solutions or answers."[55]

Of course, sometimes there are true disagreements, and no amount of listening on your part is going to change that fact. Here, according to David Stiebel, author of *When Talking Makes Things Worse! Resolving Problems When Communication Fails*, is how to identify the nature of a dispute:

■ If you only listened to the other person, would she feel satisfied and stop opposing you?

■ If you succeed in explaining yourself, would you really change the other person's mind?

■ If the other person explained himself more, would you change your mind?

When true disagreements occur, one person ultimately must be willing to change so that negotiations can begin.[56]

Being an Effective Reader

Reading shares many of the same skills as listening. You need to concentrate on the content of the message, judge the content and not the delivery, and concentrate on the main ideas. But because managers usually have to do so much reading, you also need to learn to apply some other strategies.

Realize That Speed Reading Doesn't Work   Perhaps you've thought that somewhere along the line you could take a course on speed reading. By and large, however, speed reading isn't effective. Psychologists have found that speed reading or skimming may work well with easy or familiar reading material, but it can lead to problems with dense or unfamiliar material. For instance, in one study, when questioned about their reading of difficult material, average readers got half the questions right, while speed readers got only one in three.[57]

Learn to Streamline Reading   Management consultant and UCLA professor Kathryn Alesandrini offers a number of suggestions for streamlining your reading.[58]

■ **Be savvy about periodicals and books:** Review your magazine and newspaper subscriptions and eliminate as many as possible. You can subscribe to just a few industry publications, scan and mark interesting material, later read what's marked, and pitch the rest. Read summaries and reviews that condense business books and articles.

■ **Transfer your reading load:** With some material you can ask some of your employees to screen or scan it first, then post an action note on each item that needs additional reading by you. You can also ask your staff to read important books and summarize them in four or five pages.

■ **Make internal memos and e-mail more efficient:** Ask others to tell you up front in their e-mails, memos, and reports what they want you to do. Instruct them to include a one-page executive summary of a long report. When you communicate with them, give them specific questions you want answered.

Do Top-Down Reading—SQ3R "The key to better reading is to be a productive rather than a passive reader," writes Alesandrini. "You'll get more out of what you read if you literally produce meaningful connections between what you already know and what you're reading."[59] This leads to what she calls a "top-down" strategy for reading, a variant on the SQ3R (Survey, Question, Read, Recite, Review) method we discussed in the box at the end of Chapter 1.

The top-down system has five steps:

- **Rate reasons to read:** Rate your reasons for reading ("Why should I read this? Will reading it contribute to my goals?")

- **Question and predict answers:** Formulate specific questions you want the reading to answer. This will give you reasons for reading—to get answers to your questions.

- **Survey the big picture:** Survey the material to be read so you can get a sense of the whole. Take a few minutes to get an overview so that you'll be better able to read with purpose.

- **Skim for main ideas:** Skimming the material is similar to surveying, except it's on a smaller scale. You look for the essence of each subsection or paragraph.

- **Summarize:** Summarize as you skim. Verbally restate or write notes of the main points, using your own words. Visualize or sketch the main points. Answer your initial questions as you skim the material.

Being an Effective Writer

Writing is an essential management skill, but a lot of students don't get enough practice in it, which puts them at a career disadvantage. Taking a business writing class can probably have long-term payoffs.

Following are some tips for writing more effectively. These apply particularly to memos and reports but are also applicable to e-mail messages.

Don't Show Your Ignorance E-mail correspondence has made people more relaxed about spelling and grammar rules. While this is fine among friends, as a manager you'll need to create a more favorable impression in your writing. Besides using the spelling checkers and grammar checkers built in to most word processing programs, you should reread, indeed proofread, your writing before sending it on.

Understand Your Strategy Before You Write The three strategies for laying out your ideas in writing are as follows:

- **Most important to least important:** This is a good strategy when the action you want your reader to take is logical and not highly political.

- **Least controversial to most controversial:** This builds support gradually and is best used when the decision is controversial or your reader is attached to a particular solution other than the one you're proposing.

- **Negative to positive:** This strategy establishes a common ground with your reader and puts the positive argument last, which makes it stronger.[60]

Start with Your Purpose   Often people organize their messages backward, putting their real purpose last, points out Alesandrini. You should start your writing by telling your purpose and what you expect of the reader.

Write Simply, Concisely, & Directly   Keep your words simple and use short words, sentences, and phrases. Be direct instead of vague, and use the active voice rather than the passive. (Directness, active voice: "Please call a meeting for Wednesday." Vagueness, passive voice: "It is suggested that a meeting be called for Wednesday.")

Telegraph Your Writing with a Powerful Layout   Make your writing as easy to read as possible, using the tools of highlighting and white space.

- **Highlighting:** Highlighting consists of using **boldface** and *italics* to highlight key concepts and introduce new concepts, and bullets—small colored squares like the ones in the list you're reading—to emphasize list items. (Don't overuse any of these devices, or they'll lose their effect. And particularly don't use ALL CAPITAL LETTERS for emphasis, except rarely.)
- **White space:** White space, which consists of wide margins and a break between paragraphs, produces a page that is clean and attractive.[61]

Being an Effective Speaker

Speaking or talking covers a range of activities, from one-on-one conversations, to participating in meetings, to giving formal presentations. In terms of personal oral communication, most of the best advice comes under the heading of listening, since effective listening will dictate the appropriate talking you need to do.

However, the ability to talk to a room full of people—to make an oral presentation—is one of the greatest skills you can have. A study conducted by AT&T and Stanford University found that the top predictor of success and professional upward mobility is how much you enjoy public speaking and how effective you are at it.[62]

Some brief and valuable advice is offered by speechwriter Phil Theibert, who says a speech comprises just three simple rules: (1) Tell them what you're going to say. (2) Say it. (3) Tell them what you said.[63]

AOL Time Warner's CEO Richard Parsons. When Internet company AOL merged with media goliath Time Warner in 2000, the combination was supposed to be the world's most valuable company, with an enormous market value of $290 billion. Instead, because the merger was accomplished with AOL's overinflated stock during the period known as the "Internet bubble," the empire came crashing down, and in January 2002 the company was worth only $135 billion. Parsons became the new CEO a few months later, with the task of cleaning up the messes left behind by others. How persuasive a speaker is he going to have to be to fix things? He is said to be better than his predecessors at delivering facts rather than exaggerations, but will that be enough?

1 Tell Them What You're Going to Say The introduction should take 5%–15% of your speaking time, and it should prepare the audience for the rest of the speech. Avoid jokes and such phrases as "I'm honored to be with you here today . . ." Because everything in your speech should be relevant, try to go right to the point. For example:

"Good afternoon. The subject of identity theft may seem far removed from the concerns of most employees. But I intend to describe how our supposedly private credit, health, employment, and other records are vulnerable to theft by so-called identity thieves and how you can protect yourself."

2 Say It The main body of the speech takes up 75%–90% of your time. The most important thing to realize is that your audience won't remember more than a few points anyway. Thus, you need to decide what three or four points must be remembered.[64] Then cover them as succinctly as possible.

Be particularly attentive to transitions during the main body of the speech. Listening differs from reading in that the listener has only one chance to get your meaning. Thus, be sure you constantly provide your listeners with guidelines and transitional phrases so they can see where you're going. Example:

"There are five ways the security of your supposedly private files can be compromised. The first way is . . ."

3 Tell Them What You Said The end might take 5%–10% of your time. Many professional speakers consider the conclusion to be as important as the introduction, so don't drop the ball here. You need a solid, strong, persuasive wrap-up.

Use some sort of signal phrase that cues your listeners that you are heading into your wind-up. Examples:

"Let's review the main points . . ."

"In conclusion, what CAN you do to protect against unauthorized invasion of your private files? I point out five main steps. One . . ."

Give some thought to the last thing you will say. It should be strongly upbeat, a call to action, a thought for the day, a little story, a quotation. Examples:

"I want to leave you with one last thought . . ."

"Finally, let me close by sharing something that happened to me. . . ."

"As Albert Einstein said, 'Imagination is more important than knowledge.'"

Then say "Thank you" and stop talking.

Click-Along 15.4

Taking Something Practical Away from This Chapter: Making an Effective Oral Presentation

Key Terms Used In This Chapter

Summary

15.1
The Communication Process: What It Is, How It Works

■ Communication is the transfer of information and understanding from one person to another. The process involves sender, message, and receiver; encoding and decoding; the medium; feedback; and dealing with "noise." The sender is the person wanting to share information. The information is called a message. The receiver is the person for whom the message is intended. Encoding is translating a message into understandable symbols or language. Decoding is interpreting and trying to make sense of the message. The medium is the pathway by which a message travels. Feedback is the process in which a receiver expresses his or her reaction to the sender's message. The entire communication process can be disrupted at any point by noise, defined as any disturbance that interferes with the transmission of a message.

■ For effective communication, a manager must select the right medium. Media richness indicates how well a particular medium conveys information and promotes learning. The richer a medium is, the better it is at convey-ing information. Face-to-face presence is the richest; an advertising flyer would be one of the lowest. A rich medium is best for nonroutine situations and to avoid oversimplification. A lean medium is best for routine situations and to avoid overloading.

15.2
Barriers to Communication

■ Barriers to communication are of three types: physical barriers, semantic barriers, and personal barriers.
(1) Physical barriers are exemplified by walls, background noise, and time-zone differences.
(2) Semantics is the study of the meaning of words. Jargon, terminology specific to a particular profession or group, can be a semantic barrier.
(3) Personal barriers are individual attributes that hinder communication. Nine such barriers are variable skills in communicating effectively, variations in frames of reference and experiences that affect how information is interpreted, variations in trustworthiness and credibility, oversized egos, faulty listening skills, tendency to judge others' mes-

sages, inability to listen with understanding, stereotypes (oversimplified beliefs about a certain group of people) and prejudices, and nonverbal communication. Nonverbal communication consists of messages sent outside of the written or spoken word, including body language, the kind of setting of the meeting space, and how one party or the other uses the time allotted. Men and women may show differences in the way they communicate.

15.3
How Managers Fit into the Communication Process

■ Communication channels may be formal or informal.

■ Formal communication channels follow the chain of command and are recognized as official. Formal communication is of three types: vertical, horizontal, and external. (1) Vertical communication is the flow of messages up and down the organizational hierarchy. Downward communication flows from higher levels to lower levels, upward communication from lower levels to higher levels. (2) Horizontal communication flows within and between work units; its main purpose is coordination. (3) External communication flows between people inside and outside the organization.

■ Informal communication channels develop outside the formal structure and do not follow the chain of command. Two aspects of informal channels that are important to know about are the grapevine and management by walking around. (1) The grapevine is the unofficial communication system of the informal organization. The grapevine is faster than formal channels, is about 75% accurate, and is used by employees to acquire most on-the-job information; people particularly rely on it when they are insecure. Two grapevine patterns predominate, the gossip chain and the cluster pattern. (2) In management by wandering around (MBWA), a manager literally wanders around his or her organization and talks with people across all lines of authority; this reduces distortion caused by formal communication.

15.4
Communication in the Information Age

■ This section considers five communications tools of information technology: the Internet and its associated intranets and extranets, e-mail; videoconferencing, collaborative computing, and telecommuting.

(1) The Internet is a global network of independently operating but interconnected computers, linking more than 140,000 smaller networks. Two private uses of the Internet are for intranets, organizations' private Internets, and for extranets, extended intranets that connect a company's internal employees with selected customers, suppliers, and other strategic partners.

(2) E-mail, for electronic mail, uses the Internet to send computer-generated text and documents between people. E-mail has become a major communication medium because it reduces the cost of distributing information, increases teamwork, reduces paper costs, and increases flexibility. However, e-mail has three drawbacks: wasted time; information overload, in part because of spam, or unsolicited jokes and junk mail; and it leads people to neglect other media.

(3) Videoconferencing uses video and audio links along with computers to enable people located at different locations to see, hear, and talk with one another.

(4) Collaborative computing entails using state-of-the-art computer software and hardware to help people work better together.

(5) Telecommuting involves doing work that is generally performed in the office away from the office, using a variety of information technologies.

A challenge of information technology is that it can produce information overload—the amount of information received exceeds a person's ability to handle or process it. Three ways to reduce the amount of information is to preview and ignore certain messages, filter messages, and organize your e-mail inbox. The best way to increase your information processing capacity is to use discipline, as in handling every message only once, and getting a unified messaging site for receiving all your faxes, e-mails, and voice mails.

15.5
Improving Communication Effectiveness

■ This section describes how to be more effective at listening, reading, writing, and speaking.

■ To become a good listener, you should concentrate on the content of the message. You should judge content, not delivery; ask questions and summarize the speaker's remarks; listen for ideas; resist distractions and show interest; and give the speaker a fair hearing.

■ To become a good reader, you need to first realize that speed reading usually doesn't work. You should also be savvy about how you handle periodicals and books, transfer your reading load to some of your employees, and ask others to use e-mails and reports to tell you what they want you to do. A top-down reading system that's a variant on the SQ3R system (survey, question, read, recite, review) is also helpful.

■ To become an effective writer, you can follow several suggestions. Use spelling and grammar checkers in word processing software. Use three strategies for laying out your ideas in writing: go from most important topic to least important; go from least controversial topic to most controversial; and go from negative to positive. When organizing your message, start with your purpose. Write simply, concisely, and directly. Telegraph your writing through use of highlighting and white space.

■ To become an effective speaker, follow three simple rules. Tell people what you're going to say. Say it. Tell them what you said.

Management in Action

Modern Office Designs Create Communication Problems

Excerpted from Motoko Rick, "Shut Up So We Can Do Our Jobs,"
The Wall Street Journal, *August 29, 2001, pp. B1, B8.*

Office Dwellers Nationwide have had it up to their ears.

Every couple of weeks, Michael McKay, a 33-year-old business analyst with a Santa Clara, Calif., Internet-services company, finds his concentration totally disrupted when three colleagues who sit near his workstation hop onto the same conference call—all on speakerphones.

"You get this stereophonic effect of hearing one person's voice live, and then hearing it coming out of someone else's speakerphone two or three cubes over," fumes Mr. McKay.

Incessant phone-ringing, very personal conversations, chitchat about weekend exploits, laughing at bad jokes day in and day out, office employees hear it all. The modern workplace got so loud in part after the New Economy's forward thinking surmised that open-office designs would foster creativity, communication, and collaboration among workers. Older-line companies picked up the concept and kicked workers and many managers out of private offices and into cubicles and pods.

Ever since, the aural aftershocks have been reverberating throughout U.S. offices. Now, some fed-up employees are trying to squelch the din. And architects and interior designers are heeding the call to restore some peace and quiet . . . Still, "acoustical privacy" remains the biggest concern of workstation employees, says Richard Pollack, a commercial architect in San Francisco. "Not lighting, not air conditioning, and not lack of space. It's that everything is too noisy."

In response, many offices are putting obstacles in the way of the offending sound waves. Some common approaches include wrapping cubicle panels in extra fabric; hanging decorative, sound absorbent bunting from the ceiling; and affixing cork wallboards to conference rooms and hallways.

Tom Smith, a director of facilities at Interwoven Inc., a Sunnyvale, Calif., Internet software firm, recently was in charge of moving a staff of 55 sales and engineering employees into the San Francisco offices of a failed dot-com. One of his first decisions was to retreat, somewhat, from the open-plan concept and put every worker at a desk surrounded by 64-inch-high cubicle walls. Another insightful stroke: Put the quiet people (the engineers) on one side of the office and the loud folks (the salespeople) on the other . . . More companies are installing industrial "white noise" machines. These systems, which produce low-level whooshing sounds akin to the hum of an air conditioner, help mute other ambient sounds in an office, such as a telephone conversation several cubicles away . . . Some workers though, aren't sold on that kind of quiet. Allen Shiner, a Chicago-based acoustical engineer and consultant, says that when he introduces companies to the idea of sound masking, some employees raise concerns about the technology's potential ulterior motives. At one presentation he gave at an office, "one worker was concerned that the office hierarchy would send them subliminal messages. Someone else asked if the subliminal messaging would help him stop smoking." Another question: Would the sound-masking affect workers' sex lives? (The answer presumably, is no, although no studies exist.)

Other office designers opt for lower tech, in-your-face solutions. Brigitte Preston, an interior designer for a Dallas design firm, lauckgroup, says she has introduced rolling, erasable marker boards into the new, open-plan North American headquarters of Swedish mobile-phone maker Telefon AB L.M. Ericsson. Workers who need privacy can write a message like "do not disturb" on the boards and then roll them out in front of their desks, she says.

Small conference rooms, some not much bigger than a phone booth, are making a comeback. Austin, Texas, ad agency GSD&M designed 43 conference rooms of varying sizes to give workers a chance to escape open-office noise. Most employees now work with laptops rather than desktop computers, so they can simply unplug and go into a private room.

Nancy Ryan, a 32-year-old account director, says she hops into one of the small rooms as many as eight times a day, to make a phone call to a client or to have a private conversation with a colleague . . . Some workers are just taking matters into their own hands. At 6FigureJobs.com, a Darien, Conn., executive job-search website operator, senior account manager Bill Brennan says that when his coworkers in the open-plan office talk or laugh loudly while he's on an important call, he might throw a crumpled piece of paper or a foam cell-phone holder at someone's head. If that doesn't work, the 27-year-old says, he just hits the mute button and tells his colleagues to shut up.

Questions for Discussion

1. Using Panel 15.1 as a guide, determine how modern office designs influence each stage of the communication process.

2. How do modern office designs help influence physical, semantic, and personal barriers to communication?

3. Does information technology help or hinder the accuracy of communication within and open office? Explain.

4. Do you think Bill Brennan is using an effective approach to manage the noise in his work environment?

5. Which of the approaches for reducing office noise in open work environments is most effective? Explain.

Take It to the Net

Communication is the lifeblood of an organization. Without accurate communications, minor and major mistakes can be made. But effective communication is a tricky business. Great communicators use both formal and informal communications.

According to studies on interpersonal communication, 7% of a message is verbally communicated while 93% is transmitted nonverbally. Of the nonverbal communication, 38% is through vocal tones and 55% is through facial expression. This may be why even in the age of electronic media people still fly thousands of miles to meet face to face with people with whom they are working or negotiating.

The purpose of this exercise is to give you the opportunity to learn more about communication and to assess your communication abilities, both verbal and nonverbal. Go to *http://www.queendom.com/*

cgi-bin/tests/transfer.cgi. Read all the questions and indicate which response matches how you would handle each situation. Answer honestly—as you *do* react, not as you *should* react. Do not answer how you *should* react, answer how you *do* react. There are 34 questions and the quiz should take approximately 5–10 minutes. When you are through, submit your answers for scoring.

Questions for Discussion

1. Were you surprised at your score? Why or why not? Explain.

2. Why do you think communications is so difficult for many people? Explain.

3. What can you do to improve your communication skills? Explain.

Self-Assessment

What Is Your Most Comfortable Learning Style?*

Objectives

1. To learn about your visual, auditory, and kinesthetic learning/communication style.

2. To consider how knowledge about learning/communication styles can be used to enhance your communication effectiveness.

Introduction: The purpose of this exercise is to find out what your most prominent learning style is—that is, what forms of communication can you best learn from. You should find the information of value for understanding not only your own style but those of others. Knowing your own style should also allow you to be a much more effective learner.

Instructions: Read the following 36 statements and indicate the extent to which each statement is consistent with your behavior by using the following rating scale: 1 = almost never applies; 2 = applies once in a while; 3 = sometimes applies; 4 = often applies; 5 = almost always applies.

1. I take lots of notes.	1	2	3	4	5
2. When talking to others, I have the hardest time handling those who do not maintain good eye contact with me.	1	2	3	4	5
3. I make lists and notes because I remember things better if I write them down.	1	2	3	4	5
4. When reading a novel, I pay a lot of attention to passages picturing the clothing, description, scenery, setting, etc	1	2	3	4	5
5. I need to write down directions so that I can remember them.	1	2	3	4	5
6. I need to see the person I am talking to in order to keep my attention focused on the subject.	1	2	3	4	5
7. When meeting a person for the first time, I initially notice the style of dress, visual characteristics, and neatness.	1	2	3	4	5
8. When I am at a party, one of the things I love to do is stand back and "people watch."	1	2	3	4	5
9. When recalling information, I can see it in my mind and remember where I saw it.	1	2	3	4	5
10. If I had to explain a new procedure or technique, I would prefer to write it out.	1	2	3	4	5
11. With free time I am most likely to watch television or read.	1	2	3	4	5
12. If my boss has a message for me, I am most comfortable when he or she sends a memo.	1	2	3	4	5
Total A (the minimum is 12 and the maximum is 60)					
1. When I read, I read out loud or move my lips to hear the words in my head.	1	2	3	4	5
2. When talking to someone else, I have the hardest time handling those who do not talk back with me.	1	2	3	4	5

3. I do not take a lot of notes, but I still remember what was said. Taking notes distracts me from the speaker.　　1　2　3　4　5

4. When reading a novel, I pay a lot of attention to passages involving conversations, talking, speaking, dialogues, etc.　　1　2　3　4　5

5. I like to talk to myself when solving a problem or writing.　　1　2　3　4　5

6. I can understand what a speaker says, even if I am not focused on the speaker.　　1　2　3　4　5

7. I remember things easier by repeating them again and again.　　1　2　3　4　5

8. When I am at a party, one of the things I love to do is have in-depth conversations about a subject that is important to me.　　1　2　3　4　5

9. I would rather receive information from the radio than a newspaper.　　1　2　3　4　5

10. If I had to explain a new procedure or technique, I would prefer telling about it.　　1　2　3　4　5

11. With free time I am most likely to listen to music.　　1　2　3　4　5

12. If my boss has a message for me, I am most comfortable when he or she calls on the phone.　　1　2　3　4　5

Total B (the minimum is 12 and the maximum is 60)　　————

1. I am not good at reading or listening to directions.　　1　2　3　4　5

2. When talking to someone else, I have the hardest time handling those who do not show any kind of emotional support.　　1　2　3　4　5

3. I take notes and doodle, but I rarely go back and look at them.　　1　2　3　4　5

4. When reading a novel, I pay a lot of attention to passages revealing feelings, moods, action, drama, etc.　　1　2　3　4　5

5. When I am reading, I move my lips.　　1　2　3　4　5

6. I will exchange words and places and use my hands a lot when I can't remember the right thing to say.　　1　2　3　4　5

7. My desk appears disorganized.　　1　2　3　4　5

8. When I am at a party, one of the things I love to do is enjoy activities, such as dancing, games, and totally losing myself.　　1　2　3　4　5

9. I like to move around. I feel trapped when seated at a meeting or desk.　　1　2　3　4　5

10. If I had to explain a new procedure or technique, I would prefer actually demonstrating it.　　1　2　3　4　5

11. With free time, I am most likely to exercise.　　1　2　3　4　5

12. If my boss has a message for me, I am most comfortable when he or she talks to me in person.　　1　2　3　4　5

Total C (the minimum is 12 and the maximum is 60)　　————

Scoring & Interpretation

Total A is your Visual Score _____; Total B is your Auditory Score _____; and Total C is your Kinesthetic Score _____. The area in which you have your highest score, represents your "dominant" learning style. You can learn from all three, but typically you learn best using one style. In terms of communication, communication effectiveness is increased when your dominant styles is consistent with the communication style used by others. For example, if you are primarily kinesthetic and your boss gives you directions orally, you may have trouble communicating because you do not learn or process communication well by just being told something. You must take into consideration not only how you communicate, but the learning styles of those *you* are trying to communicate with.

Questions for Discussion

1. Do you agree with the assessment? Why or why not? Explain.

2. How valuable is it to know your learning style? Does it help explain why you did well in some learning situations and poorly in others? Describe and explain.

3. How important is it to know the learning style of those you work with? Explain.

*Taken from *http://www.nwlink.com/~donclark/hrd/vak.html.*

Group Exercise

How Well Does Your Group Swim in a Fishbowl?

Objectives

1. To see how you communicate in a fishbowl setting.

2. To assess how you communicate when under pressure.

Introduction

You can learn a great deal about your communication style by receiving feedback from others. Although we communicate all day long, we do not always stop to check if we are actually communicating the intended message. By practicing our communication skills and receiving feedback, this exercise helps you become a more effective communicator. The purpose of this exercise is twofold: to see how you communicate in a group and to see how others communicate—and to learn how to develop your skills from both experiences.

Instructions

The fishbowl technique has been used for many years as a vehicle for providing feedback to individuals or groups. The class should first divide into groups of five or six people. Next these subgroups are formed into teams comprised of two groups of five or six people. Once the groups/teams are formed, one group is selected to be the discussion group, the other group will form the observing group. The seats should be arranged so that members of one group sit in the middle and members in the second group arrange their desks to form a circle around this group. The center group is the discussion group. This group will discuss a topic from the list below for approximately 10 minutes. The group surrounding the center group will observe and take notes on the center group's discussion and interaction with one another.

After time is up, the groups switch—the outer group moves to the center and begins discussion on a topic while the center group moves to the outer circle and begins observing and taking notes.

Once all of the groups have had a chance to observe and discuss, all of the two groups/teams should share their observations with one another. The feedback you receive from the group can be used or discarded by you. It is often hard to hear that we are different than we think we are in terms of how others see and hear us, but this is an opportunity to learn both.

Topics for Discussion

1. Britney Spears and Justin Timberlake should be UN Ambassadors for the United States.

2. The Internet should be regulated.

3. Gnutella and other websites that allow you to download free music should not be regulated,

and it is okay to burn CDs with music downloaded from these sites.

4. Chief executive officers who make over $10 million a year are overpaid.
5. The minimum wage should be $10 an hour.
6. All U.S. citizens should be allowed to attend college at the taxpayer's expense.

Observation Guidelines

Use the form shown below to take notes on how the center group communicates. Use the following guidelines:

What personal barriers to communication do you see in this group? That is, do any of the members have a tendency to judge others' messages? Do any of the members exhibit faulty listening skills? What types of communication styles do you see? Do some members appear to be better communicators? Do any members seem to have "the gift of gab"?

How well does this group communicate nonverbally? Do any group members look away from the speaker? Do any of the members speak too quickly or too slowly? Is there a group member that smiles and is animated? Do any of the members yawn excessively?

Questions for Discussion

1. Were you surprised at some of your behavior that your classmates noted? Explain.
2. Based on the feedback from your classmates, what are some things you can do to work on your communication style?
3. During your observation role, did you notice any gender-related communication differences? Explain.
4. Do you think the fishbowl technique is a valuable tool for obtaining feedback on interpersonal skills? Why or why not?

Group One:	Communication Styles Noted:
Student Name:	
Student Name:	
Student Name:	
Student Name:	

Group One: Student Name:	Communication Styles Noted:
Student Name:	

Ethical Dilemma

Does a Company's Communications Strategy Reflect Its Values? Learning from Arthur Andersen

Big Five accounting firm Arthur Andersen was supposed to act as independent auditor for Houston energy giant Enron, but it failed to alert analysts and stockholders to financial irregularities and then tried to put the blame on its Houston office. Excerpted from Theresa Howard, "Experts: Admission Could Have Aided Andersen," USA Today, *March 29, 2002, p. 1B.*

Publicly admitting accountability early in the Enron scandal could have helped Arthur Andersen avert a federal indictment and the departure of its 60 biggest U.S. clients, experts say.

Company executives stumbled by responding slowly to clients and trying to blame their Houston office, they say. And that left the company's image—and future—up to the Justice Department and outsiders.

"Company executives sat around and didn't react, and they let the marketplace determine their strategy rather than taking control of their image," says David Martin, executive director of client services for Interbrand, North America. "It's 89 years of goodwill thrown down the drain in three months. It shows how easy it is to blow your brand." . . .

In January, Andersen hired crisis management firm Chlopak Leonard Schechter for help. And recently it has begun to voice a defense in national newspaper ads and with employee rallies.

An ad in Thursday's *The Wall Street Journal* reprinted a letter from NCAA coaching legend John Wooden, a long-time paid speaker for Andersen, to President Bush asking for intervention on behalf of Andersen's 28,000 workers.

But the letter was Wooden's idea, not Andersen's.

Likewise, it was company employees rather than executives who decided to stage public rallies.

And its lack of a public relations strategy built it little sympathy with regulators or investors—and contributed to costing it clients such as Sara Lee, SunTrust Banks, Merck, and FedEx.

"People [at Andersen] underestimated the anger of the regulators," says Richard Edelman, president and CEO of public relations firm Edelman Worldwide.

"Too many people lost money in this [Enron's financial debacle, which Andersen was supposed to help guard against]," he says. . . .

Andersen's lack of a [communications] strategy also might have been symptomatic of more fundamental company issues, says David Schwandt, director of the Executive Leadership program at George Washington University.

"The deeper problem is evaluating the values that executives operate from," he says. "Today, there are too many illustrations of executives being centered on self and power and above how companies operate. That seems to be true of Andersen."

Solving the Dilemma

Hindsight is 20-20, of course. Nevertheless, if you had been Andersen's CEO when it was discovered that your firm had been complicit in allowing Enron investors and employees to suffer financial devastation, what would you have done?

1. To preserve the firm's 89-year image of integrity, I would have admitted partial blame—attributing responsibility to the rogue actions of the Houston office.

2. I would not have conceded responsibility for anything, least of all that the Enron debacle stemmed from any kind of Andersen policy, fearing this admission could lead to federal indictment and loss of clients.

3. I would have taken full responsibility for the firm's role in the situation and declared a top-to-bottom revision of company policy, even though this admission might cause years of Enron shareholder lawsuits.

4. Invent other options. Discuss.

Video Case

Wolinsky & Williams, Inc.

As the video case opens, account managers Joe Tanney, Cheng Jing, and Rosa Denson, along with VP of Account Management Simon Mahoney, convene their project meeting. Joe leads both the meeting and the project, and he has previously e-mailed a meeting agenda to the group. It is quickly apparent that the team members have limited time to devote to this new project. The members are apprehensive about their ability to complete the project according to schedule. However, Joe is confident the project can be completed on time.

Although Rosa is impatient to end the meeting, the group continues to discuss the relevant project tasks. Joe asks for volunteers for each task, but again the group members get off track. Again Joe attempts to redirect the meeting toward delegation of the project tasks. Since some members arrived unprepared (without the meeting agenda), Joe instead assigns tasks. However, at this point Simon abruptly leaves the meeting without committing to any project task.

Privately, Joe expresses his disappointment at the group's lack of commitment and preparedness. The members spent most of their time complaining and stressing what they could not accomplish. With Simon's abrupt departure, they were forced to adjourn the meeting without resolution. In retrospect, Joe feels he should have been more proactive and delegated the tasks to team members. Given everyone's time constraints, the process might have moved more efficiently.

It's Wednesday when the group reconvenes. All members had committed, via e-mail, to having the project tasks completed by this time, but none have done so. The project deadline is Friday. It appears there has been some miscommunication regarding the level of completion of each task. After some bickering among the group members, Joe redirects the meeting. In an attempt to meet the project deadline, Joe suggests he compile all the available information and present the findings as a preliminary report.

Privately Joe explains his philosophy on teamwork. Team members need to be able to depend on and respect each other. When commitments are broken, respect is lost. Personal difficulties only make it harder to work together as a team. A lack of commitment likely signals differing goals among team members. Joe clearly sees these problem issues in his project team.

Discussion Questions

1. Describe the group dynamic between these four individuals.

2. Assess Joe's leadership style in the two meetings. What, if anything, would you have done differently?

3. Are the team members sufficiently motivated to complete their assigned tasks? List at least three things Joe can do to improve the motivation of his team members.

4. Is this a cohesive team? Justify your response with evidence from the case.

CHAPTER 16

Control
Techniques for Enhancing Organizational Effectiveness

IMPROVING PRODUCTIVITY: GOING BEYOND CONTROL TECHNIQUES TO GET THE BEST RESULTS

How, as a manager, can you increase productivity—get better results with what you have to work with?

In this chapter we discuss control techniques for achieving better results. What are other ways for improving productivity? Following are some suggestions:

■ **Establish base points, set goals, and measure results:** To be able to tell whether your work unit is becoming more productive, you need to establish systems of measurement. You can start by establishing the base point, such as the number of customers served per day, quantity of products produced per hour, and the like. You can then set goals to establish new levels that you wish to attain, and institute systems of measurement with which to ascertain progress. Finally, you can measure the results and modify the goals or work processes as necessary.

■ **Use new technology:** Clearly, this is a favorite way to enhance productivity. With a word processor, you can produce more typed pages than you can with a typewriter. With a computerized database, you can store and manipulate information better than you can using a box of file cards. Still, computerization is not a panacea; as we have seen, information technology also offers plenty of opportunities for simply wasting time.

■ **Improve match between employees and jobs:** You can take steps to ensure the best fit between employees and their jobs, including improving employee selection, paying attention to training, redesigning jobs, and providing financial incentives that are tied to performance.

■ **Encourage employee involvement and innovation:** Companies improve productivity by funding research and development (R&D) departments. As a manager, you can encourage your employees, who are closest to the work process, to come up with suggestions for improving their own operations. And, of course, you can give workers a bigger say in doing their jobs, allow employee flextime, and reward people for learning new skills and taking on additional responsibility.

■ **Encourage employee diversity:** By hiring people who are diverse in gender, age, race, and ethnicity, you're more likely to have a workforce with different experience, outlooks, values, and skills. By melding their differences, a team can achieve results that exceed the previous standards.

■ **Redesign the work process:** Some managers think productivity can be enhanced through cost cutting, but this is not always the case. It may be that the work process can be redesigned to eliminate inessential steps.

FORECAST: WHAT'S AHEAD IN THIS CHAPTER

This final chapter explores the final management function—control. Controlling is monitoring performance, comparing it with goals, and taking corrective action as needed. In the first section, we discuss managing for *productivity*, defining what it is and explaining why it's important. We then discuss *controlling*, identify six reasons it's needed, explain the steps in the control process, and describe three types of control managers use. Next we discuss levels, areas, and styles of control. In the fourth section, we discuss financial tools for control—budgets, financial statements, ratio analysis, and audits. We then discuss total quality management (TQM), identifying its core principles and showing some TQM techniques. We conclude the chapter by describing the four keys to successful control and five barriers to successful control.

major question

How do managers influence productivity?

The Big Picture

The purpose of a manager is to make decisions about the four management functions—planning, organizing, leading, and controlling—to get people to achieve productivity and realize results. Productivity is defined by the formula of outputs divided by inputs for a specified period of time. Productivity is important because it determines whether the organization will make a profit or even survive.

In Chapter 1, we pointed out that as a manager in the 21st century you will operate in a complex environment in which you will need to deal with six challenges—managing for (1) competitive advantage, (2) diversity, (3) globalization, (4) information technology, (5) ethical standards, and (6) your own happiness and life goals.

Within this dynamic world, you will draw on the practical and theoretical knowledge described in this book to make decisions about the four management functions of planning, organizing, leading, and controlling.

The purpose is to get the people reporting to you *to achieve productivity and realize results.*

This process is diagrammed below. *(See Panel 16.1.)*

PANEL 16.1
Managing for productivity and results

What Is Productivity?

Productivity can be applied at any level, whether for you as an individual, for the work unit you're managing, or for the organization you work for. Productivity is defined by the formula of *outputs divided by inputs* for a specified period of time. Outputs are all the goods and services produced. Inputs are not only labor but also capital, materials, and energy.[1] That is,

$$\text{productivity} = \frac{\text{outputs}}{\text{inputs}} \quad \text{or} \quad \frac{\text{goods} + \text{services}}{\text{labor} + \text{capital} + \text{materials} + \text{energy}}$$

What does this mean to you as a manager? It means that you can increase overall productivity by making substitutions or increasing the efficiency of any one element: labor, capital, materials, energy. For instance, you can increase the efficiency of labor by substituting capital in the form of equipment or machinery, as in employing a bulldozer instead of laborers with shovels to dig a hole. Or you can increase the efficiency of materials inputs by expanding their uses, as when lumber mills discovered they could sell not only boards but also sawdust and wood chips for use in gardens. Or you can increase the efficiency of energy by putting solar panels on a factory roof so the organization won't have to buy so much electrical power from utility companies.

Why Increasing Productivity Is Important

"For a company and for a nation," said former General Electric CEO Jack Welch, "productivity is a matter of survival."[2]

Productivity is important to companies because ultimately it determines whether the organization will make a profit or even survive. But the productivity of the nation is important to us individually and collectively. The more goods and services that are produced and made easily available to us and for export, the higher our standard of living.

During the 1960s, productivity in the United States averaged a spectacular 2.9% a year, then sank to a disappointing 1.5% right up until 1995. Because the decline in productivity no longer allowed the improvement in wages and living standards that had benefited so many Americans in the 1960s, millions of people took second jobs or worked longer hours to keep from falling behind. Beginning in late 1995, however, during the longest economic boom in American history, the productivity rate jumped to 2.6% annually, as the total output of goods and services rose faster than the total hours needed to produce them. Most economists seem to think the recent productivity growth is the result of organizations' huge investment in high technology—computers, software, the Internet, other telecommunications advances, and computer-guided production line improvements.[3]

Productivity depends on *control*. Let's look at this.

Competing internationally for productivity. This "tank farm"—a cluster of oil storage tanks—represents the continual competition among companies and among nations to achieve productivity—"a matter of survival," as GE's Jack Welch put it. Is the United States doing everything it could to be more productive? What about taking measures to reduce dependence on foreign oil?

Why is control such an important managerial function?

The Big Picture

Controlling is monitoring performance, comparing it with goals, and taking corrective action. This section describes six reasons why control is needed, four steps in the control process, and three types of control.

Control is making something happen the way it was planned to happen. **_Controlling_ is defined as monitoring performance, comparing it with goals, and taking corrective action as needed.** Controlling is the fourth management function, along with planning, organizing, and leading, and its purpose is plain: to make sure that performance meets objectives.

- **Planning**: is setting goals and deciding how to achieve them.

- **Organizing:** is arranging tasks, people, and other resources to accomplish the work.

- **Leading:** is motivating people to work hard to achieve the organization's goals.

- **Controlling:** is concerned with seeing that the right things happen at the right time in the right way.

All these functions affect each other, and in turn affect an organization's productivity. *(See Panel 16.2.)*

PANEL 16.2

Controlling for productivity. What you as a manager do to get things done, with controlling shown in relation to the three other management functions. (These are not lockstep; all four functions happen concurrently.)

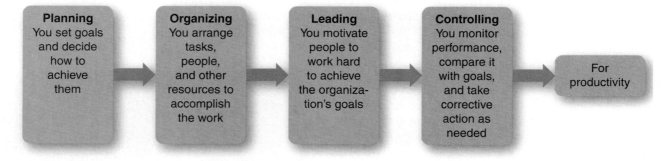

Why Is Control Needed?

There are six reasons why control is needed. *(See Panel 16.3.)*

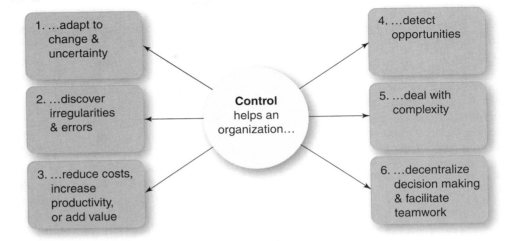

PANEL 16.3
Six reasons why control is needed

1. ...adapt to change & uncertainty

2. ...discover irregularities & errors

3. ...reduce costs, increase productivity, or add value

Control helps an organization...

4. ...detect opportunities

5. ...deal with complexity

6. ...decentralize decision making & facilitate teamwork

1 To Adapt to Change & Uncertainty Markets shift. Consumer tastes change. New competitors appear. Technologies are reborn. New materials are invented. Government regulations are altered. All organizations must deal with these kinds of environmental changes and uncertainties. Control systems can help managers anticipate, monitor, and react to these changes.[4]

Example: Suppose you're a maker of manufactured homes (mobile homes) that has been using welding techniques to connect the walls. You learn that the 3M Company has developed a tape, called VHB tape, that manufacturers of truck transport trailers use to join metal panels on the trailers. This VHB tape represents a new technology that, in the hands of your competitor, could mean a great price difference.[5]

2 To Discover Irregularities & Errors Small problems can mushroom into big ones. Cost overruns, manufacturing defects, employee turnover, bookkeeping errors, and customer dissatisfaction are all matters that may be tolerable in the short run. But in the long run, they can bring about even the downfall of an organization.

Example: You might not even miss a dollar a month looted from your credit card account. But an Internet hacker who does this with thousands of customers can undermine the confidence of consumers using their credit cards to charge online purchases at Amazon.com, Priceline.com, and other Web retailers. Thus, a computer program that monitors Internet charge accounts for small, unexplained deductions can be a valuable control strategy.

3 To Reduce Costs, Increase Productivity, or Add Value Control systems can reduce labor costs, eliminate waste, increase output, and increase product delivery cycles. In addition, controls can help add value to a product so that customers will be more inclined to choose them over rival products. For example, as we have discussed early in the book (and will again in this chapter), the use of quality controls among Japanese car manufacturers resulted in cars being produced that were perceived as being better built than American cars.

A 2002 Mitsubishi Spyder. This Japanese-built car has a reputation for being well built. Shouldn't this be so of all cars, which represent a big investment to many people? Why can't this be achieved?

4 To Detect Opportunities

Hot-selling products. Competitive prices on materials. Changing population trends. New overseas markets. Controls can help alert managers to opportunities that might have otherwise gone unnoticed.

Example: A markdown on certain grocery-store items may result in a rush of customer demand for those products, signaling store management that similar items may also sell faster if they are reduced in price.

5 To Deal with Complexity

Does the right hand know what the left hand is doing? When a company becomes larger or when it merges with another company, it may find it has several product lines, materials-purchasing policies, customer bases, even workers from different cultures. Controls help managers coordinate these various elements.

Example: Following the merger between media conglomerate Time Warner and online giant America Online, the two companies had to learn to deal with two very different cultures—an old-media, lavish-spending culture meshing with a fast-paced, highly reactive, tightwad new-media culture.

6 To Decentralize Decision Making & Facilitate Teamwork

Controls allow top management to decentralize decision making at lower levels within the organization and to encourage employees to work together in teams.

Example: At General Motors, former chairman Alfred Sloan set the level of return on investment he expected his divisions to achieve, enabling him to push decision-making authority down to lower levels while still maintaining authority over the sprawling GM organization.[6] Later GM used controls to facilitate the team approach in its joint venture with Toyota at its California plant.

Steps in the Control Process

Control systems may be altered to fit specific situations, but generally they follow the same steps. The four *control process steps* are (1) establish standards; (2) measure performance; (3) compare performance to standards; and (4) take corrective action, if necessary. (See Panel 16.4.)

PANEL 16.4
Steps in the control process

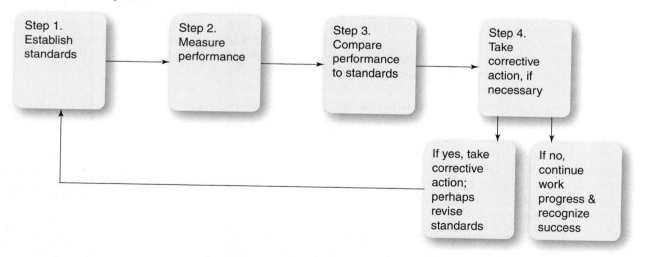

Let's consider these six steps.

1 Establish Standards: "What is the desired outcome we want?" A *control standard*, or *performance standard* or simply *standard*, is the desired performance level for a given goal. Standards may be narrow or broad, and they can be set for almost anything, although they are best measured when they can be made quantifiable. Nonprofit institutions might have standards for level of charitable contributions, number of students retained, or degree of legal compliance. For-profit organizations might have standards of financial performance, employee hiring, manufacturing defects, percentage increase in market share, percentage reduction in costs, number of customer complaints, and return on investment. More subjective standards, such as level of employee morale, can also be set, although they may have to be expressed more quantifiably as reduced absenteeism and sick days and increased job applications.

Example: United Parcel Service (UPS) establishes certain standards for its drivers that set projections for the number of miles driven, deliveries, and pickups. Because conditions vary depending on whether routes are urban, suburban, or rural, the standards are different for different routes.[7]

2 Measure Performance: "What is the actual outcome we got?" The second step in the control process is to measure performance, such as by number of products sold, units produced, or cost per item sold. Less quantifiable activities, such as new products or patents created by a research scientist or scholarly writings produced by a college professor, may be measured by opinions expressed in peer reports.

Performance measures are usually obtained from three sources: (1) written reports, including computerized printouts; (2) oral reports, as in a salesperson's weekly recitation of accomplishments to the sales manager; and (3) personal observation, as when a manager takes a stroll of the factory floor to see what employees are doing.

Example: Every day, UPS managers look at a computer printout showing the miles, deliveries, and pickups a driver attained during his or her shift the previous day.

3 Compare Performance to Standards: "How do the desired & actual outcomes differ?" The third step in the control process is to compare measured performance against the standards established. Most managers are delighted with performance that exceeds standards, which becomes an occasion for handing out bonuses, promotions, and perhaps offices with a view. For performance that is below standards, they need to ask: Is the deviation from performance significant? The greater the difference between desired and actual performance, the greater the need for action.

Comparing the sharing. Nonprofits are no more exempt from the steps in the control process than for-profits are. The Salvation Army, for instance, sets fund-raising goals based on standards from previous years. What would be the consequence if it failed to meet its targets at the end of a given Christmas holiday season?

How much deviation is acceptable? That depends on *the range of variation* built in to the standards in step 1. In voting for political candidates, for instance, there is supposed to be no range of variation; as the expression goes, "every vote counts" (although the 2000 U.S. Presidential election was an eye-opener for many people in this regard). In political polling, however, a range of 3%–4% error is considered an acceptable range of variation. In machining parts for the space shuttle, the range of variation may be a good deal less tolerant than when machining parts for a power lawnmower.

The range of variation is often incorporated in computer systems into a principle called management by exception. **_Management by exception_ is a control principle that states that managers should be informed of a situation only if data show a significant deviation from standards.**

Example: UPS managers compare the printout of a driver's performance (miles driven and number of pickups and deliveries) with the standards that were set for his or her particular route. A range of variation may be allowed to take into account such matters as winter or summer driving or traffic conditions that slow productivity.

4 Take Corrective Action, If Necessary: "What changes should we make to obtain desirable outcomes?" There are three possibilities here: (1) Make no changes. (2) Recognize and reinforce positive performance. (3) Take action to correct negative performance.

When performance meets or exceeds the standards set, managers should give rewards, ranging from giving a verbal "Job well done" to more substantial payoffs such as raises, bonuses, and promotions to reinforce good behavior.

When performance falls significantly short of the standard, managers should carefully examine the reasons why and take the appropriate action. Sometimes it may turn out the standards themselves were unrealistic, owing to changing conditions, in which case the standards need to be altered. Sometimes it may become apparent that employees haven't been given the resources for achieving the standards. And sometimes the employees may need more attention from management as a way of signaling that they have been insufficient in fulfilling their part of the job bargain.

Example: When a UPS driver fails to perform according to the standards set for him or her, a supervisor then rides along and gives suggestions for improvement. If drivers are unable to improve, they are warned, then suspended, and then dismissed.

Small business. How important is it for small businesses to implement all four steps of the control process? Do you think that employees in small companies—such as a restaurant—typically have more or less independence from managerial control than those in large companies?

Types of Control: Feedforward, Concurrent, & Feedback

There are three types of control managers use, which vary according to timing. These controls, which are established *before, during,* or *after* the workflow, are known respectively as *feedforward* (future-oriented), *concurrent* (present-oriented), and *feedback* (past-oriented) controls. *(See Panel 16.5.)*

PANEL 16.5
Three types of control: future, present, and past

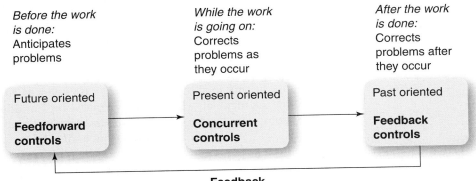

Before the work is done: Anticipates problems

While the work is going on: Corrects problems as they occur

After the work is done: Corrects problems after they occur

Future oriented
Feedforward controls

Present oriented
Concurrent controls

Past oriented
Feedback controls

Feedback

Feedforward—Control for the Future: Before the Work Begins

Feedforward control **takes place before operations begin and is intended to prevent anticipated problems.** An example is a fire drill at school or work.

This future-directed control consist of rules, policies, and procedures intended to ensure that planned performance is carried out properly. The purpose of feedforward control is to keep problems from happening so that managers won't have to fix them afterward. Of course, management may not always have the facts in hand to prevent problems from occurring anyway.

Concurrent—Control for the Present: While the Work Is in Progress

Concurrent control **takes place while operations are going on and is intended to minimize problems as they occur.** An example is a warning light in a car that indicates that the oil level is low.

This present-oriented control consists of directing, monitoring, and fine-tuning activities that can correct problems before they become too difficult or expensive.

Feedback—Control for the Past: After the Work Is Done

Feedback control **takes place after operations are finished and is intended to correct the problems that have already occurred.** An example is a standard performance appraisal review.

This past-oriented control consists of use of information about previous results to correct errors in the standard. The drawback of feedback control is that the damage has already been done. The benefit is that feedback shows how well the planning process worked and tells employees how well they performed, thereby contributing to employee motivation.

Filling orders. How do you suppose Koen Book Distributors in Moorestown, N.J., uses the three types of control?

major question

How do successful companies implement controls?

The Big Picture

This section describes three levels of control—strategic, tactical, and operational—and four areas of control—physical, human, informational, and financial resources. We also describe three approaches to implementing controls—bureaucratic, market, and clan.

How are you going to apply the steps and types of control to your own management area? Let's look at this in three ways: First, you need to consider the *level* of management at which you operate—top, middle, or first level. Second, you need to consider the *areas* that you draw on for resources—physical, human, information, and/or financial. Finally, you need to consider the *style* or control philosophy—bureaucratic, market, or clan, as we will explain.

Levels of Control: Strategic, Tactical, & Operational

There are three levels of control, which correspond to the three principal managerial levels: *strategic* planning by top managers, *tactical* planning by middle managers, and *operational* planning by first-line (supervisory) managers.

Strategic control. Joseph Berardino, then CEO of Arthur Andersen, testifying in 2002 before Congress about the accounting and consulting company's role in the Enron scandal. Should senior managers be accountable for their employees' decisions in branch offices, such as those of the Andersen Houston employees dealing with Enron?

1 Strategic Control by Top Managers <u>*Strategic control*</u> is monitoring performance to ensure that strategic plans are being implemented and taking corrective action as needed. Strategic control is mainly performed by top managers, those at the CEO and VP levels, who have an organizational-wide perspective. Monitoring is accomplished by reports issued every 3, 6, 12, or more months, although more frequent reports may be requested if the organization is operating in an uncertain environment.

2 Tactical Control by Middle Managers <u>*Tactical control*</u> is monitoring performance to ensure that tactical plans—those at the divisional or departmental level—are being implemented and taking corrective action as needed. Tactical control is done mainly by middle managers, those with such titles as "division head," "plant manager," and "branch sales manager." Reporting is done on a weekly or monthly basis.

3 Operational Control by First-Level Managers <u>*Operational control*</u> is monitoring performance to ensure that operational plans—day-to-day goals— are being implemented and taking corrective action as needed. Operational control is done mainly by first-level managers, those with titles such as "department head," "team leader," or "supervisor." Reporting is done on a daily basis.

Considerable interaction occurs among the three levels, with lower-level managers providing information upward and upper-level managers checking on some of the more critical aspects of plan implementation below them.

Areas of Control: Physical, Human, Informational, & Financial

The four resources that most organizations use are *physical*, *human*, *informational*, and *financial*. Different types of controls are used in each area.

1 Physical Resources   Physical resources include buildings, equipment, and tangible products. Thus, for example, there are equipment controls to monitor the use of computers, cars, and other machinery. There are inventory-management controls to keep track of how many products are in stock, how many will be needed, and what their delivery dates are from suppliers. There are quality controls to make sure that products are being built according to certain acceptable standards.

2 Human Resources   The controls used to monitor employees include personality tests and drug testing for hiring, performance tests during training, performance evaluations to measure work productivity, and employee surveys to assess job satisfaction and leadership.

3 Informational Resources   Production schedules. Sales forecasts. Environmental impact statements. Analyses of competition. Public relations briefings. All these are controls on an organization's various information resources.

4 Financial Resources   Are bills being paid on time? How much money is owed by customers? How much money is owed to suppliers? Is there enough cash on hand to meet payroll obligations? What are the debt-repayment schedules? What is the advertising budget? Clearly, the organization's financial controls are important because they can affect the other three types of resources.

Was this man in control? Kenneth Lay, CEO of former energy giant Enron, reads a brief statement in 2002 before Congress. Lay helped create the company in 1985 from the merger of two gas pipelines, but after a few years it was making more than 80% of its earnings by trading natural gas and electricity. It also built new markets for the trading of, for example, weather futures. For six years in a row, it was voted the most innovative of *Fortune* magazine's Most Admired Companies, and by 2000 it was the seventh-largest company in the U.S. By then Enron had also become mostly a pure trading company, an extremely volatile business to be in, although it also made some bad investments in huge overseas projects. In addition, it took equity stakes in all kinds of companies, opaque transactions that were almost impossible to understand and which finally began to adversely affect the Enron balance sheet. When Lay, who had become chairman, took back the role of CEO (relinquished to Jeffrey Skilling, who suddenly quit before things started to sour), he promised to reassure investors by improving the company's disclosure practices. "Did Lay have any idea of what he was talking about?" asks a *Fortune* article. "Or was he as clueless as Enron's shareholders? Most people believe the latter." What do you think? Can a chairman or CEO paid millions of dollars actually not know what ventures his company is engaging in or that it is failing?

Styles of Implementing Controls: Bureaucratic, Market, & Clan

There are three managerial styles or control philosophies: *bureaucratic, market,* and *clan.*[8] *(See Panel 16.6.)* Most organizations emphasize either bureaucratic or clan control, with some market control mechanisms added.

PANEL 16.6

Three styles or approaches to implementing controls

Type of approach	Characteristics
Bureaucratic control	Uses rules, regulations, formal authority to elicit employee compliance. Works well in organizations (or situations) where tasks are explicit and certain.
Market control	Uses market mechanisms—pricing, competition, market share—to guide performance. Works well in organizations (or situations) in which there is considerable competition for resources.
Clan control	Uses shared values, beliefs, rituals, and trust emanating from common culture. Works well in organizations (or situations) in which employees are allowed to make their own decisions.

1 Bureaucratic Control: Involves Formal Authority & Rules *Bureaucratic control* **is characterized by use of rules, regulations, and formal authority to guide performance.** This form of control attempts to elicit employee compliance using strict rules, a rigid hierarchy, well-defined job descriptions, and administrative mechanisms such as budgets, performance appraisals, and compensation schemes (external rewards) to get results. The foremost example of use of bureaucratic control is perhaps the traditional military organization.

Bureaucratic control works well in organizations in which the tasks are explicit and certain. While rigid, it can be an effective means of ensuring that performance standards are being met. However, it may not be effective if people are looking for ways to stay out of trouble by simply following the rules, or if they try to beat the system by manipulating performance reports, or if they try to actively resist bureaucratic constraints.

Bureaucratic control? A commercial bread bakery in which employees are expected to perform one task repetitively. A manufacturing firm need not be bureaucratic, especially if it's small.

2 Market Control: Involves Pricing Mechanisms *Market control* is characterized by use of market mechanisms—pricing, competition, market share—to guide performance. Under this philosophy, managers' performances can be evaluated according to the profit or loss attained by their business units. This approach works well in organizations in which there is considerable competition for resources and the various divisions have distinct products or services. Thus, each division can be gauged as a separate profit center and evaluated according to how well it contributes to the organization's overall profitability. General Electric, for example, has clearly differentiated divisions for different industries, ranging from light bulbs to medical imaging to financial services.

3 Clan Control: Involves Culture & Shared Values Unlike the bureaucratic and market approaches, clan control does not assume that the organization and its employees have different interests. Rather, *clan control* **is characterized by shared values, beliefs, rituals, and trusts emanating from a common culture,** and so formal controls are considered unnecessary. Clan control works best in organizations in which there is no one best way to do a job and in which employees are allowed to make many of their own decisions. Thus, this approach is found in organizations such as Microsoft Corp. or Levi Strauss in which technology or markets are changing rapidly and in which the use of teams is appropriate.

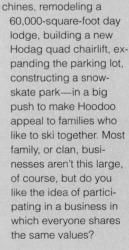

Clan control. Ski resorts, especially small ones, don't have large profit margins. But profit wasn't the main reason why Chuck Shepard (shown here at right) bought Hoodoo Ski Area at Santiam Pass, Ore., in 1999 for $1.6 million. Even though he is an accountant and real-estate investor, "I'm motivated by making something successful," he told a Eugene *Register-Guard* reporter. A central part of Shepard's decision to buy Hoodoo was that he, his wife, and six children are ardent skiers. After looking over the property, he put the proposal to buy it to a family vote, which urged him to go for it. In addition, his oldest child, Tasha, was earning a master's degree in business administration; she is now Hoodoo's general manager. The family has started a substantial upgrade of the resort—buying snow-grooming machines, remodeling a 60,000-square-foot day lodge, building a new Hodag quad chairlift, expanding the parking lot, constructing a snowskate park—in a big push to make Hoodoo appeal to families who like to ski together. Most family, or clan, businesses aren't this large, of course, but do you like the idea of participating in a business in which everyone shares the same values?

major question

Financial performance is important to most organizations. What are the financial tools I need to know about?

The Big Picture

Financial controls are especially important. These include budgets, financial statements, ratio analysis, and audits.

As you might expect, one of the most important areas for control is in regard to money—financial performance. Just as you need to monitor your personal finances to ensure your survival and avoid catastrophe, so managers need to do likewise with an organization's finances. Whether your organization is for-profit or nonprofit, you need to be sure that revenues are covering costs.

There are a great many kinds of financial controls, but here let us look at the following: *budgets, financial statements, ratio analysis*, and *audits*. (Necessarily this is merely an overview of this topic; financial controls are covered in detail in other business courses.)

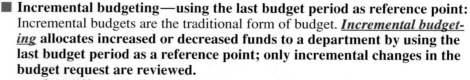

Budgets: Formal Financial Projections

A ***budget*** **is a formal financial projection.** It states an organization's planned activities for a given period of time in quantitative terms, such as dollars, hours, or number of products. Budgets are prepared not only for the organization as a whole but also for the divisions and departments within it. The point of a budget is to provide a yardstick against which managers can measure performance and make comparisons (as with other departments or previous years).

Two Budget Approaches: Incremental & Zero-Based   Managers can take essentially two budget-planning approaches—*incremental budgeting* and *zero-based budgeting.*

- **Incremental budgeting—using the last budget period as reference point:** Incremental budgets are the traditional form of budget. ***Incremental budgeting*** **allocates increased or decreased funds to a department by using the last budget period as a reference point; only incremental changes in the budget request are reviewed.**

    One difficulty is that incremental budgets tend to lock departments into stable spending arrangements; they are not flexible in meeting environmental demands. Another difficulty is that a department may engage in many activities—some more important than others—but it's not easy to sort out how well managers performed at the various activities. Thus, the department activities and the yearly budget increases take on lives of their own.

Trucks at a warehouse for Ralph's supermarkets. Clearly, the capital budget in large companies like Ralph's would be complex. What types of data would be needed to justify an expansion in the Ralph's truck fleet?

- **Zero-based budgeting—starting over at each budget period:** Developed by the U.S. Department of Agriculture and later adopted by Texas Instruments, _zero-based budgeting (ZBB)_ **forces each department to start from zero in projecting its funding needs for the coming budget period.** Thus, ZBB forces managers to reexamine their departments' activities and justify their need for funds for the coming budget period based on strategic plans for that period.

    One difficulty with ZBB is that it requires managers to spend more time rationalizing the need for more funds. Another difficulty is that it tends to work better in small work units or departments that are declining in resources.[9]

Fixed versus Variable Budgets There are numerous kinds of budgets, and some examples are listed below. _(See Panel 16.7.)_ In general, however, budgets may be categorized as two types: _fixed_ and _variable._

- **Fixed budgets—where resources are allocated on a single estimate of costs:** Also known as a _static budget_, a _fixed budget_ **allocates resources on the basis of a single estimate of costs.** That is, there is only one set of expenses; the budget does not allow for adjustment over time. For example, you might have a budget of $50,000 for buying equipment in a given year—no matter how much you may need equipment exceeding that amount.

- **Variable budgets—where resources are varied in proportion with various levels of activity:** Also known as a _flexible budget_, a _variable budget_ **allows the allocation of resources to vary in proportion with various levels of activity.** That is, the budget can be adjusted over time to accommodate pertinent changes in the environment. For example, you might have a budget that allows you to hire temporary workers or lease temporary equipment if production exceeds certain levels.

Azhar's Oriental Rugs. What types of budgeting would best suit a small business like Azhar's? What variables or factors would drive this decision?

PANEL 16.7
Examples of types of budgets

Type of budget	Description
Cash or cash-flow budget	Forecasts all sources of cash income and cash expenditures for daily, weekly, or monthly period
Capital expenditures budget	Anticipates investments in major assets such as land, buildings, and major equipment
Sales or revenue budget	Projects future sales, often by month, sales area, or product
Expense budget	Projects expenses (costs) for given activity for given period

Click-Along 16.1
Some Other Kinds of Budgets

Financial Statements: Summarizing the Organization's Financial Status

A *financial statement* **is a summary of some aspect of an organization's financial status.** The information contained in such a statement is essential in helping managers maintain financial control over the organization.

There are two basic types of financial statements: the *balance sheet* and the *income statement*.

The Balance Sheet: Picture of Organization's Financial Worth for a Specific Point in Time A *balance sheet* **summarizes an organization's overall financial worth—that is, assets and liabilities—at a specific point in time.**

Assets are the resources that an organization controls; they consist of current assets and fixed assets. *Current assets* are cash and other assets that are readily convertible to cash within one year's time. Examples are inventory, sales for which payment has not been received (accounts receivable), and U.S. Treasury bills or money market mutual funds. *Fixed assets* are property, buildings, equipment, and the like that have a useful life that exceeds one year but that are usually harder to convert to cash. *Liabilities* are claims, or debts, by suppliers, lenders, and other nonowners of the organization against a company's assets.

The Income Statement: Picture of Organization's Financial Results for a Specified Period of Time The balance sheet depicts the organization's overall financial worth at a specific point in time. By contrast, the *income statement* **summarizes an organization's financial results—revenues and expenses—over a specified period of time,** such as a quarter or a year.

Revenues are assets resulting from the sale of goods and services. *Expenses* are the costs required to produce those goods and services. The difference between revenues and expenses, called the *bottom line*, represents the profits or losses incurred over the specified period of time.

Ratio Analysis: Indicators of an Organization's Financial Health

The bottom line may be the most important indicator of an organization's financial health, but it isn't the only one. Managers often use *ratio analysis*—**the practice of evaluating financial ratios**—to determine an organization's financial health.

ANNUAL REPORT

This is Citigroup.

citigroup

Citigroup's annual report. Publicly held companies use the annual report to describe their financial health to stockholders. Some experts say the real story is in the footnotes. Have you ever carefully read an annual report? If so, did you find anything surprising?

Among the types of financial ratios are those used to calculate liquidity, debt management, asset management, and return. *Liquidity ratios* indicate how easily an organization's assets can be converted into cash (made liquid). *Debt management* ratios indicate the degree to which an organization can meet its long-term financial obligations. *Asset management* ratios indicate how effectively an organization is managing its assets, such as whether it has obsolete or excess inventory on hand. *Return ratios*—often called return on investment, ROI, or return on assets—indicate how effective management is generating a return, or profits, on its assets.

Audits: External versus Internal

When you think of auditors, do you think of grim-faced accountants looking through a company's books to catch embezzlers and other cheats? That's one function of auditing, but besides verifying the accuracy and fairness of financial statements it also is intended to be a tool for management decision making. **_Audits_ are formal verifications of an organization's financial and operational systems.**

Audits are of two types—*external* and *internal*.

External Audits—Financial Appraisals by Outside Financial Experts An *external audit* is a formal verification of an organization's financial accounts and statements by outside experts. The auditors are certified public accountants (CPAs) who work for an accounting firm (such as PricewaterhouseCoopers) that is independent of the organization being audited. Their task is to verify that the organization, in preparing its financial statements and in determining its assets and liabilities, followed generally accepted accounting principles.

Internal Audits—Financial Appraisals by Inside Financial Experts An *internal audit* is a verification of an organization's financial accounts and statements by the organization's own professional staff. Their jobs are the same as those of outside experts—to verify the accuracy of the organization's records and operating activities. Internal audits also help uncover inefficiencies and thus help managers evaluate the performance of their control systems.

Accountants at the Academy Awards? No, these clearly are Oscar-winning Denzel Washington, who in 2002 was voted Best Actor (for his role in *Training Day*), and Halle Berry, voted Best Actress (for her role in *Monster's Ball*). But every year since 1929 the secret ballots for Oscar nominees voted by members of the Academy of Motion Picture Arts and Sciences have been tabulated by a pair of accountants from the firm now known as PricewaterhouseCoopers. The accounting firm takes this event very seriously; secrecy is tight, and there is no loose gossip around the office water cooler. Two accountants tally the votes, stuff the winners' names in the envelopes—the ones that will be handed to award presenters during the Academy Awards—and then memorize the winners' names, just in case the envelopes don't make it to the show. The so-called Big Five accounting firms—PricewaterhouseCoopers, Deloitte & Touche, Ernst & Young, KPMG, and Arthur Andersen—came in for a lot of scrutiny in 2002 after Andersen's document shredding became headline news. Accounting is an important business because investors depend upon independent auditors to verify that a company's finances are what they are purported to be.

major question

How do top companies improve the quality of their products or services?

The Big Picture

Total quality management (TQM) is dedicated to continuous quality improvement, training, and customer satisfaction. Two core principles are people orientation and improvement orientation. Some techniques for improving quality are employee involvement, benchmarking, outsourcing, reduced cycle time, and statistical process control.

The Ritz-Carlton Hotel Co., LLC, a luxury chain of 43 hotels that is an independently operated division of Marriott International, puts a premium on doing things right. First-year managers and employees receive 250–310 hours of training. The president meets each employee at a new hotel to ensure he or she understands the Ritz-Carlton standards for service. The chain has also developed a database that records the preferences of more than 1 million customers, so that each hotel can anticipate guests' needs.[10]

Because of this diligence, the Ritz-Carlton has twice been the recipient (in 1992 and in 1999) of the Malcolm Baldrige National Quality Award. As we mentioned in Chapter 1, the Baldrige awards were created by Congress in 1987 to be the most prestigious recognition of quality in the United States, which is given annually to U.S. organizations in manufacturing, service, education, health care, and small business.

The Baldrige award is an outgrowth of the realization among U.S. managers in the early 1980s that three-fourths of Americans were telling survey takers that the label "Made in America" no longer represented excellence—that they considered products made overseas, especially Japan, equal or superior in quality to U.S.-made products. As we saw in Chapter 1, much of the impetus for quality improvements in Japanese products came from American consultants W. Edwards Deming and Joseph M. Juran, whose work led to the strategic commitment to quality known as total quality management.

Putting on the Ritz. Executives for the Ritz-Carlton hotel chain accept the Malcolm Baldrige National Quality Award as President Bill Clinton (right) looks on.

Core TQM Principles: Deliver Customer Value & Strive for Continuous Improvement

Total quality management (TQM) is defined as a comprehensive approach—led by top management and supported throughout the organization—dedicated to continuous quality improvement, training, and customer satisfaction.

In Chapter 1 we said there are four components to TQM:

1. Make continuous improvement a priority.
2. Get every employee involved.
3. Listen to and learn from customers and employees.
4. Use accurate standards to identify and eliminate problems.

These may be summarized as ___two core principles of TQM___—namely, **(1)** *people orientation*—**everyone involved with the organization should focus on delivering value to customers, and (2)** *improvement orientation*—**everyone should work on continuously improving the work processes.**[11] Let's look at these further.

1 People Orientation—Focusing Everyone on Delivering Customer Value

Organizations adopting TQM value people as their most important resource—both those who create a product or service and those who receive it. Thus, not only are employees given more decision-making power, so are suppliers and customers.

This people orientation operates under the following assumptions:

■ **Delivering customer value is most important:** The purpose of TQM is to focus people, resources, and work processes to deliver products or services that create value for customers.

■ **People will focus on quality if given empowerment:** TQM assumes that employees and suppliers will concentrate on making quality improvements if given the decision-making power to do so. Customers can also be a valuable part of the process if they are allowed to express choices.

■ **TQM requires training, teamwork, and cross-functional efforts:** Employees and suppliers need to be well trained, and they must work in teams. Teamwork is considered important because many quality problems are spread across functional areas. For example, if car-cellphone design specialists conferred with marketing specialists (as well as customers and suppliers), they would find the real challenge of using a cellphone in a car is not talking on it but pushing 11 tiny buttons to call a phone number while driving 65 miles an hour.

2 Improvement Orientation—Focusing Everyone on Continuously Improving Work Processes

Americans seem to like big schemes, grand designs, and crash programs. While these approaches certainly have their place, the lesson of the quality movement from overseas is that the way to success is through continuous small improvements. ___Continuous improvement___ **is defined as ongoing small, incremental improvements in all parts of an organization**—all products, services, functional areas, and work processes.

This improvement orientation has the following assumptions:

■ **It's less expensive to do it right the first time:** TQM assumes that it's better to do things right the first time than to do costly reworking. To be sure, there are many costs involved in creating quality products and services—training, equipment, and tools, for example. But they are less than the costs of dealing with poor quality—those stemming from lost customers, junked materials, time spent reworking, and frequent inspection, for example.[12]

Continuous improvement. When tuna glutted the market so that StarKist Tuna found it couldn't price a can of tuna high enough to be profitable, it turned to developing new forms of packaging, such as this resealable pouch. Not only does the pouch make it easier to save leftovers, there is also no need to drain the tuna, and the product has a firmer texture. Have you noticed other packaging innovations that are more convenient?

■ **It's better to do small improvements all the time:** This is the assumption that continuous improvement must be an everyday matter, that no improvement is too small, that there must be an ongoing effort to make things better a little bit at a time all the time.

■ **Accurate standards must be followed to eliminate small variations:** TQM emphasizes the collection of accurate data throughout every stage of the work process. It also stresses the use of accurate standards (such as benchmarking, as we discuss) to evaluate progress and eliminate small variations, which are the source of many quality defects.

■ **There must be strong commitment from top management:** Employees and suppliers won't focus on making small incremental improvements unless managers go beyond lip service to support high-quality work.

Some TQM Techniques

Several techniques are available for improving quality. Here we describe *employee involvement, benchmarking, outsourcing, reduced cycle time*, and *statistical process control*.

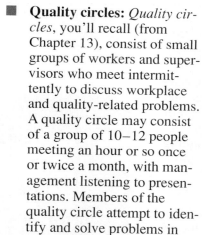

Click-Along 16.2
What Is "Six Sigma"?

Employee Involvement: Quality Circles, Self-Managed Teams, & Special-Purpose Teams As part of the TQM people orientation, employees (and often suppliers and customers) are given more decision-making power than is typical in non-TQM organizations. The reasoning here is that the people actually involved with the product or service are in the best position to detect opportunities for quality improvements.

Three means for implementing employee involvement are as follows:

■ **Quality circles:** *Quality circles*, you'll recall (from Chapter 13), consist of small groups of workers and supervisors who meet intermittently to discuss workplace and quality-related problems. A quality circle may consist of a group of 10–12 people meeting an hour or so once or twice a month, with management listening to presentations. Members of the quality circle attempt to identify and solve problems in production and quality in the work performed in their part of the company.

■ **Self-managed teams:** *Self-managed teams*, also described in Chapter 13, are groups of workers who are given administrative oversight of activities such as planning, scheduling, monitoring, and staffing for their task domains. A common feature of self-managed teams is cross-functionalism—that is, a team is made up of technical specialists from different areas.

■ **Special-purpose teams:** Quality circles and self-managed teams usually meet on a regular basis. Sometimes, however, an organization needs a ***special-purpose team*** **to meet to solve a special or one-time problem.** The team then disbands after the problem is solved. These teams are often cross-functional, drawing on members from different departments.

Bridgestone/Firestone plant. Despite being "certified" for high standards, this Decatur, Ill., plant produced most of the tires that were later recalled, causing the tire company (and Ford) so much grief. Clearly, quality standards are meaningless if managers and employees don't rigorously adhere to them.

Benchmarking: Learning from the Best Performers   We discussed benchmarking briefly in Chapter 10. As we stated there, *benchmarking* is a process by which a company compares its performance with that of high-performing organizations. For example, at Xerox Corp., generally thought to be the first American company to use benchmarking, it is defined as, in one description, "the continuous process of measuring products, services, and practices against the toughest competitors or those companies recognized as industry leaders."[13]

Example of Benchmarking: How Xerox Emulated Competitors

Southwest Airlines studied auto-racing pit crews to learn how to reduce the turnaround time of its aircraft at each scheduled stop. Toyota managers got the idea for just-in-time inventory deliveries by looking at how U.S. supermarkets replenish their shelves. Ford got ideas from Mazda (in which Ford had ownership) to learn how to create an invoiceless accounts-payable system. All these are instances of benchmarking.

THE DOCUMENT COMPANY
XEROX

One of the most famous examples, however, occurred in 1979, when Xerox found itself up against Japanese photocopiers being sold in the U.S. for prices substantially below even the production costs for Xerox copiers. Xerox managers learned through a Japanese joint-venture partner, Fuji-Xerox, that Xerox's costs were excessive owing to gross inefficiencies in its manufacturing and business practices. As a result, Xerox began a program to benchmark 67 of its key work processes against competitors identified as having the "best practices" in those processes.

Benchmarking isn't everything, however. In recent times, Xerox has found itself falling behind other technology companies.[14]

Outsourcing: Let Outsiders Handle It   *Outsourcing* **is the subcontracting of services and operations to an outside vendor.** Usually this is done because the subcontractor vendor can do the job better or cheaper. Or, stated another way, when the services and operations are done in-house, they are not done as efficiently or are keeping personnel from doing more important things. For example, when Eastman Kodak farmed out its computer operations to IBM, it found it got higher-quality computing operations at less cost.[15] Outsourcing is also being done by many state and local governments, which, under the banner known as privatization, have subcontracted traditional government services such as fire protection, correctional services, and medical services.

practical action

Outsourcing Public Services: Does Privatization Always Work?

Do public services work better when they're privatized? Privatization has been a popular idea in the last several years. As the term is used in the United States, this means farming out, or outsourcing, to private-sector companies traditional public-sector services such as prison supervision, fire protection, and road maintenance.

The driving force behind privatization is the idea that the for-profit sector is more *motivated* than the nonprofit sector to deliver services in a more customer-friendly, cost-efficient way. However, private companies can also make expensive, bad decisions. One has only to look at
continued

the example of Texas-based energy giant Enron, once the seventh-largest company in the U.S., whose off-books investments led it into bankruptcy. Or consider such money-losing private-sector projects as New Coke or the movie *A.I.* or *Talk* magazine. As one writer points out, "Is there much difference, after all, between the Defense Department paying $600 for an ordinary toilet seat and a private-sector corporation paying $600 a share for an Internet start-up with no assets, no profits, and no plan for producing either?"[16]

In Elliott Sclar's book *You Don't Always Get What You Pay For: The Economics of Privatization*, the Columbia University economist and urban planning professor points out that privatization alone is not a substitute for good public management.[17] For example, in the 1980s, the Metro-Dade Transit Agency in Florida hired a private company to run 10 of its bus routes, keeping 10 comparable routes in public operation for comparison. The result after 18 months, when the experiment was abandoned: Complaints had more than doubled on the private-sector routes, and ridership had plummeted. Moreover, the 40 new buses that the agency

Neither fish nor fowl. Is the U.S. Postal Service a government agency? Or now a self-supporting non-governmental entity? It's neither—it's a creation of Congress, points out the *Atlanta Journal-Constitution*. Thus, it can't close any of its 38,000 post offices—two-thirds of which are not profitable—because voters would howl. Congress also insists on six-day mail delivery to every U.S. address. Do you think UPS or FedEx could operate as well with restraints like these?

gave the contractor were so poorly maintained that only 10 could be kept in service.

Another example that Sclar gives is that of a mutual-aid pact among several small-town fire departments, in which one town had hired a private corporation to provide fire protection. Responding to its profit motive, the corporation kept smaller crews on each shift than the surrounding nonprofit fire companies did. The effect was to increase the reliance of that department on its public-sector neighbors for reinforcements. And on a day when the reinforcements could not show up, the for-profit department was unable to quell the fire in a $1 million home, which burned to the ground.

The lesson: Municipalities letting out contracts to the private sector have to make sure that the contracts are carefully drawn, that the contractor's performance is adequately monitored, and that the costs are measured against accurate internal costs to protect the public's interest against the company's overzealous pursuit of profit.

In other words, there must be effective *controls*.

Reduced Cycle Time: Increasing the Speed of Work Processes Another TQM technique is the emphasis on increasing the speed with which an organization's operations and processes can be performed. This is known as **_reduced cycle time_, or reduction in steps in a work process,** such as fewer authorization steps required to let a contract to a supplier. The point is to improve the organization's performance by eliminating wasteful motions, barriers between departments, unnecessary procedural steps, and the like.

Example of Reduced Cycle Time: Shorter Patient Waits

Dr. Mark Murray, a family practice physician at the Kaiser Permanente medical center in Roseville, Calif., realized that patients' waiting time had become nearly intolerable, with the wait for patients seeking nonemergency appointments having stretched to an average of 55 days.

The reason was that the center's clerical staff was scheduling two or three patients for the same time slots, hoping some wouldn't show up, then fitting in emergency patients anywhere they could.

In addition, delays produced nasty tensions in the waiting room. By the time patients finally got into the doctor's office, they were so annoyed that Murray and his colleagues found themselves spending a third of their time apologizing or discussing the reasons for the long waits and rushed visits.

Thinking about the problem, Murray reasoned that the crush of patients was like a warehouse full of goods. The doctors could clear out the warehouse by working longer hours for a while to whittle down the backlog of oldest appointments, then thereafter offer patients appointments with their own doctors the day they called for any problem. This proved doable, he found, because, although there was a heavier patient load in the winter, doctors could manage it by working late on some winter days. If a doctor took care of 2,500 patients, 21 of them wanted to be seen on a given day, and 90% of the time there were 16–25 patients calling for an appointment, a manageable number.

Murray convinced clinic administrators to give his "open-access scheduling" system a try, and within a year the backlog was gone. With more time, doctors could treat the whole patient rather than do just a rushed check of blood pressure and pulse. The bottom line: happier patients, physicians, and staff members.

Of course, Murray said, the doctors never had to have a backlog in the first place, but their attitude was that waiting patients assured them of an income. "They think the warehouse is filled with money," he said. But by reducing cycle time, the new system led to more satisfied patients who were not inclined to look elsewhere for medical care. And open access ended up providing the same revenue as the old system.[18]

More waiting, higher blood pressure? The concept of physicians in one Kaiser Permanente medical center was that there was no need for a patient backlog.

Statistical Process Control: Taking Periodic Random Samples   As the pages of this book were being printed, every now and then a press person would pull a few pages out of the press run and inspect them (under a bright light) to see that the consistency of the color and quality of the ink were holding up. This is an ongoing human visual check for quality control.

All kinds of products require periodic inspection during their manufacture: hamburger meat, breakfast cereal, flashlight batteries, wine, and so on. The tool often used for this is *statistical process control*, **a statistical technique that uses periodic random samples from production runs to see if quality is being maintained within a standard range of acceptability.** If quality is not acceptable, production is stopped to allow corrective measures.

Statistical process control is the technique that McDonald's uses, for example, to make sure that the quality of its burgers is always the same, no matter where in the world they are served. Companies such as Intel and Motorola use statistical process control to ensure the reliability and quality of their products.

What are the keys to successful control, and what are the barriers to control success?

The Big Picture

This section describes four keys to successful control and five barriers to successful control.

How do you as a manager make a control system successful, and how do you identify and deal with barriers to control? We consider these topics next.[19]

The Keys to Successful Control

Successful control systems have a number of common characteristics: (1) They are strategic and results oriented. (2) They are timely, accurate, and objective. (3) They are realistic, positive, and understandable and they encourage self-control. (4) They are flexible.[20]

1 They Are Strategic & Results Oriented. Control systems support strategic plans and are concentrated on significant activities that will make a real difference to the organization. Thus, when managers are developing strategic plans for achieving strategic goals, that is the point at which they should pay attention to developing control standards that will measure how well the plans are being achieved.

Example: "In the 1970s and 1980s, environmental groups did a great job of making people aware that the environment was in trouble," said Marcelo Carvalho de Andrade. "In the [new] millennium, we must direct our efforts toward solutions that don't depend on charity." Solutions, Andrade realized, need money, "and corporations have it." In 1986, the 40-year-old Brazilian mountain climber, former fashion model, and orthopedic surgeon had persuaded enough corporations—including Coca-Cola, Shell, Goodyear, and Christian Dior—to create Pro-Natura. One of its strategic goals is to arrest global warming. One results-oriented project intended to reduce carbon in the rain forest is to plant 10 million trees.[21]

One of 10 million trees. Established in 1986, Pro-Natura is a nongovernmental organization that specializes in sustainable development. The mission of the organization is to conserve biodiversity through integrated sustainable development projects adapted as models that can be replicated at regional levels.

2 They Are Timely, Accurate, & Objective Good control systems—like good information of any kind—should . . .

- **Be timely—meaning when needed:** The information should not necessarily be delivered quickly, but it should be delivered at an appropriate or specific time, such as every week or every month. And it certainly should be often enough to allow employees and managers to take corrective action for any deviations.

- **Be accurate—meaning correct:** Accuracy is paramount, if decision mistakes are to be avoided. Inaccurate sales figures may lead managers to mistakenly cut or increase sales promotion budgets. Inaccurate production costs may lead to faulty pricing of a product.

- **Be objective—meaning impartial:** Objectivity means control systems are impartial and fair. Although information can be inaccurate for all kinds of reasons (faulty communication, unknown data, and so on), information that is not objective is inaccurate for a special reason: It is biased or prejudiced. Control systems need to be considered unbiased for everyone involved so that they will be respected for their fundamental purpose—enhancing performance.

3 They Are Realistic, Positive, & Understandable & Encourage Self-Control
Control systems have to focus on working for the people who will have to live with them. Thus, they operate best when they are made acceptable to the organization's members who are guided by them. Thus, they should . . .

- **Be realistic:** They should incorporate realistic expectations. If employees feel performance results are too difficult, they are apt to ignore or sabotage the performance system.

- **Be positive:** They should emphasize development and improvement. They should avoid emphasizing punishment and reprimand.

- **Be understandable:** They should fit the people involved, be kept as simple as possible, and present data in understandable terms. They should avoid complicated computer printouts and statistics.

- **Encourage self-control:** They should encourage good communication and mutual participation. They should not be the basis for creating distrust between employees and managers.

4 They Are Flexible Control systems must leave room for individual judgment, so that they can be modified when necessary to meet new requirements.

Timely, accurate, objective. Wouldn't you wish that all numbers were this way?

Barriers to Control Success

Among the several barriers to a successful control system are the following:[22]

1 Too Much Control Some organizations, particularly bureaucratic ones, try to exert too much control. They may try to regulate employee behavior in everything from dress code to timing of coffee breaks. Allowing employees too little discretion for analysis and interpretation may lead to employee frustration—particularly among professionals, such as college professors and medical doctors. Their frustration may lead them to ignore or try to sabotage the control process.

2 Too Little Employee Participation As we've noted elsewhere in the book (Chapter 12), employee participation can enhance productivity. Involving employees in both the planning and execution of control systems can bring legitimacy to the process and heighten employee morale.

Temptation. Because legal gambling is a heavy cash business, casinos need to institute special controls against employee theft. One of them is the "eye in the sky" over card and craps tables.

3 Overemphasis on Means Instead of Ends We said that control activities should be strategic and results oriented. They are not ends in themselves but the means to eliminating problems. Too much emphasis on accountability for weekly production quotas, for example, can lead production supervisors to push their workers and equipment too hard, resulting in absenteeism and machine breakdowns. Or it can lead to game playing— "beating the system"—as managers and employees manipulate data to seem to fulfill short-run goals instead of the organization's strategic plan.

4 Overemphasis on Paperwork A specific kind of misdirection of effort is management emphasis on getting reports done, to the exclusion of other performance activity. Reports are not the be-all and end-all. Undue emphasis on reports can lead to too much focus on quantification of results and even to falsification of data.

Example: A research laboratory decided to use the number of patents the lab obtained as a measure of its effectiveness. The result was an increase in patents filed but a decrease in the number of successful research projects.[23]

5 Overemphasis on One Instead of Multiple Approaches One control may not be enough. By having multiple control activities and information systems, an organization can have multiple performance indicators, thereby increasing accuracy and objectivity.

Example: An obvious strategic goal for gambling casinos is to prevent employee theft of the cash flowing through their hands. Thus, casinos control card dealers by three means. First, they require they have a dealer's license before they are hired. Second, they put them under constant scrutiny, using direct supervision by on-site pit bosses as well as observation by closed-circuit TV cameras and through overhead one-way mirrors. Third, they require detailed reports at the end of each shift so that transfer of cash and cash equivalents (such as gambling chips) can be audited.[24]

Click-Along 16.3

Taking Something Practical Away from This Chapter: More on Productivity, Benchmarking, & Other Control Matters

major question

What are four keys to personal managerial success?

The Big Picture

As we end the book, this section describes some life lessons to take away.

We have come to the end of the book, our last chance to offer some suggestions to take with you that we hope will benefit you in the coming years. Following are some life lessons pulled from various sources that can make you a "keeper" in an organization and help you be successful.[25]

- **Initiative is always in short supply:** Many people still hold back in showing initiative because they have the unreasonable fear of getting reprimanded. That may still be possible with short-sighted supervisors, and of course it never hurts to put your boss in the best possible light. But here's a life lesson: "If you set the bar high, even if you don't reach it, you end up in a pretty good place—that is, achieving a pretty high mark."

- **If you have an active desire to learn new things, you'll be ready for the next step:** You should always be learning—whether through classes, on-the-job training, getting tips from a coworker, or reading a book. Learning makes you more valuable to your current employer and gives you more options in the wider work world. Here's a life lesson: "Be brutally honest with yourself about what you know or don't know, and ask what skills you need to take the next step."

- **Think ahead, understand what your obstacles are, and develop a strategy to win:** Ask for the most difficult job, study how to master it, and be willing to be accountable for outcomes. A life lesson: "Remove 'It's not my job' from your vocabulary." And another: "Don't sacrifice understanding for speed."

- **Be flexible, keep your cool, and take yourself lightly:** Things aren't always going to work out your way, so flexibility is important. In addition, the more unflappable you appear in difficult circumstances, the more you'll be admired by your bosses and coworkers. Having a sense of humor helps, since there are enough people spreading gloom and doom in the workplace. Life lesson: "When you're less emotional, you're better able to assess a crisis and develop a workable solution."

We wish you the very best of luck. And we mean it!

Angelo Kinicki
Brian K. Williams

Key Terms Used in This Chapter

Summary

16.1
Managing for Productivity

■ A manager has to deal with six challenges—managing for competitive advantage, diversity, globalization, information technology, ethical standards, and his or her own happiness and life goals. The manager must make decisions about the four management functions—planning, organizing, leading, and controlling—to get people to achieve productivity and realize results. Productivity is defined by the formula of outputs divided by inputs for a specified period of time. Productivity is important because it determines whether the organization will make a profit or even survive. Productivity depends on control.

16.2
Control: When Managers Monitor Performance

■ Controlling is defined as monitoring performance, comparing it with goals, and taking corrective action as needed. There are six reasons why control is needed: (1) to adapt to change and uncertainty; (2) to discover irregularities and errors; (3) to reduce costs, increase productivity, or add value; (4) to detect opportunities; (5) to deal with complexity; and (6) to decentralize decision making and facilitate teamwork.

■ There are four control process steps. (1) The first step is to set standards. A control standard, or performance standard, is the desired performance level for a given goal. (2) The second step is to measure performance, based on written reports, oral reports, and personal observation. (3) The third step is to compare measured performance against the standards established. Some range of variation may be permitted, often incorporated in a principle called management by exception, which states that managers should be informed of a situation only if data shows a significant deviation from standards. (4) The fourth step is to take corrective action, if necessary, if there is negative performance.

■ There are three types of control that managers use. (1) Feedforward control takes place before operations begin and is intended to prevent anticipated problems. (2) Concurrent control takes place while operations are going on and is intended to minimize problems as they occur. (3) Feedback control takes place after operations are finished and is intended to correct problems that have already occurred.

16.3
Levels, Areas, & Styles of Control

■ In applying the steps and types of control, managers need to consider (1) the level of management at which they operate, (2) the areas they can draw on for resources, and (3) the style of control philosophy.

■ There are three levels of control, corresponding to the three principal managerial levels. (1) Strategic control, which is done by top managers, is monitoring performance to ensure that strategic plans are being implemented and taking corrective action as needed. (2) Tactical control, done by middle managers, is monitoring performance to ensure that tactical plans— those at the divisional or departmental level—are being implemented and taking corrective action as needed. (3) Operational control, done by first-level or supervisory managers, is monitoring performance to ensure that operational plans—day-to-day goals—are being implemented and taking corrective action as needed.

■ Most organization have four areas that they can draw on for resources. (1) Physical resources include buildings, equipment, and tangible products; these use equipment control, inventory-management controls, and quality controls. (2) Human resources use personality tests, drug tests, performance tests, employee surveys, and the like as controls to monitor people. (3) Information resources use production schedules, sales forecasts, environmental impact statements, and the like to monitor the organization's various resources. (4) Financial resources take various kinds of financial controls, as we discuss in Section 16. 4.

■ There are three managerial styles or control philosophies. (1) Bureaucratic control is characterized by use of rules, regulations, and formal authority to guide performance. (2) Market control is characterized by use of market mechanisms—pricing, competition, market share—to guide performance. (3) Clan control is characterized by shared values, beliefs, rituals, and trusts emanating from a common culture, and so formal controls are considered unnecessary.

16.4
Some Financial Tools for Control

■ Financial controls include (1) budgets, (2) financial statements, (3) ratio analysis, and (4) audits.

■ A budget is a formal financial projection. There are two budget-planning approaches, incremental and zero-based. (1) Incremental budgeting allocates increased or decreased funds to a department by using the last budget period as a reference point; only incremental changes in the budget request are reviewed. (2) Zero-based budgeting (ZBB) forces each department to start from zero in projecting the funding needs for the coming budget period. Whether incremental or zero-based, budgets may be categorized as two types: fixed and variable. A fixed budget allocates resources on the basis of a single estimate of costs. A variable budget allows the allocation of resources to vary in proportion with various levels of activity.

■ A financial statement is a summary of some aspect of an organization's financial status. There are two types of financial statements: the balance sheet and the income statement. A balance sheet summarizes an organization's overall financial worth—that is, assets and liabilities—at a specific point in time. An income statement summarizes an organization's financial results—revenues and expenses—over a specified period of time.

■ Ratio analysis is the practice of evaluating financial ratios. Managers may use this tool to determine an organization's financial health, such as liquidity ratios, debt management ratios, or return ratios.

■ Audits are formal verifications of an organization's financial and operational systems. Audits are of two types: external and internal. An external audit is formal verification of an organization's financial accounts and statements by outside experts. An internal audit is a verification of an organization's financial accounts and statements by the organization's own professional staff.

16.5
Total Quality Management

■ Total quality management (TQM) is defined as a comprehensive approach—led by top management and supported throughout the organization—dedicated to continuous quality improvement, training, and customer satisfaction. The two core principles of TQM are people orientation and improvement orientation.

■ In the people orientation, everyone involved with the organization is asked to focus on delivering value to customers. People orientation operates under the assumption that delivering customer value is most important; that employees and suppliers will focus on quality if they are given power to do so; and that TQM requires training, teamwork, and cross-functional efforts.

■ In the improvement orientation, everyone involved with the organization is supposed to make ongoing small, incremental improvements in all parts of the organization. This orientation assumes that it's less expensive to do things right the first time than to fix them later, that it's better to do small improvements all the time, that accurate standards must be followed to eliminate small variations, and that there must be strong commitment from top management.

■ Several techniques are available for improving quality, including employee involvement, benchmarking, outsourcing, reduced cycle time, and statistical process control. (1) Employee involvement can be implemented through quality circles, self-managed teams, and special-purpose teams—that is, teams that meet to solve a special or one-time problem. (2) Benchmarking is a process by which a company compares its performance with that of high-performing organizations. (3) Outsourcing is the subcontracting of services and operations to an outside vendor. (4) Reduced cycle time consists of reducing the number of steps in a work process. (5) Statistical process control is a statistical technique that uses periodic random samples from production runs to see if quality is being maintained within a standard range of acceptability.

16.6
Managing Control Effectively

■ There are four keys to successful control and five barriers to successful control.

■ Successful control systems have four common characteristics: (1) They are strategic and results oriented. (2) They are timely, accurate, and objective. (3) They are realistic, positive, and understandable and they encourage self-control. (4) They are flexible.

■ Among the barriers to a successful control system are the following: (1) Organizations may exert too much control. (2) There may be too little employee participation. (3) The organization may overemphasize means instead of ends. (4) There may be an overemphasis on paperwork. (5) There may be an overemphasis on one approach instead of multiple approaches.

Management in Action

Working in Small Business

Excerpted from Jim Hopkins, "Big Business Can't Swallow These Little Fish," USA Today, March 27, 2002, pp. 1B, 2B.

Conventional wisdom says . . . consolidation is squeezing virtually every industry—what with the rise of Wal-Mart, AOL Time Warner, Bank of America, and other corporate giants.

But, in fact, scores of U.S. industries remain staunchly independent. Of 290 industries, 28% have a superhigh concentration of very small companies with fewer than 20 employees, a *USA Today* computer analysis of new employment data shows.

As in the past, the mom-and-pops fuel entrepreneurship, a bedrock of the U.S. economy. They create jobs and technologies, and they spread the wealth that often comes with business ownership to a broad array of people.

Yet that independence is being steadily eroded. For the first time, a majority of the U.S.A.'s 111 million workers work for big companies instead of small ones—a switch that probably occurred in 2000, experts say. Consolidation has hit hardest in retail and manufacturing, where thousands of small firms fell to big corporations in the past decade. The number of drugstore companies, for example, plummeted 28% from 1990 to 1998, the latest data show. . . .

Consolidation is especially harmful to struggling urban areas and rural Main Streets that depend on small firms for the jobs and wealth they create, experts say. Small companies—defined as those with fewer than 500 employees—produce 75% of new jobs and are a major source of new technologies. Entrepreneurship is the best way to amass wealth, says Federal Reserve Chairman Alan Greenspan.

Some industries are proving better at staying independent: 81 of 290 industries in *USA Today*'s analysis are still heavily dominated by mom-and-pops. For example, 98% of all dentists, 97% of florists, and 95% of funeral companies are very small businesses, with fewer than 20 employees. These 81 industries share common traits:

They largely sell services, not things. In addition to dentists and funeral homes, the least consolidated U.S. industries include law and accounting. . . . Whether it's preparing taxes or a funeral, the work is customized. It cannot be done in advance and stocked on a shelf to be sold in huge volumes to achieve economies of scale.

Many rely on consumer trust and proximity. Patients choose dentists they trust because they don't want pain. In large part—and helped by health insurance—the cost of the service is secondary. . . .

While trust is key in health care, proximity is a big factor for other still-independent industries. Home-appliance repair, for example, must be done where the customer lives. The business owners don't want to travel far. The same force appears to be at work with dry cleaners. Nationwide, there are almost 37,000 dry cleaners and laundries. About 91% are very small neighborhood stores. . . .

Overhead is low. Independent industries require small upfront start-up costs. That draws a constant supply of new players. Tim Buckles, 43, started his one-man hair salon in Louisville in 1997. It cost him just $15,000 to buy equipment and inventory and renovate his salon space. . . .

In contrast, industries dominated by big corporations—such as carmakers and hospitals—require enormous capital investments for machinery and other assets.

For Discussion

1. Would you think that controlling would be particularly important in small businesses? Why?

2. Give examples of feedforward, concurrent, and feedback controls for a particular small business.

3. Which of the three styles of implementing controls—bureaucratic, market, or clan—is most appropriate to the small businesses described in the article?

4. Do you think the types of budgets that would be most useful would vary depending on what kind of small business you are in?

5. What kind of TQM matters would you apply in running a hairdresser's? a dental practice? a funeral home?

Take It to the Net

As we discussed in this chapter, benchmarking is an important tool for organizations to compare their performance with those of high-performing organizations. Companies such as Xerox, Southwest Airlines, Toyota, and Ford all use benchmarking to emulate the best practices of their competitors. The purpose of this exercise is to gain familiarity with benchmarking and to learn how to use information derived from it.

Go to your college's website. Look over the section for student services. What services does the website provide? Can you register for classes online? Purchase parking passes? Does this section contain information for new student orientation? Now go to the website of another college in your area. If you are attending a community college, the site should be for another community college; if you are attending a state university, choose another state university. Go to the section for student services for this school. How does this section differ from your college's? Are there any similarities? Are there any services this website provides that your college does not? Compare the student services section to your college's and see if there are any areas in which your school could improve.

Questions for Discussion

1. What criteria did you use to benchmark your school's student services? Explain why you chose these areas.

2. What changes to your school's student services would you recommend based on your benchmarking?

3. Do you think it would be more beneficial to study the practices of a larger university (such as a state school if you are attending a community college or a larger state college if you are attending a state school) or to study schools relatively similar to your own? Explain.

Self-Assessment

Do You Have Good Time-Management Skills?*

Objectives

1. To determine how productive you are.
2. To look at ways in which you can gain better time-management skills.

Introduction: As we learned in this chapter, productivity is important to companies because it ultimately determines whether or not they make profits and survive. As a student, it is important that you too be productive. Of course there are times when you would rather watch, say, Jerry Springer than write your 15-page term paper, and there are definitely times when a few hours at the mall sounds more appealing than a few hours with your Spanish/English dictionary. But establishing good time management skills now will help you be more productive in all aspects of life. Productive people are important assets to an organization.

The purpose of this exercise is to determine whether or not you have good time-management skills.

Instructions: Read each question and mark your response under the relevant column—"Yes," "No," or "Sometimes." Answer the questions honestly; that is, don't answer as you feel you *should* but rather as you feel you really *would*.

1. Do you make a conscious effort to separate urgent tasks from other ones?	Yes	No	Sometimes
2. Do you take time to think about a situation so you can make the best possible decision?	Yes	No	Sometimes
3. Do you take at least one hour each day for uninterrupted time for thinking, studying, reading, or creative work?	Yes	No	Sometimes
4. Do you spend a lot of time maintaining relationships?	Yes	No	Sometimes
5. Do you work hard to be your best rather than trying to obtain perfection?	Yes	No	Sometimes

Interpretation: If you answered "Yes" to all five questions, your time-management skills are excellent (at least in these areas). If you answered "No" or "Sometimes" to one or more questions, you could definitely benefit by improving your time-management skills.

Questions for Discussion

1. Were you surprised by the results? Why or why not?

2. Even if you answered "Yes" to all of these questions, are there some areas where you feel you could improve your time-management skills? Explain.

3. What are some ways you can improve these skills? Discuss.

*Adapted from J. Yager. "Could Your Time Management Skills Use Improvement?" *Creative Time Management for the New Millennium,* http://www.janyager.com/self-quiz-time_management_.htm, June 2002.

Keeping an Eye on Employee Performance

Objectives

1. To look at ways in which companies monitor employee productivity.
2. To look at how monitoring productivity can be used as a control mechanism.

Introduction

In this chapter you learned that monitoring can be an effective tool for managers to identify ways to improve productivity. This control device can help them establish standards, measure performance, compare performance to goals, and assess whether corrective action is needed. The purpose of this exercise is to gain familiarity about ways managers can monitor employee productivity.

Instructions

Break into groups of five or six people. Read the following scenario, which your group is then to role-play. Discuss with your group the concerns listed in the scenario. The group should then decide whether or not your organization should use Pro-Max software to monitor employee productivity. Once all of the groups in the class have reached their decisions, the various groups should have a class discussion comparing their decisions and their reasoning to those of other groups.

Scenario

Your group is a team of managers for a large organization. Each of you represents a different department. Recently your CEO, who has not been happy with the organization's performance, learned from a golfing friend that that the latter's company had spent $1,000 installing a software program—Pro-Max, made by Replicon Inc.—to monitor employee productivity. Your CEO likes the idea, but he has learned that because your company is bigger, with 2,000 employees, it would cost $20,000 to install the software. Unsure about spending this amount, he has charged all the managers with deciding whether or not the software would work for your company.

He is open to all feedback because he wants to improve the company's productivity, though not at the employees' expense. He wants all of you to do some research and decide whether or not the software would be an effective monitoring tool. He understands that each manager has a different department and that the software might not meet the needs of some of them. Among the concerns he

wants you to consider: Will the software really increase productivity? In a company of 2,000 employees, will increased productivity justify the software's cost of $20,000? What are some of the ethical issues involved with using this software? What other concerns should he be made aware of?

Your group does some research and finds the following article: E. Goodridge, "Replicon Keeps a Close Watch on Employee Performance: ProMax Software Provides Managers with a Reliable Barometer of Worker's Productivity," *Information Week.com*, November 2001. *http://www.informationweek.com/story/WK20011101S0023*, June 2002.

Measuring the amount of time an employee spends on a job is easy. Measuring employee productivity is another matter, one that poses a challenge for project managers trying to determine accurate time expenditures when billing clients or projects. Workforce-management software supplier Replicon Inc. says it can help with an Internet-based application that tracks employee productivity in real time.

ProMax lets managers set productivity goals for employees, contract workers, projects teams, and departments. When employees enter their billable hours for the day into the software, they can immediately see how their time on the job measures up against expectations set for each individual or project team. Managers receive real-time notifications of employee productivity from the software and can immediately see if a project is running on time and spot potential problems.

While managers may appreciate the hands-on knowledge, the software's ability to measure productivity could raise concerns about employee privacy issues. Replicon CEO John Eddy insists the software will be well received by both managers and employees. "It's a barometer to let an employee know 'where do I stand this month,' and 'where do I need to focus?'" he says. "We've found employees have a natural curiosity to compare their work performance against peers."

ProMax is the latest addition to an application suite from Replicon that tracks and manages time and expense data. FundTech Ltd., a Jersey City, N.J., developer of cash-management infrastructure software, recently implemented Replicon's Web-TimeSheet 4.0, an application that tracks billable employee and project hours across international time zones and foreign currencies.

FundTech needed the software to manage its international professional services group, which develops software for clients such as Citigroup and Merrill Lynch, says Cenk Ipeker, FundTech's director of information systems and financial analysis.

Installing ProMax "is the natural progression for the company next quarter," Ipeker says. "My job is a hybrid of installing and maintaining systems while tracking project reporting. Having a tool that acts like a scorecard, offering immediate insight to worker productivity, would be helpful."

ProMax . . . will be bundled with TimeSheet software, which is used by major companies such as AT&T, Charles Schwab, Compaq, Kraft, and Sony Music Entertainment. Pricing will range from $1,000 for up to 50 users to $20,000 for up to 2,000 users.

Questions for Discussion

1. Refer to Panel 16.4. Which steps in the control process would use this software? Do you feel this software could make any of these steps easier? How? Discuss and explain.

2. What type of control is this software: feedforward, concurrent, or feedback? Explain.

3. What level of control would this software be most effective in: strategic, tactical or operational? Explain.

4. Do you feel the ethical concerns with this software outweigh the positive aspects of improving productivity? Why or why not?

Ethical Dilemma

Controls to Keep Employees from Temptation

From Shirley Leung, "McDonald's Game Scheme Thrived on Lax Security," The Wall Street Journal, *September 6, 2001, p. B8.*

Following the August 21 [2001] arrest of one of its employees in an alleged $13 million scam against McDonald's Corp., Simon Worldwide Inc. publicly called itself a "victim."

But game-promotion firms and fraud experts said that scams of the sort that a Simon employee allegedly perpetrated are hardly acts of God, and can succeed only amid inadequate security. These experts said that a tight system of checks and balances either would prevent such a scam or catch it quickly. The alleged Simon-employee scam against McDonald's lasted six years.

McDonald's had hired Simon to run such promotions as "Monopoly" and "Who Wants to Be a Millionaire," in which consumers search newspaper inserts and McDonald's products for rare winning game pieces that can be valued at $1 million each. Simon handled the printing and distribution of all game pieces, placing the winning ones in the hands of its head of security, Jerome P. Jacobson, a 58-year-old former police officer.

Mr. Jacobson was supposed to make certain that the winning pieces entered the distribution system in a random and fair way. Instead, according to the Federal Bureau of Investigation, he diverted those pieces to friends and acquaintances, who over six years claimed more than $13 million in prizes, kicking back a portion of the proceeds to Mr. Jacobson. Mr. Jacobson and seven others were arrested late last month. . . .

"This is a poster child of how not to do things," said Bill Behm, executive vice president of research and development at Scientific Games Corp., a New York firm that designs and prints instant state lottery tickets for 26 states.

Mr. Behm said there shouldn't be any employee involvement with winning tickets. At Scientific Games, a computer program generates the winning tickets and randomly shuffles them among the others. No one at the company knows which tickets are the winners . . .

"We don't place a person in the awkward position of being in physical control of the winning ticket," Mr. Behm said. "The bottom line is everyone has their price, some more than others." . . .

Carl Pergola, national director of fraud investigation and recovery services at New York accounting firm BDO Seidman LLP, said that if human handling of the winning tickets was necessary, Simon should have rotated Mr. Jacobson and other Simon employees in monitoring the distribution of those tickets.

"Preventing fraud isn't about finding someone you trust," Mr. Pergola said. "It's about finding proper controls."

Solving the Dilemma

If you were a manager from McDonald's, how would you prevent this type of unethical behavior from occurring?

1. I would continue to use Simon, but would not allow any employees from Simon to have physical contact with the winning tickets.

2. I would administer the game by using McDonald's employees and would modify the procedures so that no employees have physical contact with the winning tickets.

3. I would fire Simon, and find another company to administer the game.

4. Invent other options. Discuss.

Video Case

McDonalds: Made for You

In the early 1980s, McDonalds was struggling to meet its own internal standards. Examination of the production process reveled a lack of consistent, repeatable processes within one store or from store to store. The old production system was designed to produce large quantities of a few products during two peak periods. In response to changing customer demands, McDonalds implemented an organization-wide "kitchen changeover" to a faster, more flexible system called "Made For You" (MFY).

Implementation of the MFY system was initially hampered by structural changes within the organization. Staff support functions were removed from the central home office and placed within the five regional divisions. Research and development remained the responsibility of the home office, but implementation became the sole responsibility of the field offices. However, it quickly became apparent that this new structure was inappropriate for implementation of the MFY system. In response, top management created a cross-functional restaurant systems team. The key strategies of the team included establishment of the MFY Board. The board provided central coordination and aligned resources among the five divisions. The team also constructed the MFY database, which tracked the progress of the implementation process. Finally, the team created the Document Library containing all information regarding the MFY system.

With these changes in place, the implementation of the kitchen changeover process proceeded, with 98% completion by the target date. Importantly, the success of this process required skilled cooperation and coordination between the central and division offices.

Discussion Questions

1. Did structural changes within the organization aid or hamper implementation of the MFY system? Be able to justify your response with evidence from the case.

2. Describe the control systems evident in the case.

3. List at least three ways in which top management could assess the effectiveness of the changeover process.

APPENDIX

The Project Planner's Toolkit
Flowcharts & Gantt Charts

How can you use planning tools to enhance your performance and utmost success?

The Big Picture

Two tools used in project planning, which was covered in Chapter 5, are flowcharts and Gantt charts. A third tool, break-even analysis, was discussed in Chapter 5.

Project planning may begin (in the definition stage) as a back-of-the-envelope kind of process, but the client will expect a good deal more for the time and money being invested. Fortunately, there are various planning and monitoring tools that give the planning and execution of projects more precision. Two tools in the planner's tool kit are (1) flowcharts and (2) Gantt charts. We discussed a third tool, break-even analysis, in Chapter 5, Section 5.6.

Tool #1: Flowcharts—for Showing Event Sequences & Alternate Decision Scenarios

A *flowchart* is a useful graphical tool for representing the sequence of events required to complete a project and for laying out "what-if" scenarios. Flowcharts have been used for decades by computer programmers and systems analysts to make a graphical "road map," as it were, of the flow of tasks required. These professionals use their own special symbols (indicating "input/output," "magnetic disk," and the like), but there is no need for you to make the process complicated. Generally, only three symbols are needed: (1) an oval for the "beginning" and "end," (2) a box for a major activity, and (3) a diamond for a "yes or no" decision. (*See Panel A.1, opposite.*)

Computer programs such as Micrographix's ABC Flow Charter are available for constructing flowcharts. You can also use the drawing program in word processing programs such as Microsoft Word.

Benefits Flowcharts have two benefits:

- **Planning straightforward activities:** A flowchart can be quite helpful for planning ordinary activities—figuring out the best way to buy textbooks or a car, for example. It is also a straightforward way of indicating the sequence of events in, say, thinking out a new enterprise that you would then turn into a business plan.

- **Depicting alternate scenarios:** A flowchart is also useful for laying out "what-if" scenarios—as in if you answer "yes" to a decision question you should follow Plan A, if you answer "no" you should follow Plan B.

Flowchart: Website, print, or television? Example of a flowchart for improving a company's advertising

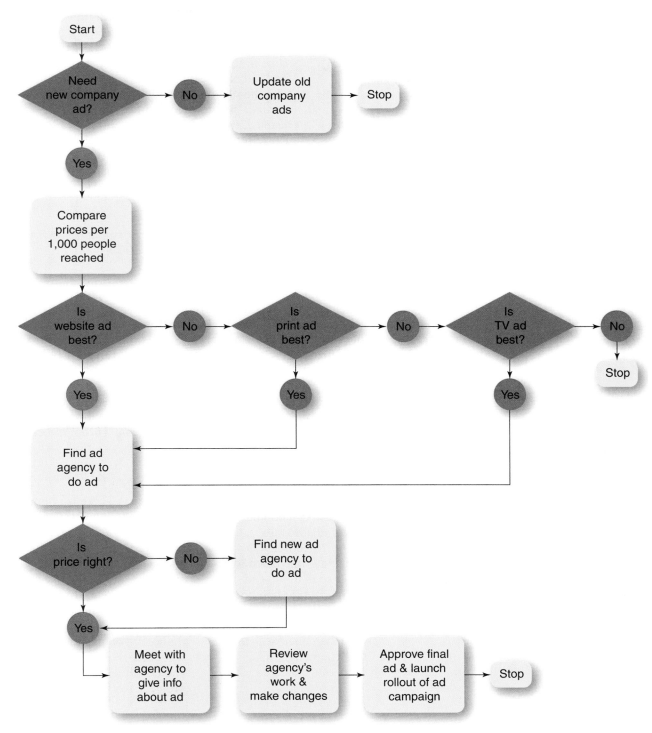

Limitations

Flowcharts have two limitations:

- **No time indication:** They don't show the amounts of time required to accomplish the various activities in a project. In building a house, the foundation might take only a couple of days but the rough carpentry might take weeks. These time differences can't be represented graphically on a flowchart (although you could make a notation).

- **Not good for complex projects**: They aren't useful for showing projects consisting of several activities that must all be worked on at the same time. An example would be getting ready for football season's opening game, by which time the players have to be trained, the field readied, the programs printed, the band rehearsed, the ticket sellers recruited, and so on. These separate activities might each be represented on their own flowcharts, of course. But to try to express them all together all at once would produce a flowchart that would be unwieldy, even unworkable.

Tool #2: Gantt Charts—Visual Time Schedules for Work Tasks

We have mentioned how important deadlines are to making a project happen. Unlike a flowchart, a Gantt chart can graphically indicate deadlines.

The Gantt chart was developed by **Henry L. Gantt**, a member of the school of scientific management (discussed in Chapter 2).[1] **A _Gantt chart_ is a kind of time schedule—a specialized bar chart that shows the relationship between the kind of work tasks planned and their scheduled completion dates.** *(See Panel A.2, opposite.)*

There are a number of software packages available to help you create and modify Gantt charts on your computer. Examples are CA-SuperProject, Microsoft Project Manager 98, SureTrak Project Manager, and TurboProject 3.0 Professional.

Benefits   There are three benefits to using a Gantt chart:

- **Express time lines visually**: Unlike flowcharts, Gantt charts allow you to indicate visually the time to be spent on each activity.

- **Compare proposed and actual progress:** A Gantt chart may be used to compare planned time to complete a task with actual time taken to complete it, so that you can see how far ahead or behind schedule you are for the entire project. This enables you to make adjustments so as to hold to the final target dates.

- **Simplicity**: There is nothing difficult about creating a Gantt chart. You express the time across the top and the tasks down along the left side. As Panel A.2 shows, you can make use of this device while still in college to help schedule and monitor the work you need to do to meet course requirements and deadlines (for papers, projects, tests).

Gantt chart for designing a website. This shows the tasks accomplished and the time planned for remaining tasks to build a company website.

Accomplished: ‖‖‖‖‖‖

Planned: \\\\\\\\\

Stage of development	Week 1	Week 2	Week 3	Week 4	Week 5
1. Examine competitors' websites	‖‖‖‖‖‖‖‖‖‖‖‖‖‖ ‖‖‖‖‖‖‖	‖‖‖‖‖‖‖‖‖			
2. Get information for your website	‖‖‖‖‖‖‖‖‖‖‖‖‖‖ ‖‖‖‖‖‖‖	‖‖‖‖‖‖‖‖‖‖‖‖‖‖ ‖‖‖‖‖‖‖			
3. Learn web authoring software		‖‖‖‖‖‖‖‖‖‖‖‖‖‖ ‖‖‖‖‖‖‖	‖‖‖‖‖‖‖‖‖‖‖‖‖‖ ‖‖‖‖‖‖‖		
4. Create (design) your website			\\\\\\\\\	\\\\\\\\\\\\\\\ \\	\\\\\
5. "Publish" (put) website online					\\\\\\\\\\\\\\

Limitations   Gantt charts have two limitations:

■ **Not useful for large, complex projects:** Although a Gantt chart can express the interrelations among the activities of relatively small projects, it becomes cumbersome and unwieldy when used for large, complex projects. More sophisticated management planning tools may be needed, such as PERT networks.

■ **Time assumptions are subjective:** The time assumptions expressed may be purely subjective; there is no range between "optimistic" and "pessimistic" of the time needed to accomplish a given task.

chapter notes

CHAPTER 1

1. P. Nakache, "Can You Handle the Truth About Your Career?" *Fortune,* July 7, 1997, p. 208.

2. H. Lancaster, "If Your Career Needs More Attention, Maybe You Should Get an Agent," *The Wall Street Journal,* October 20, 1998, p. B1.

3. R. L. Knowdell, "The 10 New Rules for Strategizing Your Career," *The Futurist,* June–July 1998, pp. 19–24.

4. D. Kreneck, quoted in M. W. Thompson, "In the Maelstrom," *American Journalism Review,* December 1998, pp. 38–44.

5. Thompson, 1998.

6. M. P. Follett, quoted in J. F. Stoner and R. E. Freeman, *Management,* 5th ed. (Englewood Cliffs, NJ: Prentice Hall, 1992), p. 6.

7. "Frustrated Bank Customer Lets His Computer Make Complaint," *Los Angeles Times,* October 20, 1993, p. A28.

8. The Segal Co., *2001 Officer Compensation* Report (New York: Aspen Publishers, 2001).

9. O. Pollar, "Are You Sure You Want to Be a Manager?" *San Francisco Examiner,* October 4, 1998, p. J-3.

10. M. Csikszentmihalyi, *Flow: The Psychology of Optimal Experience* (New York: HarperCollins, 1990), and *Beyond Boredom and Anxiety* (San Francisco: Jossey-Bass, 1975).

11. P. M. Reilly, "In the Age of the Web, a Book Chain Flounders," *The Wall Street Journal,* February 22, 1999, pp. B1, B4.

12. U.S. Census Bureau.

13. W.-T. Kwok, "Online Sensitivity," *San Jose Mercury News,* November 29, 1998, p. 2E.

14. D. Tapscott, "New Universe Forming as Business Between Businesses Explodes," *USA Today,* November 16, 1998, pp. 1E, 2E.

15. S. Cabot, reported in D. Jones, "Sales Reps Must Watch Step When Rapping Rivals," *USA Today,* June 17, 1997, p. 3B.

16. M. Murray, "A Software Engineer Becomes a Manager, with Many Regrets," *The Wall Street Journal,* May 14, 1997, pp. A1, A14.

17. S. Armour, "Management Loses Its Allure," *USA Today,* October 15, 1997, pp. 1B, 2B.

18. Murray, 1997.

20. P. Drucker, reported in R. L. Knowdell, "A Model for Managers in the Future Workplace: Symphony Conductor," *The Futurist,* June–July 1998, p. 22.

21. J. Falvey, *After College: The Business of Getting a Job* (Charlotte, VT: Williamson, 1986).

22. B. Karlin, quoted in S. Spring, "Job Titles of the Future: Director of Great People," *Fast Company,* February–March, 1999, p. 46.

23. S. Spring, "Job Titles of the Future: Chief Travel Scientist," *Fast Company,* February–March, 1999, p. 68.

24. C. Sittenfeld, "Hope Is a Weapon," *Fast Company,* February–March, 1999, pp. 179–184.

25. H. Mintzberg, *The Nature of Managerial Work* (New York: Harper & Row, 1973).

26. Mintzberg, 1973.

27. J. P. Kotter, "What Effective General Managers Really Do," *Harvard Business Review,* March–April 1999, pp. 145–159.

28. L. Stroh, quoted in A. Muoio, "Balancing Acts," *Fast Company,* February–March 1999, pp. 83–90.

29. S. MacDermid, Purdue University, and M. D. Lee, McGill University, two-year study cited in R. W. Huppke, Associated Press, "Take This Job, and Love It," *San Francisco Chronicle,* January 28, 1999, p. B2.

30. A. Deutschman, "The CEO's Secret of Managing Time," *Fortune,* June 1, 1992, pp. 135–146.

31. D. G. Lepore, quoted in Muio, 1999.

32. H. Lancaster, "Managing Your Time in Real-World Chaos Takes Real Planning," *The Wall Street Journal,* August 19, 1997, p. B1

33. R. E. Kelley, quoted in S. Shellenbarger, "You Don't Have to Be Chained to Your Desk to Be a Star Performer," *The Wall Street Journal,* August 12, 1998, p. B1.

34. B. Graham, quoted in Shellenbarger, 1998.

35. R. L. Katz, "Skills of an Effective Administrator," *Harvard Business Review,* September–October, 1974, p. 94.

36. Barbara Ross, quoted in Thompson, 1998.

37. C. Cotts, "Press Clips," *Village Voice,* March 29, 2000, ccotts@villagevoice.com.

38. D. Shoemaker, quoted in I. DeBare, "The Incredible Growing Work-week," *San Francisco Chronicle,* February 12, 1999, pp. B1, B2.

39. E. B. Zechmeister and S. E. Nyberg, *Human Memory: An Introduction to Research and Theory* (Pacific Grove, CA: Brooks/Cole, 1982).

40. B. K. Bromage and R. E. Meyer, "Quantitative and Qualitative Effects of Repetition on Learning from Technical Text," *Journal of Educational Psychology,* 1982, vol. 78, pp. 271–278.

41. F. P. Robinson, *Effective Study,* 4th ed. (New York: Harper & Row, 1970).

42. H. C. Lindgren, *The Psychology of College Success: A Dynamic Approach* (New York: Wiley, 1969).

43. R. J. Palkovitz and R. K. Lore, "Note Taking and Note Review: Why Students Fail Questions Based on Lecture Material," *Teaching of Psychology,* 1980, vol. 7, pp. 159–161.

44. J. Langan and J. Nadell, *Doing Well in College: A Concise Guide to Reading, Writing, and Study Skills* (New York: McGraw-Hill, 1980), pp. 93–110.

45. Palkovitz and Lore, 1980, pp. 159–161.

CHAPTER 2

1. E. J. Langer, *The Power of Mindful Learning* (Reading, MA: Addison-Wesley, 1997), p. 4.

2. E. J. Langer, *Mindfulness* (Reading, MA: Addison-Wesley, 1989), pp. 12–13.

3. Langer, 1989, p. 69.

4. A. Webber, "The Best Organization Is No Organization," *USA Today,* March 6, 1997, p. 13A.

5. A. Maslow, "A Theory of Human Motivation," *Psychological Review,* July 1943, pp. 370–396.

6. D. McGregor, *The Human Side of Enterprise* (New York: McGraw-Hill, 1960).

7. See J. T. Delaney, "Workplace Cooperation: Current Problems, New Approaches," *Journal of Labor Research,* Winter 1996, pp. 45–61; H. Mintzberg, D. Dougherty, J. Jorgensen, and F. Westley, "Some Surprising Things About Collaboration—Knowing How People Connect Makes It Work Better," *Organizational Dynamics,* Spring 1996, pp. 60–71; R. Crow, "Institutionalized Competition and Its Effects on Teamwork," *Journal for Quality and Participation,* June 1995, pp. 46–54; K. G. Smith, S. J. Carroll, and S. J. Ashford, "Intra- and Interorganizational Cooperation: Toward a Research Agenda," *Academy of Management Journal,* February 1995, pp. 7–23; M. E. Haskins, J. Liedtka, and J. Rosenblum, "Beyond Teams: Toward an Ethic of Collaboration," *Organizational Dynamics,* Spring 1998, pp. 34–50; and C. C. Chen, X. P. Chen, and J. R. Meindl, "How Can Cooperation Be Fostered? The Cultural Effects of Individualism-Collectivism," *Academy of Management Review,* April 1998, pp. 285–304.

8. A. Kohn, "How to Succeed without Even Vying," *Psychology Today,* September 1986, pp. 27–28. Sports psychologists discuss "cooperative competition" in S. Sleek, "Competition: Who's the Real Opponent?" *APA Monitor,* July 1996, p. 8.

9. D. W. Johnson, G. Maruyama, R. Johnson, D. Nelson, and L. Skon, "Effects of Cooperative, Competitive, and Individualistic Goal Structures on Achievement: A Meta-Analysis," *Psychological Bulletin,* January 1981, pp. 56–57. An alternative interpretation of the foregoing study that emphasizes the influence of situational factors can be found in J. L. Cotton and M. S. Cook, "Meta-Analysis and the Effects of Various Reward Systems: Some Different Conclusions from Johnson et al.," *Psychological Bulletin,* July 1982, pp. 176–183. Also see A. E. Ortiz, D. W. Johnson, and R. T. Johnson, "The Effect of Positive Goal and Resource Interdependence on Individual Performance," *The Journal of Social Psychology,* April 1996, pp. 243–249; and S. L. Gaertner, J. F. Dovidio, M. C. Rust, J. A. Nier, B. S. Banker, C. M. Ward, G. R. Mottola, and M. Houlette, "Reducing Intergroup Bias: Elements of Intergroup Cooperation," *Journal of Personality and Social Psychology,* March 1999, pp. 388–402.

10. E. Perkins, "How to Book Hotel Rooms at Half the Price," *San Francisco Examiner,* December 13, 1998, p. T-2.

11. S. F. Brown, "Wresting New Wealth from the Supply Chain," *Fortune,* November 9, 1998, pp. 204[C]–204[Z].

12. J. Strasburg, "Shaking the Blues," *San Francisco Chronicle,* February 3, 2002, pp. G1, G3; N. Munk, "How Levi's Trashed a Great American Brand," *Fortune,* April 12, 1999, pp. 83–90; and E. Neuborne, K. Kerwin, and bureau reports, "Generation Y," *Business Week,* February 15, 1999, pp. 80–88.

13. A. Field, "Hyping Investors . . . Cruising for Customers . . . Gen X Slackers," *Fortune,* October 12, 1998, pp. 188[J]–188[K].

14. J. Case, *Open-Book Management: The Coming Business Revolution* (New York: HarperBusiness, 1996).

15. J. Pfeffer, in A. M. Webber, "Danger: Toxic Company," *Fast Company,* November 1998, pp. 152–161.

16. J Pfeffer, *The Human Equation: Building Profits by Putting People First* (Cambridge, MA: Harvard Business School Press, 1996).

17. C. Kleiman, "Companies Embracing 'Open-Book' Management," *San Jose Mercury News,* May 18, 1997, pp. PC1, PC2.

18. G. T. Brown, quoted in Kleiman, 1997.

19. K. Carney, "How to Keep Staff in a Boom Economy," *Inc.,* November 1998, p. 110.

20. I. Mochari, "How Motley Fools Talk Back," *Inc.,* June 1999, p. 108.

21. G. Bylinksy, "How to Bring Out Better Products Faster," *Fortune,* November 23, 1998, pp. 238[B]–238[T].

22. P. Senge, *The Fifth Discipline* (New York: Doubleday, 1990), p. 1.

23. R. Hodgetts, F. Luthans, and S. Lee, "New Paradigm Organizations: From Total Quality to Learning to World-Class," *Organizational Dynamics,* Winter 1994, pp. 5–19D; and A. Garvin, "Building a Learning Organization," *Harvard Business Review,* July/August 1993, pp. 78–91.

24. A. S. Miner and S. J. Mezias, "Ugly Duckling No More: Pasts and Futures of Organizational Learning Research," *Organization Science,* January–February 1996, pp. 88–99; and R. P. Mai, *Learning Partnerships: How Leading American Companies Implement Organizational Learning* (Chicago: Irwin, 1996).

25. R. Schultz, quoted in J. Martin "Are You as Good as You Think You Are?" *Fortune,* September 30, 1996, p. 146.

26. D. M. Noer, *Breaking Free: A Prescription for Personal and Organizational Change* (San Francisco: Jossey-Bass, 1996); S. F. Slater, "Learning to Change," *Business Horizons,* November–December 1995, pp. 13–20; and D. Ulrich, T. Jick, and M. Von Glinow, "High-Impact Learning: Building and Diffusing Learning Capability," *Organizational Dynamics,* Autumn 1993, pp. 52–66.

27. N. A. Wishart, J. J. Elam, D. Robey, "Redrawing the Portrait of a Learning Organization: Inside Knight-Ridder, Inc.," *Academy of Management Executive,* February 1996, pp. 7–20; C. Argyris, "Good Communication that Blocks Learning," *Harvard Business Review,* July–August 1994, pp. 77–85; and D. A. Garvin, "Building a Learning Organization," *Harvard Business Review,* July–August 1993, pp. 78–91.

28. Excerpted from J. L. Lunsford, "Lean Times: With Airbus on Its Tail, Boeing Is Rethinking How It Builds Planes," *The Wall Street Journal,* October 5, 2001, pp. A1, A16.

CHAPTER 3

1. Survey by Caliper, Princeton, NJ, 1998. Cited in A. Fisher, "Am I Too Old to Be a Tech Expert?. . . What Are Employers Really Looking For?" *Fortune,* May 25, 1998, p. 202.

2. O. Pollar, "Keeping Sane in Workplace Full of Change," *San Francisco Examiner,* July 27, 1997, p. J-3.

3. P. Sellers, "Can Chainsaw Be a Builder?" *Fortune,* January 12, 1998, pp. 118–120; Daniel Kadlec, "Is That You, Al?" *Time,* March 16, 1998, p. 38; M. Brannigan and J. S. Lublin, "Dunlap Faces a Fight Over His Severance Pay," *The Wall Street Journal,* June 16, 1998, pp. B1, B3; J. R. Hagerty and T. Parker-Pope, "A Veteran Perelman Fireman Sets Out to Resuscitate Sunbeam," *The Wall Street Journal,* June 16, 1998, pp. B1, B3; G.Strauss, T. Lowry, and D. Henry, "Sagging Profits Sink Iron-Fisted Chairman," *USA Today,* June 16, 1998, pp. 1A, 2A; D. Canedy, "Next Job? Dunlap Has Chain Saw, Will Travel," *New York Times,* June 21, 1998, sec. 3, p. 4; D. Morrison and K. Mundt, "'Chainsaw Al' Gets the Ax. What's Next for Sunbeam?" *The Wall Street Journal,* June 22, 1998, p. A22; N. Deogun and T. D. Schellhardt, "Some Lessons Learned from Two Who Felt the Ax of Al Dunlap," *The Wall Street Journal,* June 23, 1998, p. B1; H. W. Jenkins Jr., "Untalented Al? The Sorrows of a One-Trick Pony," *The Wall Street Journal,* June 24, 1998, p. A19; A. Sloan, "Chainsaw Massacre," *Newsweek,* June 29, 1998; and M. Shaffer, "'Chainsaw Al' Just Followed Orders," *San Francisco Chronicle,* June 30, 1998, p. A21.

4. R. B. Reich, "The Company of the Future," *Fast Company,* November 1998, pp. 124–150.

5. M. J. Driver, "Careers: A Review of Personnel and Organizational Research," in C. L. Cooper and I. Robertson, eds., *International Review of Industrial and Organizational Psychology* (New York: Wiley, 1988).

6. Lieber, 1998.

7. Christopher Hart, author of *Extraordinary Guarantees,* quoted in A. Comarow, "Broken? No Problem," *U.S. News & World Report,* January 11, 1999, pp. 68–69.

8. R. Langreth, M. Waldholz, S. D. Moore, "Big Drug Firms Discuss Linking Up to Pursue Disease-Causing Genes," *The Wall Street Journal,* March 4, 1999, pp. A1, A8.

9. U.S. Bureau of Labor Statistics.

10. R. Pollin, "In Politics: Savvy Organizers Win 'Living Wage' Across U.S.," *San Jose Mercury News,* December 6, 1998, pp. 1P, 6P.

11. J. Brooke, "Telemarketing Finds a Ready Labor Market in Hard-Pressed North Dakota," *New York Times,* February 3, 1997, p. A8.

12. L. Atkinson and J. Galaskiewicz, "Stock Ownership and Company Contriubtions to Charity," *Administrative Science Quarterly,* vol. 33, 1988, pp. 82–100.

13. E. Brazil, "300 Protest Gap in S.F.," *San Francisco Examiner,* March 7, 1999, p. A-2.

14. S. H. Verhovek, "Across 10 Years, Exxon Valdez Casts a Shadow," *New York Times,* March 6, 1999, pp. A1, A8; and G. Strauss, "Exxon's PR Mess Still Isn't Cleaned Up," *USA Today,* March 4, 1999, pp. 1B, 2B.

15. Bureau of Labor Statistics, report of growth rate of output per hours, 1990–2000 selected service sector industries, reported by M. J. Mandel, "Service Sector Surprises," *Business Week,* May 27, 2002, p. 30.

16. Doug, quoted in C. Sutton, "Designing Women Show Off Their Marks," *San Francisco Examiner,* March 7, 1999, p. W-33.

17. D. Foote and A. Murr, "Back on the Block," *Newsweek,* May 6, 2002, pp. 42–47.

18. M. Galanter, reported in W. Glaberson, "When the Verdict Is Just a Fantasy," *New York Times,* June 6, 1999, sec. 4 pp. 1, 6.

19. American Council on Education, reported by P. Wingert, "'F' in Global Competence," *Newsweek,* May 20, 2002, p. 11.

20. G. Allred, quoted in S. Armour, "Facing a Tough Choice: Your Ethics or Your Job," *USA Today,* September 21, 1998, p. B1.

21. L. T. Hosmer, *The Ethics of Management* (Homewood, IL: Irwin, 1987).

22. B. Kabanoff, "Equity, Equality, Power, and Conflict," *Academy of Management Review,* April 1991, pp. 416–441.

23. D. Fritzsche and H. Baker, "Linking Management Behavior to Ethical Philosophy: An Empirical Investigation," *Academy of Management Journal,* March 1984, pp. 166–175.

24. S. H. Verhovek, "Northwest Confronts Its Growth: Wild Salmon Called Endangered," *New York Times,* March 16, 1999, pp. A1, A13.

25. American Management Association, reported in M. Jackson, "Most Firms Spy on Employees, Survey Finds," *San Francisco Chronicle,* May 23, 1997, pp. B1, B4; and D. Hawkins, "Who's Watching Now?" *U.S. News & World Report,* September 15, 1997, pp. 55–58.

26. M. C. Gross, quoted in C. Hymowitz, "CEOs Set the Tone for How to Handle Questions of Ethics," *The Wall Street Journal,* December 22, 1998, p. B1.

27. A. Bennett, "Ethics Codes Spread Despite Criticism," *The Wall Street Journal,* July 15, 1988, p. 13.

28. C. Wiley, "The ABC's of Business Ethics: Definitions, Philosophies, and Implementation," *Industrial Management,* January/February 1995, pp. 22–27.

29. T. R. Mitchell, D. Daniels, H. Hopper, J. George-Falvy, and G. R. Ferris, "Perceived Correlates of Illegal Behavior in Organizations," *Journal of Business Ethics,* April 1996, pp. 439–455.

30. R. Pear, "Whistleblowers Likely to Get Stronger Federal Protections," *NewYork Times,* March 15, 1999, pp. A1, A17.

31. Study by C. C. Masten, inspector general, U.S. Department of Labor, reported in Pear, 1999.

32. R. French, quoted in R. D. Schatz and C. Poole, "The Two Bottom Lines: Profits and People," *Business Week,* December 7, 1998, pp. ENT 4, ENT 6.

33. Roper Starch Worldwide Inc. and Cone Communications 1996 survey, reported in Schatz and Poole, 1998.

34. A. B. Caroll, "The Pyramid of Corporate Responsibility: Toward the Moral Management of Organizational Stakeholders," *Business Horizons,* July/August 1991, p. 42.

35. M. Friedman, *Capitalism and Freedom* (Chicago: University of Chicago Press, 1962).

36. P. Samuelson, "Love that Corporation," *Mountain Bell Magazine,* Spring 1971.

37. A. B. Carroll, *Business & Society: Ethics and Stakeholder Management* (Cincinnati: South-Western, 1989), p. 60.

38. E. Gatewood and A. B. Carroll, "The Anatomy of Corporate Social Response," *Business Horizons,* September–October, 1981, pp. 9–16.

39. D. Eisenberg, "Eyeing the Competition," *Time,* March 22, 1999, pp. 58–59.

40. "Tech Companies to Customers: Privacy Is History" [editorial], *USA Today,* March 12, 1999, p. 14A.

41. J. Collins and J. Porras, *Built to Last: Successful Habits of Visionary Companies* (London: Century Business, 1996).

42. W. Davison, D. Worrell, and C. Lee, "Stock Market Reactions to Announced Corporate Illegalities," *Journal of Business Ethics,* December 1994, pp. 979–988.

43. M. Baucus and D. Baucs, "Paying the Piper: An Empirical Examination of Longer-Term Financial Consequences of Illegal Corporate Behavior," *Academy of Management Journal,* vol. 40, 1997, pp. 129–151.

44. R. Gildea, "Consumer Survey Confirms Corporate Social Action Affects Buying Decisions," *Public Relations Quarterly,* Winter 1994, pp. 20–21.

45. D. Turban and D. Greening, "Corporate Social Performance and Organizational Attractiveness to Prospective Employees," *Academy of Management Journal,* vol. 40, 1997, pp. 658–672.

46. J. Cloud, "Why Coors Went Soft," *Time,* November 2, 1998, p. 70.

47. O. Pollar, "Why Diversity Improves the Bottom Line," *San Francisco Examiner,* November 1, 1998, p. J-1.

48. M. Loden, *Implementing Diversity* (Chicago: Irwin, 1996), pp. 14–15.

49. H. Collingwood, "Who Handles a Diverse Work Force Best?" *Working Woman,* February 1996, p. 25.

50. B. Schlender, "Peter Drucker Takes the Long View," *Fortune,* September 28, 1998, pp. 162–173.

51. R. H. Elliott, "Human Resource Management's Role in the Future Aging of the Workforce," *Public Personnel Administration,* Spring 1995, pp. 5–7.

52. T. G. Exter, "In and Out of Work," *American Demographics,* June 1992, p. 63.

53. M. Galen and A. T. Palmer, "Diversity: Beyond the Numbers Game," *Business Week,* August 14, 1995, pp. 60–61.

54. Survey by Catalyst Inc., New York, reported in M. Deibel, "Glass Ceiling Gets Higher," *San Francisco Examiner,* March 7, 1999, pp. B-1, B-6.

55. Study by AFL-CIO and the Institute for Women's Policy Research, reported in T. Lewin, "Union Links Women's Pay to Poverty Among Families," *New York Times,* February 25, 1999, p. A17.

56. Catalyst Inc., reported in Deibel, 1999.

57. Catalyst Inc., reported in Deibel, 1999.

58. J. S. Lublin, "Women at the Top Are Still Distant from CEO Jobs," *The Wall Street Journal,* February 28, 1996, pp. B1, B4.

59. R. Sharpe, "As Leaders, Women Rule," *Business Week,* November 20, 2000, pp. 75–84.

60. Exter, 1992.

61. Galen and Palmer, 1995.

62. C. Farell, G. DeGeorge, R. A. Melcher, and S. Anderson, "Is Black Progress Set to Stall?" *Business Week,* November 6, 1995, pp. 68, 72, 76.

63. J. I. Sanchez and P. Brock, "Outcomes of Perceived Discrimination among Hispanic Employees: Is Diversity Management a Luxury or a Necessity?" *Academy of Management Journal,* June 1996, pp. 704–719.

64. F. J. Milliken and L. L. Martins, "Searching for Common Threads: Understanding the Multiple Effects of Diversity in Organizational Groups," *Academy of Management Review,* April 1996, pp. 402–433.

65. M. Conlin, "Taking Precautions—or Harassing Workers?" *Business Week,* December 3, 2001, p. 84.

66. B. E. Whitley, Jr., and M. E. Kite, "Sex Differences in Attitudes toward Homosexuality: A Comment on Oliver and Hyde (1993)," *Psychological Bulletin,* January 1995, pp. 146–154.

67. J. M. Croteau, "Research on the Work Experiences of Lesbian, Gay, and Bisexual People: An Integrative Review of Methodology and Findings," *Journal of Vocational Behavior,* April 1996, pp. 195–209; and L. Badgett, "The Wage Effects of Sexual Orientation Discrimination," *Industrial and Labor Relations Review,* July 1995, pp. 726–739.

68. D. Braddock and L. Bachelder, *The Glass Ceiling and Persons with Disabilities* (Washington, D.C.: Glass Ceiling Commission, U.S. Department of Labor, 1994).

69. K. Springen, "A Boost for Braille," *Newsweek,* May 20, 2002, p. 13.

70. D. L. Stone and A. Colella, "A Model of Factors Affecting the Treatment of Disabled Individuals in Organizations," *Academy of Management Review,* April 1996, pp. 352–401; and G. C. Pati and E. K. Baily, "Empowering People with Disabilities: Strategy and Human Resource Issues in Implementing the ADA," *Organizational Dynamics,* Winter 1995, pp. 52–69.

71. D. C. Feldman and W. H. Turnley, "Underemployment among Recent Business College Graduates," *Journal of Organizational Behavior,* November 1995, pp. 691–706.

72. "High School Dropouts by Age, Race, and Hispanic Origin: 1979 to 1993," *Statistical Abstract of the United States,* September 1995, p. 174; and S. Reese, "Illiteracy at Work," *American Demographics,* April 1996, pp. 14–15.

73. T. L. Smith, "The Resource Center: Finding Solutions for Illiteracy," *HRFocus,* February 1995, p. 7. See also A. Bernstein, "The Time Bomb in the Workforce: Illiteracy," *Business Week,* February 25, 2002, p. 122.

74. M. Loden, 1996; E. E. Spragins, "Benchmark: The Diverse Work Force," *Inc.,* January 1993, p. 33.; and A. M. Morrison, *The New Leaders: Guidelines on Leadership Diversity in America* (San Francisco: Jossey-Bass, 1992).

75. G. Dell'Orto, "Special Classes Help 3M Workers Learn How to Get Along," *San Francisco Chronicle,* June 2, 2000, p. B4.

76. S. Shellenbarger, "Please Send Chocolate: Moms Now Face Stress Moving In and Out of Work Force," *The Wall Street Journal,* May 9, 2002, p. D1. See also A. Bernstein, "Too Many Workers? Not for Long," *Business Week,* May 20, 2002, pp. 126–130.

77. J. Wise, "Manufacturing the Next Extreme Sport," *New York Times Magazine,* March 21, 1999, pp. 60–61.

78. N. Templin, "Boutique-Hotel Group Thrives on Quirks," *The Wall Street Journal,* March 18, 1999, pp. B1, B9.

79. J. M. Higgins, "Innovate or Evaporate: Seven Secrets of Innovative Corporations," *The Futurist,* September–October 1995, pp. 42–43; K.Yakal, "Now You Can Use Your Post-It Notes Electronically," *Computer Shopper,* June 1997, p. 547; and "A Notable Idea," *Selling Power,* May 1998, p. 81.

80. P. F. Drucker, *Innovation and Entrepreneurship* (New York: Harper & Row, 1986), pp. 27–28.

81. Webber, 1998.

82. Bureau of Labor Statistics, cited in Clark, 1998.

83. D. C. McClelland, *The Achieving Society* (New York: Van Nostrand, 1961); D. C. McClelland, *Human Motivation* (Glenview, IL: Scott, Foresman, 1985); D. L. Sexton and N. Bowman, "The Entrepreneur: A Capable Executive and More," *Journal of Business Venturing,* vol. 1, 1985, pp. 129–140; D. Hisrich, "Entrepreneurship/Intrapreneurship," *American Psychologist,* February 1990, p. 218; T. Begley and D. P. Boyd, "Psychological Characteristics Associated with Performance in Entrepreneurial Firms and Smaller Businesses," *Journal of Business Venturing,* vol. 2, 1987, pp. 79–93; and C. R. Kuehl and P. A. Lambing, *Small Business: Planning and Management* (Fort Worth, TX: Dryden Press, 19

84. Global Entrepreneurship Monitor, 2002 study by London Business School and Babson College, reported in J. Bailey, "Desire—More Than Need—Builds a Business," *The Wall Street Journal,* May 21, 2002, p. B4.

CHAPTER 4

1. Survey by the Zimmerman Agency for Residence Inn by Marriott, in "Things You Love to Miss," *USA Today,* March 1, 1999, p. 1B.

2. C. Bowman, "Commuter Flier Is No Longer a Rare Bird," *San Francisco Chronicle,* April 12, 1999, pp. A1, A15.

3. P. Saffo, quoted in G. P. Zachary, "It's a Bird. It's a Plane. It's a Commuter!" *San Francisco Examiner,* September 20, 1998, pp. J-1, J-2; reprinted from *The Wall Street Journal.*

4. V. Schubert-Martin, quoted in S. Armour and K. L. Alexander, 1997.

5. H. Lancaster, "Global Managers Need Boundless Sensitivity, Rugged Constitutions," *The Wall Street Journal,* October 13, 1998, p. B1.

6. These events are described in K. Maney, "Economy Embraces Truly Global Workplace," *USA Today,* December 31, 1998, pp. 1B, 2B.

7. Cellular Telecommunications Industry Association, cited in A. Dunkin, "Smart, Useful—and They Won't Put a Sag in Your Suit," *Business Week,* May 30, 1994, p. 141.

8. See J. Quittner, "Tim Berners-Lee," *Time,* March 29, 1999, pp. 193–194.

9. M. Pastore, "Online Consumer Sales Keep Increasing," *Markets Retailing,* April 23, 2000 (http://cyberatlas.internet.com/markets/retailing/article); and Forrester Research Inc., reported in "E-Commerce: It's Clicking" [editorial], *Business Week,* January 11, 1999, p. 154.

10. Odyssey, reported in S. Lohr, "Survey Suggests Consumers Are Taking to E-Commerce," *New York Times,* March 22, 1999, p. C4.

11. R. M. Kantor, quoted in K. Maney, 1998.

12. Maney, 1998.

13. N. Birdsall, quoted in C. Kleiman, "Global Knowledge Helps in Making Career Decisions," *San Jose Mercury News,* September 24, 1995, p. 1PC.

14. K. Pennar, "Two Steps Forward, One Step Back," *Business Week,* August 31, 1998, pp. 116–119.

15. C. Smadja, "Living Dangerously," *Time,* February 22, 1999, pp. 94–95.

16. N. Negroponte, quoted in Maney, 1998.

17. A. Sloan, "In the Land of Giants," *Newsweek,* August 10, 1998, pp. 42–43.

18. Sloan, 1998.

19. J. Beckett, "Going, Going, Gone—'Bay Traders' Sold on Auctions," *San Francisco Chronicle,* April 12, 1999, pp. B1, B3.

20. L. M. Hughes, quoted in C. Kleiman, "Women Can Raise Their Visibility by Pursuing Overseas Assignments," *San Jose Mercury News,* November 29, 1998, p. PC1; reprinted from *Chicago Tribune.*

21. Windham International, New York, cited in Kleiman, 1998.

22. L. O. Hallstein, reported in Kleiman, 1998.

23. The Wats House for Select Appointments, North America, in "Skills in Demand," *USA Today,* July 7, 1998, p. 1B.

24. Hallstein, reported in Kleiman, 1998.

25. A. B. Isaacs, "Tact Can Seal a Global Deal . . .," *New York Times,* July 26, 1998, sec. 3, p. 13.

26. T. L. Speer, "Gender Barriers Crumbling, Traveling Business Women Report," *USA Today,* March 16, 1999, p. 5E.

27. S. Dunung, *Doing Business in Asia: The Complete Guide* (San Francisco: Jossey-Bass, 1998), quoted in Speer, 1999.

28. The Wats House for Select Appointments, North America, 1998.

29. Anne Fisher, "Readers Weigh In on Work and Women Abroad," *Fortune,* March 29, 1999, p. 200.

30. J. Schmit, "Software Industry Grows in India," *USA Today,* February 24, 1999, pp. 1B, 2B.

31. D. A. Heenan and H. V. Perlmutter, *Multinational Organization Development* (Reading, MA: Addison-Wesley, 1979).

32. R. Kopp, "International Human Resource Policies and Practices in Japanese, European, and United States Multinationals," *Human Resource Management,* Winter 1994, pp. 581–599.

33. D. Barboza, "Pluralism under Golden Arches," *New York Times,* February 12, 1999, pp. C1, C7.

34. P. Sellters, "Who's in Charge Here?" *Fortune,* December 24, 2001, pp. 76–86.

35. M. Mendenhall, B. J. Punnett, and D. Ricks, *Global Management* (Cambridge, MA: Blackwell, 1995).

36. United Nations, *World Population Prospects: The 1996 Revision,* reported in *The Futurist,* February 1999, p. 39.

37. R. J. Bowman, "Are You Covered?" *World Trade,* March 1995, pp. 100–104.

38. Associated Press, "Punitive Tariffs Are Approved on Imports of Japanese Steel," *New York Times,* June 12, 1999, p. B3.

39. P. Visclosky, quoted in K. Klee, "The Price of Prosperity," *Newsweek,* March 29, 1999, p. 40. See also A. Mitchell, "By a Wide Margin, the House Votes Steel Import Curb," *New York Times,* March 18, 1999, pp. A1, C23.

40. J. Bhagwati, *Protectionism* (Cambridge, MA: MIT Press, 1988).

41. "WTO Telecoms Deal Will Ring in the Changes on 5 February 1998," *World Trade Organization,* January 26, 1998.

42. C. Koch, "It's a Wired, Wired World," *Webmaster,* March 1997, pp. 50–55.

43. F. Vivano, "EU Nations Seek Harmony on Immigrants," *San Francisco Chronicle,* March 5, 1999, p. A10.

44. S. Porjes, "Strengthening Diversity," *International Business,* November 1996, pp. 18–24; and M. Elliott, "Hey, Can You Spare a 'Euro'?" *Newsweek,* February 17, 1997, pp. 48–49.

45. "Fair's Fair" [letters], *West, San Jose Mercury News,* April 4, 1999, pp. 3–4.

46. "Going Global? Stifle Yourself!" *Training,* August 1995, p. 14.

47. "How Cultures Collide," *Psychology Today,* July 1976, p. 69.

48. See P. R. Harris and R. T. Moran, *Managing Cultural Differences,* 4th ed. (Houston: Gulf Publishing, 1996), pp. 223–228; and M. Hilling, "Avoid Expatriate Culture Shock," *HR Magazine,* July 1993, pp. 58–63.

49. This list is based on E. T. Hall, "The Silent Language in Overseas Business," *Harvard Business Review,* May–June 1960, pp. 87–96; and R. Knotts, "Cross-Cultural Management: Transformations and Adaptations," *Business Horizons,* January–February 1989, pp. 29–33.

50. A discussion of Japanese stereotypes in America can be found in L. Smith, "Fear and Loathing of Japan," *Fortune,* February 26, 1990, pp. 50–57.

51. G. A. Michaelson, "Global Gold," *Success,* March 1996, p. 16.

52. Harris Poll, National Foreign Language Center, reported in "Lingua Franca?" *USA Today,* February 23, 1999, p. 1A.

53. Translation services are discussed in D. Pianko, "Smooth Translations," *Management Review,* July 1996, p. 10. CompuServe's online translation service for English, French, Spanish, and German is briefly discussed in L. Alderman, "Step into Cyberspace with an E-mailbox," *Money,* April 1995, p. 174.

54. W. D. St. John, "You Are What You Communicate," *Personnel Journal,* October 1985, p. 40.

55. The importance of nonverbal communication is discussed by D. Arthur, "The Importance of Body Language," *HRFocus,* June 1995, pp. 22–23; and N. M. Grant, "The Silent Shroud: Build Bridges, Not Barriers," *HRFocus,* April 1995, p. 16.

56. Guidelines taken from R. E. Axtell, *Gestures: The Do's and Taboos of Body Language Around the World* (New York: John Wiley & Sons, 1991).

57. "How Cultures Collide," 1976.

58. Norms for cross-cultural eye contact are discussed by C. Engholm, *When Business East Meets Business West: The Guide to Practice and Protocol in the Pacific Rim* (New York: Wiley, 1991).

59. See J. A. Russell, "Facial Expressions of Emotion: What Lies Beyond Minimal Universality?" *Psychological Bulletin,* November 1995, pp. 379–391.

60. Related research is summarized by J. A. Hall, "Male and Female Nonverbal Behavior," in *Multichannel Integrations of Nonverbal Behavior,* eds. A. W. Siegman and S. Feldstein (Hillsdale, NJ: Lawrence Erlbaum, 1985), pp. 195–226.

61. A thorough discussion of cross-cultural differences is provided by Axtell, 1991. Problems with body language analysis also are discussed by C. L. Karrass, "Body Language: Beware the Hype," *Traffic Management,* January 1992, p. 27; and M. Everett and B. Wiesendanger, "What Does Body Language Really Say?" *Sales & Marketing Management,* April 1992, p. 40.

62. Results can be found in Hall, 1985.

63. J. Burgoon, "Types of Touch in Cross-Sex Relationships between Coworkers," *Applied Communication Research,* reported in D. Jones, "Females Bosses Can Touch More Freely," *USA Today,* February 19, 2002, p. 9B.

64. E. T. Hall, *The Hidden Dimension* (New York: Doubleday, 1966).

65. R. W. Moore, "Time, Culture, and Comparative Management: A Review and Future Direction," in *Advances in Comparative Management,* vol. 5. ed. S. B. Prasad (Greenwich, CT: JAI Press, 1990), pp. 7–8.

66. R. Wartzman, "In the Wake of NAFTA, a Family Firm Sees the Business Go South," *The Wall Street Journal,* February 23, 1999, pp. A1, A10.

67. Results adapted from and value definitions quoted from S. R. Safranski and I.-W. Kwon, "Religious Groups and Management Value Systems," in *Advances in International Comparative Management,* vol. 3, eds. R. N. Farner and E. G. McGoun (Greenwich, CT: JAI Press, 1988), pp. 171–183.

68. J. Pohl, "Readers' Views Differ on Buying Japanese ," letter to the editor, *Reno Gazette-Journal,* December 5, 2001, p. 9A.

CHAPTER 5

1. P. Sandman, reported in C. J. Farley, "Guarding Against Day-to-Day, Often Deadly Risks," *USA Today,* March 28, 1991, p. 6D.

2. W. F. Vitulli, quoted in R. Bahr, "Stack the Deck," *Men's Health,* August 1991, pp. 82–84.

3. Bahr, 1991.

4. Bahr, 1991.

5. D. G. Myers, *The Pursuit of Happiness: Who Is Happy—and Why* (New York: William Morrow, 1992).

6. R. Kreitner, *Management,* 7th ed. (Boston: Houghton Mifflin, 1998), p. 160.

7. M. Dell, quoted in C. Farkas and P. DeBacker, *Maximum Leadership: The World's Leading CEOs Share Their Five Strategies for Success* (New York: Henry Holt, 1996).

8. Kreitner, 1998, p. 162.

9. M. Specter, "The Phone Guy," *The New Yorker,* November 26, 2001, pp. 62–72; and J. Guyon, "Nokia Rocks Its Rivals," *Fortune,* March 4, 2002, pp. 115–118.

10. R. E. Miles and C. C. Snow, *Organizational Strategy, Structure, and Process* (New York: McGraw-Hill, 1978).

11. D. Leider, "Purposeful Work," *Utne Reader,* July/August 1988, p. 52; excerpted from *On Purpose: A Journal about New Lifestyles & Workstyles,* Winter 1986.

12. P. F. Drucker, *The Practice of Management* (New York: Harper & Row, 1954), p. 122.

13. J. Bezos, "From Zero to 10 Million in Less Than Four Years: Amazon.com to Pass E-Commerce Milestone Today," June 7, 1999, PRNewswire, Amazon.com online press release.

14. Amazon.com Web site, "About Amazon.com: Amazon.com Company Information"; and P. de Jonge, "Riding the Wild, Perilous Waters of Amazon.com," *New York Times Magazine,* March 14, 1999, pp. 36–41, 54, 68, 79–80.

15. Amazon.com 1997 Annual Report.

16. T. A. Stewart, "A Refreshing Change: Vision Statements That Make Sense," *Fortune,* September 30, 1996, pp. 195–196.

17. Gibney Jr., 1999.

18. de Jonge, 1999.

19. J. Bezos, quoted in D. Eisenberg, "Now It's One Big Market," *Time,* April 5, 1999, pp. 64–65.

20. Amazon.com 1998 Annual Report.

21. P. J. Below, G. L. Morrisey, and B. L. Acomb, *The Executive Guide to Strategic Planning* (San Francisco: Jossey-Bass, 1987), p. 2.

22. S. Khan and B. Hansen, "Routes, Type of Fliers Affect Range in Airfare Costs," *USA Today,* May 11, 1999, p. 9B; and B. De Lollis,

"Southwest Plans Non-stop, Coast-to-Coast Flights," *USA Today,* May 8, 2002, p. 1B.

23. "How Herb Keeps Southwest Hopping," *Money,* June 1999, pp. 61–62.

24. H. Kelleher, quoted in "How Herb Keeps Southwest Hopping," 1999.

25. Adapted from E. A. Locke and G. P. Latham, *A Theory of Goal Setting and Task Performance* (Englewood Cliffs, NJ: Prentice-Hall, 1990).

26. Adapted from Kreitner, 1998, p. 172, Fig. 6.4.

27. Adapted from M. Shnayerson, "Dick Snyder's Tarnished Crown," *Vanity Fair,* May 1999, pp. 110–129.

28. See Locke and Latham, 1990.

29. Drucker, 1954.

30. G. P. Latham, T. R. Mitchell, and D. L. Dossett, "Importance of Participative Goal Setting and Anticipated Rewards on Goal Difficulty and Job Performance," *Journal of Applied Psychology,* April 1978, pp. 163–171.

31. R. Rodgers and J. E. Hunter, "Impact of Management by Objectives on Organizational Productivity," *Journal of Applied Psychology,* April 1991, pp. 322–336.

32. J. W. Weiss and R. K. Wysocki, *5-Phase Project Management* (Reading, MA: Addison-Wesley, 1992), pp. 3–4.

33. A. Toffler, *Powershift: Knowledge, Wealth, and Violence at the Edge of the 21st Century* (New York: Bantam Books, 1990), pp. 196–197.

34. M. Castells, *The Rise of the Network Society* (Malden, MA: Blackwell, 1996), p. 44.

35. M. Campbell-Kelly and W. Aspray, *Computer: A History of the Information Machine* (New York: Basic Books, 1996), pp. 253–256.

36. Adapted from Weiss and Wysocki, 1992; J. K. Pinto and O. P. Kharbanda, *Successful Project Managers: Leading Your Team to Success* (New York: Van Nostrand Reinhold, 1995), pp. 17–21; and Kreitner, 1999.

37. C. Wahlstrom and B. K. Williams, *Learning Success: Being Your Best at College & Life,* 3rd ed. (Belmont, CA: Wadsworth, 2002).

38. U.S. Department of Transportation study, 1999, reported in Khan and Hansen, 1999.

39. M. Boyd, quoted in Khan and Hansen, 1999.

40. C. Shavers, "Detail vs. Strategic Thinking Can Put Workers at Odds," *San Jose Mercury News,* November 1, 1998, p. 3E.

CHAPTER 6

1. D. K. Rigby, "What's Today's Special at the Consultant's Café?" *Fortune,* September 7, 1998, pp. 162–163.

2. A. J. Slywotzky and D. J. Morrison, quoted in G. Colvin, "The Most Valuable Quality in a Manager," *Fortune,* December 29, 1997, pp. 279–280.

3. John A. Byrne, "Going Where the Money Is," *Business Week,* January 26, 1998, p. 14; review of A. J. Slywotzky and D. J. Morrison, with B. Andelman, *The Profit Zone* (New York: Times Business, 1998).

4. Colvin, 1997.

5. M. R. Porter, "What Is Strategy?" *Harvard Business Review,* November–December 1996, pp. 61–78.

6. R. Rumelt, *Strategy, Structure, and Economic Performance* (Boston: Harvard University, Graduate School of Business, 1974).

7. W. K. Schilit, "An Examination of the Influence of Middle-Level Managers in Formulating and Implementing Strategic Decisions," *Journal of Management Studies,* May 1987, pp. 271–293.

8. B. W. Barry, "A Beginner's Guide to Strategic Planning," *The Futurist,* April 1998, pp. 33–36; from B. W. Barry, *Planning Workbook for Nonprofit Organizations* (St. Paul, MN: Amherst H. Wilder Foundation, 1997).

9. A. A. Thompson Jr. and A. J. Strickland III, *Strategic Management: Concepts and Cases,* 6th ed. (Homewood, IL: BPI/Irwin, 1992); and Barry 1998.

10. Nanette Byrnes and Paul C. Judge, "Internet Anxiety," *Business Week,* June 28, 1999, pp. 79–88.

11. A. Busch III, quoted in interview with G. Hamel, "Turning Your Business Upside Down," *Fortune,* June 23, 1997, pp. 87–88.

12. Barry, 1998.

13. H. Mintzberg, "The Strategy Concept II: Another Look at Why Organizations Need Strategies," *California Management Review,* vol. 30, no. 1, 1987, pp. 25–32.

14. G. Hamel, "Killer Strategies That Make Shareholders Rich," *Fortune,* June 23, 1997, pp. 70–84.

15. Byrne, 1998.

16. C. R. Schwenk and C. B. Shrader, "Effects of Formal Strategic Planning on Financial Performance in Small Firms: A Meta-Analysis," *Entrepreneurship Theory and Practice,* Spring 1993, pp. 53–64.

17. S. V. Brull, "DVD and Conquer: Why One Technology Prevailed," *Business Week,* July 5, 1999, p. 34; J. Brinkley, "Few Tears Are Shed as Divx Joins the 8-Track," *New York Times,* June 24, 1999, p. D6; M. Fleeman, "Net Flics Soon Will Be Mouse Click Away," *San Francisco Chronicle,* May 31, 1999, pp. E1, E3; and L. Wiener, "New TVs and DVD: Wait or Buy Now?" *U.S. News & World Report,* November 24, 1997, p. 96.

18. F. R. David, "How Companies Define Their Mission," *Long Range Planning,* February 1989, pp. 90–97.

19. W. Disney, quoted in B. Nanus, *Visionary Leadership: Creating a Compelling Sense of Direction for Your Organization* (San Francisco: Jossey-Bass, 1992), p. 28; reprinted from B. Thomas, *Walt Disney: An American Tradition* (New York: Simon & Schuster, 1976), p. 247.

20. J. R. Baum, E. A. Locke, and S. A. Kirkpatrick, "A Longitudinal Study of the Relation of Vision and Vision Communication to Venture Growth in Entrepreneurial Firms," *Journal of Applied Psychology,* 1998, Vol. 83, No. 1, pp. 43–54.

21. Nanus, 1992, pp. 28–29.

22. R. Kreitner, *Management,* 7th ed. (Boston: Houghton Mifflin, 1998), p. 206.

23. C. H. Roush Jr. and B. C. Ball Jr., "Controlling the Implementation of Strategy," *Managerial Planning,* November–December 1980, p. 4.

24. Barry, 1998.

25. Barry, 1998, p. 36.

26. Booz, Allen & Hamilton study, cited in S. Winston, *The Organized Executive: New Ways to Manage Time, Paper, People & the Electronic Office,* updated and revised for the nineties (New York: W. W. Norton, 1994), p. 152.

27. O. Pollar, "Questions on Peers, Time, and Meetings," *San Francisco Examiner,* June 27, 1999, p. J-3.

28. Winston, 1994, pp. 152–157, 163–164; G. English, "How About a Good Word for Meetings?" *Management Review,* June 1990, pp. 58–60; and L. G. McDougle, "Conducting a Successful Meeting," *Personnel Journal,* January 1981.

29. R. Gibson, "Starbucks Holders Wake Up, Smell the Coffee and Sell," *The Wall Street Journal,* July 2, 1999, p. B3; C. Emert, "Why Starbucks Bid for Williams-Sonoma," *San Francisco Chronicle,* June 29, 1999, pp. C1, C7; N. Deogun, "Joe Wakes Up, Smells the Soda," *The Wall Street Journal,* June 8, 1999, pp. B1, B16; C. Burress, "Coffee Heavyweight Rattles Berkeley's 'Gourmet Ghetto,'" *San Francisco Chronicle,* June 1, 1999, p. A12; N. D. Schwartz, "Still Perking After All These Years," *Fortune,* May 24, 1999, pp. 203–210; H. Schultz and D. J. Yan, "Starbucks: Making Values Pay," *Fortune,* September 29, 1997, pp. 261–262; and J. Reese, "Starbucks: Inside the Coffee Cult," *Fortune,* December 9, 1996, pp. 190–200.

30. Kreitner, 1998, p. 214.

31. T. Mack, "Time, Money, and Patience," *Forbes,* August 21, 1989, pp. 60–62.

32. A. P. De Geus, "Planning as Learning," *Harvard Business Review,* March–April 1988, pp. 70–74; C. Knowlton, "Shell Gets Rich by Beating Risk," *Fortune,* August 26, 1991, pp. 79–82; and P. Dwyer, "The Passing of 'The Shell Man,'" *Business Week,* April 24, 1995, p. 134P.

33. J. Surowiecki, "The Return of Michael Porter," *Fortune,* February 1, 1999, pp. 135–138.

34. M. E. Porter, *Competitive Strategy* (New York: The Free Press, 1980).

35. Porter, 1980; and M. E. Porter, *The Competitive Advantage of Nations* (New York: The Free Press, 1990).

36. J. Greenberg, quoted in B. Horovitz, "Restoring the Golden-Arch Shine," *USA Today,* June 16, 1999, p. 3B.

37. Horovitz, 1999.

38. P. Connors, "J&J Decides to Discontinue Its Hismanal," *The Wall Street Journal,* June 22, 1999, p. B9.

39. R. S. Kaplan and D. P. Norton, "The Balanced Scorecard—Measures that Drive Performance," *Harvard Business Review,* January–February 1992, pp. 71–79.

40. Adapted from Kaplan and Norton, 1992, p. 72.

41. Kaplan and Norton, 1992.

42. R. Quinn, quoted in J. H. Lingle and W. A. Schiemann, "From Balanced Scorecard to Strategic Gauges: Is Measurement Worth It?" *American Management Association,* March 1996, pp. 56–61.

43. Lingle and Schiemann, 1996.

CHAPTER 7

1. H. Lancaster, "How Life Lessons Have Helped a Successful Manager," *San Francisco Sunday Examiner & Chronicle,* August 15, 1999, p. CL-33; reprinted from *The Wall Street Journal.*

2. R. L. Keeney, reported in D. Murphy, "When to Make Decisions—or Delay Them," *San Francisco Examiner,* December 6, 1998, p. J-2.

3. O. Pollar, "Six Steps for Making Tough Choices," *San Francisco Examiner & Chronicle,* April 4, 1999, p. J-3.

4. D. Canedy, "After 102 Years, Campbell Alters Soup Labels," *New York Times,* August 26, 1999, pp. C1, C7.

5. A. S. Grove, *High Output Management* (New York: Random House, 1983), p. 98.

6. The discussion of styles was based on material contained in A. J. Rowe and R. O. Mason, *Managing with Style: A Guide to Understanding, Assessing and Improving Decision Making* (San Francisco: Jossey-Bass, 1987), pp. 1–17.

7. See Rowe and Mason, 1987; and M. J. Dollinger and W. Danis, "Preferred Decision-Making Styles: A Cross-Cultural Comparison," *Psychological Reports,*1998, pp. 755–761.

8. Q. Hardy, "Iridium Shares Fall After News of Missed Goals," *The Wall Street Journal,* May 17, 1999, p. B6; D. Barboza, "Motorola Rolls Itself Over," *New York Times,* July 14, 1999, pp. C1, C2; S. Rosenbush, "Iridium Bets on New Structure," *USA Today,* August 4, 1999, p. 3B; and L. Cauley, "Iridium's Downfall: The Marketing Took a Back Seat to Science," *The Wall Street Journal,* August 18, 1999, pp. A1, A6.

9. H. A. Simon, *Administrative Behavior,* 3rd ed. (New York: Free Press, 1996); and H. A. Simon, "Making Management Decisions: The Role of Intuition and Emotion," *The Academy of Management Executive,* February 1987, pp. 57–63.

10. T. Abate, "Novell's Comeback Chief," *San Francisco Chronicle,* September 12, 1997, pp. B1, B2.

11. G. Klein, quoted in T. Petzinger Jr., "Gary Klein Studies How Our Minds Dictate Those 'Gut Feelings,'" *The Wall Street Journal,* August 7, 1998, p. B1.

12. P. Bronson, "What's the Big Idea?" *Stanford,* October 1999, pp. 70–74; excerpted from P. Bronson, *The Nudist on the Late Shift* (New York: Random House, 1999).

13. K. Liebeskind, "In the Fast Lane," *Selling Power,* September 1997, pp. 16–17.

14. A. Farnham, "Teaching Creativity Tricks to Buttoned-Down Executives," *Fortune,* January 10, 1994, pp. 94–100.

15. M. L. Woodell, "Fraud? Imagine You're in the Spotlight," *New York Times,* November 14, 1991, sec. 3, p. 11.

16. D. Canedy, "Beanie Move Giving Rise to Skepticism," *New York Times,* September 2, 1999, pp. C1, C19.

17. J. Strasburg, "Abercrombie Loses Its Shirt," *San Francisco Chronicle,* April 19, 2002, pp. B1, B3.

18. G. W. Hill, "Group versus Individual Performance: Are *n* + 1 Heads Better Than 1?" *Psychological Bulletin,* May 1982, pp. 517–539.

19. N. F. R. Maier, "Assets and Liabilities in Group Problem Solving: The Need for Integrative Function," *Psychological Review,* vol. 74, 1967, pp. 239–249.

20. Maier, 1967.

21. Methods for increasing group consensus were investigated by R. L. Priem, D. A. Harrison, and N. K. Muir, "Structured Conflict and Consensus Outcomes in Group Decision Making," *Journal of Management,* December 22, 1995, pp. 691–710.

22. See D. L. Gladstein and N. P. Reilly, "Group Decision Making under Threat: The Tycoon Game," *Academy of Management Journal,* September 1985, pp. 613–627.

23. These conclusions were based on the following studies: J. H. Davis, "Some Compelling Intuitions about Group Consensus Decisions, Theoretical and Empirical Research, and Interpersonal Aggregation Phenomena: Selected Examples, 1950–1990," *Organizational Behavior and Human Decision Processes,* June 1992, pp. 3–38; and J. A. Sniezek, "Groups Under Uncertainty: An Examination of Confidence in Group Decision Making," *Organizational Behavior and Human Decision Processes,* June 1992, pp. 124–155.

24. Supporting results can be found in J. R. Hollenbeck, D. R. Ilgen, D. J. Sego, J. Hedlund, D. A. Major, and J. Phillips, "Multilevel Theory of Team Decision Making: Decision Performance in Teams Incorporating Distributed Expertise," *Journal of Applied Psychology,* April 1995, pp. 292–316.

25. See D. H. Gruenfeld, E. A. Mannix, K. Y. Williams, and M. A. Neale, "Group Composition and Decision Making: How Member Familiarity and Information Distribution Affect Process and Performance," *Organizational Behavior and Human Decision Processes,* July 1996, pp. 1–15.

26. These guidelines were derived from Huber, 1980, p. 149. See also P. Chalos and S. Pickard, "Information Choice and Cue Use: An Experiment in Group Information Processing," *Journal of Applied Psychology,* November 1985, pp. 634–641.

27. "Jack Welch's Lessons for Success," *Fortune,* January 25, 1993, p. 86.

28. See D. Pojidaeff, "Human Productivity and Pride in Work: The Core Principles of Participative Management," *Journal for Quality and Participation,* December 1995, pp. 44–47; and N. A. Holland, "A Pathway to Global Competitiveness and Total Quality: Participative Management," *Journal for Quality and Participation,* September 1995, pp. 58–62.

29. Results are presented in J. T. Delaney, "Workplace Cooperation: Current Problems, New Approaches," *Journal of Labor Research,* Winter 1996, pp. 45–61.

30. For an extended discussion, see M. Sashkin, "Participative Management Is an Ethical Imperative," *Organizational Dynamics,* Spring 1984, pp. 4–22.

31. Supporting results can be found in C. R. Leana, R. S. Ahlbrandt, and A. J. Murrell, "The Effects of Employee Involvement Programs on Unionized Workers' Attitudes, Perceptions, and Preferences in Decision Making," *Academy of Management Journal,* October 1992, pp. 861–873; and D. Plunkett, "The Creative Organization: An Empirical Investigation of the Importance of Participation in Decision Making," *Journal of Creative Behavior,* Second Quarter 1990, pp. 140–148. Results pertaining to role conflict and ambiguity can be found in C. S. Smith and M. T. Brannick, "A Role Replication and Theoretical Extension," *Journal of Organizational Behavior,* March 1990, pp. 91–104.

32. See J. A. Wagner III, "Participation's Effects on Performance and Satisfaction: A Reconsideration of Research Evidence," *Academy of Management Review,* April 1994, pp. 312–330.

33. A through discussion of this issue is provided by W. A. Randolph, "Navigating the Journey to Empowerment," *Organizational Dynamics,* Spring 1995, pp. 19–32.

34. Employee involvement training was investigated by P. E. Tesluk, J. L. Farr, J. E. Mathieu, and R. J. Vance, "Generalization of Employee Involvement Training to the Job Setting: Individual and Situational Effects," *Personnel Psychology,* Autumn 1995, pp. 607–632.

35. See R. Rodgers, J. E. Hunter, and D. L. Rogers, "Influence of Top Management Commitment on Management Program Success," *Journal of Applied Psychology,* February 1993, pp. 151–155.

36. Results can be found in S. A. Mohrman, E. E. Lawler III, and G. E. Ledford Jr., "Organizational Effectiveness and the Impact of Employee Involvement and TQM Programs: Do Employee Involvement and TQUM Programs Work?" *Journal for Quality and Participation,* January/February 1996, pp. 6–10.

37. G. M. Parker, *Team Players and Teamwork: The New Competitive Business Strategy* (San Francisco: Jossey-Bass, 1990).

38. These recommendations were obtained from G. M. Parker, *Team Players and Teamwork: The New Competitive Business Strategy* (San Francisco, CA: Jossey-Bass, 1990).

39. A complete description of the nominal group technique can be found in A. L. Delbecq, A. H. Van de Ven, and D. H. Gustafson, *Group Techniques for Program Planning: A Guide to Nominal Group and Delphi Processes* (Glenview, IL: Scott, Foresman, 1975).

40. See N. C. Dalkey, D. L. Rourke, R. Lewis, and D. Snyder, *Studies in the Quality of Life: Delphi and Decision Making* (Lexington, MA: Lexington Books, 1972).

41. Benefits of the Delphi technique are discussed by N. I. Whitman, "The Committee Meeting Alternative: Using the Delphi Technique," *Journal of Nursing Administration,* July/August 1990, pp. 30–36.

42. A through description of computer-aided decision-making systems is provided by M. C. Er and A. C. Ng, "The Anonymity and Proximity Factors in Group Decision Support Systems," *Decision Support Systems,* May 1995, pp. 75–83; and A. LaPlante, "Brainstorming," *Forbes,* October 25, 1993, pp. 45–61.

43. Results can be found in J. S. Valacich and C. Schwenk, "Devils' Advocacy and Dialectical Inquiry Effects on Face-to-Face and Computer-Mediated Group Decision Making," *Organizational Behavior and Human Decision Processes,* August 1995, pp. 158–173; R. B. Gallupe, W. H. Cooper, M. Grise, and L. M. Bastianutti, "Blocking Electronic Brainstorms," *Journal of Applied Psychology,* February 1994, pp. 77–86; and A. R. Dennis and J. S. Valacich, "Computer Brainstorms: More Heads Are Better Than One," *Journal of Applied Psychology,* August 1993, pp. 531–537.

44. A description of the work of Daniel Gilbert appears in P. J. Hilts, "In Forecasting Their Emotions, Most People Flunk Out," *New York Times,* February 16, 1999, p. D2.

45. D. D. Wheeler and I. L. Janis, *A Practical Guide for Making Decisions* (New York: Free Press, 1980), pp. 34–35; and I. L. Janis and L. Mann, *Decision Making: A Psychological Analysis of Conflict, Choice, and Commitment* (New York: The Free Press, 1977).

46. H. Lancaster, "Academics Have to Do Their Own Homework on Job Opportunities," *The Wall Street Journal,* July 13, 1999, p. B1.

47. J. S. Lublin, "In the Race to Fill Job Vacancies, Speed Demons Win," *The Wall Street Journal,* July 13, 1999, pp. B1, B12.

48. A. Levin and L. Parker, "Human, Mechanical Flaws Cut Off Path to Survival," *USA Today,* July 12, 1999, pp. 1A, 8A, 9A.

49. Wheeler and Janis, 1980.

50. J. Drape, "For the Best Thoroughbreds, It Quickly Pays Not to Race," *New York Times,* May 2, 2002, pp. A1, C19.

51. D. Kahnemann and A. Tversky, "Judgment under Uncertainty: Heuristics and Biases," *Science,* vol. 185, 1974, pp. 1124–1131; A. Tversky and D. Kahneman, "Availability: A Heuristic for Judging Frequency and Probability," *Cognitive Psychology,* vol. 5, 1975, pp. 207–232; A. Tversky and D. Kahneman, "The Belief in the Law of Numbers," *Psychological Bulletin,* vol. 76, 1971, pp. 105–110; C. R. Schwenk, "Cognitive Simplification Processes in Strategic Decision Making," *Strategic Management Journal,* vol. 5, 1984, pp. 111–128; K. McKean, "Decisions," *Discover,* June 1985, pp. 22–31; J. Rockner, "The Escalation of Commitment to a Failing Course of Action: Toward Theoretical Progress," *Academy of Management Review,* vol. 17, 1980, pp. 39–61; D. R. Bobocel and J. P. Meyer, "Escalating Commitment to a Failing Course of Action: Separating the Roles of Choice and Justification," *Journal of Applied Psychology,* June 1994, pp. 360–363; and B. M. Shaw, "The Escalation of Commitment to a Course of Action," *Academy of Management Review,* October 1981, pp. 577–587.

52. W. Goodman, "How Gambling Makes Strange Bedfellows," *New York Times,* June 10, 1997, p. B3.

53. P. Slovic, "The Construction of a Preference," *American Psychologist,* vol. 50, 1995, pp. 364–371; and K. J. Dunegan, "Framing, Cognitive Roles, and Image Theory: Toward an Understanding of a Glass Half Full," *Journal of Applied Psychology,* vol. 78, 1993, pp. 491–503.

54. M. H. Bazerman, *Judgment in Managerial Decision Making* (New York: Wiley, 1990); D. E. Vell, H. Raiffa, and A. Tversky, *Decision Making* (Cambridge: Cambridge University Press, 1988).

55. H. J. Einhorn and R. M. Hogarth, "Confidence in Judgment: Persistence in the Illusion of Validity," *Psychological Review,* vol. 85, 1978, pp. 395–416.

56. B. Fischoff, "Hindsight ≠ Foresight: The Effect of Outcome Knowledge on Judgment under Uncertainty," *Journal of Experimental Psychology: Human Perception and Performance,* vol. 1, 1975, pp. 288–299.

CHAPTER 8

1. C. Dahle, "Women's Ways of Mentoring," *Fast Company,* September 1998, pp. 186–195; "Mentors Wanted," *Fast Company,* September 1998, p. 192; "Deadly Sins of Mentoring," *Fast Company,* September 1998, p. 194; M. Cottle, "Minding Your Mentors," *New York Times,* March 7, 1999, sec. 3, p. 8; C. Dahle, "HP's Mentor Connection," *Fast Company,* November 1998, pp. 78–80; and I. Abbott, "If You Want to Be an Effective Mentor, Consider These Tips," *San Francisco Examiner,* October 18, 1998, p. J-3.

2. A. E. Hayden, quoted in Cottle, 1999.

3. C. Dahl, *My First 60 Days,* *Fast Company,* June–July, 1998, p. 190.

4. E. H. Schein, "Organizational Culture," *American Psychologist,* vol. 45, 1990, pp. 109–119; E. H. Schein, *Organizational Culture and Leadership* (San Francisco: Jossey-Bass, 1985); and E. H. Schein, "The Role of the Founder in Creating Organizational Culture," *Organizational Dynamics,* Summer 1983, pp. 13–28.

5. R. D. Hof, "Scott McNeal's Rising Sun," *Business Week,* January 22, 1996, p. 70.

6. S. S. Watkins, in testimony before the Oversight and Investigations Subcommittee of the House Energy and Commerce Committee, U.S. Congress, February 14, 2002.

7. D. C. Hambrick and S. Finkelstein, "Managerial Discretion: A Bridge Between Polar Views of Organizational Outcomes," in L. L. Cummings and B. M. Staw, eds., *Research in Organizational Behavior* (Greenwich, CT: JAI Press, 1987), pp. 384–385.

8. P. Burrows, "Carly's Last Stand?" *Business Week,* December 24, 2001, pp. 63–70.

9. T. E. Deal and A. A. Kennedy, *Corporate Cultures: The Rites and Rituals of Corporate Life* (Reading, MA: Addison-Wesley, 1982), p. 22.

10. R. Jacob, "Corporate Reputations: The Winners Chart a Course of Constant Renewal and Work to Sustain Cultures that Produce the Very Best Products and People," *Fortune,* March 6, 1995, pp. 54–64.

11. D. Maraniss, "Lombardi's Way," *Vanity Fair,* September 1999, pp. 206–226, 231–246; excerpted from D. Maraniss, *When Pride Still Mattered: A Life of Vince Lombardi* (New York: Simon & Schuster, 1999).

12. A. Farnham, "Mary Kay's Lessons in Leadership," *Fortune,* September 20, 1993, pp. 68–77.

13. Deal and Kennedy, 1982.

14. Adapted from L. Smircich, "Concepts of Culture and Organizational Analysis," *Administrative Science Quarterly,* September 1983, pp. 339–358.

15. S. McCarney, "Airline Industry's Top-Rated Woman Keeps Southwest's Small-Fry Spirit Alive," *The Wall Street Journal,* November 30, 1996, pp. B1, B11.

16. D. Anfuso, "3M's Staffing Strategy Promotes Productivity and Pride," *Personnel Journal,* February 1995, pp. 28–34.

17. L. Seale, quoted in C. Dahle, "Fast Start: Your First 60 Days," *Fast Company,* June–July 1998, pp. 182–190.

18. D. Murphy, "Surviving and Thriving in a First Job," *San Francisco Examiner,* September 13, 1998, p. J-3.

19. Dahle, 1998; Murphy, 1998; and S. Gruner, "Lasting Impressions," *Inc.,* July 1998, p. 126.

20. R. Ailes, in "Your First Seven Seconds," *Fast Company,* June–July 1998, p. 184.

21. L. P. Frankel, in "Your First Impression," *Fast Company,* June–July 1998, p. 188.

22. P. Burrows, "The Hottest Property in the Valley?" *Business Week,* August 30, 1999, pp. 69–74.

23. C. I. Barnard, *The Functions of the Executive* (Cambridge, MA: Harvard University Press, 1938), p. 73.

24. P. M. Blau and W. R. Scott, *Formal Organizations* (San Francisco: Chandler, 1962).

25. S. E. Reed, "Helping the Poor, Phone by Phone," *New York Times,* May 26, 2002, sec. 3, p. 2.

26. S. Plant, "On the Mobile," study reported in L. Moseley, "Lords of the Ring," *Newsweek,* June 10, 2002, p. 32P.

27. S. Steklow, "Management 101," *The Wall Street Journal,* December 9, 1994, p. B1.

28. O. Pollar, "Don't Overlook the Importance of Delegating," *San Francisco Examiner,* August 8, 1999, p. J-3; D. Anderson, "Supervisors and the Hesitate to Delegate Syndrome," *Supervision,* November 1992, pp. 9–11; and E. Raudsepp, "Why Supervisors Don't Delegate," *Supervision,* May 1979, pp. 12–15.

29. R. T. Nel, "What You Say to Your Employees When You Delegate," *Supervisory Management,* December 1993, p. 13; T. Pollock, "Secrets of Successful Delegation," *Production,* December 1994, pp. 10–12; S. Caudron, "Delegate for Results," *Industry Week,* February 6, 1995, pp. 27–30; R. Morgan, "Guidelines for Delegating Effectively," *Supervision,* April 1995, pp. 20–22; J. Ninemeier, "10 Tips for Delegating Tasks," *Hotels,* June 1995, pp. 20–22; and Pollar, 1999.

30. E. H. Schein, *Organizational Psychology,* 3rd ed. (Englewood Cliffs, NJ: Prentice-Hall, 1980).

31. For an overview of the span of control concept, see D. D. Van Fleet and A. G. Bedeian, "A History of the Span of Management," *Academy of Management Review,* July 1977, pp. 356–372.

32. T. A. Stewart, "CEOs See Clout Shifting," *Fortune,* November 6, 1989, p. 66.

33. Pollar, 1999.

34. D. Machalaba, "After Crippling Chaos, Union Pacific Can See the Proverbial Light," *The Wall Street Journal,* August 25, 1999, pp. A1, A8.

35. J. Lippman, "In the Wings: Time Warner's Next Generation," *The Wall Street Journal,* July 22, 1999, pp. B1, B12.

36. L. Grant, "New Jewel in the Crown," *U.S. News & World Report,* February 28, 1994, pp. 55–57; H. Rothman, "The Power of Empowerment," *Nation's Business,* June 1993, pp. 49–52; and J. Galbraith, *Designing Complex Organizations* (Reading, MA: Addison-Wesley, 1973);

37. J. A. Byrne, "The Virtual Corporation," *Business Week,* February 8, 1993, pp. 98–102; G. Lorenzoni and C. Baden-Fuller, "Creating a Strategic Center to Manage a Web of Partners," *California Management Review,* Spring 1995, pp. 146–163.

38. R. Walker, quoted in B. Richards, "The Business Plan," *The Wall Street Journal,* November 18, 1996, pp. R10, R16.

39. P. F. Drucker, quoted in J. A. Byrne, "Advice from the Dr. Spock of Business," *Business Week,* September 28, 1987, p. 61.

40. K. Deveny, "Bag Those Fries, Squirt That Ketchup, Fry That Fish," *Business Week,* October 13, 1986, p. 86.

41. T. Burns and G. M. Stalker, *The Management of Innovation* (London: Tavistock, 1961).

42. T. J. Peters and R. H. Waterman, *In Search of Excellence* (New York: Harper & Row, 1982).

43. P. R. Lawrence and J. W. Lorsch, *Organization and Environment* (Homewood, IL: Irwin, 1967).

44. D. S. Pugh and D. J. Hickson, *Organization Structure in Its Context: The Aston Program* (Lexington, MA: D. C. Heath, 1976); and R. Z. Gooding and J. A. Wagner III, "A Meta-Analytic Review of the Relationship between Size and Performance: The Productivity and Efficiency of Organizations and Their Subunits," *Administrative Science Quarterly,* December 1985, pp. 462–481.

45. L. Smith, "Does the World's Biggest Company Have a Future?" *Fortune,* August 7, 1995, p. 124.

46. Peters and Waterman, 1982, pp. 272–273.

47. P. Parker, quoted in C. Palmeri, "A Process that Never Ends," *Forbes,* December 21, 1992, p. 55.

48. J. Woodward, *Industrial Organization: Theory and Practice* (London: Oxford University Press, 1965).

49. J. R. Kimberly, R. H. Miles, and associates, *The Organizational Life Cycle* (San Francisco: Jossey-Bass, 1980).

50. P. Gruber, quoted in A. Muoio, ed., "My Greatest Lesson," *Fast Company,* June–July 1998, pp. 83–92.

51. D. A. Garvin, "Building a Learning Organization," *Harvard Business Review,* July/August 1993, pp. 78–91; and R. Hodgetts, F. Luthans, and S. Lee, "New Paradigm Organizations: From Total Quality to Learning to World-Class," *Organizational Dynamics,* Winter 1994, pp. 5–19.

52. P. Senge, *The Fifth Discipline* (New York: Doubleday, 1990), p. 1.

53. J. B. Keys, R. M. Fulmer, and S. A. Stumpf, "Microworlds and Simuworlds: Practice Fields for the Learning Organization," *Organizational Dynamics,* Spring 1996, pp. 36–49; and F. Kogman and P. M. Senge, "Communities of Commitment: The Heart of Learning Organizations," *Organizational Dynamics,* Autumn 1993, pp. 5–23.

54. J. Case, "A Company of Businesspeople," *Inc.,* April 1993, p. 86.

CHAPTER 9

1. K. Lingle, national work-life director for KPMG, an accounting and consulting firm, quoted in C. Kleiman, "Work-Life Rewards Grow," *San Francisco Examiner,* January 16, 2000, p. J-2; reprinted from *Chicago Tribune.*

2. T. A. Stewart, "A New Way to Think about Employees," *Fortune,* April 13, 1998, pp. 169–170.

3. M. Buckingham and C. Coffman, *First, Break All the Rules: What the World's Greatest Managers Do Differently* (New York: Simon & Schuster, 1999).

4. Kimberly Scott, project leader for Hewitt Associates, which helps compile the *Fortune* list, reported in D. Murphy, "Can Morale Contribute to Safer Skies?" *San Francisco Examiner,* February 11, 200, p. J-1.

5. R. Levering and M. Moskowitz, "The 100 Best Companies to Work For," *Fortune,* January 10, 2000, pp. 82–102; and *Fortune,* January 8, 2001, pp. 148–168.

6. K. Maney, "SAS Gets Off on Right Foot with Workers, but What Does It Do?" *USA Today,* May 23, 2001, p. 3B.

7. T. D. Schellhardt, "An Idyllic Workplace Under a Tycoon's Thumb," *The Wall Street Journal,* November 23, 1998, pp. B1, B4.

8. J. Welch, quoted in N. M. Tichy and S. Herman, *Control Your Destiny or Someone Else Will: How Jack Welch Is Making*

General Electric the World's Most Competitive Corporation (New York: Doubleday, 1993), p. 251.

9. K. Connors, quoted in S. Lawrence, "Voices of HR Experience," *Personnel Journal,* April 1989, p. 69; reported in R. Kreitner, *Management,* 7th ed. (Boston: Houghton Mifflin, 1998), pp. 319–320.

10. P. Cappelli and A. Crocker-Hefter, "Distinctive Human Resources Are Firms' Core Competencies," *Organizational Dynamics,* Winter 1996, pp. 7–22.

11. R. J. Mirabile, "The Power of Job Analysis," *Training,* April 1990, pp. 70–74; and S. F. Mona, "The Job Description," *Association Management,* February 1991, pp. 33–37.

12. J. Useem, "For Sale Online: You," *Fortune,* July 5, 1999, pp. 67–78.

13. E. Wasserman, "Human Resources Using Net Resources," *San Jose Mercury News,* May 25, 1997, pp. 1D–2D.

14. S. Armour, "Companies Put Web to Work as Recruiter," *USA Today,* January 25, 2000, p. 1B.

15. B. Schneider and N. Schmitt, *Staffing Organizations,* 2nd ed. (Glenview, IL: Scott, Foresman, 1986).

16. G. McWilliams, "The Best Way to Find a Job," *The Wall Street Journal,* December 6, 1999, pp. R16, R22.

17. D. E. Terpstra, "The Search for Effective Methods," *HRFocus,* May 1996, pp. 16–17; and J. P. Kirnan, J. A. Farley, and K. F. Geisinger, "The Relationship between Recruiting Source, Applicant Quality, and Hire Performance: An Analysis by Sex, Ethnicity, and Age," *Personnel Psychology,* Summer 1989, pp. 293–308.

18. B. M. Meglino, A. S. DeNisi, S. A. Youngblood, and K. J. Williams, "Effects of Realistic Job Previews: A Comparison Using an Enhancement and a Reduction Preview," *Journal of Applied Psychology,* vol. 73, 1981, pp. 259–266.

19. Data from American Psychological Association and Certified Reference Checking Co. reported in S. McManis, "Little White-Collar Lies," *San Francisco Chronicle,* October 1, 1999, pp. B1, B3.

20. McManis, 1999.

21. S. Armour, "Firms Key Up PCs for Job Screening," *USA Today,* October 20, 1997, p. 6B.

22. B. Weinstein, "Prescreened Interviews Are Catching On," *San Francisco Sunday Examiner & Chronicle,* February 21, 1999, p. CL-21.

23. M. Messmer, quoted in "Honesty Counts in Job Interview," *The Futurist,* July–August 1997, p. 49.

24. D. Stamps, "Cyberinterviews Combat Turnover," *Training,* August 1995, p. 16.

25. E. D. Pursell, M. A. Campion, and S. R. Gaylord, "Structured Interviewing: Avoiding Selection Problems," *Personnel Journal,* November 1980.

26. E. D. Pursell, M. A. Campion, and S. R. Gaylord, "Structured Interviewing: Avoiding Selection Problems," *Personnel Journal,* November 1980, pp. 907–912; J. M. Jenks and B. L. P. Zevnik, "ABCs of Interviewing," *Harvard Business Review,* July–August 1989, pp. 38–42; T. F. Case, "Making the Most of a Selection Interview," *Personnel,* September 1990, pp. 41–43; T. Mullins, reported in "How to Land a Job," *Psychology Today,* September/October 1994, pp. 12–13; S. Urquhart-Brown, "When You're Ready to Hire an Employee," *San Francisco Examiner,* March 28, 1999, p. J-3; and D. Murphy, "Choice Advice," *San Francisco Examiner,* November 15, 1998, pp. J-1, J-2.

27. H. Lancaster, "Making a Good Hire Takes a Little Instinct and a Lot of Research," *The Wall Street Journal,* March 3, 1998, p. B1.

28. M. P. Cronin, "This Is a Test," *Inc.,* August 1993, pp. 64–68.

29. S. Adler, "Personality Tests for Salesforce Selection: Worth a Fresh Look," *Review of Business,* Summer/Fall 1994, pp. 27–31.

30. S. Shellenbarger, "Companies Are Finding It Really Pays to Be Nice to Employees," *The Wall Street Journal,* July 22, 1998, p. B1.

31. Brookings Institution, cited in Shellenbarger, 1998.

32. MCI Communications surveys, reported in Shellenbarger, 1998.

33. G. R. Jones, "Organizational Socialization as Information Processing Activity: A Life History Analysis," *Human Organization,* vol. 42, no. 4, 1983, pp. 314–320.

34. E. Lawler, reported in S. Ross, "Worker Involvement Pays Off," *San Francisco Examiner,* November 15, 1998, p. J-2.

35. "1996 Industry Report," *Training,* October 1996, pp. 37–39.

36. "1996 Industry Report," 1996.

37. L. Koss-Feder, "Brushing Up from the Boardroom to the Back Office," *Time,* July 20, 1998, p. B5.

38. A. C. Oberg, "Surfing for a Degree on the Internet," *USA Today,* June 10, 1999, p. 13A.

39. B. Muirhead, "Looking at Net Colleges" [letter], *USA Today,* November 12, 1999, p. 14A.

40. C. Hymowitz, "Why Managers Take Too Long to Fire Employees," *San Francisco Examiner,* February 21, 1999, p. J-2; reprinted from *The Wall Street Journal.*

41. L. B. Combings and D. P. Schwab, *Performance in Organizations: Determinants and Appraisal* (Glenview, IL: Scott, Foresman, 1973).

42. H. Lancaster, "Why Bosses Are Encouraging Workers to Review Themselves," *San Francisco Examiner,* February 28, 1999, p. J-2; reprinted from *The Wall Street Journal.*

43. F. Hazucha, S. A. Hezlett, and R. J. Schneider, "The Impact of 360-Degree Feedback on Managerial Skills Development," *Human Resource Management,* Summer/Fall 1993, p. 42.

44. J. R. Morris, *Employee Benefits* (Washington, DC: U.S. Chamber of Commerce, 1986).

45. Adapted from D. L. McClain, "Tricks for Motivating the Pay to Motivate the Ranks," *New York Times,* November 15, 1998, sec. 3, p. 5.

46. A. Etzioni, "Americans Could Teach Austrians about Diversity," *USA Today,* February 14, 2000, p. 19A.

47. A. Fisher, "Dumping Troublemakers, and Exiting Gracefully," *Fortune,* February 15, 1999, p. 174.

48. Hymowitz, 1999.

49. R. Moss Kanter, "Show Humanity When You Show Employees the Door," *The Wall Street Journal,* September 21, 1997, p. A22.

50. Moss Kanter, 1997.

51. G. Skoning, "Explanations of Sexual Harassment: Are They Viable Defenses?" *HRMagazine,* July 1998, pp. 130–134; D. R. Sandler, "Sexual Harassment Rulings: Less Than Meets the Eye," *HRMagazine,* October 1998, pp. 136–143; M. Maremont, "A Case Puts a Value on Touching and Fondling," *The Wall Street Journal,* May 25, 1999, pp. B1, B4; and R. Ganzel, "What Sexual Harassment Training Really Prevents," *Training,* October 1998, pp. 86–94.

52. *Public Health Report,* U.S. Department of Health and Human Services, June 1991, pp. 280–292.

53. "Prevent Sexual Harassment," California University, www.cup.edu/women/prsh.htm.

CHAPTER 10

1. T. J. Fadem, quoted in O. Port and J. Carey, "Getting to 'Eureka!'" *Business Week,* November 10, 1997, pp. 72–75.

2. C. Hymowitz, "Task of Managing in Workplace Takes a Careful Hand," *The Wall Street Journal,* July 1, 1997, p. B1.

3. T. Peters, "A Brawl with No Rules," *Forbes ASAP,* February 21, 2000, p. 155.

4. M. McGuinn, quoted in Hymowitz, 1997.

5. G. Kawasaki with M. Moreno, *Rules for Revolutionaries: The Capitalist Manifesto for Creating and Marketing New Products and Services* (New York: HarperBusiness, 1999); P. Carbonara, "What Do You Do with a Great Idea?" *Your Company,* August/September 1998, pp. 26–31; Port and Carey, 1997; and Hymowitz, 1997.

6. L. Jennings and J. Minerd, "Cybertrends Shaping Tomorrow's Marketplace," *The Futurist,* March 1999, pp. 12–14; N. D. Schwartz, "The Tech Boom Will Keep on Rocking," *Fortune,* February 15, 1999, pp. 64–80; and P. Drucker, "The Future that Has Already Happened," *The Futurist,* November 1998, pp. 16–18;

7. P. Robertson, D. Roberts, and J. Porras, "Dynamics of Planned Organizational Change: Assessing Empirical Support for a Theoretical Model," *Academy of Management Journal,* vol. 36, no. 3, 1993, pp. 619–634.

8. "J&J Is on a Roll," *Fortune,* December 26, 1994, pp. 178–192; S. Siwolop and C. Eklund, "The Capsule Controversy: How Far Should the FDA Go?" *Business Week,* March 3, 1986, p. 37; and "After Its Recovery, New Headaches for Tylenol," *Business Week,* May 14, 1984, p. 137.

9. K. Kerwin, M. Stepanek, and D. Welch, At Ford, E-Commerce Is Job 1," *Business Week,* February 28, 2000, pp. 74–78; and D. Welch, "Fear and Loathing in the Showroom," *Business Week,* February 28, 2000, p. 78.

10. J. Waggoner, "Information Age Losing Memory," *USA Today,* October 22, 1999, pp. 1B, 2B.

11. P. Dusenberry, "The Challenges of Managing Creative People," *USA Today,* November 20, 1997, p. 4B.

12. D. Carvajal, "Virtual Publishing: From Arthur Clarke to Psoriasis Tales," *New York Times,* December 7, 2000, pp. A1, A16; K. Terrell, "E-Books Struggle to Replace Type on Paper," *U.S. News & World Report,* January 31, 2000, pp. 58–59; V. Hua, "Doing Business by the Book," *San Francisco Examiner,* January 16, 2000, pp. B-1, B-3; A. Klein, "Will the Future Be Written in E-Ink?" *The Wall Street Journal,* January 4, 2000, pp. B1, B4; D. Carvajal, "Racing to Convert Books to Bytes," *New York Times,* December 9, 1999, pp. C1, C27; and L. Guernsey, "Beyond Neon: Electronic Ink," *New York Times,* June 3, 1999, p. D11.

13. This three-way typology of change was adapted from discussion in P. C. Nutt, "Tactics of Implementation," *Academy of Management Journal,* June 1986, pp. 230–261.

14. Radical organizational change is discussed by T. E. Vollmann, *The Transformational Imperative* (Boston: Harvard Business School Press, 1996); and J. A. Neal and C. L. Tromley, "From Incremental Change to Retrofit: Creating High-Performance Work Systems," *Academy of Management Executive,* February 1995, pp. 42–53.

15. L. N. Spiron, T. J. Mullaney, and L. Lee, "Bullish on the Internet," *Business Week,* July 14, 1999, pp. 45–46; M. J. Mandell, "Can Merrill Be a Maverick?" *Business Week,* July 14, 1999, p. 46; and C. M. Christensen, *The Innovator's Dilemma: When New Technologies Cause Great Firms to Fail* (Cambridge, MA: Harvard Business School Press, 1997).

16. K. Lewin, *Field Theory in Social Science* (New York: Harper & Row, 1951).

17. The role of learning within organizational change is discussed by C. Hendry, "Understanding and Creating Whole Organizational Change through Learning Theory," *Human Relations,* May 1996, pp. 621–641; and D. Ready, "Mastering Leverage, Leading Change," *Executive Excellence,* March 1995, pp. 18–19.

18. C. Goldwasser, "Benchmarking: People Make the Process," *Management Review,* June 1995, p. 40.

19. R. Kreitner and A. Kinicki, *Organizational Behavior,* 4th ed. (Burr Ridge, IL: Irwin/McGraw-Hill, 1998), p. 619.

20. J. P. Kotter, "Leading Change: Why Transformation Efforts Fail," *Harvard Business Review,* March–April 1995, pp. 59–67; and J. P. Kotter, *Leading Change* (Boston: Harvard Business School Press, 1996).

21. M. B. Grover, "Preshrunk," *Forbes,* March 6, 2000, pp. 82–84.

22. M. Fugate, A. Kinicki, and C. L. Scheck, "Coping with an Organizational Merger over Four Stages," *Personal Psychology,* in press.

23. An historical overview of the field of OD can be found in J. Sanzgiri and J. Z. Gottlieb, "Philosophic and Pragmatic Influences on the Practice of Organization Development, 1950–2000," *Organizational Dynamics,* Autumn 1992, pp. 57–69.

24. W. W. Burke, *Organization Development: A Normative View* (Reading, MA: Addison-Wesley, 1987), p. 9.

25. The role of values and ethics in OD is discussed by M. McKendall, "The Tyranny of Change: Organizational Development Revisited," *Journal of Business Ethics,* February 1993, pp. 93–104.

26. W. L. French and C. H. Bell Jr., *Organization Development: Behavioral Interventions for Organizational Improvement* (Englewood Cliffs, NJ: Prentice-Hall, 1978); and E. F. Huse and T. G. Cummings, *Organizational Development and Change,* 3rd ed. (St. Paul: West, 1985).

27. D. A. Nadler, *Feedback and Organizational Development: Using Data-Based Methods* (Reading, MA: Addison-Wesley, 1977).

28. P. J. Robertson, D. R. Roberts, and J. I. Porras, "Dynamics of Planned Organizational Change: Assessing Empirical Support for a Theoretical Model," *Academy of Management Journal,* June 1993, pp. 619–634; and G. A. Neuman, J. E. Edwards, and N. S. Raju, "Organizational Development Interventions: A Meta-Analysis of Their Effects on Satisfaction and Other Attitudes," *Personnel Psychology,* August 1989, pp. 461–489.

29. J. M. Nicholas, "The Comparative Impact of Organization Development Interventions on Hard Criteria Measures," *Academy of Management Review,* October 1982, pp. 531–542.

30. W. W. Burke, L. P. Clark, and C. Koopman, "Improve Your OD Project's Chances for Success," *Training and Development Journal,* September 1984, pp. 62–68.

31. R. J. Schaffer and H. A. Thomson, "Successful Change Programs Begin with Results," *Harvard Business Review,* January–February 1992, pp. 80–89.

32. R. Rodgers, J. E. Hunter, and D. L. Rodgers, "Influence of Top Management Commitment on Management Program Success," *Journal of Applied Psychology,* February 1993, pp. 151–155.

33. Neuman, Edwards, and Raju, 1989.

34. W. G. Dyer, *Team Building: Current Issues and New Alternatives,* 3rd ed. (Reading, MA: Addison-Wesley, 1995).

35. C. C. Mann, "The SlashDot Effect," *Forbes ASAP,* February 21, 2000, pp. 43–50.

36. S. Baker, "How to Keep the Idea Pot Bubbling," *Business Week,* October 20, 1997, pp. 15–18.

37. G. C. O'Connor, quoted in Port and Carey, 1997.

38. A. V. Bhidé, quoted in G. Gendron, "The Origin of the Entrepreneurial Species," *Inc.,* February 2000, pp. 105–114.

39. J. Yaukey, "Disposable Cell Phones Will Reach Retail Soon," *Reno Gazette-Journal,* October 22, 2001, p. 1E; and D. Pogue, "Cellphones for a Song, Just in Case," *New York Times,* September 27, 2001, pp. D1, D7.

40. B. Evangelista, "Movies by Mail: Netflix.com Makes Renting DVDs Easy," *San Francisco Chronicle,* January 26, 2002, p. B1.

41. R. Moss Kanter, *The Change Masters* (New York: Simon & Schuster, 1983).

42. T. Kuczmarski, "Inspiring and Implementing the Innovation Mind-Set," *Planning Review,* September–October 1994, pp. 37–48; and L. K. Gundry, J. R. Kickul, and C. W. Prather, "Building the Creative Organization," *Organizational Dynamics,* Spring 1994, pp. 22–36.

43. T. J. Martin, "Ten Commandments for Managing Creative People," *Fortune,* January 16, 1995, pp. 135–136; B. Schneider, S. K. Gunnarson, and K. Niles-Jolly, "Creating the Climate and Culture of Success," *Organizational Dynamics,* Spring 1994, pp. 22–36; T. Katauskas, "Follow-Through: 3M's Formula for Success," *R&D,* November 1990; and R. Mitchell, "Masters of Innovation: How 3M Keeps Its New Products Coming," *Business Week,* April 10, 1989, pp. 58–63.

44. Adapted from eight steps in K. M. Bartol and D. C. Martin, *Management,* 3rd ed. (Burr Ridge, IL: Irwin/McGraw-Hill, 1998), pp. 360–363.

45. Carbonara, 1998.

46. T. J. Allen and S. I. Cohen, "Information Flow in Research and Development Laboratories," *Administrative Science Quarterly,* March 1969, pp. 12–19.

47. Moss Kanter, 1983.

CHAPTER 11

1. Survey by Gallup Organization, reported in S. L. Lynch, "Gen Xers Sharpen Work Skills," *San Francisco Chronicle,* September 7, 1998, p. A2.

2. O. Pollar, "Managing the MTV Generation," *San Francisco Examiner & Chronicle,* June 15, 1997, p. J-3.

3. R. Zemke, C. Raines, and B. Filipczak, *Generations at Work: Managing the Clash of Veterans, Boomers, Xers and Nexters in Your* Workplace (New York: AMACOM, 1999); J. Minerd, "Bringing Out the Best in Generation X," *The Futurist,* January 1999, pp. 6–7; "19 to 33 Years Old," *San Francisco Examiner,* March 7, 1999, special section, pp. W-1–W-34; Lynch, 1998; Pollar, 1997; S. Armour, "Xers Mark the Workplace," *USA Today,* October 13, 1997, p. 5B; and M. Hornblower, "Great Xpectations," *Time,* June 9, 1997, pp. 58–68.

4. See M. Rokeach, *Beliefs, Attitudes, and Values* (San Francisco: Jossey-Bass, 1968), p. 168.

5. M. Rokeach, *The Nature of Human Values* (New York: Free Press, 1973).

6. Families and Work Institute, cited in C. Shavers, "Qualities that Make Working with Gen Xers a Special Challenge," *San Jose Mercury News,* December 6, 1998, p. 3E.

7. For a discussion of the difference between attitudes and values, see B. W. Becker and P. E. Connor, "Changing American Values—Debunking the Myth," *Business,* January–March 1985, pp. 56–59.

8. J. Schaubroeck, D. C. Ganster, and B. Kemmerer, "Does Trait Affect Promote Job Attitude Stability?" *Journal of Organizational Behavior,* March 1996, pp. 191–196.

9. B. M. Shaw and J. Ross, "Stability in the Midst of Change: A Dispositional Approach to Job Attitudes," *Journal of Applied Psychology,* August 1985, pp. 469–480.

10. J. S. Becker, "Empirical Validation of Affect, Behavior, and Cognition as Distinct Components of Attitude," *Journal of Personality and Social Psychology,* May 1984, pp. 1191–1205.

11. L. Festinger, *A Theory of Cognitive Dissonance* (Stanford, CA: Stanford University Press, 1957).

12. Described in R. Plotnik, *Introduction to Psychology,* 3rd ed. (Pacific Grove, CA: Brooks/Cole, 1993), p. 602; based on account in *Los Angeles Times,* June 14, 1989.

13. S. Bok, cited in E. Venant, "A Nation of Cheaters," *San Francisco Chronicle,* January 7, 1992, p. D3; reprinted from *Los Angeles Times.*

14. A. Dobrzeniecki, quoted in D. Butler, "MIT Students Guilty of Cheating," *Boston Globe,* March 2, 1991, p. 25.

15. I. Jacobsen, Jacobsen Consulting, "IanSights, New Years, 2002– e-mail version," January 7, 2002, ian@jacobsenconsulting.com

16. For a review of the development of the JDI, see P. C. Smith, L. M. Kendall, and C. L. Hulin, *The Measurement of Satisfaction in Work and Retirement* (Skokie, IL: Rand McNally, 1969).

17. R. Kreitner and A. Kinicki, *Organizational Behavior,* 5th ed. (Burr Ridge, IL: Irwin/McGraw-Hill, 2001), p. 227.

18. See C. Ostroff, "The Relationship between Satisfaction, Attitudes, and Performance: An Organizational Level Analysis," *Journal of Applied Psychology,* December 1992, pp. 963–974.

19. See S. P. Brown, "A Meta-Analysis and Review of Organizational Research on Job Involvement," *Psychological Bulletin,* September 1996, pp. 235–255.

20. See R. P. Tett and J. P. Meyer, "Job Satisfaction, Organizational Commitment, Turnover Intention, and Turnover: Path Analysis Based on Meta-Analytic Findings," *Personnel Psychology,* Summer 1993, pp. 259–293.

21. See J. E. Mathieu and D. Zajac, "A Review and Meta-Analysis of the Antecedents, Correlates, and Consequences of Organizational Commitment," *Psychological Bulletin,* September 1990, pp. 171–194.

22. 2000 study by Development Dimensions International, Pittsburgh, reported in "Replacing Key People Has Many Hidden Costs," *San Francisco Chronicle,* December 24, 2000, p. J1; reprinted from *Boston Globe.*

23. For evidence of the stability of adult personality dimensions, see R. R. McCrae, "Moderated Analyses of Longitudinal Personality Stability," *Journal of Personality and Social Psychology,* September 1993, pp. 577–585. Adult personality changes are documented in L. Kaufman Cartwright and P. Wink, "Personality Change in Women Physicians from Medical Student to Mid-40s," *Psychology of Women Quarterly,* June 1994, pp. 291–308.

24. The landmark report is J. M. Digman, "Personality Structure: Emergence of the Five-Factor Model," *Annual Review of Psychology,* vol. 41, 1990, pp. 417–440. Also see M. R. Barrick and M. K. Mount, "Autonomy as a Moderator of the Relationships between the Big Five Personality Dimensions and Job Performance," *Journal of Applied Psychology,* February 1993, pp. 111–118; J. A. Johnson and F. Ostendorf, "Clarification of the Five-Factor Model with the Abridged Big Five Dimensional Circumplex," *Journal of Personality and Social Psychology,* September 1993, pp. 563–576; and M. Zuckerman, D. M. Kuhlman,

J. Joireman, P. Teta, and M. Kraft, "A Comparison of Three Structural Models for Personality: The Big Three, the Big Five, and the Alternative Five," *Journal of Personality and Social Psychology,* October 1993, pp. 757–768.

25. M. R. Barrick and M. K. Mount, "The Big Five Personality Dimensions and Job Performance: A Meta-Analysis," *Personnel Psychology,* Spring 1991, pp. 1–26.

26. Barrick and Mount, 1991, p. 18.

27. See M. P. Cronin, "This Is a Test," *Inc,* August 1993, pp. 64–68.

28. For an overall view of research on locus of control, see P. E. Spector, "Behavior in Organizations as a Function of Employee's Locus of Control," *Psychological Bulletin,* May 1982, pp. 482–497; the relationship between locus of control and performance and satisfaction is examined in D. R. Norris and R. E. Niebuhr, "Attributional Influences on the Job Performance–Job Satisfaction Relationship," *Academy of Management Journal,* June 1984, pp. 424–431; salary differences between internals and externals were examined by P. C. Nystrom, "Managers' Salaries and Their Beliefs about Reinforcement Control," *The Journal of Social Psychology,* August 1983, pp. 291–292.

29. See, for example, V. Gecas, "The Social Psychology of Self-Efficacy," in *Annual Review of Sociology,* eds. W. R. Scott and J. Blake (Palo Alto, CA: Annual Reviews, 1989), vol. 15, pp. 291–316; and C. K. Stevens, A. G. Bavetta, and M. E. Gist, "Gender Differences in the Acquisition of Salary Negotiation Skills: The Role of Goals, Self-Efficacy, and Perceived Control," *Journal of Applied Psychology,* October 1993, pp. 723–735.

30. J. Barling and R. Beattle, "Self-Efficacy Beliefs and Sales Performance," *Journal of Organizational Behavior Management,* Spring, 1983, pp. 41–51.

31. For more on learned helplessness, see M. J. Martinko and W. L. Gardner, "Learned Helplessness: An Alternative Explanation for Performance Deficits," *Academy of Management Review,* April 1982, pp. 195–204.

32. W. S. Silver, T. R. Mitchell, and M. E. Gist, "Response to Successful and Unsuccessful Performance: The Moderating Effect of Self-Efficacy on the Relationship between Training and Newcomer Adjustment," *Journal of Applied Psychology,* April 1995, pp. 211–225.

33. See P. C. Earley and T. R. Lituchy, "Delineating Goal and Efficacy Effects: A Test of Three Models," *Journal of Applied Psychology,* February 1991, pp. 81–98.

34. The positive relationship between self-efficacy and readiness for retraining is documented in L. A. Hill and J. Elias, "Retraining Midcareer Managers: Career History and Self-Efficacy Beliefs," *Human Resource Management,* Summer 1990, pp. 197–217.

35. J. Brockner, *Self-Esteem at Work* (Lexington, MA: Lexington Books, 1988); and V. Gecas, "The Self-Concept," in *Annual Review of Sociology,* eds. R. H. Turner and J. F. Short Jr. (Palo Alto, CA: Annual Reviews, 1982), vol. 8.

36. J. L. Pierce, D. G. Gardner, L. L. Cummings, and R. B. Dunham, "Organization-Based Self-Esteem: Construct Definition, Measurement, and Validation," *Academy of Management Journal,* September 1989, p. 625.

37. Practical steps are discussed in M. Kaeter, "Basic Self-Esteem," *Training,* August 1993, pp. 31–35.

38. J. W. McGuire and C. V. McGuire, "Enhancing Self-Esteem by Directed-Thinking Tasks: Cognitive and Affective Positivity Asymmetries," *Journal of Personality and Social Psychology,* June 1996, p. 1124.

39. Adapted from discussion in J. K. Matejka and R. J. Dunsing, "Great Expectations," *Management World,* January 1987, pp. 16–17.

40. M. Snyder and S. Gangestad, "On the Nature of Self-Monitoring: Matters of Assessment, Matters of Validity," *Journal of Personality and Social Psychology,* July 1986, p. 125.

41. Data from M. Kilduff and D. V. Day, "Do Chameleons Get Ahead? The Effects of Self-Monitoring on Managerial Careers," *Academy of Management Journal,* August 1994, pp. 1047–1060.

42. See F. Luthans, "Successful vs. Effective Managers," *Academy of Management Executive,* May 1988, pp. 127–132.

43. J. Pierson, "Preparing for 2000, Census Bureau Tests Carrots vs. Sticks," *The Wall Street Journal,* May 2, 1996, p. B1.

44. D. Dearborn and H. Simon, "Selection Perception: A Note on the Departmental Identification of Executives," *Sociometry,* vol. 21, 1958, pp. 140–144.

45. I. K. Broverman, S. Raymond Vogel, D. M. Broverman, F. E. Clarkson, and P. S. Rosenkrantz, "Sex-Role Stereotypes: A Current Appraisal," *Journal of Social Issues,* 1972, p. 75.

46. B. P. Allen, "Gender Stereotypes Are Not Accurate: A Replication of Martin (1987) Using Diagnostic vs. Self-Report and Behavioral Criteria," *Sex Roles,* May 1995, pp. 583–600.

47. J. Landau, "The Relationship of Race and Gender to Managers' Ratings of Promotion Potential," *Journal of Organizational Behavior,* July 1995, pp. 391–400.

48. S. R. Rhodes, "Age-Related Differences in Work Attitudes and Behavior: A Review and Conceptual Analysis," *Psychological Bulletin,* March 1983, pp. 38–367.

49. See G. M. McEvoy, "Cumulative Evidence of the Relationship between Employee Age and Job Performance," *Journal of Applied Psychology,* February 1989, pp. 11–17; D. A. Waldman and B. J. Avolio, "Aging and Work Performance in Perspective: Contextual and Developmental Considerations," in *Research in Personnel and Human Resources Management,* ed. G. R. Ferris (Greenwich, CT: JAI Press, 1993), vol. 11, pp. 133–162; and B. J. Avolio, D. A. Waldman, and M. A. McDaniel, "Age and Work Performance in Nonmanagerial Jobs: The Effects of Experience and Occupational Type," *Academy of Management Journal,* June 1990, pp. 407–422.

50. M. C. Healy, M. Lehman, and M. A. McDaniel, "Age and Voluntary Turnover: A Quantitative Review," *Personnel Psychology,* Summer 1995, pp. 335–345; and J. J. Martocchio, "Age-Related Differences in Employee Absenteeism: A Meta-Analysis," *Psychology and Aging,* December 1989, pp. 409–414.

51. M. Galen and A. T. Palmer, "Diversity: Beyond the Numbers Game," *Business Week,* August 14, 1995, pp. 60–61.

52. See E. Hatfield and S. Sprecher, *Mirror, Mirror . . . The Importance of Looks in Everyday Life* (Albany, NY: State University of New York Press, 1986); K. Dion, "Stereotyping Based on Physical Attractiveness: Issues and Conceptual Perspectives," in *Physical Appearance, Stigma, and Social Behavior: The Ontario Symposium on Personality and Social Psychology,* eds. C. P. Herman, M. P. Zanna, and E. T. Higgins (Hillsdale, NJ: Erlbaum), vol. 3; J. C. Brigham, "Limiting Conditions of the 'Physical Attractiveness Stereotype': Attributions About Divorce," *Journal of Research and Personality,* vol. 14, 1980, pp. 365–375; M. M. Clifford and E. H. Walster, "The Effect of Physical Attractiveness on Teacher Expectation," *Sociology of Education,* vol. 46, 1973; pp. 248–258; and G. R. Adams and T. L. Huston, "Social Perception of Middle-Aged Persons Varying in Physical Attractiveness," *Developmental Psychology,* vol. 11, 1975, pp. 657–658.

53. Clifford and Walster, 1973.

54. T. Cash and L. H. Janda, "The Eye of the Beholder," *Psychology Today,* December 1984, pp. 46–52.

55. R. P. Quinn, "Physical Deviance and Occupational Mistreatment: The Short, The Fat, and the Ugly," master's thesis, University of Michigan Survey Research Center, University of Michigan, Ann Arbor, 1978.

56. See D. Eden and Y. Zuk, "Seasickness as a Self-Fulfilling Prophecy: Raising Self-Efficacy to Boost Performance at Sea," *Journal of Applied Psychology,* October 1995, pp. 628–635. For a thorough review of research on the Pygmalion effect, see D. Eden, *Pygmalion in Management: Productivity as a Self-Fulfilling Prophecy* (Lexington, MA: Lexington Books, 1990), ch. 2.

57. See B. Schlender, "How Bill Gates Keeps the Magic Going," *Fortune,* June 18, 1990, pp. 82–89.

58. These recommendations were adapted from J. Keller, "Have Faith—in You," *Selling Power,* June 1996, pp. 84, 86; and R. W. Goddard, "The Pygmalion Effect," *Personnel Journal,* June 1985, p. 10.

59. H. H. Kelley, "The Processes of Causal Attribution," *American Psychologist,* February 1973, pp. 107–128.

60. S. J. Linton and L.E. Warg, "Attributions (Beliefs) and Job Satisfaction Associated with Back Pain in an Industrial Setting," *Perceptual and Motor Skills,* February 1993, pp. 51–62.

61. W. S. Silver, T. R. Mitchell, and M. E. Gist, "Responses to Successful and Unsuccessful Performance: The Moderating Effect of Self-Efficacy on the Relationship between Performance and Attributions," *Organizational Behavior and Human Decision Processes,* June 1995, pp. 286–299; and D. Dunning, A. Leuenberger, and D. A. Sherman, "A New Look at Motivated Inference: Are Self-Serving Theories of Success a Product of Motivational Forces?" *Journal of Personality and Social Psychology,* July 1995, pp. 58–68.

62. *The Wirthlin Report,* reported in "Job Stress Can Be Satisfying," *USA Today,* April 19, 1999, p. 1B.

63. Study by The Medstat Group appearing in the *American Journal of Health Promotion,* October 3, 2000, reported in K. Fackelmann, "Stress, Unhealthy Habits Costing USA," *USA Today,* October 3, 2000, p. 5A.

64. Study in *Circulation,* March 1998, reported in "Managers at Risk from Work Stress," *San Jose Mercury News,* April 12, 1998, p. 5E; reprinted from *New York Times.*

65. R. S. Schuler, "Definition and Conceptualization of Stress in Organizations," *Organizational Behavior and Human Performance,* April 1980, p. 1980; and R. S. Lazarus, *Psychological Stress and Coping Processes* (New York: McGraw-Hill, 1966).

66. H. Selye, *Stress without Distress* (New York: Lippincott, 1974), p. 27.

67. R. S. Lazarus and S. Folkman, "Coping and Adaptation," in *Handbook of Behavioral Medicine,* ed. W. D. Gentry (New York: Guilford, 1982).

68. R. S. Lazarus, "Little Hassles Can Be Hazardous to Health," *Psychology Today,* July 1981, p. 61.

69. Selye, 1974, pp. 28–29.

70. T. D. Schellhardt, "Company Memo to Stressed-Out Employees: 'Deal with It,'" *The Wall Street Journal,* October 2, 1996, pp. B1, B4.

71. J. A. Davy, A. J. Kinicki, and C. L. Scheck, "A Test of Job Security's Direct and Mediated Effects on Withdrawal Cognitions," *Journal of Organizational Behavior,* July 1, 1997, p. 323.

72. G. Graen, "Role-Making Processes within Complex Organizations," in *Handbook of Industrial and Organizational Psychology,* ed. M. D. Dunnette (Chicago: Rand McNally, 1976), p. 1201.

73. T. D. Wall, P. R. Jackson, S. Mullarkey, and S. K. Parker, "The Demands-Control Model of Job Strain: A More Specific Test," *Journal of Occupational and Organizational Psychology,* June 1996, pp. 153–166; and R. C. Barnett and R. T. Brennan, "The Relationship between Job Experiences and Psychological Distress: A Structural Equation Approach," *Journal of Organizational Behavior,* May 1995, pp. 250–276.

74. "Lousiest Bosses," *The Wall Street Journal,* April 4, 1995, p. A1.

75. G. Stern, "Take a Bite, Do Some Work, Take a Bite," *The Wall Street Journal,* January 17, 1994, pp. B1, B2; R. F. Fettendorf, "Curing the New Ills of Technology: Proper Ergonomics Can Reduce Cumulative Trauma Disorders Among Employees," *HRMagazine,* March 1990, pp. 35–36, 80; and S. Overman, "Prescription for a Healthier Office," *HRMagazine,* February 1990, pp. 30–34.

76. J. Schaubroeck and D. C. Ganster, "Chronic Demands and Responsivity to Challenge," *Journal of Applied Psychology,* February 1993, pp. 73–85.

77. J. M. Plas, *Person-Centered Leadership: An American Approach to Participatory Management* (Thousand Oaks, CA: Sage, 1996).

78. N. E. Adler, T. Boyce, M. A. Chesney, S. Cohen, S. Folkman, R. L. Kahn, and S. L. Syme, "Socioeconomic Status and Health: The Challenge of the Gradient," *American Psychologist,* January 1994, pp. 15–24.

79. The link between stress and depression is discussed by P. Freiberg, "Work and Well-Being: Experts Urge Changes in Work, Not the Work," *The APA Monthly,* January 1991, p. 23.

80. Absenteeism and stress are discussed by S. Shellenbarger, "Work & Family: Was That 24-Hour Flu That Kept You Home Really Just the Blahs?" *The Wall Street Journal,* July 24, 1996, p. B1.

81. Recommendations for reducing burnout are discussed by M. Wylie, "Preventing Worker Burnout while Supporting the Users," *MacWeek,* October 4, 1993, pp. 12–14; and "How to Avoid Burnout," *Training,* February 1993, pp. 15, 16, 70.

82. These examples and techniques are discussed by R. L. Rose, "Time Out: At the Menninger Clinic, Executives Learn More About Themselves—and Why They're So Unhappy," *The Wall Street Journal,* February 26, 1996, p. R5; and L. Landon, "Pump Up Your Employees," *HRMagazine,* May 1990, pp. 34–37.

83. F. Luthans, *Organizational Behavior* (New York: McGraw-Hill, 1985), pp. 146–148.

CHAPTER 12

1. A. Zipkin, "The Wisdom of Thoughtfulness," *New York Times,* May 31, 2000, pp. C1, C10; L. Brenner, "Perks that Work," *Business Week Frontier,* October 11, 1999, pp. F.22–F.30; L. Alderman, "And We'll Even Throw In . . .," *Business Week Frontier,* October 11, 1999, pp. F.34–F.37; L. Stern, "Talent Trawl: What's the Best Bait?" *Business Week Enterprise,* December 7, 1998, pp. ENT22–ENT24; and S. Schafer, "Battling a Labor Shortage? It's All in Your Imagination," *Inc.,* August 1997, p. 24.

2. D. Katz and R. L. Kahn, *The Social Psychology of Organizations* (New York: Wiley, 1966).

3. K. Down and L. Liedtka, "What Corporations Seek in MBA Hires: A Survey," *Selections,* Winter 1994, pp. 34–39.

4. T. Van Tassel, "Productivity Dilemmas," *Executive Excellence,* April 1994, pp. 16–17.

5. A. Maslow, "A Theory of Human Motivation," *Psychological Review,* July 1943, pp. 370–396.

6. C. C. Pinder, *Work Motivation: Theory, Issues, and Applications* (Glenview, IL: Scott, Foresman, 1984), p. 52.

7. D. E. Meyerson, *Tempered Radicals: How People Use Difference to Inspire Change at Work,* quoted in J. N. Lynem, "New Breed Wants to Rock the Boat but Still Stay in It," *San Francisco Chronicle,* "Sunday," November 11, 2001, pp. J1, J3.

8. F. Herzberg, B. Mausner, and B. B. Snyderman, *The Motivation to Work* (New York: Wiley, 1959); and F. Herzberg, "One More Time: How Do You Motivate Employees?" *Harvard Business Review,* January–February 1968, pp. 53–62.

9. D. C. McClelland, *Human Motivation* (Glenview, IL: Scott, Foresman, 1985).

10. D. McClelland and H. Burnham, "Power Is the Great Motivator," *Harvard Business Review,* March/April 1976, pp. 100–110.

11. D. C. McClelland and R. E. Boyatsis, "The Leadership Motive Pattern and Long Term Success in Management," *Journal of Applied Psychology,* vol. 67, 1982, pp. 737–743.

12. C. Ansberry, "Shock Absorber: Bob Stadler Has Lived All the Business Trends of the Past 50 Years," *The Wall Street Journal,* July 11, 1996, p. A1.

13. V. H. Vroom, *Work and Motivation* (New York: Wiley, 1964).

14. J. S. Adams, "Toward an Understanding of Inequity," *Journal of Abnormal and Social Psychology,* November 1963, pp. 422–436; and J. S. Adams, "Injustice in Social Exchange," in L. Berkowitz, ed., *Advances in Experimental Social Psychology,* 2nd ed. (New York: Academic Press, 1965), pp. 267–300.

15. E. Nelson, "Work Week: A Special News Report about Life on the Job—and the Trends Taking Shape There," *The Wall Street Journal,* February 6, 1996, p. A1.

16. See M. A. Korsgaard and L. Roberson, "Procedural Justice in Performance Evaluation: The Role of Instrumental and Non-Instrumental Voice in Performance Appraisal Decisions," *Journal of Management,* 1995, pp. 657–669.

17. E. A. Locke and G. P. Latham, *Goal Setting: A Motivational Technique that Works!* (Englewood Cliffs, NJ: Prentice-Hall, 1984); and E. A. Locke, K. N. Shaw, L. A. Saari, and G. P. Latham, "Goal Setting and Task Performance, *Psychological Bulletin,* August 1981, pp. 125–152

18. B. F. Skinner, *Walden Two* (New York: Macmillan, 1948); *Science and Human Behavior* (New York: Macmillan, 1953); and *Contingencies of Reinforcement* (New York: Appleton-Century-Crofts, 1969).

19. S. Melamed, I. Ben-Avi, J. Luz, and M. S. Green, "Objective and Subjective Work Monotony: Effects on Job Satisfaction, Psychological Distress, and Absenteeism in Blue-Collar Workers," *Journal of Applied Psychology,* February 1995, pp. 29–42.

20. M. A. Campion and C. L. McClelland, "Follow-Up and Extension of the Interdisciplinary Costs and Benefits of Enlarged Jobs," *Journal of Applied Psychology,* June 1993, pp. 339–351.

21. S. Phillips and A. Dunkin, "King Customer," *Business Week,* March 12, 1990, p. 91.

22. J. R. Hackman and G. R. Oldham, *Work Redesign* (Reading, MA: Addison-Wesley, 1980).

23. Adapted from Hackman and Oldham, 1980, p. 90.

24. A. Taylor III, "Rally of the Dolls: It Worked for Toyota. Can It Work for Toys?" *Fortune,* January 11, 1999, p. 36.

25. Zipkin, 2000.

26. Gallup Organization study, reported in Zipkin, 2000.

27. B. E. Graham-Moore and T. L. Ross, *Productivity Gainsharing* (Englewood Cliffs, NJ: Prentice-Hall, 1983).

28. J. Lardner, "OK, Here Are Your Options," *U.S. News & World Report,* March 1, 1999, pp. 44–46.

29. Lewis, 2000.

30. PricewaterhouseCoopers survey, reported in S. Shellenbarger, "What Job Candidates Really Want to Know: Will I Have a Life?" *The Wall Street Journal,* November 17, 1999, p. B1.

31. Walker Information survey, reported in Lewis, 2000.

32. Spherion and Louis Harris Associates 1999 survey, reported in Zipkin, 2000.

33. B. L. Ware, quoted in Zipkin, 2000.

34. B. Moses, quoted in Lewis, 2000.

35. K. Lingle, quoted in C. Kleiman, "Work-Life Rewards Grow," *San Francisco Examiner,* January 16, 2000, p. J-2; reprinted from *Chicago Tribune.*

36. C. Kleiman, "CEO of Family-Friendly Firm Tells Others to 'Just Do It,'" *San Jose Mercury News,* September 19, 1999, p. PC-1; and D. Dallinger, "Battling for a Balanced Life," *San Francisco Chronicle,* November 14, 1999, "Sunday" section, p. 9.

37. A. Hedge, quoted in P. Wen, "Drab Cubicles Can Block Workers' Creativity, Productivity," *San Francisco Chronicle,* March 10, 2000, pp. B1, B3; reprinted from *Boston Globe.*

38. H. Lancaster, "Sabbaticals Can Help You Improve Your Job or Spur a New Career," *The Wall Street Journal,* February 13, 1996, p. B1.

CHAPTER 13

1. K. W. Thomas, "Conflict and Conflict Management," in *Handbook of Industrial and Organizational Psychology,* M. Dunnette, ed. (Chicago: Rand McNally, 1976), pp. 889–935; K. W. Thomas "Toward Multiple Dimensional Values in Teaching: The Example of Conflict Behaviors," *Academy of Management Review,* July 1977, pp. 484–490; and M. A Rahim, "A Strategy for Managing Conflict in Complex Organizations," *Human Relations,* January 1985, p. 84.

2. Rahmin, 1985.

3. B. Rosner, "How to Avoid Violence from a Fired Worker," *San Francisco Sunday Examiner & Chronicle,* November 15, 1998, p. CL-13.

4. "Job Violence: A Global Survey," *Business Week,* August 17, 1998, p. 22.

5. J. A. Wall Jr. and R. Robert Callister, "Conflict and Its Management," *Journal of Management,* no. 3, 1995, p. 517.

6. C. Alter, "An Exploratory Study of Conflict and Coordination in Interorganizational Service Delivery Systems," *Academy of Management Journal,* September 1990, pp. 478–502; S. P. Robbins, "'Conflict Management' and 'Conflict Resolution' Are Not Synonymous Terms," *California Management Review,* Winter 1978, p. 70. .

7. Cooperative conflict is discussed in D. Tjosvold, *Learning to Manage Conflict: Getting People to Work Together Productively* (New York: Lexington, 1993); and D. Tjosvold and D. W. Johnson, *Productive Conflict Management Perspectives for Organizations* (New York: Irvington, 1983). See also A. C. Amason, K. R. Thompson, W. A. Hochwarter, and A. W. Harrison, "Conflict: An Important Dimension in Successful Management Teams," *Organizational Dynamics,* Autumn 1995, pp. 20–35; and A. C. Amason, "Distinguishing the Effects of Functional and Dysfunctional Conflict on Strategic Decision Making: Resolving a Paradox for Top

Management Teams," *Academy of Management Journal*, February 1996, pp. 123–148.

8. S. Flax, "The Toughest Bosses in America," *Fortune*, August 6, 1984, p. 21.

9. J. B. Treece, "Richard LeFauve," *The 1990 Business Week 1000*, April 13, 1990, p. 130. For a Saturn update, see M. Maynard, "Automaker's Influence Takes Orbit," *USA Today*, October 2, 1996, pp. 1B–2B.

10. A. M. O'Leary-Kelly, R. W. Griffin, and D. J. Glew, "Organization-Motivated Aggression: A Research Framework," *Academy of Management Review*, January 1996, pp. 225–253.

11. L. R. Pondy, "Organizational Conflict: Concepts and Models," *Administrative Science Quarterly*, vol. 2, 1967, pp. 296–320.

12. P. Burrows, "Carly's Last Stand?" *Business Week*, December 24, 2001, pp. 63–70. See B. Pimentel, "Heftier HP Is Ready to Forge Ahead," *San Francisco Chronicle*, May 5, 2002, pp. G1, G4.

13. R. A. Cosier and C. R. Schwenk, "Agreement and Thinking Alike: Ingredients for Poor Decisions," *Academy of Management Executive*, February 1990, p. 71. Also see J. P. Kotter, "Kill Complacency," *Fortune*, August 5, 1996, pp. 168–170.

14. See "Facilitators as Devil's Advocates," *Training*, September 1993, p. 10; and C. R. Schwenk, "Devil's Advocacy in Managerial Decision Making," *Journal of Management Studies*, April 1984, pp. 153–168.

15. S. G. Katzenstein, "The Debate on Structured Debate: Toward a Unified Theory," *Organizational Behavior and Human Decision Processes*, June 1996, pp. 316–332.

16. W. Kiechel III, "How to Escape the Echo Chamber," *Fortune*, June 18, 1990, p. 130.

17. T. Kelley, quoted in P. Sinton, "Teamwork the Name of the Game for Ideo," *San Francisco Chronicle*, February 23, 2000, pp. D1, D3.

18. J. Katzenback and D. Smith, "The Discipline of Teams," *The Harvard Business Review*, March-April 1993, pp. 111–120.

19. See P. F. Drucker, "The Coming of the New Organization," *Harvard Business Review*, January-February 1988, pp. 45–53.

20. Data from "HR Data Files," *HRMagazine*, June 1995, p. 65.

21. J. K. Bennett, "The 12 Building Blocks of the Learning Organization," *Training*, June 1994, p. 41; and R. Jacob, "The Search for the Organization of Tomorrow," *Fortune*, May 18, 1992, pp. 93–94.

22. P. Sinton, "The Enemy Within," *San Francisco Chronicle*, February 23, 2000, pp. D1, D3.

23. E. E. Lawler III, *From the Ground Up* (San Francisco: Jossey-Bass, 1996).

24. Sinton, 2000.

25. A. Deutschman, "The Managing Wisdom of High-Tech Superstars," *Fortune*, October 17, 1994, pp. 197–206.

26. B. Dumaine, "Why Do We Work?" *Fortune*, December 26, 1994, p. 202.

27. This definition is based in part on one found in D. Horton Smith, "A Parsimonious Definition of 'Group': Toward Conceptual Clarity and Scientific Utility," *Sociological Inquiry*, Spring 1967, pp. 141–167.

28. E. H. Schein, *Organizational Psychology*, 3rd ed. (Englewood Cliffs, NJ: Prentice-Hall, 1980), p. 145.

29. J. R. Katzenbach and D. K. Smith, *The Wisdom of Teams: Creating the High-Performance Organization* (Boston: Harvard Business School Press, 1993), p. 45.

30. J. R. Katzenbach and D. K. Smith, "The Discipline of Teams," *Harvard Business Review*, March–April 1995, p. 112.

31. D. Krackhardt and J. R. Hanson, "Informal Networks: The Company Behind the Chart," *Harvard Business Review*, July–August 1993, p. 104.

32. Study by Center for Workforce Development, Newton, MA, reported in M. Jackson, "It's Not Chitchat, It's Training," *San Francisco Chronicle*, January 7, 1998, p. D2.

33. E. Sundstrom, K. P. DeMeuse, and D. Futrell, "Work Teams," *American Psychologist*, February 1990, pp. 120–133.

34. See K. Buch and R. Spangler, "The Effects of Quality Circles on Performance and Promotions," *Human Relations*, June 1990, pp. 573–582; and G. R. Ferris and J. A. Wagner III, "Quality Circles in the United States: a Conceptual Reevaluation," *The Journal of Applied Behavioral Science*, no. 2, 1985, pp. 155–167.

35. E. E. Lawler III and S. A. Mohrman, "Quality Circles: After the Honeymoon," *Organizational Dynamics*, Spring 1987, pp. 42–54. Also see E. E. Lawler III, "Total Quality Management and Employee Involvement: Are They Compatible?" *Academy of Management Executive*, February 1994, pp. 68–76.

36. Lawler and Mohrman, 1987.

37. Good background discussions can be found in P. S. Goodman, R. Devadas, and T. L. Griffith Hughson, "Groups and Productivity: Analyzing the Effectiveness of Self-Managing Teams," in *Productivity in Organizations*, eds. J. P. Campbell, R. J. Campbell and Associates (San Francisco: Jossey-Bass, 1988), pp. 295–327; C. Lee, "Beyond Teamwork," *Training*, June 1990, pp. 25–32; and S. G. Cohen, G. E. Ledford Jr., and G. M. Spreitzer, "A Predictive Model of Self-Managing Work Team Effectiveness," *Human Relations*, May 1996, pp. 643–676.

38. For an instructive case on this topic, see C. C. Manz, D. E. Keating, and A. Donnellon, "Preparing for an Organizational Change to Employee Self-Management: The Managerial Transition," *Organizational Dynamics*, Autumn 1990, pp. 15–26.

39. Review of J. Lipnack and J. Stamps, *Virtual Teams: Reaching Across Space, Time, and Organization with Technology* (New York: John Wiley, 1997), in "Virtual Teams Transcend Space and Time," *The Futurist*, September-October 1997, p. 59

40. W. Arnold, "Cathay Pacific Is Lesson in Culture, Computing," *The Wall Street Journal*, November 25, 1998, p. B6.

41. Adapted from "Managing the Challenge of a Virtual Workplace," box in C. Sandlund, "Remote Control," *Business Week Frontier*, March 27, 2000, pp. F.14–F.20.

42. See B. W. Tuckman, "Developmental Sequence in Small Groups," *Psychological Bulletin*, June 1965, pp. 384–399; and B. W. Tuckman and M. A. C. Jensen, "Stages of Small-Group Development Revisited," *Group & Organization Studies*, December 1977, pp. 419–427. An instructive adaptation of the Tuckman model can be found in L. Holpp, "If Empowerment Is So Good, Why Does It Hurt?" *Training*, March 2995, p. 56.

43. Practical advice on handling a dominating group member can be found in M. Finley, "Belling the Bully," *HRMagazine*, March 1992, pp. 82–86.

44. J. Case, "What the Experts Forgot to Mention," *Inc.*, September 1993, pp. 66–78.

45. M. Erez, "Is Group Productivity Loss the Rule or the Exception? Effects of Culture and Group-based Motivation," *Academy of Management Journal*, vol. 39, 1996, pp. 1513–1537.

46. "A Team's-Eye View of Teams," *Training*, November 1995, p. 16.

47. M. E. Shaw, *Group Dynamics*, 3rd ed. (New York: McGraw-Hill, 1981); G. Manners, "Another Look at Group Size, Group Problem-Solving and Member Consensus," *Academy of Management Journal*, vol. 18, 1975, pp. 715–724.

48. H.-S. Hwang and J. Guynes, "The Effect of Group Size on Group Performance in Computer-Supported Decision Making," *Information & Management,* April 1994, pp. 189–198.

49. Deutschman, 1994.

50. S. J. Karau and K. D. Williams, "Social Loafing: Research Findings, Implications, and Future Directions," *Current Directions in Psychological Science,* October 1995, pp. 134–140; and S. J. Zacarro, "Social Loafing: The Role of Task Attractiveness," *Personality and Social Psychology Bulletin,* vol. 10, 1984, pp. 99–106.

51. K. D. Benne and P. Sheats, "Functional Roles of Group Members," *Journal of Social Issues,* Spring 1948, pp. 41–49.

52. D. C. Feldman, "The Development and Enforcement of Group Norms," *Academy of Management Review,* January 1984, pp. 47–53.

53. D. Kahneman, "Reference Points, Anchors, Norms, and Mixed Feelings," *Organizational Behavior and Human Decision Processes,* March 1992, pp. 296–312.

54. G. L. Miles, "The Plant of Tomorrow Is in Texas Today," *Business Week,* July 28, 1986, p. 76.

55. Feldman, 1984.

56. See, for example, P. Jin, "Work Motivation and Productivity in Voluntarily Formed Work Teams: A Field Study in China," *Organizational Behavior and Human Decision Processes,* vol. 54, no. 1, 1993, pp. 133–155.

57. L. Janis, *Groupthink,* 2nd ed. (Boston: Houghton Mifflin, 1982), p. 9.

58. V. H. Palmieri, quoted in L. Baum, "The Job Nobody Wants," *Business Week,* September 8, 1986, p. 60.

59. J. Flynn, "Giving the Board More Clout," *Business Week,* Bonus Issue: Reinventing America, 1992, p. 74.

60. Janis, 1982, pp. 174–175.

61. M. R. Callway and J. K. Desser, "Groupthink: Effects of Cohesiveness and Problem-Solving Procedures on Group Decision Making," *Social Behavior and Personality,* no. 2, 1984, pp. 157–164.

CHAPTER 14

1. R. E. Kelley, *How to Be a Star at Work: Nine Breakthrough Strategies You Need to Succeed* (New York: Times Books, 1999); R. E. Kelley interview with Webber, 1998; C. Shavers, "Being a Star at Work Requires Self-Management," *San Jose Mercury News,* December 13, 1998, p. 4E; I. DeBare, "How to Become a Star in the Workplace," *San Francisco Chronicle,* July 20, 1998, p. D2; L. M.Sixel, "So You Want to Be a Star at Your Job," *San Francisco Examiner & Chronicle,* September 13, 1998, p. CL-17; reprinted from *Houston Chronicle*; and C. Smith, "'Star' Traits Aren't Always Obvious Ones," *San Francisco Examiner & Chronicle,* August 15, 1999, p. CL-17.

2. T. Peters and N. Austin, *A Passion for Excellence* (New York: Random House, 1985), pp. 5–6.

3. B. M. Bass, *Bass & Stogdill's Handbook of Leadership: Theory, Research, and Managerial Applications,* 3rd ed. (New York: Free Press, 1990), p. 383.

4. J. P. Kotter, "What Leaders Really Do," *Harvard Business Review,* December 2001, pp. 85–96.

5. F. Smith, quoted in "All in a Day's Work," *Harvard Business Review,* December 2001, pp. 54–66.

6. N. Tichy and C. DeRose, "Roger Enrico's Master Class," *Fortune,* November 27, 1995, pp. 105–106.

7. L. H. Chusmir, "Personalized versus Socialized Power Needs among Working Women and Men," *Human Relations,* February 1986, p. 149.

8. D. Leonhardt, "Don't Mess with This Maytag Repairman," *Business Week,* August 9, 1999, p. 70.

9. C. H. Deutsch, "G.E. Taps Successor to the Chief," *New York Times,* November 28, 2000, pp. C1, C14; T. A. Stewart, "See Jack. See Jack Run Europe," *Fortune,* September 27, 1999, pp. 124–136; G. Colvin, "The Ultimate Manager," *Fortune,* November 22, 1999, pp. 185–187; C. H. Deutsch, "GE's Chief Sets a Date to Step Down," *New York Times,* November 3, 1999, pp. C1, C2; M. Allen, "Another Jack Welch Isn't Good Enough," *The Wall Street Journal,* November 22, 1999, p. A22; A. Sloan, "Judging GE's Jack Welch," *Newsweek,* November 15, 1999, p. 67; R. Slater, *Jack Welch and the GE Way* (New York: McGraw-Hill, 1999); and J. A. Byrne, "Jack," *Business Week,* June 8, 1998, pp. 90–106.

10. "Management 101: Motivation Matters" [editorial], *Business Week,* June 8, 1998, p. 130.

11. "Push-Button Age," *Newsweek,* July 9, 1990, p. 57.

12. D. Kipnis, S. M. Schmidt, and I. Wilkinson, "Intraorganizational Influence Tactics: Explorations in Getting One's Way," *Journal of Applied Psychology,* August 1980, pp. 440–452. Also see C. A. Schriesheim and T. R. Hinkin, "Influence Tactics Used by Subordinates: A Theoretical and Empirical Analysis and Refinement of the Kipnis, Schmidt, and Wilkinson Subscales," *Journal of Applied Psychology,* June 1990, pp. 246–257.

13. G. Yukl, H. Kim, and C. M. Falbe, "Antecedents of Influence Outcomes," *Journal of Applied Psychology,* June 1996, pp. 309–317.

14. B. Schlender, "A Conversation with the Lords of Wintel," *Fortune,* July 8, 1996, p. 44.

15. R. M. Stogdill, "Personal Factors Associated with Leadership: A Survey of the Literature," *Journal of Psychology,* 1948, pp. 35–71; and R. M. Stogdill, *Handbook of Leadership* (New York: Free Press, 1974).

16. B. Bass, *Stogdill's Handbook of Leadership,* rev. ed. (New York: Free Press, 1981).

17. J. M. Kouzes and B. Z. Posner, "The Credibility Factor: What Followers Expect from Their Leaders," *Business Credit,* July–August 1990, pp. 24–28; J. M. Kouzes and B. Z. Posner, *The Leadership Challenge: How to Get Extraordinary Things Done in Organizations* (San Francisco: Jossey-Bass, 1995); and J. M. Kouzes and B. Z. Posner, *Credibility* (San Francisco: Jossey-Bass, 1993).

18. L. Bossidy, "The Job No CEO Should Delegate," *Harvard Business Review,* March 2001, pp. 47–49.

19. D. Goleman, *Emotional Intelligence* (New York: Bantam, 1995).

20. D. Goleman, "What Makes a Leader," *Harvard Business Review,* November–December 1998, pp. 93–102.

21. "Get Happy, Carefully," box in D. Goleman, R. Boyatzis, and A. McKee, "Primal Leadership: The Hidden Driver of Great Performance," *Harvard Business Review,* December 2001, p. 49.

22. Goleman, Boyatzis, and McKee, 2001, pp. 42–51.

23. S. Fox and P. E. Spector, "Relations of Emotional Intelligence, Practical Intelligence, General Intelligence, and Trait Affectivity with Interview Outcomes: It's Not All Just 'G,'" *Journal of Organizational Behavior,* March 1, 2000, pp. 203–220.

24. M. D. Davies, L. Stankov, and R. D. Roberts, "Emotional Intelligence: In Search of an Elusive Construct," *Journal of Personality & Social Psychology,* October 1, 1998, pp. 989–1015.

25. R. Sharpe, "As Leaders, Women Rule," *Business Week,* November 20, 2000, pp. 75–84.

26. Study by Hagberg Consulting Group, Foster City, Calif., reported in Sharpe, 2000, p. 75.

27. Data from Hagberg Consulting Group, Management Research Group, Lawrence A. Pfaff, Personnel Decisions International Inc., and Advanced Teamware Inc., in table in Sharpe, 2000, p. 75.

28. B. R. Ragins, B. Townsend, and M. Mattis, "Gender Gap in the Executive Suite: CEOs and Female Executives Report on Breaking the Glass Ceiling," *Academy of Management Executive,* February 1, 1998, pp. 28–42.

29. R. Likert, *New Patterns of Management* (New York: McGraw-Hill, 1961); and R. Likert, *The Human Organization* (New York: McGraw-Hill, 1967).

30. C. A. Schriesman and B. J. Bird, "Contributions of the Ohio State Studies to the Field of Leadership," *Journal of Management Studies,* vol. 5, 1979, pp. 135–145; and C. L. Shartle, "Early Years of the Ohio State University Leadership Studies," *Journal of Management,* vol. 5, 1979, pp. 126–134.

31. V. H. Vroom, "Leadership," in *Handbook of Industrial and Organizational Psychology,* ed. M. D. Dunnette (Chicago: Rand McNally, 1976).

32. H. Lancaster, "New Managers Get Little Help Tackling Big, Complex Jobs," *The Wall Street Journal,* February 10, 1998; and C. Hymowitz, "New Top Managers Often Find They Miss Close Peers, Counsel," *The Wall Street Journal,* November 25, 1997, p. B1.

33. The Leadership Grid® figure is adapted from R. R. Blake, J. S. Mouton, L. B. Barnes, and L. E. Greiner, "Breakthrough in Organization Development," *Harvard Business Review,* November–December 1964, p. 136.

34. P. C. Nystrom, "Managers and the Hi-Hi Leader Myth," *Academy of Management Journal,* June 1978, pp. 325–331; and L. L. Larson, J. G. Hunt, and R. N. Osborn, "The Great Hi-Hi Leader Behavior Myth: A Lesson from Occam's Razon," *Academy of Management Journal,* December 1976, pp. 628–641.

35. F. E. Fiedler, "Assumed Similarity Measures as Predictors of Team Effectiveness," *Journal of Abnormal and Social Psychology,* vol. 49, 1954, pp. 381–388; F. E. Fiedler, *Leader Attitudes and Group Effectiveness* (Urbana, IL: University of Illinois Press, 1958); and F. E. Fiedler, *A Theory of Leadership Effectiveness* (New York: McGraw-Hill, 1967).

36. R. J. House, "A Path-Goal Theory of Leader Effectiveness," *Administrative Science Quarterly,* September 1971, pp. 321–338.

37. R. J. House and T. R. Mitchell, "Path-Goal Theory of Leadership," *Journal of Contemporary Business,* Autumn 1974, p. 83.

38. A. C. Filley, R. J. House, and S. Kerr, *Managerial Process and Organizational Behavior* (Glenview, IL: Scott, Foresman, 1976).

39. A thorough discussion is provided by P. Hersey and K. H. Blanchard, *Management of Organizational Behavior: Utilizing Human Resources,* 5th ed. (Englewood Cliffs, NJ: Prentice-Hall, 1988).

40. Results can be found in J. R. Goodson, G. W. McGee, and J. F. Cashman, "Situational Leadership Theory," *Group & Organization Studies,* December 1989, pp. 446–461.

41. See D. C. Lueder, "Don't Be Misled by LEAD," *Journal of Applied Behavioral Science,* May 1985, pp. 143–154; and C. L. Graeff, "The Situational Leadership Theory: A Critical View," *Academy of Management Review,* April 1983, pp. 285–291.

42. J. M. Burns, *Leadership* (New York: HarperCollins, 1978); and N. M. Tichy and D. O. Ulrich, "The Leadership Challenge—A Call for the Transformational Leader," *Sloan Management Review,* Fall 1984, pp. 59–68.

43. W. Bennis and B. Nanus, *Leaders* (New York: Harper & Row, 1985).

44. B. M. Bass, *Leadership and Performance Beyond Expectations* (New York: Free Press, 1985); Bass, 1990; and G. Yukl and D. D. Van Fleet, "Theory and Research on Leadership in Organizations," in M. D. Dunnette and L. M. Hough, eds., *Handbook of Industrial and Organizational Psychology,* 2nd ed., vol. 3 (Palo Alto, CA: Consulting Psychologists Press, 1992), pp. 147–197.

45. An overall summary of servant leadership is provided by L. C. Spears, *Reflections on Leadership: How Robert K. Greenleaf's Theory of Servant-Leadership Influenced Today's Top Management Thinkers* (New York: Wiley, 1995).

46. D. L. Moore, "Wooden's Wizardry Wears Well," *USA Today,* March 29, 1995, pp. 1C, 2C.

47. B. Saporito, "And the Winner Is Still . . . Wal-Mart," *Fortune,* May 2, 1994, pp. 62–70.

48. F. F. Reichheld, *Loyalty Rules! How Today's Leaders Build Lasting Relationships* (Cambridge, MA: Harvard Business School Press, 2001); and *The Loyalty Effect: The Hidden Force Behind Growth* (Cambridge, MA: Harvard Business School Press, 1996).

49. F. F. Reichheld, "Lead for Loyalty," *Harvard Business Review,* July–August 2001, pp. 76–84.

50. K. Western, "No Matter What It Takes, I'll Do It," *The Arizona Republic,* August 1, 1993, p. F1.

51. B. L. Clark, "Slavish Devotion to the Cult of Customer Service," *FSB,* November 2001, p. 42.

CHAPTER 15

1. See C. Kanchier, "Telephone Skills Crucial for Success," *San Francisco Examiner,* May 2, 1999, p. J-2; C. Kanchier, "How to Make Effective Phone Calls," *San Francisco Examiner,* September 26, 1999, p. J-3; B. Roserner, "The Right Tone for When You Use the Phone," *San Francisco Examiner & Chronicle,* August 29, 1999, p. CL-13; and O. Pollar, "How to Be a Winner at Phone Tag," *San Francisco Examiner & Chronicle,* May 2, 1999, p. J-3.

2. R. Todd, quoted in A. Fisher, "Readers Speak Out on Illiterate MBAs and More," *Fortune,* March 1, 1999, p. 242.

3. September 1998 survey by OfficeTeam, reported in S. Armour, "Failure to Communicate Costly for Companies," *USA Today,* September 30, 1998, p. B1.

4. J. R. Hinrichs, "Communications Activity of Industrial Research Personnel," *Personnel Psychology,* Summer 1964, pp. 193–204.

5. J. Kotter, "Power, Dependence, and Effective Management," *Harvard Business Review,* vol. 55, 1977, pp. 125–136.

6. R. L. Daft, and R. H. Lengel, "Information Richness: A New Approach to Managerial Behavior and Organizational Design," in *Research in Organizational Behavior,* eds. B. M. Staw and L. L. Cummings (Greenwich, CT: JAI Press, 1984), p. 196; and R. H. Lengel and R. L. Daft, "The Selection of Communication Media as an Executive Skill," *Academy of Management Executive,* August 1988, pp. 225–232.

7. E. Goode, "Old as Society, Social Anxiety Is Yielding Its Secrets," *New York Times,* October 20, 1998, pp. D7, D11.

8. Goode, 1998.

9. P. Post and P. Post, *Emily Post's The Etiquette Advantage in Business* (New York: HarperCollins, 2000); J. Flaherty, "Finding Your Manners," *New York Times,* February 13, 1999, pp. B1, B14;

E. White, "Lessons in Shaking Hands, Twirling Spaghetti Await Some Workers," *The Wall Street Journal,* December 7, 1999, pp. B1, B16; H. Lancaster, "Workday Etiquette: Know the Right Fork and Watch that Email," *The Wall Street Journal,* April 21, 1998, p B1; J. Blais, "Mind Your Manners, Even If You're at Work," *USA Today,* January 17, 2000, p. 5B; B. Rosner, "Giving Thanks without Looking Like a Phony," *San Francisco Examiner & Chronicle,* March 7, 1999, p. Cl-13; and C. Smith, "How Clean Underwear Aids Your Career," *San Francisco Examiner,* February 28, 1999, p. CL-13.

10. Some of these barriers are discussed in J. P. Scully, "People: The Imperfect Communicators," *Quality Progress,* April 1995, pp. 37–39.

11. A. Farnham, "Trust Gap," *Fortune,* December 4, 1989, p. 70.

12. C. R. Rogers and F. J. Roethlisberger, "Barriers and Gateways to Communication," *Harvard Business Review,* July–August 1952, pp. 46–52.

13. Rogers and Roethlisberger, 1952, p. 47.

14. This statistic was provided by A. Warfield, "Do You Speak Body Language?" *Training and Development,* April 2000, pp. 60–61.

15. See N. Morgan, "The Kinesthetic Speaker: Putting Action into Words," *Harvard Business Review,* April 2001, pp. 113–120.

16. W. D. St. John, "You Are What You Communicate," *Personnel Journal,* October 1985, p. 43.

17. St. John, 1985.

18. Derived from D. Tannen, "The Power of Talk: Who Gets Heard and Why," *Harvard Business Review,* September–October 1995; pp. 138–148; and D. Tannen, *You Just Don't Uinderstand: Women and Men in Conversation* (New York: Ballantine Books, 1990).

19. J. C. Tingley, *Genderflex: Men & Women Speaking Each Other's Language at Work* (New York: American Management Association, 1994), p. 16.

20. D. Tannen, "The Power of Talk: Who Gets Heard and Why," in *Negotiation: Readings, Exercises, and Cases,* 3rd ed., eds. R. J. Lewicki and D. M. Saunders (Burr Ridge, IL: Irwin/McGraw-Hill, 1999), pp. 147–148.

21. R. Sharpe, "As Leaders, Women Rule," *Business Week,* November 20, 2000, pp. 75–84.

22. P. Gogoi, "Teaching Men the Right Stuff," *Business Week,* November 20, 2000, p. 84.

23. D. Jones, "Male Execs Like Female Coaches," *USA Today,* October 24, 2001, p. 3B.

24. D. Katz and R. Kahn, *The Social Psychology of Organizations* (New York: Wiley, 1966).

25. E. Planty and W. Machaver, "Upward Communications: A Project in Executive Development," *Personnel,* vol. 28, 1952, pp. 304–318.

26. T. Petzinger Jr., "The Front Lines: Two Executives Cook Up Way to Make Pillsbury Listen," *The Wall Street Journal,* September 27, 1996, p. B1.

27. G. M. Goldhaber, *Organizational Communication,* 4th ed. (Dubuque, IA: W. C. Brown, 1986).

28. S. J. Modic, "Grapevine Rated Most Believable," *Industry Week,* May 15, 1989, pp. 11, 14.

29. Early research is discussed by K. Davis, "Management Communication and the Grapevine," *Harvard Business Review,* September–October 1953, pp. 43–49; and R. Rowan, "Where Did *That* Rumor Come From?" *Fortune,* August 13, 1979, pp. 130–137. The most recent research is discussed in "Pruning the Company Grapevine," *Supervision,* September 1986, p. 11; and R.

Half, "Managing Your Career: 'How Can I Stop the Gossip?'" *Management Accounting,* September 1987, p. 27.

30. K. Davis and J. W. Newstrom, *Human Behavior at Work: Organizational Behavior,* 7th ed. (New York: Mc-Graw-Hill, 1985).

31. H. B. Vickery III, "Tapping into the Employee Grapevine," *Association Management,* January 1984, pp. 59–60.

32. A thorough discussion of organizational moles is provided by J. G. Bruhn and A. P. Chesney, "Organizational Moles: Information Control and the Acquisition of Power and Status," *Health Care Supervisor,* September 1995, pp. 24–31.

33. T. J. Peters and R. H. Waterman Jr., *In Search of Excellence* (New York: Harper & Row, 1982); and T. Peters and N. Austin, *A Passion for Excellence: the Leadership Difference* (New York: Random House, 1985).

34. S. Branch, "The 100 Best Companies to Work for in America," *Foturne,* January 11, 1999, pp. 118–144.

35. J. B. White, "How Detroit Diesel, Out from Under GM, Turned Around Fast," *The Wall Street Journal,* August 16, 1991, p. A1.

36. W. H. Bulkeley, "The View from the Top," *The Wall Street Journal,* June 21, 1999, p. R6.

37. Information Data Corp., reported in A. Petersen, "A Fine Line: Companies Face a Delicate Task When It Comes to Deciding What to Put on Their Intranets: How Much Is Too Much?" *The Wall Street Journal,* June 21, 1999, p. R8.

38. Results are summarized in S. Armour, "Boss: It's in the E-mail," *USA Today,* August 10, 1999, p. 3B.

39. The benefits of using email were derived from discussion in R. F. Federico and J. M. Bowley, "The Great E-Mail Debate," *HRMagazine,* January 1996, pp. 67–72.

40. S. Schafer, "Operations: 'E-Mail, or Else!'" *Inc.,* January 1996, p. 94.

41. Results can be found in M. L. Markus, "Electronic Mail as the Medium of Managerial Choice," *Organization Science,* November 1994, pp. 502–527.

42. Reported in J. Yaukey, Gannett News Service, "E-mail Out of Control for Many," *Reno Gazette-Journal,* May 7, 2001, p. 1E.

43. S. Shostak, "You Call This Progress?" *Newsweek,* January 18, 1999, p. 16.

44. M. Feschner, "Bold Goals: How Pinacor Wraps Itself Around the Customer," *Selling Power,* June 1999, p. 57.

45. Results can be found in M. S. Thompson and M. S. Feldman, "Electronic Mail and Organizational Communication: Does Saying 'Hi' Really Matter?" *Organization Science,* November–December 1998, pp. 685–698.

46. R. Balu, "Work Week: A Special News Report about Life on the Job," *The Wall Street Journal,* July 20, 1999, p. A1.

47. In-StatMDR, May 2002, www.instat.com

48. D. Clark, "Managing the Mountain," *The Wall Street Journal,* June 21, 1999, p. R4.

49. J. Kaye, "The Devil You Know," *Computer Weekly,* March 19, 1998, p. 46; D. Shenk, "Data Smog: Surviving the Info Glut," *Technology Review,* May–June 1997, pp. 18–26; C. Hymowitz, "Flooded with E-Mail? Try Screening, Sorting, or Maybe Just Phoning," *The Wall Street Journal,* September 26, 2000, p. B1; M. Irvine, "You've Got Too Much E-Mail," *San Francisco Chronicle,* July 20, 2000, p. B3; S. G. Thomas, "Online In-boxes Aim to Simplify Our Harried Lives," *U.S. News & World Report,* March 6, 2000, p. 54; J. Yaukey, "Take Control of Your E-Mail Now," *Reno Gazette-Journal,* October 16, 2000, pp. 1E, 2E; C. Hymowitz, "Taking Time to Focus on the Big Picture Despite Flood of Data," *The Wall Street Journal,* February 27, 2001,

p. B1; and R. Strauss, "You've Got Maelstrom," *New York Times,* July 5, 2001, pp. D1, D9.

50. Estimates are provided in both J. H. Seibert, "Listening in the Organizational Context," in *Listening Behavior: Measurement and Application,* ed. R. N. Bostrom (New York: The Guilford Press, 1990), pp. 119–127; and D. W. Caudill and R. M. Donaldson, "Effective Listening Tips for Managers," *Administrative Management,* September 1986, pp. 22–23.

51. C. G. Pearce, "How Effective Are We as Listeners?" *Training & Development,* April 1993, pp. 79–80; and R. A. Luke Jr., "Improving Your Listening Ability," *Supervisory Management,* June 1992, p. 7.

52. See the discussion on listening in G. Manning, K. Curtis, and S. McMillen, *Building Community: The Human Side of Work* (Cincinnati, OH: Thomson Executive Press, 1996), pp. 127–154.

53. Derived from G. Manning, K. Curtis, and S. McMillen, *Building the Human Side of Work Community* (Cincinnati, OH: Thomson Executive Press, 1996), pp. 127–154; P. Slizewski, "Tips for Active Listening," *HRFocus,* May 1995, p. 7; and J. R. Goldon, *A Diagnostic Approach to Organizational Behavior,* 2nd ed. (Boston: Allyn and Bacon, 1987), p. 230.

54. C. Vinzant, "Messing with the Boss' Head," *Fortune,* May 1, 2000, pp. 329–331.

55. M. Price, "Effective Communication Begins with Listening," *Reno Gazette-Journal,* November 27, 2000, p. 1F.

56. D. Stiebel, *When Talking Makes Things Worse! Resolving Problems When Communication Fails,* reported in O. Pollar, "Talk Is Cheap If You Have Big Disagreements," *San Francisco Examiner & Chronicle,* February 21, 1999, p. J-3.

57. M. Just, P. A. Carpenter, and M. Masson, reported in J. Meer, "Reading More, Understanding Less," *Psychology Today,* March 1987, p. 12.

58. K. Alesandrini. *Survive Information Overload* (Homewood, IL: Irwin, 1992), pp. 191–202.

59. Alesandrini, 1992, p. 197.

60. T. Alessandra and P. Hunsaker, *Communicating at Work* (New York: Fireside, 1993), p. 231.

61. Alessandra and Hunsaker, 1993, p. 241.

62. Alessandra and Hunsaker, 1993, p. 169.

63. P. Theibert, "Speechwriters of the World, Get Lost!" *The Wall Street Journal,* August 2, 1993, p. A16. This section adapted from C. Wahlstrom and B. Williams, *Learning Success: Being Your Best at College & Life,* 3rd ed. (Belmont, CA: Wadsworth, 2002), pp. 243–245.

64. L. Waters, *Secrets of Successful Speakers: How You Can Motivate, Captivate, and Persuade* (New York: McGraw-Hill, 1993), p. 203.

CHAPTER 16

1. W. A. Ruch, "Productivity Measurement," *Arizona Business,* February 1981, p. 20.

2. J. Welch, quoted in T. A. Stewart, "U.S. Productivity: First but Fading," *Fortune,* October 1992, p. 54.

3. G. Hager, "Computers Complicate Productivity," *USA Today,* April 12, 2000, p. 3B; L. Uchitelle, "Productivity Finally Shows the Impact of Computers," *New York Times,* March 12, 2000, sec. 3, p. 4; J. Reingold, M. Stepanek, and D. Brady, "Why the Productivity Revolution Will Spread," *Business Week,* February 14, 2000, p. 112–118; S. Silverstein, "U.S. Productivity Up 2.9% in '99, Best in 7 Years," *Los Angeles Times,* February 9, 2000, pp. A1A8; L. Uchitelle, "U.S. Productivity Rose at 5% Rate in 2nd Half of '99," *New York Times,* February 9, 2000, pp. A1, C2; and G. Hager, "Worker Output Spurts, Helps Control Inflation," *USA Today,* December 8, 1999, p. 1B.

4. W. Taylor, "Control in an Age of Chaos," *Harvard Business Review,* November–December 1994, pp. 64–70.

5. "Coming Up Next: Joining," *Time,* December 4, 2000, p. 79.

6. A. P. Sloan Jr., *My Years with General Motors* (New York: Doubleday, 1964).

7. "Behind the UPS Mystique: Puritanism and Productivity," *Business Week,* June 6, 1990, pp. 66–73.

8. R. D. Robey and C. A. Sales, *Designing* Organizations (Burr Ridge, IL: Irwin, 1994); W. G. Ouchi, "Markets, Bureaucracies, and Clans," *Administrative Science Quarterly,* March 1980, pp. 129–141; and W. G. Ouchi, "A Conceptual Framework for the Design of Organizational Control Mechanisms," *Management Science,* August 1979, pp. 833–838.

9. L. J. Shinn and M. S. Sturgeon, "Budgeting from Ground Zero," *Association Management,* September 1990, pp. 45–58; J. V. Pearson and R. J. Michael, "Zero-Based Budgeting: A Technique for Planning Organizational Decline," *Long Range Planning,* June 1981, pp. 68–76; P. A. Pyhrr, "Zero-Based Budgeting," *Harvard Business Review,* November–December 1970, pp. 111–118; and "Zero-Based Budgeting," *Small Business Report,* April 1988, pp. 52–57.

10. D. Jones, "Baldrige Winners Named," *USA Today,* November 24, 1999, p. 3B.

11. R. N. Lussier, *Management: Concepts, Applications, Skill Development* (Cincinnati, OH: South-Western College Publishing, 1997), p. 260.

12. O. Port, "The Push for Quality," *Business Week,* June 8, 1987, pp. 130–136.

13. H. Rothman, "You Need Not Be Big to Benchmark," *Nation's Business,* December 1992, pp. 64–65.

14. Rothman, 1992; O. Port and G. Smith, "Beg, Borrow, and Benchmark," *Business Week,* November 30, 1992, pp. 74–75; and J. Main, "How to Steal the Best Ideas Around," *Fortune,* October 19, 1992, pp. 102–106.

15. J. B. Quinn and F. Hilmer, "Strategic Outsourcing," *Sloan Management Review,* Summer 1994, pp. 43–52; and S. Tully, "You'll Never Guess Who Really Makes . . .," *Fortune,* October 3, 1994, pp. 124–128.

16. D. B. Henriques, "'Privatized' Doesn't Always Mean Perfect," *San Francisco Examiner,* May 14, 2000, p. B-10; reprinted from *New York Times.*

17. E. Sclar, *You Don't Always Get What You Pay For: The Economics of Privatization* (Ithaca, NY: Cornell University Press, 2000).

18. G. Kolata, "Harried Doctors Try to Ease Big Delays and Rushed Visits," *New York Times,* January 4, 2001, pp. A1, A16.

19. See R. J. Aldag and T. M. Stearns, Management (Cincinnati, OH: South-Western Publishing, 1987), pp. 653–654; D. Robertson and E. Anderson, "Control System and Task Environment Effects on Ethical Judgment: An Exploratory Study of Industrial Salespeople," *Organizational Science,* November 1993, pp. 617–629.

20. K. A. Merchant, *Control in Business Organizations* (Boston: Pitman, 1985), pp. 10–11; K. M. Bartol and D. C. Martin, *Management,* 3rd ed. (Burr Ridge, IL: Irwin/McGraw-Hill, 1998), pp. 533–534; and J. R. Schermerhorn Jr., *Management for Productivity,* 3rd ed. (New York: John Wiley & Sons, 1993), p. 592.

21. J. Epstein, "Corporations Enlisted in Battle to Save Rain Forests," *San Francisco Chronicle,* July 7, 1999, pp. A8, A10.

22. Bartol and Martin, 1998, pp. 532–533; S. C. Certo, *Modern Management,* 8th ed. (Upper Saddle River, NJ: Prentice Hall, 2000), pp. 435–436; and Griffin, 1997, pp. 384–386.

23. J. P. Kotter, L. A. Schlesinger, and V. Sathe, *Organization: Text, Cases, and Readings on the Management of Organizational Design and Change* (Homewood, IL: Irwin, 1979).

24. K. Merchant, *Control in Business Organizations* (Boston: Pitman, 1985).

25. D. Murphy, "A Show of Initiative," *San Francisco Examiner,* February 13, 2000, pp. J-1, J-2; H. Lancaster, "Take on Tough Jobs, Assess Your Own Work, and Other Life Lessons," *The Wall Street Journal,* December 7, 1999, p. B1; O. Pollar, "These Crucial Skills Make You a 'Keeper,'" *San Francisco Examiner & Chronicle,* November 28, 1999, p. J-3; B. Weinstein, "Define What Product You Can Deliver," *San Francisco Examiner & Chronicle,* January 17, 1999, p. CL-21; and D. Murphy, "To Manage Well, Break a Few Rules," *San Francisco Examiner,* May 24, 1999, p. J-1.

APPENDIX

1. H. L. Gantt, *Organizing for Work* (New York: Harcourt, Brace and Howe, 1919).

glossary

Terms and definitions printed in italic are considered business slang, or jargon.

A

Absenteeism When an employee doesn't show up for work.

Accommodative Approach An approach by managers to do more than the law requires, if asked, and to demonstrate moderate social responsibility.

Acquired-Needs Theory This states that there are three needs—achievement, affiliation, and power—which are the major motives determining people's behavior in the workplace.

Action Plan The course of action needed to achieve the stated goal.

Adjourning The stage in which members prepare for disbandment.

Administrative Management Administrative management is concerned with managing the total organization.

Affective Component of an Attitude The feelings or emotions one has about a situation.

Affirmative Action This focuses on achieving equality of opportunity within an organization.

American dream Americans' hope for a better quality of life and a higher standard of living than their parents'.

Americans with Disabilities Act An act that prohibits discrimination against the disabled.

Analyzers They allow other organizations to take the risks of product development and marketing and then imitate (or perhaps slightly improve on) what seems to work best.

Anchoring and Adjustment Bias The tendency to make decisions based on an initial figure.

Assessment Center Some companies have management candidates participate in activities for a few days while being assessed by evaluators.

Association of Southeast Asian Nations (ASEAN) A trading bloc consisting of nine countries in Asia.

Attitude A learned predisposition toward a given object.

Authority The right to perform or command.

Authority The rights inherent in a managerial position to make decisions, give orders, and utilize resources.

Availability Bias Where managers use information readily available from memory to make judgments.

B

B2B Business to business.

B2C Business to consumer.

Balance Sheet A summary of an organization's overall financial worth—assets and liabilities—at a specific point in time.

Balanced Scorecard This gives top managers a fast but comprehensive view of the organization via four indicators: (1) customer satisfaction, (2) internal processes, (3) the organization's innovation and improvement activities, and (4) financial measures.

Base Pay Consists of the basic wage or salary paid employees in exchange for doing their jobs.

been there, done that Having prior experience with a situation or task.

Behavior Actions and judgments.

Behavioral Component of an Attitude Also known as intentional component, this refers to how one intends or expects to behave toward a situation.

Behavioral Leadership Approach Attempts to determine the distinctive styles used by effective leaders.

Behavioral Science Behavioral science relies on scientific research for developing theories about human behavior that can be used to provide practical tools for managers.

Behavioral Viewpoint This viewpoint emphasizes the importance of understanding human behavior and of motivating employees toward achievement.

Behavioral-Description Interview The interviewer explores what applicants have actually done in the past.

Behaviorally Anchored Rating Scale (BARS) Employee gradations in performance rated according to scales of specific behaviors.

Benchmarking A process by which a company compares its performance with that of high-performing organizations.

Benefits, Fringe Benefits Additional nonmonetary forms of compensation.

Big Five Personality Dimensions They are (1) extroversion, (2) agreeableness, (3) conscientiousness, (4) emotional stability, and (5) openness to experience.

Birth Stage The nonbureaucratic stage, the stage in which the organization is created.

bit of kick A rather strong or spicy taste added to a product or beverage.

black mark A negative evaluation.

blue flu Calling in sick when you're really not. The blue refers to the color of the uniform some workers wear.

Bonuses Cash awards given to employees who achieve specific performance objectives.

bossy Telling employees what to do and not listening to their suggestions.

bottom line The last line in a profit and loss statement; it refers to net profit.

bought into To have accepted completely.

Bounded Rationality A concept that suggests the ability of decision makers to be rational is limited by numerous constraints.

bowing to competition Following what competition does.

Break-Even Analysis A way of identifying how much revenue is needed to cover the total cost of developing and selling a product.

Break-Even Point The amount of sales revenue at which there is no profit but also no loss to your company.

brick-and-mortar store Stores with traditional physical buildings as opposed to stores on the Internet.

Budget A formal financial projection.

Buffers Administrative changes that managers can make to reduce the stressors that lead to employee burnout.

Bureaucratic Control The use of rules, regulations, and formal authority to guide performance.

Burnout A state of emotional, mental, and even physical exhaustion.

C

cannibalized business One franchise pulls business away from another franchise.

Cascading Objectives are structured in a unified hierarchy, becoming more specific at lower levels of the organization.

Causal Attribution The activity of inferring causes for observed behavior.

celebrity stargazers Customers that attend the opening of a new business hoping to see or meet a celebrity.

Centralized Authority Where important decisions are made by higher-level managers.

Change Agent A person inside or outside the organization who can be a catalyst in helping deal with old problems in new ways.

Charismatic Leaders Visionaries who challenge people to perform above and beyond what's expected of them—to pursue organizational goals over self-interests.

Clan Control Shared values, beliefs, rituals, and trusts emanating from a common culture.

Classical Viewpoint A classical viewpoint emphasizes finding ways to manage work more efficiently and has two branches—scientific and administrative.

climbed the ladder Promoted to higher-level jobs.

Closed System A system that has little interaction with its environment.

Coalitional Model In this style of decision making, managers band together in groups favoring different alternatives, and the groups bargain, negotiate, and compromise on a particular problem.

Code of Ethics A formal written set of ethical standards guiding an organization's actions.

Coercive Power All managers have this power, which results from their authority to punish their subordinates.

Cognitive Component of an Attitude The beliefs and knowledge one has about a situation.

Cognitive Dissonance This describes the psychological discomfort a person experiences between his or her cognitive attitude and incompatible behavior.

Cohesiveness The tendency of a group or team to stick together.

Collaborative Computing Using state-of-the-art computer software and hardware to help people work better together.

Collective Bargaining Negotiations between management and employees regarding disputes over compensation, benefits, working conditions, and job security.

Command Economy In a planned economy or a central-planning economy, the government owns most businesses and regulates the amounts, types, and prices of goods and services.

Common Purpose Unifies employees or members and gives everyone an understanding of the organization's reason for being.

Communication The transfer of information and understanding from one person to another.

Compensation Composed of three parts: wages or salaries, incentives, and benefits.

Competitive Advantage The ability of an organization to produce goods or services more effectively than its competitors do, thereby outperforming them.

Competitors People or organizations that compete for customers or resources.

Computer-Assisted Instruction (CAI) Training in which computers are used to provide additional help or to reduce instructional time.

Conceptual Skills Skills that consist of the ability to think analytically, to visualize an organization as a whole and understand how the parts work together.

Concurrent Control A control that takes place while operations are going on and is intended to minimize problems as they occur.

Conflict The process in which one party perceives that its interests are being opposed or negatively affected by another party.

Conglomerate Structure Group divisions around similar businesses or activities.

Consensus This occurs where members are able to express their opinions and reach agreement to support the final decision.

Constructive Conflict Functional conflict that benefits the main purposes of the organization and serves its interest.

Contemporary Perspective A contemporary perspective includes three viewpoints—systems, contingency, and quality-management.

Contingency Approach to Leadership The belief that effective leadership behavior depends on the situation at hand.

Contingency Design The process of fitting the organization to its environment.

Contingency Leadership Model This determines if a leader's style is (1) task oriented or (2) relationship oriented and that style is effective for the situation at hand.

Contingency Planning, Scenario Planning, Scenario Analysis The creation of alternative hypothetical but equally likely future conditions.

Contingency Viewpoint This viewpoint emphasizes that a manager's approach should vary according to—that is, be contingent on—the individual and environmental situation.

Continuous Improvement Ongoing, small, incremental improvements in all parts of an organization.

Continuous-Process Technology A highly routinized technology in which machines do all of the work.

Control Process The four control steps are (1) to establish standards; (2) to measure performance; (3) to compare performance to standards; and (4) to take corrective action, if necessary.

Control Standard A performance standard, or simply standard, is the desired performance level for a given goal.

Controlling Monitoring performance, comparing goals, and taking corrective action as needed.

Coordinated Effort The coordination of individual efforts into a group or organizational-wide effort.

Core Principles of TQM (1) People orientation—everyone involved with the organization should focus on delivering value to customers and (2) improvement orientation—everyone should work on continuously improving the work processes.

Cost Leadership Strategy Keeping the costs, and hence prices, of a product or service below those of competitors and targeting the wider market.

Cost-Focus Strategy To keep the costs, and hence prices, of a product or service below those of competitors and to target a narrow market.

couch potatoes *People who sit and watch TV for hours at a time.*

Countertrading Bartering goods for goods.

counting on it *Expecting it.*

Cross-Functional Team A team that is staffed with specialists pursuing a common objective.

Culture A shared set of beliefs, values, knowledge, and patterns of behavior common to a group of people.

Culture Shock Feelings of discomfort and disorientation associated with being in an unfamiliar culture.

Customer Division A division with group activities around common customers or clients.

Customers Those who pay to use an organization's goods or services.

D

360-Degree Assessment A 360-degree feedback appraisal in which employees are appraised not only by their managerial superiors but also by peers, subordinates, and sometimes clients.

dead duck *Something doomed to failure.*

a deal *A special price or some other benefit that all people don't get.*

Decentralized Authority Where important decisions are made by middle-level and supervisory-level managers.

Deciding to Decide A manager agrees that he or she must decide what to do about a problem or opportunity and take effective decision-making steps.

Decision A choice made from among available alternatives.

Decision Making The process of identifying and choosing alternative courses of action.

Decision-Making Style A style that reflects the combination of how an individual perceives and responds to information.

Decisional Roles Managers use information to make decisions to solve problems or take advantage of opportunities.

The four decision-making roles are entrepreneur, disturbance handler, resource allocator, and negotiator.

Decline Stage The period in which the product falls out of favor, and the organization withdraws from the marketplace.

Decoding Interpreting and trying to make sense of a message.

Defenders Experts at producing and selling narrowly defined products or services.

Defensive Approach An approach by managers to make the minimum commitment to social responsibility—obeying the law but doing nothing more.

Defensive Avoidance When a manager cannot find a good solution and follows by (a) procrastinating, (b) passing the buck, or (c) denying the risk of any negative consequences.

Defensive Strategy/Retrenchment Strategy This strategy involves reduction in the organization's efforts.

Delegation The process of assigning managerial authority and responsibility to managers and employees lower in the hierarchy.

Delphi Group A group using physically dispersed experts who fill out questionnaires to anonymously generate ideas; the judgments are combined and in effect averaged to achieve a consensus of expert opinion.

Democratic Governments These governments rely on free elections and representative assemblies.

Demographic Forces Influences on an organization arising from changes in the characteristics of a population, such as age, gender, ethnic origin, and so on.

Developed Countries Countries with a high level of economic development and generally high average level of income among their citizens.

Development This term describes the education of professionals and managers in the skills they will need to do their jobs in the future.

Devil's Advocacy The process of assigning someone to play the role of critic.

Diagnosis Analyzing the underlying causes.

Dialectic Method The process of having two people or groups play opposing roles in a debate in order to better understand a proposal.

Differentiation The tendency of the parts of an organization to disperse and fragment.

Differentiation Strategy To offer products or services that are of a unique and superior value compared to those of competitors and to target a wide market.

Discrimination When people are hired or promoted—or denied hiring or promotion—for reasons not relevant to the job.

Distributor A person or organization that helps another organization sell its goods and services to customers.

Diversity This represents all the ways people are unlike and alike—the differences and similarities in age, gender, race, religion, ethnicity, sexual orientation, capabilities, and socioeconomic background.

Division of Labor Also known as work specialization, this is an arrangement of having discrete parts of a task done by different people. The work is divided into particular tasks that are assigned to particular workers.

Divisional Structure An organization where people with diverse occupational specialties are put together in formal groups by similar products or services, customers or clients, or geographic regions.

downsizing *The process of eliminating managerial and nonmanagerial positions.*

Downward Communication Communication that flows from a higher level to a lower level.

duck the opportunity *Avoid the opportunity.*

ducks in row *To have all one's tasks lined up and ready to be executed.*

dug down *Worked hard and diligently.*

Dumping A foreign company's practice of exporting products abroad at a lower price than the price in the home market, or even below the costs of production, in order to drive down the price of the domestic product.

E

E-commerce The buying and selling of products and services through computer networks.

Economic Forces General economic conditions and trends—unemployment, inflation, interest rates, economic growth—that may affect an organization's performance.

economic pie *The money available in the economy.*

Effect Uncertainty When the impacts of environmental changes are unpredictable.

Effective To achieve results, to make the right decisions and successfully carry them out so that they achieve the organization's goals.

Efficient To use resources—people, money, raw materials, and the like—wisely and cost-effectively.

E-mail Electronic mail, using the Internet to send computer-generated text and documents between people.

e-mail snooped *When someone other than the addressee reads e-mail messages.*

Embargo A complete ban on the import or export of certain products.

Emotional Intelligence The ability to cope, empathize with others, and be self-motivated.

Employee Assistance Program A program to help employees overcome personal problems affecting their job performance.

Employment Tests Tests that are legally considered to consist of any procedure used in the employment selection decision process.

Encoding Translating a message into understandable symbols or language.

Entrepreneur Someone who sees a new opportunity for a product or service and launches a business to try to realize it.

Entrepreneurship The process of taking risks to try to create a new enterprise.

Equal Employment Opportunity (EEO) Commission Their job is to enforce anti-discrimination and other employment-related laws.

Equity Theory Employee perceptions as to how fairly they think they are being treated compared to others.

Escalation of Commitment Bias When decision makers increase their commitment to a project despite negative information about it.

Ethical Behavior Behavior that is accepted as "right" as opposed to "wrong" according to those standards.

Ethical Dilemma A situation in which you have to decide whether to pursue a course of action that may benefit you or your organization but that is unethical or even illegal.

Ethics Standards of right and wrong that influence behavior.

Ethnocentric Managers Managers who believe that their native country, culture, language, and behavior are superior to others.

Ethnocentrism The belief that one's native country, culture, language, abilities, or behavior is superior to those of another culture.

European Union (EU) The EU consists of 15 trading partners in Europe.

Exchange Rate This is the rate at which one country's currency can be exchanged for anther country's currency.

Expatriate Manager A manager living or working in a foreign country.

Expectancy The belief that a particular level of effort will lead to a particular level of performance.

Expectancy Theory A theory that suggests that people are motivated by two things: (1) how much they want something, and (2) how likely they think they are to get it.

Expert Power Power resulting from one's specialized information or expertise.

Exporting Producing goods domestically and selling them outside the country.

Expropriation A government's seizure of a foreign company's assets.

External Audit A formal verification of an organization's financial accounts and statements by outside experts.

External Dimensions of Diversity Human differences that have an element of choice; they consist of the personal characteristics that people acquire, discard, or modify throughout their lives.

External Recruiting Attracting job applicants from outside the organization.

External Stakeholders People or groups in the organization's external environment that are affected by it.

Extinction The withholding or withdrawal of positive rewards for desirable behavior, so that the behavior is less likely to occur in the future.

Extranet An extended intranet that connects internal employees with selected customers, suppliers, and other strategic partners.

Extrinsic Reward The payoff, such as money, a person receives from others for performing a particular task.

F

the Fed *Refers to the Federal Reserve Bank.*

Feedback The receiver expresses his or her reaction to the sender's message. The information about the reaction of the environment to the outputs which affect the inputs.

Feedback Control A control that takes place after operations are finished and is intended to correct problems that have already occurred.

Feedforward Control A control that takes place before operations begin and is intended to prevent anticipated problems.

Financial Statement This is a summary of some aspect of an organization's financial status.

First-Line Managers Also called supervisory managers. They make the short-term operating decisions, directing the daily tasks of nonmanagerial personnel.

Fixed Budget Allocating resources on the basis of a single estimate of costs.

Focused-Differentiation Strategy To offer products or services that are of unique and superior value compared to those of competitors and to target a narrow market.

Forecast A vision or projection of the future.

Foreign Corrupt Practices Act of 1977 An act that makes it illegal for employees of U.S. companies to bribe political decision makers in foreign nations.

Formal Appraisals Appraisals conducted at specific times throughout the years and based on performance measures that have been established in advance.

Formal Communication Channels Communications that follow the chain of command and are recognized as official.

Formal Group A group established to do something productive for the organization and is headed by a leader.

Forming The process of getting oriented and getting acquainted.

Four Management Functions Performing the planning, organizing, leading, and controlling necessary to get things done.

Franchising This is a form of licensing in which a company allows a foreign company to pay it a fee and a share of the profit in return for using the first company's brand name and a package of materials and services.

Free Market Economy The production of goods and services are controlled by private enterprise and the interaction of the forces of supply and demand rather than by the government.

Free Trade The movement of goods and services among nations without political or economic obstruction.

freelancers People who work independently of a firm and offer their work to anyone who is willing to pay.

from scratch To make something completely new.

Functional Managers Managers who are responsible for just one organizational activity.

Functional Structure An organization where people with similar occupational specialties are put together in formal groups.

Fundamental Attribution Bias Where people attribute another person's behavior to his or her personal characteristics rather than to situational factors.

G

Gainsharing The distribution of savings or "gains" to groups of employees who reduce costs and increase measurable productivity.

Garbage-Can Model In this style of decision making, managers make virtually random decisions.

General Environment (Macroenvironment) Includes six forces: economic, technological, sociocultural, demographic, political-legal, and international.

General Managers Managers who are responsible for several organizational activities.

Geocentric Managers Managers who accept that there are differences and similarities between home and foreign personnel and practices and that they should use whatever techniques are most effective.

Geographic Division A division with activities grouped around defined regional locations.

Glass Ceiling The metaphor for an invisible barrier preventing women and minorities from being promoted to top executive jobs.

Global Economy The increasing tendency of the economies of the world to interact with each other as one market instead of many national markets.

Global Outsourcing Using suppliers outside the United States to provide labor, goods, or services.

Global Village The "shrinking" of time and space as air travel and the electronic media have made it easier for the people of the globe to communicate with each other.

Globalization The trend of the world economy toward becoming a more interdependent system.

go for the gold To work to be the very best (figuratively winning a gold medal).

Goal Displacement This occurs when the primary goal is subsumed to a secondary goal.

Goal, Objective A specific commitment to achieve a measurable result within a stated period of time.

Goal-Setting Theory The suggestion that employees can be motivated by goals that are specific and challenging but achievable.

goof off (1) To take unauthorized time off from work. (2) Doing things at work not associated with the job, such as talking with others at the drinking fountain.

Government Regulators Regulatory agencies that establish ground rules under which organizations may operate.

Grand Strategy A grand strategy explains how the organization's mission is to be accomplished. Three common grand strategies are growth, stability, and defensive.

Grapevine The unofficial communication system of the informal organization.

Greenfield Venture A foreign subsidiary that the owning organization has built from scratch.

Group Two or more freely interacting individuals who share collective norms, share collective goals, and have a common identity.

Group Cohesiveness A "we feeling" binding group members together.

Groupthink A cohesive group's blind unwillingness to consider alternatives. This occurs when group members strive for agreement among themselves for the sake of unanimity and avoid accurately assessing the decision situation.

Growth Stage This, the most profitable stage, is the period in which customer demand increases, the product's sales grow, and later competitors may enter the market.

Growth Strategy This strategy involves expansion—as in sales revenues, market share, number of employees, or number of customers or (for nonprofits) clients served.

H

Halo Effect An effect in which we form a positive impression of an individual based on a single trait.

heavy hitters People with power and influence—and probably money.

helped turn around Helped reverse the downward trend.

Hero A person whose accomplishments embody the values of the organization.

Heuristics Strategies that simplify the process of making decisions.

Hierarchy of Authority, Chain of Command This is a control mechanism for making sure the right people do the right things at the right time.

Hierarchy of Needs Theory People are motivated by five levels of needs: (1) physiological, (2) safety, (3) belongingness, (4) esteem, and (5) self-actualization.

high gear Going at full strength.

high tech Anything having to do with advances in technology, such as computers, computer software, pagers, scanners, and the like.

Historical Perspective The historical perspective includes three viewpoints—classical, behavioral, and quantitative.

Horizontal Communication Communication that flows within and between work units; its main purpose is coordination.

hot second Immediately.

Human Relations Movement This movement proposed that better human relations could increase worker productivity.

Human Resource (HR) Management The activities managers perform to plan for, attract, develop, and retain a workforce.

Human Skills   Skills that consist of the ability to work well in cooperation with other people in order to get things done.

Hybrid Structure   An organizational form using functional and divisional structures in different parts of the same organization.

Hygiene Factors   Factors associated with job dissatisfaction—such as salary, working conditions, interpersonal relationships, and company policy—all of which affect the job context or environment in which people work.

I

Import Quota   A trade barrier in the form of a limit on the numbers of a product that can be imported.

Importing   Buying goods outside the country and reselling them domestically.

in the black   *Profitable*

in the red   *Unprofitable*

in the right hands   *To the person who can give you the most help.*

Incentives   Many organizations offer incentives such as commissions, bonuses, profit-sharing plans, and stock options.

Income Statement   A summary of an organization's financial results—revenues and expenses—over a specified period of time.

Incremental Budgeting   Allocating increased or decreased funds to a department by using the last budget period as a reference point; only incremental changes in the budget request are reviewed.

Incremental Innovations   The creation of products, services, or technologies that modify existing ones.

Incremental Model   Where managers take small, short-term steps to alleviate a problem.

Indigenization Laws   Laws that require that citizens within the host country must own a majority of whatever company is operating within that country.

Individual Approach   Ethical behavior guided by what will result in the individual's best long-term interests, which ultimately is in everyone's self-interest.

Informal Appraisals   Appraisals conducted on an unscheduled basis and consisting of less rigorous indications of employee performance.

Informal Communication Channels   Communication that develops outside the formal structure and does not follow the chain of command.

Informal Group   A group formed by people seeking friendship that has no officially appointed leader, although a leader may emerge from the membership.

Information Overload   An overload that occurs when the amount of information received exceeds a person's ability to handle or process it.

Informational Roles   Managers receive and communicate information with other people inside and outside of the organization as monitors, disseminators, and spokespersons.

Infrastructure   This consists of the physical facilities that form the basis of a country's level of economic development.

Innovation   Finding ways to deliver new or better goods or services.

Inputs   The people, money, information, equipment, and materials required to produce an organization's goods or services.

Instrumentality   The expectation that successful performance of the task will lead to the outcome desired.

Integration   The tendency of the parts of an organization to draw together to achieve a common purpose.

Interacting Group   A group in which members interact and deliberate with each other to reach a consensus.

Internal Audit   A verification of an organization's financial accounts and statements by the organization's own professional staff.

Internal Dimensions of Diversity   Those human differences that exert a powerful, sustained impact throughout every stage of our lives.

Internal Locus of Control   The belief that you control your own destiny.

Internal Recruiting   Hiring from the inside, or making people already employed by the organization aware of job openings.

Internal Stakeholders   Employees, owners, and the board of directors, if any.

International Forces   Changes in the economic, political, legal, and technological global system that may affect an organization.

International Management   Management that oversees the conduct of operations in or with organizations in foreign countries.

International Monetary Fund (IMF)   The purpose of the International Monetary Fund is to assist in smoothing the flow of money between nations.

Internet   A global network of independently operating but interconnected computers, linking more than 140,000 smaller networks.

Interpersonal Roles   Managers interact with people inside and outside of their work units. The three interpersonal roles include figurehead, leader, and liaison activities.

Intervention   An attempt to correct the diagnosed problem.

Intranet   An organization's private Internet.

Intrapreneur   Someone who works inside an existing organization who sees an opportunity for a product or service and mobilizes the organization's resources to try to realize it.

Intrinsic Reward   The satisfaction, such as a feeling of accomplishment, a person receives from performing the particular task itself.

Introduction Stage   The stage in the product life cycle in which a new product is introduced into the marketplace.

Intuitive Model   This style consists of a manager quickly sizing up a situation and making a decision based on his or her experience or practice.

IOUs   *Debt; abbreviation for "I owe you."*

is the heart   *The most important part of something; the central force or idea.*

J

Jargon   Terminology specific to a particular profession or group.

Job Analysis   The determination, by observation and analysis, of the basic elements of a job.

Job Characteristics Model   This consists of (1) five core job characteristics that affect (2) three critical psychological states of an employee that in turn affect (3) work outcomes—the employee's motivation, performance, and satisfaction.

Job Description   A summary of what the holder of the job does and how and why he or she does it.

Job Design The division of an organization's work among its employees and the application of motivational theories to jobs to increase satisfaction and performance.

Job Enlargement Increasing the number of tasks in a job to increase variety and motivation.

Job Enrichment Building into a job such motivating factors as responsibility, achievement, recognition, stimulating work, and advancement.

Job Involvement The extent to which you identify or are personally involved with your job.

Job Posting Placing information about job vacancies and qualifications on bulletin boards, in newsletters, and on the organization's intranet.

Job Satisfaction The extent to which you feel positively or negatively about various aspects of your work.

Job Simplification The process of reducing the number of tasks a worker performs.

Job Specification The minimum qualifications a person must have to perform the job successfully.

Joint Ventures A U.S. firm may form a joint venture, also known as a strategic alliance, with a foreign company to share the risks and rewards of starting a new enterprise together in a foreign country.

joke around Tell jokes and generally act less than professional.

jump at the idea Respond positively to a new idea.

jumped headfirst Began quickly and eagerly, without hesitation.

Justice Approach Ethical behavior guided by respect for impartial standards of fairness and equity.

K

key player Important participant.

kick back and relax To take a rest.

knowledge walk out the door Lose knowledge that employees have because they don't share it with others before they leave the company.

L

Large-Batch Technology Mass-production assembly-line technology.

the last laugh This comes from the expression, "He who laughs last, laughs loudest" because he or she has been proven right.

Leadership The ability to influence employees to voluntarily pursue organizational goals.

Leadership Grid Model The ideal leadership style having a high concern for (1) production, the job aspects of subordinates' behavior, and (2) people, the human aspects of their behavior.

Leading Motivating, directing, and otherwise influencing people to work hard to achieve the organization's goals.

Learned Helplessness The debilitating lack of faith in one's ability to control one's environment.

Learning Organization An organization that actively creates, acquires, and transfers knowledge within itself and is able to modify its behavior to reflect new knowledge.

Legitimate Power All managers have this power, which results from their formal positions with the organization.

Less-Developed Countries Also known as developing countries, they consist of nations with low economic development and low average incomes.

Licensing When a company allows a foreign company to pay it a fee to make or distribute the first company's product or service.

Line Managers Managers who have the authority to make decisions and usually have people reporting to them.

Locus of Control An indication of how much people believe they control their fate through their own efforts.

Loss Your total costs exceed your total sales revenue.

M

Maintenance Role A relationship-related role consisting of behavior that fosters constructive relationships among team members.

Management The pursuit of organizational goals efficiently and effectively by integrating the work of people through planning, organizing, leading, and controlling the organization's resources.

Management by Exception A control principle that states that managers should be informed of a situation only if data shows a significant deviation from standards.

Management by Objectives (MBO) This is a four-step process in which (1) managers and employees jointly set objectives for the employee, (2) managers develop action plans, (3) managers and employees periodically review the employee's performance, and (4) the manager makes a performance appraisal and rewards the employee according to results.

Management by Wandering Around (MBWA) A style of management in which a manager literally wanders around the organization and talks with people across all lines of authority.

Management Process Performing the planning, organizing, leading, and controlling necessary to get things done.

Management Science This focuses on using mathematics to aid in problem solving and decision making.

Maquiladoras Manufacturing plants allowed to operate in Mexico with special privileges in return for employing Mexican citizens.

Market Control The use of market mechanisms—pricing, competition, market share—to guide performance.

marriage of software, hardware, etc. Combination of various technologies.

Matrix Structure An organizational form which combines functional and divisional chains of commands in a grid so that there are two command structures—vertical and horizontal.

Maturity Stage A stage when the organization becomes very bureaucratic, large, and mechanistic.

Maturity Stage The period in which the product starts to fall out of favor and sales and profits fall off.

Means-End Chain In the chain of management (operational, tactical, strategic) the accomplishment of low-level goals are the means leading to the accomplishment of high-level goals or ends.

measuring stick Tool used to evaluate or compare something.

Mechanistic Organization An organization where authority is centralized, tasks and rules are clearly specified, and employees are closely supervised.

Media Richness An indication of how well a particular medium conveys information and promotes learning.

Medium The pathway by which a message travels.

Mercosur The largest trade bloc in Latin America, with four members.

Message The information to be shared.

Middle Managers They implement the policies and plans of the top managers above them and supervise and coordinate the activities of the first-line managers below them.

Midlife Stage A period of growth evolving into stability when the organization becomes bureaucratic.

mine the knowledge Make maximum use of the knowledge employees have.

Mission An organization's mission is its purpose or reason for being.

Mission Statement A mission statement expresses the purpose of the organization.

Mixed Economy In a mixed economy, most of the important industries are owned by the government, but others are controlled by private enterprise.

money laundering When illegal money is made to appear legal by passing it through a bank or legal business.

Monochronic Time A preference for doing one thing at a time.

Moral-Rights Approach Ethical behavior guided by respect for the fundamental rights of human beings.

more than meets the eye There's more to something than can be seen.

Most Favored Nation This trading status describes a condition in which a country grants other countries favorable trading treatment such as the reduction of import duties.

Motivating Factors Factors associated with job satisfaction—such as achievement, recognition, responsibility, and advancement—all of which affect the job content or the rewards of work performance.

Motivation May be defined as the psychological processes that arouse and direct goal-directed behavior.

muddy the water Make things unclear.

Multinational Corporation A business firm with operations in several countries.

Multinational Organization A nonprofit organization with operations in several countries.

N

National Labor Relations Board As legislated in 1935, it enforces the procedures whereby employees may vote to have a union and for collective bargaining.

Need-Based Perspectives Also known as content perspectives, these are theories that emphasize the needs that motivate people.

Needs Physiological or psychological deficiencies that arouse behavior.

Network Structure An organizational form with a central core that is linked to outside independent firms by computer connections, which are used to operate as if all were a single organization.

no haggle pricing Situation where prices are fixed and cannot be negotiated with the seller.

Noise Any disturbance that interferes with the transmission of a message.

Nominal Group A group to generate ideas and evaluate solutions by writing down as many ideas as possible. The ideas are then listed on a blackboard, then discussed, then voted upon.

Nonprogrammed Decisions Decisions that occur under nonroutine, unfamiliar circumstances.

Nonrational Models of Decision Making A style that explains how managers make decisions; they assume that decision making is nearly always uncertain and risky, making it difficult for managers to make optimum decisions.

Nonverbal Communication Messages sent outside of the written or spoken word.

Norming The stage in which conflicts are resolved, close relationships develop, and unity and harmony emerge.

Norms General guidelines or rules of behavior that most group or team members follow.

North American Free Trade Agreement (NAFTA) A trading bloc consisting of the United States, Canada, and Mexico.

not bat an eye To not seem to see; to not react.

O

Objective Appraisals, Results Appraisals Appraisals that are based on facts and are often numerical.

Obstructionist Approach An approach by managers to put economic gain first and resist social responsibility as being outside the organization's self-interest.

Open System A system that continually interacts with its environment.

Operational Control Monitoring performance to ensure that operational plans—day-to-day goals—are being implemented and taking corrective action as needed.

Operational Goals Goals that are set by and for first-line managers and are concerned with short-term matters associated with realizing tactical goals.

Operational Planning Managers determine how to accomplish specific tasks with available resources within the next 1-week to 1-year period.

Operations Management Operations management focuses on managing the production and delivery of an organization's products or services more effectively.

Opportunities Situations that present possibilities for exceeding existing goals.

Organic Organization An organization where authority is decentralized, there are fewer rules and procedures, and networks of employees are encouraged to cooperate and respond quickly to unexpected tasks.

Organization A group of people who work together to achieve some specific purpose. A system of consciously coordinated activities or forces of two or more people.

Organization Chart A box-and-lines illustration showing the formal lines of authority and the organization's official positions or division of labor.

Organization Development (OD) A set of techniques for implementing planned change to make people and organizations more effective.

Organizational Behavior (OB) Behavior that is dedicated to better understanding and managing people at work.

Organizational Culture Sometimes called corporate culture, this is a system of shared beliefs and values that develops within an organization and guides the behavior of its members.

Organizational Life Cycle A four-stage cycle with a natural sequence of stages: birth, youth, midlife, and maturity.

Organizational Opportunities The environmental factors that the organization may exploit for competitive advantage.

Organizational Size This is usually measured by the number of full-time employees.

Organizational Strengths The skills and capabilities that give the organization special competencies and competitive advantages in executing strategies in pursuit of its mission.

Organizational Threats The environmental factors that hinder an organization's achieving a competitive advantage.

Organizational Weaknesses The drawbacks that hinder an organization in executing strategies in pursuit of its mission.

Organizing Arranging tasks, people, and other resources to accomplish the work.

Orientation This helps the newcomer fit smoothly into the job and the organization.

out of the office loop *Not included in everyday workplace communication.*

Outputs The products, services, profits, losses, employee satisfaction or discontent, and the like that are produced by the organization.

Outsourcing Subcontracting of services and operations to an outside vendor. Using suppliers outside the company to provide goods and services.

Owners Those who can claim the organization as their legal property.

P

Panic A situation where a manager reacts frantically to get rid of a problem that he or she cannot deal with realistically.

Paradigm Generally accepted way of viewing the world.

Participative Management (PM) The process of involving employees in (1) setting goals, (2) making decisions, (3) solving problems, and (4) making changes in the organization.

Path-Goal Leadership Model Contingency approach that holds that the effective leader clarifies paths through which subordinates can achieve goals, both organizational and personal.

Pay for Knowledge The employees' pay is tied to the number of job-relevant skills or academic degrees they earn.

Pay for Performance Pay based on one's results.

Perception The process of interpreting and understanding one's environment.

Performance Appraisal Assessing an employee's performance and providing him or her with feedback.

Performing The stage in which members concentrate on solving problems and completing the assigned task.

perks *Short for perquisites; compensation in addition to salary, such as day care or a company car.*

Personality The stable psychological traits and behavioral attributes that give a person his or her identity.

Personalized Power Power directed at helping oneself.

Philanthropy Donating money to worthwhile recipients.

pick up the tab *Pay for something.*

piece of the action *Part of the opportunities.*

Piece Rate Pay based on how much output an employee produces.

pink slip *To be fired from a job; derived from the days when employers gave workers written notices (on pink paper) that their jobs were terminated.*

pitch in *To help as needed.*

Planning Setting goals and deciding how to achieve them. Also coping with uncertainty by formulating future courses of action to achieve specified results.

Planning/Control Cycle A cycle that has two planning steps (1 and 2) and two control steps (3 and 4), as follows: (1) Make the plan. (2) Carry out the plan. (3) Control the direction by comparing results with the plan. (4) Control the direction by taking corrective action in two ways—namely, (a) by correcting deviations in the plan being carried out, or (b) by improving future plans.

played his last card *Tried the last thing he could think of.*

Political Risk The risk that political changes will cause loss of a company's assets or impair its foreign operations.

Political-Legal Forces Changes in the way politics shape laws and laws shape the opportunities for and threats to an organization.

Polycentric Managers Managers who take the view that native managers in foreign offices best understand native personnel and practices, and so the home office should leave them alone.

Polychronic Time A preference for doing more than one thing at a time.

pool their creative juices *To combine their talents; to work together.*

Porter's Four Competitive Strategies (Four Generic Strategies) (1) Cost-leadership, (2) differentiation, (3) cost-focus, (4) focused-differentiation.

Positive Behavior The use of positive consequences to encourage desirable behavior.

Power The extent to which a person is able to influence others so they respond to orders.

Privatization Privatization occurs where state-owned activities are performed by private enterprise.

Proactive Approach An approach by managers to actively lead the way in being socially responsible for all stakeholders, using the organization's resources to identify and respond to social problems.

Proactive Change Proactive or planned change involves making carefully thought-out changes in anticipation of possible or expected problems or opportunities.

Problems Difficulties that inhibit the achievement of goals.

Process Innovation A change in the way a product or service is conceived, manufactured, or disseminated.

Process Perspectives Perspectives concerned with the thought processes by which people decide how to act.

Product Division A division with activities grouped around similar products or services.

Product Innovation A change in the appearance or performance of a product or service or the creation of a new one.

Product Life Cycle A model that graphs the four stages of a product or service during the "life" of its marketability: (1) introduction, (2) growth, (3) maturity, and (4) decline.

Profit The amount by which total revenue exceeds total costs.

Profit Sharing The distribution to employees of a percentage of the company's profits.

Program A single-use plan encompassing a range of projects or activities.

Programmed Conflict Conflict designed to elicit different opinions without inciting people's personal feelings.

Programmed Decision Decisions that are repetitive and routine.

Project A single-use plan of less scope and complexity than a program.

Project Life Cycle A cycle with four stages from start to finish: definition, planning, execution, and closing.

Prospectors Managers who develop new products or services and seek out new markets, rather than waiting for things to happen.

provided the spark *Supplied the energy that motivated others.*

Punishment The application of negative consequences to stop or change undesirable behavior.

Q

Quality The total ability of a product or service to meet customer needs.

Quality Assurance This focuses on the performance of workers, urging employees to strive for "zero defects."

Quality Circles Control circles consisting of small groups of volunteer workers and supervisors who meet intermittently to discuss workplace and quality-related problems.

Quality Control The strategy for minimizing errors by managing each state of production.

Quality-Management Viewpoints Viewpoints that include quality control, quality assurance, and total quality management.

Quantitative Management This is the application to management of quantitative techniques, such as statistics and computer simulations. Two branches of quantitative management are management science and operations management.

quite a stir *A situation where people are all excited about something.*

R

Radical Innovations The creation of products, services, or technologies that replace existing ones.

Ratio Analysis The practice of evaluating financial ratios.

Rational Model of Decision Making/ Classical Model This style of decision

making explains how managers should make decisions; it assumes that managers will make logical decisions that will be the optimum in furthering the organization's best interests.

Reactive Change Making changes in response to problems or opportunities as they arise.

Reactors Managers who make adjustments only when finally forced to by environmental pressures.

Readiness The extent to which a follower possesses the ability and willingness to complete a task.

Realistic Job Preview Giving a candidate a picture of both positive and negative features of the job and organization before he or she is hired.

Receiver The person for whom a message is intended.

Recruiting The process of locating and attracting qualified applicants for jobs open in the organization.

Reduced Cycle Time A reduction of steps in the work process.

Referent Power Power deriving from one's personal attraction.

Reinforcement Anything that causes a given behavior to be repeated or inhibited.

Reinforcement Theory An attempt to explain behavior change by suggesting that behavior with positive consequences tends to be repeated whereas behavior with negative consequences tends not to be repeated.

Relaxed Avoidance A condition in which a manager decides to take no action in the belief that there will be no great negative consequences.

Relaxed Change A condition in which a manager realizes that complete inaction will have negative consequences but opts for the first available alternative that involves low risk.

Representativeness Bias The tendency to generalize from a small sample or a single event.

Response Uncertainty When the consequences of a decision are uncertain.

Responsibility The obligation you have to perform the tasks assigned to you.

the rest is history *What happens next is well known.*

Reward Power All managers have this power, which results from their authority to reward their subordinates.

Rites and Rituals The activities and ceremonies, planned and unplanned, that celebrate important occasions and accomplishments in an organizations' life.

Role A socially determined expectation of how an individual should behave in a specific position. Set of behaviors that people expect of occupants of a position.

roller coaster ride *Volatile; refers to the resemblance to the rapid change between extreme high and low points on an amusement park ride.*

rookie mistakes *A newcomer's errors; errors made by someone inexperienced.*

run on the banks *When people are uncertain whether or not their funds are safe in banks, they may rush to take their money out before other people do and there is none left for them.*

S

Sales Commissions Where sales representatives are paid a percentage of the earnings the company made from their sales.

Satisficing Model Where managers seek alternatives until they find one that is satisfactory, not optimal.

scab *A person who crosses a union picket line to assume the job of a striking worker.*

Scientific Management Scientific management emphasizes the scientific study of work methods in order to improve the productivity of individual workers.

sea of information *Lots of information; often too much to process.*

seat-of-the-pants start-up *A new business that has very few resources.*

second thoughts *Rethinking a decision based on more information being available.*

Selection Process The screening of job applicants to hire the best candidate.

Selective Perception The tendency to filter out information that is discomforting, that seems irrelevant, or that contradicts one's beliefs.

Self-Efficacy Personal ability to do a task.

Self-Esteem The extent to which people like or dislike themselves.

Self-Fulfilling Prophecy Also sometimes known as the Pygmalion effect; it is the phenomenon in which people's expectations of themselves or others leads them to behave in ways that make those expectations come true.

Self-Managed Teams Groups of workers who are given administrative oversight for their task domains.

Self-Monitoring The extent to which people are able to observe their own behavior and adapt it to external situations.

Self-Serving Bias Where people tend to take more personal responsibility for success than for failure.

Semantics The study of the meaning of words.

Sender The person wanting to share information.

Servant Leaders One who focuses on providing increased service to others—meeting the goals of both followers and the organization—rather than themselves.

Sexual Harassment Unwanted sexual attention that creates an adverse work environment.

sift through mountains of information *Sort through large volumes of information.*

Simple Structure An organization with authority centralized in a single person, a flat hierarchy, few rules, and low work specialization.

Situational Interview The interviewer focuses on hypothetical situations.

Situational Leadership Theory Leadership behavior reflecting how leaders should adjust their leadership style according to the readiness of the followers.

Skunkworks A project team whose members are separated from the normal operation of an organization and asked to produce a new, innovative product.

Small-Batch Technology This is often the least complex technology; goods are custom-made to customer specifications in small quantities.

SMART Goal A goal that is Specific, Measurable, Attainable, Results oriented, and has Target dates.

Social Loafing The tendency of people to exert less effort when working in groups than when working alone.

Social Responsibility A manager's duty to take action that will benefit the interests of society as well as of the organization.

Socialized Power Power directed at helping others.

Sociocultural Forces Influences and trends originating in a country, society, or culture; human relationships and values that may affect an organization.

Spam Unsolicited e-mail jokes and junk mail.

Span of Control The number of people reporting directly to a given manager.

Special-Interest Groups Groups whose members try to influence specific issues.

Special-Purpose Team A team that meets to solve a special or one-time problem.

squeezing franchisees' profits *Tightening or reducing profits.*

Stability Strategy This strategy involves little or no significant change.

Staff Personnel Staff with advisory functions; they provide advice, recommendations, and research to line managers.

Stakeholders People whose interests are affected by an organization's activities.

start-up business *A new company.*

State Uncertainty When the environment is considered unpredictable.

Statistical Process Control A statistical technique that uses periodic random samples from production runs to see if quality is being maintained within a standard range of acceptability.

Stereotype Oversimplified beliefs about a certain group of people.

Stereotyping The tendency to attribute to an individual the characteristics one believes are typical of the group to which that individual belongs.

Stock Options Certain employees are given the right to buy stock at a future date for a discounted price.

Storming The emergence of individual personalities, roles, and conflicts within the group.

Story A narrative based on true events, which is repeated—and sometimes embellished upon—to emphasize a particular value.

Strategic Allies Describes the relationship of two organizations that join forces to achieve advantages neither can perform as well alone.

Strategic Control Monitoring performance to ensure that strategic plans are being implemented and taking corrective action as needed.

Strategic Goals Goals that are set by and for top management and focus on objectives for the organization as a whole.

Strategic Human Resource Planning The development of a systematic, comprehensive strategy for (1) understanding current employee needs and (2) predicting future employee needs.

Strategic Management A process that involves managers from all parts of the organization in the formulation and implementation of strategies and strategic goals.

Strategic Planning Plans to determine what the organization's long-term goals should be for the next 1–10 years with the resources it expects to have available.

Strategy A large-scale action plan that sets the direction for an organization.

Strategy Formulation The process of choosing among different strategies and altering them to best fit the organization's needs.

Strategy Implementation Putting strategic plans into effect.

Stress The tension people feel when they are facing or enduring extraordinary demands, constraints, or opportunities and are uncertain about their ability to handle them effectively.

Stressor The source of stress.

Structured Interview Asking each applicant the same questions and comparing their responses to a standardized set of answers.

Subjective Appraisals Appraisals based on a manager's perceptions of an employee's traits or behaviors.

Subsystems This is a collection of parts making up the whole system.

Supplier A person or organization that provides supplies—raw materials, services, equipment, labor, or energy—to other organizations.

SWOT Analysis The search for the Strengths, Weaknesses, Opportunities, and Threats affecting the organization.

Symbol An object, act, quality, or event that conveys meaning to others.

System A system is a set of interrelated parts that operate together to achieve a common purpose.

Systems Viewpoint This viewpoint regards the organization as a system of interrelated parts.

T

Tactical Control Monitoring performance to ensure that tactical plans—those at the divisional or departmental level—are being implemented and taking corrective action as needed.

Tactical Goals Goals that are set by and for middle managers and focus on the actions needed to achieve strategic goals.

Tactical Planning Managers determine what contributions their departments or similar work units can make with their given resources during the next six months to two years.

take the plunge *To finally get started.*

talking the talk *Promising things to people, but not following through with action.*

Tariff A tariff is a trade barrier in the form of a customs duty, or tax, levied mainly on imports.

Task Environment Eleven groups that present you with daily tasks to handle: customers, competitors, suppliers, distributors, strategic allies, employee groups, local communities, financial institutions, government regulators, special-interest groups, and mass media.

Task Role Behavior that concentrates on getting the team's task done.

Team A small group of people with complementary skills who are committed to a common purpose, performance goals, and approach to which they hold themselves mutually accountable.

Team-Based Structure An organizational form where teams or workgroups, either temporary or permanent, are used to improve horizontal relations and solve problems throughout the organization.

Technical Skills Skills that consist of the job-specific knowledge needed to perform well in a specialized field.

Technological Forces New developments in methods for transforming resources into goods or services.

Technology All the tools and ideas for transforming material, data, or labor (inputs) into goods or services (outputs). It applies not just to computers but any machine or process that enables an organiza-

tion to gain a competitive advantage in changing materials used to produce a finished product.

telecom *Short for telecommunications.*

Telecommuting Doing work that is generally performed in the office away from the office, using a variety of information technologies.

telephone tag *To leave a telephone message when you attempt to return a message left for you.*

thorny issue *An issue that can cause pain (as a thorn on a rose bush may).*

time in the trenches *Working out with the other employees and experiencing what they contend with as opposed to managing from an office and relying solely on reports about what is happening in the workplace.*

tip of the iceberg *There is much more to the issue than what appears on the surface.*

Top Managers They make the long-term decisions about the overall direction of the organization and establish the objectives, policies, and strategies for it.

Total Quality Management (TQM) This is a comprehensive approach—led by top management and supported throughout the organization—dedicated to continuous quality improvement, training, and customer satisfaction.

Totalitarian Governments These governments are ruled by a dictator, a single political party, or a special-membership group.

Trade Protectionism The use of government regulations to limit the import of goods and services.

Trading Bloc Also known as an economic community; it is a group of nations within a geographical region that have agreed to remove trade barriers with each other.

Training Educating technical and operational employees in how to better do their current jobs.

Trait Approaches to Leadership Attempts to identify distinctive characteristics that account for the effectiveness of leaders.

Transactional Leader One who focuses on the interpersonal transactions between managers and employees.

Transformation Processes The organization's capabilities in management

and technology that are applied to converting inputs into outputs.

Trend Analysis A hypothetical extension of a past series of events into the future.

Turnover When employees leave their jobs.

Two-Factor Theory Proposes that work satisfaction and dissatisfaction arise from two different work factors—work satisfaction from so-called motivating factors and work dissatisfaction from so-called hygiene factors.

U

Underemployed People working at jobs that require less education than they have.

Unstructured Interview Using ordinary conversation to ask probing questions to find out what the applicant is like.

up front *To be forthcoming, to be honest from the start.*

Upward Communication Communication that flows from lower levels to higher levels.

Utilitarian Approach Ethical behavior guided by what will result in the greatest good for the greatest number of people.

V

Valence The value or importance a worker assigns to the possible outcome or reward.

Value System The pattern of values within an organization.

Values Abstract ideals that guide one's thinking and behavior across all situations. The relatively permanent and deeply held underlying beliefs and attitudes that help determine a person's behavior.

Variable Budget Allowing the allocation of resources to vary in proportion with various levels of activity.

Variable Costs Expenses that vary directly depending on the numbers of the product that you produce and sell.

Videoconferencing Video and audio links along with computers to enable people located at different locations to see, hear, and talk with one another.

virtual bank *A bank with no building to go to; an Internet bank.*

Vision Statement A statement that expresses what the organization should become, and where it wants to go strategically.

W

walking the walk *Doing what you say you will do.*

wannabes *Individuals who want to be something.*

watching over your shoulder *Someone looking at everything you do.*

Whistleblower An employee who reports organizational misconduct to the public.

Wholly Owned Subsidiary This is a foreign subsidiary that is totally owned and controlled by an organization.

Work Teams Teams that engage in collective work requiring coordinated effort; they are of four types, which may be identified according to their basic purpose: advice teams, production teams, project teams, and action teams.

World Bank The purpose of the World Bank is to provide low-interest loans to developing nations for improving transportation, education, health, and telecommunications.

World Trade Organization (WTO) An organization designed to monitor and enforce trade agreements.

Y

you get what you pay for *If you pay a low price, you'll probably get a low-quality product.*

Youth Stage The stage in which the organization is in a prebureaucratic stage, a stage of growth and expansion.

Z

zero sum game *A game in which, if one side wins, the other side must lose—as opposed to a game where both sides can win, which is called a win-win game.*

Zero-Based Budgeting (ZBB) Forcing each department to start from zero in projecting its funding needs for the coming budget period.

credits

CHAPTER 1

Photo/Illustration: Courtesy of Burrston House; Photo Disc; Photo Disc; AP Wide World Photo; Courtesy of Fed Ex; Photo Disc; Courtesy of Burrston House; © Brian Williams & Stacey Sawyer; AP Wide World Photo; Photo Disc; Courtesy of Microsoft; Photo Disc; Photo Disc; Rosemary Hedger; Photo Disc; AP Wide World Photo; © Martin E. Klimek; Courtesy of Focus: Hope; Photo Disc; Courtesy of Handspring, Inc.; AP Wide World Photo; AP Wide World Photo; Photo Disc; Barbel Schmidt; Photo Disc.

Text: Management in Action: Aftermath of the World Trade Center Terrorist Attacks, from *The Wall Street Journal,* Eastern Edition by Carol Hymowitz. Copyright © 2001 by Dow Jones & Co., Inc. Reproduced with permission of Dow Jones & Co., Inc. via Copyright Clearance Center; Ethical Dilemma: Waddell & Reed Financial Inc., from *The Wall Street Journal,* Eastern Edition by Susanne Craig and Kara Scannell. Copyright © 2001 by Dow Jones & Co., Inc. Reproduced with permission of Dow Jones & Co., Inc. via Copyright Clearance Center.

CHAPTER 2

Photo/Illustration: Photo Disc; Photo Disc; Bettmann/CORBIS; Bettmann/CORBIS; Underwood & Underwood/CORBIS; Photo by Piotr Malecki/Liaison; Photo Disc; Joan C. Tonn/Unwich Management Center; Courtesy of AT&T Corporate Archives; Bettmann/CORBIS; Courtesy of Debra's Natural Gourmet; Kent Dayton Photography; Photo Disc; Courtesy of Fed Ex; Courtesy of Costco; Photo Disc; Philippe Gontier/The Image Works; Photo Disc; Courtesy of Burrston House; Photo Disc; Cyndy Freeman/© Starbuck Coffee Co. All rights reserved; Photo Disc; Courtesy of the Department of Commerce; with permission of the W. Edwards Deming Institute; Photo Disc; Courtesy of EDS.

Text: Management in Action: Boeing Relies on a Variety of Management Theories, from *The Wall Street Journal,* Eastern Edition by J. Lynn Lunsford. Copyright © 2001 by Dow Jones & Co., Inc. Reproduced with permission of Dow Jones & Co., Inc. via Copyright Clearance Center; Ethical Dilemma: Recycling Automobile Air Bags, reprinted from August 6, 2001 issue of *Business Week* by special permission. Copyright © 2001 by The McGraw-Hill Companies, Inc.

CHAPTER 3

Photo/Illustration: Photo Disc; AP Wide World Photo; Courtesy of United Airlines Archives; Photo Disc; Courtesy of Burrston House; Debra McClinton; Cleve Bryant/PhotoEdit; Tony Freeman/PhotoEdit; AP Wide World Photo; Photo Disc; AP Wide World Photo; AP Wide World Photo; Courtesy of Nike; AP Wide World Photo; Photo Disc; Courtesy of Bagel Works; AP Wide World Photo; © Brian Williams & Stacey Sawyer; AP Wide World Photo; Photo Disc; Michael Newman/PhotoEdit; AP Wide World Photo; Bob Daemmrich/Stock Boston; Courtesy of Eastman Kodak Company; Myrleen Ferguson Cate/PhotoEdit; Photo Disc; Courtesy of Line Skis; Courtesy of Post-It® Flags from 3M; © 2002 Morton Buildings, Inc./Courtesy of Woodward Camp; Courtesy of Ebay.

Text: Management in Action: New Roles are Required, from Laird Harrison, "We're All The Boss," *Time,* April 2002. Copyright © 2002 Time Inc. Reprinted by permission; Ethical Dilemma: A Teacher Faces the Problem of Dealing with Cheating Students, from Clayton Bellamy, "Teacher Resigns as School Backs Plagiarizing Kids," *The Arizona Republic,* February 10, 2002. Reprinted with permission of The Associated Press.

CHAPTER 4

Photo/Illustration: Photo Disc; Bob Daemmirch/ Stock Boston; Courtesy of Amazon.com, Inc.; © Brian Williams & Stacey Sawyer; © AFP/CORBIS; Photo Disc; Photo Disc; Photo Disc; Courtesy of Burrston House; Photo Disc; Courtesy of Home Depot © Homer TLC, Inc.; MANDM, Inc./The Image Works; Courtesy of Burrston House; Photo Disc; Photo Researchers/P. Chickering; Deborah Harse/The Image Works; AP Wide World Photo; Photo Disc; AP Wide World Photo; James Marshall/The Image Works; Photo Disc; Aaron C. Anderer; Rosemary Hedger; © John B. Moore, Jr./The Image Works; Courtesy of Mercedes Benz.

Text: Management in Action: The Daimler-Benz and Chrysler Merger . . ., reprinted from September 17, 2001 issue of *Business Week* by special permission. Copyright © 2001 by The McGraw-Hill Companies, Inc.; Ethical Dilemma: Dawn Raids Are Used. . ., from *The Wall Street Journal,* Eastern Edition by Philip Shishkin. Copyright © 2002 by Dow Jones & Co., Inc. Reproduced with permission of Dow Jones & Co., Inc. via Copyright Clearance Center.

CHAPTER 5

Photo/Illustration: Photo Disc; Rachel Epstein/The Image Works; Jim Sulley/Wire; Pix/The Image Works; Courtesy of Nokia; Courtesy of Rubbermaid; Photo Disc; Courtesy of Intel Corporation; Photo Disc; Courtesy of Southwest Airlines; Photo Disc; Rosemary Hedger; Photo Disc; © R.W. Jones/CORBIS; Bill Bachmann/The Image Works; Photo Disc; Courtesy of UPP Business Systems; Courtesy of IBM; Frank Pedrick/The Image Works; Courtesy of Lear Corporation; Photo Disc; Photo Disc; Courtesy of Wal-Mart; Panel 5.2, Adapted from Locke/Latham, *A Theory of Goal Setting and Task Performance,* Prentice-Hall, 1990; Panel 5.3, Adapted from C. Shavers, "Detail vs. Strategic Thinking Can Put Workers at Odds," *San Jose Mercury News,* November 1, 1998.

Text: Practical Application Box: Detail Thinkers versus Strategic Thinkers, adapted from C. Shavers, "Detail vs. Strategic Thinking Can Put Workers at Odds," *San Jose Mercury News,* November 1, 1998; Management in Action: Mondavi's French Venture, reprinted from September 3, 2001 issue of *Business Week* by special permission. Copyright © 2001 by The McGraw-Hill Companies, Inc.; Ethical Dilemma: Retention Bonuses, from *The Wall Street Journal,* Eastern Edition by Joann S. Lubin. Copyright © 2002 by Dow Jones & Co., Inc. Reproduced with permission of Dow Jones & Co., Inc. via Copyright Clearance Center.

CHAPTER 6

Photo/Illustration: Kevin Lee/Getty Images; Photo Disc; Courtesy of Ford Motor Company; © Brian Williams & Stacey Sawyer; Courtesy of Swatch; Courtesy of Ateco, Inc.; Rosemary Hedger; Photo Disc; Courtesy of McGraw-Hill; Syracuse Newspapers/The Image Works; AP Wide World Photo; AP Wide World Photo; Matthew Borkoski/Stock Boston; Photo Disc; Photo Disc; Rosemary Hedger; AP Wide World Photo; Courtesy of Shell Oil; Photo Disc; Rosemary Hedger; © Brian Williams & Stacey Sawyer; Courtesy of Southwest Airlines; Photo Disc; Photo Disc; Bob Daemmrich/Stock Boston; Panel 6.5, Adapted R.S. Kaplan and D.P. Norton, "The Balanced Scorecard—Measures That Drive Performance," *Harvard Business Review,* January-February 1992.

Text: Management in Action: Intel Adopts a Many-Pronged Strategy, reprinted from October 15, 2001 issue of *Business Week* by special permission. Copyright © 2001 by The McGraw-Hill Companies, Inc.; Ethical Dilemma: Some American Companies Follow Strategy . . ., from David Cay Johnston, "Senators Assail Corporate Use of Bermuda as Tax Shelter," *The New York Times*, March 22, 2002. Copyright © 2002 by the New York Times Co. Reprinted by permission.

CHAPTER 7

Photo/Illustration: Photo Disc; Rosemary Hedger; Tina-Marie Lacava/Courtesy of Camden County College; Gary A. Conner/PhotoEdit; Courtesy of Southwest Airlines;, Eric Draper/White House/Getty Images; Photo Disc; AP Wide World Photo; Photo Researchers, Inc./Joseph Sohm; Courtesy of Novell, Inc.; AP Wide World Photo; Photo Disc; AP Wide World Photo; Courtesy of NASCAR; Courtesy of Whirlpool Corporation; Rosemary Hedger; AP Wide World Photo; Photo Disc; Photo Disc; Ford Motor Corporation; Rosemary Hedger; Photo Disc; Rudi Meisel/Visum; Photo Disc; AP Wide World Photo; AP Wide World Photo; AP Wide World Photo; Roger Ressmeyer/CORBIS.

Text: Management in Action: Nike's Decision making Impacts . . ., reprinted from July 2, 2001 issue of *Business Week* by special permission. Copyright © 2001 by The McGraw-Hill Companies, Inc.; Ethical Dilemma: UBS Paine Webber, from Richard A. Oppel, Jr., "The Man Who Paid the Price for Sizing Up Enron," *The New York Times*, March 27, 2002. Copyright © 2002 by the New York Times Co. Reprinted by permission.

CHAPTER 8

Photo/Illustration: Photo Disc; Courtesy of Sun Microsystems; Courtesy of Hewlett-Packard Company; Courtesy of Mary Kay; Photo Disc; Photo Disc; Courtesy of Hewlett-Packard Company; Courtesy of Allstate Insurance Company; Courtesy of the Democratic National Committee; Courtesy of the Republican; National Committee; Photo Disc; Photo Disc; Rosemary Hedger; Photo Disc; Photo Disc; AP Wide World Photo; Courtesy of Burrston House; © Brian Williams & Stacey Sawyer; Photo Disc; Courtesy of JetBlue Airlines; Courtesy of McDonald's; Melanie Dunea/Cpi; Courtesy of Mitsubishi; © Auntie Anne's, Inc.; Courtesy of Krispy Kreme Doughnuts, Inc.; Photo Disc; Courtesy of Peter Guber.

Text: Management in Action: How Accounting Firms Arthur Andersen Changed Its Culture; from *The Wall Street Journal*, Eastern Edition by Ken Brown and Jonathan Weil. Copyright © 2002 by Dow Jones & Co., Inc. Reproduced with permission of Dow Jones & Co., Inc. via Copyright Clearance Center; Ethical Dilemma: Enron's Organizational Culture, reprinted from February 25, 2002 issue of *Business Week* by special permission. Copyright © 2002 by The McGraw-Hill Companies, Inc.

CHAPTER 9

Photo/Illustration: Photo Disc; Photo by Stef Barber-Mueller, SAS; The Container Store; Courtesy of Burrston House; Courtesy of Wachovia; Photo Disc; Photo Disc; DVC Worldwide; Eileen Anderer; Courtesy of McGraw-Hill; Lafayette Instrument Company, Inc.; Photo Disc; Courtesy of FedEx; Photo Disc; Photo Disc; Photo Disc; Rosemary Hedger; Photo Disc; Courtesy of Internation Paper Company; Larry Kolvoord/The Image Works; Photo Disc; Photo Disc; Photo Disc; Photo Disc; AP Wide World Photo.

Text: Management in Action: Workforce Shifts to Big Companies, from Jim Hopkins, "Workforce Shifts to Big Companies," *USA Today*, March 19, 2002. Copyright © 2002 USA TODAY. Reprinted with permission; Ethical Dilemma: More Companies Want the FBI to Screen, from *The Wall Street Journal*, Eastern Edition by Ann Davis. Copyright © 2002 by Dow Jones & Co., Inc. Reproduced with permission of Dow Jones & Co., Inc. via Copyright Clearance Center.

CHAPTER 10

Photo/Illustration: Photo Disc; Courtesy of IBM Corporation; Courtesy of Johnson & Johnson; Courtesy of Ford Motor Company; Courtesy of AT&T Global Info/Solution; AP Wide World Photo; Photo Disc; AP Wide World Photo; Courtesy of Burrston House; Courtesy of Southwest Airlines; Photo Disc; Courtesy of Burrston House; AP Wide World Photo; Esbin-Anderson Photography/The Image Works; Photo Disc; AP Wide World Photo; Courtesy of Burrston House; Courtesy of UPS; Photo Disc; Courtesy of 3M; Thomas Strand Photography/TEC Interface Systems.

Text: Management in Action: A Man with No Experience, from Steve Lohr, "He Loves to Win. At IBM, He Did," *The New York Times*, March 10, 2002. Copyright © 2002 by the New York Times Co. Reprinted by permission; Ethical Dilemma Chapter 10: Is This Innovation for Real?, from Todd Wallack, "Sample 'New' Cell Phone Really Just Modified Nokia," *San Francisco Chronicle*, March 29, 2002. Copyright © 2002 San Francisco Chronicle. Reprinted by permission.

CHAPTER 11

Photo/Illustration: Photo Disc; Steve Mason/Photo Disc; Courtesy of New School University, NY, NY; Bill Tarver; Photo Disc; Courtesy of Principal Financial Group; Ben Van Hook; Photo Disc; Peter L. Chapman/Stock Boston; Steve Mason/Photo Disc; Photo Disc; Photo Disc; Photo Disc; Courtesy of Nova Wines, Inc.; Photo Disc; Courtesy of USA Today; Photo Disc; Martin Rogers/Stock Boston; Steve Mason/Photo Disc; Photo Disc; Andrew Levine/Photo Researchers, Inc.; Vic Bider/PhotoEdit; Photo Disc; Michael Stravato, USA Today.

Text: Management in Action: Having Friends at Work, from *The Wall Street Journal*, Eastern Edition by Sue Shellenbarger. Copyright © 2002 by Dow Jones & Co., Inc. Reproduced with permission of Dow Jones & Co., Inc. via Copyright Clearance Center; Ethical Dilemma: Enron Employees Create a Positive Impression, from *The Wall Street Journal*, Eastern Edition by Jason Leopold. Copyright © 2002 by Dow Jones & Co., Inc. Reproduced with permission of Dow Jones & Co., Inc. via Copyright Clearance Center.

CHAPTER 12

Photo/Illustration: Photo Disc; Mark Richards/PhotoEdit; Photo Disc; Mark Burnett/Stock Boston; Photo Disc; Michael Newman/PhotoEdit; Courtesy of Burrston House; Courtesy of O.C. Tanner Company; Photo Disc; James Schnepf/Liaison Agency; Photo Disc; Nina Leen/TimePix; Photo Disc; Photo Disc; Chuck Kennedy/Knight Ridder Tribune; Photo Disc; Courtesy of Goodwill Industries International, Inc.; Photo Disc; Bob Daemmrich/Stock Boston; Photo Disc; Photo Disc; Bo Daemmrich/Stock Boston; Geostock/Photo Disc; Reprinted with of the Principal Financial Group © 2002; Photo Disc; Panel 12.10, Adapted from J.R. Hackman and G.R. Oldham, *Work Redesign*, Addison-Wesley, 1980.

Text: Management in Action: Technology Professionals Corp., from *Inc: The Magazine for Growing Companies* by L. Buchanan. Copyright © 2001 by Business Innovator Group Resources/Inc. Reproduced with permission of Business Innovator Group Resources/Inc. via Copyright Clearance Center; Ethical Dilemma Chapter 12: Would You Fire Someone . . ., reprinted from December 17, 2001 issue of *Business Week* by special permission. Copyright © 2001 by The McGraw-Hill Companies, Inc.

CHAPTER 13

Photo/Illustration: Photo Disc; Fabian Falcon/Stock Boston;Courtesy of KPGM; Courtesy of Burrston House; Photo Disc; Published Image; Courtesy of Boeing; Photo Disc; Rosemary Hedger; Kevin Horan/Stock Boston; Courtesy of Volvo Car Corporation; Courtesy of PeopleSoft;

Photo Disc; Photo Disc; Courtesy of NASCAR Public Relations; Courtesy of GM Saturn; Photo Disc; Courtesy of Texas Instruments; Courtesy of Burrston House; AP Wide World Photo; AP Wide World Photo; Karen Nein.

Text: Management in Action: Virtual Teamwork, reprinted from February 28, 2002 issue of *Business Week* by special permission. Copyright © 2002 by The McGraw-Hill Companies, Inc.; Ethical Dilemma: Virtual Morality, from *The Wall Street Journal,* Eastern Edition by Michael J. McCarthy. Copyright © 1999 by Dow Jones & Co., Inc. Reproduced with permission of Dow Jones & Co., Inc. via Copyright Clearance Center.

CHAPTER 14

Photo/Illustration: Photo Disc; AP Wide World Photo; AP Wide World Photo; AP Wide World Photo; AP Wide World Photo; Photo Disc; AP Wide World Photo; Photo Disc; Rosemary Hedger; Photo Disc; Photo Disc; Photo Disc; Michael Newman/Photo Edit; Photo Disc; Photo Disc; Photo Disc; AP Wide World Photo; AP Wide World Photo; Photo Disc; Photo Disc; AP Wide World Photo; AP Wide World Photo; Panel 14.5, Reprinted from November 20, 2000 issue of *Business Week* by special permission. Copyright © 2002 by The McGraw-Hill Companies, Inc.; Panel 14.6, Adapted from The Leadership Grid® R.R. Blake, J.S. Mouton, L.B. Barnes, and L.E. Greiner, "Breakthrough in Organization Development," *Harvard Business Review,* November-December 1964. Panel 14.7, Adapted from P. Hersey and K.H. Blanchard, Management of Organizational Behavior: *Utilizing Human Resources, 5th edition,* Prentice-Hall, 1988.

Text: Management in Action: The New Xerox Chief Shakes . . ., reprinted from August 6, 2001 issue of *Business Week* by special permission. Copyright © 2001 by The McGraw-Hill Companies, Inc.; Ethical Dilemma: Cashing in on Expense Accounts, from Mary McNamara and Martin Miller, "Brothel or Wedding Gown: Putting It on the Company Tab," *Los Angeles Times,* March 5, 20002. Copyright © 2002 Los Angeles Times. Reprinted by permission.

CHAPTER 15

Photo/Illustration: Photo Disc; Photo Disc; Photo Disc; Photo Disc; Rosemary Hedger; Photo Disc; Photo Disc; Photo Disc; Photo Disc; Courtesy of Burrston House; Photo Disc; Photo Disc; Jamie Tanaka Photography; Photo Disc; Photo Disc; Courtesy of General Mills; Courtesy of Burrston House; Photo Disc; Photo Disc; Courtesy of Sun Microsystems; Courtesy of CIDCO; Zigy Kaluzny/Getty Images; Photo Disc; Photo Disc; Photo Disc; Photo Disc; Photo Disc; AP Wide World Photo.

Text: Management in Action: Modern Office Designs, from *The Wall Street Journal,* Eastern Edition by Motoko Rick. Copyright © 2001 by Dow Jones & Co., Inc. Reproduced with permission of Dow Jones & Co., Inc. via Copyright Clearance Center; Ethical Dilemma: Does a Company's Communications Strategy Reflect . . ., from Theresa Howard, "Experts: Admission Could Have Aided Andersen," *USA Today,* March 29, 2002. Copyright © 2002 USA TODAY. Reprinted with permission

CHAPTER 16

Photo/Illustration: Photo Disc; Photo Disc; Photo Disc; Courtesy of Mitsubishi; Courtesy of the Salvation Army; Photo Disc; Courtesy of Burrston House; Photo Disc; AP Wide World Photo; AP Wide World Photo; David Frazier/Photo Researchers, Inc.; Courtesy of Hoodoo Ski Area/Leon Pearson; Photo Disc; Michael Newman/PhotoEdit; Courtesy of Burrston House; Courtesy of Robert Cormack; AP Wide World Photo; Photo Disc; Courtesy of Ritz Carlton; AP Wide World Photo; Herald and Review/Kelly J. Huff; Courtesy of Xerox Corporation; Rosemary Hedger; Photo Disc; Photo Disc; Courtesy of Instituto Pro-Natura; Charles Thatcher/Getty Images; Massimo Borchi/Photo Researchers; Photo Disc.

Text: Management in Action: Working in Small Business, from Jim Hopkins, "Big Business Can't Swallow These Little Fish," *USA Today,* March 27, 2002. Copyright © 2002 USA TODAY. Reprinted with permission; Ethical Dilemma: Controls to Keep Employees from Temptation, from *The Wall Street Journal,* Eastern Edition by Shirley Leung. Copyright © 2001 by Dow Jones & Co., Inc. Reproduced with permission of Dow Jones & Co., Inc. via Copyright Clearance Center.

name index

company & organization index

subject index

Continuous-process technology, **270**
Control, 520–556
  areas of, 531
  barriers to, 545–546
  definition of, 524
  dissonance and, 350
  ethics and, 555
  financial tools for, 534–537
  levels of, 530–531
  locus of, 95, 356
  need for, 525–526
  productivity and, 523, 524
  quality, 54
  small companies and, 528, 551
  span of, 255–256
  steps in process of, 526–528
  strategic, 186, 202
  styles of implementing, 532–533
  successful systems of, 544–545
  summary of, 548–550
  total quality management and, 538–543
  types of, 529
  video case on, 556
Controlling, **13,** 524
Control/planning cycle, 156–157, 169
Control process steps, 526–528
Control standard, **527**
Cooperation vs. competition, 45, 273
Cooperative conflict, 414
Coordinated effort, **254**
Core culture, 247
Corporate culture. *See* Organizational culture
Cost-focus strategy, **193**
Cost-leadership strategy, **193**
Costs, fixed vs. variable, 165
Countertrading, **116**
Country-club management, 461
Cramming, 24
Creativity, 232
Credibility, 491
Crises
  deadlines vs., 219
  strategic management and, 182
  as stressors, 364
Crisis management, 29–30
Cross-cultural communication, 486
Cross-functional teams, **424**
Cubicles, 403, 488, 512–513
Cultural differences, 126–131, 135
  group exercise on, 140–141
  language and, 127
  national culture and, 126–127
  nonverbal communication and, 128–129
  religion and, 131
  time orientation and, 130
Cultural skills, 112
Culture, **126**–127
Culture shock, 126–127
Currency exchange rates, 120
Current assets, 536
Customer divisions, 260, **261**
Customer-relations management (CRM), 407
Customers, **72**
  perspective of, 198
  responsiveness to, 8

Customers—*Cont.*
  taking care of, 72
Customer service, 198
Customs, 140–141

D

Dawn raids, 141
Deadlines, 163
  crises vs., 219
  stress of, 364
Debt management ratios, 537
Decentralized authority, **257**
Deciding to decide, **230**
Decisional roles, **21**
Decision making, 208–242
  biases in, 231–232, 233
  computer-aided, 227
  definition of, **210**
  effective reactions to, 230, 236
  ethical behavior and, 220, 240, 241
  example of, 237–238
  general strategies for, 209
  group, 222–227, 235–236
  group exercise on, 240–241
  ineffective reactions to, 229, 236
  Internet resource on, 238
  nonprogrammed decisions and, 210
  nonrational models of, 215–217
  overcoming barriers to, 228–232, 236
  participative management and, 225
  programmed decisions and, 210
  rational model of, 214–215
  self-assessment of, 238–239
  steps in process of, 218–221, 235
  styles of, 212–213
  summary of, 234–236
  video case on, 242
Decision-making style, **212**–213, 234
  self-assessment of, 238–239
  using knowledge of, 213
Decisions, **210,** 234
  programmed vs. nonprogrammed, 211
  reactions to situations requiring, 229–230
Decline stage of product life cycle, **195**
Declining career, 71
Decoding communications, **485,** 489
Defenders, **149**
Defensive approach, **84**
Defensive avoidance, **229**
Defensive strategy, **185**
Definition stage of project life cycle, 162, 163
Delegation, 253, **256,** 467
Delphi groups, **227**
Democratic governments, **121**
Democratic National Committee, 251
Demographic forces, **77,** 320
Demotions, 305
Departmental objectives, 159
Department of Agriculture, 535
Deposition test, 220
Detail thinkers, 167
Devaluation, 108
Developed countries, **119**
Developing countries, 119

Development process, 296–297, 309
  definition of, **296**
  methods used in, 296–297
  See also Training process
Devil's advocacy, **419**
Diagnosis, **219,** 330, 399
Dialectic method, **419**
Differential rate system, 40
Differentiated organization, **268**
Differentiation strategy, **193**
Digital books, 323
Dilbert cartoons, 11
Dining tips, 490
Directive decision making, 212, 213
Directive leadership, 464, 465
Disabled people, 89
Disagreements. *See* Conflict
Disciplining employees, 305
Discrimination, 90, **287**
Dismissals, 305, 306
Dissatisfaction, 383
Disseminator role, 21
Distance learning, 210, 211, 297
Distinctiveness, 363
Distributors, **73**
Disturbance handler role, 21
Diversity, 10, **86**–91, 98
  barriers to, 90–91
  external dimensions of, 87
  internal dimensions of, 87
  productivity and, 521
  workplace trends in, 87–89
Diversity programs, 90
Divisional objectives, 159
Divisional structure, **260**–261
Division of labor, **254, 432**
Divorce, 411
Divx disks, 182–183
Doing Business in Asia: The Complete Guide
  (Dunung), 111
Downsizing, 305
Downward communication, **497**
Drinking behavior, 362
Driving Force Analysis, 192
Drug abuse, 306–307
Dubai, 251
Dumping, **123**
DVD disks, 182–183
Dysfunctional conflict, 414

E

E-books, 323
Echo Boomers, 51
E-commerce (electronic commerce), **107**
Economic communities, 125
Economic development, 119
Economic differences, 118–120, 133
Economic forces, **76**
Economic systems, 118–119
Educational levels, 89
Educational opportunities, 403
Effectiveness, **5,** 28
  of communications, 504–509, 512
  of control systems, 544–546

Formulating strategy—*Cont.*
   product life cycle and, 194–195
   summary of, 201–202
For-profit organizations, 251
Fortune 500 companies, 179
Fortune, 15, 17, 52, 63, 67, 112, 151, 219, 281, 282, 283, 436, 454, 531
Four generic strategies, 192–193
Four management functions, **12**–**13**, 28
Fragmentation, 273
Franchising, **117**
Free-market economy, **118**
Free trade, **122–125**, 134
   barriers to, 122–123
   major trading blocs for, 125
   most favored nation status and, 125
   organizations promoting, 123–124
Freeze magazine, 92
Fringe benefits. *See* Benefits
Functional conflict, 414
Functional managers, **17**
Functional structure, **259**
Fundamental attribution bias, **363**

G

Gainsharing, **401**
Gambling casinos, 546
Gantt charts, **A4**-**A5**
   benefits of, A4
   example of, A5
   limitations of, A5
Garbage-can model of decision making, **216**
Gay employees, 89
"Gazelle" companies, 94
Gazing, 128
Gender diversity, 88
   communication and, 494–495
   leadership traits and, 457
   overseas assignments and, 111
   sex-role stereotypes and, 360
   wage gap and, 359
   See also Women
General Agreement on Tariffs and Trade (GATT), 124
General and Industrial Management (Fayol), 40
General environment, **76**–**77**, 97
General managers, **17**
Generation X, 51
Generation Y, 51
Geocentric managers, **113**
Geographic divisions, 260, **261**
Gestures, 129
Glass ceiling, **88**
Global economy, **108**
Globalization, 10, 104–141
   cultural differences and, 126–131
   definition of, **106**
   e-commerce and, 107
   economic differences and, 118–120
   ethical dilemma related to, 141
   free trade and, 122–125
   global economy and, 108
   international expansion and, 114–117

Globalization—*Cont.*
   international management and, 110–113
   Internet resources on, 137–138
   megamergers and, 109, 135–137
   methods of, 116–117
   minifirms and, 109
   overview of, 106, 132
   political-legal differences and, 120–121
   reasons for, 114–115
   summary of, 132–135
   travel and, 105
   See also International management
Global outsourcing, **116**
Global village, **107**
Goal displacement, **223**
Goals, 153–155
   hierarchy of, 153
   inconsistent, 417
   motivational, 390–391
   path-goal leadership, 464
   perspectives on, 196–198
   SMART, 155
   types of, 154
   See also Objectives
Goal-setting theory, **390**–**391**
Gorillas in the Mist (film), 272
Gossip chain, 499
Governmental systems, 121
Government regulators, **74**
Grand strategies, **185**, 201
   common types of, 185
   establishing, 188–191
Grapevine, **498**–**499**
Graphic method, 165
Greenfield venture, **117**
Group behavior
   developmental stages of, 428–429
   organizational behavior and, 348
   See also Individual behavior; Workplace behavior
Group cohesiveness, **429**, 435
Group decision making, 222–227, 235–236
   advantages and disadvantages of, 222–223
   characteristics of groups and, 224
   participative management and, 225
   practical guidelines for, 224
   problem-solving techniques and, 226–227
Group demands, 366
Group-driven computer-aided decision systems, 227
Group exercises
   on communication, 516–517
   on conflict management, 443
   on decision making, 240–241
   on designing an organization, 278–279
   on ethical behavior, 101, 240
   on human resource management, 314–315
   on identifying values, 373–374
   on international customs, 140–141
   on leadership, 479–481
   on managerial planning, 173–174
   on monitoring productivity, 553–554
   on most-admired companies, 63–64
   on motivation, 409–410
   on organizational change, 342–343

Group exercises—*Cont.*
   on strategic planning, 206
   on time management, 32–33
Group problem solving, 226–227
Groups, **422**, 438
   cohesiveness of, 429, 435
   formal vs. informal, 423
   stages of development, 428–429
   See also Teams
Groupthink, **223**, 418, **435**–**437**
   preventing, 437
   results of, 436–437
   symptoms of, 436
Growth stage of product life cycle, **195**
Growth strategy, **185**

H

Halo effect, 360–**361**
Handshakes, 490
Happiness, 11
Harvard Business Review, 449
Hassles, 364
Hawthorne effect, 43
Health and safety issues, 286
Helplessness, learned, 356
Heroes, **247**
Heuristics, **231**, 236
Hierarchy
   of authority, 252, **254**–**255**
   of human needs, 44, 380–382
Hierarchy of needs theory, **380**–**382**
High-control situations, 463
Highlighting, 508
"High road" companies, 473
High-school dropouts, 89
High-tech industries, 14
Highway Loss Data Institute, 64
Hindsight bias, 233
Hispanics, 88, 360
Historical perspective, **37**
   behavioral viewpoint and, 42–45
   classical viewpoint and, 38–41
   overview of, 38, 39
   quantitative viewpoint and, 46–47
Honesty, 455
Horizontal communication, **498**
Horizontal loading, 397
Horizontal specialization, 252
Horn-and-halo effect, 361
Hostile environment sexual harassment, 307
Hotel discounts, 47
Human Equation: Building Profits by Putting People First, The (Pfeffer), 53
Human relations movement, **44**
Human resource (HR) management, 280–315
   benefits and, 302–303
   compensation and, 302–303
   definition of, **283**
   demotions and, 305
   development process and, 296–297
   discipline process and, 305
   dismissals and, 305, 306
   employment tests and, 292–293
   ethical dilemma in, 315
   group exercise on, 314–315

Management theory—*Cont.*
 behavioral viewpoint and, 42–45
 classical viewpoint and, 38–41
 contemporary perspective and, 37, 48, 49
 contingency viewpoint and, 52–53
 example of applying, 60–61
 historical perspective and, 37, 38, 39
 learning organizations and, 56–57
 quality management viewpoint and, 54–55
 quantitative viewpoint and, 46–47
 systems viewpoint and, 48–51
 video case on, 65
Managerial Decision Making (Rowe, Boulgaides, and McGrath), 239
Managerial Grid, 460
Managers
 entrepreneurs vs., 94–95
 ethnocentric, 113
 expatriate, 113
 first-line, 16
 functional, 17
 general, 17
 geocentric, 113
 leaders vs., 448–449
 line, 257
 middle, 16
 polycentric, 113
 psychological rewards of, 7
 roles played by, 18, 20–21, 29
 skills required by, 22–23, 29
 top-level, 15
 wages for, 6–7
Manager's Toolbox, 3
Mandatory Retirement Act (1978), 287
Manners, 490
MAPP (Motivational Appraisal of Personal Potential), 31
Maquiladoras, **115**
Marital breakups, 411
Market changes, 320
Market control, **533**
Mass media, 75
Matrix structure, **263**
Maturity stage
 of organizational life cycle, **271**
 of product life cycle, **195**
MBA Jungle Online, 32
MBO. *See* Management by objectives
Mean Business (Dunlap), 68
Means-end chain, **153**
Measurable goals, 155
Measurement management, 198–199
Mechanistic organizations, **267**
Media richness, **487**
Medium of communications, **485,** 486–487, 489
Meetings, 187
Megamergers, 109
Memorization, 24
Memory improvement, 24
Men's Health, 93
Mental imagery, 24
Mentally disabled people, 89
Mentoring relationship, 245
Mercosur, **125**

Mergers
 adapting to, 329
 management challenge of, 135–137
 megamergers and, 109
Merit pay, 401
Message, **485**
Mexico
 maquiladoras in, 115
 NAFTA and, 125
 time orientation in, 130
Middle managers, **16,** 153
Middle-of-the-road management, 461
Midlife stage of organizational life cycle, **271**
Millennium Generation, 51
Million Mom March, 75
Mindfulness, 35
Mindguards, 436
Mindlessness, 35
Minifirms, 109
Minimum wage requirements, 286
Mission, **151,** 183
Mission statement, **151,** 177, 183–184
Mixed economy, **119**
Moderate-control situations, 464
Moles, 499
Momentum, 180
Monitoring performance, 13, 524, 548, 553–554
Monitor role, 21
Monochromatic time, **130**
Monster.com website, 238, 311–312, 441
Moods, 456
Moonshine shops, 60
Moral-rights approach, **79**
Most-admired companies, 63–64
Most favored nation status, **125**
Mothers Against Drunk Driving (MADD), 469
Motion studies, 40
Motivating factors, **383**–384
Motivating potential score (MPS), 399
Motivation, 376–411
 compensation and, 400–401
 definition of, **378**
 employee benefits and, 378, 403
 equity differences and, 408–409
 ethical dilemma related to, 411
 explanation of, 378–379
 flexible workplace and, 377, 402
 group exercise on, 409–410
 importance of, 379
 Internet resource on, 408
 job design and, 396–399
 leadership and, 449
 mutual accountability and, 431
 need-based perspectives on, 380–385
 nonmonetary incentives and, 402–403
 process perspectives on, 386–391
 reinforcement theory of, 392–395
 rewards and, 379, 407
 simple model of, 378–379
 summary of, 404–406
Multinational corporations, **110**
Multinational organizations, **110**
Multiplier effect, 6

Multitasking, 1, 130
Mutual accountability, 431
Mutual-benefit organizations, 251
Mutual stakeholders, 273

N

Narrow markets, 192–193
National Center for Employee Ownership, 62, 99
National culture, 126–127
 See also Cultural differences
National Highway Traffic Safety Administration, 64
National Labor Relations Board, **286**
Necessity entrepreneurs, 95
Need-based perspectives, **380**–385, 404–405
 acquired-needs theory, 384–385
 hierarchy of needs theory, 380–382
 two-factor theory, 382–384
Needs, **380**
Negative conflict, **414**
Negative reinforcement, **393**
Negotiator role, 21
Networking, 447
Network structure, **265**
New Mexico State University, 206
New York Daily News, 4, 18, 22–23, 36
New Yorker, The, 93
New York Post, 23
New York Stock Exchange, 364
New York Times, 75, 114, 207, 241, 340
Noise, **486**
Nominal groups, **226**
Nonmonetary incentives, 402–403
Nonprofit organizations, 251
Nonprogrammed decisions, **211,** 234
Nonrational models of decision making, **215**–217, 235
 bounded rationality and, 215
 examples of, 216, 217
Nonverbal communication, **128**–129, **492**–493
 group exercise on, 140–141
 international examples of, 128
 noise in, 486
Nonwork demands, 366
Norming stage, **429**
Norms, **433**–434
North American Free Trade Agreement (NAFTA), **125**
Note-taking skills, 25–26

O

Objective appraisals, **298**
Objectives, 153
 cascading, 159
 management by, 158–159
 three types of, 158
 See also Goals
Objective tests, 26–27
Observable culture, 247
Obstructionist approach, **84**
Occupational Safety and Health Act (OSHA), 81, 286, 287

Trait approaches to leadership, **454**–457, 474–475
  Bossidy's observations, 455
  gender studies, 457
  Goleman's emotional intelligence, 456
  Kouzes & Posner's five traits, 454
Transactional leaders, **468**, 476
Transfers, 305
Transformation processes, **49, 50**
Transitory career, 71
Translators, 127
Transparent company, 61
Transportation
  business travel and, 105
  globalization and, 107
Travel issues, 105
Trend analysis, **191**
Trucking industry, 315
Trust, 469, 491, 551
Turnover, **353**
20-20 hindsight bias, 233
Two core principles of TQM, **539**
Two-factor theory, **382**–384
Tylenol contamination crisis, 319, 469

U

Ultimate Travel and Savings Directory, 47
Uncertainty
  organizational responses to, 149
  planning and, 146–149, 168
  three types of, 148
Underemployment, **89**
Understanding Organizations (Handy), 32, 33
Unfreezing stage, 326, 327
Unified hierarchy, 159
Unions, 73
University of Michigan Leadership Model, **458**
Unrepresentative sample bias, 233
Unstructured interview, **291**
Upward appeals, 452
Upward communication, **497**
USA Today, 75, 108, 310, 518, 550, 551
U.S. Bureau of Labor Statistics, 6, 76, 94, 285
U.S. Census Bureau, 6, 285, 358
U.S. Department of Commerce, 113
U.S. News and World Report, 359
U.S. Postal Service, 542
U.S. Small Business Administration, 310–311
Utilitarian approach, **79**

V

Valence, **387**
Validity of tests, 293
Value orientation, 212
Values, **78**, 348–349
  group exercise on, 373–374
  workplace behavior and, 351
Value system, **78**
Variable budgets, **535**

Variable costs, 165
Verbal communication, 19
Vertical communication, 496–497
Vertical hierarchy, 252
Vertical loading, 397
Videoconferencing, 187, **502**
Video disks, 182
Vienna, Austria, 190
Violent behavior, 414
Virtual meetings, 187
Virtual morality, 444
Virtual teams, 424, 427, 440
Visible culture, 247
Vision, **151**–152, 184, 449, 455, 469
Vision statement, **152**, 177, 184
Visual imagery, 24
Volunteers, 425

W

Wages
  for employees, 302
  for managers, 6–7
  See also Compensation
Wagner Act (1935), 286
Wall Street Journal, The, 29, 60, 141, 174, 276, 298, 370, 374, 444, 459, 512, 518, 555
Warfare, 415
Weaknesses, 188, 189
Wealth of Nations, The (Smith), 38
Websites
  Brefi Group, 171
  Grolier, 478
  Interlink Training and Coaching, 479
  iUniverse.com, 323
  Journal of Comparative International Management, 138
  MAPP Assessment, 31
  Microsoft, 277
  Monster.com, 238, 311–312, 441
  Morrisey Group, 204
  National Center for Employee Ownership, 62
  New Mexico State University, 206
  OD-Online Organization Health Survey, 100
  Outofservice.com, 371
  Queendom.com, 513
  Self-Directed Search, 31
  Southwest Airlines, 408
  3M Corporation, 341
  Wet Feet, 31
  See also Internet resources; World Wide Web
"What-if" scenarios, 166
"What Would Your Parents Say?" test, 220
When Talking Makes Things Worse! Resolving Problems When Communication Fails (Stiebel), 506

Whistleblowers, **81**
White Men Can't Jump (film), 90
"White noise" machines, 512–513
Whiz Kids, 46
Wholly-owned subsidiary, **117**
Wide markets, 192–193
Women
  communication and, 494–495
  international management and, 110, 111
  leadership traits in, 457
  sex-role stereotypes and, 360
  top managers as, 473
  wage gap and, 359
  workforce diversity and, 88
  See also Gender diversity
Word games, 24
Work assignment, 160
Worker Adjustment and Retaining Notification Act (1988), 287
Worker-owned companies, 99
Workforce demographics, 310–311
Work-life benefits, 281, 403
Workplace behavior, 351
  conflict and, 414–415
  ethics of faking, 374
  etiquette and, 490
  evaluation of, 353
  flexible workplace and, 377, 402
  Internet use and, 444
  office design and, 403, 488, 512–513
  personality traits and, 356–357
  workplace friends and, 370
  See also Group behavior; Individual behavior
Work specialization, 253
Work teams, 424
World Bank, **124**
World Trade Center attack, 29–30, 228
World Trade Organization (WTO), **124**
World Wide Web
  e-commerce and, 107
  employee policies about, 444
  origin of, 107
  productivity and, 52
  recruiting employees via, 289
  See also Internet; Websites
Writing skills, 507–508
Written communications, 19, 507–508

Y

You Don't Always Get What You Pay For: The Economics of Privatization (Sclar), 542
Young workers, 347
Youth stage of organizational life cycle, **271**

Z

Zero-based budgeting (ZBB), **535**